English Constitutional
and Legal History

ENGLISH CONSTITUTIONAL AND LEGAL HISTORY

A SURVEY

Colin Rhys Lovell

University of Southern California

New York
OXFORD UNIVERSITY PRESS
1962

Copyright © 1962 by Oxford University Press, Inc.
Library of Congress Catalogue Card No. 62-9825
Printed in the United States of America

Dedicated to
JEAN KATHRYN McCAMMOND LOVELL
My Wife

CONTENTS

FOREWORD

There have been many texts on English constitutional history, but from time to time there must be a rewriting of that history. New researches have changed former interpretations; and the great changes wrought by the extension of state-interest, a process accelerated by two world wars, have added much to the constitution in this present century.

This book is designed for beginning students and does not pretend to detailed treatment·of any one phase of the constitution and its development. Avenues of further investigation are provided by suggested readings at the close of each chapter, though these lists furnish only approaches and are not intended as complete bibliographical guides.

The development of the English constitution has proceeded by means which lend themselves to disagreement among scholars, using the same materials to support their different views. This text has either presented these various interpretations or the one which seems most logical to the writer. The reading lists at the end of chapters include selections disagreeing with the views of the text on these controversial matters.

This volume attempts to fill the needs of both student and teacher in a beginning course. Scottish and Irish constitutional developments are mentioned only where they affect England. The constitutional history of the British Empire and of the subsequent emergence of the present Commonwealth has not been included. This is the constitutional history of only one part, if for a long time the most important part, of that evolving group of states resting on the principle of unity through diversity.

The author acknowledges his considerable obligation to John W. Lovell, II, for assistance in preparing the Index.

C.R.L.

Los Angeles, California
January 1962

INTRODUCTION TO STUDENTS

MOST introductions are ignored, but if an exception is made for this one, certain problems may be avoided later. For most students English constitutional history is a first encounter with what is called *institutional* history, which aims at telling what and why something occurred, and also asks *how* it occurred. English constitutional history, therefore, is a demonstration of the whys, whats, and hows of the development of modern English governmental and legal institutions and practices.

The American student will immediately recognize the essential relevance of the subject. With all American representative bodies derived from English practice and tradition, the historical background in England is vital for understanding their workings in modern America. With the notable exception of the civil law of Louisiana, based upon the Code Napoleon, all sections of the United States have a body of law resting on the English common law, the origins of which can be traced back until they are lost in the mists of some early Anglo-Saxon community. To understand the history of law is to know much about its present meaning and purpose, as Justice Oliver Wendell Holmes of the United States Supreme Court knew when he once tartly informed counsel that with a little history his brief would have been briefer.

The astute student will realize at once that there is a certain unreality about studying the development of any system of government and law without considering the changes in social, economic, and political conditions. Yet this text can take only passing notice of these other factors. They are dealt with only insofar as is necessary to understand the institutional developments clearly.

Few things in English constitutional history can be said to have started at a particular moment; "first causes" usually remain unknown, and exact dates cannot be given when we come to discuss the origins of such institutions as Parliament or the cabinet. It is usually better to accept the principle that most of the English institutions grew up gradually, almost imperceptibly, and that by the time men became aware of their constitutional significance they had already been in existence for a long time. When this is understood, it will be seen why there are inevitably differing interpretations, each with equally strong support, of the origins of any specific constitutional change. This divergency of opinion is particularly true for the earlier periods. Faced by the problems of the moment, Englishmen applied pragmatic solutions and found no need for verbal explanations to their contemporaries. They were like the signpost painter who, when informed that he had painted the direction to Bangor incorrectly, replied testily, "Any fool knows the way to Bangor." Thus the meaning of a certain set of words in a constitutional document was plain to the persons who put them down. That the same words have later become matters of disagreement is only because the original implication has been forgotten.

C.R.L.

English Constitutional
and Legal History

1

THE ANGLO-SAXON BASIS

THE unbroken continuity of English constitutional history begins with the Anglo-Saxons. Few if any traces of the old Celtic society survived their invasions, and the 350 years of Roman occupation failed to introduce into England any forms of government or law strong enough to withstand the impact of the Anglo-Saxons in the fourth and fifth centuries. Roman law entered England after the Norman Conquest as the canon law of the church courts, and in the fifteenth and sixteenth centuries there were echoes of it in the inquisitional procedures of such courts as the Star Chamber. But these were later importations, always essentially alien, for in contrast to some other European countries, there were no remnants of the ancient Roman law still surviving with which they could be assimilated. The Romans governed Britain in the same way as they governed Gaul and other portions of the Empire. But this forms no part of English constitutional history, so thoroughly did the Anglo-Saxons eliminate the traces of their predecessors.

We have no contemporary records of the kind of constitution that the Anglo-Saxons brought with them into England during the migrations of the fourth and fifth centuries, but we do know a little about the way they organized their society in earlier times on the Continent, and we know also how the Anglo-Saxon constitution emerged in the centuries to come. Like most simple societies, that of the Anglo-Saxons seems to have been relatively stable, even though for centuries they had been a restless, marauding people, the terror of the civilized world.

The Continental Anglo-Saxons

The Anglo-Saxons came from central and western Germany and consisted of two major groups and a minor one, all from the same broad Germanic ethnic-cultural group: Angles, Saxons, and Jutes.

Similar in language and institutions, these tribes had been briefly described by Caesar in his *Commentaries* and later in A.D. 98 more fully
by Tacitus in his *Germania*. The latter source needs to be used with
some care, however, for Tacitus hoped to set an example to Romans
and ascribed to the Germanic tribesmen heroic virtues it is hardly
likely they possessed. From these two works it is clear that when not
fighting the Anglo-Saxons were subsistence farmers. All their political
institutions, therefore, were based on landholding and use. A significant
feature of their land law was the *annual redistribution of arable land*
among all freemen. This annual redistribution was based on the assumption that the ultimate ownership of land lay with the tribe; individual
land possession had not hardened into ownership, as it was to do later.

The social structure, while not rigid, had definite gradations. Classes
did not rest upon wealth per se, but the upper classes were entitled to
more wealth in cattle and land to support their rank. The *nobility* gained
its status by both birth and service, because certain offices automatically
ennobled their holders; and members of the nobility enjoyed a larger
share of tribal wealth. The bulk of the tribe, however, consisted of
freemen. All adult free males had the obligation of bearing arms and
therefore the right to participate as equals in the tribal assembly and to
hold a share of the tribal land. Below the freemen lay a quasi-free group,
the *freedmen*, former slaves who had been manumitted, usually for
special heroism which had saved their masters' lives. Manumission included this transitional stage, but the children of these former slaves
became fully free on reaching adulthood. As a freedman an individual
shouldered all the obligations and had all the rights of the fully free,
except that he was not permitted to participate in the tribal council.

The unfree were of two types. There were *former freemen*, or their
descendants, who had surrendered their free status to a master in return
for protection. Although not obligated for personal services, they had
to till his fields, and supply him with produce from plots which he gave
them. In time of crisis their master could call on them to bear arms,
and it was from this element of the unfree that the freedmen were
recruited. But they did have some legal rights. They could not be
killed with impunity or sold as chattels apart from the land, because they
were bound to it.

The second group of the unfree was the true *slave* class. Very small
on the Continent, it disappeared rapidly after the Anglo-Saxons reached
England. Slaves had no legal, political, or economic rights and performed

personal services for masters who bought and sold them as chattels. Although largely hereditary, this class was also recruited from other sources, from prisoners-of-war and those condemned to slavery by the tribal council, and even from those who would stake and lose their own freedom in the Anglo-Saxon passion for gambling.

The organs and functions of government in Anglo-Saxon society were by no means clearly defined, and imprecision in varying degrees has been a characteristic of the English constitution ever since. Caesar and Tacitus as Romans looked for a "system," neatly separating the government into functional agencies. But to the Anglo-Saxons such classifications would have been meaningless.

Freemen (both ordinary freemen and nobles) supplied the officials whose names and functions varied among the different tribes, depending upon their size and whether or not they were at war. As they usually were, most officials had military duties. All, however, were named by and were responsible to the tribal council. Tacitus discovered a hierarchy of *duces, principes, sacerdotes,* and *reges,* the last being priests[1] and kings. But the word "king" has connotations that make it an inaccurate term for the head of a tribe so "chief" is a better word. The difference between duces and principes is not clear, except that the latter probably headed larger military formations; but it is unlikely that there was a consistent chain of command and responsibility in this hierarchy. Only the largest tribes could, in any case, have had the full complement of officials, and most must have contented themselves with a chief and a few lesser leaders in battle. With the exception of the hereditary priests, these officials usually, though not always, came from the nobility; this meant that all officials were nobles although not all nobles were officials.

The *chief* owed his office to the tribal assembly, which selected and could also depose him. His authority was limited at every turn, and though he no doubt commanded respect his opinion carried no more weight in the debates of the assembly than that of any freeman. Even his primary duty of military leadership he shared with other chieftains responsible not to him but to the assembly. Every chief had a personal

---

[1] Neither Caesar nor Tacitus is very clear about the status and functions of this priestly class except that it was hereditary. Possibly priests occasionally presided at smaller tribal meetings and undoubtedly made intercession for the tribe with the proper deities. Anglo-Saxon priests, however, do not appear to have enjoyed the same prestige as Celtic druids. After the Anglo-Saxons were in England, they became dissatisfied with paganism generally so that their conversion to Christianity was one of the most easily accomplished of any European people.

bodyguard, *comitatus*, whose members he selected for their valor and whose duty was to fight around him in battle. This was their honor; their shame was to survive him in battle. The chief was responsible for the members of the comitatus, supervising the division of booty among them and presiding over meetings of the full comitatus when disputes needed to be settled. Though this bears some resemblance to a rudimentary military feudalism, the relation between individual members and the chief was in fact a strictly personal one without the essential ingredient of feudalism — land. Honor, glory, booty were the rewards for the bodyguard, never land; land came from the tribal assembly. Even after the Anglo-Saxon comitatus fighter had become the *thegn* in England, this essential element of feudalism was still lacking.

The principal instrument of government was the tribal council, in which all freemen participated. Meeting at the full of the moon with its members usually under arms to show their right to participate, the tribal assembly had in theory full powers over every aspect of tribal life. It named the chief and lesser chiefs, or if necessary, deposed them, and appointed all other officials. It decided on war and peace, annually redistributed the arable land, and tried important cases. The size of the assembly, particularly in larger tribes, must however have made it unwieldy and potentially unmanageable. No doubt for that reason its agenda was prepared by a meeting of the lesser chieftains. This smaller body is often overlooked in describing the primitive democracy of the Anglo-Saxons. Probably an individual freeman could raise another issue in the full assembly; but the primary interest of most freemen was fighting, their distant secondary one farming, and as a very poor third, government. Thus, although theoretically the chief could not dominate the tribal assembly, in practice he and his lesser lights might control it by their power to prepare its agenda. There is also some evidence that this smaller meeting had the full powers of the assembly during the intervals between its monthly (lunar) meetings.

Tribal subdivisions came to exist in those tribes which enlarged their territories. Originally personal in nature, these subdivisions had lost this characteristic even before the migrations to England. The most important subdivision was the *pagus*, or *hundred*, to use the name employed in England. Perhaps originally the term indicated that a hundred freemen occupied this land. By the time the Anglo-Saxons embarked for England, however, the term was designating a territorial unit without regard to the number of freemen in it. The hundred had an assembly under the chairmanship of a lesser chief.[2] Its chief business was what later times would consider judicial, with a jurisdiction concurrent with that of the full tribal council, except for capital charges which could be tried only by the latter. Otherwise the deciding factor as to what court tried a case was the importance of the people concerned. This was a pragmatic principle; a great man was less easily brought to accept the jurisdiction of a small group than he would accept that of a larger one. In some of the largest and most complex tribes there was also, under the hundred, the *vicus*, or *vill*, again with a communal assembly having the same powers as other larger bodies.[3]

The law applied by any of these Anglo-Saxon assemblies was customary. Until the Anglo-Saxon conversion to Christianity it was unwritten and like all customary law was considered *immutable*. Even the all-powerful tribal assembly had no legislative power, and this theory of legislative impotence endured for a long time in the development of the English constitution and disappeared only very gradually; even many centuries later the fiction that specific legislation was not making new law but reinforcing ancient customs was preserved. Most of the great steps forward in the development of the English constitution have been taken with loud assertions that nothing new was being contemplated, only the old was being restored.

In its substantive aspects, if that term can be used, the law was one of damages for injury to person or property; that is, by modern legal terminology, it was exclusively a law of torts, with no distinction between civil and criminal wrongs. Yet certain actions hurt the tribe in its fundamental purpose as a fighting force and so were met with the death penalty — treason, cowardice, desertion, and, because of its threat to the tribal population, sexual perversion.

All other actions were the personal affairs of individuals. But the Anglo-Saxons realized that personal vengeance for wrongs could lead to family blood feuds, inevitably draining the vitality of the tribe. For its own protection, therefore, the tribe interposed itself between the principals and provided an alternative to a feud by a procedure (to be described in more detail as it is known to have existed later in England) for the peaceful settlement of the dispute. Although in modern practice a decision for the plaintiff results in compensation by the defendant,

---

[2] Named occasionally by the hundred assembly, but more often by that of the full tribe, this official thus provided a tenuous link between these two bodies.

[3] The vill must not be thought of as even a small urban unit; Anglo-Saxon society was rural, and the vill a rural unit.

this was not the case with such payments by the early Anglo-Saxons. Instead a certain price attached itself to any injury that might cause an imbalance in society; payment of that price not merely atoned for the injury, but actually cancelled it, so that it could (or at least should) never be a cause for further dispute between the principals, their friends, or families. So strong was this concept that even homicide, when "paid for" to the survivors of the deceased, ceased to be an injury. Until the reign of Alfred the Great (871–99) in England even regicide meant only a higher payment to the royal survivors than would have been the case if the victim had been an ordinary freeman.

Two things stand out in the Continental Anglo-Saxon constitution. The first is the informal, fluid nature of government. The second is the strong element of personal relationship underlying all tribal organization and functions. Although invested with territorial connotations, the tribe, nevertheless, still had rights and duties attached to persons rather than to more abstract entities.

The Migration to England

The migration of the Anglo-Saxons to England began in the late fourth century and continued for about 300 years. At first it took the form merely of raids by small bands, but gradually larger family groups began to arrive and to carve out enclaves for themselves at the expense of the defeated Celts. These groups then consolidated and extended their holdings at the expense of other Anglo-Saxons. By the sixth century this process had reduced the number of divisions in the country to seven kingdoms, the *Heptarchy:* Kent (settled largely by Jutes), Sussex, Wessex, and Essex (the Saxon kingdoms), and East Anglia, Mercia, and Northumbria (peopled by Angles). Each of these kingdoms in turn had an ill-defined and unstable dominance over the others, when it was said to *hold the imperium*, and its ruler became *bretwalda*, lord of Britain. What this meant is vague, but it rested almost exclusively upon the personal strength of individual rulers. In the late eighth and early ninth centuries a series of able rulers in Wessex gave that kingdom dominance for several generations. During this time Wessex administration became quite elaborate and records were kept. Most of our knowledge about the Anglo-Saxon constitution in England comes from this later Wessex experience and practice, but the very complexity of its constitution makes it an exception, and there is no reason to suppose that the earlier kingdoms were organized in the same way.

The Danish invasions of the ninth century enabled Wessex rulers to enlarge their kingdom. The Danes had conquered the rivals of Wessex north of the river Thames and administered them as the *Danelaw*, where Danish law applied. When the successors of Alfred reconquered the Danelaw, they did not restore the former Saxon kingdoms but added them to their own, so that their holdings ceased to be Wessex and became England. The Danish invasions also forced the Anglo-Saxons to modify their constitution for greater military efficiency, with the result that the king acquired more authority and a class of nobles was created which was eventually to challenge the power of the crown. But the Danes, from the same basic Germanic cultural group as the Anglo-Saxons, had a constitution essentially similar, and after the Danes had accepted Christianity in the Treaty of Wedmore in 878, Danish variations began to be submerged. Moreover, unlike the people of the earlier Anglo-Saxon migrations, the Danes were bachelors, so the process of assimilation was further facilitated. Later, when the Danish Cnut was king (1017–35), he took pride in retaining English customs, which were quite familiar to him. The importance of the Danish invasions for the English constitution, therefore, does not lie in any uniquely "Danish" contributions to it but in the changes which the Anglo-Saxons had to make in government to meet the Danish threat.

With no "Danish" elements complicating Anglo-Saxon constitutional development, it is possible to look at the Anglo-Saxon period of English constitutional history as a single unit from about A.D. 600, when written materials became available, to 1066 and the Norman Conquest. Local variations always existed even within Wessex. Nevertheless, the basic elements of the English constitution are the same for about four centuries.

Central Government

Of all the changes made in their constitution by the Anglo-Saxons during the invasions, the most important was the transformation of the chief into the king. He and his *Witan*, or council of advisers, became the central government.

A condition of almost constant warfare, first with Celts, then with rival Anglo-Saxons, then with the Danes, made it essential that the chief should have special and superior authority. He was leader of the national army, the *fyrd*, in which all freemen were bound to serve, and upon his power to command their loyalties everything might depend. Moreover, there could be no long intervals between chiefs, while the tribal council considered the merits of several candidates. There had to be a mode of rapid succession, which would also reduce the chances of rivals disputing for the office and thus dissipating tribal strength.

Another reason for the change from chief to king was the psychological need of a people, uprooted from their past environment, to have one element of stability in a hostile land. Etymology reveals much here. In their need for some degree of security, the *cyn* (kin) required a focal point in a person representing them as a group, a *cyning* (king), a title retaining the older implication of personal relationship rather than indicating territorial sovereignty. No doubt the chiefs themselves saw the advantages of a title emphasizing their greater power and majesty as well. Finally, the Church, which exercised a great influence over the Anglo-Saxons after their conversion, also sought to advance the dignity of kingship. With their links to a Roman past, the missionaries raised tribal headship to kingly status and gave it a quasi-divine significance. The clergy hoped that a powerful and respected king might not only ensure longer periods of peace and order, but also, once converted to Christianity, he would be able to order the baptism of his subjects too. Thus the Church transformed the pagan custom in which tribal warriors held their new chief aloft on their shields into the religious ceremony of coronation, where priests anointed the new ruler with holy oil and he in turn took a solemn oath upon sacred relics to protect the Holy Church and the poor, to punish evil but yet show mercy. With the strong faith of the Anglo-Saxons, the link between Church and crown assured to the latter a much greater degree of veneration than had previously been accorded to a mere chief.

The need for strong military leadership in the face of the Danish threats of the eighth and ninth centuries led to the acceptance of the Wessex kings as the special defenders of all the English. The recovery of the Danelaw placed them in a unique position among their rivals; they could logically claim the title of *Rex Anglorum* (King of the English). It is worth noting, however, that they did not claim the title of *Rex Angliae* (King of England), a title with connotations of territorial sovereignty, which was not to be assumed until John's accession in 1199.

Though the office of kingship had thus emerged, it would be misleading to think of it in terms of constitutional theory. Everything depended on the abilities of the individual monarch. A strong king might extend the royal power; a weak one might allow it to recede. But it was one of the traditions of the Anglo-Saxon peoples that there were limits to the authority of their rulers. The king had certain specific powers and no more. This sense of the "limitation" of royal power is nowhere more clearly seen than in the principle that the king came to his high place not by birthright but by selection of the Witan. This elective element in English kingship continued and survived the Norman Conquest, albeit on a different basis of approval.

In the early period the Witan, like the older tribal council, felt free to name anyone king. As the dignity of the office grew, there was a tendency to make selections from within a single family. This tendency hardened when for several generations the house of Cedric provided very able rulers for Wessex. Thus a broad hereditary principle of royal succession came to be accepted, although the Witan still retained some freedom of choice because the primogeniture principle was lacking. It rarely happened during this period that a king came to the throne by immediate inheritance, and it was often hard to determine which member of a royal house should succeed. It was widely recognized that it was the duty of the council in these circumstances to decide, and in the last analysis it was the relative military ability of the several candidates to the throne that determined its choice. In 871 the Witan preferred Alfred to his young nephew, son of the late king; and in 1066 the choice fell on Harold, a great noble but the brother-in-law and not a direct heir of the late king, Edward the Confessor. Even when the succession appears to have been decided in practice by military action, formal ratification by the Witan was very often sought. In 1017 Cnut was not satisfied with his victory and hastened to have the Witan declare him king. In 1066, as its last act, the Witan named Duke William king as he approached London after his victory at Hastings.

The Witan could also depose the monarch, who thus always remained "on approval," as Ethelrede II, the Redeless (978–1016), discovered. After Hastings, the Witan named Edgar Atheling to succeed the slain Harold, only to depose him as the Normans neared London. Although such depositions, it is true, usually occurred under the force of military circumstances, it is significant that prevailing attitudes required formal deposition of the defeated ruler before victory had full legality.

A further aspect of the limitation of royal power was the Anglo-Saxon land law, which vested ultimate ownership of all land vaguely in the people and not the king, in great contrast to later feudal law which stated flatly that *only* the king owned land. In Anglo-Saxon law everyone, including the king, merely possessed his lands.

Nevertheless, in spite of these limitations there are signs that Anglo-Saxon kingship was on the road to what Norman and particularly Angevin kingship became. Thus the penalty for regicide had changed from a high wergeld to death by the time of Alfred the Great, although treason remained an offense against the realm and not the crime against the king that it became after the Norman Conquest. Further evidence of growing kingship was the concept of the *king's peace*, giving royal protection to certain people so that they enjoyed greater security than those in the "peace" of a lesser man. To break the king's peace meant a heavy fine to him over and above other penalties. The Church encouraged this *pax regis*, and by the close of the Anglo-Saxon period certain crimes, regardless of their victims, were always violations of the king's peace. Ultimately, long after Anglo-Saxon times, the concept was carried to the point at which all crimes were regarded as personal affronts to the sovereign. This concept is expressed in criminal trial citations; thus "Rex (Regina) *v.* William Smith": republican countries have replaced the sovereign in the formula with the artificial person of the "State" (People or Commonwealth).[4]

In the development of the king's peace, Anglo-Saxons recognized that violence was most unseemly in certain places. Churches, churchyards, abbeys, cathedral closes, the royal dwelling of the moment, and all within these places were under the king's protection. Those particularly vulnerable to attack stood always in the king's peace: women, children, and the clergy. The king could extend his protection to a person for a specific purpose and time: the foreign merchant while trading in his realms, the foreign emissaries coming to and from his court. The effectiveness of the king's peace depended ultimately upon his willingness

---

[4] This constitutional-legal principle of the king's peace has gone even further. Whenever an English schoolboy shouts, "Pax!" or his American counterpart demands, "King's X," each is appealing to that highest protection of the king's peace, which alone can save him from his adversary, who should likewise honor the concept by desisting immediately.

and ability to enforce it, and at times it might become entirely ineffectual. Nevertheless, the concept of a special peace owed to and
maintained by the king indicates that kingship had come to be something more than the old office of chief.

Further evidence of the enhancement of Anglo-Saxon kingship was
the introduction in England of the *wite*, the king's *share* of all judicial
payments for personal damages, such as *bots* for bodily injuries and
wergelds for murders. This had quite a different origin from the concept that certain actions as affronts to royal dignity required special
payments to the king. The wite initially represented the successful claim
by the king to a portion of judicial revenues, and as such, by itself was
an indication of growing royal power. The wite may have appeared as
early as the seventh century; it was certainly accepted by the ninth. By
that time, however, the wite was inevitably being confused with the
special penalties due to the king for violations of his peace. When a
man made a payment to the king, it mattered little whether it was a
wite for a bot or a wergeld paid to another, or a special fine for breaking
the king's peace. All the payer knew was that he had to pay the king
money for something that he had done. By the time of the *Laws of
Alfred the Great* wites were clearly regarded as penalties, and under
Edgar the Peaceful (959–75) the confusion between wites and fines
for violations of the king's peace was almost complete; wites from bots
and wergelds for harm done to persons under royal protection were
larger than wites from bots and wergelds for persons not under royal
protection. The combination of wite and king's peace was strong evidence of the growth of Anglo-Saxon kingship.

The greatest restraint on the power of the monarch at this time, as
indeed for many centuries to come, was his lack of large financial resources. The concept of a national revenue apart from the personal
funds of the king did not exist, and would not for a long time in England. The king had wites and fines for violations of his peace, both of
which were considered his personal moneys. But the bulk of his income came from manorial dues and rents, and like everyone else the
king was expected to "live of his own." That there might be expenses
for the king in his public capacity beyond those for an ordinary lord
no one was prepared to admit. That freemen might have an obligation
to pay taxes for governmental activities, Englishmen would begin to
accept only very haltingly and grudgingly in the early seventeenth
century. There was only one national tax in Anglo-Saxon England,

and it was accepted as a temporary measure to meet a dire emergency, although — as usual — the tax continued long after the emergency had ceased. This was the *Danegeld*, first levied in 991 to finance defense against the renewed Danish threat, although Ethelrede the Redeless used the money to buy off the Danes. His successors continued to call for the money, setting the amount at a flat 12d. per *hide* of land.[5] It is interesting to note that Anglo-Saxon kingship, whatever its vicissitudes, never surrendered this "temporary" tax.

All money received by the king belonged to him personally, and he was not accountable to anyone for it. There was a sort of rudimentary royal treasury, where a certain technique known as "blanching" (and that is about all that is known about it) kept some semblance of order in royal financial records.

It has been argued that the development of Anglo-Saxon kingship was retarded by the lack of a large trained civil service. What might be termed public administration was largely in the hands of ecclesiastics, as it was later in Norman and Angevin times. The effort of Alfred to introduce a lay element into it was not continued by his successors, and in any case the employment of the clergy for this purpose was inevitable at a time when so few people outside the Church were literate. In general, Saxon clergy, particularly toward the end of the period, and the administrative techniques of the Anglo-Saxon central government, could not compare in efficiency with their Norman and Angevin successors.

After the interlude of the Danish dynasty of 1017 to 1042, Anglo-Saxon kingship declined sharply because of the weak personality of Edward the Confessor and the growing power of the *earls*, once *ealdormen*, heading one or more shires. Cnut, for greater administrative efficiency, had grouped all shires into four earldoms, each under a powerful earl. He had kept these earls in strict subordination, but his weaker successors had permitted them to challenge the crown. The challenge reached its height during the reign of Edward the Confessor, when the Godwin family interest held all four earldoms and defied the crown.[6]

---

[5] Anglo-Saxon land measurements were little more precise than their public administration and varied with localities, so that a hide was usually 100 to 120 acres, depending upon particular local custom. A unit of both size and type of land, but scarcely more accurate, was the *carucate*, about 100 acres of plowed land.

[6] The title of "earl," indicating the noble head of a district, should not be confused with the social rank of "eorl," or noble. Although the official title would appear derived from the social designation, actually "earl" comes from the Danish "jarl," having nearly the same meaning as "ealdorman." After the Norman Conquest "earl" lost its official connotation to become a rank of the nobility.

His successor, Harold, although head of the Godwin family, found his royal authority challenged by these earls. Whether kingship would have surmounted this challenge is problematical. Certainly, in its later days Anglo-Saxon kingship failed to measure up to its potentialities or to continue its earlier promise.

The Witan, the other part of the central government, appeared after the Anglo-Saxon invasions of England. As tribes developed into kingdoms, the full meeting of all freemen became impractical, although the theory remained that any freeman might approach the king with advice. That the Witan was the descendant and remnant of the older full tribal council is also unlikely. The tribal council had been self-selective, that is, all freemen who wished might attend, but this was no longer the case with the Witan. It is possible that the tribal council continued to exist for a time in England, but that the king named a smaller and more wieldy body to replace it.

It is a mistake to regard the Witan as a counterpart of the Parliament of later times, or as the original source from which Parliament sprang. Neither view is now accepted. Unlike Parliament, the Witan was not a representative body; its members represented nobody but themselves. And it had no elective principle, its fluctuating membership being named by the king for each meeting. The origins of Parliament, as we shall see, lie elsewhere.

In theory the king named Witan members, and a summons to one meeting did not entitle its recipient to a future one. In practice, however, the king was far from having complete freedom in his selections. He could hardly avoid summoning great men of the realm, and after the conversion of the Anglo-Saxons to Christianity, he also felt compelled to summon the great prelates because of their greater learning and also because the Witan dealt in ecclesiastical as well as secular affairs. Certain officials were necessarily present in their administrative capacities, and other male members of the royal family would also be there. Thus the king had real freedom of summons only for persons other than those noted above. It was these "nonofficial" persons who received the occasional summons, and their influence must have been slight in comparison with that of the more permanent members.

The functions of the Witan cannot be precisely defined. It was not a legislature; the Anglo-Saxons lacked the concept of legislation. It had judicial functions but not of an appellate nature; Anglo-Saxon law did not provide for appeals. The Witan acted judicially when cases involved great persons, but its jurisdiction as to subject (*res*) and its procedures in reaching a decision were precisely the same as those in other courts. The Witan had an elective function in naming the king, although, as we have seen, this function might be more nominal than real. It could similarly depose the king, but this was rare and usually in response to outside pressure.

The basic duty of the Witan was advisory. Here we encounter a difficulty inherent in the Anglo-Saxon constitution. The king consulted his councillors on many important matters. Whether in practice it was their advice he sought, or rather their ratification of decisions he had already made, we do not know; nor whether if they offered advice, the king was under any obligation to accept it. They approved the radical innovation of the Danegeld, though this does not mean that they had any financial power; they were consulted on military projects, relationships with foreign powers, the prosecution of traitors. But the occasions on which members of the Witan opposed royal policy must have been rare. All, in theory at least, owed their seats to the king, and it was the king who decided what questions should be submitted to them. It seems most likely that under a strong monarch fear or respect must have made the Witan fairly subservient to his wishes; on the other hand there were members whose standing and importance in the country were such that a weak king could not have afforded to ignore whatever advice they might have offered.

The two major components of central government were neither particularly strong nor particularly efficient, and it is not at all surprising that Anglo-Saxon institutions of central government failed to survive the Norman Conquest. The lack of a permanent seat of government has been suggested as a possible explanation of governmental weakness. Although Winchester had a special status as the location of the permanent treasury, the central government was wherever the king happened to be at the time. Not until long after the Norman Conquest did London become the capital. But this in itself is significant, for the want of such a permanent seat of government did not prevent the Normans and Angevins from building a strong central administration. There was in fact no need for a permanent capital until government had amassed enough filing cabinets to require one.

Anglo-Saxon central government contributed little to the later constitution, and then only indirectly and by routes so devious that later forms of central government and procedures owe little to any particular Anglo-Saxon source. It was in local government that the Anglo-Saxons were most active; this was their most important contribution to the political development of England. Their work in this field survived the Norman Conquest with very little change.

The Landed Basis of Local Government

One reason the system of local government survived the Conquest is that beforehand there had been remarkably little connection with the central government; on the local level the events of 1066 did not make very much difference. Local government, based firmly on Anglo-Saxon land law, proved itself both efficient and durable. Its influence on the emerging constitution, moreover, was not only at the level of local administration; it was also a source for certain later developments in central government, notably for the initiation of Parliament.

Individual land possession in Anglo-Saxon England was permanent. The violent dispossession of the Celts placed more land at the disposal of the Anglo-Saxons than they had ever known. This apparent abundance of land meant that in England the annual redistribution of land ceased, with the result that possession took on a different meaning, without however developing into the conception of full ownership. The lack of a precise concept of land ownership meant that the law of ownership for everything else was similarly hazy.

Cultivation was by the strip system, each person holding individual strips within larger fields, usually rotating with the same crops on either a two- or three-field basis. Forest land, pasturage, and water rights were used by the community generally. Strip-holding was not ownership, but because such holding was far more than mere temporary possession two types of land titles developed.

Folkland was the earlier type. There are very few references to this type of possession in the written records, and scholars have long disputed the exact meaning of the word. But it seems most likely that folkland meant land held according to custom. Thus everyone in the village knew that Ethelwulf's father had tilled a particular strip, so had his grandfather; and as far as anyone knew, the family of Ethelwulf had always farmed that particular piece of land. Thus the title by which Ethelwulf was now holding it was registered in the memories of people, the folk, and so its formal title of folkland. Ethelwulf did not own his land; ownership lay in the community as proven by his inability to part with any part of it, that is *alienate* it, without community consent, thereby indicating its ultimate owner. Thus folkland could not meet the criterion of full, or *allodial*, ownership of free alienation, which oddly enough cannot be tested until something is passed by its possessor to another.

Bookland was a later and much more sophisticated title. It came to the Anglo-Saxons with their conversion to Christianity by the monks, who also taught them the Roman method of conveyancing land by a written charter. The recipient of such a charter held his land by this written grant, often from the king. The chief beneficiaries of bookland were the Church (including its monastic foundations) and the great lords. It is obvious that the ability to grant land by charter had at least implications of ownership on the part of the grantor; but they remained implications. His associates, a segment of the community, had to approve his grant by charter — the Witan for the king, and the shire and hundred courts for grants by lesser men. Special witnesses, individually or in groups, observed the formal transfer of land, either as continuing folkland or as folkland conveyed by charter and so transformed into bookland. Their oaths on land transfers were incontrovertible. They were witnesses, however, only in a notarial or registry sense, and were not witnesses in the sense of giving testimony. Whenever folkland became bookland, all folkland titles in it were in the event of any dispute about land possession cast into doubt by the superior bookland title. In most instances where folkland became bookland, the people most immediately affected were not consulted.

The bookland holder had several advantages over the folkland possessor. The main one was that once land was held by bookland, its subsequent alienation, by whatever means, did not require the consent of the community. This loss by the community of control over the land was, as will be seen, a major reason why certain older communal courts lost out to manorial courts. If any dispute arose as to which party had the better right to a certain parcel of land, the man producing a charter had the advantage. Obviously the bookland holder could defeat the rights of his own heir by both real and artificial grants outside his family, such as to monasteries. Yet even bookland had its limitations in alienation.

The ability to alienate land determines the extent to which its possessor is its owner. The allodial owner can part with his land *freely* and *unconditionally;* his ownership is called *fee simple*, first of land and later of anything. The Anglo-Saxons never had this full ownership, though they came near to it at times. The folkland holder was more closely checked than the bookland possessor, who in practice was often able to alienate freely. But neither folkland nor bookland could meet the next part of the fee simple test — to alienate unconditionally. Both folkland and bookland could be alienated only for the length of three generations, when the land returned to the original line of descent. Whether from folkland or bookland, alienated land was only on loan, making it *laenland*.

Laenland had superficial resemblances to later feudal subordinate land holdings. However, there was actually little real similarity. Bookland was one type of laenland, which even if freely granted by its holder, by pure logic and law should return in time to the original line of descent of the grantor. In practice, of course, such pure logic was asking rather too much from the Anglo-Saxons. Whatever the original theory about bookland, its holders tended to retain their possession of it. This must have happened to most laenland, whether from folkland or bookland, by oral agreement or written charter. The return of the land, or *reversion* to the original line, at the end of three generations, must have been most difficult to enforce if only because in the course of so long a period the original transaction must often have been forgotten. It was not only difficult but impossible if the recipient were the Church or one of its corporations, because these had no generations but were perpetual.

Laenland was usually given by the grantor for previous services by the grantee, and it was hoped, but not demanded, that similar services would be performed in the future. During the reconquest of the Danelaw, Wessex kings rewarded their followers in this manner. The Church received large grants for its prayers. All this seems to hint of later feudal practice, but a closer examination shows that laenland was very far from being an Anglo-Saxon feudalism. The grantor of laenland could not *demand* services in the future, whereas feudal grants were couched solely in terms of the future performance of precise duties, even though the grant itself might be a reward for past services. Another difference, which seems theoretical but which was very real to persons who knew both systems, was the treatment of obligations, *servitudes*, on the land. The recipient of laenland took over these obligations, vested in the land regardless of its extent and type. Both grantor and grantee knew these servitudes, and neither could vary them. Obligations if owed, were to the land, possibly the community, but

definitely not to the person of the grantor. Thus if Cedric conveyed
some of his holdings as laenland to Athelstane, Cedric was obligated for
the duties of a smaller area, while Athelstane took over the obligations
on the land he received. This is in great contrast to feudalism where the
grantor, regardless of the amount of his grant to another, was still
responsible for the same amount of service as prior to the grant. Finally,
laenland grants presumed no neat pyramid of downward flowing
alienation and upward moving obligations. This theory was possible
only when feudalism declared the king the owner of all land. Without
such a theory, the pyramid was impossible to construct in Anglo-Saxon
England. These distinctions between laenland and feudal grants may
seem unreal, but to people who knew about both systems they were
both real and important.

The *trinoda necessitas* rested on all land. The Normans continued
these obligations for the repair of bridges and later the upkeep of roads
(or payment of the commutation of *brycgbot*), for the maintenance of
local fortifications (commuted by paying *burghbot*), and for service
in the national militia, *fyrd-fare*. These duties were servitudes on all
land, regardless of its particular title or holder, who, therefore, had to
assume them. All of them were what could be termed "community"
duties, not personal ones.

The manorial system grew from bookland grants. It was simultaneously a method of agriculture, a social institution, and a system of
government, and its last two aspects make it a part of English constitutional history. Here the most crucial aspect of the bookland charter
was that it bestowed upon the recipient the rights of *sac* and *soc* over
his land, that is, jurisdiction over the people on the land and the right
to summon them to his private court. This did not mean that the
grantee sat in judgment; the manorial court like all others was an assembly court with the lord of the manor (or his steward) merely presiding. The important thing was that judicial revenues went to the
lord. When, as increasingly occurred, these manorial courts had a territorial and personal jurisdiction concurrent with those of the older
communal hundred courts, the latter disappeared into the court of the
manor, a process which in turn accelerated the decline in social status
of people whose folkland holdings were subordinated to the bookland
charter of a greater man. The bookland holder permitted the folkland
occupier to retain his holding *if* he performed services for him, including the cultivation of the lord's own land, both regularly, *week*

work, and additionally at seeding and harvest, *boon work*. The manorial lord was also entitled to a share of the crops produced by the folkland occupiers. Thus in the manorial system it was usual for two men to hold the same land by different titles. Athelstane, the cultivator, held his strip by the older customary folkland title. Cedric, his lord, held the same plot as part of his larger manorial grant in bookland.

Although two titles governed the possession of the same piece of land, inevitably the rights of the customary one declined before those of bookland. In a society where personal status and landholding were ultimately related, the man who held by something less than a free title became less than free himself. Although only one of the reasons for the increase of servile persons during the latter Anglo-Saxon period, this growth of the manorial system via bookland grants was probably the most important of them.

The manorial system which had been emerging in England for many generations before the Norman Conquest, again seems to be an incipient feudalism, but again the similarity is superficial. Manorialism was a land organization and a system of government for servile lands and servile persons. Feudalism was interested only in free tenures and people. The fact that they co-existed after 1066 indicates there was a real separation between manorial and feudal arrangements, and contemporaries had no difficulty in distinguishing between them.

The Social Basis of Local Government

The Anglo-Saxon land system, including the manorial system, determined not only the forms of local government but also the whole structure of society and the relationships between classes. These changed drastically with the Anglo-Saxon invasions of England, particularly among the lower social groups.

The slave class, never large among the Anglo-Saxons, declined rapidly after the invasions. Constant warfare and the rapid slaughter of freemen meant that slaves were needed as fighting men, and so they ceased to be slaves. The apparently unlimited supply of land also meant that a slave who had been armed to fight could be rewarded with land by his chief, thereby removing him still further from his old status. Celts remaining in the southeastern plain region were sometimes enslaved, as well as prisoners from other Anglo-Saxon tribes. But even this indigenous slave class did not last long, because after the conversion the Church persuaded the Anglo-Saxons that manumission was a good work. The Church also declared free all slaves who entered the clergy. Although masters' permission was required, it was usually forthcoming under the teaching of the Church that this, too, was a good work. All the evidence suggests that the truly slave class was at its largest during the invasions but declined quite rapidly afterwards.[7] A *theow*, or *esnas*, was originally a chattel, without oath or land. Injuries to him required payment to his master as damages to his property. After the Anglo-Saxon conversion the Church established the point that a slave had a soul, and slave-killing resulted in the payment by the slayer not of wergeld but of *manwryth*, of lesser amount, to his family. When this principle entered the law, the slave was something more than a chattel. Most slaves were born in their status, but freemen convicted of certain crimes might be made slaves or could suffer the same fate if they did not make payments ordered by a court, which declared them *wite-theows*. Any person could sell himself at thirteen, or his children at seven, into slavery, though the Church frowned on this practice.

Freemen with folkland titles overridden by superior bookland grants sank in social status to become *serfs*. When bookland grants gave private jurisdiction to manorial lords, the transition from freeman to serf was even more rapid, and the freeman on a manor saw its court absorb his older hundred court and so further depress his status. The supply of land was not in fact inexhaustible, moreover, and there were landless men upon whom society looked with the gravest suspicion. If Cedric had land, he could be made to conform to communal opinion, as expressed in the decisions of the local assembly, which might deprive him of his holding. Such a threat meant nothing to Edwig, who as a *laet* was landless. Edwig's kind constituted a potential threat to social order. Therefore, society required such men to have a landed man to guarantee their behavior and to produce them in court if summoned; in short to be their guarantor, or *borh*. A law of Edgar the Peaceful ordering all laets to have borhs, whose own land was the actual pledge for the laet's proper behavior, also required services of them in return for this guarantee. A series of involved relations binding laets to borhs

---

[7] Although the Domesday Survey of 1086, after the Norman Conquest, listed 25,000 persons — about one-eleventh of the estimated total population — as *servi*, as used in the surveys this Latin word included a variety of men who were less than fully free. Other evidence shows that slaves in the true sense of chattels were by this time negligible.

reduced the former to serf status — a process which was even more rapid when the borh was also the lord of a manor with private jurisdiction.

The practice of *commendation* also tended to reduce the ranks of the genuine freemen. In times of disorder individual freemen commended themselves to a protector, a *hlaford* (soon to become "lord"), who in turn demanded certain menial services. This practice grew during the Danish threat until finally Wessex kings ordered that every man not himself a hlaford should have one. If the individual freeman did not make a selection, his family was to do it for him. Thus public law forced many freemen down. Commendation may look like a simple feudalism again, but the vast gulf between manorialism and feudalism lay in the requirement of the former of *menial* service — week work, boon work, crop-sharing — in contrast to the honorable services demanded by the latter. With both hlaford and borh systems in operation it was natural to combine their functions in the same man, logically the lord of the manor where the former freemen lived. With such pressures being brought to bear upon him, a freeman might survive for a time, but within a generation or so he was likely to fall into serfdom.

Serfs did have certain legal rights. They were not chattels to be sold apart from the land, but they were bound to it. Their oaths either had small value or were not permitted. Wrongs done them required smaller payments than those done to freemen. Yet so long as they performed their required duties they could not be dispossessed of their holdings — at least legally.

A freeman, a *ceorl*, held in a completely free manner at least one hide of land. He had full political and legal rights, including that of participation in assemblies. The number of freemen, however, was probably at its highest during the first four centuries following the Anglo-Saxon invasions of England. Thereafter, particularly during and after the Danish invasions, the number declined, and those remaining in this class did not fully exercise their political rights, preferring to have other men represent them in the courts. By the time of the Norman Conquest many English freemen had been reduced by political and economic insecurity to servitude.

The nobility, or *eorl* class, was partly hereditary, but far from being a closed group. Any ceorl holding five hides of land became an eorl. Certain posts ex-officio gave their holders noble status, and apparently this status continued regardless of whether they remained in office. The most important of these offices was that of the *ealdorman*, who was in charge of a shire. By the tenth century, however, custom required an ealdorman to possess forty hides of land, thereby ensuring his being an eorl prior to appointment. Other offices, the possession of which had once meant acquisition of noble status, increasingly went to men who were nobles already.

The obvious relationship between landholding and social position did not apply so immediately to other elements of the nobility. Any merchant who crossed the sea [8] three times at his own expense became a noble. In a subsistence agrarian economy the number of such nobles could not have been large. More important was a nobility of service, a direct reflection of the rise of kingship. After the initial battles a member of the chief's comitatus became the *gesith*, the companion of the king; and this relationship made the gesith a noble. Rewards of land for past services then reinforced his noble position. Later in the period, the gesith became the *thegn*, who had the same personal relationship with the king and had received a grant of land in return for his services. However, in order to be "thegnworthy," that is, capable of being created one, a man had to possess five hides of land, which meant that he was already a noble. Thegns performed services ordinarily menial but now honorable in that they were for the king, who had *dish-thegns*, *bower-thegns*, and *horse-thegns*. The decline of kingship can be seen in the claims of bishops and ealdormen that persons performing similar services for them were also thegns.

There was another type of noble, the *atheling*, a male member of the immediate royal family, and therefore of the eorl class. It was possible, certainly if he were young, that he might not hold any land. Whether his noble status passed to his children is uncertain.

The high veneration accorded the clergy by the Anglo-Saxons made them consider parish priests as "thegnworthy," and rank bishops with athelings. Beyond mere veneration was the fact that the upper clergy received broad acres to support their dignity.

In contrast to the Anglo-Saxon Continental nobility, that in England had special rights over ordinary freemen. Noble oaths carried more weight; their personal injuries required higher payments. These differences reflected the rise of the eorl class with the Danish wars, the manorial system, and the hlaford and borh organizations. During the

[8] Apparently the North Sea and not the English Channel.

reconquest of the Danelaw the nobility benefited from large bookland grants made by royal charters of the most recently annexed portions. By the close of the Anglo-Saxon period the nobility had extended its holdings, reduced the status of many freemen to serfs, and was challenging the crown. The results for the government system were most obvious in the central administration, but they also appeared on the local level.

Local Government

The three major divisions of Anglo-Saxon local government in ascending order were: tun, hundred, and shire. The last, after the Norman Conquest, became the county, although the older term was and still is in general usage.[9] There were also a few boroughs, none of great importance in the government of an essentially rural society. The names and functions of these units varied from time to time, and from place to place.

The tun, or town, was in no sense an urban center. Urban areas were very rare in Anglo-Saxon England and were called boroughs. The nearest modern approximation to the tun is perhaps the New England town, or township. Probably each tun had its own meeting, or *moot*, although there is some disagreement on this point. Often called a court, this moot dealt with all types of local public business, and its judicial duties were little more than police functions. The court named the *tun-reeve*, a quasi-executive officer, who with four other freemen originally represented the tun, *not* at the hundred court, as might be expected, but at the *shire* moot, and only later at both courts. The tun court does not seem to have been particularly active, despite the formal requirement that all tun freemen should attend. This and the smallness of its area of concern made it one of the first courts to be absorbed in private manorial jurisdiction.

The origins of the hundred are extremely obscure and it appears to have emerged, at least in the form in which we know it, comparatively late in the period. In England it was always a territorial designation,

[9] Omitted here is the unit of the vill, which although as ancient and durable as the major three units, was not as important. Smaller than the tun, the vill was essentially the village community. As an administrative unit it was being used as late as the Angevins, Henry II (1154–89) specifically basing part of the presentment jury system upon it (below, p. 109). It was, however, not as vital an organ of Anglo-Saxon local government as the three cited here. See also above, p. 7, note 3.

possibly referring originally to a unit of 100 hides, though as time went on the hundred came to vary considerably in size. Those areas in the south and southeast of the country first conquered by the Anglo-Saxons had more hundreds, and with greater population density, than the later subjugated and more sparsely settled regions of the west and north. The occupation of eastern England by the Danes appears to have left this unit intact, and it was known by the Danes as the *wapentake*. After the recovery of the Danelaw, the laws of Edgar the Peaceful recognized that "hundred" and "wapentake" were synonymous. These territorial units formed the basis of the administration of public justice and the control of public finance throughout most of the country.

Where there were a large number of hundreds in a shire, they might be grouped into larger units. Kentish hundreds were in six *laethes*, a Jute word derived from "lething," a military force, indicating that at one time these laethes were territorial subdivisions of the national forces. Sussex grouped its 61 hundreds into six *rapes*, a Saxon word with the same meaning. Yorkshire and Lincolnshire, once part of the Danelaw, organized their wapentakes into three groups, *trithings*, later corrupted to "ridings." Where such units were superimposed over hundreds (or wapentakes) the larger units took on functions normally belonging to their component hundreds. However, since these larger groupings were infrequent, the term "hundred" is used here to describe units with different names, occasionally with different composition, but all having about the same functions.

Each hundred had a moot composed originally of all freemen who met monthly (by lunar calculation). This assembly dealt with all affairs of the hundred, including ecclesiastical matters, with each freeman having an equal voice, *not* vote. No formal vote was taken; instead a consensus was reached by discussion. The hundred court selected the hundred man, who had some executive duties. Originally he presided at the monthly meetings; but as the shadows of manorial jurisdiction fell on the court, the steward of the manorial lord began to replace him. When this happened, the hundred court was on its way toward being absorbed into the manor court, particularly when the steward collected judicial revenues for his employer. When the hundred court dealt with ecclesiastical matters, the local parish priest presided to explain the law of the Church; but the assembly reached decisions in the same manner as for secular business.

Although all freemen could attend the hundred court, and may originally have done so, by the reign of Edgar the Peaceful laws were needed to order the presence at the hundred court of all lords, or their stewards, having manors within the hundred, the parish priest, and four men named by each tun moot. While these laws did not formally absolve other persons from attendance, they indicate that many freeman were not attending the court. The growing practice of naming twelve of its number to exercise all its powers between monthly meetings further reduced participation in the hundred court, because the natural tendency was for this group to become identical with that required to attend the moot. Thus the affairs of the hundred tended in the course of time to fall into the hands of a few men.

The hundred court enjoyed a certain amount of independence of any superior authority, even though theoretically it was supposed to report all of its actions to the shire ealdorman or the shire reeve. The frequent meetings of several hundreds within a shire often precluded either such reports to, or close supervision by, these officials. The king's interest in the hundred court ended with his receiving the portion of its judicial revenues to which he was entitled; but lacking effective supervisory agents, the king probably often failed to collect all that was due to him. Royal collection agents might sometimes visit the hundred courts, but so rarely and haphazardly that their efforts were of little avail.

The hundred court members handled judicial questions, no distinction being made between civil and criminal matters. They witnessed transfers of folkland title and gave community approval to granting folkland by charter and so transforming it into bookland. While in session the court had its own "peace" for members and litigants, which usually covered their travel time to and from the assembly. The efficacy of this peace, lower than that of the king's, depended upon the willingness and ability of the hundred court to enforce it. The same limitation applied to the power of the hundred court to assess and collect fines from people ignoring its summons. Still another function of the court was to enroll all adult males in *tithings*, groups of ten to twelve men collectively responsible for each other's conduct and appearance in court when summoned. The sheriff, or shire reeve, on his own circuit, or *tourn*, through the shire met with the several hundred courts to verify this enrollment in his *view of the frankpledge*. When the Normans made the sheriff more powerful, the frankpledge system came to have real strength.

The hundred was also a unit for the collection of revenue. The king was entitled to wites from its court's fines. The hundred moot saw that the obligations of the *trinoda necessitas* were met and collected monetary commutations of them. Ethelrede the Redeless (978–1016) grouped all hundreds into units of three, each to supply a ship to fight the Danes. Curiously enough these were not collection units for the Danegeld, which was collected at the shire moot by the sheriff.[10]

It is not known just how or when the shire system developed in England, but it was evidently a creation of the Anglo-Saxons after their conquest, for there is no Continental counterpart for it. Wessex had been divided into shires before the end of the eighth century and by the eleventh century all England south of the river Tees was divided into these administrative units. Some of the shires, like Kent or Suffolk, were former kingdoms, ancient territorial divisions. In Wessex a group of shires emerged around particular towns, Dorsetshire centering on Dorchester, Wiltshire on Wilton. In the midlands, many of the shires were based on the areas occupied by the various Danish armies. With the reconquest of the Danelaw, the former headquarters of the Danish forces became the shire capital and gave its name to the whole—Leicester, Derby, Nottingham, for instance. In the west midlands some of the shires, like Shropshire and Warwickshire, seem to have been artificially created by a king powerful enough to overrule traditional boundaries and local feeling. In all these districts the shire capitals assumed a special importance, as military, administrative, and judicial centers, seats of the shire courts presided over by the king's representatives. In the far north, it was not until Norman times that the divisions into shires occurred: Durham, Northumberland, and Cumberland were special areas for military defense.

Shire administration was shared unequally by the *ealdorman* and the shire reeve, the *sheriff*, with the bishop of the diocese participating in matters concerning the Church. The shire reeve arrived late on the scene, but in the end pushed out all rival authorities. Originally much of the work had fallen to the ealdorman, usually an appointee of the central government, although there is some evidence to suggest that occasionally the shire courts presented their own nominees for the approval of the central government. Normally, however, the king and

---

[10] The collection of the Danegeld at the shire level was possibly a royal recognition that the hundred was not very efficient as a revenue-producing unit.

Witan jointly named him. His official role in the shire gave to the ealdorman, who was frequently a noble at the time of his appointment and a member of the Witan, high social standing. Burglarizing his home required the same compensation, *burgbryce*, as breaking into the house of the bishop himself. The fine was much higher than for breaking and entering the homes of ordinary noblemen — to whose houses prudent burglars no doubt turned their attention. In the early days the ealdorman commanded his shire section of the fyrd and presided at its shire moot, receiving a third of its judicial revenues; generally, the ealdorman was responsible for the administration of his shire, where the central government gave him a fairly free hand.

It might be thought that as the ealdorman sat in the Witan and the shire courts he would have been an invaluable agent of the central administration. But the ealdorman's prior noble status, together with a series of weak rulers in the later Anglo-Saxon period, made him less effective in controlling local affairs than the central government could have wished. Often the ealdorman operated as a free agent and increasingly held his office on an hereditary basis. This hereditary principle appeared early in the Anglo-Saxon period when the royal family of a recently extinguished kingdom was allowed to remain as ealdormen of the shire. The hereditary principle became stronger with the reconquest of the Danelaw, when there was a need for experienced administrators with military talent to run the new territories. Such men were able to wield much power with a central government dependent upon their abilities.

During the reign of Ethelrede the Redeless great ealdormen flouted the royal wishes. Cnut restored them briefly to subordination, dividing the realm into four major districts for greater efficiency, each headed by an *earl*, the Saxon equivalent of the Danish "jarl," who was therefore administrator of an earldom. However, Cnut's successors were unable to cope with these officials, who by the time of Edward the Confessor were again openly defying the crown. Thus the office of ealdorman, or earl, was more of a hindrance than a help to the central government in its attempts to keep control over local affairs.

It was the very power of the ealdorman that eventually was to lead to his replacement by the royal sheriff. The process began when a great ealdorman, in charge of several shires, delegated certain of his functions to the sheriff in each of them. Thereafter, central government control over local matters came to be exercised by the sheriff, who gradually assumed most of the ealdorman's duties, including that of presiding at the shire court.

The shire court, less active than the hundred court, met only twice a year. Both administrative and judicial matters were handled by it without differentiation in procedure. If ecclesiastical questions came before the court, which like the hundred court was competent to consider them, the bishop presided to explain Church law and so guide the members. The bishop retained his functions in the shire court until after the Norman Conquest, when William I (1066–87) ordered that all ecclesiastical issues be handled by separate Church courts. Regardless of the official presiding at the shire moot, it was not he but the assembly which made the decisions, again by consensus.

Composed in theory of all freemen of the shire, the shire court, even with its fewer meetings, must have been an irksome duty to many men, who did not wish to travel or to assume duties above those imposed by their frequent attendance at their hundred court. In a systematic organization of government, the various hundred courts of a shire would have sent representatives to its moot, but Anglo-Saxon government was not hierarchical. The representative element at the shire moot was the reeve and four men from the tuns. The requirement that all nobles of the shire attend must have been impossible to enforce. Certainly, the mass of freemen sought to avoid attendance at a court which dealt with the same type of matters as their local hundred court.

For people accustomed to "systematic" notions of government this duplication may be difficult to understand, but it was something the Anglo-Saxons took for granted. They regarded the shire and its component hundreds as co-ordinate and concurrent in all things. Whether an issue came before hundred or shire court depended upon the rank of the particular persons concerned. The greater their importance, the more likely that the matter would come before the shire court, but no decision of the latter could direct or determine the activities of the hundred court. Nor did the shire court have appellate review of hundred court decisions. In practice, however, great people were less inclined to accept decisions of the hundred court, because it had fewer resources with which to enforce them.

If an individual asked the hundred court three times to hear his case without success, he might then bring it before the shire court, which was presumably better able to enforce attendance and compliance by the other party. If even with its greater resources the shire court were powerless, the aggrieved person could go to the Witan and the king, who were in an even stronger position to compel the other party to attend upon them for the disposition of the case. This custom might seem to regularize the various courts' jurisdictions, but undoubtedly many cases came before the shire court or even before the Witan and the king without invoking this procedure. Certainly, this was no crude appellate system, because the essential element of any appeal — prior decision by a lower court — was lacking. On the contrary, it was because a lower court, for one reason or another, had not heard a case that it came before a court of a larger territorial unit.

The manorial system may be traced back to the gifts of land by the king to his followers. Later, bookland grants transferred not so much land as the right of the lord to exact dues and services from the local peasantry which had previously gone to the king. It was not until the establishment of manorial courts, however, that the system began to have important consequences for local government. Manorial grants were sometimes on such a scale that whole tuns, or even whole hundreds, were included in them. By the time of the Norman Conquest the political and economic functions of the manor were thoroughly established, and the private jurisdiction of the manorial courts had supplanted many hundred courts altogether and sapped the vigor of others. After the Conquest, the feudal and manorial systems existed side by side, two quite distinct and unrelated forms of social organization.

Even when a particular manor did not include all of a tun or hundred, it often embraced so much land that many people found themselves obligated to attend at three courts: tun, hundred, and manor. Such a burden forced the individual freeman to choose one of them, and inevitably the choice was the manorial court, since absence from it might result in the loss of his holding within the manor. The gradual confusion of free holdings, both in and out of the manor, with the unfree holdings within it, meant that freemen increasingly found that all of their land within a manor was considered unfree and they along with it. When this stage was reached, freemen had no choice — they had to attend the manorial court.

The change, however, may seem larger than it actually was from the point of view of local government. It is true that the tendency for a man to decline to servile status within a manor gave to its court a different character from the tun and hundred moots of freemen. But private manorial jurisdiction did not have a different procedure or jurisdiction from the older "public" courts. It did not mean that a manorial lord sat in judgment. He or his agent merely presided over a moot composed of all persons on the manor, and they made decisions in the same way as in any Anglo-Saxon assembly court. But it did mean that judicial revenues, previously retained by the community, now went into private hands. The income from these revenues, rather than control over the court's decisions, made it important to the manorial lord. On the other hand, it may be doubted that servile tenants, whose holdings practically depended upon the will of the lord, were as independent in reaching decisions as freeholders in a public court. The manorial courts moreover reduced the resources of the crown, inasmuch as wites often went to the lord instead of the king. Ealdormen, who as great nobles held large manors, benefited from this diversion of funds, which swelled their revenues beyond their third of the judicial revenues of the shire. The manor courts endured throughout many centuries of English history. Their power gradually diminished from the fourteenth century onwards, but it was not until 1926 that manorial rights, long since dead in reality, were formally abolished.

It may be said that organized town-planning began during the Danish wars, although important boroughs such as Canterbury, Rochester, and London had existed for a long time before then. The growth of trade would also no doubt have led in due course to the creation of more English boroughs, but as it was the majority owed their existence to military necessities. During the reconquest of the Danelaw by the Wessex kings more strategic points were fortified. In the comparative security of these defensive positions, commercial activities could be carried on. As well as being a military and trading center, however, the borough remained an agricultural unit, lacking many of the characteristics of urban life we would expect to find in later times. The king retained a close interest in the boroughs, which very often were his own creation. He received rents and services from the inhabitants and most of the burgesses were his men. In time these centers separated from the other units of local government, the shire and hundred councils. They acquired courts of their own, and their merchants elected a *port reeve* (*port* meant originally a market town), with general supervisory powers over trade. Long before London became the political capital it was regarded as quite independent of nearby shires and hundreds. Its size, the volume of its trade, and the part it played as the center of resistance to the Danes set it apart from other boroughs and gave its citizens a feeling of special responsibility. The freemen of the city, largely merchants, joined the Witan in naming the king, and, indeed, on more than one occasion claimed the nominations as their own exclusive right. William the Conqueror, after entering the city, thought it wise to confirm its privileges. Though it was to be some time before the conception of a national capital arose, London was already in the Anglo-Saxon period assuming a position which would later make it a natural choice.

The Sheriff

One of the most important offices developed by the Anglo-Saxons was that of the sheriff, who became the king's chief executive agent in the shires. At first the minor of the two links between central and local government, his importance grew steadily at the expense of the ealdorman. After the Norman Conquest the encouragement of strong monarchs accelerated the process.

The sheriff was the personal servant of the king, a man usually of the freeman class or belonging to the lower nobility. His office was the creation of the Anglo-Saxons in England and did not exist among them on the Continent, though the Normans had similar officials known as the *vicomes*, who were created to meet similar needs and appeared at about the same time. The origins of the English office are very obscure.[11] The great lords needed agents, stewards, or reeves to supervise their manorial administration and the king likewise had reeves for this purpose. Between the lord, or king, and his reeve there was thus the personal, private relationship of employer and employee; and the office retained this characteristic long after the sheriff was immersed in public duties. As the king's personal steward the reeve had general responsibility for the king's *personal*, rather than public, interests in each shire. He supervised the efficient working of royal manors, collected royal rents, and did anything else his employer ordered.

[11] The *shirman* mentioned in the laws of the mysterious Ine of Wessex was less likely the sheriff than the ealdorman, still actively heading the shire at this time, the late seventh century.

With the extension of his public duties, the sheriff assumed the position formerly occupied by the ealdorman. In the late tenth century, the growing power and independence of the ealdormen, who might be in charge of several shires, made it both more convenient for themselves that they should delegate certain of their functions to the sheriffs, and also very much to the advantage of the king that their duties should be transferred to his own personal servants, who would be more dependable and loyal. Their importance grew, but not to the extent that they could ever break free from royal control. Unlike the ealdorman, a great noble in his own right, the sheriff's fortunes were dependent upon the king. While the ealdorman increasingly made good his claim for hereditary succession to office, the sheriff never put forward such a demand until after the Norman Conquest, and then without success.

It was through the sheriffs that the king could most effectively assert his authority in the shires. But even when the power of the monarch declined, the sheriff remained an important figure. By the close of the Anglo-Saxon period he was collecting all revenues due the king from the shire. Money from royal estates, wites, Danegeld, and fines for breaking the king's peace — all went into his hands for transmission to his royal employer. There is evidence that in these payments the Anglo-Saxon sheriff had his *ferm*, or farm, the lump-sum payment of post-Norman Conquest times.

Gradually the ealdorman's duties of leading the shire levy and presiding at its moot passed to the sheriff, often with the approval of the ealdorman, who was thus spared certain burdensome responsibilities while at the same time retaining his right to one-third of the shire's judicial revenues — the famous third penny. It was the sheriff, not the ealdorman, who on his tourn through the shire met the hundred courts to check the enrollment of all adult males in tithings. With this growth of the sheriff's power, his continued personal relations with the king, plus the increasing inability of the king to control the ealdorman, it was natural that the central government should have seized upon this personal official as the important link between itself and local administration. These developments were not complete during the Anglo-Saxon period, and the full flowering of the sheriff's office belongs to Norman times. But even before then, the Anglo-Saxon sheriff was receiving royal instructions to keep a special eye on violations of the king's peace, both for reasons of internal order and for the revenue accruing to the king from special fines. As presiding officer at the shire moot the sheriff was in a good position to note these violations, as well as to ensure that all wites from other fines went to the crown. The king quickly appreciated that the sheriff could keep him informed on local affairs generally. His reports would be more complete and more accurate than those of the ealdorman, who was sometimes remote from local affairs or might well have reasons for concealing the truth about them. The Anglo-Saxon sheriff, the agent of royal administration, was not a great lord with whom the ordinary person hardly ever came in contact, but an ordinary man himself, an official who might be approached at any time. Had there been stronger monarchs in the later Anglo-Saxon period, the sheriff might have assumed the full powers he was to acquire in Norman and Angevin times. Even so, the office was sufficiently well-established to provide the Normans with a valuable instrument of government ready to hand.

ANGLO-SAXON LAW

Just as Anglo-Saxon government, especially on the local level, was inextricably bound up with land, so also was its law. Portions of Anglo-Saxon law have already been described in previous sections, notably those on landholding. Here Anglo-Saxon law is being considered apart from other Anglo-Saxon institutions. To the Anglo-Saxons, however, land, society, and government were parts of the seamless garment of law.

Substantive Law

Law is generally divided into two very broad and not always clearly separated categories — substantive and procedural. *What* the law can do, prescribes, and proscribes, is substantive; *how* it does these things is procedural. This distinction, here briefly made, is a modern sophistication, however. It cannot be stressed too much that Anglo-Saxon law did not differentiate between its substantive and procedural aspects. To the Anglo-Saxons, law was law; and more important, like the land to which it was related in every aspect, it was immutable.

Anglo-Saxon law was folk law and unwritten until after the conversion to Christianity. Monks then wrote down *some* of this customary law, previously handed down orally from generation to generation, in *dooms*, or judgments. Setting customary law into written form must not be confused with legislation. To most Anglo-Saxons the law was either divinely inspired or the work of their ancestors, of such antiquity that it was unthinkable that it should be changed. Alfred the Great, who had rather advanced ideas on government and public administration, was one of the few rulers of the period who issued new laws, but he too regarded the body of traditional Anglo-Saxon law as sacred and God-given. Cnut's great code of laws also constantly looks back to the laws of earlier kings for guidance; it was clearly his wish not to be regarded as an innovator.

At the outset only a few fragmentary, disconnected portions of the law reached written form, usually those parts which were at variance with each other and in need of clarification. Later, more complete and elaborate expressions were attempted with some degree of systematic organization. But even these later dooms did not represent the totality of Anglo-Saxon law, certain parts of which must have been so well known that there seemed little point in committing them to parchment. As in all aspects of the Anglo-Saxon period, our knowledge of their law is very far from complete.

The idea that God gave the law, which was above and beyond the interference of sinful men, is quite typical of any people living under customary law. Perhaps beneath this supposition lay the feeling that God was the only safe person to do this. The Anglo-Saxons could not feel quite confident that the maker of the law might not be above it, and so not bound by it. It was highly undesirable, therefore, to have human agencies of legislation that might override their own law.

Whatever the theory, negative legislation was inevitable. Whenever kings ordered that laws should be written down as dooms so as to resolve local variations, only one version survived. The customary laws of a particular community were thus overruled and a theoretical change in the law had been achieved. In practice, however, the want of an effective judicial system to apply these dooms often meant that the communities concerned never learned of them and they continued to apply their old customary law.

The dooms give some knowledge of Anglo-Saxon law. They usually appeared shortly after the mass conversion of a kingdom. The first dooms were those of Kent, the kingdom first converted in the sixth century, and the last dooms appear to be those of Cnut in the eleventh.[12] No set of dooms, however, gave the complete body of law of any kingdom at any time. Even the fuller and more carefully arranged dooms of the later Wessex kings left much law still in customary, unwritten form.

The law was a slender barrier between community order and direct personal vengeance. Anglo-Saxons recognized that feuds weakened the community internally, and therefore provided in their law a required alternative for satisfying personal claims for justice. Yet the effort to secure acceptance of this alternative must have been difficult. The numerous stern prohibitions in the dooms against direct personal action to satisfy wrongs are eloquent testimony to their frequent ineffectiveness, when men in passion seized their nearest weapons and called upon their friends to assist them in getting a direct justice in equity.

The law was variable in its application because of its theoretical immutability. Since all people shuddered at the thought of making law, it was always necessary to make certain adjustments in it in any particular case and to bring it into line with current ideas of equitable justice. Any moot, or court, could *declare the law*, that is, state what the law was on a particular matter. As time wore on, however, a court might come to declare a different law from that which had been known by earlier generations, particularly if customary law offended its sense of justice in a specific issue. Local, as well as temporal, variations in the law were also numerous. What the law said in Sussex about a certain matter might not be what the people of Kent *knew* to be the law. Within a single shire there were variations from hundred to hundred. The written attempts to codify and resolve these variations were crude and had little real effect. Convenience and the exigencies of the moment swayed courts of freemen far more than the dooms of kings who had no judicial agents to apply them or even proclaim them to the people.

In no court did the presiding officer rule on the law; the people of the court declared it. Thus lay amateurs, always maintaining that

[12] Careful search has failed to uncover any dooms produced after that reign so that the phrase "Laws of Edward the Confessor" refers only to legal custom on the eve of the Norman Conquest. Usage of the phrase actually made it an appeal to the "good old days," rather than to any specific set of laws.

For an excerpt from the later, more symmetrical dooms see the example from the Dooms of Alfred, in David C. Douglas, gen. ed., *English Historical Documents*, I, 372–80 (henceforth to be cited as Douglas).

they had to apply the law as given by God, did so with a twofold effect. One was to increase tremendously the possibilities for legal variation. Laymen untrained in legal discipline find it much easier to bend the law to fit pragmatic ideas of justice on a specific issue than does the legal expert, to whom the purity of the law, apart from the issue to which it is applied, may be all important. With the exception of the Witan, all Anglo-Saxon courts were composed solely of these legal amateurs; and even the Witan had few "experts." If for laymen to declare the law, largely unwritten, was difficult, it was almost impossible in local courts where few men could ever have seen a set of dooms, and would not have been able to read them if they had. But every local court had a group of older men, repositories of community knowledge, who were supposed to know the law. These *doomsmen* declared the law upon the request of the assembly, which doubtless accorded their views great respect. But the assembly was not bound by their declaration, and they themselves in their formal statement of the law must have shared communal attitudes as to what was justice in a certain case. The tendency would be to treat each case on its merits, to make allowances and to distort the law by a readiness to regard the particular circumstances as exceptional.

From this followed the second important consequence of the layman's administration of the law in Anglo-Saxon England. If it was variable in application, for that reason it was vital, living law which continued because it could be modified to fit new situations. Had the Anglo-Saxons used bureaucratic justices responsible to the central government, their law would have had much less malleability. Because the old English law was flexible — even though everyone maintained that it was not — it remained vigorous enough to survive the Norman Conquest; on the death of William the Conqueror the law observed by Englishmen was still essentially the same as it had been a hundred years before.

Property law was primarily concerned with possession of land. For both land and for movable property, or chattels, the law consistently favored the current possessor; and the old saw that "possession is nine-tenths of the law" is an echo of the hard fact that the Anglo-Saxon community found it easier to let possession, even wrongful possession, remain undisturbed than to recover property for its rightful possessor. With land law not recognizing full individual ownership, other property laws also could not be clear about ownership, a concept foreign to the Anglo-Saxons. This haziness concerning the law of property penetrated other aspects of the law as well. A man could not devise folkland, or rarely bookland, by a will. Land law generally favored a descent by male *partage*, all sons sharing equally the holding of their father, rather than by primogeniture, except possibly in Kent. The willing of *chattels* was usually done orally to the priest at the time of extreme unction on the deathbed. England had no separate Church courts to handle the probate of wills — either oral or written — until after the Norman Conquest. Until then the communal court either approved or disapproved the distribution of the deceased's chattels by the priest as reported by him.

With property law less than precise, it is not surprising that the law of contract, warranty, and other related phases was nebulous in Anglo-Saxon England, whose primarily rural society had little need for much law relating to commerce. Certainly, the dooms show little concern about such matters.

The concern of the dooms was avoidance of the feud for personal injuries. The dooms regarded all injuries as personal damage cases. Like modern tort actions the remedies of the dooms were monetary damages. Differentiation between civil and criminal actions was just beginning at the close of the Anglo-Saxon period and then not on the *res* but the *persona* of the injury. To kill Cedric meant a payment to his family; to murder the king, death. It was less the deed than the status of the victim that determined the penalty. There was a practical reason for this principle. A great man who was injured would be less willing to accept for the blood feud the required alternative provided by the community, unless he was assured that his compensation would be large.

Remedies were largely monetary. At first glance to meet murder by wergeld or to meet personal injuries less than death by a bot might seem lenient. However, in a society where hard money was rare these penalties were harsh enough; if a person failed to pay, he was declared an outlaw and in that state could be killed on sight with impunity. In its attempt to put a stop to all personal feuding, the law sought to make these payments a virtual cancellation of the wrong done, so that the injured party would have no further cause for vengeance. A very elaborate table of such payments developed with gradations according to the person injured and the degree of his injury.

Anglo-Saxon law had few other penalties. Imprisonment was extremely rare. The death penalty, usually inflicted by hanging, although there were a few instances of beheading, was invoked only for cowardice and, after Alfred, regicide. The later brutalities of English criminal law were not devised by the Anglo-Saxons.

The Anglo-Saxons stressed the concept, which has entered into modern law, that a man was responsible for injuries caused by his property, whether or not within his immediate control. Even if the injury were entirely accidental, he was not absolved from this responsibility. Thus if Cedric in tripping over a branch knocked down Esgar's spear, which in falling punctured Edwin's left eye, Esgar was liable to pay Edwin a bot and his spear was accursed and had to be surrendered to some court, which would destroy it. The custom, derived from primitive animism, received reinforcement with the conversion of the Anglo-Saxons to Christianity by monks who knew the pagan Roman practice of *deodand*, whereby weapons causing death or injury had to be dedicated to the gods for purification. Seeking any method to reduce disorder, the clergy brought forward this Roman concept, but modified it so that such weapons went to the king. The principle of deodand became so firmly entrenched in English law that in the nineteenth century there was some question as to whether railway trains involved in accidents might not be liable to confiscation by the crown as deodand! Many states in the United States confiscate all guns involved in hunting fatalities, obviously to encourage safety habits, but the principle involved runs back to the ancient practice of deodand.

Procedural Law

Essentially it was procedural law which was the required alternative to the feud. However, it was far from a complete alternative. If the law forbade a person to wreak direct vengeance, it required him, in concert with his friends, to do almost everything else. The summoning of the other party, compelling his appearance in court if he were recalcitrant, even executing the court's decision — all were duties for the individual, not the community as embodied in the court. All that the law did was to provide a decision by the community in one phase of the required procedure.

Group action and responsibility were essential. The law had no agencies of its own to bring men to court or enforce its decisions. Originally the law made a man's kinsmen the guarantors of his behavior and responsible for producing him in a moot when summoned. As the kin group faded, the law devised artificial groups and agencies for these purposes. The borh method [13] appears to have been reasonably effective, and by the tenth century the law required that men not borhs themselves should have one. Since the borh was a landowner and man of substance, the community could seize his property if he failed to produce one of his men on summons to a court or failed to enforce its decision against him. The laws of Edgar the Peaceful encouraged borhs in this latter duty by imposing upon them the penalties adjudged for one of their men if they failed to enforce them. The growth of the manorial system where one man was both lord and borh of other men meant that usually the borh could fulfill his duties without too much difficulty.

The tithing, originally a company of ten householders, coincided with and supplemented the borh system. To modern minds it is illogical to have two agencies performing precisely the same functions for exactly the same individuals. To the Anglo-Saxons in a time when public order was difficult to maintain, two devices for the same purpose often seemed better than one, and three were better still. The laws of Edgar the Peaceful formally sanctioned this duality by requiring at one and the same time that every man over twelve should be in a tithing and also have a borh, unless he himself was a borh. The tithing, probably on the basis of general agreement, selected the *tithing man* to head this artificial substitute for the older kin group. A man used his tithing to summon an individual of another tithing to court and to execute its judgments. A court could order all tithings within its territorial jurisdiction to pursue criminals with *hue and cry*. Later the sheriff could order as many tithings as were needed to pursue malefactors. Long afterward in a distant land the sheriff would swear in a posse and announce that "They went that 'a way!" Still later a police officer would leap into a private automobile and order its driver to "Follow that car!" Anglo-Saxons have traveled far since they first put foot on English soil.

The importance of the individuals joined in a case determined which court acted on it. All Anglo-Saxon courts thus had concurrent jurisdiction *in rem* but varied in their effective jurisdiction *in personam*. It was useless for Cedric to have his tithing summon Earl Godwin to a hundred court. Its resources simply could not compel the

[13] Above, p. 22.

attendance of so great a man. Practical considerations meant that any-one having a dispute with the earl would have to try the shire court and probably the Witan itself.

From this arose a legal theory which was to present a grave problem for a long time to come. With agencies of public order only barely accepted, it was necessary for any court to secure the *voluntary* acceptance of its competence by both parties before it could act. Long after the Anglo-Saxons, when the crown had powerful agencies to enforce its courts' decisions, the theory, which was regarded as axiomatic, remained. One of the most difficult steps in a criminal action was to arraign the accused man and get his plea, that is, his acceptance of the jurisdiction of the court. If he refused to plead, the court was powerless. The obvious remedy for the dilemma, the abolition of tne theory, was not acceptable to the English until the late eighteenth century. Before then courts had to order physical coercion of the accused to make him plead and so accept their jurisdiction.[14]

However, though an Anglo-Saxon court could act only after both parties had accepted its competence, the court then exercised complete and final jurisdiction over every aspect of the case. This totality of jurisdiction *in rem*, plus the idea that proof came as a sign from God, made it impossible for any Anglo-Saxon court to have appellate functions.

As the summoning of parties and the execution of court decisions were matters for the principals of a dispute, their tithings, and their borhs, it was only in the trial procedure itself that the community as a corporate entity acted. This procedure followed very precise and exact formulas, which were essential for its success. The essentially formal nature of Anglo-Saxon legal procedure can be seen by looking at the case between Cedric and Esgar.

There had been bad blood between them for some time when one day Esgar called Cedric a liar and Cedric retorted by drawing his knife. In the ensuing scuffle Esgar lost his right thumb — a very serious loss. Bleeding, Esgar called in his tithing, which agreed that Cedric should be dealt with by the local hundred court. When Esgar's tithing set forth to summon their man, Cedric's tithing looked at the crops ready for harvest and decided that it would be better to bring him to

---

[14] The most common method was *peine forte et dure*, with heavy weights successively laid on the accused until he was willing to plead or die. This was not torture for judicial proof, because the case had not yet begun.

the next monthly meeting of the hundred court rather than lose time in a feud.

Up to now everything had been personal; but the moment the two men appeared in the hundred court, the community had to take notice. The hundred court did not consider that Cedric had committed a "crime," a word and conception with which it was not acquainted. It was just another damage suit, or tort action to use modern parlance. The procedures now used by the hundred court were exactly the same as any court, public or private, would have employed once Esgar and Cedric had agreed to having their dispute judged at all.

The hundred court, like any other court, was a partial judge of fact only; theoretically it had to accept and apply the law as it stood. In reaching a decision of fact the members had to follow a highly rigid procedure, because the court was not going to arrive at its decision by any rational process but by a revelation from heaven as to where right lay. Eye-witness testimony was worse than useless as proof. Who could believe sinful man, particularly if he were one of the principals of the case?

As the plaintiff, Esgar, accompanied by his tithing or friends, or *secta*, began with a foreoath, couched in elaborate phraseology, stating precisely his allegations. These had to include how, when, by whom, and with what he had been injured. Any faltering, misstating, or the least verbal slip might immediately cost him the case; God would not let a man swear falsely without some sign that he was lying.[15] Esgar managed to make his foreoath properly, and at once the hundred court assembly had a strong predisposition in his favor, which increased when two men of his secta, who had seen the brawl with Cedric, took supporting oaths — *not* as eye-witnesses of what had actually happened but to guarantee and bear witness to Esgar's *oath*, something quite different from modern testimony.

Cedric had his chance to deny everything, or, in later legal terms, to plead the general issue. This he did by an elaborate oath of rebuttal, which again had to be given perfectly. To the amazement of the court Cedric met this test. God had not yet shown where the right lay, so the hundred court had to invoke divine guidance. It was at this point, and *only* at this point, that the assembly really decided anything. Everything else, supposedly, was decided for it. But here the

---

[15] Modern psychology would not brush aside the idea that a man, strongly believing in direct and immediate divine intervention, would lie glibly.

assembly gave what amounted to a temporary or *medial* judgment when it proceeded to *award the proof.*

The award of proof consisted of two phases: who should have it, and what it should be. Although only a medial judgment, this decision about proof was important, because it indicated the prevailing view of the court and so, possibly, its eventual judgment. To the Anglo-Saxons, proof was no "burden" but a benefit in that he who received it could prove the veracity of his original oath, while his adversary could only hope that heaven would do the right thing by him. In the case of Esgar *v.* Cedric the men of the hundred court as members of a small community knew both parties well. Both men had successfully taken their oaths, but since Cedric's was one of rebuttal, there was a slight margin in his favor; and so the hundred court awarded him the proof.

To the Anglo-Saxons and their later Norman and Angevin rulers any sworn evidence, particularly oral testimony, was useless and an affront to God, who alone knew the truth and would reveal it to men. Even if Cedric and Esgar had fought before fifty people, the court would not have called any of them to give sworn evidence. Proof for the hundred court was the testing by divine revelation of the veracity of the oath given by the man who was awarded the proof.

Operating on this principle, the hundred court had at its disposal two modes of proof: *compurgation* and the *ordeal.* In the present case the court selected the former and ordered Cedric to have twelve compurgations to support his rebuttal oath at the court's next monthly session. Compurgation was the affirmation of the original oath, sometimes called *oath-helping.* Thus Cedric's rebuttal oath would be strengthened by the oaths of other men. However, their value varied according to social rank, so that the requirement was for compurgations, not compurgators. If Cedric could get the oath of a great noble, a "twelve-oath" man, his would be the only oath needed to meet this requirement. If Cedric were a member of the ordained clergy, his own rebuttal oath would have been sufficient to clear him. However, Cedric was no clergyman and his lord was meeting in the Witan with the king, perhaps fortunately for Cedric; for had his lord refused to be a compurgator, the hundred court would have been so shocked that it would have tripled the required compurgations.

During the month's interval between court sessions, Cedric was not looking for witnesses to the fight. He was trying to find men willing to risk their own immortal souls against hell-fire by swearing that his oath was true. Although an eye-witness might be willing to take such an oath, this was not sworn testimony about the row with Esgar. Actually, there was no need for the compurgator to know anything about the case. His only consideration was whether to gamble his soul by supporting Cedric's oath; because should it be false, all compurgators fell into mortal sin. Although compurgation might seem futile as a mode of proof, Cedric lived in a small community where much was common knowledge and his own reputation already thoroughly assessed. A man living in such a community in an age of faith would hesitate before consenting to be a compurgator.

By the time the hundred court met again Cedric had picked up five men with oaths equal to twelve compurgations. The court moved into the parish church, where the priest in full vestments was waiting before the candle-lit altar, wherein were sacred relics, two teeth of St. Ethelwold. Each compurgator came to kneel before the altar, with his hands resting on its surface while reciting the compurgation oath formula. Three of Cedric's compurgators blithely swore in this elaborate manner to the truth of his rebuttal oath taken a month ago. But the fourth tripped over a word, and at once a murmur ran through the church. The fifth approached the altar with a ghastly face, started to kneel, and then suddenly fainted in a twitching fit. Heaven had given its decision twice over to an awed hundred court, which declared that Cedric had lost his case — not on the basis of any assembly action but because God had shown the truth.

The court now consulted its doomsmen as to the proper payment for the loss of a right thumb of a man of Esgar's class. The doomsmen reported that the law required Cedric to pay Esgar five shillings and also forfeit his knife to the king as deodand. This seemed reasonable to the other freemen, who ordered Cedric to do these things, not because they so decided, but because the law said so. The hundred court had now finished with the case, wherein its only real action had been to award the proof; in all else it had been moved either by God or by His law.

The court had no responsibility nor agents for collecting the payment due to Esgar; that was his affair. If his tithing or borh helped him, this would be better than direct action on his account; but the hundred court itself was not interested. If Cedric refused to obey its order, and was guilty in our sense of contempt of court, the hundred court could order Esgar's friends to go on the *bloody morth*, which was a legal feud, against Cedric and his group. But the court would naturally be very unwilling to do this, because its procedure was for the very purpose of preventing feuds. The court could declare Cedric an outlaw if he were contumacious about paying, but again it would hesitate to invoke this extreme measure. Although killing an outlaw incurred no penalty, it could easily lead to a feud. Thus the hundred court would probably prefer to hear no more about the case of Esgar *v.* Cedric.

As society became more complex, however, the practice of compurgation tended to die out. Local communities were less closely knit; people knew less about their neighbors. There were even those who were cynical enough to act as compurgator for anyone in return for a small fee, at the risk of their immortal souls. But the resources of the law were not exhausted. It had the proof of ordeal, which was increasingly favored as a method of ascertaining heaven's will. Sometimes the court had no choice and had to select the ordeal as proof. Anyone caught in the very act of a crime, in *flagrante delicto*, had to go to the ordeal to prove his innocence. At first glance this seems ridiculous; was he not seen committing the crime? But Anglo-Saxon society recognized that direct justice was dangerous; there had to be an intervening stage. Besides, could sinful and fallible men be sure that even the apparently guilty man was in truth guilty?

Perjurers could only receive the ordeal if they won the proof. Perjury was a serious matter with far-reaching affects. Thus not only Cedric but all his compurgators who took their oaths were now branded as perjurers and henceforth could have only the ordeal as proof. Had Cedric failed to secure the requisite number of compurgations, the hundred court might have given him another chance to use his proof by changing it to the ordeal. However, if it came out that among those refusing to be a compurgator for him had been his lord, the ordeal would have been of triple difficulty. Generally, the court would order all men of bad repute, should they win the proof, to the ordeal to test their oaths. Any unfree man awarded proof could have only the ordeal, because as a landless man his original oath was without value.

From a modern view, proof by ordeal was a true burden, but the hundred court felt that proof was still a benefit, even if it involved physical pain. A man who must otherwise have lost his case still had a chance to succeed via an ordeal, which even more than compurgation was a direct appeal to heaven to show by a miracle where the right lay.

The hundred court had four types of ordeals available. After much deliberation between the perfectly spoken oaths of Edwin and Harthe, two notorious brawlers who accused each other of theft, the court gave the proof to Edwin and made it the ordeal of *cold water*. Taken to the river, Edwin heard the priest bless the water, which thereby became doubly pure, before he was bound hand and foot and hurled into the stream. Since this pure body would reject anything guilty, somewhat to the surprise of the freemen, Edwin sank, showing his essential purity. God had spoken plainly, and the freemen rushed to rescue Edwin from the river. Although he was dead, the assembly knew that even now his soul was in heaven. To complete justice, the court formally declared Harthe a perjurer.

The freemen then turned to Athelstane, who had secured only five of his required eight compurgations to clear himself of housebreaking. The court permitted him to clear himself by the ordeal of *hot water*. But because his lord was among those refusing to risk their souls for him, Athelstane was to have the ordeal in triple difficulty, which meant that he had to plunge his arm into boiling water up to the shoulder instead of merely to his wrist or elbow as the ordeal required of only single or double difficulty. Athelstane and some of the court retired to the churchyard, holy ground, where a large cauldron was bubbling. After special prayers by the priest, Athelstane plunged his arm into the kettle and rapidly withdrew it. The priest then wrapped his entire arm in cloth. Three days later Athelstane presented himself to the priest, who was to declare if God had intervened with a miracle to show Athelstane's innocence, in this case the lack of any blisters. When the priest unwrapped the arm, however, it was a mass of corruption, a fact he reported at the next meeting of the hundred court. No one was surprised, and Athelstane had to pay a bot to his victim as well as a wite to the king.

The case of Harold was much more serious, the charge of slaying a merchant under royal protection, during a fight seen by the hundred man himself, who was now presiding at the court. Having been seized *in flagrante*, Harold could have only the proof of ordeal, which had to be in triple measure because the crime had touched the king's peace. The hundred court selected the ordeal of the *hot iron*. Again the churchyard was the place for the ordeal, which involved Harold's carrying a 27-pound weight, heated until glowing, for 27 feet. If the king's peace had not been concerned, Harold would have had to carry a nine-pound weight only nine feet, but royal dignity had been touched. The priest blessed the glowing ingot and gave a sign to Harold, who seized the metal with both hands and walked the prescribed distance rapidly before dropping the iron. At the end of the course stood the priest, who bound up his seared hands. Three days later Harold presented himself before the altar for inspection by the priest, who reported at the next session of the hundred court that Harold's hands were without blemish. The assembly was amazed, but plainly God had wrought a miracle to show Harold's innocence.

One more ordeal was ordered by the hundred court that day. Wulfang was accused by Agatha, widow of Cyrnic, who had supposedly fallen upon the former's spear at the last ale feast, the reason for her present status. Wulfang answered flatly that although Cyrnic undoubtedly had fallen on a spear and was in consequence dead, the spear did not belong to him. In modern terms, Wulfang entered a special plea, almost a demurrer. The members of the assembly were not concerned about such niceties. They wanted to get the case settled quickly before there was a feud, because Agatha's brother, who was having to support her, was looking at Wulfang grimly. The court therefore immediately ordered Wulfang to the ordeal of *morsel* as the proof for his oath. Wulfang repaired to the churchyard, where the priest had already blessed a large piece of dough,[16] which he gave to Wulfang to swallow in one gulp. As all expected, Wulfang choked and spluttered so that the court knew it was right in declaring Wulfang a perjurer and ordering him to pay proper wergeld to Agatha according to her late husband's social station, as well as a wite to the king, to whom Wulfang also had to surrender his spear as deodand.

And so the freemen of the hundred court wound up their business for another month. The temptation to smile at their simplicity should be resisted. Neither the Normans nor the more sophisticated Angevins added anything to methods of proof except the additional ordeal by battle, with God giving the victory to the right in a combat between the principals or their hired champions. This ordeal was available only to the French-speaking upper classes, not the Anglo-Saxons. Long

---

[16] There should be no confusion here between this blessing and the form of consecration of the wafer in the Mass. Their forms and purposes were entirely different, and the wafer was never used in this ordeal.

after the Norman Conquest, compurgation, now called "wager of law," and the ordeal lingered on. In 1215 the papal prohibition against clerical participation in ordeals robbed this method of proof of its validity, but it took much trial and plenty of error before the jury method of proof finally emerged. Even then the jury only gradually supplanted these older modes of proof, which remained, nearly forgotten but legally intact. Suddenly, in 1817, the ordeal of battle was revived to the intense embarrassment of justices, who, however, had to admit its validity. It took an act of Parliament in 1819 to abolish it; and compurgation lived on, even if unused, for another fourteen years.

Apart from these interesting fragments of Anglo-Saxon procedural law which survived long after the Anglo-Saxon period, there were other elements which became essential parts of English law. Anglo-Saxon doubt about testimony as proof was shared by both Normans and Angevins, so that even after the introduction of trial by jury the later common law courts refused to accept evidence as proof until the late fourteenth century, and then only very grudgingly. Gradually the common law courts accepted more testimony but under such rigid conditions that the modern law of evidence is one of the most complex aspects of jurisprudence.

The Anglo-Saxon refusal to allow a man to testify for himself led to a fundamental common law dictum before the close of the Middle Ages that a man could not be *forced* to testify against himself. So vigorous was this rule that in criminal cases the accused might not testify even if he so wished until 1898.[17]

The vigor of Anglo-Saxon law came from its application by local government agencies, which were so closely related to the land and the basic social structure that they escaped the Norman Conquest more or less unscathed. Norman administrators found that Anglo-Saxon local government arrangements worked well. One of the fundamental principles underlying these arrangements was the theory that all freemen should participate in the affairs of their community. Although this had certainly ceased to be true long before Hastings, the theory was sufficiently vital to survive and reappear centuries later in the town meetings of New England. Even where local government seemed to be in the private hands of manorial lords, the people still had responsible functions to perform. It was in local government that the Anglo-Saxons

[17] Below, p. 510.

made their most important contribution to the English constitution. Their armies defeated, their country occupied by a foreign power, they handed on their English traditions of local government to their conquerors. In return they were to enjoy the novel experience of a strong monarchy and efficient central government, benefits that they were most reluctant to receive.

READING LIST

HOLDSWORTH, SIR WILLIAM S. *History of English Law*, Vol. II, Book II.

JOLLIFFE, J. E. A. *Pre-Feudal England*.

OLESON, TRYGVE J. *The Witenagemot in the Reign of Edward the Confessor*.

PLUCKNETT, THEODORE F. T. *A Concise History of the Common Law*, 4th ed., Book I, Part I, Chap. 1, Part II, Chap. 2.

POLLOCK, SIR FREDERICK, and FREDERIC W. MAITLAND. *The History of English Law*, 2nd ed., Vol. I, Book I, Chap. II.

STENTON, SIR FRANK M. *Anglo-Saxon England*, 2nd ed.

STEPHENSON, CARL. *Borough and Town*.

VINOGRADOFF, PAUL. *Growth of the Manor*, 2nd ed.

2

THE NORMAN FEUDAL ADDITIONS

As THE SUN set on Hastings and Saxon hopes, the army of Duke William moved from the hill of victory it had won by stratagem and around the Kentish coast toward Canterbury and London. From our day we look back and draw a heavy line under 1066, one of the "two memorable dates" in English history.[1] The keepers of the *Anglo-Saxon Chronicle* were not so impressed and with almost cold detachment noted that Duke William landed, defeated Harold, and was then crowned on Christmas Day, 1066. That was all.

This was not simply the English habit of understatement. The clerks of the *Chronicle* were recording a political event which at first made very little impact upon probably the majority of the people in the country. It is true that for the upper levels of English society it was a disaster — they lost land after the Conquest if they did not lose their lives during it. But to the ordinary man it did not make very much difference that the new king was a foreigner, nor was he greatly concerned that the new lord of the manor spoke French, provided he himself was allowed to carry on in the way to which he was accustomed. And this he was allowed to do. The Normans were not innovators and saw no reason to change the forms of local government that the natives understood and used well.

There was no violent upheaval of society as a whole. It was moreover royal policy to preserve the constitutional framework of the old English state. Although he owed his position entirely to military force, William was particularly anxious that he should be recognized by Englishmen as the legitimate successor to the throne of King Edward. At the beginning of his reign it was his ambition that Frenchmen and Englishmen should associate in his government on equal terms. Although this turned out to be impossible, 1066 came and went without

[1] W. C. Sellar and R. J. Yeatman, *1066 and All That* (New York, 1931), I, n. 1; 17.

any essential break in the continuity of English life. To emphasize this continuity, and his own legality, one of William's first acts was to have himself elected king by the Witan — the last act of that august assembly. He confirmed all Anglo-Saxon law for his English subjects, and to begin with, until the rebellion of 1069 at least, made a serious effort to govern the country through what was left of the old English ruling class. Yet when all this has been said, the fact remains that the Normans did eventually bring about in England a social revolution which by the end of William's reign was beginning to affect the whole structure of the state. This was very largely the result of the introduction of feudalism.

Norman Feudalism

The feudalism imported into England by William was developed by Norman dukes to fit their particular needs. This type of feudalism now became the basis of English central government. The origins of feudalism are obscure, and the theory of it is still a matter for much controversy among historians. It developed into an exceedingly complex system, with many ramifications. At one level it was a method of conducting what later would be termed public or state functions at a time when government agencies were few and the state in its modern concept did not exist. Individuals performed these functions as *personal* duties owed by them as *vassals* to a *lord*. These obligations were the result of a contract (usually unwritten and customary) between subordinates and superior which had as its "valuable consideration" the land held by vassals of a lord and for which they owed him *honorable* services. Thus, simultaneously, feudalism was a system of government, a complex of contract law, and a landholding system. Its main object during the Norman period was to achieve a state of military preparedness.

Feudalism, as Viking raiders on the West French coast encountered it, was a product of the post-Carolingian disintegration of political and social order in western Europe. It may be said to have consisted of three elements. From above came the element of *beneficium*, whereby the king or some great man gave land to a loyal follower in return for specific services. From below came the element of *commendation*, by which an individual, seeking protection, gave his land and with it himself to a greater man, who would provide protection in return for services. The link between the two men, whether generated from above or below, determined the manner by which the subordinate held his land; and feudal law was always more interested in the tie and its conditions than in the persons joined by this link. The third element was *private jurisdiction*, whereby the lord permitted a vassal to hold a court for his own vassals, freemen like himself, who would decide cases brought by other men of their own level.

This all bears a superficial resemblance to the English manorial system.[2] But in feudalism every holder of land was a freeman, whereas in the manorial system only the lord of the manor was free and those holding manorial land tended to be servile. Moreover, as seen, the Anglo-Saxon manorial lord had received his land for *past* services, and his future obligations were either very hazy or nonexistent: a man holding his land by a feudal tenure might hold it as the reward for past services, but his obligations lay solely in the future. The two systems existed side by side, and in their different ways were equally characteristic of the rural life of England in the Middle Ages.

By 1066 Norman feudalism had already assumed an hereditary character; the duties of lord and vassal were not for the single life of either but for the duration of a tenure, which could endure for several generations. The reciprocity of duties between lord and vassal should be remembered, because it is too easy to think of the duties as all flowing one way. Feudal law obliged the lord to protect his vassal and neither lord nor vassal could alone vary the contract between them in the slightest.

The introduction of Norman feudalism into England led to a revision of the basic principle of land law. Anglo-Saxon law had been vague about land ownership; feudalism said flatly that the king was lord of all the land and everyone else merely held of him. This principle stood William in good stead in 1066. In Normandy, as a vassal himself, he was limited by feudal law in his relations with his lord, the King of France. The limitations might be more formal than real, but they represented some check upon his ducal authority over the Norman vassals. Not so in England, which William held of no man. There he was free to carry out the great redistribution of land in the years following the Conquest, and in due course most of the larger estates throughout the country passed into the hands of the Norman aristocracy.

The lands of Englishmen who had fallen in the wars naturally reverted to the king. Others who survived the battles but failed to come

[2] Above, pp. 23, 31.

to terms with William had their lands confiscated. The dissatisfaction of the English lords, on finding themselves gradually falling into a position of inferiority, expressed itself in the rebellion of 1069. Sternly put down by William, this led to further large-scale confiscations and opened the northern part of the country to Norman settlement. That William succeeded in bringing about this huge redistribution of land as smoothly and rapidly as he did was a remarkable achievement. Within a few years thousands of small estates had been divided among the Norman barons, who held them as *fiefs* or *fees* of the king. As it has been estimated that the number of these barons cannot have exceeded 180, it is obvious that some of the new baronial fees must have been very large indeed. Manorial estates scattered throughout the country might also be included in the king's endowments, so although in most cases the baron's *honor*, as his lands were also called, was largely concentrated in one district, it sometimes consisted entirely of isolated manors with no geographical unity whatsoever.

There were several kinds of feudal tenure, but quite the most important in the Middle Ages, in an essentially military society, was that which provided military forces. This was achieved by tenure in *chivalry*, or by *knight's service;* the holder was obliged to provide knights, men who fought on horse, when called upon by his lord to do so, to the number laid down in the original grant, or *enfeoffment*. The number of these knights to be thus provided was called the *knight's fees* of the vassal's fief. Thus if Aimeric held fiefs of the king to the extent of twenty knight's fees, he would have to send twenty fully trained and equipped knights to the king upon his call.

William also needed supplies. If he had larger demesne lands than other lords, he also had larger obligations, which he partially met by grants of fiefs in the tenure of *grand serjeanty*. Holders in this tenure had to supply their lords with goods, of a type and quantity specified in the original enfeoffment. Obviously, serjeanty duties were not as honorable as those of chivalry, but grand serjeanty was a free tenure. Equally honorable, if not as vital, were the duties of those holding land in *petty serjeanty* — which involved such personal services as carrying the lord's banner and helmet or his cup.[3] Serjeanty tenure did not survive very long for the king soon found better ways to secure supplies

---

[3] King John made a grant in petty serjeanty for the not inconsiderable service by its recipient of holding the royal head whenever he crossed the choppy Channel.

and services,[4] and with the growth of a money economy the whole system became out of date.

As a son of the Church, William was concerned for the care of his soul. His personal chaplain, Lanfranc, became Archbishop of Canterbury and received large grants in chivalry. Like other ecclesiastical holders in this tenure, Lanfranc was not himself expected to mount a horse and fight — but he had to furnish knights. On the other hand, William's half-brother, Odo, Bishop of Bayeux and also Earl of Kent, noticed that the Latin verb in canon law forbidding clerical shedding of blood was "to cut." And so the Bishop of Bayeux rode forth to battle carrying a mace, adhering to the letter of the law by employing a blunt instrument. Indeed, churchmen could hold by any feudal tenure, but only they might receive grants in *frankalmoign,* literally "free alms." Here the vassal's only duty was to pray for the soul of the grantor; and the Church and its foundations, such as the monasteries, received generous grants in frankalmoign. However, William and his successors also needed literate men for administration, and in the grant of frankalmoign was the tacit but nonetheless effective presumption that the Church would provide royal clerks.

Although William's revenue from his own demesne and the customary payments of the shires was considerable, he sought to increase it by making frequent grants in *socage* tenure. The socage vassal had to make an annual cash payment for his holding. Yet this least honorable of tenures survived feudalism to become the modern *fee simple,* because what William and later kings ultimately wanted were not men-at-arms, supplies, banner carriers, clerical help, or even prayers — but *money* with which to buy all these things without the feudal limitations on them. By the late thirteenth century royal courts were only too ready to convert other tenures into free and common socage.

Within the manors of these free vassals, serfs tilled the soil, holding their strips of land by various unfree tenures, which feudalism, with its indifference toward manorial matters, lumped together as tenure in *villeinage.* The only feudal personage interested in these servile tenures

---

[4] Petty serjeanty still survives in parts of Cornwall, where holders of royal lands must annually give a token sheaf of grain or bundle of faggots to the sovereign. Certain serjeanty tenures were created long after feudalism, notably for the Dukes of Marlborough and Wellington, who each year deliver to the sovereign a French flag (fleur-de-lis and tricolor respectively) and then receive it back to place in their ancestral halls, built to commemorate the victories of their ancestors by a grateful nation, which now taxes the present dukes out of house and home.

was the particular vassal who was the manorial lord. Thus for the feudal lord and his vassals the law was feudal; for the manorial lord and his serfs it was manorial.

Feudal obligations lay on the various tenures, not the land. The distinction may appear puristic, but it is important and the Normans saw it clearly. If a tenure ceased to exist, the land reverted to the grantor, who might retain it or regrant part or all of it on any tenure; but the land per se remained unchanged. William I made it a point to continue the Anglo-Saxon obligations, or servitudes, on all land, notably the Danegeld and the *trinoda necessitas*, whose obligations were apart from duties arising from feudal tenures.

The first duty of the holder of any tenure was the fulfillment of its particular purpose — fighting, supplying, praying, or paying. There was also the obligation of *homage* and *fealty*. Homage required the vassal on receiving his fief from his lord to kneel before him and, placing his own hands in his, to say, "Je deviens votre homme" — that is, the vassal became the lord's man. Whereupon the vassal then rose to swear loyalty (fealty) to the lord. Vassals also had the duty, except for those holding in frankalmoign, of *suit of court*, which required them to appear with other vassals on the lord's summons to compose his *court baron*. Like the Anglo-Saxon courts, the court baron handled judicial work, but also anything else required within the feudal framework. Sometimes called the *court of honor*, this feudal assembly must not be confused with the manorial court, composed largely of servile people and dealing with manorial matters. A lord could have only one feudal court baron but several manorial courts.

Feudal incidents were services that the vassal might be called upon to render occasionally. Feudal obligations were continuous for the duration of a tenure, but the incidents were what their name suggests — incidental duties which probably, but not necessarily, would crop up during the life of a tenure. Fewer incidents applied to socage and frankalmoign than to chivalry, but for all tenures these demands tended to become particularly irksome, as they were open to abuse. There was, for instance, the incident of *wardship*. The lord, naturally, had to be certain that a fief would always perform the duties of the tenure on which he had granted it, but the fief could not fulfill its basic function when it passed to a minor. Therefore, the lord might re-enter and administer the fief during the period of minority, when he might take all its profits, except for those moneys required to educate the minor according to his station in life. However, this amount the lord determined: feudal law gave the heir no rights against his guardian either during or after minority, which ended at age 14, although this figure slowly rose.

When he became of age, the heir was entitled to *ousterlemain*, quite literally to "oust the hand" of the lord from his fief, or more elegantly, to "sue out his livery," that is, declare his coat of arms. At this time feudal law permitted the lord to demand a payment from the heir equal to half of the annual profits of the fief, whose revenues he was now losing. The new vassal received no accounting from his lord for his management of the fief, which might have been sadly neglected, unless he were a socage tenant. Fiefs in socage held by minors were under the administration of the nearest male relative, who had to give a full accounting when the heir became of age. Of all the feudal incidents, wardship was the most profitable to the lord and the most capable of abuse, and therefore gave rise to the greatest number of complaints.

Again, an unmarried minor heiress of a chivalry fief was in a very invidious position. Wardship applied and also the incident of *marriage*, which meant that the lord had the right to dispose of her hand. There were sound reasons for this feudal principle. A woman tenant in chivalry could not be expected to fight; but when she married, her fief went to her husband. No lord, least of all the king, could allow her to marry a man incapable of performing the duties of the tenure, nor under any circumstances could he permit an enemy to become his vassal by the simple expedient of marrying such an heiress. Even after the heiress reached her majority, therefore, the incident of marriage continued to apply. This too could provide revenue for a lord. In practice, heiresses were frequently sold in marriage to the highest bidder. A lord could also make money by deliberately arranging a marriage between an heiress and a man of lower social standing. Rather than accept a marriage of such disparagement, the heiress often preferred to pay her lord the required fine. There were a number of other ways in which this incident could be abused — fines could be exacted if the girl refused to marry or married against the wishes of her lord — and as time went on the marriages of male as well as female heirs were controlled by the lord. All this was in contrast to the marriage of the heiress to a socage fief. In her case, her relatives as guardians had to find her a suitable husband, and if his assets were less than he represented, they were liable to reimburse her.

Chivalry, socage, possibly serjeanty, but not frankalmoign, were also obligated for the *three aids,* designed to assist the lord in meeting special expenses. Vassals of a lord captured in battle were liable to contribute to his *ransom,* which might be large. They also had to share expenses incurred by their lord for *knighting* his *eldest son.* Their third "customary" aid was to provide the *dowry* of the lord's *eldest daughter* on her *first* marriage. Her younger sisters did not require this assistance; and neither did she if she survived her husband and remarried, in that case her marriage portion became her new dowry. Although feudal law said that the lord should be "reasonable" in setting the amounts of these three customary aids, it left their determination solely to him.

When an heir, including one who had been a minor and had so paid for ousterlemain, succeeded to his fief, he paid *relief* to his lord as fixed by him. Originally this incident was a token reminder to the vassal that he only held the land of the lord, but by the time of William II (1087–1100) lords were regarding relief as a source of revenue, and vassals were finding it a burden. Henry I (1100–1135) at the outset of his reign promised reasonable reliefs, but reliefs continued to rise until Magna Carta in 1215, when "customary" rates were fixed at 100 shillings per knight's fee for chivalry (and possibly serjeanty) fiefs and a sum equal to a year's rent from socage holders, with a maximum for all reliefs of £100.

A royal tenant-in-chief had not only to pay relief to the king, but also had to pay a fee for the performance of the incident of *primer seisin.* Again beginning as a token payment in recognition of the fact that the vassal was merely holding land owned by the king, the incident quickly became a source of royal revenue. After payment, which could be as high as a year's profits from the fief over and above the relief payment, the king (or his agent) walked with the new vassal through his lands. The king bent down and picked up a leaf, twig, or piece of dirt, which he placed in the vassal's hands to symbolize delivery of the fief. Only after this symbolic act might a tenant-in-chief do homage and fealty and so enter his fief. The double payment of relief and primer seisin applied to all royal tenants-in-chief except those holding in frankalmoign. The opportunities for extortion were clearly manifold. An unscrupulous king exploited his barons or tenants-in-chief; the unscrupulous baron exacted aids and reliefs from his vassals, and exploited and abused various feudal incidents. The vassal in his turn passed on the burden to his own feudal tenants, and they in their turn to those under them.

Feudal law permitted a holder of a fief to exercise the right of *subinfeudation* freely, that is, to make grants to others of such extent and by such tenures as he chose. This rule might be logical, but it permitted what feudal law said was impossible — the alienation of land out of its normal line of descent. Legally, regardless of the amount of subinfeudation from it, a specific fief carried the same obligations as when originally granted. But the heir might not be left with any fief or one so small that he could not perform the services upon which his lord depended. These facts were painfully clear when the subinfeudation was in frankalmoign to the Church. The lord who suffered most in the end from subinfeudation was the greatest, the king; but feudal law afforded him no more protection than it did to any other lord.

Fiefs descended according to primogeniture, with males having precedence over females. If a vassal had no legitimate children, the incident of *escheat* applied to his fief, that is, it reverted to the grantor (or his line) and again became part of his demesne. Every lord, but particularly the king, was vitally concerned that lands due to escheat did so revert. In a time when title registration offices did not exist this was not easily discovered. The lords' stewards and the king's sheriffs had instructions to keep close watch and report all escheats.

A vassal violating feudal law made his fief liable to *forfeiture*. Any vassal guilty of treason lost his head and, regardless of his immediate lord, his lands reverted to the king. If guilty of a mere felony, the vassal forfeited his lands to the king only for a year and a day, after which they returned to the vassal's immediate lord. Any vassal toying with the idea of rebellion, particularly against the king, was well advised to make the *diffidatio* before putting his idea into practice. In a solemn ceremony the nascent rebel declared that his lord had not fulfilled his part of the feudal contract and that therefore he renounced his homage and fealty; if he should then go to war with his former lord, it need not be regarded as an illegal act. Obviously, however, the legality of the diffidatio depended upon the success of any subsequent rebellion.

Feudal society became increasingly complex. Far from being the simple pyramid it was ideally supposed to be, with the king as the apex, descending through clear-cut gradations, the shape of feudalism became more and more distorted and confused. *Multiple tenures* of vassals, produced largely from subinfeudation but also stemming from collateral inheritance and marriage, introduced complications which were eventually to undermine the whole system — a system which after all had been designed to meet the needs of a fairly simple and predominantly military society.

Feudal law regarded the king as a lord, who granted land to vassals, who then by subinfeudation became lords of other vassals, and so on, until finally there was the tenant who was only a vassal. With the exception of this man and the king, all feudal holders were simultaneously lords and vassals. Thus the king granted land to Aimeric, who then subinfeudated some to Giles. This established a very neat relationship among the three men. The king was the lord of Aimeric, his vassal, who was also the lord of Giles. Aimeric was a tenant-in-chief of the king, and Giles a tenant-in-chief of Aimeric but a *rear tenant* of the king. If Giles granted land to Fitzpeter, the scale of relationships extended. Giles was now the royal *mesne tenant*, while Fitzpeter was a royal rear tenant. Aimeric became the *mesne lord* of Giles, and the king his *overlord*, or *suzerain*. For Fitzpeter and other tenants of Giles the scale was lowered by one degree, with Giles their mesne lord and Aimeric their suzerain. Thus, according to the theory of feudalism, there was still what might be termed a vertical relationship among these four people, and the pyramid appeared to be taking shape.

But in practice this was not the way things turned out. Aimeric, although a royal tenant-in-chief, might receive a grant from Fitzpeter. If Aimeric held of the king and of Fitzpeter by different tenures, as was possible, there might be some confusion. Multiply this instance numerous times, and there would certainly be confusion. Feudal law tried to provide a remedy in the principle of the *liege lord*, to whom a vassal, regardless of his immediate lord, or lords, had an overriding duty. In carrying this principle of liegeancy to England, William I insisted that the king was the liege lord of every feudal tenant. In every oath of homage and fealty, a saving clause declared that the first loyalty of the new vassal was to the king. At times vast concourses of feudal tenants of different lords swore fealty to the king, the best-known occasion being the Oath of Salisbury in 1086. Once this principle was established, no vassal could ever plead that he had fought the king solely on his own lord's orders. Furthermore, the only time a lord could legally call upon a tenant in chivalry for knights was when the king had sent this order down the feudal chain; English feudal monarchs sternly forbade the use of feudal military resources for private warfare.

Royal liegeancy did not give the king autocratic power, however. Though in practice he might often come close to absolutism, feudal law insisted that the king, albeit lord of all, was subject to the same limitations as any other lord in his relations with his vassals. Thus, said the law, the king was only *primus inter pares*, first among equals. This again was the theory, and it did not always coincide with the facts. But it was a useful theory with which to curb the aspirations of powerful kings and keep weaker kings in their place. It took the Tudors to dislodge the preconception from the minds of the king's subjects. But in practice, during the reign of William the Conqueror, the royal voice did count for more and the royal tenants-in-chief knew it to their cost.

The king certainly possessed considerable advantages over his vassals. His manors were more numerous, larger, and wealthier than those of anybody else, so that he received much larger manorial revenues than his vassals; he was also the ultimate recipient of all feudal dues. He had therefore this important advantage over his rivals, though it might not be sufficient to maintain the royal authority under a weak king, as the reign of Stephen (1135–54) showed. But Stephen was the exception to a succession of vigorous and effective monarchs during the first century and a half following the Conquest. Norman rulers were able to insist upon the principle of liegeancy, the most practical application of which was the sternly enforced rule that no castle might rise except with royal permission, and then the local lord was to be merely its governor for the king. Stephen's failure to prevent the building of "adulterine" castles was recognized as a threat to the crown by his successor Henry II (1154–89), who had them pulled down.

Central Government

The Norman equivalent of the Anglo-Saxon Witan was the Great Council, or *Magnum Concilium*, a meeting of all the great lords of the land held three times a year at Easter, Whitsuntide, and Christmas. It was an occasion on which the king could assure himself of the loyalty of his tenants-in-chief and in general keep an eye on them. Though it met more regularly than the Witan, the Great Council probably transacted less business. It was much more of a ceremonial occasion, when the king sought to impress his vassals by his superior wealth and dignity, and he and his vassals together sought to impress the common people and any foreign observers who happened to be present by the might and splendor of their assembly.

The Great Council, however, was not and could not be an effective instrument of central government. The Norman kings needed the kind of institution the Anglo-Saxons had never managed to develop, to perform the administrative and executive functions of central government. William, therefore, introduced, as the principle institution of the Anglo-Norman state, the king's court, or *curia regis*. This may be said to derive from the Magnum Concilium, or to have been the Magnum Concilium in miniature, but its powers became much more clearly defined and it emerged as a distinctive organ of government.

The nucleus of this court was a body of from ten to thirty persons who belonged to the royal household; a number of the great lay and ecclesiastical barons would also be present, either by virtue of the offices they held or because they were visiting the king at the time or had been specially invited by him to assist in business that was their particular concern. The group of household officers was in constant attendance on the king, and the court could be summoned at any time and in any place. It was a flexible and adaptable institution that could be expanded to meet whatever demands were made on it. It could be an informal social gathering of the king and a few men he knew well; it could also be a fully representative assembly at which the king equipped himself in all the paraphernalia of royalty, as at the thrice yearly meetings of the Great Council. But it was in its former aspect that it marked a significant break with Anglo-Saxon traditions and became the novel and effective organ of the central government of the Norman and early Angevin kings. It acquired important judicial, advisory, administrative, and financial functions.

Curia regis acted as a feudal court. It performed the functions of any such court — the settlement of all questions arising from feudal law. The decision in such matters came from the assembly as a whole, though the king had great influence. As vassals, the members of curia regis had to advise their lord, the king, on wardships, marriages, and the disposition of escheats and forfeitures. But these feudal matters interested curia regis only where they applied to tenures held of the king. Feudal law gave neither the king nor curia regis any competence over matters arising from tenures held of other lords.

Curia regis advised the king. Although it offered advice only on such topics as the king submitted to it, and although under a strong king it was likely that members hesitated to offer advice that might displease him, the opinion of men of such importance in the realm when it was forthcoming could not be safely ignored. The king's position was in fact the same as that of his barons in their own baronial courts. They might ride roughshod over the opinions of their counsellors; but if they did so, they must expect to face the consequences — the worst of which would be the tenants' renunciation of their homage and fealty to the lord, and rebellion. Curia regis was consulted on all kinds of public business and the very range of its interests had important consequences. It intimated that there was a sphere of government outside the closed system of feudalism, a sphere in which the king with the help of his court might extend his powers and gradually escape the limitations imposed upon him by feudal custom. Further, by exercising "government" in the larger sense, curia regis began a major process of political evolution. It was from the court that subsequent government departments emerged. It would not be too fanciful to see it as a primitive ancestor of the civil service and the whole bureaucratic apparatus of the modern state.

The administrative functions of curia regis developed rapidly under the first Norman king. The first department of state to emerge was the royal Chancery, the office in which the clerks produced the charters and writs, our most important records of the period, under the control of the Chancellor, a distinguished officer of the king's household. The Exchequer appeared later in the reign of Henry I as a separate department, and there was an officer known as the Justiciar who assumed some responsibility for judicial matters. The specific allocation of duties to members of the court, however, was at this time the exception rather than the rule: the court was an assembly, and all its members were expected to turn their attention to whatever business was before them.

Curia regis also supervised revenue collection. This function did not as a rule involve taxation, a concept hardly recognized in the eleventh century; the money due the king was his by feudal or Anglo-Saxon law. The collection of royal revenues was naturally the special concern of the Treasurer, but other members of curia regis assisted him. As a feudal lord, William had income from feudal dues and socage payments. He also had large manorial revenues from *tallages* — payments arbitrarily exacted by him as by any other manorial lord. All of these sums went into the royal treasury as the *personal* funds of the king, who was not accountable to anyone for their expenditure. On at least three occasions William imposed a *geld,* a general land tax, that, according to Anglo-Saxon traditions, the king had a right to levy in emergencies. William I is supposed to have been the wealthiest ruler of his time in Europe.

Centralizing Tendencies

However often William might insist that he was the lawful king and heir of Edward the Confessor, the fact remained that he was the Conqueror and Norman rule was that of an alien power over a fundamentally hostile and untrustworthy population. The establishment of an essentially military society with a powerful central authority was an inevitable basis of his policy. To some extent feudalism also implied centralization. The concept of royal liegeancy, the picture of society as pyramidal with the king at its apex, enhanced royal power, despite the theoretical limitations imposed upon it. There were, however, more important reasons for the growing tendency toward centralization.

The Domesday Survey resulted from William's desire to know the essential facts about his new realm. It was decided to undertake it at a meeting of the Great Council on Christmas Eve, 1085, the immediate cause being the threat of a Danish invasion and the need to know the resources available to repel it. The survey had been completed by the end of the following year. It had utilized the strongest devices for centralization yet seen in England. Commissioners, themselves members of curia regis, armed with specific royal instructions, went to every shire moot, where they put certain men under oath to answer precise questions truthfully. The sheriff and all feudal tenants of the shire (or "county," as the Normans called it) were interrogated on feudal matters. The reeve and six freemen from each tun, together with all priests, similarly gave information on nonfeudal subjects. The questions covered a wide range of topics. The circumstances of the royal tenants-in-chief and their vassals, and of all freeholders and villeins in the shire, were investigated. Who held the land now; who had possessed it in the days of Edward the Confessor? What was its size and obligations, now and in the days of that sovereign? What was the extent of the wastelands? How many livestock were there on each manor? In this way William collected a great mass of information about his realm, and eventually bequeathed to historians a remarkable and inexhaustible document, the great *Domesday Book*.[5]

A striking feature of this inquiry, or *inquest*, is that it was initiated and controlled by the king acting not in his feudal capacity, but through his *prerogative*. It was one early instance of the growth of the crown at the expense of the baronage and the assimilation of feudal interests into the larger national interest. That such a survey could be carried out in so brief a time, with the help of ordinary people, many of whom were hostile to the regime conducting it, is striking proof of the effectiveness of William's rule. The only portions of England not covered were the four northern counties, where ecclesiastics conducted similar surveys and also sent their results to curia regis.

Commissioners from the central, or capitalis, curia regis at times presided at county courts. These commissioners, who usually included the sheriff, appeared irregularly and for a specific purpose as indicated in their royal orders; they might be seeking particular information about local matters or attempting to make the shire court more efficient or conscientious. Again, these commissioners were acting as prerogative not feudal agents. Only the king might use these commissioners; no other lord might avail himself of this device, except the palatine bishops, who exercised regal powers in the counties bordering Scotland and Wales. Indeed, when the commissioners sat at the shire court, it ceased for the moment to be one; it took on the character of its presiding officers to become a branch of curia regis. Thus local and central government could by these means be very closely integrated. During their sojourn at the shire court all feudal jurisdictions in the county were in abeyance, and all freemen had to attend this temporary local royal court.

The momentary transformation of a simple shire court into a royal court was not as drastic to contemporaries as it seems to us. Only freemen could attend the shire court, and all free tenures were in the feudal structure. Thus people of the time did not see the procedure as essentially nonfeudal, particularly since all feudal persons had the king

[5] There are various explanations about the name "Domesday." Some feel it was from the word "doom," a judgment, a decision; thus the survey and book by which all would be judged for taxes. Such an explanation, even with the lack of a national tax system, appears more reasonable than the idea that the word was a corruption of "doomsday," a day of reckoning. Another view is that the name came from the chapel of *Domus Dei* in Winchester Cathedral, where the data was stored. The book and portions of the survey are in Douglas, II, 854-93.

in any case as their liege lord. Nevertheless, the king was doing what feudal law said he could not do — his court was dealing with the affairs of men who were not his immediate vassals. The continuing sessions of capitalis curia regis did not affect other feudal jurisdictions, but the temporary local curia regis momentarily cancelled them and was thus a powerful agency of centralization.

The earl ceased to be an agent of the central government. Only the title, usually held by a Norman, remained. He may possibly have retained his right to the third penny of the shire's judicial revenues, but his territorial designation had no administrative implications. With the title hereditary, it was deemed unwise to permit its holders a dominant position in local affairs.

The sheriff was the most important single agent of Norman centralization. This official now rapidly assumed the position that had already been prepared for him in Anglo-Saxon times. The Normans knew the office of the *vicecomes*, with functions similar to those of the sheriff. Although the word would eventually become "viscount" to designate a rank in the peerage, neither in Normandy nor in post-Conquest England did the office carry noble status with it; on the other hand, it usually went to a person who was already a minor noble. The sheriff after 1066 was still a personal employee of the king, with whose interests his own were linked. He carried out the same duties as he had before Hastings, but with the added prestige and authority that a powerful king could bestow upon his servant. He presided at the shire court, occasionally, as seen, as one of a commission transforming it into a royal court. He gathered information for the king, either personally or as a member of such a commission. The shire fyrd was his responsibility as in the past, and he continued his tourn throughout the county to verify the enrollment of all adult males in tithings. Now called *viewing the frankpledge*, this duty took the sheriff twice a year to each of the various hundred courts. The Norman rulers regarded frankpledge as a police measure and not as something touching on their powers, so they occasionally included the right to view it in grants of private feudal jurisdiction. In such cases, the sheriff was naturally not responsible for this duty.

The sheriff paid into the royal treasury his shire *ferm*, a lump sum set by the king. The ferm consisted of several items. Most important were revenues from the royal manors, which the sheriff collected as the royal steward. Wites and fines for violations of the king's peace and the

newer feudal payments due the king also went into the ferm. The practice of selling the right to collect the ferm was short-lived in England
and did not exist during the reign of William I. Not part of his ferm,
but also collected by the sheriff, were the Danegeld and the fines ordered by the shire court when it was momentarily part of curia regis.

The process of centralization did not extend to the palatine counties.
These counties were areas of particular importance for defense along
the Scottish and Welsh borders. Here the earl remained important and
was almost a viceroy. All feudal tenures ran from him, not the king;
and unlike other lords he possessed criminal jurisdiction. All judicial
revenues were his, and no royal writ ran in his county. To allow such
large powers to an earl was of course contrary to William's general
policy, and only the most urgent military considerations could have
induced him to make such concessions. Even so, William entrusted
palatine powers only to bishops.

The Conquest and the Church

The Norman Conquest brought the practices of the Norman Church
into England. These practices separated the Church from secular government, but also meant the ultimate control of the Church by the
crown.

The Church had the dual character of a spiritual and a feudal
corporation. As the former, it was a supranational body, extending over
western Europe; as the latter, it played a major part in the feudal organization of the country and was vital to the interests of the crown. While
its spiritual and feudal characteristics appeared unrelated, in practice
it was not at all easy to distinguish them. If the Archbishop of Canterbury was Primate of All England, he was also a great vassal of the
king, who regarded him not so much as a father-in-God as a tenant-in-
chief. Ecclesiastics were essential for the workings of the central government, for only the clergy had the literacy, the administrative experience, and hierarchical organization needed to make it function effectively. Furthermore, although the Church held in frankalmoign, it
also held by other tenures, particularly chivalry, which bound it as
much as any lay vassal. William and his successors insisted that tenure
and not persons determined feudal obligations; and although this policy
did not mean that bishops donned armor and rode into battle — Bishop
Odo always excepted — it did mean that the Church and its foundations,

such as abbeys and monasteries, were to send knights for fiefs in chivalry and to meet all obligations of any of its tenures. That feudal duties might conflict with the spiritual character of churchmen was recognized by Norman rulers, who had a very simple solution — that feudal obligations should override spiritual ones.

William I and his chaplain, Lanfranc, were strong supporters of ecclesiastical reforms, and they found much in the old English Church that required their attention. Where Church reforms involved clerical freedom from secular control, however, there was only partial royal support; where the aim was ecclesiastical superiority over lay authority, there was implacable royal opposition. In Normandy William's ecclesiastical supremacy had been firmly established and he had every intention of maintaining secular authority in England.

It was during this period of the Hildebrandine reforms that the papacy was establishing itself as the supreme authority over the Western Church, and was seeking to impose its own religious aims on secular rulers. After the Conquest it looked hopefully toward England, a country that had always shown considerable respect for the papacy; and its new leader, William, had put himself in a somewhat false position. He had first submitted his claim to the English kingdom to the papal curia, which had decided in his favor; the Pope had sent him a blessed banner just before the invasion and had rejoiced later in its success. William, therefore, had implicitly recognized the papacy as a superior court and thus had given both Alexander II and Gregory VII the opportunity to claim his feudal homage and fealty. This, however, William firmly refused to give.

In 1070, the king's chaplain, Lanfranc, was elected Archbishop of Canterbury. Formerly a monk in Normandy, he accepted this dignity with the greatest reluctance and evidently did not find his onerous new office in a foreign and to his mind backward land at all to his taste. Nevertheless, he proved a most able administrator, a fine churchman, and a wise counsellor of the king, whose taste for efficient organization he shared. It was largely through the combined efforts of the king and his archbishop that important reforms in the Church were carried out. The English sees and monasteries were quickly filled with Norman bishops and abbots, more learned than their English predecessors, with greater administrative abilities and a taste for reform. As part of their administrative policy, the Norman bishops transferred their seats from older to newer centers of population. With full royal support they reinvigorated cathedral chapters,[6] and the general effect of their efforts was an improvement in both learning and piety among the clergy.

William was willing to implement papal demands that Church administration should be by purely ecclesiastical bodies, but he insisted on maintaining ultimate control over them. All ecclesiastical matters were henceforth to be handled in separate Church courts, and bishops and archdeacons were not to hold pleas in shire and hundred moots.

The new courts of ecclesiastical jurisdiction had several functions. In the *cure of souls*, that is, matters relating to the spiritual welfare of the people, they could admonish, fine, or even excommunicate the offender; and by royal order the sheriff would enforce such judgments. Church courts also acted in matters relating to *ecclesiastical economy*, the maintenance of the fabric of churches by tithes and other payments due the Church by the laity and which its courts collected. Since the priest heard the dying man's last words and wishes, ecclesiastical courts handled the *probate of wills*, usually oral, occasionally written. From the duty of the Church to protect the helpless came ecclesiastical judicial control of *wardship* of the *physical persons* of minors. This function might conflict with feudal law on wardship dealing with a fief, but generally there were few problems about severing the *personam* of canon law from the *rem* of feudal law. It was at this time also that the Church established its claim to exclusive jurisdiction over *matrimonial* cases.

Canon law was more sophisticated than either Anglo-Saxon or Norman feudal customary law. A generation after William I it was so developed that Gratian could codify it, and even in the late eleventh century it was fast approaching a symmetry, partly due to its Roman law basis, but also because of the judicial skill of the clergy in making the law apply to new situations, which secular law could not match. In their decisions, clerical judges were guided by several laws, each derived from the one superior to it. Thus at the summit was the Bible, particularly the New Testament, below which were decisions of early Church councils and later the papal decretals. This was a formidable and complex law, but persons accustomed to theological problems were competent to handle it.

[6] Cathedral chapters were composed of clergy attached to a cathedral foundation and not assigned to a specific parish. Both Canterbury and York Provinces had cathedral chapters of regular (monastic) and secular clergy. Although only the latter was strictly a chapter of "canons," the term was used to cover both types of cathedral chapter clergy.

By the time of the Norman Conquest, canon law had lost some of its connections with Roman law, and popes were beginning to question that part of Roman law that made the will of the secular emperor supreme. For a time the papacy actually forbade clerics to study Roman law, in spite of the canon law debt to the principles of Roman law.

Ecclesiastical courts were hierarchical. In ascending order the courts of the archdeacon, bishop, and archbishop applied canon law, with the latter two courts largely appellate in jurisdiction. Appeal from the archbishop's court was to the papal curia, but this was extremely rare. The hierarchical arrangement of ecclesiastical tribunals and the right of appeal through them made them very different from their secular counterparts; in both Anglo-Saxon and Norman law every court legally possessed concurrent final jurisdiction. The burden of other duties usually prevented archbishop and bishop from presiding in their own courts. Instead they delegated this duty to a chancellor, a cleric who was expert in canon law. Consequently, Church courts, unlike the lay assemblies, often consisted of a judge sitting alone, though he might call in others if he wished. These courts and their law were quite distinct from any others existing in England. Eventually they were to pose a serious challenge to royal authority. But this challenge did not come in the days of William I, whose Archbishop was no advocate of papal supremacy and who willingly accepted the principle that appeals to the papal court could only be made with royal permission.

William I consistently resisted any threat to his ecclesiastical powers, either from his own clergy or from the Pope. Alexander II claimed that William had promised to do fealty to the Pope for his new land: William made no move. In 1080 Pope Gregory VII instructed his legate to inquire when William proposed to do this fealty and also pay *Peter's Pence*, a special tax to the papacy, which he alleged had traditionally been paid by the English. Through Lanfranc, who had coldly correct relations with Gregory, William replied that the Pope was in error about his having promised to do fealty. However, William was willing to pay Peter's Pence, including its arrears, to the papacy; perhaps for this reason it did not press the matter of fealty further.

At the same time William, in co-operation with Lanfranc, defined certain basic rules which should govern relationships between Church and crown. Misleadingly termed the "triple concordat" (for that implies negotiation and agreement), these principles were uncompromisingly laid down by William, and every English monarch afterwards who was strong enough to do so insisted on their observance. The English clergy should recognize no pope without royal approval, which would also be necessary for the admission of papal legates and bulls into the realm. No ecclesiastical council should meet, discuss anything, or have its decisions binding without royal approval. No royal tenant-in-chief should be excommunicated without royal approval. This final precaution was necessary because by a few well-placed anathemas the Church might disrupt his entire administration. The excommunicate was not only damned in the next world but ostracized in this.

The Growth of Kingship

The crown steadily extended its powers at the expense of the baronage until the last of the Norman monarchs, Stephen (1135–54). His failings created such anarchy that only by accelerating the growth of monarchy could his Angevin successor hope to restore order. Before Stephen, however, the sons of William I had succeeded in tipping the feudal balance of power very much in favor of the king.

William II (1087–1100) turned feudal law to the advantage of the crown. The second son of the Conqueror, he owed his crown to his father. Normandy as a fief had to pass by primogeniture to his elder brother, Robert. But England was not a fief, and William I doubted the ability of Robert to control its barons. He therefore, in a sense, "willed" England to his second son, as the only man able to deal with these nobles. The title of William II rested on the homage and fealty given him by royal tenants-in-chief as their lord. Some of them rebelled subsequently and without success, and Duke Robert of Normandy failed to take advantage of their rising. William II broke the rebellion by using the English fyrd and by making fair promises, most of which he soon broke.

From the point of view of constitutional history, what is most interesting about William II's reign is the skill with which, under the guidance of his astute friend, Ranulf Flambard, Bishop of Durham, he succeeded in distorting and exploiting the feudal contract. As a theologian, Ranulf knew how to interpret law for specific purposes, and for his master the fundamental purpose was money. All feudal incidents soared in amount, their objects twisted to serve royal ends. Reliefs became things to be dreaded, and the incident of marriage downright extortion. More important, Ranulf pressed upon the king the feudal principle that tenure, not the persons holding by it, governed the feudal relationship between lord and vassal.

In no place was the application of this principle so important as in the fiefs of the Church, which, although including frankalmoign, were largely in knight's service. By applying this legal principle to Church holdings it was plain how feudal law, in so far as it was unwritten, consistently favored the king. When the king applied the rule of "tenure, not persons" to Church lands, he was dealing with an enormously wealthy and potentially rebellious corporation; but William was not the man to be deterred by the latter consideration.

By feudal law a vacant military fief reverted to the lord until its new tenant performed homage and fealty. It was assumed that this interval would be brief; but William II, by demanding exorbitant payments for relief and primer seisin, lengthened it. He kept ecclesiastical fiefs vacant by refusing permission to chapters to fill vacant Church offices. While these fiefs were thus "temporarily" in his hands, he granted portions of them (viewing them now as part of his demesne) to friends, so that when the cleric was finally allowed to enter his fief, he found its extent and resources greatly reduced but its obligations the same as before. By a strictly legalistic view the king had not broken feudal law, but he had certainly distorted it.

The most famous example of this royal practice was the Province of Canterbury, vacant for four years after the death of Lanfranc in 1089. During that time the king refused to let the Canterbury chapter elect a successor and retained the fiefs of the primate, taking all of the revenues. In 1093, on what he thought was his deathbed, William in an agony of apprehension about his doubtful welcome in the next world, permitted the chapter to act. The election went to Anselm, who promptly raised in the issue of his investiture, the first of the great quarrels between Church and crown.[7]

Throughout his reign William II did all he could to make feudal incidents yield more money. When heirs could not pay the enormous reliefs demanded by him, the king had curia regis declare their lands forfeited to him. Wardship usually left fiefs drained dry. Marriage meant the sale of royal permission at a high price. Escheats and forfeitures were rigidly interpreted. Tenants-in-chief might groan, but feudal law gave them little remedy. Rebellion seemed futile. Then on

[7] Below, p. 75.

2 August 1100, William II went hunting in New Forest and was found with an arrow in his throat — dead.

Henry I (1100–1135) continued the Norman policy of centralization. A member of the hunting party, he wasted no time mourning, but spurred to Winchester and seized the treasury, an action typical of the man. If William II personified the brawling, roistering Norman, Henry I was the cold, shrewd Norman administrator. The barons were willing to have Henry as their lord, but their recent experiences made them set conditions, which Henry met with many vague promises and considerable political artistry.

The *Coronation Charter* [8] was a generalized statement of the feudal contract. It is of fundamental importance in English constitutional history because it placed the king under law (although Henry I, once safely crowned, continued to adapt feudal law to his own purposes), and also because it was the antecedent of the more precise expression of feudal custom set forth in Magna Carta. The Coronation Charter was based on the contract for conveyancing land, the most binding contract of that time. To the Church the new king promised that while one of its fiefs was vacant he would not sell, rent, or otherwise reduce it. In addition he assured the Church that he would demand no "unjust" exactions. The issue that was now disturbing all Europe, whether the king or the Pope was the supreme head of the Church, was not referred to.

Lay tenants of the king received similar promises. They would not be liable to "illegal" exactions under the guise of feudal incidents. Reliefs would not be so high as to amount to a redemption of fiefs. Heiresses holding of the king had to receive his permission to marry, but he promised never to deny it unless the proposed match were to one of his enemies. The king also promised never to force a minor heiress into marriage, or even arrange one for her, without the approval of the baronage — a move in the direction of marriage arrangements for socage heiresses. Widows of tenants-in-chief would not be forced into remarriage and while unmarried would retain their dower rights. Although the king retained the right to revenues from a fief in wardship, he promised that the personal control of the minor should be by the mother. Henry also declared that he would drop his brother's practice of demanding serfs from his military tenants to labor on the royal manors. Personal property (not land) might be willed — a reasonable

[8] Or Charter of Liberties. For the text of the charter see Douglas, II, 400–402.

concession, in that feudal law was not interested in chattels. If a man died intestate, his survivors would apportion his personal effects, a concession to laymen but also a setback to the ecclesiastical courts, which had hopes of securing jurisdiction over intestate property. An odd concession in the charter was its promise of "reasonable" fines as defined by "English" custom, which suggests that the Norman aristocracy was gradually being anglicized. The king also promised to restore the Laws of Edward the Confessor, that is, the good old ways of the good old days.

Henry enjoined his vassals to do for their tenants what he had already done for them. Setting an example of lenience toward tenants, he cancelled all debts that any of them might have owed to his brother. To please the English he also remitted all outstanding murder fines (the *murdrum*)[9] and promised that in future these amounts should be the same as in the Laws of Edward the Confessor, though as the murdrum had not existed before Hastings this was rather a vague assurance. Finally, while the charter retained royal forest rights, it significantly added that it was with the consent of the baronage.

Although not as precise as later constitutional documents, the Coronation Charter began the tradition of declarations citing wrongs — wrongs being defined as what was contrary to ancient custom. Although Henry I ignored the charter at his convenience, the fact remained that a formal document had declared that certain things, even when done by the king, were illegal.

The relationship between Church and state inevitably became strained with the growing power of the king. Papal pretentions increased the rivalry between them. The crux of the issue was the Church's claim to complete independence of all lay authorities. No strong feudal monarch was likely to admit this claim. If the Church were essentially a spiritual force, it also occupied a vital place in the feudal system. Furthermore, spiritual lords did not hesitate to employ spiritual weapons in secular affairs, and in an age of faith these weapons were powerful. With Church and king equally jealous of their powers, a collision was bound to occur sooner or later.

Church-crown relations in England were based upon the policies of William I, which assumed co-operation between the two institutions; such co-operation had been possible while he and Lanfranc lived. Under William II, however, relations with the Church steadily de-

[9] Below, pp. 79–80.

teriorated, until the *investiture* struggle, a source of bitter controversy throughout Christendom, brought matters to a head. The issue was expressed in symbolic terms — whether ecclesiastics should receive their symbols of authority from the spiritual or lay powers. Behind this symbolic quarrel was the issue, clearly seen by the principals, as to the ultimate authority for churchmen — Pope or king.

England became involved in the quarrel with the election of Anselm as Archbishop of Canterbury in 1093. With the uncompromising zeal of the scholar, Anselm requested William II to waive his obligation of performing homage and fealty for lands which the Archbishop held of him, and simultaneously refused to receive his symbols of office — ring and crozier — from the king. William II would not yield on either point, and Anselm soon left England.

Henry I, wanting the support of the Church, asked the wandering Archbishop to return and found him co-operative in all things except the crucial ones of homage, fealty, and investiture. Characteristically, Henry did not press these matters with Anselm; instead he arrived at a compromise with the Pope, whom Anselm had declared to be his only superior. By this agreement Henry abandoned his claim to invest prelates, and in return the Pope ordered English prelates — including Anselm, who must have been bewildered — to do homage and fealty to the king for their temporalities *before* their spiritual investiture. In consequence the king retained an effective veto over the selection of prelates, in that his refusal to accept their homage and fealty precluded their investiture and denied them entry to their lands, without which they could not support their ecclesiastical dignity.

For the rest of his reign Henry I remained on good terms with the Church. He permitted cathedral chapters to elect bishops, according to his Coronation Charter promise, but always in his presence. The rules of William I were continued without comment from either side.

Royal Finances

Beyond the revenues available to William I, Henry I added those of the *auxilium*, or *donum*, from boroughs, a fixed payment to the king, often in return for the grant of borough status. Royal revenues also greatly increased from the practice of *scutage*, a monetary commutation of military service. William I had used it as an act of grace for ecclesiastical vassals with military fiefs. Henry I extended the practice to lay holders in chivalry. Although theory still held that scutage was only a mark of favor and did not imply that the obligation to supply knights was permanently waived, Henry I invoked it increasingly. Scutage gave cash to buy mercenaries, weakened the military potential of the baronage, could be demanded by the king as he chose, and used for any purpose — not merely for men at arms.

The greater the royal revenues, the greater the need for some system of accounting, so the Treasury became an increasingly important department of the government. Two forms existed: one permanently established in Winchester Cathedral; the other traveling with the king. The safest place for this traveling Treasury was under the royal bed or in the adjoining wardrobe, where were also stored his rich robes and strong chests for jewels. Bedchamber (or just Chamber) and Wardrobe were side by side, each with personal attendants and guards. With the increase of royal funds, the permanent Treasury at Winchester expanded and developed a more elaborate system of finance. Professionals were employed to do this important work, and the distinguished members of the Fitz Neal family, which included Richard Fitz Neal, Bishop of London, Roger of Salisbury, and Nigel, Bishop of Ely, all held the office of Treasurer. But even so, the king's Chamber remained of importance. It was a private exchequer where he could receive sums of money paid to him directly, without having them pass through the hands of Treasury officials. In later days it allowed the king a certain cherished independence of the great ministers of the crown. In general, however, the king's personal control of the royal funds diminished as the responsibilities of the professional Treasury officials grew.

The Exchequer dealt with the vital *collection* of royal revenue. Originally a part of the Treasury, the Exchequer with the Treasurer at its head gradually detached itself from the parent body and eventually came to absorb it.[10] It was an excellent example of the growing administrative efficiency of the central government, and the power of the crown was greatly enhanced by the development of an effective system of revenue collection.

The name "Exchequer" came from a system of abacus computation developed at Laon in France; members of the English clergy, including Roger of Salisbury, the Treasurer, had attended a school there. The

[10] Thus in modern times it is the Chancellor of the Exchequer and not the First Lord of the Treasury (usually the Prime Minister) who is the head of the Treasury.

system used a cloth with squares resembling a checkerboard and was probably introduced into England early in the reign of Henry I. A writ of 1118 concerning payments into the Treasury of fines for violations of the king's peace refers to the method, and certainly when Richard Fitz Neal wrote the famous *Dialogue of the Exchequer* (*Dialogus de Scaccario*) in 1179, he was describing something already in operation. The *Dialogue*, between master and pupil, explained in detail the workings of the system.

At Easter the sheriffs came to curia regis, where certain of its members (Treasurer and Justiciar always included) usually sat at one side of a table covered by the checkered cloth, while the sheriffs gave a preliminary accounting. At Michaelmas (29 September) they appeared again for a final reckoning. Amounts due and paid were computed by tallies, or counters, moved on the squares of cloth. At the close of the accounting the board was cleared and a receipt prepared in duplicate. This receipt was a wooden tally with a hole in one end for "filing," with notches of different depths carved on either side to indicate by their depth the amount paid in by the sheriff, who was thus discouraged from whittling on his own. Thus doubly carved, the receipt was split down its middle, half going to the sheriff and half being retained by the Treasury as a permanent record.[11]

After the annual accounting Exchequer clerks under the direction of the Treasurer made up the yearly record of royal income on tightly rolled parchment, the *Pipe Roll*. Only the roll of 1130 remains from the reign of Henry I, and the disorderly reign of Stephen left none. But beginning with the Pipe Roll of 1155 there is a complete series, a mine of information about medieval royal administration and revenue.[12]

Modern minds, accustomed to double-entry bookkeeping, I.B.M. computers, and deficit financing, find the Exchequer system rudimentary. For the twelfth and thirteenth centuries the system's intricacies

[11] Over the years these tax receipts piled up in the Treasury, and long after the Exchequer system was gone the wooden paddles were retained; it is no light thing to destroy tax records. Ultimately they were stored in the Houses of Parliament, where in 1834 — now well-seasoned — they ignited from an overheated flue and burned the Parliament buildings to the ground. Perhaps the ghosts of those once gouged by the Exchequer system danced in savage glee around the flames, as the records of their agony sent the modern source of taxation to destruction.

[12] Besides the *Dialogue of the Exchequer* two other works, possibly by the same author, on financial practice of the twelfth century survive, the *Black Book of the Treasury* and the *Red Book of the Exchequer*. Neither of these two latter works reaches the standard of the *Dialogue*, which may be found in Douglas, II, 400–569. Selections from the Pipe Rolls may be found in Douglas, II, 569–83.

and efficiency were almost terrifying. Certainly it revealed a very wealthy king; no other would have needed such a system. It showed the diversification of governmental functions, primarily to meet problems arising from such large revenues. The Exchequer system of accounting gave a great impetus to centralization in the vital matter of finance.

Initially, the Exchequer was only a function of curia regis, but by the time of Henry I it demanded special training, so that only those members thus qualified sat at the *Exchequer sessions* of curia regis. In a relatively brief time the Exchequer separated from curia regis, but there remained a large duplication of personnel, and it is difficult to find a precise date at which the Exchequer finally "emerged."

It was as part of curia regis that the Exchequer developed judicial functions relating to revenue collection as early as the reign of Henry I, when men normally performing the judicial work of curia regis, notably the Justiciar and other legal experts, dealt with these subjects. Later these experts would become "Barons of the Exchequer," so as to meet feudal lords as equals in settling revenue disputes. In 1178 Henry II established a permanent court of five justices to hear and determine certain issues. Some see in this court the Court of the Exchequer, while others regard it as the Court of Common Pleas. The duplication of personnel, so characteristic of medieval administration, makes the difference of opinion almost impossible to resolve. The matter was not vital in terms of the twelfth century, when the court dealt with whatever came before it.

NORMAN LAW IN ENGLAND

Many of the legal changes wrought by the Norman Conquest have already been discussed in connection with feudalism and central government. At this point, however, we must consider the law per se.

Juridical Dualism

The Conquest did not mean the supplanting of Anglo-Saxon law by Norman law. The earlier law continued in full force, duly confirmed by William I for his English subjects and applied in their customary courts. Alongside of the older law, however, was now also the feudal law for Normans, operating in different courts. To modern minds legal dualism within a single jurisdiction is impossible, but to eleventh- and twelfth-century men there was no single jurisdiction but a series of laws for different people and purposes. For a good two centuries after Hastings this legal dualism continued, and the *Leges Henrici Primi* [13] (compiled about 1116) show the two laws co-existing without ever coinciding. Only when the assimilation of Normans and Saxons was complete would such legal unity emerge.

Norman feudal law was customary and unwritten, and this perhaps was even more characteristic of Norman law than Anglo-Saxon. Feudal law as such was very rarely written down. The Anglo-Saxons had presented parts of their law formally as dooms, but the Normans set down portions of their feudal law only indirectly in charters. It was only after much bitter experience that the barons, realizing that unwritten law always tended to favor the interests of the crown, sought to define some aspects of it in Magna Carta.

The Normans had no more concept of legislation than the Anglo-Saxons. They, too, saw their law as a once-given, perfect, and immutable body. Indeed, feudal law was less susceptible than Anglo-Saxon law to formal change because it was essentially contract law and so not easily modified.

Substantive feudal law was a law of contracts and torts. Truly criminal actions, that is, *pleas of the crown*, remained largely unchanged after 1066. As in Anglo-Saxon law, wrongful actions below this degree resulted in monetary payments by those committing them to the injured.

Procedural feudal law similarly resembled its Anglo-Saxon counterpart. The court baron of a lord, whose vassals fulfilled their obligation of suit of court by composing it, applied this law, with the lord merely presiding. By himself, in theory at least, he could not apply any phase of feudal law. However, a strong lord, particularly the king, would find it relatively easy to bend the assembly's decisions to his will. *Modes of proof* were the same as in Anglo-Saxon courts, with the additional ordeal of *wager of battle*. [14]

The *presentment of Englishry* was a legal expression of the inferior status of the English. In a country basically hostile to the new regime

---

[13] Douglas, II, 459–62. The title of this compilation merely indicates the laws were operating in the reign of Henry I, not that he made them.

[14] Above, p. 48.

the assassination of Normans was not uncommon. William I, in the interests both of public order and the safety of his regime, commanded that every man murdered by stealth should be presumed Norman, with the burden of proving otherwise lying on his relatives. Unless they could prove that the victim was English, the hundred where the killing occurred was liable to a heavy *amercement* (fine) to the king, known as the murdrum. In the next century Normans and English so inter-mingled that it was often impossible to prove that the dead man was English. In any case, the system was so much abused by the later Norman kings that the fine was often exacted when no murder had been committed and the death had occurred by accident. It was no doubt the royal greed for extra revenue that kept the murdrum in force for so long, but it must also have had some usefulness as a police measure. The hundred would certainly make every effort to bring the murderer to justice in order to avoid paying the fine itself. It was not abolished until 1340.

Forest laws were a Norman innovation that had serious consequences for the average man. Until the reign of Cnut, freemen could hunt any-where. Cnut reserved certain areas solely for his use, but permitted freemen to hunt on their own land. William I and his successors set aside vast areas as forests, a generic term, since much of it was "forest" only in a legal sense. It has been estimated that by Henry II's reign al-most one-third of the country had been converted by royal proclama-tion into this enormous game-preserve, all in order to gratify the royal passion for hunting, particularly the red stag. In these preserves only the king and his guests might hunt, and special forest laws dealt savagely with violators. Inhabitants of these vast areas might not legally take any game, a great hardship when hunting was less a sport than a neces-sity, to exterminate noxious animals. The tradition of these laws sur-vived into the early nineteenth century and was responsible for the extremely severe penalties for poaching.

The King's Justice

Neither Anglo-Saxons nor Normans acknowledged that the king was capable of modifying the law, and neither Anglo-Saxon nor Norman rulers ever explicitly made such a claim. Yet the king was nevertheless a legislator, with more power perhaps than either he or his subjects knew.

Legislation was infrequent, but it was certainly possible. In curia regis it was unlikely that a strong ruler would permit formal feudal law to balk his purposes of the moment, and the members of curia regis were present because he wanted them to be there. The unwritten nature of feudal law lent itself to this type of tacit, negative legislation, particularly when the issue before curia regis was of great importance to the king. The king and his curia might not break existing feudal law, but in applying it to meet royal needs, they created precedents that assumed the force of new law.

Itinerant justices spread this modified feudal law throughout the country. These agents of the crown, members of curia regis, made their appearance shortly after 1066. Their duties were largely administrative — as in the Domesday Survey — but they also had a judicial function. Their presence in the shire courts, whereby the shire court was momentarily transformed into a branch of curia regis, had important consequences. As agents of the central government, with the prestige of a strong ruler behind them, their voice carried great weight; and though it was assumed that law was law wherever it was administered, the fact was that these itinerant justices were interpreting it in a particular way. They were introducing the law of the king and curia regis into the local courts, and in consequence many of the traditional local variations in the law began to disappear. It was a slow process, but by the time of Henry II (1154–89) it had gone far enough to assure him of advantages unknown to his predecessors.

The most important changes that the Norman Conquest brought about in the English constitution were in the area of central government, largely because of the introduction of feudalism. In local government the Anglo-Saxon system remained relatively untouched, except that through the Norman sheriffs and the itinerant justices its relationship with the central government became very much more intimate. The Exchequer system consolidated the authority of the central government, which was reaching the stage at which it could no longer accept the feudal, rigidly contractual relationship between the king and his vassals. In its relations with the Church, the Norman monarchy had asserted its authority over that of the Pope. By the end of Henry I's reign the crown had established a position which even the follies and failures of Stephen were unable completely to undermine. When Henry

II became king in 1154, he had the resources with which to assert the royal authority more strongly than ever before.

READING LIST

BARLOW, FRANK. *The Feudal Kingdom in England*, Chaps. I–III.

BROOKE, Z. N. *The English Church and the Papacy from the Conquest to the Reign of John*, Chaps. I–II.

JOHNSON, C., trans. & ed. *The Course of the Exchequer.*

MORRIS, W. A. *The Mediaeval English Sheriff to 1300.*

POLLOCK, SIR FREDERICK, and FREDERIC W. MAITLAND. *History of English Law*, 2nd ed., Vol. I, Book I, Chaps. III–IV.

POOLE, A. L. *From Domesday Book to Magna Carta*, 1087–1216, Chaps. I–II.

——. *Obligations of Society in the Twelfth and Thirteenth Centuries.*

POOLE, R. L. *The Exchequer in the Twelfth Century.*

STENTON, SIR FRANK M. *The First Century of English Feudalism.*

3

THE ANGEVIN INNOVATIONS

DURING the reign of Henry II (1154–89) the foundations of central government were finally laid down; this proved to be a remarkable achievement, for some of these foundations have hardly been disturbed throughout the subsequent course of English history. Some of Henry's administrative and legal innovations give to his government a curiously modern look.

Financial Efficiency

Henry II recognized that his power was directly dependent on his wealth and that his wealth depended on effective centralization. Finance, therefore, was the main preoccupation of his administrative policies.

Judicial revenues increased. Henry insisted on the collection of old fines and fees, such as wites and fines for breaking the king's peace. He also placed his special judicial machinery at the people's disposal in return for a suitable fee. These judicial policies of the king had other far-reaching effects,[1] but they were important from the financial point of view as well.

Scutage became systematized. By 1158 the practice was sufficiently common to acquire this name scutage, which meant "shield-money," the term being used to describe a levy imposed by Henry in the War of Toulouse. Actually, in this instance the name was not too accurate, in that the demand was more nearly a tallage. The baronage paid *and* went to war. The clergy stayed home but paid heavily. Holders in chivalry of the Church, contrary to feudal law, also had to pay scutage directly to the king.

However, during the reign of the first Angevin the entire meaning of

---

[1] For these juridical effects see below, pp. 85, 102.

scutage changed. Formerly a favor by royal grace, whereby a tenant in particular circumstances might commute his military obligations for a monetary payment, it now became the preferred mode of service from military fiefs. Increasingly, vassals were asked for scutage without the alternative of active service. In dire situations the king demanded both scutage and service. Scutage, however, became divorced from immediate military needs. In 1160 and 1161 Henry called for scutage because of a *threatened* war with France. The war did not break out, but the money remained with the king; and scutage was on its way to becoming a regular levy.

New sources of revenue were opened up by the crusades. In 1166 and 1185 the king required all vassals to pay an aid for a crusade. There was no crusade, but three years later the demand was dignified by the name, *Saladin tithe,* and set at one-tenth of the value of all property (both immovable and chattels) and income. The money from this tax was never used to fight the Saracen leader, whose name was thus used. The importance of the Saladin tithe was that it marked the beginning of setting tax incidence by fractions rather than demanding fixed sums as with the older Danegeld.

Royal wealth was vast. The Pipe Rolls showed a steady increase in royal income, until in 1187 it touched £34,000. The next year tax cancellations lowered the annual figure to £22,000. These were enormous sums for the twelfth century. Add to the royal income from English sources the money coming to Henry from vassals and demesne lands in his large holdings in France, and it is easy to see why the first Angevin outdistanced all other European rulers in wealth.

Royal financial agencies became increasingly departmentalized. The growth in royal revenue made it necessary to define clearly the functions of officials entrusted with it. The Treasurer ceased to be a mere custodian of cash. Because he knew what the royal funds would bear, his influence was great in the determination of policy. He and the Justiciar knew, from their sessions in the Exchequer, now beginning to break away from curia regis, what further sources of revenue might be tapped and how older ones could be made more lucrative. Reports of sheriffs on shire finances given to the Exchequer involved a general review of local affairs. The Exchequer was the center for the collection of both revenue and information.

Administrative-Juridical Innovations

The major constitutional changes of Henry II came from certain administrative practices. Whether considered as basically administrative — as they appeared to Henry II and his contemporaries — or essentially juridical — as they appear to us — these practices brought central and local government into much closer relationship with each other. They also produced, in due course, a new form of law, which could be administered only by the royal courts. These courts eventually swept aside all rivals, until there was only one system of law, common to the entire realm. Of more immediate importance, these changes were brought about by the king acting by virtue of royal prerogative, as an independent ruler unfettered by feudal customs and constraints.

In the eyes of the king the devices by which he asserted his prerogative were essentially administrative. The *writ* was a written royal order to someone to do something. The *inquest* was a method by which the king secured information on a particular matter. Crucial to the inquest was the *jury*, whose origins lay in the practice by the Carolingian monarchs of France of having their agents put certain men under oath to report truthfully on specific topics. Norman kings had used the inquest and jury in England on several occasions, the most notable being the Domesday Survey. Henry II developed this fact-finding agency and added to its functions, for example, by using juries to assess the Saladin tithe. Broadly speaking, the juries were still largely for the purpose of gathering information but they could also be used in a judicial capacity, particularly in disputes concerning the possession of land. Every person on a jury took a solemn oath before royal agents, beginning *"Iuro"* (I swear), to tell the truth. The sworn findings of a jury were thus a true saying, a *verdictum*, a *verdict*. It was not until trial by ordeal began to die out after 1215, however, that criminal cases were decided in this way. The jurors, unlike the witnesses to land transfers in Anglo-Saxon courts,[2] were named directly by the king or his agents. Unlike the modern juryman, on the other hand, who is supposed to know nothing about the issues in dispute before he is empaneled, the Angevin juror was selected on the presumption that a man of his standing in the community would know the relevant facts. If he and his fellows did not, they were supposed to go out and get them. Nor

[2] See above, p. 18.

should the juror be confused with the Anglo-Saxon doomsman. The doomsman stated customary law, never facts, whereas the juror cared nothing for the law and was concerned only with the facts. Thus there appeared in the twelfth century that principle which is the essence of modern English law, wherever it is used: the jury is concerned with facts, not law; it is the duty of the professionals to apply the law to the facts. These amateurs were vital in the development of English jurisprudence. They were cheap — for a long time, in fact, they were unpaid — and the king never had much reason to use paid officials for securing information, as was common practice under Roman civil law systems.

It was not until later that the jury became established as a body of twelve good men and true. At this period there was no fixed number, and as many jurors were summoned as the king or his agents thought to be necessary. The principle of unanimity was, however, always accepted; the jury represented the community as a whole and was to express its true and undivided opinion on any given matter.

Though often regarded as the sure shield of the subject against royal tyranny, the jury was an institution deriving directly from the royal prerogative and with the sole purpose of furthering royal ends. In time the jury came to be something else, but Henry II was not thinking of the liberties of his subjects when he turned the old inquest to new purposes.

Somewhat broader than inquest or jury was the *assize*. Originally, as implied by the word, it was the sitting of some body, usually in fact curia regis. It soon came to be used to describe the written decision of that sitting, as in the *Assize* of Clarendon, and eventually to mean the regular sessions of the courts held throughout the country to administer civil and criminal justice. In the twelfth century the assize covered the entire process of inquest as ordered by the king for a particular situation. Not feudal institutions in any sense, the various assizes enlarged the scope of royal jurisdiction and struck directly at the basic feudal conception of a single immutable law. The assizes worked extremely well, and their procedure proved to be very much more popular than that of the feudal courts, which came to appear antiquated in comparison. Many people sought justice in the assizes, particularly in disputes over possession of land, and as the revenues from this royal justice went into the royal Exchequer, the king had good reason to encourage them to do so.

Assize procedures could be used only before *royal justices,* the final element in the new administrative-juridical system that the Angevins devised. Royal justices received writs ordering them to have a jury sworn in to answer certain questions on a specific case. This was not new. Royal commissioners had received orders in the past to use the inquest in order to secure information for the king, as in the Domesday Survey. Henry I had used them in financial transactions, as is seen from his sole surviving Pipe Roll. These men went through the country on the march, *iter;* and during the reign of Henry II they became known as *itinerant justices.* Despite this name, their major duties were for a long time primarily administrative. Henry II regarded them as administrators, even when enforcing the Assize of Clarendon on criminal accusation. Their administrative character was obvious when checking on the work of sheriffs, as in the famous Assize of Sheriffs in 1170. So valuable were they to the king that in the Assize of Northampton in 1176 (dealing with criminal justice), Henry divided the realm into six regular circuits, with three justices assigned to each annually.

The justices were the final link between central and local government. Because they were all members of curia regis, each in himself represented curia regis, whether he was traveling with the king or by himself in the wilds of Norfolk. Their appearance at a shire court transformed it during their presence into a local segment of curia regis with royal administrative duties. At such times no other court might sit in the county, and all lords and freemen and clergy had to appear before the justices to perform their duty and serve their king. Most of the important business of the county came to be transacted at the local royal court, with the result that private jurisdictions within the shire languished.

At the local royal court the justices checked on the sheriff, usually included among the justices until 1194; they swore in all juries as ordered by their writs; they checked on escheats due to the king, vacant churches for which the king had *advowson* (the right of nominating a man to a Church post for the bishop's approval), wardships, marriages, criminals, aids, usurers, wine sold contrary to law, property of dead crusaders, and other things. They held the grand assize [3] for any property dispute involving land of £5 value. They also laid tallages on royal demesne lands and boroughs in the shire as ordered by the king. In addition to their other duties, they were to do anything else the king

[3] See below, pp. 107–8.

required. So large were these duties that in 1179 Henry II increased the number of itinerant justices to twenty-one, grouped into four annual circuits. From these circuits the justices returned to capitalis curia regis, bearing the record of its local segments and giving any explanations needed.[4]

With the development of these administrative juridical methods . the influence of the central government in local administration was very greatly increased. While the sheriff remained an important link between the two levels, his role declined as members of curia regis came into his county, regularly, checking on everything in it. The jury also provided the central government with an agency to implement its administrative policy. When the central government decided to reorganize the fyrd, the *Assize of Arms* in 1181 made it the responsibility of the jury to decide what military equipment each man, according to his social and economic status, ought to possess.

By these methods the victory of royal justice was assured. To modern minds a single system of courts may appear logical, but to people in the twelfth century it was a novel development unsanctioned by custom. Courts "belonged" to certain persons, who therefore had the right to their revenues. In the sweep of royal justice, Englishmen of the twelfth century were seeing the triumph of one private court baron over all others. Lords, who watched business dwindle at their courts baron as their vassals waited for royal justices, found this astounding and unpleasant. The fact that the king was the liege lord of all freemen might suggest that the expansion of his court baron could occur within the feudal framework, but people rapidly came to view the traveling curia regis not as the court baron of their liege lord but as the royal court of their sovereign, to whom they increasingly turned. Yet the barons were powerless before these prerogative, nonfeudal acts of kingship, and further prejudiced their own cause by themselves having recourse to the royal courts; indeed, so useful did they find them that they inserted a clause in Magna Carta designed to perpetuate the system. Thus all members of the feudal society of the twelfth century were conspiring toward its end, at least in so far as the principles of private jurisdiction were concerned.

Residual jurisdiction lay with the central curia regis. Any matter of

[4] It is unlikely that the justices in the twelfth century were regarded as actually *being* the monarch; but this is certainly the modern view, which receives symbolic application in justices' *not* rising when the national anthem is played at the opening of a court's term.

particular importance to the king came before it for action. With private litigants wishing to use royal courts but not wanting to wait until the itinerant justices appeared in their locality, curia regis, that much overworked body which traveled with the king, was swamped. Private parties, moreover, might have difficulty reaching this normal curia regis, which moved rapidly with the king through his far-flung territories. Unless a litigant were willing to rush after Henry II, he would have to wait for the itinerant justices to appear in his shire. This meant delay and also a possible loss of judicial revenue — both things equally abhorrent to Henry II. The remedy was obvious.

A *central court* was established by Henry II in 1178. Staffed by five men (three lay and two clerical) of the royal household, it was still a part of curia regis. But instead of following the king, it remained at Westminster where it handled all cases brought before it, with the help of a jury. Only cases of peculiar difficulty might pass on to the king and his traveling curia regis. By 1189 this branch of curia regis, performing only judicial work, had separated from the parent body, as is indicated by the acquisition of its own seal in that year. In time the financial jurisdiction of the court moved into the hands of fiscal experts, so as to divide it further into the Courts of the Exchequer and of Common Pleas.

The central court did not end the work of itinerant justices, but merely relieved it. But soon it came to be accepted that the central court would handle any case unless (*nisi*) the itinerant justices were to reach the shire where the issues arose before (*prius*) the central court could take it up. Those cases were stuffed into the saddle bags of the itinerant justices for determination in the particular county. In later centuries the central court included with such cases certain directions for the justices to follow in their local determination of them, so that the *nisi prius* cases became an important feature of the growth of common law.[5]

Chancery partially emerged from curia regis. The volume of paper work entailed by royal administrative policies was enormous. Originally the royal chaplain had also been the royal clerk because of his confidential relationship with the king, whose soul he shrived and whose letters he wrote. Edward the Confessor introduced the Norman technique (in turn learned from Carolingian monarchs) of authenticating the royal signature by a seal; and William I required the royal seal to

[5] Below, pp. 136-7.

pass over all documents emanating from curia regis. The royal seal — a heavy chunk of metal showing the king on horseback on one side, and seated and encircled by his titles on the other — could do many things. It was, however, a nuisance for the king to carry constantly on his person. Thus he gave custody of this powerful artifact to a man he could trust, his chaplain, who produced it whenever the king wished to use it. During the reign of Henry I the chaplain ceased to bring the seal to the king and instead affixed it himself to documents on the royal order. This shift in practice marked the chaplain's transformation from a personal to a governmental functionary. By that time royal business had swollen to such an extent that it was beyond the ability of the chaplain to handle it alone. He therefore organized a secretarial office, the *scriptorium*, where one of the more gifted clerks, the *magister scriptorii*, supervised details, while he busied himself with matters of more general concern.

The great increase in paper work as a result of Henry II's policies made it impractical for the king to send a separate order to the chaplain each time a document needed the royal seal. At first the king sent blanket orders to pass the seal on broad categories of documents; and soon the chaplain, who knew the royal mind and royal policies, frequently affixed the seal without any reference to the king. The chaplain, however, found it impossible to care for both the royal soul and the royal business being handled by the scriptorium, which accompanied the king. He was usually to be found in whatever castle he happened to be resident working behind the screen, or *cancelli;* this name soon indicated the writing area itself. The chaplain, therefore, became the *Chancellor* in charge of the *Chancery;* and though still an ecclesiastic, he was no longer the royal confessor but a key figure in royal government.

Chancery remained part of the traveling royal household until the death of Henry II, when the long absence of Richard I (1189–99) from England and then the loss by John (1199–1216) of most of his French territories caused it to come to rest near the central court at Westminster. Even before that time Chancery had formalized much of its work by classifying its documents into broad categories. The most solemn were charters, usually grants from the king attested by witnesses, with seals impressed upon silk or leather hanging below. Judicial writs were a large part of the flood of parchment, as were also proclamations to people generally, *letters patent* (open letters). More private matters were so sealed as to close the parchment in *letters close*. Chancery clerks of Henry II were too busy to employ elegant phraseology. Their documents got right down to the business at hand, and they reached that stage of bureaucracy characterized by blank forms.

The multiplication of royal seals was a measure of the increase of royal business. William I found one seal sufficient; Henry II feared that the necessity of having his Chancellor pass the seal over all papers flowing through Chancery would create a bottleneck. Financial matters were so vital that they could not wait for the Chancellor to seal pertinent documents. In a radical innovation Henry II gave the Exchequer a smaller royal seal, held by the Treasury and brought out at the Justiciar's command for the Easter and Michaelmas sessions. The possession by the Exchequer of its own seal marked its separation from curia regis, although its top officials still sat in the parent body.

The original *great seal* remained with the Chancellor, whose duties were so large that occasionally he fell behind in them. The impatient Henry II ordered a *privy seal*, which he held himself and used for personal matters, but also at times for public ones. By the thirteenth century it had become a burning question which matters were proper for the privy seal, still held by the king, though being used more and more often in the transaction of public business, and which for the great seal, which was still in the Chancellor's possession.

There was also the royal *signet*, which the king wore on his finger. Although Henry II may not have had one, Richard I used the signet for sealing personal documents of a more intimate nature; and since the signet continued to authenticate only such matters, it remained in the sovereign's personal control.

Although the multiplication and particular uses of seals may appear somewhat trivial, for twelfth- and thirteenth-century officials they were vital. Their multiplication proved how widely royal government had enlarged its purview. Had royal literacy been more widespread in Carolingian times, perhaps seals would have loomed less large. But though initially a matter of primitive necessity, later they symbolized power and dignity, and have thus remained a part of modern administrative practice.

Church and Crown

The one institution capable of resisting the expanding royal administrative system and also of competing with it was the Church. The drive for centralization by Henry II was certain to produce a clash between Church and crown.

The opposition of the Church rested on its claims to a unique spiritual authority. Since it was also at the same time a great international feudal corporation, the monarch had strong political reasons for resisting any such ecclesiastical claims. The clergy on the other hand, seeing that few feudal prescriptive rights could for long resist the encroachment of the royal power, took their stand on the grounds of their independence of all secular authority. Although in theory it might be thought that crown and miter moved in different orbits, the practice of William I and his successors, and indeed feudal custom itself, had always insisted that, whatever claims the Pope and some of his clergy might make for the supremacy of the spiritual over the lay authorities, in the last resort the Church was subordinate to the crown. This position was maintained in England for the first fifty years or so after the Conquest.

During Stephen's reign, however, the Church was able to take advantage of his weaknesses to win large concessions from him. At Oxford in 1136 he granted the clergy a large measure of freedom from secular interference and restored to the Church all the possessions it had lost since the time of William I. Though these concessions were wrung from the king when he was in a weak bargaining position and he may have hoped to be able to withdraw them later, by the time Henry II came to the throne the Church had secured certain permanent advantages and was in a position to challenge the Angevin policy of centralization. The immediate issue concerned the jurisdiction of the Church courts.

The scope of ecclesiastical jurisdiction had greatly increased during the reign of Stephen. He permitted it to include all clerical *persons* and any case involving such a person. This jurisdiction encompassed such a vast area that it is inconceivable that any of the first three Normans would ever have consented to it. Moreover, the Church extended the definition of "clergy" during the reign of Stephen to include not only ordained and monastic clergy but also the "unordained," which was any person connected with the Church. Thus sextons, vergers, gravediggers, bell-ringers, serfs on the demesne lands of the Church, and perhaps its free vassals — all were "unordained" clergy. Since clerics were literate, by inference all literates were clerics, so that students fell into this broad definition of "clergy." Taken together these claims gave a vast field of jurisdiction to the Church courts and placed many feudal tenants beyond the control of their liege lord, the king.

The *res* jurisdiction of Church courts had similarly grown when Stephen allowed them the right to declare whether lands held by the Church and its subsidiary corporations were in frankalmoign or in some lay tenure. Not surprisingly, the ecclesiastical courts usually found for frankalmoign; whereupon all issues arising from such lands fell to the Church courts, even if the Church regranted portions of them in lay tenures to laymen. The total jurisdictional claims by the Church were enormous, and had they been admitted by Henry II would have left the Church an *imperium in imperio* and himself with greatly diminished power. The Church courts were quite independent of the king, and their appeals culminated in the papal court. Henry knew moreover, that people's loyalties went to authorities whose courts decided their cases. Again, ecclesiastical judicial procedure was more advanced than that of the royal courts. Church courts employed oral, sworn testimony, proof by paper (sworn depositions), and pleading. The procedure of appeal through several ranks of courts required a careful system of court reporting and judicial records. The very efficiency of ecclesiastical jurisprudence was an argument in favor of those who sought greater independence for the Church.

Henry II's policy was to restore the Church to the position it had occupied during the reign of William I. Inevitably, this led to conflicts, the most dramatic of which revolved round the issue of the "criminous clerks." These were criminals who either genuinely belonged to the clergy, or else had claimed and been granted clerical status with, in many cases, quite insufficient justification — sometimes merely on the grounds of their literacy. Such offenders were thus tried by the episcopal courts. These courts sometimes pardoned or acquitted criminals who in lay courts would certainly have been less fortunate. Moreover, even if found guilty, the penalties imposed by Church courts were not nearly so severe. Canon law forbade the death penalty, but the admonitions, fines, and degradations imposed by the episcopal courts seemed far too mild to the lay authorities. The king, therefore, claimed the right to punish criminous clerks after they had been convicted by the ecclesiastical courts; the clergy on the other hand claimed that the offending cleric should continue to be under the protection of the Church after his conviction. The issue of the criminous clerks therefore gave rise to a number of vital questions concerning the relationship between Church and crown.

In the early years of his reign, while Theobald was still Archbishop of Canterbury, Henry bided his time. His close friend, Thomas Becket, was his Chancellor and trusted adviser, and there can be little doubt that he expected Becket's support in his attempt to recover some of the ground lost to the Church during Stephen's reign. Becket was Archdeacon of Canterbury, but a worldly man and sufficiently sympathetic toward royal policy to be exceedingly useful to Henry during this period. When Theobald died Henry had no difficulty naming a successor: Becket duly became Archbishop of Canterbury in 1162.

No sooner had he been elected than he ceased entirely to do what Henry must have expected of so loyal and tried a friend. A perfectionist in any duty he undertook, he became the complete churchman and devoted all his great energies and abilities toward strengthening the position of the Church. The interests of the crown were no longer his concern. To Henry, who had depended upon him to help work out a *modus vivendi* with the Church, it was a severe blow. Becket demanded complete ecclesiastical independence, emphasized the point by at once resigning the chancellorship. At a meeting of curia regis at Woodstock in 1163 he successfully flouted the royal wishes. Henry had demanded a change in the method of paying sheriffs, who had been levying two shillings on every hide both within and out of the royal demesne for their salaries. The king planned to continue this levy making it part of the sheriff's ferm, to be paid to the Exchequer, which would then reimburse the sheriff and so bring him under closer royal control. Becket said that while the lands of the Church would pay the amount, it would be in the form of an aid and contributed only if the Church had received good services from a sheriff. This high tone provoked an angry royal reply, but in the end the king had to withdraw his demand. It was probably the first occasion on which the central government was successfully opposed on a matter of taxation.

Friction between the king and Archbishop increased. Their vigorous personalities were now committed to two incompatible and irreconcilable theories. Henry maintained that he was not molesting the

Church by innovations, but trying to restore the position that had existed under Henry I, which in turn had been based upon the policies of the Conqueror. To Becket it was a matter of indifference whether the king's views on what constituted that situation were correct or not; nothing could limit Holy Church in any manner. Thus when Henry raised the issue of criminous clerks at another meeting of curia regis in 1163, Becket resisted all royal proposals. Significantly, however, the other prelates at that meeting did not support the Archbishop. After hot words between king and Archbishop, Becket was willing to have the clergy agree to the customs current in the days of Henry I, but always "saving their order," which practically nullified their assent.

The king now summoned the articulate elements of the nation to meet in curia regis at Clarendon in 1164. At the meeting Henry asked the members to act as a jury of inquest and state what had been the customs of Henry I in so far as relations between Church and crown were concerned. Although the "jurors" knew what the king wanted, they did not give him all he desired. Furthermore, among the fact-finders were the great spiritual barons. But all of the council agreed to abide by these customs except Becket, who entered his demurrer that it was of no import if these customs were those of Henry I; no earthly power could bind the Church. After a stormy session the other prelates persuaded Becket to give a halting acceptance of the "jury's" verdict, but with so many conditions as to render it meaningless. Later Becket sought to evade even this partial assent by securing a papal dispensation from his promise, as having been wrung from him by threats. But the other churchmen worked with the king and produced the sixteen items of the famous *Constitutions of Clarendon*.[6]

The Constitutions of Clarendon were an attempt to codify the customs that were believed to have been enforced by the Norman kings. In general, they governed the relations between Church and crown until the sixteenth century. Thus they repeated the rules of William I and the solution of the investiture controversy. However, royal permission was now required for ecclesiastical interdict (withholding sacraments from a region) as well as for excommunications; and royal approval for excommunication now extended to demesne officials as well as to tenants-in-chief. The royal courts were to decide by what tenure the Church and its bodies held land and were also to have jurisdiction over cases of debt; and the right of sanctuary for pursued

[6] Douglas, II, 718-22.

criminals was not to cover debtors' goods. When a case had both spiritual and temporal issues, the Justiciar would sever them and send them to the proper courts. No appeals could be made beyond the archbishop's court to the Court of Rome, however, without the king's consent.

These clauses in the Constitutions reduced the purview of Church courts to that enjoyed prior to Stephen. Certain administrative matters were decided in a feudal manner, and so in the royal favor. Royal permission was required for the granting of churches lying in the royal demesne, and for the departure from the realm of ecclesiastical as well as for lay tenants-in-chief. Similarly, spiritual lords were equally obligated with lay vassals for the duty of suit of court, although they might withdraw where a matter involved life and limb. Revenues from vacant Church fiefs should go to the king, but he had to meet ecclesiastical requests to fill such vacant posts promptly. However, the resultant election should be in the royal chapel. The interests of secular barons generally were protected by the provision that they must approve the entrance of any of their serfs into the clergy.

The king, in his turn, made certain concessions. The Constitutions gave the Church the benefit of the royal administrative machinery. Upon ecclesiastical request, the sheriff could seize the goods of a contumacious excommunicated person, who might give no oath but had to give security that he would abide by the judgment of the Church court. Bishops received what no other lord had, nothing less than the royal machinery of accusation by a jury, which they could empanel for spiritual offenses, subsequently triable in the archdeacon's court. Bishops could also use sheriffs to force attendance at ecclesiastical courts, although they could not excommunicate persons refusing to obey a summons until they had requested the sheriff to act. However, they could force royal courts to try barons for interfering with ecclesiastical tribunals.

Once again it was the question of the criminous clerks that caused the greatest controversy. Becket had violently opposed any suggestion that the king might have the right to try criminous clerks in his royal courts, and in the Constitutions Henry was more moderate in his demands. He asked only that a clerk, once convicted by the ecclesiastical court, should no longer be under the protection of the Church, but should be sentenced by a secular court.

Becket for the moment accepted this solution and instructed his bishops to do the same. It was a compromise, whereby royal justices were to rule upon the status of any person claiming clerical privileges: they might deny that Church hangers-on were clergy, but were most unlikely to rule unfavorably on the plea by a member of the monastic or ordained clergy. The trial of the criminous clerk therefore was left solely in the hands of the Church court, which could in the last resort render the royal court impotent by finding the accused innocent.

But though Becket had for the moment accepted the Constitutions, he had managed to avoid setting his seal to the document, and very soon he had second thoughts. These were confirmed when the Pope declared most of the clauses intolerable. Becket reversed his decision, and his relations with Henry went from bad to worse, until he was in such danger that he fled the country. He remained in exile in France for the next six years.

In December 1170, Henry II was on the Continent and met Becket, who was everything the king remembered before their quarrel. Henry believed that Becket wanted to return to England; and although the Archbishop did not mention the Constitutions, the king was certain that he tacitly accepted them. Unwilling to humiliate his old friend by demanding a formal acceptance of the Constitutions, Henry urged Becket to return. Becket took ship to England, while Henry remained in France. On arriving at Canterbury, the Archbishop excommunicated all the bishops who had earlier that year participated in the coronation of Henry's son and heir, in a ceremony which only the Archbishop of Canterbury had the right to perform and which had been forbidden by the Pope. This had disastrous effects upon the English Church and gravely endangered the royal administration.

Henry's reaction to Becket's astonishing move was frenzied rage, during which he was said to have exclaimed, "Is there none will rid me of this turbulent priest?" Some knights crossed the Channel and spurred to Canterbury, where they entered the cathedral. By the high altar the conflict reached its dramatic climax. "Where is the foul traitor, Thomas Becket?" demanded the knights. With his own sense of the dramatic, the Archbishop, clad in full vestments, gave his answer of defiance, but one also revealing his own dichotomy and that of his Church, "Here stands no traitor but a loyal subject of the king; but also of God's Holy Church." The knights were no experts in casuistry; drawing their swords they dispatched the "turbulent priest" into martyrdom and sainthood. "No man can serve two masters."

Henry's victory after this tragedy proved his strength. With his whole program endangered by the murder, he underwent a humiliating penance for having instigated, even if inadvertently, the deed. He promised to conquer Ireland as a papal fief. Then he promised Pope Alexander III that he would cancel all the customs introduced during his reign to the detriment of the Church. This presumably implied the Constitutions of Clarendon, but as he had always insisted that the Constitutions were the "customs of his grandfather," it made little difference. The shaken king had, however, to cancel the procedure for trials of criminous clerks. Yet even here the crown was soon to limit ecclesiastical jurisdiction by declaring that misdemeanors and treasons did not fall under this *benefit of clergy* and so could be tried only by royal courts.

Benefit of clergy continued to apply to felonies without much change until the religious transformations of Henry VIII's reign. By that time almost all literate persons were enjoying the privilege. With the religious changes, Parliament began the dual process of narrowing the benefit as to crimes but enlarging it as to persons, beginning with peers, who received the privilege for their first conviction of a felony other than murder. The process continued through the seventeenth century when the number of "clergyable" crimes fell, but the number of persons eligible for the "benefit" increased. Temporary acts of Parliament, commencing with the reign of James I (1603–25) and made permanent with William III (1689–1702), extended the benefit to all women upon their first conviction of a "clergyable felony." The reduction of clergyable crimes, however, was so steady that when benefit of clergy was finally abolished in 1827 there were very few such crimes left.

Until that time, however, criminal training included memorizing the "neck verse" of the Bible, which saved the convicted person's neck if the crime were clergyable. By the sixteenth century, royal courts had entire control of criminal proceedings. Upon conviction, the felon was asked why he should not receive sentence of death. If he could, the wretch "pleaded his clergy" and proved his clerical status by literacy, tested by Holy Writ. The Bible was allowed to fall open at random, and the convicted person read the first verse catching his eye. Over the years court Bibles ever more frequently fell open at a page in Psalms, where lay the verse so carefully memorized by professional law-breakers, and carrying echoes of the fierce struggle of the

twelfth century between two proud men, each heading a powerful institution, "How long will ye judge unjustly, and accept the persons of
the wicked? Selah." [7]

The Proof of Royal Power

During the reign of Henry II, kingship had steadily grown at
the expense of the baronial element of the feudal scheme and had
checked the power of the Church. English monarchy was thus established and though the power of the monarch may still have been far
from absolute, the machinery of central government had come into
existence and was sufficient to maintain royal power through such
vicissitudes as rebellions, minorities, and royal absence. The work of
the first Angevin gave it a momentum which permitted the system
to operate for the next decade without a resident king.

During his ten-year reign (1189–99) Richard I was only six months
in England, which he regarded as a source of revenue and of supplies
for his crusades. His officials in England had to accept this royal policy,
which entailed heavy burdens on the realm. From the view of administration the reign of Richard I saw the highest development of the
role of the Justiciar.

The Justiciar had both judicial and administrative duties. Henry II
had depended on him more and more as the amount of business transacted in the royal courts increased, and the office acquired new dignity
when, unable to trust his wife or sons, Henry made the Justiciar his
regent in England during his frequent and long absences on the Continent. Acting on his father's example, Richard kept administration
out of the hands of his brother, John, and entrusted it during his
absences to a series of remarkable men who held the post of Justiciar.[8]
During Richard's absentee reign these Justiciars gathered all the business of government into their hands. The control over them exercised in
theory by curia regis did not in practice extend to their policies,
which were designed essentially to meet Richard's heavy financial demands.

[7] Psalms, 82:2.
[8] William Longchamp (Bishop of Ely) held the office, 1190–91; Walter of
Coutances (Archbishop of Rouen), 1191–93; Hubert Walter (Archbishop of Canterbury), possibly the most able of these able administrators, 1193–98; and Geoffrey
Fitzpeter, the only layman, who ran out the remainder of Richard's reign and into
that of John until 1212.

Royal financial exactions pressed hard on the nation. Richard sold offices, although his first Justiciar soon put a stop to the practice. The royal demesne lands were sold, and then their purchasers ejected and the lands sold again. The government pressed the Saladin tithe and the old Danegeld with vigor. More significant constitutionally were the sales by the government of *charters* to *boroughs* giving them a corporate status. In 1191 London gained such a charter, by which it acquired the right to elect its mayor. As a manorial lord, Richard, or more accurately his regents, laid heavy tallages on his demesne lands; but no baron could complain of this action.

When, in 1193, the news came that Archduke Leopold of Austria was holding Richard for a ransom of 70,000 marks in gold, one Justiciar resigned rather than incur the odium attendant upon raising the sum. His successor, Hubert Walter, addressed himself to the task with energy in the course of the next year. The resources of tenants-in-chief, who were obligated to pay the ransom, were insufficient. The new Justiciar therefore sent letters to *all* clergy, barons, and freemen, regardless of their feudal position *or* of their previous contributions to the ransom, informing them that they were obliged to pay 150,000 marks. People assumed that this was the ransom figure, but the government had decided to build up a backlog for future needs. For most people the exactions for this "ransom" were tallages. Every knight's fee was liable for twenty shillings. The same land often paid a tallage, a hidage, and a carucage. The government was not content and seized the wool of the Cistercian and Gilbertine orders and sold it. Over and above its other obligations, the Church had to contribute jewels and plate. Finally, every person had to pay one-quarter of his income and property.

Although the amount raised fell short of the ransom demanded by Leopold, he accepted it as a down payment; and Richard promised to pay the balance on his return to England, a promise which this later beau-ideal of chivalry promptly forgot. On his return the king demanded a new carucage plus a fine from the Cistercians to get back part of their wool.

In 1194 came a tallage on the realm and the next year a scutage on tenants-in-chief, some of whom were in the field with the king. Richard was dissatisfied and threatened an audit of the Exchequer accounts. Walter stiffly offered to resign, and the king reconsidered. When in

1198 the king demanded another large sum immediately, Walter was at his wits' end. In curia regis he proposed an *annual* carucage assessed by juries. The lay barons howled in anguish, but it was the regular clergy who flatly refused to pay their carucage assessment that year. From abroad the king retorted by declaring the monks outlaws and guaranteeing immunity to laymen for any injuries done them. Walter, papal legate and Archbishop of Canterbury, had the unenviable duty of enforcing the proclamation, which soon produced the monastic payment.

In 1194 Walter, partly with a view to getting more money, and partly to curb a certain tendency toward independent action on the part of the sheriffs, overhauled administrative machinery so as to extend pleas of the crown, and to bar sheriffs from holding them, even if named among the itinerant justices. The sheriff soon ceased to be a justice in consequence because he could not hear cases where the crown was vitally interested, and in any case was not permitted by Walter's reforms to act as a justice in his own county, where he might be biased. At the same time Walter established the new office of *Coroner*, responsible to the central government for keeping track of crown pleas pending the visitation of the royal justices. If the matter were especially important, the Coroner could send it to the central court for immediate action.

ANGEVIN LAW

The structural and procedural changes made by Henry II in the law were enormous, and this practical refutation of the theory of legal immutability was a measure of the strength and vitality of kingship. The administrative aspects of these changes have already been seen; like the legal changes now to be considered, they were part of a single process which was both a cause and a consequence of the expansion and development of central government and justice. In the course of Henry's reign, the true foundations of English common law were laid down. The old, unsatisfactory methods of trial by ordeal or compurgation were gradually superseded by the system of trial by jury. Crime, instead of being regarded as an injury to an individual, became a violation of the king's peace, an affront to his dignity. The jurisdiction of curia regis was extended throughout the realm. Henry found England in a state of anarchy; he left it with deeply rooted principles of law and order.

The Growth of Royal Law

Royal law was nonfeudal and frequently antifeudal. The legal machinery by which it was administered was much more popular than that of the feudal courts, with the result that the royal jurisdiction was greatly sought after by private litigants.

Royal law was attractive to litigants for several reasons. The person who got his case into a royal court received a "package deal," where royal agents took over the entire process the moment he bought a writ. No longer did Geoffrey have to think of the risks attendant upon summoning Fitzroy to court; because the royal writ ordered the sheriff, a royal employee, to bring Fitzroy before a royal court under pain, *subpoena,* of the royal displeasure. Although the personnel in the royal court appeared similar to that of the shire court, there was a vast difference in their duties. The assembly did not act as a shire court; instead the justices empaneled juries from it for specific purposes. There was no need to worry about correct-speaking of foreoaths and oaths of rebuttal; the justices ordered the jury to give its sworn statement about the central facts of the case. Upon its answer the justices ordered the sheriff to take the appropriate administrative action, by which to enforce the judgment. At no point did the principals of the case have to do anything in the procedure. It was little wonder that private persons petitioned the king to let them use this royal court machinery.

Jurisdiction of royal courts also increased because royal agents constantly devised new judicial processes for the king's purposes, which, however, might also be useful to private litigants. Thus royal jurisdiction extended both in area and in depth, a fact clearly observed by one of the royal justices, Rannulf Glanvil, when writing his *Tractatus de Legibus Angliae,* some time between 1187 and 1189.[9]

Glanvil dealt only with royal law. He had been sheriff of Yorkshire

[9] Doubts have been cast upon Glanvil's authorship of the *Tractatus,* some ascribing it to Roger Hoveden or Hubert Walter. The authorship is less important than what the work reveals about the condition of the law in the late twelfth century, and the ultimate praise is bestowed upon it by its being merely cited as Glanvil. To be found in Douglas, II, 462–79.

prior to becoming an itinerant justice and later Justiciar, during the last years of the reign of Henry II. The very name of his book, *Treatise on the Laws of England*, was significant, in view of the fact that the only law in the work was the law as applied in the royal courts. There were other laws, but Glanvil regarded them as unimportant. The legal dualism of the *Leges Henrici Primi* had disappeared; the law of the royal courts covered Normans and English equally. Glanvil did not attempt substantive classifications of this law except under the broadest headings. For the most part, he found that the only way to classify royal law was by actions, which rested on the procedural rules of the king's courts. Thus he began the modern method of legal classification in Anglo-American jurisprudence. The law he classified was already very complex, and too complex for amateurs even when acting with the best of intentions; this was one reason why sheriffs ceased to be named as royal justices after 1194.

The influences of Roman law were comparatively few. Glanvil borrowed from it the distinction between civil and criminal actions, and the law of *personal status* showed traces of Roman influence. It also revealed a large unfree class, though the royal duty of protecting the life and limb of all men, stressed by Glanvil, was reducing the size of the truly unfree section of society. Furthermore, any man charged with a crime which was a plea of the crown was in the *king's mercy*, whether duke or slave. Thus what became criminal law took notice only of the act, *res*, not *persona;* the law was no respecter of persons. Roman law ideas may also have influenced Glanvil in his rough *constitutional law*, wherein he insisted that the law was superior to all men, including the king. This principle, however, existed as much in Anglo-Saxon and Norman feudal law as in Roman law, although Glanvil used the terminology of Roman law to express the concept.

Forms of action and procedure were the law to Glanvil. Glanvil saw several types of writs here. *Original writs* not only began actions; they described precisely every step of their procedures. Justices issued *judicial writs* permitting or compelling one or both of the parties to an action to do something. A person refusing to attend a royal court would find justices ordering the sheriff to seize his land. At the close of a case the justices issued a *writ of judgment*, essentially more administrative that judicial, telling the sheriff to do something for one of the parties to the recent case.

Writs and the Multiplication of Actions

The law, therefore, consisted of writs, each designed for a specific purpose. Taken together, the writs thus determined substantive law. To know the law required knowledge of the writs and what each would do.

The writ was the core of royal justice and strictly nonfeudal. The king ordered a royal agent to do something by writ. For Glanvil and his contemporaries the writ was an administrative device with judicial overtones. A private person petitioned the king as the fountain of justice for the use of his judicial machinery in an action. Upon receiving the petition (and a fee), curia regis had the Chancellor issue a writ commanding royal administrative-judicial agents to handle the matter along the specific lines set forth in the writ. Initially, the king and curia regis acted upon every petition, but the volume of petitions soon made this impossible. The easiest thing was to funnel them to the Chancellor as head of the Chancery, the writ-issuing agency. The Chancellor, however, was soon just as swamped with petitions, so that he and his clerks answered certain petitions with writs as a matter of course. These *writs in course* were often prepared in blank, ready for a formal reply.

Certain petitions, however, described matters not quite met by writs currently available on Chancery's *register of writs*. Nothing daunted, the Chancellor drew up a new writ, *describing* the action apparently needed by the petitioner, often using some of the very words of his petition. Thus new writs appeared and in time also became writs in course, initiating and defining legal actions, while conducting them through all their stages. Simultaneously, they were enlarging and enriching the royal law. Upon receiving a petition, the Chancellor and his clerks decided what writ was appropriate by asking the question repeated to this day by attorneys in countries with English law, "What is the remedy?"

In the time of Henry II the writs most frequently issued were those putting in motion the judicial machinery of the various assizes, and dealing with that most crucial matter of the Middle Ages — the possession of land and the resultant rights and obligations. First employed by Henry II to recover crown lands lost during the reign of Stephen, these writs became very popular with Henry's subjects. All dealt with *free tenures* only — servile tenures were matters for manorial courts. The actual operation of the assizes made the possessor something approaching the "owner." It was to the royal advantage, as the royal justices knew, that everyone should look toward the king rather than to his own immediate lord.

The assizes were classified according to specific actions: Assize divided into Petty and Grand, with the former either Utrum or Possessory; this latter was further subdivided into Novel Disseisin, Mort d'Ancestor, and Darrein Presentment.[10] Although this classification may appear simple, it was far more elaborate than anything devised by either Normans or Anglo-Saxons. From it has flowed, because of expert differentiation, practically every action known in English law.

Petty assizes dealt with precise matters of land possession. They were certainly not unimportant. Like other assizes the *assize utrum* received its name from the opening words of the royal order (likewise an assize) describing this action. Henry II employed the assize largely to determine claims of the Church that land was held by frankalmoign, and so owed no duty except prayer. The assize utrum ordered the sheriff of the county where the land lay to swear in a jury which would say *whether* (utrum) the land was held by the Church in frankalmoign or in some lay tenure. Initially the sheriff reported the answer to curia regis, but soon the itinerant justices put this question to the jury, upon whose answer they then based their administrative decisions. If land in dispute was held by frankalmoign, the matter was referred to the Church court.

Although theoretically in this and other assizes it was the royal court baron acting, the fact was that the real decision came from a royal prerogative agency, the jury, acting in a feudal matter. Nevertheless, other lords confronted by similar ecclesiastical claims turned to the assize utrum, which could be applied only by royal courts. When the Constitutions of Clarendon gave royal courts sole jurisdiction over questions concerning the specific tenure by which the Church held certain lands, the victory of the king's courts was not only over those of the Church but also over other courts baron.

The *possessory* assizes were more directly concerned with land possession and resultant rights. Again devised by the king to recover royal lands, they were sought after by private persons. After the anarchy of Stephen's reign these assizes were badly needed. Although the precise order of their appearance is uncertain, the entry on the Pipe Roll of 1167, for the first time, of revenue from amercements for

[10] For examples of the various writs instituting these assizes see Appendix I.

unlawful disseisin may mean that the assize of novel disseisin was worked out at the meeting of curia regis the previous year. However, the new entry may mean only that by 1167 amercements for unlawful disseisin had become sufficiently large to warrant a new bookkeeping category.

In the assize of *novel disseisin* there appeared the principle that royal justice would protect the holding of any freeman. A person believing himself wrongfully dispossessed of his free holding could secure a writ from Chancery ordering royal justices to empanel a jury to answer the simple question as to whether the plaintiff at the time of his dispossession had been lawfully *seised* (in possession) of the land. If the jury's verdict was affirmative, the justices ordered the defendant to return the land and pay a fine to the king in his capacity of fountain of justice. If the verdict was negative, the king still had the plaintiff's fee for borrowing the machinery of his court.

While all this may seem straightforward enough, it was actually undermining the entire feudal structure. Feudal tenants could refuse to meet their obligations to their lords (always excepting the king) in the certainty that even if courts baron declared their fiefs forfeited, the royal court would order their return by virtue of this assize; because the only interest of the assize of novel disseisin was the lawful possession of the land by the plaintiff *prior* to his ejectment. The royal courts in applying the assize assured the possessor of land, whether on a large or a small scale, of considerable independence from his immediate lord. As its ultimate principle, novel disseisin said that only due process would permit the dispossession of a property-holder; and in effect royal courts were claiming that this due process was their monopoly. Long after the makers of the assize were dead, the fundamental principle of novel disseisin moved into the American Constitution.[11]

A plausible defense to novel disseisin was that the plaintiff never had been in possession of the land. Such a situation existed between the death of a tenant and the delivery by the lord of his fief to his heir. If the lord did not make such delivery (usually because of nonpayment of relief), the jury could not say that the plaintiff had held the land. The remedy for this situation and an answer to this defense was the assize of *mort d'ancestor*, apparently "made" at a meeting of curia regis at Northampton in 1176. In this assize the jury informed the justices whether or not the plaintiff's direct ancestor had been in lawful

---

[11] Fifth and Fourteenth Amendments.

possession of his holding at the time of his death. If the jury replied affirmatively, the justices ordered the immediate delivery of the land to the plaintiff, who henceforth ceased to concern himself much about his immediate lord, in the knowledge that the king would defend his land now, and, when he died, that of his heirs. Mort d'ancestor thus struck another blow against feudalism.

When persons claimed the right of *presentation*, or *advowson*, of nominees to Church posts in which the king had an interest, the answer by Henry II was the assize of *darrein presentment*. The assize was important because presentation could be a valuable right of patronage. Although the nominee had to be canonically qualified for the post, this was not an onerous condition; and the practice of presentation circumvented canon law prohibitions against *simony*, the sale and purchase of Church offices, in that the sale and purchase was only of the *right to nominate*. The Constitutions of Clarendon had declared that litigation over advowsons belonged to the royal courts. The assize was originally designed to settle royal disputes in such cases but other holders of ecclesiastical patronage found the assize useful. When a dispute arose about advowson, one of the parties secured a writ of darrein presentment commanding the justices to ask a jury which party had made the presentation to the post when it was last vacant. Upon the answer, the justices ordered, "Let him who presented last present again." This administrative action, ignoring the question of who had the better right to nominate, meant that in darrein presentment possession was not nine-tenths, but all of the law.

The larger question of land title, however, was not the concern of the possessory assizes. Proprietary actions were dealt with by the *grand assize*. Feudal law provided for the settlement of disputes over title by trial by battle or the judicial combat, occasionally between the disputants, but more often between hired champions, with God giving victory to the right. Although the possessory assizes made these title actions less necessary, they could still occur. As a king it was beneath the dignity of Henry II to brawl for his land rights or hire champions to do so. Therefore, he and curia regis provided an alternative, the grand assize, which provided that no one should be dispossessed of his free holding without due process, and also that no judgment would be sufficient to support such a dispossession unless it was the result of a procedure initiated by a royal summons — that is, a royal court had to hear the case. This was a bold move by the crown, aimed directly at the feudal courts baron, and more was to follow. The grand assize declared that no one should be forced to defend his possession of land by wager of battle. Instead, he (originally the king, but soon many another man) could have the entire question of title decided by a jury of indirectly elected knights. Taken together, the provisions of the grand assize practically ensured that nearly all land cases would come within the jurisdiction of the royal courts.

Private feudal courts were seriously affected by the assize system. Only the feudal court of the king profited from it. Feudal obligations came to mean little if they were not owed to the king, because his courts would enforce these and also prevent other feudal courts from enforcing others. Increasingly, therefore, people were concerned with their obligations to their sovereign and less interested in their ties of fealty to other lords. Yet instead of resisting these encroachments of the crown, lords yielded to temptation and used the system against their own lords, thereby contributing to the ever-widening purview of the royal justices.

As a feudal lord himself, the king was able to exploit the concept of royal liegeancy to the embarrassment of his rivals. The king was supposed to protect the interests of all vassals, regardless of whom they held. Judicial implementation of this doctrine was in the *writ of right*,[12] which any man could buy from Chancery, and which directed the lord to do right to the plaintiff. If he failed to do so, the case could be transferred to a royal court. This in itself was a bold intrusion into the sphere of private feudal jurisdiction. Often the purchaser of the writ either anticipated losing or had already lost his case in a court baron; either way that court lost the action to a royal court. But the king might act in an even more arbitrary fashion. Although the writ of right was technically within, although only barely, feudal legal limits, the royal *writ praecipe* (command) was clearly outside them. This writ instructed the sheriff, a personal employee of the king, to see that the lord returned the land of a man buying the writ or else appear in a royal court and show cause why he had not. The writ praecipe thus ignored the court baron; in fact, the defendant in the resultant action in the royal court was usually the lord of a feudal court baron which had previously decided against the purchaser of the writ. The writ praecipe was a serious denial of the rights of the private feudal courts, and the whole question was to be raised by the barons in

[12] See Appendix I.

Clause 34 of the Magna Carta.[13] But if they believed that this writ was the reason for their loss of judicial business, they were mistaken; by the time of Magna Carta private feudal jurisdictions were beyond rescue.

Criminal accusation received collective security from the *presentment jury*. The *Assize of Clarendon* in 1166 may have devised the machinery, or it may have merely described something already in operation. When the itinerant justices appeared at the shire court, now royal, they swore in juries from the hundreds and vills of the county to report men suspected of being robbers, murderers, or thieves, or of harboring such malefactors. Upon receiving these names, the justices ordered the sheriff to bring those thus accused before them. Men so accused went at once to the ordeal; no other proof was available to them. If they failed the ordeal, they were hanged — not by sentence of the justices but by the administrative orders they carried with them. Even if heaven cleared those accused by presentment juries, they still had to quit the realm at once on pain of death.

The advantages of accusation by this forerunner of the grand jury were so great for both the king and private persons that the older method of individual accusation, now called an *appeal* (from the Latin verb meaning "to name"), dwindled rapidly, as the list of crimes for presentment juries grew; but the older method did not finally disappear until 1819.

A *"Common"* Law

The law administered by the royal courts was known as *common law*, because it was a law common to the whole of England. Not until Henry II's reign, when curia regis became supreme over all its rivals, the sheriff's courts and the feudal courts, could the law really answer to this description.

The essence of common law was case law. This was true for Glanvil and has been for every law student since. Glanvil explained the law in terms of writs, actions, and judicial decisions. There was (and is) no single repository for the entire law on any subject. Specific cases and the recorded decisions of the courts were the law; thus the common law can be said to be unwritten only in a limited sense. There was no codi-

[13] Below, p. 115.

fied system of legislation, but there were the innumerable decisions of the judges of the English courts. From time to time judges may have argued that there was a "natural" justice which lay behind the law and determined particular decisions. But generally they worked from precedent, from case law; their duty was not to make new laws but to "declare" the law as it had been known in the past.

Angevin justices had little in common with modern trial judges. The latter conduct the trial according to the correct procedural rules, keep order between the contending parties, and finally explain to the jury what it should or should not consider. The justices of Henry II, on the other hand, were *administrative agents* of the monarch, acting under strict instructions from him. Thus inherent in Angevin jurisprudence was the danger that justices, essentially bureaucrats, might adjust the law to suit the government's convenience. For this reason the rigidity imposed upon the law by stare decisis was much to be preferred, from the point of view of the private litigant to the potentially arbitrary conceptions of "natural" law. Essentially, Angevin justices were collectors of verdicts, upon which they issued administrative orders according to their instructions. The great trial justices appeared only when the common law accepted proof by evidence, which it did under pressure from rival systems of jurisprudence in the fourteenth and fifteenth centuries. Until then the jury found fact on its own, not from sworn evidence in court, and the itinerant justices did not rule on admissibility of evidence because there was none. Nor did they rule on points of law raised in trial pleading; there was none of this either until the common law grudgingly admitted oral testimony. Until that time pleading was allowed only in the central court, where during the thirteenth century bench and bar worked out the issues to be submitted by the itinerant justices to juries for their determination. The real founders of the common law were not so much the justices on iter as those of the central court, who were beginning to hammer out precedents when Glanvil wrote.

By the end of Henry's reign they had gone far toward creating a uniform legal system throughout England. Unlike many other countries, England did not need to introduce Roman law in order to achieve legal uniformity.

THE REACTION: MAGNA CARTA

Inevitably, the Angevin drive for royal centralization produced a violent baronial reaction and a desire to confine monarchy within its feudal limits. Magna Carta, often regarded as the source of English liberties, was in many ways an assertion or restatement of feudal laws and customs.

The Background

John (1199–1216) was a powerful monarch, whatever the shortcomings in his character. He had enormous wealth and the most efficient administrative machine in Europe. But early in his reign things began to go wrong. First, he became involved with one of his French vassals over the exercise of the incident of marriage, John exercising it so that the heiress, his vassal's betrothed, became his queen. The vassal appealed to their common feudal lord, Philip Augustus, king of France, who was delighted to accept the case. Upon John's refusal to attend his court, the king of France had his court baron declare that John had forfeited his French fiefs. John was unsuccessful in his attempt to recover them by force and by 1205 retained only Aquitaine. This meant that barons holding fiefs in both England and Normandy had to decide between them, because they could no longer hold both; and those who chose to reside in England were not likely to forget that John was responsible for the loss of their French fiefs.

Then, in his quarrel with the Church, John began with a good case, but he prejudiced it by violent behavior. In violation of the rules of William I and the Constitutions of Clarendon, the Canterbury cathedral chapter had secretly elected one of their number as Archbishop upon Walter's death in 1205. When John learned of this, he forced the chapter to hold a second election, which named another churchman to the post. Both men hastened to Rome to secure papal approval. At Rome, Innocent III, one of the most able popes, saw in the situation an ideal opportunity to exercise the papal claim of being able to make direct appointments to Church posts. Ignoring both candidates from England, Innocent named Stephen Langton the Archbishop of Canterbury. John refused to recognize the appointment or permit Langton to enter England. Had he been content to remain on what was strong legal ground, he might eventually have forced the papacy to recognize the man named in the second and legal election by the Canterbury monks.

Instead he took violent reprisals, seized the revenues of Canterbury and persecuted those of the clergy who had accepted Langton. Innocent's drastic reply was to place an interdict on England; though this meant in theory the suspension of all ecclesiastical rites, John remained unmoved.[14] When, however, the Pope took the even more drastic step of excommunicating John and absolving his subjects from allegiance to him, the king's position became precarious. Ecclesiastics in administrative positions who had stood by him through the interdict could no longer associate with him without risking excommunication themselves. Finally, Innocent commissioned the French king to lead a crusade against England.

John gave way. He accepted Langton as Archbishop, promised to make amends for his spoliation of the Church, and then became a papal vassal with the duty of paying a thousand marks annually to the Pope, of whom he therefore held England in socage.[15] Feudal law required John's lord to protect him, and Innocent ordered the king of France to drop his plans for an invasion. In his first promise, however, John accepted his due; for Langton united the baronage, giving them a basis of action in the Coronation Charter of Henry I. In the end John stood alone except for some particularly vicious advisers.

Magna Carta

On 15 June 1215 John met his barons at Runnymede, a pleasant meadow on the Thames between Windsor and Staines. The charter he there granted became one of the most notoriously misinterpreted documents in English history, largely because succeeding generations of Englishmen read into its provisions meanings relevant to their own times. Essentially a manifesto of feudalism, the charter has been termed the "palladium of English liberties," "the foundation of freedom," and

[14] The interdict was less serious than it sounds, since it did not apply on feast days, including Sundays. The greatest inconvenience from it was the difficulty of having the dead buried. Monkish chroniclers bitterly recorded that not all of the secular clergy obeyed the interdict.

[15] Post-Reformation writers viewed John's commendation of England to the Pope as the absolute nadir of his misrule. However, contemporaries did not feel that way. To be a vassal was to enjoy a perfectly honorable status, and the greater the lord, the more honorable the position of a vassal. And what could be higher status than to be a vassal of the Vicar of Christ?

the like. Misinterpretation may often have been fruitful but the importance of Magna Carta in English history is to be found in the uses to which it was put in the succeeding centuries and the image it created in the minds of Englishmen. But the historian wishing to interpret the charter as it was written at Runnymede must always bear in mind the feudal frame of reference within which it was drawn up.

The legal form of Magna Carta was that of a charter conveyancing land. This was the most binding and solemn type of a contract, in this instance between the king and certain persons named specifically, together with the community of the realm generally. The physical charter was a single, long block paragraph in medieval Vulgate Latin; the division of the charter into chapters came much later. Copies of the charter, sealed by the king and the barons, went to the public depositories of that time, the cathedrals. One of those copies ultimately came to a strange land, whose very existence was unknown to the men of Runnymede.[16]

The drafters of the charter hoped that explicit and precise statements of hitherto unwritten feudal law would end royal encroachments on it. With this purpose in mind, the barons set the amounts of *reliefs* and made detailed regulations about *wardship*, which the king was not to exercise over socage (including *burgage*) fiefs, nor over fiefs held of other lords. Royal exercise of the incident of *marriage* was to be controlled by the relatives of the heiress. The king promised that he would not use this incident to force widows of tenants-in-chiefs, who also secured protection in their dower rights, to remarry.[17]

The heavy royal financial demands beginning with Henry II led to provisions in Magna Carta which, while accepting royal unilateral determination of the amounts for the three customary *aids*, restated the feudal dictum that only bilateral agreement could modify contractual relations or, in other words, that the king could not levy extraordinary aids or any scutages "except by the common counsel of the realm." The great barons, both spiritual and lay, were very careful to ensure that the king should not circumvent this requirement, and they insisted that they should receive individual summonses to curia regis when it met to

[16] This copy was on exhibition at the British Building at the New York World's Fair, 1939–40, and remained on display in the Library of Congress in Washington during World War II prior to its return to Great Britain in 1947.

[17] Chapters 2–8, 37, 46, 59. The 1217 version of the charter set dower at one-third of the husband's property, a fraction still obtaining in certain state jurisdictions in the United States. These and subsequent chapter references are to the 1215 edition of the charter as given in George Burton Adams and H. Morse Stephens, eds., *Select Documents of English Constitutional History*, 42.

discuss extraordinary aids and scutages. The drafters of the charter were willing to have other royal feudal tenants summoned generally by the king via the sheriff to such meetings.[18]

American colonial leaders of the eighteenth century, appealing to these provisions of Magna Carta in their slogan of "No taxation without representation," were characteristically reading into the charter a meaning suited to the needs of their times. At most, in 1215 these provisions merely reinforced the feudal theory of bilateral *consent* between lord and vassal to any modification of the terms of their contract. So generally was this understood, that the 1216 version of the charter omitted this chapter on consent as unnecessary. Feudalism had no conception of representation, the essence of which is that certain men can speak for and bind others. By feudal law each member of a court baron spoke only for himself and could bind no one — not even other members of the assembly, and certainly not men who were absent; and the charter was significantly silent about these aspects of the representative principle. So foreign was it to feudal principles that during much of the thirteenth century members of curia regis who did not agree to extraordinary aids and scutages were not obliged to pay them!

The financial resources of the crown remained considerable. The king still had the normal feudal payments due him, and the charter did not touch his nonfeudal exactions of tallages on his demesne, the Danegeld, and the Saladin tithe. The barons had little interest in limiting royal financial arrangements that did not directly affect them.

The barons did protect mesne royal tenants against having their obligations suddenly increased by virtue of the escheat of their lord's fief to the king; and they forbade the king to collect fines from tenants obligated to garrison castles after he had filled them with mercenaries. The charter formally stated the feudal rule that the land of a vassal convicted of a crime other than treason should be held by the king only for a year and a day, after which it had to return to the vassal's lord. For their part, the barons accepted the same limitations themselves in their relations with their own vassals, who should enjoy the same rights accorded by the king to the great barons.[19] Measures were taken to guard against the arbitrariness of royal officials in commandeering goods and services in *purveyance*, although complaints about purveyance continued into the seventeenth century.[20]

[18] Chapters 12, 14.
[19] Chapters 15–16, 29, 32, 43, 60.
[20] Chapters 28, 30–31.

Mercantile interests received cursory attention. London, like other boroughs, had its charter confirmed, and also benefited from the removal of navigational obstacles from the Thames. The charter reinstated Walter's assize of uniform weights and measures and promised merchants generally freedom from "evil tolls" and royal observance of "right custom" — generous sentiments, though no provision was made for their implementation.[21] Anglo-Saxon custom was indirectly recognized in a chapter dealing with the repair of bridges. In another the king promised to observe ancient custom in levying demands on local subdivisions, although specifically saying that this promise did not affect his right to tallage his demesne lands.[22]

The judicial clauses of Magna Carta were the most important. In their moment of triumph the barons accepted nearly all of the administrative and judicial machinery of Angevin government and also the legal innovations which were in fact shaking the very foundations of the feudal system. With the notable exception of the writ praecipe, whose issuance it forbade, Magna Carta actually endorsed the Angevin juridical system, either by tacit acceptance or by explicit sanction. It indirectly approved the jury system and called for qualified justices, regulated the procedure of the possessory assizes, and insisted that the central court should remain permanently at Westminster.[23] Taken together, these judicial provisions admitted that private courts baron had lost their jurisdiction over land cases to the royal courts.

However, though the barons accepted this fact, they tried to set some limits to the judicial discretion of the crown and therefore, in defiance of feudal theory, made additions to the law. Thus with regard to amercements the charter stated the principle, still vigorous wherever English law runs, that a judicial order should never deprive a man of his essential means of livelihood.[24]

The indifference of feudal law to chattels also made it necessary for the framers to include in the charter protection to chattels against the rapacity of royal tax collectors,[25] and to transfer the administration of intestates' chattels to Church courts.[26]

[21] Chapters 12–13, 33, 35, 41.
[22] Chapters 23, 25.
[23] Chapters 17–19, 24.
[24] Chapters 20, 22.
[25] Chapters 9, 26.
[26] Chapter 27. Although omitted in 1216, this chapter continued to have tacit application.

The charter also made law about interest payments in a section drafted by the barons as debtors. The Church forbade Christians to lend at interest, and thus gave the unhappy Jewish community, always at the mercy of the king, a monopoly of this function. In their perilous situation, Jewish moneylenders demanded high interest rates. The barons placed a moratorium on interest payments from fiefs under wardship and freed dower lands altogether of them.[27]

Contrary to popular misinterpretation Magna Carta did not provide for criminal trial by jury. Although sanctioning the method of accusation by the presentment jury,[28] the barons had no wish to be rushed off to the ordeal as provided by the Assize of Clarendon. They therefore laid down that resultant trials for themselves after accusation by a jury should be by their equals, their *peers*. For other men's trials the barons were vague saying that they should be tried according to the law of the land.[29] Whatever may have been the barons' original intention, these provisions, by the end of the thirteenth century, had come to mean that unless a man were accused by the older method of appeal, that is, at the suit of a private accuser, his indictment by a grand jury required his trial by another jury; or if he were a peer, by his fellow peers. The mistaken belief that Magna Carta established the "right" to trial by jury had profound consequences in English law and is reflected in the United States Constitution.[30]

Taken as a whole, the judicial chapters of Magna Carta accepted the great legal innovations of the Angevins. This was not due to baronial ignorance of their ramifications. The barons knew them very well; many of them had used the royal courts for their own purposes. This was one reason why they showed such forbearance. Moreover, royal justice was popular with their own vassals. Thus the great barons at Runnymede, who were trying to confine monarchy within its feudal limits, had to accept the one thing above all others that was extending the monarchial power beyond them. Perhaps for this reason those who drew up the charter tried to make the operation of royal juridical machinery a subject of public law. In the clause that said "right and justice shall not be sold or denied or delayed,"[31] which did not mean that writs instituting actions in royal courts should be free but that

---

[27] Chapters 10–11. Not until 1624 would the maximum interest rate be set statutorily at 8 per cent.
[28] Chapter 38.
[29] Chapters 21, 39.
[30] Fifth and Sixth Amendments.
[31] Chapter 40.

their prices should be reasonable, they were insisting that the issue of writs should be automatic upon payment of such fees. What had initially been the king's own personal justice thus fell under public law.

The severity of the forest laws and the arbitrary way in which they were applied had long been grounds for complaint. John, moreover, used his forest courts to deal with persons living beyond the forests. Magna Carta limited the jurisdiction of these courts to the forests as they had existed at John's accession in 1199, and denied to the king the right to extend the forest borders. Having done this much, the charter's drafters made an ineffective attempt to mitigate the severity of the forest laws.[32] These forest sections became a separate charter in 1217, the Forest Charter, or *Parva* (Little) *Carta*. The frequent "confirmation of the *charters*" during the thirteenth century referred to both Magna Carta and the Forest Charter, indicating their close connection in the popular mind.

The clause relating to the enforcement of the charter [33] has often been called crude, but in fact it contained elements of considerable sophistication. The machinery employed was naturally the feudal *diffidatio;* but in its operation the barons clearly distinguished between king and kingship. At Runnymede they chose 25 of their number to act as a committee with power to co-opt to vacancies. This committee was to supervise the implementation of the temporary provisions of Magna Carta, but its permanent duty was the enforcement of the charter. Persons injured by royal nonobservance of the charter could bring their complaints to any four of the committee for transmittal to the king or his Justiciar. If no action was taken, the four barons would inform the full committee, which would then issue a diffidatio in the name of the realm and call upon all loyal men to fight — not the king personally, but the king as the government. Men remaining loyal to him or neutral would be considered rebels.

These provisions established a remarkable legal right to rebellion. Furthermore, in startling contrast to their vagueness about the ability of a majority in curia regis to bind the minority in regard to royal financial demands, the barons explicitly declared that a majority of the baronial committee would make its decisions. Thus, though the barons chose a feudal method of enforcing their charter, they provided for its exercise in a nonfeudal manner.

From the point of view of constitutional history, the charter was the

[32] Chapters 44, 47–48.
[33] Chapter 61.

watershed between the days when the barons sought a strictly feudal kingship and the days when their main effort was to control nonfeudal kingship. The very arrangement of the charter's provisions indicated this development; whereas the earlier clauses aimed at restoring feudal monarchy, the later ones, particularly the enforcement chapter, hinted at the thirteenth-century attempt by the barons to control kingship by committee.

As the provisions of the charter became increasingly less capable of precise application, men came to regard it not in a literal sense but as a symbolic statement of the limitations upon monarchy. This was one reason for the frequent confirmations of the charter, together with the Forest Charter, throughout the Middle Ages. The precise form of Magna Carta, thus confirmed, varied with new editions. The reissues of 1216 and 1217 had substantial changes; but in the reign of Henry III the two charters reached their final form. The reissue of 1225 later became one of the first statutes in English law in 1297.

Eventually Parliament made itself the guardian of Magna Carta, forbidding in 1369 any alteration of its provisions without parliamentary consent. By that time many of the provisions were literally meaningless, but Parliament viewed the charter as a living symbol of royal limitation.

The charter also survived because of its essential moderation, something too often overlooked. The great barons had John in their grip at Runnymede. Yet they did not exercise their undoubted feudal right to depose him, and they left almost untouched the powerful Angevin administrative and judicial machine. This very moderation made Magna Carta a "practical" document, capable of living beyond feudalism for the benefit of later generations who could interpret it according to their needs.

Magna Carta thus became a symbol of the vital principle that there is a definite body of law superior to all men, including the king and his government. Those who break that law will be proceeded against — by the government if ordinary men, by ordinary men if the government. The ultimate guardian of the law is the community of the realm. Long after feudalism has disappeared, Magna Carta still emphasizes that "The Law is no respecter of persons." The implications of this familiar phrase are vast. The achievement of those desperate barons facing an angry king at Runnymede may be seen reflected in the words emblazoned on the lintel of a white marble building in the capital of a land unknown to those men — "Equal Justice under Law."

Angevin constitutional innovations were large and meant vigorous centralization under the king, whose central government began to be differentiated into departments. These developments sapped feudal vigor, and not even the power of the Church could check them. So strong did royal machinery become that it operated without the presence and immediate direction of the king during the reign of Richard I. As part of royal administrative centralization there developed a single law in the royal courts, which pressed on all rivals. The misrule of John dramatically emphasized the power of this centralized kingship, and in Magna Carta the barons sought to restore the feudal balance. The task proved impossible, so the future importance of the charter was in its emphasis on the supremacy of law.

READING LIST

HASKINS, C. H. *The Normans in European History*, espec. Chap. IV.
MCKECHNIE, W. S. *Magna Carta*, 2nd ed.
POLLOCK, F. and F. W. MAITLAND. *History of English Law*, Vol. I, Chap. VI.
POOLE, R. L. *The Exchequer in the Twelfth and Thirteenth Centuries*.
THOMPSON, F. *The First Century of Magna Carta*.
TOUT, T. F. *Chapters in the Administrative History of Mediaeval England*, Vol. I.

4

THE CONTEST FOR GOVERNMENT

MAGNA Carta marked a change in baronial policy. Instead of seeking to restore a limited feudal kingship, the barons henceforth tried to control the workings of an ever growing nonfeudal monarchy. The crux of the constitutional issue of the thirteenth century was whether the barons collectively or the king personally would operate the increasingly complex institution of monarchy, which had so many ramifications that it lost many of the personal connotations it had once had and became the impersonal "crown" or "government." This impersonal crown expanded rapidly during the thirteenth century, when for much of that century Henry III (1216–72) ruled. Henry was a minor when he came to the throne, and upon reaching his majority was neither particularly able nor particularly popular. Yet the crown continued notwithstanding to extend its functions and powers.

The Minority

Soon after Magna Carta the barons were in a position to control the government. They had anticipated that John would break his word, and they were not mistaken. When the king secured a papal dispensation from his promise at Runnymede, claiming that it had been given under duress, and began gathering mercenaries, the barons in an attempt to forestall royal plans went to war. Baronial unity, achieved with so much difficulty at the time of Magna Carta, now broke down over the question of who should become the military commander; the only solution to that problem in the end was to call in Prince Louis of France. The kingdom was on the verge of anarchy, when suddenly the major cause of the war disappeared — in 1216 John died.

The guardians of Henry III came to terms with the barons. Under the leadership of William Marshal they reissued Magna Carta, with certain omissions, in the name of the young king. At once baronial ranks wavered. The barons had no animosity against the new king, who was nine years old, and no love for Louis. They also knew that Marshal was basically in sympathy with their position. By 1217 Louis found himself alone and unwanted and was glad to return to France under a safe-conduct from Marshal. The war came to an end, and the government again reissued the charter to show its good faith.

Theoretically, feudal law supplied a regency in the person of the Pope, who as the lord of John's minor son made certain claims to wardship over the papal fief of England. However, curia regis would have none of this and acted as a regency council. This council was the normal smaller curia regis, which always included the Justiciar, the Chancellor, and the Treasurer. Marshal was dominant until his death in 1219, but then factions began to appear and the council was seriously divided. Some stability was regained, however, under the last of the great Justiciars, Hubert de Burgh, who was supported by the Archbishop of Canterbury, Stephen Langton. As far as the barons were concerned curia regis was a committee exercising the royal powers; and for the rest of the thirteenth century, whenever the barons were at odds with the king, they looked back on this system of committee rule as an admirable way out of their difficulties.

The baronage was quiet during the royal minority. Great barons were assured of participation in the regency council if they so desired, and some of the more turbulent of them were working off their energies in Palestine against the Saracens. It was during the minority that the dictum "The king can do no wrong" was first heard. It was literally true, for with Henry still a minor it was his council that formed policy. The theory persisted, however, after Henry III had attained his majority, and proved useful in justifying baronial efforts to control the government, as they had grown accustomed to doing during the minority.

The Majority

Although the Pope declared his ward, Henry III of England, to be of age at sixteen, in 1223, the regency council ignored this "foreign" action and delayed until 1227 before ending the royal minority. The long duration of the minority made it difficult for the barons to grasp the fact that curia regis had ceased to be a governing body and was once again only an advisory group.

Friction between the king and barons was almost certain. It was made the more likely by fundamental differences in attitudes between Henry and his great vassals. The barons disliked losing control over the *appointment of officials*, and so they believed (not unreasonably) over policy. They resented it therefore when the king used his *household officials*, who were for the most part under his control, rather than the "great officers" for what had once been personal duties for the king but which were now, with the extension of royal power, of a quasi-public nature. In this connection the barons accused the king of being under *foreign influences*, in that he drew these household officials from the members of his mother's and wife's French suites. This charge was also leveled at Henry because of his support of *papal policies* involving heavy exactions on the English Church and interference with its personnel.

Undoubtedly the barons in their dissatisfaction with these royal policies were motivated by more than sheer altruistic concern for the realm, but significantly they couched their protests in just such terms. During the thirteenth century the thriving wool trade gave to England a new prosperity which was particularly evident among the smaller feudal tenants and the mercantile group. These people, as well as the great barons, were also filled with a new spirit of English nationalism, which, like most nascent nationalisms, exhibited itself chiefly in the negative form of "anti-foreign" feeling.

With Henry's coming of age, de Burgh found his position invidious. A moderate baron, he had dominated the government in the last years of the minority and found it difficult to adjust himself to the new situation in which the king was supposed to rule and his Justiciar merely to administer and advise. He did not conceal his feelings when royal policy ran counter to his own, and the king was eventually persuaded by Peter des Roches, his former guardian, to dismiss de Burgh in 1232. After de Burgh, the post of Justiciar was filled by minor personages until the office was finally abolished by Edward I.

Though the barons had made no attempt to save de Burgh, his dismissal rendered the king very vulnerable to their criticisms. No matter what the dictum, it now *was* the king who was doing wrong in their eyes. Nevertheless, they persisted in the fiction that the fault lay with "evil" and "foreign" advisers.

One of the major objectives of the barons was to acquire control over the appointment of officials. This was radical enough. The very name, "royal official," implied royal appointment; and until Henry III every monarch had exercised that right without question. The policies of Henry III, together with the experience the barons had already had in curia regis during the minority, now encouraged them to claim the right at least to supervise the royal appointment of major officials. They realized that their own occasional and brief appearances at the full curia regis were insufficient if they were to retain any sort of control and therefore they wanted their interests represented in the normal, smaller curia regis. After his dismissal of de Burgh, the king made a point of filling great offices with subservient men of low social status or else of leaving offices vacant. Either way, the king was free from baronial pressure. He had shown in 1237 and again in 1242 that he would not allow the barons' refusal to sanction extra aids to influence his policy. On both occasions he had borrowed money and had sold royal demesne lands. To the barons, therefore, the best way of influencing policy seemed to be to secure some control over the appointment of royal advisers. Thus they proposed that the king should fill major offices from their ranks, and that major officials should be responsible to curia regis. This proposal came to naught, but in 1244 the baronage made another attempt. They claimed that only the full curia regis of all tenants-in-chief should name the Chancellor, Treasurer, and Justiciar (although the last office was rapidly declining) and that these officials should act for the king in all matters. Again Henry managed to resist his importunate barons. He assigned to servants of his *Wardrobe*, who were amenable to royal orders, functions that had come to be regarded as public. Having lost control of the great seal to the Chancellor, he had a Wardrobe servant authenticate public documents with the royal privy seal. Money did not flow to the Treasury but to the Wardrobe, where a personal servant of the king disbursed it according to his employer's orders. The barons looked down on members of the household as "low-born men" and as "foreigners" and demanded that the Wardrobe should cease to perform public functions.

It was Henry's acceptance of papal policies that brought the constitutional issue to a crisis. The Pope had been eager to take advantage of the situation in England, a prosperous country over which he was the feudal lord, and where a pious king, who believed wrongly that papal wardship had saved his realm for him, appeared ready to play into his hands.

The heavy papal financial demands made upon the English Church, particularly in 1199 and 1215, when the clergy were called upon to contribute to the latest crusade, were met, but only with the greatest reluctance and after much grumbling. During the royal minority Langton and de Burgh had managed to resist papal demands or at least to keep them within bounds. But the English Church found to its dismay that, having reached his majority, Henry III actively supported these demands and gave royal protection to the extremely unpopular papal tax-collectors who were soon swarming throughout the kingdom. In 1229 many clergy were disgusted by a papal call for money to support a "crusade" against the Holy Roman Empire, yet it was on this occasion that the king dismissed de Burgh for not proceeding against the rioters who had mobbed the collectors. De Burgh's dismissal removed the last defender of the English clergy against the exactions of Rome.

The king also went so far as to approve of the papal practice of *provisors*, whereby the Pope made direct appointments to any vacant Church office. The most famous such appointment, that by Innocent III of Langton to the archbishopric of Canterbury, had produced a storm; but Henry consistently supported these appointments. Although some appointees were men of ability, many were Italian hangers-on at the papal court. There they remained, drawing the revenues of their English ecclesiastical offices, and sending underpaid and underqualified vicars to act in their stead. If the appointees appeared in England, they usually had little in common with the laity. Above all, the practice of papal provisions deprived both ecclesiastical and lay barons of their vested rights of nomination to Church positions. The legal action of darrein presentment was of little use when the king would not permit one of his personal servants to issue the necessary writ. In 1229 the barons protested in curia regis about provisions, but to no effect.

In 1254 Henry accepted the Pope's suggestion that he should conquer Sicily for his son, Edmund, who would then hold it of the Pope. The current holder of the island had successfully resisted papal claims of lordship, and the papacy had already spent £90,000 (an enormous sum for the time) in a vain effort to oust him. Henry now agreed to the papal plan for his son and also to reimburse the Pope the sum of £90,000. These promises involved financial commitments that could not be met out of the normal revenues of the crown. The king therefore summoned the great barons to a meeting of curia regis at Oxford in

1258, in order to secure their assent to the necessary aids and scutages. The barons had never approved of the king's Sicilian venture, which they felt to be extravagant and foolish. Like their fathers before them at Runnymede, the barons now resolved that the king must once again be made subject to their will. It was not only the Sicilian affair that had enraged them but also the breakdown of a Welsh truce and the formation of a Welsh-Scottish alliance, both of which they attributed to mismanagement by the king. The clergy had a bill of complaints prepared by the brilliant Bishop Grossteste of Lincoln, wherein they blamed the king for allowing *foreign* influences to corrupt the *English* Church. The barons were in an ugly temper and armed; the king had few forces and few funds. When the barons presented their demands for a general reform, Henry could only give way.

Government by Committee

The way in which the barons hoped to curb and control their misguided king was by reviving the system of government by committee. The enforcement clause in Magna Carta, together with the satisfactory arrangement of affairs during the minority, had firmly established the precedents for this form of baronial supervision. At Oxford in 1258 the barons forced the king to agree to a committee of twenty-four, half of whom would be chosen by the baronage and half by the king, to make ordinances for the reform of the realm and to have a plan of government ready for curia regis later in the year. In June a large number of barons, the knights, and smaller feudal tenants gathered in curia regis. They complained of the maladministration of justice and alleged that the king's refusal to fill great offices from the baronage was a violation of Magna Carta.[1] In this last complaint the barons revealed that their fundamental purpose was to gain control of the government. Their other grievances, about the misuse of feudal incidents (particularly of wardship, marriage, and escheats) and purveyance, were secondary. The committee of twenty-four believed that their main purpose would be achieved by the plan that was now approved by curia regis (sometimes called a "parliament" because of the presence of knights) and accepted by Henry as the *Provisions of Oxford*.[2]

[1] This last is an interesting, early typical example of how any group with a grievance seized on the charter, whose literal phrases said nothing about how the king should name his officials, or from what class he should draw them.

[2] B. Wilkinson, *Constitutional History of Medieval England*, I, 167. Henceforth cited as Wilkinson.

At Oxford the barons restored the office of Justiciar and insisted that the great officers of the royal household, like the Treasurer and the Chancellor, should be subjected to the control of the council. But the most important provisions were those that elaborated the baronial conceptions of committee rule. The business of government was to be conducted in the royal name by several committees. One of fifteen, nine named by the barons and six by the king from the royal household, would advise the king and make appointments to all major offices. This committee would be supplemented by another committee of twelve men named entirely by the barons, which would meet with the first committee each first of June and Candlemas (2 February). The barons would also name yet another committee of twenty-four to discuss the immediate problem of the Sicilian expedition, and join the original committee of twenty-four in hearing grievances and directing them toward the proper authority, which might be the committee of fifteen. Matters concerning the Church, however, were to be referred to the original committee of twenty-four for action.

At all points in this complex committee system the baronial party had the advantage. Officers of the royal household formed a minority in the crucial committee of fifteen, and had already shown in the first committee of twenty-four that they could be overawed by the barons despite equality in numbers. If the plan had worked, there would have been oligarchical rule, with the king at best *primus inter pares*. The plan, however, was too complex and unwieldy, and it also neglected nonbaronial interests and was seriously weakened as a result. If Henry III ignored the force of nationalism, so too did the barons at Oxford.

When the barons met again at Westminster Hall in 1259, they made a number of concessions to the smaller feudal tenants in the *Provisions of Westminster*.[3] In the royal name the barons guaranteed them the same rights accorded to tenants-in-chief by the Provisions of Oxford. More important, the Provisions of Westminster practically ended feudal jurisdictions by declaring that only those feudal tenants whose charters of enfeoffment specifically required suit of court owed it to their lords. For most vassals the duty lay in unwritten, customary feudal law; consequently suit of court became unnecessary and their duty to submit issues to private courts baron came to an end. The great barons, now in control of government, including the courts, were willing to concede the final consequences of their acceptance at Runnymede of the juridical innovations of the Angevins.

[3] Wilkinson, I, 172.

The smaller feudal landholders, the knights, and the merchants were excluded from the baronial schemes for maintaining control over the government. The committees compelled the king to make peace with Wales, Scotland, and France and replaced foreigners in government posts by their own men; but having done that their enthusiasm waned, and the barons seemed to have run out of constructive ideas. Splits appeared within their ranks. A conservative section headed by the Earl of Gloucester opposed any changes in the *status quo* and sought to preserve baronial domination at all costs. A more liberal element aimed at accepting knights and merchants as members of the baronial committees. The leader of the latter group was Simon de Montfort who, as a foreigner and a brother-in-law of Henry III, might have been expected to belong to the royal party. But his idealism and ambition combined to make de Montfort leader of the baronial reform group.

Between the two baronial factions stood Henry III, opposed to each and biding his time. Within a year the two factions in the various committees disliked each other so intensely that the king could make an attempt to recover control of local government by naming new sheriffs, loyal to himself and contemptuous of the sheriffs named previously by the committees. By 1261 Henry III felt strong enough to ask for a papal dispensation from his oath to observe the Provisions of Oxford, and the Pope obliged. This was a clear enough indication of Henry's future plans, but the barons were by this time so riven with dissension that the committee of fifteen, the core of the entire baronial arrangement, took no positive steps to forestall the royal designs. With the futility of the barons now revealed, Henry enlisted foreign mercenaries. When the committee of fifteen objected, the king dismissed all the advisers the barons had named at Oxford.

Civil War

Having failed to retain control of the machinery of government, the barons now tried to sabotage it. In the rivalry between themselves and the king for the glittering prize of government both sides appealed to force, but not before they had also taken the unusual step of appealing to a section of the population that had hitherto generally been left out of account.

Two rival governments were striving for the kingdom. The barons under Gloucester's leadership tried to prevent the new justices appointed by the king from holding assizes, and some shire courts refused to meet them. But the barons also saw that the Provisions of Oxford and their claim that the king was still bound by them were futile unless their program had a wider base. In the royal name, therefore, the committee of fifteen summoned three knights from each shire to meet with it at St. Albans. The royal reply was prompt, a countersummons to these knights to come to meet with curia regis at Windsor. Just how many knights went to the rival meetings is uncertain, but each side was now obviously appealing to a minor and previously neglected element in the feudal hierarchy. Realizing that even if the barons were to succeed in their present conflict with the king they would have to share the spoils of victory with lesser men, Gloucester chose to compromise with Henry. The younger barons charged Gloucester with duplicity and looked to de Montfort for leadership.

De Montfort, however, was disgusted by the debacle and thought of going on a crusade. Some of the barons, hoping to retrieve something from the wreckage, were willing to concede to the king the sole right to name sheriffs, but their offer came too late. His plans already laid, Henry III formally repudiated the Provisions of Oxford in 1262. The conciliatory barons offered to renounce everything else if only their committee system might be retained; but the younger and more ambitious barons saw how far they had fallen and at last persuaded de Montfort to commit himself to their cause. This action in turn alarmed the king, who offered to submit the Provisions of Oxford and the whole question of the relations between crown and baronage to the interpretation and arbitration of Louis IX of France. De Montfort, for the sake of peace, agreed to the proposal.

Louis would undoubtedly have liked to weaken the English monarchy, but he was hardly in a position to do so without undermining his own position in regard to his own vassals. Thus his decision, given in the *Mise of Amiens*,[4] was in favor of strong, personal kingship and Henry III's right to name his own advisers freely. De Montfort, who had sworn to accept the decision, protested that instead of interpreting the Provisions of Oxford the mise had canceled them. He and his followers declared that their earlier oath to uphold the provisions was superior to their later oath to accept the mise, and now things finally came to a head. Gathering large forces, de Montfort in 1264 defeated and captured the king and Prince Edward at Lewes in Sussex. A con-

[4] Wilkinson, I, 175.

stitution framed by de Montfort, the *Mise of Lewes*,[5] was dictated to them.

Despite his oath, de Montfort did not revert to the earlier baronial propositions, but devised what was on the whole a more workable plan. A board of arbitrators, named by the king and de Montfort, was to settle all issues and name a council. The council was to fill government posts and regulate royal expenditures until current debts had been paid. The most significant restrictions in an otherwise flexible arrangement were that the arbitrators and members of the council should all be English and should faithfully observe Magna Carta and the Forest Charter.

This plan received the sanction of a council composed of the barons of de Montfort's faction and four knights from each shire. Sometimes called a "parliament," [6] this body made revisions in the Mise of Lewes and declared the new plan the *forma regiminis*. This written constitution resembled the mise with the addition that the council should name nine men as royal advisers, three always to be with the king, who would be bound in all matters by their advice.

All might have been well, from the point of view of the barons, had it not been for the escape of Prince Edward. Unlike his father, Edward was a shrewd and able man. In 1265, in order to broaden his support, de Monfort summoned in the king's name a carefully picked parliament of lay and spiritual lords, together with knights from the shires *and* borough representatives. Often hailed as the first true *Parliament*,[7] it represented only the followers of de Montfort, and it is very doubtful whether it ever merited this distinction. What is significant, however, is that it did include the mercantile section of the population, and this reveals more about de Montfort's awareness of the political and economic realities of his time than it does about any idealistic conceptions he may have had on the subject of representative government.

But meanwhile Edward had gathered an army. He defeated de Montfort at Evesham in 1265, and the baronial leader was left dead on the field. Henry III was again free, but the real ruler was his son. The royalist victory doomed de Montfort's plan, and for a time Edward conducted a policy of terror against those who had supported it until he realized that there was a better policy.

[5] Wilkinson, I, 181.
[6] Below, p. 162.
[7] Below, p. 163.

Strong Monarchy

After Evesham, Prince Edward ruled the realm so well for his father that the latter's death in 1272, while Edward was on a crusade, did not give rise to any internal disturbance. The nation quietly waited for the return of Edward I, whose reign (1272–1307) was a continuation of his unofficial regency. A shrewd, not to say crafty, man, Edward I was one of the great molders of the English constitution.

Edward submitted all outstanding issues to a group of arbitrators named jointly by himself and the barons. Since the defeat and disintegration of the baronial party, however, there was no danger of any organized opposition to the king, and in the *Dictum of Kenilworth* [8] of 1266 he secured full control over government and ended the committee system devised by the baronage. All acts of de Montfort and his parliaments, even if in the royal name, were declared void. The Church received its usual guarantee that it would be "free," though by this time it was little more than a gesture, as was the royal promise to observe the two charters. All barons, except some of the ringleaders and de Montfort's family, regained their property, and the king promised to proceed against individuals only for specific crimes and not by blanket charges. Yet the fallen baronial leader had come close enough to success and had so captured the popular imagination that the Dictum of Kenilworth ended with the significant clause that de Montfort was not to be worshipped as a saint.

Edward's policies rested on a tacit but real alliance between the crown on the one hand and the lesser feudal and mercantile personages on the other. In 1267, in his father's name, Edward summoned a parliament, consisting of his council and a number of knights, to reaffirm the legal clauses of the Provisions of Westminster of eight years before. In this *Statute of Marlborough* [9] the king repeated the guarantees of the great barons to their vassals, including that which freed them from suit of court. Smaller feudal tenants thus had reason to be grateful for a strong crown.

In 1267 and for a long time to come, a *statute* was only a particularly solmen and binding promise by the king, who might call in interested groups to help frame it but was not under any obligation to do so. Thus like all other Edwardian statutes, that of Marlborough might be legis-

[8] Wilkinson, I, 184.
[9] Ibid., III, 179.

lative both in intention and result, but not so in the method of its formulation.

Feudalism also declined because the crown had less need for its services. Mercenaries had won the royal victory, demonstrating that the king no longer required the military resources of the barons. It was now scutage and not mounted men that the king demanded of his military tenants. The baronial debacle in the civil war made it quite unnecessary for the king to get baronial consent to scutage, which he was now able to levy at his own discretion and which the barons meekly paid, thereby reducing their military strength still further. Some years later when Edward demanded by what warrant certain private feudal rights were held, the Earl of Pembroke took down his sword and stormily declared that here was his warrant — but it was too late: the sword was rusty.

The crown also ceased to be dependent for supplies and services upon holders in serjeanty, who were encouraged to commute these obligations by a money payment, *arrentation*. Inevitably this payment became confused with the normal feudal obligation of socage, so that serjeanty and socage became one and the same thing, usually described by the name of the latter.

In 1275 Edward, now king, set out the precise obligations of honorable tenures in the *Statute of Westminster I*,[10] which was expanded the next year by the *Statute of Rageman*. Though in their content these statutes might appear to be an affirmation of feudal principles, the way in which they were granted was contrary to the spirit of feudalism. Feudal law made obligations a bilateral matter between lord and vassal. The statutes were a unilateral declaration by the king of the duties of *all* vassals, regardless of whom they held. Henceforth a vassal's obligations to his lord rested upon this royal statement; it was to the king, therefore, that he would turn for any definition of his rights.

Three years later Edward made a frontal assault on feudal prescriptive rights, including the control of hundred courts and viewing of frankpledge, as well as a few franchise jurisdictions weakly granted by Henry III. At Runnymede, the barons had wanted these rights defined, particularly those of private jurisdiction, as a measure of independence from the king. At Oxford, the baronial desire to maintain prescriptive rights had derived largely from financial considerations, and the same considerations prompted Edward's attack on them. At the

[10] Wilkinson, III, 312.

opening of his reign he instructed commissioners to find out from juries just what were the private rights held by specific persons in every county. This information went on the *Hundred Rolls,* a monumental source of information on later thirteenth-century England. In 1278 his *Statute of Gloucester* [11] instituted *quo warranto* proceedings, whereby royal commissioners summoned holders of prescriptive rights to show *by what warrant,* or right, they exercised them. The commissioners, who were otherwise common law justices, heard the crown legal serjeants plead the common law doctrine that a prescriptive right, even if exercised continuously, could not stand against royal wishes without a specific grant. Few holders of these private rights could produce such a charter for them, and consequently the commissioners cancelled scores of them, to the accompaniment of a growing rumble of baronial discontent. In 1290 Edward compromised, accepting the doctrine of the *limit of legal memory,* which both placated holders of private rights and also modified the prerogative nature of this phase of the common law. Any right exercised continuously since the coronation of Richard I in 1190, even without specific support for it, was valid. This doctrine was quickly extended to include all branches of the law, so that any legal precedent after 1190, not otherwise modified or overruled by subsequent judicial or legislative action, may be pleaded in modern English courts.

The decline of feudalism was also reflected in developments in the royal council. With William I all tenants-in-chief were bound to attend curia regis, although in practice only those few actually needed by the king normally appeared. With Henry III the barons had complained that too many persons at curia regis came from the royal household. With Edward I, however, the old feudal curia regis ceased to advise the king and began to move away from the royal person to become the core of the new Parliament and eventually one of its houses — the House of Lords. But for the time being the weakness of the barons permitted Edward to summon to his council whomever he wished, regardless of his feudal position or lack of it.

In the necessary reorganization after the war Edward was guided by the principle that the royal will should prevail through the realm by means of an efficient civil service. Neither feudal nor household personnel held important positions in the new administration; the former were ignored, and the latter returned to their household duties. Thus the Lord Chamberlain, who had been a great public personage with

[11] Wilkinson, III, 312.

Henry III, found his duties restricted once again to announcing the royal presence. Daily administration was in the hands of anonymous experts, named for their administrative abilities but with no responsibilities for the formation of policy.

Local administration too was tightened up. The new sheriffs were emphatically king's men, but their authority was being limited to the execution of royal court orders. The coroner, now named by the shire court subject to royal approval, continued to help the sheriff check on pleas of the crown. Barons were forbidden to interfere in local administration by the Statute of Westminster I. In 1285 the *Statute of Winchester* [12] revitalized the old assize of arms of Henry II and made all subjects responsible for clearing roadside brush, wherein robbers might lurk. Town gates were to be closed at night, and a watch posted, while "strangers" — always suspect — would be checked on by borough officials and sheriffs. In the statute a new official was named, although he may have existed previously, the *conservator of the peace*, whose duties included checking on crown pleas. That sheriff and coroner also had this duty did not preclude a third official's performing the task. For Edward I there could never be enough crown pleas. The conservators of the peace went on to assume ever greater importance and to become men of all work under their later title of *justices of the peace*.[13]

Edward came to an understanding with the rising, nonfeudal mercantile class. In 1283 his able Chancellor, Robert Burnell, Bishop of Bath, assembled some merchants at his manor of Acton Burnell to work out the statute of that name, or *De Mercatoribus*.[14] Although common law courts could collect private debts, they were powerless if the creditor lacked a sealed bond to prove the debt. The boom in trade, especially in wool, had created a need for credit; but more than once creditors, particularly foreign merchants, had burned their fingers on debts without seal so that credit became difficult to obtain. The *Statute of Acton Burnell* permitted merchants to *register* their debts with royal officials; and in the event of nonpayment, creditors could have these officials distrain (seize and sell) the goods of *English* debtors. The statute was a radical departure from previous law, and not all English merchants were happy about it. Nevertheless, the law was generally satisfying to the new merchant princes.

[12] Wilkinson, III, 180.
[13] Below, pp. 207–8.
[14] Wilkinson, III, 317.

Royal Jurisprudence

That the troubled reign of Henry III should be one of the great periods in the extension of royal jurisdiction is proof enough of the inherent vitality of the institution of monarchy. When the barons in the Provisions of Westminster ended suit of court for their vassals, they recognized that the king's courts had become those of the realm and the king's law the *common* law. The danger from Church courts had long disappeared, and their jurisdiction was no more than that allowed them by royal justices. Manorial courts for serfs were losing their business as the ranks of the servile diminished in the late thirteenth century. Thus the royal common law and courts grew, even during the reign of a weak king. Under Edward I the common law was finally crystallized in a form which was not to be substantially modified for over four centuries.

Common Law: Expansion and Differentiation

The enlargement of the law of the royal courts made it impossible for the king to exercise direct personal control over its application. The main characteristics of this common law, as has been seen,[15] became intensified during the thirteenth century. During that time, although some local customs may have been accepted, the common law in its application by the courts steadily eliminated local variations and created legal uniformity as to issues, persons, time, and place.

Such uniformity implied the supremacy of law. Although this ideal had existed in Anglo-Saxon and Norman feudal justice, Angevin law had an extra authoritarian quality inasmuch as it emanated from the king and his agents, and in its application partook of the majesty of royalty. During the thirteenth century, however, the law of the royal courts also began to acquire that fundamental characteristic of Anglo-Saxon and feudal law, the assumption that the law was supreme over all men, *including* the king. This was in part because the law of the royal courts became popular in the true sense of the word; people made royal courts and law *their* courts and law. Yet, paradoxically, the two measures through which the law chiefly developed during this period in

[15] Above, pp. 103-4, 108.

response to public demand were essentially royal measures — the issue of new writs from Chancery and the appointment of royal justices.

New writs extended and differentiated the law. They were issued in large numbers during the thirteenth century when the royal courts had a rush of business, much of it concerned with new problems which older writs would not meet. Chancery therefore constantly enlarged its register of writs to create new actions and thus extend the law. The baronial complaint at Oxford that these new writs made the law uncertain was in vain; too many people (including the barons) were asking Chancery for them. The flow did not stop until Parliament in the early fourteenth century wrung from the king a promise that no new writ should be issued under either the great or privy seal without its approval. This parliamentary guardianship of the law made for more certainty but less flexibility, because Parliament proved very unwilling to change the basic national law.

Theoretically, new writs were only refinements of old ones, but they quickly produced new actions. A typical example of such differentiation was the action of *debt*, whereby the Exchequer Court collected private debts.[16] However, when the debtor had no cash, a court order to pay was of little use to the creditor. Chancery met the problem by the writ of *detinue*, which initiated an action at law whereby the justices, upon the verdict of a jury that the debt existed, permitted the plaintiff to seize and hold the debtor's goods until he paid. In short order the justices were allowing the plaintiff to sell such goods to satisfy the debt. Wise creditors purchased both writs of debt and detinue, and Chancery soon sold them as one.

The new action of *debt and detinue* was further refined to meet the case of a man who could not recover chattels he had loaned, because a favorite defense of the person holding them was that he retained them to force payment of a debt. For people obstructed in this way Chancery devised the writ of *replevin*, which began the action of that name. If the purchaser of the writ gave security to the court to pay the debt if a jury found that he did in fact owe it, the justices would swear in a jury not to answer the question about the debt (that was another matter for which another writ would have to be brought), but to report whether the chattels in question belonged to the plaintiff in the replevin action. If the jury's verdict were in the affirmative, the justices would order the return of the goods to the plaintiff.

[16] Above, p. 78.

But this was not the end. The holder of the chattels could put forward the defense that he had just *found* the chattels; and "finders keepers, losers weepers." At first glance it might seem that justices would brush aside such a specious defense, but thirteenth-century justices had little power to brush aside anything. As a result, Chancery produced the writ of *trover*, which began an action in which a jury would decide whether the chattels supposedly found (*trouvé*) by the defendant in fact belonged to the plaintiff. If this was the verdict, the justices issued an order for their return to him. Thus from the simple action of debt, there grew three others.

Again, there was the problem of the person injured by a criminal act. Punishment of the offender might satisfy the king, but it did little to compensate the victim. Chancery, therefore, produced its writ of *trespass*, instituting an action which lay somewhere between a modern civil and criminal suit, the plaintiff alleging that he had been injured by a criminal act of the defendant for which he had been convicted. If a jury found the allegations correct, the defendant (or his survivors) had to pay damages to the plaintiff. It soon became unnecessary to show prior conviction of the defendant for a successful trespass action. From here it was only a short distance to *tort*, a wrong suffered by a person for which he could claim damages. The common law soon produced a spate of such tort actions, and most modern civil suits are actions of tort.

The royal justices during this period played an extremely important part in establishing legal uniformity by their rulings on writs. These rulings became part of a growing body of precedent which the justices followed in subsequent decisions in similar cases. Pre-trial judicial rulings determined the specific issues to be submitted to the jury by the itinerant justice and what administrative order he would issue according to the verdict on these issues.

The work of the five royal justices in the central court, now generally called Common Pleas, increased to such an extent that the court began to call in the parties to a case to assist it. The principals often found it inconvenient to come to Westminster, so the justices permitted litigants to have agents represent them, and during the thirteenth century there appeared in the central court professional pleaders who would sell their services to anyone.[17]

Initially, pleading was informal. It was "in" not "before" Common

[17] For the training of these pleaders, see below, p. 152.

Pleas, where justices and pleaders sat around a table to engage in what was actually wrangling and haggling between the pleaders, with the justices seizing on points they found significant. Pre-trial pleading was crucial in the thirteenth century, because it determined the exact issues which were to be put to the jury and the exact words in which they were framed. These proceedings were at first conducted in Latin, but later in that peculiar tongue, "Law French," which lived on in pleading until the close of the seventeenth century, by which time it was virtually unintelligible to everyone.

Pleading opened with the plaintiff's pleader producing the writ ordering the justices to hear the case, the facts of which, said the pleader, would be confirmed by a jury on the basis of local community knowledge. The defendant's pleader was then confronted by three alternatives. He could *admit* the allegations in the writ, whereupon all the justices had to do was to give judgment. He could deny the whole thing, that is, *plead the general issue* in the belief that a jury would deny the plaintiff's statements. More often, however, he did neither and instead would *except to* the writ, that is declare that the plaintiff had the wrong writ for the situation he claimed existed. If the justices agreed, the writ would not *lie* (literally, on the table of the court) but would be swept onto the floor. If the justices held that the writ did lie, the defense turned to various hypothetical issues which *might* have a bearing on the case. The defense pleader did not say that these *were* the facts, only that certain matters might be germane to the issue. The plaintiff's pleader would counter-plead, and so it went back and forth until the justices decided which hypothetical issues should be included in the question given the jury. By this procedure Common Pleas justices defined the issue — and also might very well make the action as submitted to the jury different from its statement in the original writ. By the time the central justices were through with a case, there might be just one small issue for the itinerant justice to place before the jury, but upon it the entire case would turn.

The law was thus no longer merely what the writs said; it was also (and more important) what the justices said about the writs. By the close of the thirteenth century, Common Pleas had worked out rules of pleading, the most important being that every writ governed the pleas to be entered on it, although certain pleas might be entered on several writs. These rules as to what pleas entered pleading on what writs rested on the stare decisis of Common Pleas, and the great achievement for a pleader was to persuade the court to accept a new plea on a writ. Such a triumph almost ensured his client's victory in the trial court and also enlarged the law by that much more. So valuable was nisi prius pleading in shaping the law and sharpening trial actions that it received formal recognition in 1285 in the *Statute of Westminster II*.

For the application of the principle of stare decisis, written records were essential. Court clerks entered pleas to writs on *Plea Rolls*, but these records kept no track of arguments or rulings. The recording of these important matters was a labor of love by clerks in the central court, who from 1292 to 1525 set them down in the *Year Books*, giving pleas, arguments, and rulings in the major cases for the preceding year.[18] The *Year Books* did not give the final determination of the case in the trial court; that was of no concern to their zealous compilers, who were interested only in what the central court said. Despite the rule of stare decisis, pleaders did not use the *Year Books* in the same manner or to the same extent as they did the later Law Reports. Only a few instances have come down to us where a plea was made, argued, and ruled upon in terms of past decisions in the *Year Books*, and even there only the most recent decisions were invoked. But the *Year Books* and *Plea Rolls* were essential tools for the common law pleader, who, unlike the *civilian* working in Roman and canon law, had no *a priori* maxims or codices to guide him. The common law pleader had to know what writs to buy, what pleas to enter on them, and the rules of the king's court; and this information came only from the *Year Books* and *Plea Rolls*.

The law produced by writs, pleaders, and justices was very complex. The average man simply could not be expected to understand it in all its ramifications. Henry de Bracton, who as an itinerant justice from 1248 to 1268 knew exactly what was going on, described this complexity in his *De Legibus et Consuetudinibus Angliae*, written between 1250 and 1260. Bracton recognized that the law was what the justices said it was, and he cited 2000 judicial rulings to describe it. His *Notebook* of jottings on numerous cases is scarcely less valuable as a source of thirteenth-century jurisprudence. In his larger work Bracton indicated that the law was fast becoming a series of rigid formularies for a multitude of carefully defined actions. Precise adherence to these formularies was essential if a litigant were to win his case.

The degree to which Roman and canon law influenced thirteenth-

[18] For examples of an entry in the *Year Books* see Appendix II.

THE CONTEST FOR GOVERNMENT

century English common law in a time of "anti-foreign" English nationalism is difficult to measure. But Bracton, like most justices of his time, was an ecclesiastic, albeit in minor orders, and was well acquainted with both Roman and canon law. He used Roman law for broad classification, but at the same time within these broad categories he was concerned with the particular rulings of English common law. His use of Roman legal terms to describe and explain common law actions, however, is some evidence of the influence of Roman law, which was indeed inevitable. All justices must have been familiar with it, and the Chancellor himself was invariably a great churchman. Certainly, contemporaries believed that the common law was being affected by canon law, as can be seen from the barons' statement at Merton in 1236, in which they objected to the inclusion within the common law of the canon law rule that bastards were legitimized by the marriage of their parents. When on that occasion the barons declared, "We do not want the laws of England changed," they were not objecting to the application of this particular canon law principle by the Church courts; their obvious fear was that it might enter the common law to affect property inheritance. There was certainly no reason for the barons to have voiced their objection unless they had already seen canon law influencing the common law.

The baronial opinion at Merton that each law should remain within its own court expresses the actual relationship of the common law to Roman and canon law in the thirteenth century. The medieval kingdom, in contrast to the modern state, had several systems of jurisprudence. Although the common law of the king's courts was the most important, there was room for other laws and courts.

Common Law: Crystallization

The monumental statutes of Edward I's reign crystallized the common law into a form which, despite all the changes of the nineteenth century, can still be perceived today. Should some ghostly shade of one of Edward's justices wander into any common law court now, he would quickly recover from his initial confusion and recognize the basic forms of procedure and pleading.

Statutes were originally the ultimate expression of prerogative kingship. The power to *make* law, something never claimed by Anglo-Saxon or feudal monarchs, was now exercised by a king who had transcended feudal limitations. That the new institution called Parliament had any *right* to assist in the formation of statutes did not occur to anybody, and Parliament had very little conception of the power of legislation until Henry VIII (1509–47) showed it what it could do. The theory that a statute had to have the approval of king, lords, and commons, that it should receive the "threefold assent," belongs to a later period, and there is no evidence that during the reign of Edward I the king was under any obligation to share his statute-making power. He was more independent in this respect than Henry III, and the statutory legislation of his reign expresses the victory of prerogative kingship.

A few statutes had appeared prior to Edward I, such as the Statute of Merton in 1236 [19] and the Statute of Marlborough in 1267; but during his reign they increased to such an extent that the *Statute Rolls* became necessary. The way in which these were kept shows the close connection between statutes and royal power. There was one roll for each *regnal year* of the reign, that is commencing from the date of the monarch's accession and rarely corresponding precisely with the normal year. A royal clerk indicated a particular statute of that year as a heading, *capitulum*. The modern method of English statute citation recalls how statutes were once the royal will: "1 Eliz. II, cap. 3" indicates the third law to receive the royal assent during the first regnal year of the reign of Queen Elizabeth II. Nowhere in the citation is there any hint that the queen had to wait until Parliament passed the measure before she could give her assent, nor of the even more significant fact that once Parliament had passed the measure she was virtually compelled to give her assent. In the reign of Edward I, however, what went on the Statute Rolls was a matter for royal determination, and the mechanical definition of a statute was therefore anything that appeared on the rolls. The 1225 edition of Magna Carta went on the Statute Rolls in 1297 simply because Edward I wished to emphasize the solemn nature of his confirmation of it. Although the modern method of citation can be used for these statutes, they are more commonly indicated by the name of the place where the king issued them or by their opening words.

By the late thirteenth century the land law was in need of revision. The disintegration of feudalism, together with some peculiar features of the common law, had created a situation which was often prejudicial to royal interests. Edward I met the problem by prerogative statute.

[19] Wilkinson, III, 257.

The greatest landholder was the Church, an eternal corporation, which, regardless of the tenure by which it held land, forever kept it. The land of the Church never escheated, was rarely forfeited, and never came under wardship. Instead, the Church held its land with the grip of a dead hand, *mortmain*. This was unsatisfactory to the ultimate beneficiary of all escheats, forfeitures, and wardships — the king. Edward might not have needed to take action had not the excessive piety of his father resulted in large grants to the Church and its subsidiary corporations, usually in frankalmoign. Vast areas of the realm had no obligation to the king except that of prayer, which Edward valued but only up to a point. Other feudal tenants had similarly granted land to the Church. Edward did not cancel previous grants, but in 1279 his *Statute of Mortmain* [20] forbade any layman in the future to grant or otherwise alienate land to the Church, which in its turn was forbidden to receive it, without license by the grantor's *overlord*, who by virtue of the crumbling of the feudal pyramid was more and more likely to be the king. The requirement of license was an extension of the older feudal rule of fines for alienation of land by tenants-in-chief, and it by no means ended grants to the Church. Edward and his successors were liberal in granting licenses to alienate land — for a fee. However, the law did restrict the alienation of land, which the royal courts had hitherto encouraged.

They had encouraged it because they generally favored the man in possession. But although this attitude had helped to undermine baronial power, it had reached the point where it was harming the greatest lord, the king. His courts were interpreting charters granting land in a re-markable way. By feudal law these grants were always conditional, in that the recipient held the land on condition that he performed certain services for the grantor. However, common law pleaders and justices had seized on a phrase in all charters which gave the land to the grantee and the heirs of his body lawfully begotten, and were interpreting *this* as the condition of the grant; consequently, as soon as a grantee had a child born in wedlock, he had fulfilled the conditions of the grant and could henceforth alienate his land. This judicial doctrine thus created the title of *fee simple conditional*. The courts were careful not to say that the donee, upon becoming a lawful father, had acquired an estate in fee for all purposes. If his issue predeceased him, his land still reverted to the donor, even if the grantee had surviving collateral relatives. Such escheats, however, did not occur often; because as soon as a man had an

[20] Wilkinson, III, 316.

heir, he began to mortgage and sell his land. Thus the common law experts, in freeing land law from the choking rules of feudal descent, almost ended the possibility of escheat.

Here was the rub for the king, who was the ultimate beneficiary of all escheats as they moved upward through the feudal hierarchy. Yet so entrenched were the doctrines of royal courts that they continued to oppose the interests of the king. The only way Edward could cut the judicial Gordian knot was by statute law, a method used by later generations for the same purpose.

In 1285 that portion of the *Statute of Westminster II* known as *De Donis Conditionalibus* [21] declared that henceforth courts were to comply with the wishes of the grantor, as indicated in the original written conveyance, in matters relating to the descent of land. Such a grant, therefore, conveyed only a limited title to the grantee, who did not receive a fee simple but a fee from which full ownership had been cut, *taillé*, so that his estate was *entailed*. The grantor could set a very broad or a very narrow line of descent in his entailing of the land in his original grant, which was to govern the movement of the land for all time. Obviously, De Donis (to use its shortened title) enhanced the possibility of escheat, because the moment that one of the conditions of the original grant checked the descent of land, it reverted to the grantor's line. Furthermore, the law by substituting for the title of fee simple conditional that of *fee tail* required the holder of entailed land, who now had only a limited estate in it, to pass it down in its *entirety* to the next in line as detailed in the original grant. At most, alienation of part or all of it could only be for the lifetime of the present possessor.

At first glance De Donis might seem to have restored feudal land law, but its ultimate effect was to return all lands to the king. Contemporaries saw this clearly and numerous petitions asking for repeal of the statutes were presented to the king. He, however, ignored them.

When De Donis was joined with *Quia Emptores* in the *Statute of Westminster III* [22] in 1290, the disintegration of the feudal system was accelerated. Quia Emptores apparently had just the opposite intention, free alienation; but Quia Emptores dealt with land to be granted in entail. Feudal law permitted subinfeudation freely and by any tenure, although it recognized possible injury to the grantor's lord by allowing him to levy fines for alienation. However, this was really no protection to the grantor's overlord, often now the king, against the day when

---

[21] Wilkinson, III, 318.
[22] Ibid., 319.

some grave abbot would inform him that his monks had once prayed for Geoffrey and also for Aimeric after the escheat of Geoffrey's fief to him, so that now after another escheat they were going to do the same thing for their new lord, the king. Magna Carta had underlined the feudal principle, repeated in the Statute of Marlborough, that obligations of tenure were unaffected by changes in lords. Thus a lord, as the incident of escheat moved upward, might find himself with a series of small vassals without any obligations, or with payments, now the most important aspect of feudal relationships, which were slight.

Since feudal law could not protect the interests of the overlord, Edward sought to remedy the situation in Quia Emptores. It began by graciously allowing every feudal holder to subinfeudate freely (providing that he did not violate De Donis, now five years old). The statute then declared that the recipient of a grant would hold it not of the grantor but of *his* lord. Immediately what remained of the feudal pyramid trembled. With the likelihood of escheats increased by De Donis, and with all future tenures brought nearer the king by Quia Emptores, it would not be long before all freemen would hold of the king. Furthermore, Quia Emptores by removing from grantors the benefits of subinfeudation in practice ended it. The legal effect of the statute was in fact to prohibit creations of new tenures; if anyone in modern England holds from a person other than the sovereign, it must be by a tenure created before 1290. But long before Elizabeth II, Quia Emptores and De Donis together leveled the feudal pyramid, leaving almost all freeholders royal tenants-in-chief.

Limitations on land alienation soon extended to chattels. If land could be entailed, so too could everything else. English property law became complicated by statutes alone, and the courts then proceeded by evasions of them to make the whole matter even more complex.

Judicial evasions accounted for some extraordinary developments in the law of property. What the king had declared in his statutes, his courts might blandly reverse. The holder of an entailed estate could have a person to whom he intended to sell land bring suit against him, alleging a better title. On the day of the trial of the collusive action the defendant-seller did not appear; and the plaintiff-purchaser won the land by default. This collusion received the dignity of a name, *common recovery*, which holders of entailed property used to *bar* or *dock* entail with the assistance of sympathetic justices. Later the name for the action became *fines and recovery* and so common that courts ceased to demand a formal action. The interested parties merely filed a deed for recording in Chancery. But the difficulty with this method of evading De Donis and Mortmain was that any person with a future interest in the property could frustrate it by filing a *caveat*. However, the method generally served its purpose before its abolition in 1833.

Long before the abolition of fines and recovery, the common law devised other means for avoiding the plain letter of royal statutes. A hopeful purchaser of entailed property would arrange a collusive action alleging better title. The possessor entered a plea that he had received the property from a third person who had guaranteed its title to be clear, so that the action should lie against this person who had vouched to warrant a clear title. The justices would summon this third individual only to discover that he was their clerk. Properly shocked at his having dared to warrant a title which he had never possessed, the justices ordered the delivery of the property, usually land, to the plaintiff-purchaser, who thus acquired a free title and also enlarged the common law by adding *vouching to warranty* as another method to bar entail. The justices soon dispensed with the services of their clerk in this action, and vouching to warranty continued, to become one of the bases of modern title insurance.

The Central Courts

Older private courts had long since fallen before the king's central courts, and the jurisdiction of the Church courts had been greatly restricted. In 1285 Edward I approved the existing jurisdiction of the latter as to *res* and *persona* in *Circumspecte Agatis,* and in doing so emphasized that the scope of ecclesiastical jurisdiction depended on the royal will. Ecclesiastical courts retained what the king wished them to retain — probate, marriage, cure of souls, and ecclesiastical economy. Benefit of clergy survived but was brought firmly under the control of royal justices, who decided who should have it and then only after a jury had found the accused guilty.

Common Pleas had taken over the central court established in 1178. As early as 1234 it had its separate plea roll, which showed its control over wide aspects of law via its nisi prius cases, largely private suits, although occasionally royal interests were involved. By 1278 it had a Chief Justice with an annual salary of 60 marks plus fees.

The Exchequer Court had moved out of the central court. It naturally attached itself first to the Treasury; although its records go back only to 1236, it is probable that the court was operating before that time, when it was handling all financial cases involving the crown and collecting private debts. However, because it employed common law procedures the court became increasingly concerned with the judicial rather than the financial side of government. Edward I emphasized this by replacing the Treasurer by a Chief Justice and when the barons objected that the court was trying them contrary to the promise in Magna Carta of trial by peers, Edward transformed the Chief Justice and justices into a Chief Baron and barons, who remained distinctly judicial personages. The Exchequer Court operated almost entirely on the central level, with little of its business going to itinerant justices.

A later development was the court of King's Bench. It appeared because of the practice by Common Pleas of sending very knotty cases, or those directly touching royal interests, to curia regis, where the king sat at his bench, *coram rege*. Litigants dissatisfied with the pre-trial rulings of the court of Common Pleas could appeal to the king in his council. The volume of this quasi-appellate, civil judicial business justified the king's naming a special group within curia regis to deal with it. Soon this group institutionalized itself as King's Bench, which then departed from the parent curia regis, just as other courts before it had. This must have occurred as early as 1234, because the court had its own plea roll by that time. Staffed by a Chief Justice and *puisne* (inferior) justices, the court retained the same jurisdiction it had held while part of curia regis. By 1278 its Chief Justice had a salary equal to that of his counterpart in Common Pleas.

King's Bench heard appeals on points of law from Common Pleas, but appeals from Exchequer were very rare. From King's Bench the routes of appeal divided. One route was to the king, as the ultimate source of justice, in curia regis. However, common law practitioners by the close of the thirteenth century were urging that appeals from King's Bench should go to the more impersonal king-in-Parliament, as the descendant of the old full curia regis. Ultimately, common law appeals did terminate in the descendant of this old feudal curia regis, the House of Lords.

Whatever the destination of appeals, they could be only on issues of law, not questions of fact. This limitation of appeal remained a major characteristic of the English common law until a very late date, and even then was only partially relaxed.

The work of the central courts inevitably overlapped and all three competed with each other for business, and thus for fees. Although Common Pleas handled most civil suits, King's Bench was only too ready to do so. Exchequer developed a set of fictions by which it also heard ordinary civil suits; and its procedure, previously applied to debt collection, was so rapid as to earn it the name, the *course of the Exchequer*. This gave it a popularity irksome to the other two courts and also in the long run damaging to its own efficiency. In 1284 Edward I issued the *Statute of Rhuddlan,* in which he forbade the Exchequer Court's hearing any ordinary common law actions *except* those directly involving royal interests. The result was that the Exchequer barons were once more confined to their former jurisdiction over debt. Nevertheless, each of the three courts was adept in devising remedies and doctrines to draw business away from the others. That there was not utter confusion and a general canceling out of each court's judgments by the others was due mainly to the role of the Chancellor.

The Chancellor, as head of the royal record office, Chancery, was familiar with all affairs of state. Chancery was also the source of all writs initiating judicial actions, so that the Chancellor, although as yet without his own court, was the functional head of the judicial system. He was the obvious person to deal with the numerous petitions flowing to the king, and as head of the clerical staff he specified, in answering these petitions with writs, which court would hear pleading on them. Thus the writ-issuing function of the Chancellor determined the jurisdiction of the three central courts on a pragmatic basis.

As the issue of new writs became more rare, the Chancellor took on a new role. In 1280 Edward I ordered that all petitions to him should pass through Chancery. Only if the Chancellor could find no remedy in the registry of writs, should he and he alone bring the matter before the overworked monarch in his council. The Chancellor and his clerks soon assisted the king and council by working out answers to these special petitions before presenting them for formal royal approval. By the close of the reign of Edward I the Chancellor was almost ready to reply to these petitions himself, without reference to the sovereign, on the basis of *equity*, fairness. What constituted fairness would soon be a matter to be determined by the Chancellor in his *Court of Chancery*,[23] which emerged from the secretarial Chancery soon after the death of Edward I in 1307.

Trial Procedure

Medieval trial procedure was almost entirely on the local level under the direction of itinerant justices. The Chancellor laid out their work for each new circuit in a *commission*, ordering them to hold assizes on specified actions. The Chancellor then went through all administrative questions requiring jury answers, and the rulings of each central court needing local verdicts, and brought them all together in a commission for a *general eyre* (circuit), which covered all royal administrative and judicial business, and imposed heavy burdens on justices and juries. Less onerous were commissions of *oyer et terminer*, which instructed justices to hear and determine the judicial actions listed in their commission either by individual actions or by categories. More straightforward still was the commission of *gaol delivery*, by which justices in criminal trials were to deliver persons from jail either to freedom or to the hangman.

The procedure in civil trials was simple enough. One of the central courts had already framed the issue for submission by the itinerant justice to the jury, whose responsibility was to answer the often very narrow question of fact previously formulated by the justices at Westminster. There was no evidence; the jury was supposed to know the facts. There was no pleading; it had already taken place in the central court. There was no summing up by the trial judge; he had nothing to sum up. Upon receiving the jury verdict, the trial justice gave judgment according to orders framed by his superiors at Westminster at the close of the pre-trial pleading.

The common law's exclusion of oral testimony in trials persisted late into the fourteenth century. Until the thirteenth century, however, the plaintiff had entered the trial lists with an offer of proof by witnesses, whose stories, strictly speaking, were not evidence but only a series of helps and hints to the jury in reporting the verdict of community knowledge. Although the defendant had to agree to this mode of proof, the procedure might well have developed into compulsory proof by evidence, except that the elaborate pre-trial pleading so narrowed the issue for the jury that there was very little need of evidence.

[23] Below, pp. 218–19.

As men of community standing jurors could be expected to know the facts on this particular issue; if they did not, they were to get the facts by their own exertions. Evidence was thus unnecessary, and soon the common law regarded it as dangerous. How could justices from distant Westminster tell whether witnesses in York were telling the truth? The law therefore thought it safer to exclude all oral evidence, and it was not until the late fourteenth century, when community knowledge had become less dependable in deciding specific local issues, that the common law very grudgingly admitted evidence as proof. One curious result of this was that until well into the seventeenth century the common law did not "know" the crime of perjury and had no way of dealing with it until Parliament made it a felony.

Pre-trial pleading also excluded the *inquisitorial* method of trial. In spite of its connotations of torture, which the common law did not accept, the term actually referred to the procedure whereby trial justices asked the jury a series of questions, inquiries, *inquisitions*, about the action at trial. Upon the jury's answers the justices then decided which party should have judgment. Pre-trial pleading, by narrowing the issues for trial, removed the need for inquisitorial trial procedure, which, however, has continued on the European continent until the present day.

Criminal trial procedure was brief and to the point. Upon the appearance of itinerant justices, the grand jury duly indicted suspects in the name of the king, whose sheriff produced them for trial. The trial had two phases: *arraignment* of the accused, and petit jury *verdict* on the indictment. The arraignment was crucial. After hearing the indictment read, the accused had to accept the jurisdiction of the court by entering a plea. If he refused to plead, the court was unable to proceed. However, for such contumacious persons the law had at its disposal a means of persuasion known as *peine forte et dure*, which involved putting him into a box with rocks piled on top. This, the common law claimed, was not torture for trial proof, for the trial had not yet begun. After 1774 the defendant who stood mute before the court was deemed to have pleaded, "Not Guilty," but in the reign of Edward I pleading by the accused was essential to his arraignment.

In pleading the accused had to accept a rigid formula. When the clerk of the court read the indictment and formally asked him, "How do you plead?" he had just two possible replies, "Guilty" or "Not Guilty." The justices would accept no other. Pleas of "Guilty with extenuating circumstances," "Not Guilty by reason of insanity," and the like only confused the issue and delayed the judges. If he pleaded guilty the justices had only to look at their commission to discover what sentence they were required to pass; they were acting *administratively* and not judicially when they formally sentenced the accused to death or imposed a fine — at this time imprisonment was rarely the penalty.

If the accused boldly answered the clerk, "Not Guilty," that functionary moved on to the next question, "How will you be tried?" Again the answer had to be very precise, because it was at this point that the accused accepted the jurisdiction of the court. If he were a baron, he answered, "By God and my peers," meaning that he wanted, and until 1948 would get, a trial by other lords.[24] If the accused were a commoner, he replied, "By God and my country." The "country" was the petit jury of twelve men of the community. The accused having thus "voluntarily" admitted the jurisdiction of the court, its clerk uttered the final part of the arraignment formula, "God send you a good deliverance."

The clerk's hopeful wish indicated how the jury would decide its verdict — by consulting God, not evidence. If common law gave short shrift to witnesses in civil cases, it had no use for them in criminal actions. Even after the law allowed some oral testimony in civil cases, this was barred from criminal trials until the late fifteenth century, when the law permitted witnesses for the crown to give testimony under solemn oath. The law only very slowly admitted testimony for the defendant, and continued to exclude him as a witness until 1898.[25] The lack of evidence in criminal trials in the thirteenth century precluded any addresses to the jury by counsel and summations by justices. As soon as the trial jury was sworn, it received the case and retired immediately to a room to listen to the voice of Heaven. All twelve jurors had to agree; they were the country, which corporately had only one voice, and God spoke only with one voice on the same subject. For practical reasons, justices refused to decide the guilt or innocence of accused men. Justices were birds of passage and could not aspire to the local knowledge that the proper settlement of a case demanded. To leave the determination of guilt or innocence to the solid

[24] In 1948 trial of peers by peers was abolished (below, p. 551). It should also be noted that peer trials for spiritual lords were not normal. In 1692 the House of Lords disclaimed jurisdiction over prelates, who, however, for that reason were not peers but merely "lords of Parliament."

[25] Below, p. 510.

citizens of York was better than deciding it themselves. The road was narrow and the woods thick, and Westminster far distant.

By modern standards the jury reached its verdict by an irrational method, but to people in the thirteenth and fourteenth centuries to have God decide was the ultimate in fairness. The jury procedure also permitted its members to mitigate the law in special cases where community knowledge saw extenuating circumstances for a crime. Jurors could thus exercise a sort of juridical-administrative clemency by finding the accused innocent; and since they received this information from God, there could be no complaints. This procedure also removed from the accused all obligation to disprove the charge. Even when both parties, including the accused himself after 1898, could submit evidence, the defendant was under no obligation to prove his innocence; the burden of proof still lay solely on the crown. Modern defense evidence *rebuts* the evidence of the prosecution; it is not for the purpose (at least legally) of *proving* the defendant's innocence.

There was no appeal from the judgments of the trial courts, either in criminal or civil cases. In the former the jury's verdict was final. In civil cases the higher courts had already worked out all the legal issues involved so that there was no point in taking an appeal on law. Only after evidence and trial pleading appeared was it possible to appeal on issues of law, and civil appeals on fact were illogical. How could a distant court in Westminster know more about a specifically local question than the county jurors who were on the spot? Even after testimony entered civil trials, appeals on fact were difficult. Most modern appellate courts refuse to reopen issues of fact, on the grounds that the jury has already heard the evidence.

The Legal Profession

The need for lawyers appeared only with the development of the bureaucratic jurisprudence of the Angevin kings. To begin with, as in Anglo-Saxon times, cases still opened with the plaintiff's foreoath and the defendant's one of rebuttal, and precision in speaking these oaths was essential. However, the principal, either plaintiff or defendant, could well be nervous about saying words upon which so much depended. The royal justices of Henry II were urbane churchmen prepared to make allowances for such human weaknesses, and so they permitted a man to have somebody else, not so directly concerned, speak the words of the oath. If he stumbled, the principal himself had a chance to retrieve the situation. Usually this was not necessary, because his agent, *attorney*, was letter perfect, a professional with no direct interest in the case but willing to sell his services. The attorney, however, was not a pleader; having spoken the words successfully, he withdrew.

Pleaders first appeared in the central courts, emerging as a professional group as the law which they were helping to mold became ever more complex. By the close of the thirteenth century they received royal recognition in the title of *serjeants at law*. The king could call upon them for advice, and only they could plead before the central courts. Such men had too much dignity to scramble for business, a function they left to attorneys, who dealt directly with clients and did the spade work on a case for the serjeants — even as today solicitors brief barristers. The medieval serjeant, however, was not the exact counterpart of the great English trial lawyers of later times. Medieval trial procedure afforded no opportunities of that kind; serjeants were confined to pleading before one of the central courts, where they wore their *coifs* (a sort of white cap). Although the order of serjeants died out in the nineteenth century, being replaced by Queen's (King's) Counsel, the symbol of their order became the name of an honorary legal society to which every American law student aspires.

The bench came to be recruited from serjeants. By the close of the thirteenth century, ecclesiastical personnel were not entirely satisfactory as justices for a king like Edward I, who wanted no divided loyalties on the bench. Henry III had caused great offense by using his household officials as justices; his son wisely named his justices from the order of serjeants, so that bench and bar became a single entity. This integration continues to distinguish English from Continental juridical systems, where persons are trained either to be judges or advocates, but not both. Such a division is possible because of the codification characteristic of Continental law. But from the very beginning English common law was case law, and only men who had soaked themselves in it while pleading at the bar were qualified for the bench. Like other royal officials justices were named at the royal pleasure; but until they became arbitrators between king and Parliament in the seventeenth century, serjeants who exchanged coif for *toque*, the round, brimless hat worn by justices,[26] were in practice assured of a post for life. The English bench was remarkably free from

[26] The modern characteristic wigs of English barristers and justices entered only with the Restoration as part of the French influences surrounding Charles II.

royal pressures. When Edward I wanted courts to change their doctrines, he had to proceed by statute.

Legal training for this integrated bench and bar was essential. There had to be future generations of serjeants and justices. Would-be pleaders hung around the central courts to pick up what they could, but this was too haphazard a method, and in 1290 and again in 1292 Edward I appointed commissions to investigate the problem of legal training. The later commission suggested that law students should follow the western circuit that year to see the operation of trials and to work with attorneys. This recommendation, however, was not particularly helpful because there was no pleading on the circuits. Seeing that serjeants might have an interest in not providing competition for themselves, Edward ordered the justices to train young men either as attorneys or pleaders.

The justices were busy during term so that their pedagogical efforts were during their vacations, when they turned to a ready-made class, the hopeful, would-be pleaders living in inns around the central courts. The *Inns of Court* claiming the greatest antiquity were those of the Outer and Middle Temple, once the London house of the Knights Templar. Hotly disputing this claim was Gray's Inn, originally the town house of the Chief Justice of the Palatine County of Chester. Whatever the oldest inn of court, all had the same educational methods. The justices explained the rules of pleading and judicial rulings on different pleas in various actions. But formal instruction was the least part of this education, which was intensely practical with numerous *moots*, where justices had students plead before them in a hypothetical case. Students were also expected to conduct practice moots among themselves (and still do on the steps of every law school in the common law world). The average student thus became saturated in case law, and his thinking was based entirely on it. If he had a text, it was the *Year Books*, not the *Institutes of Justinian*.

When the courts sat, students observed their workings. Finally came the day when serjeants and justices examined students on points of law and rules of pleading by giving them more hypothetical situations. If a student passed this test, the committee of examiners "Admitted him to the bar," before which he could now plead. To this day "practical" bar examinations are conducted by such quasi-official bodies, whose recommendations are accepted by official agencies of the state.

After Magna Carta the major desire of the barons was to control a centralized government, whose existence they accepted. Their attempts to win this control met with failure, both because of the complex devices they employed and because of the narrow base upon which they rested—their own narrow class interest, to the exclusion of rising nonfeudal groups. Baronial failure meant that Edward I had personal control of the government, whose administrative and judicial aspects were all-pervading. From the judicial aspect there was a remarkable development of the common law so that its basic rules and courts, as well as the method to learn it, were essentially those of the present time.

READING LIST

HOLDSWORTH, SIR WILLIAM S. *History of English Law*, Vol. II, Book III, Part I, Chaps. III–IV; Vol. IV, Book IV, Part I, Chaps. I–II.

PLUCKNETT, THEODORE F. T. *A Concise History of the Common Law*, 4th ed., Book I, Part I, Chaps. 3–4; Part II, Chap. 5; Book II, Part III, Chap. 5.

———. *The Legislation of Edward I*.

POLLOCK, SIR FREDERICK, and FREDERIC W. MAITLAND. *History of English Law*, 2nd ed., Vol. I, Book I, Chap. VII; Vol. II, Book II, Chaps. VIII–IX.

POWICKE, SIR MAURICE. *Henry III and the Lord Edward*.

THOMPSON, FAITH. *The First Century of Magna Carta*.

TOUT, T. F. *Chapters in the Administrative History of Mediaeval England*, Vols. II–III.

TREHARNE, R. F. *The Baronial Plan of Reform 1258–1263*.

5

THE EMERGENCE OF PARLIAMENT

OF ALL ELEMENTS in the English constitution, Parliament has had the greatest impact upon the world. The common law of England traveled far, but never beyond the confines of the Commonwealth, and it exists today in other areas because these once belonged to the Empire. Within the Commonwealth, there are non-common law jurisdictions such as the Province of Quebec in Canada with French civil law, Scotland with its own law, and the Union of South Africa, formerly a Commonwealth member, with Roman-Dutch law. The common law never spanned all these diverse territories.

The concept of Parliament on the other hand, of *representative* government, belongs to all parts of the Commonwealth; it has remained firmly fixed in areas no longer within the Empire, and has spread into areas which were never at any time part of it. This is particularly significant as a reflection of the conscious efforts of nineteenth-century European liberals to transplant British parliamentary institutions into their own countries. In Commonwealth Parliaments, whether members address "Mr. Speaker," or "Monsieur, le Speaker," they acknowledge the foundation of their legislatures. Whenever a member of the United States Congress rises to a point of *parliamentary* privilege, he links his house to a distant English past transplanted to North America by Englishmen and given its first expression in 1619 in the House of Burgesses of Virginia. The Communist member of the French Chamber of Deputies prefaces his attack upon "bourgeois capitalism" with "Monsieur, le président," and so admits the past of his body. Rules of procedure for any meeting are *parliamentary*. Truly, the "Mother of Parliament" sits in that Victorian Gothic building at Westminster on the Thames.

The understandable pride of Englishmen in their unique contribution to government has caused them to pay particularly close attention to the origins of their Parliament — with the result that probably no other aspect of the modern English constitution is lost in quite the same obscurity. Most of the various and conflicting theories, however, are based upon the crucial events of the thirteenth and fourteenth centuries, which can be interpreted in many different ways.

The Problems

The problems concerning the origins of Parliament derive from the day-to-day, entirely practical nature of its early development. Action was needed, and no one at the time was particularly interested in the implications of such action. This entirely pragmatic approach to the business of government makes it difficult to determine how far Parliament had advanced as a political institution before the death of Edward I in 1307.

The modern Parliament is a good point of departure for recognizing some of these problems. Parliament today is a bicameral, *legislative* body. The House of Lords, which also possesses appellate judicial functions, consists largely of hereditary peers, some bishops, a few representative Scottish and Irish peers, a handful of "law lords," and those with life peerages, now conferred upon both men and women. Altogether this "upper" House has over 800 members, whose attendance varies greatly. The "lower" and vastly more important house, the House of Commons, has 630 members, one elected per district by all adults. Together these Houses as Parliament can do anything except repeal the fundamental laws of nature, and there are some who would say that in recent years Parliament has pressed even on this limitation. More important, these actions by a majority of both Houses bind everyone.[1] Disagreement with such an action by, or complete lack of previous consultation with, the people does not in the least affect the application of acts of Parliament.

Nothing distinguishes the modern Parliament and its thirteenth-century ancestor more than these facts about functions and powers, because Parliament at its inception and for many years thereafter did not possess one of them. The last Parliament of Edward I and the

---

[1] It is true that since the Parliament Act of 1911 (q. v., below, p. 531) the House of Lords has had no control over money measures and can only delay other legislation. Nevertheless, all acts of Parliament formally state their approval by both Houses, although the Lords may actually have disapproved.

most recent one of Elizabeth II have little in common except their name.

The principle of representation, inherent in the modern Parliament, was lacking in its ancestor. Briefly stated, the modern representative principle implies that people elect some of their number to represent or express their views on specific subjects. However, the theory then goes on to say that these representatives, by a simple majority, can bind not only themselves and those who voted for them but also those who opposed them. Furthermore, the particular action of the majority may very well concern matters which were not considered at all by the electorate at the time it elected its representatives to Parliament. No comparable theory of representation was known at the beginning of the fourteenth century, and indeed it is easy to see why men were very slow to accept it. Again, the modern concept of representation rests upon the consent of the governed to be bound by a majority of Parliament. But this was not the "consent" of feudal law, which expected each free person to act for himself and denied that another could act for him.

To contemporaries the emergent Parliament of the thirteenth century was a matter of extreme indifference. Bracton, who saw very clearly what was happening in the law, had no interest in Parliament. Matthew Paris, the astute historian and observer at the court of Henry III, to the despair of later generations used the term "parliament" very loosely to denote all sorts of assemblies, many of them apparently not meeting even the flexible criteria of his times as to what was a true parliament.

The fact was that as late as 1307 Parliament was simply *not* important. A latecomer to the constitution, its form and powers were too vague for contemporaries to take it very seriously. In the thirteenth century the important body was curia regis, including the king. If people were aware of Parliament at all, it was only as a temporary extension of this vital core of government, playing only a very minor part in the big issues of the day.

The Conditions Required for Parliament

To trace the beginnings of Parliament we must turn back to the reign of John (1199–1216). During that reign certain facts were evident which came into sharper focus later in the thirteenth century.

Such a starting point precludes any direct relationship between the early Parliament and the Anglo-Saxon Witan. Neither in function nor personnel did the two institutions have the slightest connection.

A sense of nationhood was essential for Parliament. Prior to the thirteenth century men owed loyalty to a person, possibly to the king, but still the king as a person and not as the embodiment of the nation. Moreover, people in Somerset had little interest in or knowledge of their neighbors in Devon, except to be certain of their utter untrustworthiness. This personal allegiance and localism began to give way during the thirteenth century and to be replaced by a fiercely negative, anti-foreign nationalism. Distinctions between Normans and Saxons began to disappear and a booming trade made men look beyond their parish. In place of a series of personal loyalties and narrow local interests, there emerged a measure of cultural homogeneity and the figure of a king who somehow embodied the nation as a whole.

The wool trade was the most important business from the point of view of the developing constitution. Wool from sheep grazing on land, including that of smaller feudal tenants, now often called *knights*, flowed into such cities as London and Norwich, where *merchants* became men of importance and substance as they passed it on to the looms of Flanders. Thus the wool trade, while breaking down localism and feudal loyalties, was also linking smaller feudal tenants with nonfeudal people in a community of economic interest. The flexible minds of the thirteenth century saw that such terms as "communitas" and "commune" were coming to indicate corporate entities with connotations of national groups, groups interested less in a feudal than in a national monarch to guard their interests.

A strong monarchy was equally essential for Parliament. The quarrel between king and Parliament in the seventeenth century tends to obscure the fact that hitherto they had always worked together quite harmoniously. If Parliament depended on the emergence of national feeling, it was also a manifestation of a monarchy which had broken free from feudal limitations. Historically, Parliament was as much a creation of the royal prerogative as of the royal courts, their common law, and the great statutes of Edward I. That Parliament like statutes, laws, and courts ceased to be a royal instrument later, does not alter the fact that it originated at the royal command of a strong monarch, claiming the right to summon whom he wished to advise him in defiance of feudal custom. It was no accident that Parliament became very much more clearly defined during Edward I's reign. The very phrase "king-in-Parliament" indicates their close historical connection. The enacting formula of legislation accords the action solely to the "Queen's most gracious majesty," with only the advice and consent of lords spiritual and temporal and the faithful commons in Parliament assembled. Although the modern legislative sequence is precisely the reverse of that indicated in the formula, it is a reminder that initially Parliament was an agency of the sovereign.

Royal financial needs were not however essential for Parliament's appearance. Feudal dues from various incidents were based on land and immovables, and were therefore fixed in amount. The only movable property (chattels) which could produce revenue for the king was that on his own demesne by means of tallages. Though royal revenues might be greater than those of any other lord, so also were the demands on them. John sought to escape the feudal limitations on his sources of revenue in 1204 when he called for an aid, fixed at one-seventh of the value of movable property of earls, barons, and parish and monastic churches. Both the use of a fraction to determine the amount of an aid and its imposition upon movable property were radical innovations. In 1207 he called for another aid of one shilling per mark (thirteen shillings, four pence) value of all chattels and income. This famous Thirteenth, together with similar impositions of the Seventh, Fifteenth, Fortieth, and the like, all appeared during the thirteenth century, when these and similar exactions were named according to the fraction demanded. However, this unilateral imposition by John of a new type of aid was one of the chief reasons why the barons insisted in Magna Carta that there should be no extra aids without their consent.

Although this particular chapter was omitted from later editions of the charter, the regents of Henry III and then that king himself honored its procedure, thereby underlining the feudal theory that additional aids from vassals came from their free consent and not as a result of the lord's commands.

The financial needs of the crown were therefore always associated with the feudal principle of consent during the early thirteenth century. With the baronial debacle of 1265, however, this was no longer necessarily the case, and more than once Edward I levied extra aids unilaterally. Furthermore, in the thirteenth century the principle of consent had never applied to quite the same extent to the smaller feudal tenants, the knights. Magna Carta had provided that knights should be summoned by the sheriffs to attend curia regis in order to give their assent to extra aids and scutages; but this general summons was less likely to secure their presence than the individual summonses the great barons required for themselves. The king would hardly forgo asking knights for aids simply because they did not attend curia regis. But the knights were also the local administrators for the crown, responsible for the actual local assessment of aids to which the barons had consented in curia regis. Knights on juries of assessment naturally tended to place their own interests first, and as many of them had been made rich by wool this was a matter of some concern to the king. Royal financial administration had always used the shire as an important collection unit, and during the thirteenth century the knights as assessors made themselves the corporate shire. What the king wanted was a sure method of getting money from the knights of the shire, or from the "shire," a term that by this time had come to mean the knight class.

Traditionally, the knights had been allies of the king and were essential to his local administration. To ensure the presence of such men on juries, Henry II had ordered that every hundred should send its reeve and eight men to the local segment of curia regis during its sojourn in the shire. The duties of this knight class were further added to by Richard I, who depended upon it for his coroners, and by Edward I, who required them to be his conservators of the peace. These knights had long carried the record of the local curia regis to Westminster and certified its correctness. With their growing prosperity both barons and king had wooed them. The barons had promised immunity from suit of court in the Provisions of Westminster; the king had given it to them in the Statute of Marlborough. So important for local administration were these knights, that Edward I in his *distraint of knighthood* ordered every man holding land of £20 annual value (a comfortable sum at that time) to accept the dignity and obligations of knighthood. As smaller tenants, the knights had little interest in such matters as private jurisdiction, with its revenues, or the control of central government. Their interests lay in getting rid of their immediate lords and in making money from wool.

Taxation, to use the modern term, required consent; but it was difficult to have every knight appear at curia regis, and most knights did not want to appear. The logical thing, therefore, was to have them delegate certain of their fellows in a particular shire to express (represent) their consent and their other opinions to the king. Thus the representative principle emerged as an effective way of securing the consent of the knights.

However, at this point a difficulty arises; the principle was not applied in Parliament, except when it suited royal convenience. The principle of representation for smaller feudal tenants could equally well be expressed in other meetings — as it frequently was prior to 1307. Thus even taking into account the royal financial needs, the principles of consent and of representation, the result was still not a Parliament.

This was even more the case with the nonfeudal mercantile community. During the thirteenth century merchants, grown wealthy from the wool trade, were willing to pay handsome sums to the king for charters, giving their particular locality borough status and removing it from shire control. To the merchants the privileges given by a borough charter made it worth its price. They gained freedom from tolls, which continued to apply to "foreign" merchants (including those from other English boroughs). Merchants in a borough could organize a guild to regulate its internal trade and also elect a mayor and a council to negotiate directly with the king about aids from the borough. With financial relations between king and boroughs governed in this way, there was little need for the king to summon borough representatives to Parliament, and by 1307 they had appeared there only very infrequently. If the king wished to meet burgesses from some of the boroughs, he could summon them to a special meeting without bringing them to Parliament.

The Elements of Parliament

In the thirteenth century the word "parliament" appeared to denote a session of curia regis with more than its usual membership and with more than the usual amount of discussion — in contrast to the smaller administrative meetings of curia regis. As a rule, the purpose of these gatherings was to secure the extra aids and grants desired by the king. But discussions of royal financial needs necessarily led to considerations of the policy occasioning them, and thus to parleying: such a meeting was therefore known as a *parliamentum*. It was in this sense that Matthew Paris used the word, to describe the occasion and purpose of a special kind of session of the council.

The knights rarely appeared in these early parliaments, which consisted exclusively of feudal elements. Their relative unimportance is seen in the casual provision in Magna Carta in 1215 whereby they should be summoned generally by the sheriff to financial meetings of curia regis. The regents of Henry III and later the king himself, however anxious they may have been to secure baronial consent to extra aids and scutages, did not in fact summon knights to the council. It was not until 1258, when barons and knights met together at Oxford and formulated the Provisions of Oxford, that the functions of a parliament were to some extent clarified. Contemporaries of the meeting at Oxford, which was a particularly large session of curia regis, called it a "parliament" in the sense that the knights (feudal tenants not normally summoned) were there present as feudal persons, rather than as representatives of the shires. To these people Parliament therefore appeared as a revival of the old Magnum Concilium, summoned to discuss the great affairs of the realm.

The Provisions of Oxford marked the beginning of the shift from a parliament of the council to Parliament. As a result of the Oxford meeting, there were frequent meetings between the barons and the king's council. Chancery clerks, in issuing the writs summoning barons to attend, invariably used the writ *De Veniendo ad Parliamentum*, that is, a meeting of the council; recipients were to appear at the council to discuss with the king *and* with other magnates similarly summoned, "the king's business and the business of the king and the kingdom," an all-inclusive term reflecting the early hopes of the barons that they might control royal policy and administration. The meeting that ensued was a "parliament" of the council, and it followed that any meeting produced by the writ De Veniendo ad Parliamentum was Parliament. This may seem a mechanical and oversimplified definition, but it was precisely the definition of Parliament generally recognized after about 1250: Parliament was an *occasion* on which the council, with additional *magnates*, discussed matters of major importance. This general view of Parliament meant that an essential element in it was the magnates; without them it was simply a meeting of the normal council.

By the end of the thirteenth century, however, Parliament could no longer be defined solely by reference to its personnel; there was the additional criterion of its *function*. When the council and magnates met, the meeting was considered to be a Parliament only if its major business was judicial — the handling of pleas and petitions, collected by clerks in the *Rolls of Parliament*. Prior to Edward I, Parliament meant either a council meeting with additional barons present, or council meetings devoted largely to judicial business. Once it was recognized that it should possess both these characteristics, it was not far from becoming an institution in itself.

The barons summoned by the writ De Veniendo were always distinguished from the regular council members, and their numbers varied with each Parliament. In the brief period during which they controlled the government after 1258 most barons were in fact present, but with baronial disagreement and then war, the actual barons attending Parliament varied from session to session. When de Montfort was dominant, he was able to persuade the king to summon only his own supporters; after the victory of the crown only barons supporting the king were summoned.

The Commons initially were not an essential part of Parliament. The term "commons" certainly did not imply "common people" but rather *communities*, in a corporate sense, of the articulate elements of counties and boroughs, that is, the knights and the merchants. The growth of trade had given them prosperity and had established them as separate groups, rather than, as in feudal theory, integral parts of the same free tenant class to which the greatest barons belonged.

In the continuous constitutional crisis between 1258 and 1265 the contestants for government bid for all the support they could possibly get, and each side recognized that the wealth of the knights and merchants could tip the scales in its favor. In 1261 both the de Montfort faction and Henry III sent summonses to sheriffs to send three knights from each shire to meet and *discuss* in council the affairs of the realm. Regardless of which meeting the knights attended (or of whether they decided to play it safe and attend neither) the two summonses represented an important change in outlook: they implied that the magnates were not *the* community but only *a* community of the realm. To a large extent, of course, this was dictated by monetary expedience and the knights remained in theory feudal personages, but the two summonses were significant nevertheless.

After his victory at Lewes in 1264, de Montfort had writs issued in the king's name ordering each shire to elect four knights and send them to meet with the council and the de Montfort barons in Parliament. The next year the same thing occurred except that each shire sent only two knights. The de Montfort faction, in its desperate struggle with royalist forces, recognized the usefulness of the knights, but how far they represented their shires in the modern sense is difficult to determine. The Parliament of 1265, the importance of which has often been greatly exaggerated, was significant, however, because it included the burgesses, who for the first time were associated with feudal elements: two burgesses from every borough met with knights, five earls, eighteen barons, and some bishops to "discuss" the affairs of the kingdom.

After the defeat of the barons, Parliament developed under royal direction. The *sovereign* was vital; without him there was (and is) no Parliament. The *new council*, selected by the king, became the inner core of Parliament, which after 1272 was the king-in-council-in-Parliament, that is, in discussion with persons not usually at the council. The familiarity of councillors with the business of government made them the most important working element in Parliament. *Royal officials*, forerunners of later civil servants, assisted the council during its parliamentary sessions, their close knowledge of the daily workings of government increasing the dominance of this conciliar element in Parliament. *Royal justices* from the central courts were also summoned to Parliament, since its major business was judicial. This "official" element was joined by the *magnates,* individually summoned by the writ of De Veniendo ad Parliamentum.[2] After 1265 the king summoned barons as he chose, regardless of the size of their holdings or even of their feudal relationship to him; an individual writ of summons did not yet attach itself either to a particular piece of land or to a person. Not until Richard II (1377–99) was there any suggestion that the possession of a title of nobility carried with it an inherent right to sit in Parliament.

Knights of the shire, *burgesses* from boroughs, and *clerical proctors* for the lower clergy also appeared in Parliament from time to time, at the royal convenience. But of the thirty Parliaments summoned by Edward I up to 1297, only four actually included people belonging to these classes. His first Parliament in 1275 included four knights from each shire and four to six burgesses from every borough, who were there to report the prior consents by shire and borough courts to an aid. Such nonbaronial consent, however, did not necessarily involve the calling of a Parliament, and it was twenty years before a comparable

---

[2] Chancery practice sharply differentiated between these magnates and the regular council; and only if the two joined was the writ De Veniendo used and the meeting Parliament. When barons came together on royal orders without the core of the council, the Chancery clerks used other writs having various names, the most frequent being *colloquia*.

assembly was summoned. In the meantime the king received similar consents to aids from knights and burgesses at various meetings which Chancery clerks did not refer to as Parliaments, because the barons had not been summoned by De Veniendo.

The king's attitude toward the knights was demonstrated clearly in 1290, when he summoned only bishops and lay barons to a Parliament to consent to an aid for his eldest daughter's dowry on her first marriage, although it was in fact one of the three customary feudal aids and did not require consent by tenants.[3] This enlarged meeting of the council discussed the future statute of Quia Emptores.[4] After this work Parliament ended. Then a summons went out via the sheriffs for knights of the shire to come and give their consent to the aid for the dowry. Although knights as feudal tenants, albeit smaller ones and so less likely to subinfeudate than barons, had an interest in Quia Emptores, Edward did not feel it necessary to have them consider the proposed law.

In 1294, knights came to Parliament "to consult and consent" on the usual basis of two from each shire. Then two more were to come and "hear and do what we then enjoin upon them." This last was an indication that the king in summoning knights was trying to establish links through the machinery of the county court and Parliament with these smaller feudal tenants, whose numbers were increasing. Men, who had previously held of some other lord, were now coming to hold directly of the king, who naturally wanted some means whereby to emphasize this relationship.

The "Model Parliament" of 1295 was summoned at a time of crisis. With French and Scottish wars, as well as a Welsh rebellion, on his hands, Edward knew that his financial demands were going to be heavy, and he was concerned about the baronial, and especially the ecclesiastical, reaction to them. Above all, in this crisis he needed a united realm. Perhaps it was at the suggestion of the king that some Chancery clerk dropped into the summoning writs the Roman maxim, "What concerns all must be approved by all." This meant no more than that royal policies should have the support of articulate groups of the nation, or at least not run counter to their interests. Such might be achieved by a "talking-out" of different views until a consensus was reached. In this sense the old Roman maxim was not entirely hollow.

[3] Edward did not regard this meeting as a precedent, because in 1306 he called for another customary aid, that for knighting his eldest son, without summoning any assembly.
[4] Above, p. 143.

The term "Model Parliament" is misleading if it gives the impression that its composition governed that of succeeding ones. Barons came by individual summons. The lower clergy had proctors to represent them. Every shire sent two knights and each borough two burgesses. When it met, the Model Parliament thus represented each important class. Edward explained his needs; whereupon the Chancellor told each class what was expected of it. After hearing this doleful news, the members divided into three groups: feudal (bishops, lay barons, and knights), clerical (the proctors), and mercantile (burgesses). In these bodies there was some registering of previous class consent as in the past, but there was also an actual working out of ways and means whereby a particular class would make its own contribution to the royal needs. In this action the members of the three groups, particularly the mercantile, came very close to performing a modern representative function; it was this aspect of the Model Parliament more than its composition which made it a "model" for later ones. In other respects its methods were quite unlike those of later Parliaments. In 1295 each group assented to an aid for its own class only. The idea that all elements of Parliament had to agree to the same thing before it was binding on any of them certainly did not occur to members of the Model Parliament. Instead, as each group finished its plans to raise money, the Chancellor graciously permitted it to depart.

Of the twenty later Parliaments of Edward I only three followed the pattern of the Model Parliament: twelve were without knights or burgesses. The king-in-council-in-Parliament remained the core of the assembly, as the Rolls of Parliament of 1305 make clear. These men had the help of officials and justices from the central courts. Magnates, individually summoned, completed the essential Parliament. The variable elements of knights, burgesses, and clerical proctors continued to appear only occasionally. They had separate meetings both with and without the council; but these were not of the same importance as a meeting of Parliament. Nevertheless, the very frequency with which Parliament met under Edward I made it an accepted, if not an essential, part of the government by the time his reign came to an end.

Functions of Parliament

The work of the early Parliament consisted essentially of judicial functions. Indeed, only when it was engaged in such activities was it regarded as a Parliament; otherwise it was just another meeting of curia regis or an assembly of various people with whom the king wished to consult. The Rolls of Parliament consist almost entirely of pleas and petitions. During the reign of Henry III the central courts had begun to handle particularly difficult cases at the beginning of their terms in conjunction with the council, because this procedure made subsequent appeals from the courts to the council less likely. Some of these meetings had been called "parliaments" in that there was "parleying" about legal issues; and most of the parleying in Parliament prior to 1307 was on judicial business. Essentially, therefore, until that date Parliament was the ultimate source of justice, a supreme court; some writers feel that the only time that the king himself acted purely as the fountain of justice was in Parliament. However, this procedure was not really an innovation. Petitions to the king often went to the small council for disposition. By 1280 the procedure was already becoming established whereby the small council sent most petitions to the courts or the Chancellor for action and reserved only the most difficult ones for Parliament, when justices and councillors jointly considered them. In 1305 Edward I ordered the Chancellor and the Treasurer to bring petitions they had received previously to the parliamentary session of the council.

The fact that Parliament's main function was judicial meant that the Edwardian Parliaments before 1307 were largely controlled by the royal clerks and justices, who would inform other elements in Parliament whether a certain petition fell within the jurisdiction of a central court, or whether its answer from the king-in-council, presently in Parliament, should be a *bill in eyre*, authorizing an itinerant justice to afford equitable relief to the petitioner as outlined in the bill.

After the Provisions of Oxford there were frequent summonses to individual barons to join the parliament of the council, not to do judicial work so much as to continue their older feudal duty of tendering advice to the king on the basis of discussions with him and other magnates. By the reign of Edward I, however, these summonses nearly always coincided with the special judicial sessions of the council, with the result that all those present necessarily became involved in what was the original and primary function of Parliament. The presence of the barons lent some weight to the view that Parliament was a restored form of the old full curia regis; and this theory gave some support to the claim by common law serjeants that appeals from the central courts should terminate with the king-in-Parliament and not the truncated king-in-council.

The fact that Parliament was primarily a court of justice to some extent explains why the appearance of knights, burgesses, and proctors in it was so sporadic. These people had not only no inherent right to participate in this judicial work but they also had no desire to do so. When they did attend, they brought remarkably few petitions with them for judicial action. The knights and burgesses, summoned to Parliament in 1275 "to discuss together with the magnates the affairs of our kingdom," were being flattered. The thirteenth century was not the century of the "common man" even if we assume that wealthy knights and merchants belonged to that category; neither they nor the lower clergy could claim any share in the determination of royal policy.

Though the king was finding that his private and fixed feudal revenues were insufficient for his purposes, he could, as seen, get consent to additional aids from bodies other than Parliament. With the possible exception of the Model Parliament, the consent of shire and borough representatives in Parliament to an aid was really a reporting of the *prior* assent to that aid determined by shire and borough courts. Such a report could be given just as well at a colloquium as in a Parliament. Even in Parliament there was not a consent from all classes but a series of consents from each class included in Parliament. Naturally the king was often tempted to call for aids without asking for their consent, and Edward I did so more than once. Both he and his father also borrowed heavily, principally from the Jews, to whom Edward finally owed so much that, rather than repay his debts, he expelled these unhappy people from his kingdom in 1290.

In special negotiations with boroughs, Edward found that their growing prosperity gave them a self-assurance which made them resent arbitrary tallages. In 1283, therefore, he adopted a different tone to ask them for a "courteous aid," which they duly granted. In 1294 the boroughs made a separate agreement with the king for the payment of a Sixth, which is probably why they did not send representatives to Parliament that year. In 1295 the burgesses came to Parliament and agreed to a Seventh from the boroughs. But even after this date borough consent to aids was rarely given in Parliament.

Legislation was no part of Parliament's functions. It is possible to argue that parliamentary judicial work on petitions was legislative in a sense, but as this work merely meant sending cases to particular courts or issuing bills in eyre such a view is not really justifiable. Not one of the great statutes of Edward I was the result of formal parliamentary action. The king might occasionally consult with interested groups, but he was under no obligation to do so. The Statute of Westminster I (1275) did record the assent of the magnates to it, but there is no evidence that such assent was considered essential to the statute. In fact, there is negative evidence that it was not, for there is no record of baronial assent to any other statute. Some statutes, such as Quia Emptores in Westminster III (1290), indicated that they had been *considered* at a particular Parliament, but consideration is not assent. By their own words statutes emanated only from a single element of Parliament, and not necessarily while it was in Parliament — the king-in-council.

We do not know just how often or for how long Parliament met during these years. Between 1275 and 1298 Chancery issued writs of De Veniendo ad Parliamentum nine times, and the Rolls record fifteen sessions of Parliament; not one of them coincides with the nine occasions when the writs went out.[5] In later times the opening of Parliament was marked by the welcoming speeches by king and Chancellor, but it was still difficult to say when a session of Parliament came to an end and the council returned to its normal size and functions. There was no formal closing. As each group summoned to Parliament finished its work, which often meant merely giving instructions to the smaller council for its disposition, it departed. Although the small council was certainly not Parliament, the clerks who kept the Rolls of Parliament recorded the council's handling of business left to it on these Rolls, thus recognizing that Parliament was not so much a separate body as the occasion for an enlarged council meeting with a largely judicial agenda. It was therefore logical to record the ultimate disposition of these items on the agenda on the Rolls of Parliament, where they had first appeared.

The Changing Role of Parliament

The rudimentary, amorphous institution of Parliament was, however, about to be transformed, and to gain an assured place in the constitu-

[5] An effort to reconcile this contradiction appears in J. E. A. Jolliffe, *Constitutional History of Medieval England*, 3rd ed., p. 343, n. 4.

tion, by the king's promise that he would in future secure approval before making further financial exactions.

The wars of Edward I were a heavy burden, and the people did not, on their account, cease to believe that the king although popular should "live of his own"; when he did not do so and constantly turned to them, they became increasingly dissatisfied. The clergy saw an opportunity to escape from these royal financial demands in the bull of Pope Boniface VIII, *Clericis laicos,* which in 1296 forbade ecclesiastics to pay aids to secular persons. Edward retorted by outlawing the clergy, who in the face of such drastic action were compelled to pay. Barons and knights were no happier about the seemingly endless requests for money. However, most unhappy of all were the merchants, who were accustomed to being gouged but who also believed in contract. They had recently made an agreement with Edward about a wool toll, only to have him increase the export duty to 40 shillings a sack and damage their business with Flemish weavers. When the financial demands of the war became even more acute, the king simply ordered his officials to seize merchants' wool and give Exchequer tallies in return. To modern eyes the tallies might seem as good as gold, but thirteenth-century merchants knew that they were not; their payment depended upon the royal whim.

In July 1297, Edward put pressure on the barons and knights in an irregularly summoned meeting and received assent to an Eighth. Similar pressure produced a Fifth from the boroughs, and the clergy also agreed to a grant. These forceful negotiations by the king made the magnates fear that the older feudal idea of consent as an act of grace by the vassal was about to disappear.

A century earlier the realm might have girded itself for civil war, but now in the late thirteenth century the national reaction was a vague, ill-defined, but very effective passive resistance; it was sufficient to persuade the king that without the positive backing of the realm his policies were doomed to failure. From this remarkable national forbearance and royal understanding came the solution of the crisis in a constitutional formula which was to be vital for the future of Parliament.

In August 1297, the barons, acting no longer for their own class, as at Runnymede or Oxford, but for the *community of the realm,* presented a list of grievances to the king; they included the heavy royal financial demands, the flouting of old customs and law (symbolically joined to a complaint that the king was failing to observe the two charters), and the grievance of the merchants about the new wool duty. Edward was about to leave for the Continent on a military campaign, but he promised the barons that the Prince of Wales [6] would settle their grievances, which they had summed up in their demands for the royal confirmation of the two charters.

At a Parliament in October Prince Edward in the name of his father confirmed the two charters on 12 October 1297, an action ratified by his father on 5 November. This ratification was more comprehensive than previous ones, and in its language looked to the future.

The Confirmation of the Charters of 1297 [7] gave a new role to Parliament. Its first four chapters did no more than give the usual *pro forma* promise that the king would observe these two symbolic charters. But it went on to list specific recent royal exactions and to declare that henceforth the king would demand them only according to "ancient custom," [8] words of such generality that they might have been meaningless except for the royal promise that henceforth neither he nor his successors would take such "aides, mises, and prises except by the common consent of all the realm," always excepting customary aids and dues,[9] which included tallages on the royal demesne.

In contrast with former confirmations, and indeed with Magna Carta itself, which had consisted of well-meaning but somewhat empty generalizations, this Confirmation dealt specifically with the mercantile grievance. The recent royal export duty on wool (called the *maletote*) was canceled and henceforth duties on wool, hides, and leather were also to require the common consent of the realm.[10]

Like Magna Carta, the Confirmation of the Charters must be interpreted in the context of its times; but it must also be considered with an eye to its future significance. The baronial drafters of the Confirmation did not mean for a moment that all extra aids and nonfeudal exactions had to have the approval of Parliament, even as defined in the late

[6] Incidentally, the first to bear that title as a result of the promise by Edward I to the recently subdued Welsh that he would give them a prince who spoke no English, which he did in presenting to them at Carnarvon Castle in 1284 his infant son. Since that time the male heir to the throne has usually had the title of Prince of Wales, which, however, must be conferred by letters patent and with investiture at Carnarvon Castle.

[7] Carl Stephenson and Frederick Marcham, *Sources of English Constitutional History*, 164. Henceforth cited as Stephenson and Marcham.

[8] Chapter 5, *Confirmation of the Charters*. Stephenson and Marcham, 164.

[9] Chapter 6.

[10] Chapter 7.

thirteenth century. What they did demand, principally for themselves but inevitably for other groups, was that each group should give its consent to these additional financial obligations. Whether such consent were in Parliament or not was a matter of indifference to the magnates, although their own assent would usually be given there because of the royal practice of summoning them to meet with the council. Other groups too could, and did, give their assent to aids and the like at non-parliamentary gatherings. In 1306 knights of the shire were summoned to a colloquium to give their approval to a grant to which the magnates in Parliament had already consented. Separate negotiation with boroughs still continued. Such separate group consent therefore met the requirement of the "consent of all the realm." Emphatically, the Confirmation did not mean that all groups had to consent to a specific exaction from merely one of them.[11] It did, however, require that the particular class affected had to consent to an exaction falling on it.

The importance of the Confirmation of the Charters for the future of the new institution of Parliament was, however, great. As feudal dues provided less revenue for the king, it was necessary for him to ask for more additional aids. In the end it became more convenient for him to secure the separate assents he required simultaneously at a single meeting; and what better place than at Parliament?

In turn this meant that those groups, particularly of the knights and the burgesses, which had appeared irregularly in Parliament came to be in much greater demand; their assent was constantly being required by the king. All of this presumed, of course, faithful royal adherence to the Confirmation of the Charters. Edward I and his successors may have tried to evade his promise, but circumstances always compelled them to return to it. In this way the king emphasized the usefulness of Parliament and also extended its regular personnel, bringing into the political life of his realm a class that under the feudal order had had only a small part to play.

The origins of Parliament are diverse and hazy. The special needs of the king, the requirements of local administration, and the forces in the

[11] It is perhaps for this reason that the so-called "statute" *De tallagio non concedendo* (which was no such thing), appearing at the same time, did not receive royal approval. Whether a statement of baronial demands or a rough Latin draft version of the Confirmation (which was in French), De tallagio would have actually obligated the king to secure consent for tallages, which at this time would have been ridiculous for everyone; tallages fell largely on serfs, whose consent no lord asked. For a translation of De tallagio see Stephenson and Marcham, 164, note 1.

socio-economic situation of the thirteenth century combined to create a situation favorable to the emergence of such an institution as Parliament. The Provisions of Oxford served to define the institution as part of the baronial plans for monopolizing government. De Montfort sought to widen this government by including knights and burgesses as members of Parliament, but met with severe noble opposition. The royalist victory saw Parliament emerge as an enlargement of the newer council, certain individually summoned magnates being added. Royal convenience dictated the infrequent appearances of knights and burgesses, and even more rarely, the lower clergy. Control of Parliament by the king meant that its major duty was judicial, its advisory and financial functions small, and its legislative functions practically non-existent. The Confirmation of the Charters in 1297 increased its importance by preparing the way for its later appearance as a legislative body, with a direct interest in the finances of the crown.

By the close of the reign of Edward I in 1307 the principal organs of the modern constitution had appeared, even if they did not possess their precise modern functions. There was the crown with its multifarious attributes and duties centralized in a small council. The common law, now crystallized, had agencies of application in three central courts, which supervised itinerant justices. The very rigidity of the common law was forcing the Chancellor to nibble at equity. Parliament had appeared with an organization and functions still to be determined. Local administration, with sheriffs, coroners, and conservators (soon to be justices) of the peace, was in a form not to be substantially changed for centuries. Thus the close of the reign of Edward I marked the end of the period of gestation; although some features of the constitution would subsequently change more than others, all were visible by 1307. The most important single factor then was a powerful sovereign, who was the ultimate director of every phase of its workings. Feudal attempts to limit royal government and then to control it had failed, leaving the monarch supreme; and there was reason to doubt whether any other institution could make the king share his control of government with it.

READING LIST

Jolliffe, J. E. A. *Constitutional History of Medieval England*, 3rd ed., Chap. IV.
McIlwain, C. H. *High Court of Parliament and Its Supremacy.*

PASQUET, D. *Les Origines de la Chambre des Communes.*

PIKE, L. O. *Constitutional History of the House of Lords,* Chaps. I–II.

POLLARD, A. F. *Evolution of Parliament,* 2nd ed.

RICHARDSON, H. G. and G. O. SAYLES. "The English Parliaments of Edward I," *Bulletin of the Institute of Historical Research,* V, 129.

STEPHENSON, CARL. "The Beginnings of Representative Government in England," in the *Constitution Reconsidered,* ed. by Conyers Read.

TEMPLEMAN, GEOFFREY. "The History of Parliament to 1400 in the Light of Modern Research," *University of Birmingham Historical Journal,* I, 202. (Also in Robert Livingston Schuyler and Herman Ausubel, eds., *The Making of English History,* 109.)

6

THE REFINEMENT OF GOVERNMENT

BETWEEN the death of Edward I in 1307 and the accession of the Tudors in 1485, substantial modifications occurred in the constitution, which were less in the way of additions, although some important ones appeared, then in the refinement of older institutions and practices. These refinements gave to the constitution of 1485 a "modern" appearance. A large part of these modifications derived from administrative considerations, a fact which made the ultimate agency of administration, the king-in-council, appear to be the most important part of government. In practice it undoubtedly was, yet when any faction during this period objected to a particular administrative action or disagreed on matters of general policy, it invariably tended to turn toward Parliament. As a result disgruntled factions attributed to Parliament new powers and functions, so, although the vital center of government was the king-in-council, the supreme element in the constitution became the king-in-Parliament.

The King

The core of the constitution, legally, was the king. Neither "council" nor "Parliament" was anything without him. The law knew (and knows) each of them only as different manifestations of the sovereign. In the fourteenth and fifteenth centuries this view was not entirely a legal fiction, because the concept was generally accepted that government was the king's business.

The hereditary principle gradually superseded the older feudal notion of acceptance by tenants-in-chief of a new "lord," who was only *primus inter pares*. The decline of feudalism and the legislation of Edward I confirmed the principle of primogeniture. Although the feudal concept of "election" lingered,[1] as a legal principle it was moribund, and in 1307 Edward II claimed the crown solely by hereditary right.

With the hereditary title went certain limitations on the royal power. Edward II (1307–27), and his successors until the Tudors, ruled a medieval kingdom with numerous special exemptions from royal administration. Within these exempted areas the king at best had only influence. Thus the vast field of the *Church* was beyond direct royal control. That Henry II and Edward I had defined ecclesiastical jurisdiction actually implied the inability of the king and his officials to act within it. In addition, there were the *franchise jurisdictions* in border regions,[2] where no royal writ ran. Royal courts moreover upheld *private prescriptive rights*, even against the king, as being based either upon royal charters, or failing that, upon the doctrine of legal memory.[3]

Even in those areas admittedly falling to royal administration, the king's personal authority was legally and practically limited. *Customary law*, partially declared in statutes (including the two symbolic charters), supposedly bound the king in all his actions. Even if he chose to flout the law in specific instances, it was difficult for him to do so consistently. The *business of government* was too vast, its machinery too complicated, and above all, its bureaucracy too numerous to permit continual royal direction of its every phase. Efforts by the king to gain control over certain branches of the administration therefore usually took the form of appointing new administrative agencies which were directly under the royal eye.

The Council

In no place was the gulf between legal theory and contemporary attitudes wider than in the council, whose membership theoretically depended upon the king, who equally theoretically could request its advice and act thereon as he chose. Legal theory, however, was blunted by realities.

[1] Even to the Recognition portion of the modern coronation service, in which in response to the archbishop's question the peers "accept" their new sovereign, who has usually been in that position for about a year.

[2] Above, p. 67.

[3] One of the more practical applications of such private prescriptive rights appears in Oxford and Cambridge when the local bobbies are pursuing a hapless student, who upon reaching his college gates is safe, because of royal charters giving colleges sole disciplinary action over persons within their walls.

The personnel of the council ceased to have a feudal basis. Edward I summoned men to the council board, not because they were tenants-in-chief (as more freemen were becoming), but because he wanted them. Since the council was "continuous," a formal summons occurred only to bring a new man to it; and a man left the council equally at the royal pleasure. In practice, however, royal discretion was limited. Royal justices of the central courts and at least one of the archbishops along with other prelates normally appeared. The great officers of state, such as the Chancellor and the Treasurer, really sat ex-officio. By the fourteenth century these onetime royal personal servants had acquired large public duties and become at least quasi-public officials.

Inability either to coerce or ignore this "public" element of the council made Edward II and Edward III (1327–77) seek to counteract it by bringing to the board their *royal household* officials as men more sympathetic or amenable to pressure. The presence of this element in the council was a source of irritation to the nobility, who at various times claimed that the king should consult *all* his council, meaning every person receiving an individual summons to the council's session in Parliament. Ultimately, the claim was futile; few of the nobility had either time or ability to perform the council's essential duty of administration. What the nobility wanted was less continual membership in the council than more favorable administrative policies from it — a fact shrewdly grasped by Edward III, who after 1341 carefully balanced noble and household elements in the council.

The close relation of the council to the king and its descent from curia regis gave it residual *administrative* and *judicial*, as well as advisory, duties. It exercised a general supervision over all government agencies, occasionally by direct orders to them, but more frequently through the heads of these agencies who sat in the council. It is difficult to assess the degree of effectiveness of such supervision over daily administration; civil servants are notoriously enamored of their accustomed procedures and bitterly resentful of interference in them. However, the dangers inherent in the performance of public administration by household officials became obvious during the latter part of the reign of Richard II (1377–99), when maladministration was notorious.

The council could deal with any problem administratively, and it was in this area that royal efforts went the furthest in seeking to short-circuit the public element of the council by giving broad administrative functions to household officials. This was particularly evident in finance.

Rulers after Edward I found Wardrobe and Chamber employees more co-operative than Exchequer officials, some of whom regarded themselves as having vested rights in their posts. During the Hundred Years' War (which began during the reign of Edward III) many of its logistical and financial aspects were in the hands of these two "personal" departments. Officials of "public" departments objected to this royal practice, publicly on constitutional grounds, practically because they stood to lose importance and fees. Thus if the Chancellor refused to "pass" the great seal over a document, the king merely ordered the head of the Wardrobe to affix the royal *privy seal* of equal legal force. In due course those who resented this procedure managed to transform this seal and the post of *Keeper of the Privy Seal* into public entities, as the great seal and Chancellor had been so transformed in the past.

As the privy seal slipped from his hands, Edward II turned to the Chamber as his major administrative agency, with the Lord Chamberlain affixing the *royal signet* as the king directed. Edward III revived the controversy by giving the Chamber a special seal, the *griffin*, to be affixed at his order. Faced with strong protests from nobility and public officials, the king compromised by limiting its use to affairs connected with the war in France. Although the issue about use and custodianship of seals may appear trivial, it was a matter of real importance in medieval administration.

The council acted judicially in dealing with the numerous petitions to the king, although the Chancellor cleared as many as possible by answering them with one of the standardized common law writs, transferring their issues to one of the courts. For petitions not capable of such an answer, the council could suggest a reply to be given as a royal order under the royal seal, the control of which was therefore a vital matter. In framing answers to such petitions the council used a rough equity, which had the merit of flexibility but also the defect of variability. As these petitions increased, the council turned more over to the Chancellor, who soon had his own Court of Chancery for such matters. However, the council continued to deal with petitions, which Parliament also considered. Such a triple overlap of function among council, Chancellor, and Parliament was characteristic of medieval administration. In practice the three agencies interlocked, with Parliament often depositing petitions into the laps of the council and Chancellor, sometimes with broad directives for their disposition.

Relations between the council and Parliament were normally harmonious. The latter was, of course, no more than an enlargement of the former at the beginning of the reign of Edward II; and although during his reign Parliament gradually drew away from the council, there was always a large number of people who were both councillors and members of Parliament. It became accepted that certain nobles should always receive writs of summons to Parliament, and this meant that those nobles who belonged to the council invariably appeared in Parliament. Parliament did not regard the council as a competitor, and most members were glad to get back home and leave the business of government to the council, which had prepared Parliament's agenda and guided its members through the session. Members might come from isolated communities throughout the country and their contact with each other during a session was too brief to generate much feeling of solidarity. When there was a conflict between factions, the story was different; but otherwise Parliament and council moved in harmony.

The Use of Parliament

No part of the constitution changed more rapidly during the early fourteenth century than Parliament. The impetus for these changes came during the troubled reign of Edward II, when the opposition parties, composed of disgruntled nobles, invariably used Parliament to serve their own ends, and in doing so exalted its constitutional significance. Trained in government by his father, Edward realized that the great officers of state could not be depended on to act as his servants; he therefore entrusted large segments of administration to his household employees, who also came to dominate his council. Many public officials and members of the nobility were outraged. They formed an alliance, expressed in terms of righteous wrath against "low-born" royal favorites in their effort to recover control over public departments and a dominant position in the council. The thwarted public officials and the nobility bid for the support of those classes, notably of the knights and burgesses, which had hitherto usually come down on the royal side. The result was that the opposition to the king saw in Parliament a convenient vehicle for its purposes. Undoubtedly Edward II had serious personal weaknesses; and some of his favorites, notably Gaveston and the Despencers, were unsavory. But these personal characteristics were of little significance constitutionally. The opposition's real dislike of royal policies came from the fact that they concentrated administrative control in the hands of the king and his friends.

Matters reached a crisis in 1309 when Parliament made a grant to the king which was conditional upon his meeting eleven specified grievances, usually referred to as the *Articles of Stamford*.[4] The importance of this statement of grievances lay in its being couched in broad national terms. Thus the mercantile elements received recognition in complaints about royal purveyance, a recent wool toll unilaterally imposed by the king, and his debasement of the coinage. There was criticism about the extension of the jurisdiction of the courts of the Steward and the Marshall and the holding of common pleas by the Constable, officials previously having a legal jurisdiction over minor issues in palace administration, troops in the field, and troops in garrison respectively. The articles continued by citing the abuse of *quo warranto* proceedings and by showing how pardons and royal writs interfered in criminal and civil proceedings. Parliamentary petitions were ignored, and royal tax collectors were unusually rapacious.

The king promised to remedy these grievances, whereupon the nobles pressed their advantage and revealed their true intentions by naming twenty-one of their number as *Lords Ordainers* to supervise the implementation of the royal promise and to make ordinances for the reform of his realm and household.[5]

The Lords Ordainers were another expression of the old baronial belief in the possibility of controlling the central government by means of committees. Unlike earlier noble efforts to win control of the council, however, this committee operated on a somewhat broader social base and perhaps for that reason it endured for a decade. The twenty-one great lords became the small council and during 1310 produced 41 ordinances,[6] which Parliament approved the next year. Among other things the ordinances barred household officials from the council and required the king to receive advice only from the great officers of state, whose appointment should be approved by the barons in Parliament. Similar approval was required for measures relating to war and peace, for the royal departure from the realm, and for the appointment of a regent during such an absence.

[4] B. Wilkinson, II, 125.
[5] Wilkinson, II, 127.
[6] Stephenson and Marcham, 193.

The plan of the Ordainers assumed frequent sessions of Parliament, which was to meet once or twice annually. More important, the Lords Ordainers inadvertently revised the composition of Parliament. The Parliament of Edward I had been a meeting of his personal council with certain additional nobles individually summoned, occasionally joined by knights and burgesses; but these last two groups had not been essential to Parliament in 1307, when Edward II became king. The Parliament of 1311 which approved the ordinances, however, included knights and burgesses, and though there was no suggestion in the demand for annual Parliaments that commoners had necessarily to appear, there is no doubt that the baronage welcomed the support of these classes and found that, from the point of view of propaganda, they were most useful in securing widespread popular assent for the ordinances. Certainly, no Parliament after 1311 met without these non-noble personages and it gradually came to be accepted that Parliament was such *only* if they were present.

The baronial unity of 1311 survived for a time, but in 1318, after the fall of Thomas, Earl of Lancaster, the only figure of ability in the group, increasingly serious cleavages began to appear among them. The Ordainers administered the realm for personal ends. Their refusal to support the royal effort to hold Scotland following the debacle of Bannockburn in 1314 had already caused resentment. It was felt that they did not recognize truly national interests, and once again those who found themselves in opposition to the government sought to use the national institution of Parliament to express their discontent and bring about the reforms they believed necessary.

In 1322 Edward II defeated the noble party and summoned a Parliament at York, which duly approved the statute of that name.[7] This canceled all the ordinances of the past decade, declaring them illegal in that they had not received the formal sanction of Parliament, now defined in the statute as consisting of barons, prelates, and commoners. Only such a Parliament, declared the statute, had full powers over all affairs of the kingdom. Torrents of ink have flowed over this *Statute of York*. The interpretation of later parliamentary supporters that it gave Parliament a legislative monopoly is very suspect in view of the hazy notions concerning legislation in those days. Furthermore, running through the statute is the implication that any limit set upon royal

[7] Stephenson and Marcham, 204.

prerogative (as by the Ordainers) was illegal, a view certainly inconsistent with the dominance of Parliament.

The real constitutional significance of the Statute of York can be seen when it is viewed in its historical setting. Edward felt the need of a legal ratification of his military victory, a ratification which in terms of contemporary attitudes could come only from Parliament. In the process the Parliament at York restated formally the tacit baronial acceptance of commoners as a part of Parliament and attributed to it (this time for royal rather than for noble purposes) powers which it had not previously possessed.

With the deposition of Edward II, Parliament took a further step forward. For Parliament the royal victory had meant its separation from the council, which had again become a royal, personal agency. Although certain members of the council were in Parliament, the old Magnum Concilium appeared only in Parliament as a result of individual summonses. Moreover, Parliament to be such had to include, with the great magnates, knights and burgesses. Edward's enemies found this new definition useful when in 1327 they coalesced around his vengeful queen and her paramour, Mortimer, Earl of March, and defeated the royal forces. "Legality" then required the victors to summon Parliament in the royal name. There they drafted a bill of particulars against the monarch who, unnerved by his experiences, admitted the justice of the complaints and abdicated in favor of his minor son, whom Parliament recognized as Edward III (1327–77). In effect, Parliament had deposed Edward II. Whether it had such a right is extremely doubtful. Peers and knights might resurrect the feudal principle of *diffidatio* to support their part in the action, but the burgesses and lower clergy could not. But at least the enemies of the king had seized on Parliament to "legalize" their rebellion, which says much about the status of Parliament in 1327.

The Refinement of Parliament

It was during the early part of the reign of Edward III that Parliament began to emerge as a bicameral institution, setting a pattern to be followed by almost all subsequent national legislatures. At the outset of the fourteenth century, in structure Parliament consisted of one house, but functionally of three. After the opening greetings from the king, it divided into the feudal elements of barons (lay and spiritual) and knights, of the burgesses, and of the clerical proctors, with each group separately agreeing to exactions falling on its particular class. This operational tricameralism might have become institutionalized had it not been for certain important social and economic factors.

The king remained the innermost part of Parliament. It met only at his summons, and he and his council prepared its agenda. Yet the relationship between king and Parliament was not that between master and servant. If Parliament depended upon the king for its existence, so also did he depend upon it for his — as Edward II found out to his cost. In 1330 Edward III presented himself to a Parliament, which, disgusted by the dominance in the regency council of his mother and Mortimer, in a burst of enthusiasm declared the young king of fifteen to be of age.

It was generally accepted by this time that the great men of the realm should always be in Parliament, if only for practical reasons, and the need of Edward III to have friendly lords in Parliament made him summon many of the same nobles each time. The king also had the unquestioned right to bestow titles of honor, and normally the king would want their recipients to be in Parliament too. By the reign of Richard II (1377–99) the idea was prevalent that possessors of certain titles should always receive writs to Parliament. Such men were the equals of similar men, peers. From the older feudal concept of the baronage came the theory that the titles of such men descended to heirs, either by primogeniture or according to the entail set forth in the original patent conferring the title.

This rule of inheritance is in sharp contrast to that of the Continental nobility, all of whose legitimate children were nobles. In England only the eldest son inherited his father's title. Until he did, he was a commoner; and his younger brothers and all his sisters remained commoners. This limitation of the peerage was vital in the history of Parliament, because no peer could despise his commoner relatives; yet any commoner could hope to be raised by the king to the peerage.

By the reign of Richard II the peerage by definition was composed of those persons whose titles, hereditary or created, entitled them to writs of summons to every Parliament. These persons held titles, in descending order, of duke, marquess, earl, viscount, and baron.[8] How-

[8] Confusion is compounded in the English peerage by courtesy titles, whereby the heir of a peer takes the rank below his father, frequently with one of his titles, but remains a commoner. The second son prefixes "Lord" to his name and is also a commoner. Thus the heir of the Duke of Devonshire, a peer, is the

ever, the gradations in rank did not derogate from their equality of rights, including that of being tried for treason and felonies solely by their peers.

Assimilated to the lay peerage and sometimes erroneously termed "spiritual peers," [9] were the *lords spiritual:* archbishops, bishops, abbots, and priors, whose right to summonses attached to their benefices and was in theory due to them as onetime great feudal barons. In practice, the king summoned them because they usually supported him; and until the Tudor religious changes these prelates outnumbered lay peers in Parliament.

As has been seen, non-noble elements had become essential to Parliament. Two *knights* (although not always bearing that formal title) from each county and two *burgesses* from every borough appeared in Parliament. Selected in their respective shire and borough courts, neither group now had that reluctance to attend as had earlier been the case. Burgesses, in particular, saw in the tendency for Parliament to meet at Westminster near the booming City of London a chance to combine duty with business, which was also a pleasure.

During the reign of Edward III most of the *clerical proctors* left Parliament, although a few remained into the fifteenth century. The bitter factional struggles of the reign of Edward II and the strong punishments dealt out to the Mortimer faction in the early years of Edward III's reign made these men of God uneasy. Their departure did not disturb the king, who in any friction with the papacy could count on its most zealous supporters coming from this group, not the urbane prelates. Royal willingness for the lower clergy to absent themselves from Parliament was the more readily forthcoming because of willingness of the clergy to tax themselves in the two Convocations, an arrangement which lasted until 1664.

Bicameralism followed the departure of the lower clergy. Peers, prelates, and knights sat in one group and burgesses in another. Had this bicameralism become institutionalized, the two houses would have had little relation to each other, and the workings of bicameralism

Marquess of Hartington, a commoner, as is his younger brother, usually Lord Frederick Cavendish. Heirs of viscounts and barons merely prefix "Honorable" to their names. A baron, however, is always called "Lord," and all other peers may be, along with heirs of peers (who are not peers) and their younger brothers.

[9] As the House of Lords tartly pointed out in a resolution of 1692: "Bishops who are only Lords of Parliament are not Peers, for they are not of tryal by nobility," thereby making one of the rights of the peerage an essential qualification for membership in it.

would have been completely different from what they actually became. The vital fact about bicameralism, however, was that by the time it had become formalized its social basis had changed. Whatever the feudal theory, the thirteenth and fourteenth centuries had seen a growing divergency between the great lords and the smaller feudal landholders, or knights; while simultaneously trade, particularly in wool, was giving a growing sense of common economic, social, and even family interest between knights and merchants. Thus the association of knights with barons in Parliament had no social basis, and the community of interest between knights and merchants inevitably affected their relations in Parliament.

During the early part of the reign of Edward III individual knights found themselves preferring to meet with burgesses, often their business acquaintances and not infrequently their relatives. The burgesses welcomed these knightly additions which they may well have felt added to the social prestige of their group. The peers and prelates did not regret the departure of the knights; indeed they encouraged it. Although the knights' move was gradual, already by 1332 the Rolls of Parliament indicated that the peers and prelates were meeting in one group and knights and burgesses in another. By 1343 the magnates were meeting in the White Chamber and knights and burgesses in the Painted Chamber of Westminster Palace. Nine years later these non-noble elements were ensconced in the Chapter House of Westminster Abbey, which became their "accustomed" place until 1395, whereafter for some twenty years they used the Refectory of the Abbey. After that time it is uncertain just where they met, but in 1547 the crown acquired St. Stephen's Chapel within the Palace of Westminster and gave it to knights and burgesses as their part of Parliament. Here they sat until the Parliament buildings were burned down in 1834, when, after several years in temporary quarters, they moved into their new chamber (with the peers in another chamber opposite them), which they used until it was destroyed in the German air blitz of 1940. Following World War II a new chamber was built similar in form and size to the old one, and here the descendants of knights of the shire and burgesses from the boroughs work today.

This division of Parliament in the early fourteenth century into two houses had the most far-reaching consequences. It cut across and through class lines, inasmuch as landed elements belonged in either group, with the result that anything affecting them had to be approved by both houses; from this sprang the convention, which came to be regarded as an essential part of bicameralism, that both houses had to approve everything in the same manner before it could be said to have come from Parliament.

A further consequence of English bicameralism was that Parliament ceased to be thought of as representing separate classes and came to speak for the nation, at least for its articulate portions. The broad social and economic similarity between the peers in the one house and the knights in the other also reduced the likelihood of disagreements between the two houses; they worked together in co-operation, without being torn by class antagonisms. As a result, the system of bicameralism came to appear not only workable and practical but also finally "logical" to the English and to those who later emulated their Parliamentary practice.[10]

The social and economic facts of fourteenth-century English life, which made bicameralism workable, also underlay a practice which began as a convenience and hardened into a rigid rule. With merchants possessing the largest amounts of liquid capital, there was little point in bringing money measures, particularly those asking for revenue, through Parliament unless they approved. To save time, therefore, money proposals went first to the body where these merchants sat. This procedure was formalized in 1407, when the king recognized that money bills had to originate in the "lower" house.[11]

The lower house was known as the *House of Commons* at least as early as 1372 — in the sense that its members represented the *communi-*

[10] The story is told that in the Austrian phase of the Revolution of 1848 one enthusiastic Viennese liberal congratulated another on the emperor's having been forced to concede a two-house legislature; to which his friend, sometimes apocryphally designated as the younger Johann Strauss, replied, "Yes, but we shall not rest until he has given us a third, and even a fourth house."

The federal system easily lends itself to national legislative bicameralism, as in the United States, Australia, and the Union of Soviet Socialist Republics. Canadian federalism, however, is expressed in the Senate on a supra-provincial basis. Bicameralism is also equally the rule for unitary governments, such as in the Union of South Africa, Pakistan, France, and Italy, to name only a few, as well as 49 (Nebraska being the unicameral exception) of the state legislatures in the United States. National unicameralism in the Commonwealth is limited to New Zealand, but unicameralism is the rule for all Canadian provincial parliaments except that of French-speaking Quebec.

[11] The pertinent portion of the United States Constitution giving the sole right to the House of Representatives to initiate money bills is Article I, Section 7. The powers of "second" chambers over money measures vary from the impotency of the British House of Lords since 1911 to the co-ordinate position of the United States Senate with its full power to amend money measures coming from the House of Representatives.

ties of shires and boroughs. Early in its separate existence members were insisting that their House must concur in all measures of Parliament. As early as 1376 they were selecting a Speaker, who presided over the House and was so called because he acted as a channel of communication between the House and the king. For a long time the Speaker was a royal nominee, and failure to accept him involved the House in the risk of having its selection vetoed by the king.[12] An early description of the office gave the qualifications of its occupant as being "a well-fed and stately man with a well-filled purse, frequently open."

Usually the House of Commons worked in close harmony with the peers and the king. But during the "Good Parliament" of 1376 abuses in the government, by that time largely in the hands of John of Gaunt, Duke of Lancaster, and Alice Perrers, mistress of the now senile Edward III, were fiercely attacked by the Commons. The reformers in this "Good Parliament" attributed to the House of Commons, as representing the communities of the realm, the right of making accusation by articles of *impeachment*, as could a grand jury in its capacity of representing local opinion by indictments. The reformers were unwilling to continue the parallel and have the crown prosecute, as it did indictments. Instead, they borrowed from the older appeal procedure, whereby the accuser himself prosecuted, and similarly had the House of Commons "manage" its impeachment before the peers, who as heirs of Magnum Concilium tried the persons thus accused. By the new instrument of impeachment a number of unpopular courtiers and officials were quickly dismissed; but although the weapon of impeachment remained in its arsenal, until the seventeenth century the House of Commons usually brought it out only at the wishes of some noble party.

The *House of Lords* did not receive its name until the reign of Henry VIII (1509–47). Long before then, however, peers and prelates regarded themselves as possessing the special rights of the old Magnum Concilium. For medieval peers their most important function was to *advise* the king; at times they claimed that the king should consult only his "full council" of peers. This claim was futile; the full peerage was too unwieldy and the abilities of its members too varied to be of use to the king, who could normally safely ignore the claim and consult his smaller personal council. But the right of individual peers to *record* the

---

[12] This royal veto was last exercised in 1679, and in later times the Speaker upon presenting himself to the sovereign for approval has received royal congratulations to himself and the House for its good sense in selecting him.

reasons for their *dissent* from majority decisions (a right exercised as late as 1832) and the right of *individual access* to the sovereign, which continued until Queen Victoria effectively discouraged it, derived from this medieval function of the peers.

More important, however, were the *judicial functions* exercised by the peers as the *High Court of Parliament,* possessing both original and appellate jurisdiction. The former was entirely criminal and the latter nearly all civil. Original jurisdiction had two aspects. All peers indicted for treason and felony could be tried only by their peers, an individual right which became the right of the House of Lords to hear such cases. It came to have grave disadvantages for accused peers before its abolition in 1948.[13] The second aspect of the original jurisdiction of the High Court of Parliament was the trial of impeachments laid by the House of Commons.[14] In exercising their original jurisdiction the peers were judges equally of both law and fact, with all decisions, including verdict, reached by a simple majority. Usually the peers hesitated to act as judges of law without the advice of royal justices, who if they were not peers received a summons from the High Court of Parliament to advise it on points of law.

From the original jurisdiction of the High Court of Parliament there could be no appeal, because it was the highest court. Its appellate jurisdiction was in law only (never fact) over cases coming on writs of error from the common law courts, usually at this time King's Bench. Most of these appeals, which were not numerous, were for civil cases. Only rarely did appeals on law in criminal cases reach the peers. Common law supporters preferred the High Court of Parliament to the council as a final court of appeal, and ultimately the former gained the larger share of appellate business. As an appellate court the peers were loath to do anything to modify the common law, an attitude commended by their judicial advisers. Very soon the peers regarded them-

---

[13] Two of the important disadvantages were the inability of peers to challenge their triers and their lack of an appeal from their verdict, since it was given in the highest court of the realm. Not to be confused with this *procedural* right was the substantive one of *privilege of peerage,* a statutory extension in 1547 of benefit of clergy, with modifications, to any peer upon his first conviction of any crime save treason and murder, so that he should go free. This privilege, exercised several times in the seventeenth and eighteenth centuries, was abolished in 1841.

[14] Although never formally abolished, impeachment was last invoked by the Commons in 1805 (with trial in 1806 by the Lords); and in the light of ministerial responsibility to the Commons, it would seem that this phase of original jurisdiction of the High Court of Parliament is moribund.

selves as bound by their own precedents, a rule still differentiating the House of Lords from other final appellate tribunals.

During the fourteenth century the peers performed quasi-judicial functions as "triers" of petitions, often sent to them by the House of Commons and the Chancellor, from persons asking for relief not available at law. The peers would return these petitions to the king and the Chancellor with recommendations. The rise of equity as applied by the Court of Chancery in the mid-fifteenth century reduced the number of petitions thus examined by the Lords. However, the procedure of "trying" petitions has endured to the present in *private bill* procedure,[15] which invariably commences in the House of Lords, whose opinion after a quasi-judicial hearing always has the concurrence of the House of Commons.

The Functions of Parliament

Much of the time of the Parliaments of Edward III and Richard II was taken up with financial matters. The Hundred Years' War made heavy financial demands over and above the normal expenses of government. Parliament, however, did not underwrite the entire cost of either the war or ordinary government. Royal prerogative raised large sums from export-import duties and by negotiations with special groups, particularly foreign merchants, who were glad to pay for privileges; and the king of course also had income from feudal dues and his own estates. Parliament had no objections to these exactions, none of which in the fourteenth-century sense of the word constituted a "tax," which was a direct levy upon individuals. The medieval Parliament was uneasily aware that it could not be the sole source of revenues for the crown without imposing additional taxes upon the very classes supplying its membership.

When the king first turned to Parliament for money for the war, he found that pride in the great enterprise in France made its members generous. But some precedents were being set. If parliamentary grants authorized crown agents to collect taxes, there was also the clear implication that only parliamentary grants could authorize tax collections. Moreover, it might happen that Parliament made these grants contingent upon the royal promise to do something that the king had no wish to do. Parliament did not consistently use its power of the

---

[15] Below, pp. 425–6.

purse, but in 1339 and again in 1341 large conditions were attached to the granting of a subsidy. Parliament demanded the redress of certain grievances, specified the purposes for which the subsidy was to be used, and required the king to fill his council with men named by Parliament. The peers added a rider declaring that trial by peers extended to misdemeanors. Needing the money, the king had to agree — though he revoked his promise after Parliament rose, saying frankly that he had given it only to get the money. Upon reassembling, Parliament again voted the king a very generous sum, but on condition that he lay no charge on the realm without its consent, a condition repeated in 1362 and 1371. Each time Edward willingly agreed, because he knew that Parliament was thinking of the narrowly defined "taxes." What the king did in private bargaining and how he imposed customs duties was of little concern to Parliament. When royal deals with foreign merchants were detrimental to mercantile interests represented in the House of Commons, the House protested, as in 1372 when it persuaded the king by means of a large grant to revoke a recent agreement with foreign traders. Edward, who had already received a generous sum from these merchants, graciously obliged and got the money from Parliament. When soon afterward he entered into another arrangement with foreign merchants, which gave them less, Parliament was silent.

In 1377 Parliament made a determined attempt to control the *disbursement* of a subsidy by naming two commissioners to supervise it; this was in the hope of preventing the creatures of the Gaunt-Perrers faction, once again in power, from handling the money. Parliament did not continue the practice, and it is easy to attach too much importance to Parliament's various financial maneuvers in the fourteenth century, all of which were contrived in terms of the immediate political situation. It is true, however, that an expensive war and reduced royal personal revenues had given to Parliament real financial powers by the close of that century.

Members of Parliament in the fourteenth century still subscribed to the view that the law was a once-given, perfect, and immutable thing. Even strong kings, such as Edward I and Edward III, were careful to obscure their actual legislation by elaborate denials that they were introducing anything new; they were merely declaring and clarifying, not making, law. Parliament, therefore, did not have or desire any greater legislative responsibilities than were required for assisting the king in framing the very solemn statutes declaring previously unwritten law. But by the close of the fourteenth century it had come to be generally accepted that statutes could come only from king, Lords, and Commons. Statutes, on the other hand, were only one part of written law; royal proclamations and orders from the council carried equal weight.

Haltingly and unwillingly, nevertheless Parliament legislated. Petitions came to the peers from the Chancellor, the council, and the House of Commons to be "tried" by the magnates, who sent them on to the king and council with recommendations. Obviously if the magnates did not give a favorable recommendation to a petition from the House of Commons, the king would be unlikely to grant it; and in time such petitions did not leave Parliament. However, if the great men of the kingdom looked favorably upon a petition, it was fit to go to the king. By the close of the fourteenth century the House of Commons was insisting that royal assent to statutes could come only after the statute had been approved by both Houses. It was the royal assent to such a petition which made it law, however, and technically it was (and is) the monarch who legislated, not Parliament.

Parliament learned that the gracious granting of a petition by the king and his promise of a proclamation or an administrative order from the council to give it effect did not always coincide with what Parliament had had in mind. In drafting the proclamation or order, royal officials were adept at including certain words and omitting others so that the result was a different answer from that desired by Parliament. In 1340 Parliament named a commission, to remain after the session had closed, to put petitions which the king had granted into statutory form; the king and council, however, still made changes. In 1348 Parliament told the king that the practice would have to stop. Edward promised that it would, but went on much as before. Gradually Parliament came to the conclusion that the only way to prevent the king and his officials from tampering with measures was to have Parliament prepare them in exactly the form for which it desired the royal assent. By the close of the fourteenth century this legislating by *bill* was just beginning.

Parliament's position, as a legislative body, was stronger than it knew, however. By the latter part of the reign of Edward III certain formulas, still used, indicated the royal attitude toward measures coming from Parliament. Edward liked to say to petitions, "Soit fait comme il est désiré," and he enjoyed replying to a proposed statute, "Le roi le veult"; he was then more likely to be able to utter the most gratifying

words of all, "Le roi remercie ses bons sujets et accepte leur dons."
Rather than upset Parliament with a flat "No," a softer veto was devised, "Le roi s'avisera," suggesting that the king might "consider"
favorably later.

Control over governmental policy was exercised by Parliament only
sporadically, and usually occurred only when some noble faction was
using Parliament as a vehicle to power. When Edward II enraged certain important groups in the kingdom, they used Parliament to oust him.
Under Edward III, Parliament intervened occasionally on matters of policy formation, and then only to a limited degree. Parliament's *financial
powers* might sometimes influence policy, but only to the extent of the
conditions or specified purposes attached to a particular subsidy. During much of the reign of Edward III, Parliament was in general agreement with the policies of the king and had few occasions on which to
use even these limited financial devices to affect his policy. The Parliamentary "power of the purse" existed, but in fact Parliament rarely
used it.

The nobility found that the best way of influencing policy was by
controlling *council personnel*. However, the incident of 1341 [16] showed
that the king was in a position to flout such designs, although subsequently Edward III carefully balanced his household officials with peers
in his council. Yet the fact that Parliament existed gave to noble
factions a way to power if they chose to use it and knew how to.

On the death of Edward III the power of Parliament was, at least
potentially, considerable. It had a monopoly of taxation, even though
that was defined in a narrow sense. Such legislation as there was
had to go through both Houses. Parliament, moreover, represented
a broad national feeling, expressed in a language neither Norman-
French nor Anglo-Saxon, but in an English which partook of both. In
1258 Henry III had used this emergent tongue in a proclamation which
he hoped would have a wide audience. By 1363 the Chancellor was
addressing Parliament in this language, which was the only one for
many of its members. By 1414 the House of Commons would be using
this English, rather than French, in formal petitions. The language reflected a spirit of nationalism much more mature and profound than the
crude and negative type of the thirteenth century. It throws some
light on why Parliament had become an essential part of government.

[16] Above, p. 189.

The Proof of Parliamentary Power

In the course of Richard II's reign (1377–99) the power of Parliament was manifested. It dominated the crown; and when the king tried to regain control, Parliament proved too much for him.

Violent social upheavals lay behind the constitutional issues of the reign. The ravages of the Black Death had wrecked the manorial system; lords had to pay wages to surviving serfs, who thereby ceased to be servile. In 1381, lower-class discontent flared up in the Peasants' Revolt, in the face of which the central government found itself powerless. The Black Death took its toll of the clergy, and the Church in its haste to fill vacancies often placed unworthy men in parish posts. The result was widespread anti-clericalism, hitherto rarely known in England, to which John Wyclif and his Lollard followers gave expression. Fundamental doctrines of the Church, previously unquestioned, came under fire. The long French war had bred fighting men who were either campaigning in France or else troublemaking in England. Private persons raised forces for the war under *commissions of array*, so that private armies, to some extent legally sanctioned, were often used by the nobility to challenge administrative and judicial honesty on the local level. The uneasy times were inevitably reflected in the constitutional developments.

The minority of Richard II saw Parliament controlling the council. During the minority, from 1377 to 1389, the importance of the House of Commons was evident from the efforts of various factions to control it, even to the point of bribing sheriffs to return their men to it. As the king grew older, he came to resent this obvious parliamentary control over the crown. Efforts have been made to portray Richard as a sensitive young man whose understandings of prevailing social problems inevitably pitted him against the selfish great men who controlled Parliament. But it is less than reasonable to suppose that his background qualified him better as a social analyst than anyone else of his class and time.

Toward the end of the minority an incident occurred which gave a foretaste of the royal temper and touched off a crisis. In 1386 the older nobility, bitterly resentful of the high places attained by the upstart merchants of the De La Pole family, had the House of Commons impeach the head of this family interest, the Earl of Suffolk, who was then the Chancellor. The king was powerless to help him, and the earl was convicted by the peers and jailed. The next year certain nobles persuaded Parliament to petition the king for the removal of other men, whom they disliked, from his council. However, on this occasion Richard flatly refused. The reaction of the nobles was to resort to the old baronial committee system, giving it the new name of the *Lords Appellant,* a self-appointed, *ad hoc* committee of five peers, headed by the king's uncle, the Duke of Gloucester. In 1388 after defeating the royal forces, these peers accused royal ministers of treason by the old appeal procedure. The charge was of doubtful legality, for treason could be committed only against the king — and in this case he had already indicated his support of the accused. But this legal principle was of no moment to the nobles in the "Merciless Parliament," during which they tried the accused as quickly as possible and sent them either into exile or to the block. The Lords Appellant had so little popular support, however, and were so riven by dissension that when Richard declared himself of age in 1389 they were at once obliged to withdraw from the scene.

During the next eight years, king and Parliament co-operated in the selection of royal advisers. But the king was biding his time; he was impatient of any restraints upon his power and his ultimate aim was royal absolutism. In 1397, he struck one of his first revealing blows. Thomas Haxey, one of the last clerical proctors in the Commons, had criticized the extravagance of the royal court. Richard came before the peers to declare that all members of Parliament were responsible to him for their utterances. He then sent the Duke of Lancaster before the Commons to demand the name of the wretch who had dared to criticize the king. Such was their position in the late fourteenth century, that when confronted by a royal peer, the Commons were compelled to surrender Haxey. Richard then had the peers alone pass an ex post facto ordinance declaring Haxey's remarks to be treasonable. Under this ordinance Haxey was tried in King's Bench and condemned to death, but he was saved by his clerical status and in fact survived Richard II.

The royal attack upon free speech in the House of Commons proved that Richard did not regard the peers as a serious barrier to his plans. Anticipating the techniques of "legal" twentieth-century dictators, he summoned a carefully packed Parliament, which surrendered all its powers to a committee of eighteen named by the king, with any three to be a quorum. After this success Richard named members of his household as heads of the great state departments. The king's power was absolute, but Richard was quite unable to use it wisely. Striking fiercely at real and fancied opposition, he antagonized important elements, who in 1399 rallied around Henry Bolingbroke, Duke of Lancaster; and Richard found himself isolated.

The forces of Lancaster controlled a hastily summoned body, which, while careful not to call itself a Parliament, was so in all but name. It is significant that Lancaster felt the need for such a body. Using the precedent of Edward II in 1327, this "Parliament" allowed Richard to abdicate, but also said flatly that he had forfeited the crown. It went on to abandon the principle of primogeniture and named Lancaster successor to the throne as Henry IV.[17] Out of a reign of twenty-two years Parliament had been in control of the crown for twenty, even if usually for narrow noble purposes. When Richard broke away from that control, the great lords were only momentarily discomfited. Using the instrument of Parliament, they stripped one king of his title and found another more amenable to their parliamentary direction. The reign of Richard II, above all the way in which it ended, gives clear proof that contemporaries regarded Parliament as the supreme authority in government.

Lancastrian "Constitutionalism"

The Lancastrian period, 1399–1461, is often called the time of the "premature constitution," or of the "constitutional experiment." Neither term is quite accurate. There is always some sort of a "constitution"; and "experiment" implies the conscious exploration of new ground. The Lancastrian period saw no such development. Yet the terms are interesting and significant in their implications, because during that period, through most of the fifteenth century, Parliament was superior to the king.

The manner of the dynasty's coming to the throne irrevocably committed it to accept parliamentary direction, and its three reigns reinforced this commitment. Henry IV (1399–1413) knew that Parliament had given him the crown and could snatch it away from him. Henry V (1413–22) by renewing the Hundred Years' War made himself dependent upon parliamentary grants. The long minority and subsequent

---

[17] Henry IV was the issue of the first marriage of John of Gaunt, Duke of Lancaster (who had demanded the name of Haxey in 1397), fourth son of Edward III. By rules of primogeniture descent of the crown, the heir of Richard II was Edmund, Earl of March, descended from the third son of Edward III.

personal weakness and mental instability of Henry VI (1422–61) meant that during his reign Parliament overshadowed the crown.

This sixty-year Lancastrian dependence upon Parliament was not an unmixed blessing. The parliamentary basis of the dynasty meant that the king often had to placate strong noble factions operating through Parliament, thereby reducing the crown's administrative efficiency, particularly on the local level, where great nobles came to control its agencies, often to the detriment of public order and justice. These rifts in the lute of Lancastrian "constitutionalism" were particularly evident by the close of the period.

There was no conscious planning behind the government's arrangements; the framers of Lancastrian "constitutionalism" were not far-seeing theorists, but practical men working from day to day. Powerful nobles, through one reign of royal insecurity, another of heavy financial needs, and a third of royal minority and weakness, used Parliament to exploit each of these situations for their own immediate purposes. Yet this misuse of Parliament had important results. Frequent sessions and the many tasks assigned to it made Parliament appear a natural, eternal, and *essential* part of government.

The king's position in consequence became increasingly limited. It was significantly described largely in *negatives* by King's Bench Chief Justice Fortescue in his *De Laudibus Legum Angliae,* written between 1468 and 1470, after the Lancastrian period but in terms of its practices, as required reading for the heir of Edward IV. Writing from observation and experience, Fortescue said that without the consent of his subjects (presumably as expressed in Parliament), the king could not change the laws, levy strange (new) taxes, or reduce any of his subjects' liberties. These were broad denials of royal power, but Fortescue went on to declare that the king had no powers except those given him by his subjects, an attitude approaching the compact theory of government in John Locke's *Second Treatise on Civil Government* (1690),[18] and similar to views in another document, well known to Americans since 1776, which states that all just powers of government rest on the consent of the governed.

Once again, finance was the major business of Parliament in the Lancastrian period. It exercised a close control, although it did not attempt to interfere with royal personal revenues. The practice of forced loans, about which Parliament had vainly complained to Richard

[18] Q.v., below, pp. 363–4.

II, largely ceased. Public revenues were a parliamentary monopoly. In 1440 the members of the council agreed to give an aid to the king, but were careful to note that those members not agreeing to it were not obliged to pay. This caution contrasted strangely with Parliament's belief that its decisions were binding on the entire realm. In all matters relating to finance the House of Commons took the lead, probably because its burgesses knew the value of money and accounting methods. After Henry IV and the peers had admitted in 1407 that money bills had to begin in the "lower" House,[19] its members pressed their advantage to make appropriations for specific purposes. Occasionally, the House named some of its members as a committee of audit for expenditures of parliamentary grants.

Legislation remained a secondary function of Parliament, but legislation by bill became normal, thereby reducing, although not precluding, the danger of the king's altering the wording of a measure prior to assent. In 1414 Parliament took Henry V severely to task for this practice, and the king promised not to offend again. The Lancastrian Parliament did not regard itself as the fount of statutory law, but it was uneasy about legislation from other sources, notably proclamations. In 1391 it had said that the king might legislate by proclamation in the intervals between its sessions, but that all such proclamations lapsed with the reassembling of Parliament. The Lancastrian Parliament would not go even so far as this, saying that proclamations might only enforce existing laws, not make new ones, even for a brief period.

Parliament disapproved of the king's claims to the right of *dispensing* with certain laws for individuals and of *suspending* laws generally. Parliament also argued that the royal prerogative of mercy could be exercised only *after* a court judgment. In what was to some extent a compromise, the theory was put forward that the king might dispense with or suspend laws creating crimes, that is, *mala in legem,* but that he had neither power over a law reinforcing divine prohibitions, *mala in se.* The crown seized upon this theory to maintain that reasons of state often made dispensation or suspension of the former type of laws essential. In 1413 Parliament passed a drastic measure expelling all foreigners. Henry V gave it a reluctant consent; the statute embarrassed his efforts to build up alliances against France. For that reason he later suspended the law, to the irritation of Parliament, which, however, admitted that in this instance state policy might require such action. In

[19] Above, p. 185.

practice, the right of the king to dispense with and suspend laws varied with the relations between king and Parliament. The crown could tacitly suspend laws by not enforcing them, and the royal power of pardon (which Parliament did not challenge) could be exercised in such a manner as to nullify a law.[20]

Despite its increased importance during this period, Parliament still exercised only a very small influence on the actual formation of policy. While the Lancastrians all realized their dependence upon Parliament in the long run, yet they and their council were hardly more concerned about parliamentary attitudes in formulating their policies than their Angevin predecessors had been. When a policy required parliamentary grants for its implementation, of course, the opinion of Parliament could not be wholly ignored: some sort of harmony between king and Parliament was necessary. However, there were numerous policies not dependent upon parliamentary grants for their effectiveness, and when this was the case, Parliament's say in matters of state counted for little.

Even when it came to votes of money, the control over the king which the nobles were able to exercise through Parliament was not as great as they sometimes wished. In 1404 Henry IV dismissed a number of councillors, representatives of a dissatisfied noble faction. Two years later this disgruntled group persuaded Parliament to demand their restoration to the council. They then pressed upon the king a plan designed to recover control of the royal council for the barons: Parliament was to name sixteen of its members as the council, from which household officials were to be barred and not even receive petitions addressed to the king. This new council would have the sole right to advise the king, to whom its members would have access at *their* request. The plan also empowered Parliament to imprison "wicked" councillors, that is those who would not give voice to the opinions of a dominant parliamentary noble group. To the new council Parliament gave complete jurisdiction over any matter touched by the common law, which members of Parliament were to swear to observe.

This scheme for a more direct control of royal policy by peers seems to indicate an extreme form of parliamentary control; and as the same

[20] The royal prerogative of mercy undoubtedly applied where convictions were on indictments laid and prosecuted in the king's name. There were some doubts as to whether the royal pardon could issue on convictions prosecuted by appeal, although their prosecution in a royal court would probably permit such intervention. Very doubtful was the royal right to issue a pardon for a conviction on impeachment, in that technically the king-in-Parliament had been the judge.

men were to sit in both the council and in Parliament (which presumably would be able to change councillors as it chose) it has the appearance of a rudimentary cabinet system. Closer examination, however, reveals that this was by no means the case. In the first place the plan of 1406 was not new; it was only a slight modification of the abortive plan put forward in 1341.[21] Moreover, the system of 1406 was scarcely more enduring, not even lasting throughout the reign of Henry IV. But beyond these immediate considerations are broader ones which reveal how vast was the gulf between the arrangement of 1406 and the later cabinet system. The nobles' plan made royal advisers individually, directly, and legally responsible to Parliament; whereas the cabinet was (and is) collectively, indirectly, and only extra-legally responsible to the House of Commons. In 1406 the sixteen councillors could be held to criminal responsibility by Parliament, whereas the modern cabinet has no legal responsibility, criminal or noncriminal, to the House of Commons; in law ministers are named by and responsible solely to the sovereign.

Apart from the short-lived plan of 1406, parliamentary control of royal policy was much less than is sometimes claimed by those historians who regard the Lancastrian period as the cradle of modern constitutional democracy. Certainly the crown saw no need to secure a vote of confidence on policy, and Parliament approved it only tacitly by voting funds where necessary. Thus the control of policy by the Lancastrian Parliament was essentially negative; it might formally denounce a policy, but rarely initiated or formulated one.

The king did not consult Parliament before launching a new venture, even though it might involve grave issues of policy, though no doubt he had calculated to some extent what Parliament's reaction would be. Thus Henry V renewed the Hundred Years' War on his own initiative, only later securing indirect parliamentary approval for his decision in the form of generous grants. In 1420, at the height of his triumphs, Henry V flattered Parliament by submitting the Treaty of Troyes (making him regent of the King of France and his heir) to it for ratification. Parliament approved the treaty and went on to forbid negotiations with the "pretended" Dauphin of France, and in an interesting attempt at extra-territorial legislation, forbade the French Estates-General to meet without *its* approval. But the field of foreign policy was still, as a general rule, far outside the scope of Parliament's activities.

[21] Above, p. 189.

What little authority Parliament enjoyed in these matters was diminished still further during the reign of Henry VI. Noble factions
struggled for control of Parliament, but the average member became
hesitant about committing himself too far to any one of them; the
penalty for error was high. The efficient working of Parliament depended upon a well-ordered realm, prepared to accept Parliament as the
ultimate authority. After 1450 the realm was anything but well ordered,
and fundamental law and order were crumbling. When three years later
the Hundred Years' War came to an inglorious end and Henry VI, to
the surprise of all, became a father, Parliament was in no position to
take action. Instead the great nobles seized the initiative and put the
Duke of York, until recently heir to the throne, in charge of the
government — Henry VI having lapsed for the first, though not the
last, time, into insanity. When the king briefly recovered, again it was
not Parliament but the queen, the iron-willed Margaret of Anjou, who
ejected York and replaced him with the Duke of Somerset. In the Wars
of the Roses that followed, Lancastrians and Yorkists sought to resolve
their problems outside the law, and the possibility of a constitutional
settlement, in which Parliament might have guided the foundering ship
of state into harbor, disappeared.

The problem of honest elections to the lower House had appeared as
early as 1275, when Edward I had said that elections should be "free," a
pious hope which did little to prevent sharp practices on the part of
sheriffs. The Lancastrian period was filled with complaints about dishonest elections. According to the proposals of 1406, Parliament was
to regulate *county* elections; this began the tradition which continued
until 1832, that Parliament would not intervene in borough elections,
where merchants believed (wrongly) that they could resist both noble
and royal pressures. In 1406 Parliament was chiefly concerned about the
rabble which tended to hang around the county elections meetings,
where voting was open. Sheriffs used to bring in "ringers" to vote for
favored candidates, and in order to check this practice it was decided
that election returns made by the sheriff to Chancery should be endorsed by two knights duly elected at the shire meeting. This, however, met with little success, and in 1410 Parliament asked the crown to
order the justices to inquire into the legality of election returns and to
fine sheriffs £100 if their returns were false. This was a heavy penalty,
but nevertheless sheriffs were exposed to many temptations. In 1445 a
law provided that the sheriff should transmit election writs to bailiffs

and mayors of counties and boroughs respectively, who should return
the results to the sheriff; if he then falsified them, he would be liable to
a fine of £100 and for damages to any person proving injury by such
falsification. This last might be difficult to prove and, when joined with
noble pressures on the sheriff to select favorable jurors, was practically
worthless. The Lancastrian Parliament found it difficult to prevent election frauds, which is not surprising since some of the worst offenders
were its own members, who might tolerate severe statutory prohibitions
against dishonesty so long as they were not enforced.

A second method of preventing abuses in county elections was to
reduce the number of voters who were susceptible to bribery and intimidation. This involved the imposition of county franchise qualifications, because again merchants were satisfied that the franchise requirements set forth in royal borough charters guaranteed their continued
control of borough elections. Traditionally, in the counties, all freemen
were entitled to attend the shire court for any purpose, including elections; thus, so long as land tenure determined social status, all persons
holding by free tenures could vote. Henry III in issuing a summons
to knights to attend Parliament in 1254, had provided for their election
by *freeholders*. By 1376, however, the Good Parliament was trying to
limit county electors to the "better folk," a category so vague that it
was soon impossible to define. The next year Parliament proposed that
any *freeman* should have the vote. By the late fourteenth century, the
connection between land tenure and social status was no longer so
clear-cut, and there were in fact many more freemen than freeholders.
Landless freemen, however, were peculiarly susceptible to the tactics
used by the great to manipulate county elections. In 1430 Parliament
reversed its previous policy and drastically reduced the county franchise to persons *owning* land of a clear annual value of 40 shillings, a
rather substantial sum at that time. Many smaller freeholders thus lost
the suffrage, and other men holding by other tenures land of greater
value lost it too.[22] The 40-shilling freeholders, however, determined
county elections until 1832.

One consequence of joining the franchise to freehold was *plural
voting*. In 1413 the law required that a man should be a resident in the
county within which he used his vote, but after 1430 this law was no
longer enforced. A man was allowed to vote in any county or borough
wherein he met the franchise qualifications. This, in spite of the 1413

[22] For the law see 8 Hen. VI, cap. 7.

residency requirement, came to be conventionally accepted: great nobles could get more votes for their candidates by such an arrangement than under law. The convention eventually became law in 1773 with the statutory "legalization" of plural voting and nonresidency of voters.[23]

A number of qualifications for membership in the House of Commons were also laid down during these years. The residency requirement for voters in 1413 extended to members and was similarly ignored in the interests of the great lords who could thereby get more of their men into the lower House. In justification of such illegality, it was claimed that nonresidency of members was in fact a good thing, making for broad, "national" thinking in the House instead of "parish pump" politics. Whatever the merits of the theory, it endured, and in 1773 received statutory approval.[24] Nonresidency of members of Parliament has come to be the general rule in most nations of the Commonwealth.

The Lancastrian idea that only "gentlemen" should sit in Parliament was an indication of the fact that "knight of the shire" was no longer a sufficiently clear definition of social status. In 1445 a law limited membership in the Commons to persons of "good birth," a term with no legal meaning; practical considerations ensured that members would be men of substance, as only such men could afford to leave their business and serve in the House without remuneration from the crown. But not until 1711 were positive steps taken to ensure that only men of landed wealth should be members.[25]

Payment of members was no concern of the crown. All loyal subjects were supposed to be delighted to serve the king. Edward II, however, did require counties and boroughs to pay their respective members four and two shillings (a differential reflecting the greater liquid wealth of merchants) per day while Parliament was in session. Constituencies of both types were so unenthusiastic about the duty that they petitioned the crown to relieve them either of the payment or of parliamentary representation. By the time of Henry VI, the crown had granted so many such exemptions that few members were receiving any payment, although the borough of Hull faithfully reimbursed its two members until 1678.

[23] Below, p. 426.
[24] In 1541 an unsuccessful bill tried to resurrect the residence qualification for members in order, said its supporters, to permit artisans to be members of the House of Commons.
[25] Below, p. 426.

The concept of parliamentary privilege emerged during the Lancastrian period — though the term is misleading, as the House of Commons claimed them as of *right*. Some were not firmly established until the seventeenth century, but already in the fifteenth century Parliament was becoming conscious of the precedents on which its claims of privilege were based. It was also insisting that the interpretation and enforcement of privileges were matters for the *sole* determination of each House, without recourse to the other House or to any agency outside Parliament.

The most vital, of course, was the privilege of *free speech*. Although Henry IV pardoned the unfortunate Haxey, who had fallen foul of Richard II,[26] Parliament was not willing to have the privilege rest on royal grace alone and passed a law canceling the Haxey judgment, not because it was founded upon an ordinance of dubious legality, but because it had violated parliamentary privilege, now by inference superior to any ordinance or judicial decision. This statutory basis was sufficient to ensure the privilege until the reign of Henry VI, when uncertainty about the succession and the wranglings between Beauforts and Yorkists militated against the privilege of free speech. In 1450, Sir Thomas Yonge proposed in the House of Commons that should the then still childless Henry VI die without issue the crown should pass to the Duke of York. This proposal infuriated the Beauforts, who hoped one of their number would become king [27] and who were momentarily dominant with the king. Yonge, in consequence, found himself in the Tower of London and remained there, despite pleas from the Commons, for two years until released by a general amnesty. In 1455 he was again in the House and the next year demanded damages for illegal imprisonment, a violation of the privilege of free speech. Both Houses sent his petition to the king asking for the desired relief, but Henry VI merely turned the matter over to the council. It is not known what action it took, but it is doubtful whether Yonge received damages; and it was certainly to be some time before this privilege became firmly and finally established.

Two corollaries followed from the privilege of free speech: one was that the king should take *no notice* of the actions of either House until they were reported to him officially, and the other that he should then

---

[26] Above, p. 193.
[27] The Beauforts were descended from the third marriage of John of Gaunt, Duke of Lancaster (to Catherine Swynford). The issue of that marriage antedated it; and although Parliament had legitimatized that issue, it was with the proviso that it should not inherit, or transmit claims to, the crown.

place the *best interpretation* on them. In 1400 Henry IV confirmed the second claim and seven years later the first. In practice, however, neither House had means to enforce either claim, and royal interference in parliamentary business was common enough right up until the end of the eighteenth century.[28]

The fact that Parliament began as an agency of the crown entitled its members to *freedom from arrest* and *from assault*. The "arrest" was for civil process; Parliament never claimed for its members immunity from criminal arrest. Traditionally, persons summoned to the royal presence, as were members of Parliament, were under the king's peace. The dooms of Ethelbert and Cnut had provided bots three times the usual ones for injuries done to people summoned to the Witan, both while at its meeting and while traveling to and from it, along with a special wite of 50 shillings for violating this phase of the king's peace. These rules, said the Lancastrian Parliament, had been the "Laws of Edward the Confessor," and it also claimed that the protection extended 40 days on either side of the session (to cover the travel of far-distant members) and included the members, their servants, and their property.

For some time the implementation and enforcement of these privileges lay with the crown. In 1290 Edward I refused leave to the Master of the Temple to distrain the house of a bishop, because he was then in Parliament. In 1315 when the Prior of Moulton was arrested on his way to Parliament, a royal writ released him. As Parliament moved away from the crown, enforcement of the privilege became the responsibility of either or both Houses. In 1404 a certain Cheddar, a servant of a member, was beaten by John Savage. Parliament promptly passed a law ordering Savage to pay a fine to be fixed by King's Bench, or to be liable for double damages to Cheddar. In 1411 another statute repeated the essential features of the doom of Ethelbert and extended its protection to members of the Convocations as well as of Parliament.

---

[28] One of the difficulties of enforcing the claims was that there was no clear prohibition against the king's attending either House, although during the seventeenth century it was regarded as sufficiently unusual for the king to appear in the Commons that when Charles I did enter the chamber in 1641, the members declared that he had violated their privilege; and this was the last time the monarch did come into the lower House. Charles II liked to attend the debates in the Lords, saying that they were better than a play. However, he was the last king to do this. During the eighteenth century ministers reported parliamentary doings to the king. In the nineteenth century the leader of the government in each House informed the sovereign on its activities by brief letters (some by Disraeli being quite witty). Actually, the sovereign today can learn what Parliament did the previous evening by reading the *Times* at breakfast.

During the Yorkist-Lancastrian dispute both privileges lapsed to some extent, or at least became very difficult to enforce. In 1453 no less a personage than the Speaker of the House of Commons, Thomas Thorpe, was jailed by the Exchequer Court for nonpayment of a fine. When the Commons asked King's Bench for an order of release, the justices hedged, admitting the privilege but saying that in the present case a writ of release could come only from the peers, whose action is not known. It was obvious that only if each House enforced the privileges could they be assured. The House of Commons took this step in 1477, when it asked the jailers of a member, Atwyll, to release him. The action was successful, but probably only because Edward IV supported it.

Constitutional forms of government could barely survive in times of increasing disorder and lawlessness. In 1399 petitions from the Commons urged Henry IV to take strong action against the illegal occupation of land by nobles, but the fact that such pleas were repeated so often during the Lancastrian period shows how futile they were. The evil of livery and maintenance, which had caused complaints in the days of Richard II, became even more vicious. In 1404 the Earls of Northumberland and Westmorland used their armies for a private war, which by the law was treason. Eventually Northumberland was brought to trial and convicted of trespass! In 1411, Parliament passed a very severe law against forays and riots, but such a law was meaningless when in the same year a justice of Common Pleas, upon being charged with laying an ambush for a rival, pleaded ignorance that it was an offense! The re-enactment of the law three years later again showed its ineffectuality. This was not because these laws were not in themselves perfectly clear, but because the administration was too weak to enforce them. Herein perhaps lay the final weakness of Lancastrian "constitutionalism." It was the duty of the crown to administer, but the Lancastrian crown was the gift of Parliament, among whose peers were some of the worst violators of the law. In such a situation the crown dared not administer the laws vigorously enough, and until the great of the kingdom ceased to use Parliament to protect themselves against the laws this situation was bound to continue.

"Strong" Government

The Yorkists were no parliamentarians; nor were they on the other hand, as some historians have suggested, particularly anti-parliamentarian. They wished to keep Parliament in its place, a necessary but not the central part of government. Both Edward IV (1461–83) and Richard III (1483–85) recognized its powers in granting taxes and enacting statutes, but they had no intention of allowing it to dictate or supervise their policies. Edward called Parliament seven times in a reign of twenty-two years; and the intervals between his Parliaments lengthened as the reign progressed. Such infrequent meetings caused later Englishmen, on the basis of their experiences in the seventeenth century, to regard Yorkist rule as tyrannical. But this is hardly a very sound criterion, especially when writs for a new Parliament meant only new taxes. Edward IV sought to avoid such occasions as much as possible by tightening up the collection of old taxes, using forced loans, and by directly engaging in the thriving mercantile business of his time. Richard III summoned but one parliament, and that one, according to his enemies, was packed — royal "management" of elections was by no means unusual.

Both Yorkist monarchs named persons to the council without regard to Parliament. The major duties of the Yorkist council were administrative with judicial overtones,[29] and its efficiency in performing these duties helped to restore the royal power. This was also seen in the rise of the royal *secretary*. Once in charge of the king's personal correspondence and records as well as the royal signet, he followed the example of other royal private employees before him, such as the Chancellor and the Treasurer, and acquired a number of public duties and was usually in the council. By the time of Elizabeth I (1558–1603) he was the Secretary of State, from whom the various modern secretaries of state have descended.[30]

In spite of the very much more efficient system of administration of the Yorkists, the essential weakness of their position was revealed when Parliament abandoned the principle of primogeniture it had invoked to declare Edward IV king and passed over his minor son, Edward V, in favor of his uncle, Richard III. This action, although a reassertion of Parliament's right to determine the succession, had the effect of once again exposing the throne to the machinations of rival claimants. Rich-

[29] Below, pp. 215–18.
[30] Their descent from this single secretary permits the legal fiction that there is still only one Secretary of State, whose duties are shared by several persons, each capable of performing the functions of any of the others. However, implementation of this theory would undoubtedly produce at least a question in the House of Commons.

ard III in his own time was not generally so unpopular as later legend would have us suppose, but with his defeat on Bosworth Field the Yorkist dynasty came to an end.

Local Administration

In the years between 1307 and 1485 local administration underwent few major changes. It continued to work smoothly and well, and even the Tudors in their turn saw little need to alter arrangements that had lasted for centuries.

The disintegration of private jurisdictions at the beginning of the period had been swift. Only vestigial remnants of feudal jurisdictions existed after the thirteenth century, and manorial jurisdictions crumbled when the social basis of serfdom was swept away by the Black Death. The dwindling of private jurisdictions meant that local public administration agencies had to extend their functions over people and things hitherto considered in private courts. Local administration naturally felt the strain of this adjustment. However, it is necessary to add that in isolated regions private jurisdictions continued, and palatine administration still operated. An extension of this palatine principle to other areas might have been the solution for increased burdens upon local government, but such an extension would have precluded royal control over it. Even so, such control diminished toward the end of the Lancastrian period.

Public assembly courts did not revive. Trade had widened men's affairs beyond the ability of these small local administrative units to deal with them. Even attendance in the shire courts, despite the increase in the freeman class, declined. Only its use as an electoral body for county members of Parliament kept it alive, and the drastic reduction of the franchise in 1430 meant a further drop in attendance even at election meetings. Borough courts continued with little change, except that there were tendencies for their membership to shrink. Crown charters, which eventually would give most borough governments into the hands of mercantile oligarchies, furthered this tendency by fixing their various franchises in explicit and restrictive terms.

The sheriff lost his old functions to the itinerant justices, whose agent he now became. Treasury agents collected taxes, although they could call on the sheriff for help. The Hundred Years' War, with its need for men in France, reduced his military importance in that he led the shire levy only in England. The decline of the shire court reduced his importance as its presiding officer, except when he acted as returning officer at elections. As the office had tended to become hereditary, the crown preferred itinerant justices and agents from various central departments as its local agents. Finally, the loss of the sheriff's old police powers in 1461 completed his decline.

The coroner at one time looked as if he might take the place of the sheriff. Initially, he duplicated certain of his duties, but as his election was by the county court, his loyalties were divided between king and the local magnates — or so at least the king feared. Thus, in due course, his duties were limited to the holding of inquests into suspicious deaths, when, together with his jury, he enjoyed a fairly free hand. He transmitted verdicts of his jury to royal justices or to the new justices of the peace for further action; but he himself had no power to act on them.

The *justices of the peace* proved to be the agents of the crown in, but also *of*, local affairs. This dichotomy was crucial in the history of their office. The financial burdens of the Hundred Years' War made the crown look for unpaid agents, which it found in the landed gentry, who as jurors had been accustomed to doing the king's work without pay for over two centuries. The dual character of the justice of the peace made for administrative flexibility. The old conservators of the peace had done well as men of all work, and sometime during the latter part of the reign of Edward III had become *justices* of the peace. The change of name did not reflect any change of duties, some judicial, many more administrative. As sheriff and coroner became less important, the crown gave more of their duties to these justices of the peace, who remained as unpaid as ever.

Sir John Rogers, to take an imaginary case, owed his position as justice of the peace to his *previous* social standing in the county, where he was highly respected. His office might be one of honor but not of profit and with much work, work which took Sir John away from his own affairs. Sir John had been born and brought up in the county, and he *knew* what was best for it, far better than those distant figures on the council, whose orders he followed if he thought them feasible and ignored if he did not think so. If this last irritated the king, he could dismiss Sir John, who would lose only office, not income or social standing.

Sir John and his fellows performed petty police work, which they took over from the sheriff in 1461. In their small judicial work, Sir John and his colleagues did not try to apply the rarified subtleties of the common law of Westminster courts. Instead, the justices of the peace preferred a rule of thumb justice, the "laws of England," which anyone having common sense naturally knew.

The main business of Sir John and his kind was administrative. Anything and everything which the crown needed done on the local level came to them. As early as 1351 they had the duty of administering the Statute of Laborers, which by restoring wages to pre-Black Death levels Sir John, as a landlord with labor problems, fully supported. In 1362 their administrative duties received institutional expression in the *quarter sessions;* four times a year all the justices of the peace of the county met at one of their manors to handle administrative matters. It might be clearing brush away from the roads, or seeing that all corpses had woolen shrouds (an item which Sir John as a wool grower viewed as very important). Some Lollards, who had been stirring up trouble, had to be apprehended, a duty causing Sir John some uneasiness, since at one time he had been not unsympathetic to Lollardy, until it advocated the abolition of private property.

In short, Sir John and his friends — fine fellows, all good men — ran the gamut of county administration. Naturally, they decided what was best for the county. Some of the orders from the council were so foolish that they were doing the king a service in not applying them to their people, for whom they had a paternalistic feeling. Sir John was pleased that the council did not insist upon its folly, for such it would be if its members insisted on certain policies, which Sir John knew his people would never accept. If the council wished to dismiss him, Sir John would be glad to use the time thus gained to deal with his workers, whose dependability was the reverse of their wage demands since the Black Death. But dismissal never came. The council knew that if Sir John and his fellows were sometimes cantankerous, they did a great deal of work for nothing. If they thought that their shire was not a fit area for the application of a particular policy, why, perhaps they were right.

Juridical Additions

Between the reigns of Edward I and Henry VII, while kings and dynasties rose and fell, the common law survived them all with little change. It took little notice of the great social and economic changes of the fourteenth and fifteenth centuries, remaining fixed in the form it had

had in 1307. English jurisprudence, in order to meet these changes, developed supplementary forms of law, notably conciliar jurisdiction, equity, and admiralty — none applicable in common law courts and all bitterly resented by them.

Treason

One addition to the common law resulted from the royal victory over the baronage in the late thirteenth century. The legal definition of treason became possible only when it was clear where the ultimate authority in the kingdom resided.

Anglo-Saxon England had possessed a number of strong rulers, but the crime of treason was never formally defined. It was only a little clearer conceptually in feudal England, when though every free person owed loyalty to the king, he owed it to him as liege lord and not as king. Feudal law indirectly sanctioned treason, at least in so far as it was successful, in its provision for the *diffidatio*.[31] After the victory of prerogative kingship, however, treason clearly became a crime against the king, and it was for the king to determine precisely what it involved. Edward I and Edward II interpreted the crime somewhat freely, and in protest against the excessive flexibility of the royal definition Parliament intervened in 1352.

The treason law of 1352 laid down the substantive law of treason. It made clear that treason was more than a felony, in that certain felonies when committed against the king as a person became treason, and treason legally remained a crime against the person — of the king.[32] Although the list of treasonable actions in the 1352 law was lengthy, it actually included fewer crimes than had previously been classified as treasonable by the royal prerogative. The first category consisted of actions of a peculiarly direct nature against the king as a person: "compassing" (planning or executing) his death, or that of his consort or eldest son. This last crime endangered the succession, and the second category was also concerned with crimes that put the succession in doubt: the violation of the queen's chastity,[33] and that of his eldest

[31] Above, p. 59.
[32] So strong did this personal nature of the crime remain that in 1641 the House of Lords would have no part of an impeachment by the House of Commons against the Earl of Strafford, who had the confidence of Charles I, for treason "against the nation." For text of the law see Wilkinson, III, 108.
[33] If this violation were by the queen's consent, she was an accomplice and equally guilty of treason, as in the cases of Queens Anne Boleyn and Katherine Howard, consorts of Henry VIII.

daughter, if unmarried, or of his eldest son's wife. The third type of treason was less injurious to the king personally, but still very harmful to him, levying war against him *in his kingdom*. This limitation of place, however, had little meaning; because the fourth category was simply adhering to the king's enemies, without respect either to place or time.

These four categories remain as the modern definition of treason. The fifth type mentioned in the 1352 statute was counterfeiting the coinage or the royal seals, and forging the royal signature. A sixth category was the introduction of "false money" into the realm. Finally, to murder the Chancellor, Treasurer, or royal justices while in the performance of their duties was also treason. By the close of the seventeenth century these last three categories had reverted to the level of simple felony, although all remained capital offenses until the early nineteenth century.

The law of 1352 provided a simple penalty for treason — death and forfeiture of all property, real and personal, to the king to compensate him for such grave injuries. Society demanded a savage retribution for treason. Commoners were hanged and disemboweled (frequently while still alive) and their bodies quartered. The crown usually commuted this sentence for nobles to mere beheading. Women were liable to be burned, but might be hanged or beheaded according to their social station.[34]

Shifts in the Common Law

Although the common law showed a certain inertia to change, differing social conditions and the competition of newer courts did give rise to a number of modifications.

Land law remained complicated. There was some simplification when, with the decline of feudalism, the common law became less concerned about particular types of tenures and tended to view all free tenures as at least similar if not identical. With the disintegration of the manorial system, these free tenures increased, and the common law ceased to know servile tenures or persons and accepted the fact that most tenures, and therefore men, were free.

The most important procedural change in the law was the admission of evidence as proof, which completely reversed the earlier practice.

---

[34] The normal method for inflicting the death penalty since 1747, when Simon Fraser, Lord Lovat, was beheaded, has been hanging. The full text of the treason laws of 1352 may be found in Stephenson and Marcham, 227.

The modern idea that sworn testimony affords a rational method of arriving at the truth did not commend itself to justices before the mid-fourteenth century; they shared King David's low opinion of human veracity and preferred to rely on community knowledge as the basis for jury verdicts. As local communities lost some of their self-sufficiency and solidarity with expanding trade, the Hundred Years' War, and the Black Death, community knowledge tended to become either faulty or nonexistent. Litigants hesitated to have their suits decided by the frailties of public opinion and looked to newer tribunals, notably that of the Chancellor, which accepted sworn testimony as proof. Faced with this loss of business to rival courts, common law justices were less hostile to offers by litigants to present sworn testimony to "guide" the jury in its statement of community knowledge. By the mid-fifteenth century, oral evidence was commonly accepted in trial courts, and by the sixteenth it had ceased to be merely a guide and a supplement to communal knowledge and was instead the *sole* evidence on which juries should base their verdicts. Affidavits and depositions came to be regarded as "paper-proof," because they did not afford an opportunity for justices and juries to observe the demeanor of witnesses. The refusal by justices to *admit* such sworn, written statements revealed a new discretionary power for trial justices.

The rules of evidence, deriving from the decisions of trial justices about what they would and would not allow the jury to hear, came to determine trial procedure. Originally, as a result of their long prejudice against oral evidence, the justices only allowed witnesses to testify to things they knew *personally*. What they heard from others was worthless, mere *hearsay;* nor did the opinion of witnesses have any merit. The questions asked witnesses should be so phrased that they did not *lead* them to give the desired answers. Above all, evidence had to bear directly on the issue at trial and not be *incompetent, irrelevant,* or *immaterial.* What fell into these categories was a matter for judicial determination. Inevitably, individual judicial rulings on evidence combined to form a large and complex body of precedent, which became a new branch of the common law. The law of evidence has always been based on such precedents, and the legislature has rarely intervened, even to give statutory effect to these judicial rules.

Certain people were not permitted to give evidence. The mentally incompetent were obviously incapable of telling a true story, as were children "below the age of discretion," which the justices, borrowing from canon law, set at eight. The law also viewed testimony of the principals in a case with grave suspicion. How could they be expected to tell the truth? Gradually and very grudgingly the law permitted them to testify in *civil* actions, but in criminal cases the law would not accept their testimony. One principal was the king, who was prosecuting the case. Obviously, in most instances he knew nothing about the facts personally; but the law had another reason for barring him. The justices theoretically *were* the sovereign, who could hardly be a justice and a witness simultaneously. Again, law was unwilling to accept evidence for the accused. It was assumed that witnesses for the defendant would lie to save his neck, which was usually in danger. Until well into the seventeenth century they could only give unsworn statements that would not endanger their souls by perjury, which the law fully expected of them. For this very reason, the worst and most unreliable witness for the defense was the defendant; the law reluctantly permitted him to give an unsworn statement, but he was not allowed to appear in the witness box until 1898.[35]

With the growing acceptance of oral testimony in trial courts, pleading also came to be admitted. The principals wanted to be certain that the justices would admit their evidence and that the juries understood it. The logical thing for litigants was to bring their pleaders down from the central courts to the trial court to persuade justices and convince jurors. When pleaders appeared at the trial court, they found that their legal subtleties, so impressive at Westminster, might interest the justices but not the jury. It was therefore less important for them to win on points of law than to influence the jury by a skillful examination of witnesses, the cross-examination of opposition witnesses, and the marshaling of evidence. By the seventeenth century pre-trial pleading no longer occurred in the central courts.

The character of the jury changed with the introduction of testimony. The original Angevin jury, composed of men who were supposed to know the facts of an issue, would no longer work once oral evidence had become the sole basis of proof. It was, instead, essential that jurors should not have, before the trial, any preconceived notions about the case. If counsel for either side believed that a prospective juror had such ideas, he could challenge his competence to be one. Whether to "excuse" such a man from the jury was, however, solely for the justice's discretion; and again, a body of precedent developed as to who was and was not competent to sit on a jury.

[35] Below, p. 510.

Trial procedure, therefore, changed completely. Pleading the issues and presenting the facts about them to the jury became the responsibility of counsel, with the trial justice acting as a referee between the parties according to a growing body of procedural rules. Counsel and judge summed up the evidence for the jury, whose verdict was to rest solely upon it. By the seventeenth century the great English trial justices and barristers were beginning to appear.

Appellate jurisdiction became the function of the central courts. In civil cases, however, grounds for appeal from trial courts were few; and in criminal actions they were almost nonexistent, for they depended largely on rulings by the trial judge on issues and evidence, never on fact, which was fixed for all time by the jury's verdict. Justices in the particular central court, either of Exchequer, Common Pleas, or King's Bench according to the issues of a case, reviewed these rulings.

This reversal in common law procedure had by the sixteenth century produced new writs to bring cases from the trial courts to one of the central courts. The appellant from the former could purchase a *writ* of *error*, permitting him to argue before a central court that certain rulings of the trial justice had been legally incorrect. If the particular central court were satisfied, it issued a writ of *certiorari*, ordering the trial court to submit for review its record of the case (until stenographic reporting developed in the nineteenth century this meant little more than the judge's notes). In a central court pleading was no longer hypothetical, as it had been in the older pre-trial argument; pleading now had to limit itself to trial rulings. After hearing pleas on the record of a civil suit, the central court could *affirm* the trial court's judgment, *reverse* it, or in rare instances *remand* the case to the lower court for retrial according to its directions.

The loser in a civil appeal had a further right of appeal, which was reasonable if a central court disagreed with the legal views of a trial justice. All central court justices gathered in the *Exchequer Chamber*, soon the name for this further appellate court (and not to be confused with either the Exchequer or the Exchequer Court) to hear and rule on further arguments. Nor was this the end. The peers, as the High Court of Parliament, had the duty of guarding the purity of the common law, so that further appeal was possible from the Exchequer Chamber to the peers, who in certain instances would hear appeals directly from a central court.

In contrast to the elaborate appellate hierarchy for civil actions was the short shrift given to criminal appeals, severely limited to narrow points of law for the defense alone. King's Bench heard such infrequent appeals, and in extremely rare instances the peers would entertain a further appeal. Normally, however, there were no criminal appeals. The facts were clear; a jury had stated them in its verdict, beyond which no justice, either in a trial or an appellate court, would go.

This judicial hierarchy, which began with the introduction of oral testimony in the fourteenth century and was completed only by the late seventeenth, consolidated the common law and fixed it in a more rigid form. Although the principle of stare decisis required only that each court should honor its own precedents, the fact that appellate courts (applying their own stare decisis) could reverse the decisions of lower courts meant that the latter incorporated the precedents of the higher courts into their own body of precedents to be applied in future cases by the principle of stare decisis. This process made the law more precise, authoritative, and uniform; but it also made the common law less amenable to change by judicial action. Lower courts hesitated to make changes in the law because of the ability of higher tribunals, applying stare decisis, to reverse them. This rigidity in the common law was ensured by the attitude of the court at the apex of the judicial system, the High Court of Parliament, which regarded itself bound by its own decisions, one of the few final appellate courts to have such a doctrine.

The administration of the law, however, often left much to be desired. Justices like Fortescue might uphold the ideal of the supremacy of the law, but local pressures on sheriffs and juries often proved irresistible. Henry VI's anxiety to please all factions during his reign led to an issue of new writs, not all of which were in the interests of true justice. One such writ actually ordered a sheriff to empanel a jury favorable to its purchaser. The Yorkists sought to tighten up legal administration, Edward IV even sitting occasionally with the justices of King's Bench to encourage them; and the Yorkist Common Pleas gave fair justice between private litigants. But there was always the tendency for the government to devise means of circumventing the common law when it did not serve its interests, or prevented the government from getting its own way. The Yorkists had no compunction about using the arbitrary and summary military courts of the Constable and the Marshall to deal with persons suspected of disloyalty to the regime. The same considerations made the Yorkists yield to the temptation of inflicting torture to elicit proof. Fortescue (ignoring *peine forte et dure*) complacently claimed that the common law would not accept as proof evidence obtained under torture; and justices were certainly reluctant to do so. The crown, however, beginning with Edward IV, had no such misgivings; the Tudors did not hesitate to order it. James I (1603–25), with the ready approval of his council, had Guy Fawkes put to the torture to force a full revelation of the Gunpowder Plot.

Conciliar Jurisprudence

The council, in its quasi-judicial work of processing the numerous petitions coming before it, developed more clearly defined forms of jurisdiction, particularly in order to meet problems beyond the reach of the common law. In exercising this jurisdiction, the council was guided by the needs of state policy rather than by any fixed legal principles.

The criminal jurisdiction of the council was considerably extended. Intimidation of sheriffs and juries at times made the enforcement of the law at the local level almost impossible, but bribery and rioting were unknown to the common law except in terms of violations of the king's peace. During the late Angevin period the council began to summon persons accused of such actions before them for examination. Malefactors, who in their own neighborhoods might have enjoyed great power, found themselves very much reduced in stature when facing the council of the king, sitting in the safety of Westminster, or traveling under the panoply of royal power. Conciliar criminal jurisprudence could be extremely arbitrary; a man might languish in prison merely on the council's orders. As early as 1350 Parliament passed a law forbidding the council to interfere in criminal matters; it did so again in 1352 and 1358, so it is evident that these measures had little effect. The truth was that the council acted because the common law courts did not. Without power to impose sentences of life and limb, the council usually ordered heavy fines and imprisonment for failure to pay them. The Lancastrian council for a time was very active in cases of intimidation and riots in the courts, but some of the worst offenders either sat in the council or had friends in Parliament. The Yorkist council, less concerned about Parliament, dealt vigorously with such cases; but it was at the expense of due process and individual rights as established by the common law. Certain members of the council became expert in this criminal equity and heard such cases apart from other members in a room with stars on its ceiling. It is probable that the name of the *Court of Star Chamber* attached itself to this section of the council at least by the Yorkist period and possibly earlier. The court remained very close to the council so that it is often difficult to tell from records whether Star Chamber or the full council acted in a particular case.

The judicial procedure of the council was summary and also extremely flexible. Members of the council were judges equally of law and fact, so that they had no need for a jury. The law, however, was of less interest to them than the facts and there was therefore no need to have pleading by legal professionals — who in time came to resent the judicial work of the council and denounce it as tyrannical. The council discovered the facts by *inquisitorial* methods — by either oral or written inquiries, the answers to which came in sworn affidavits and depositions, the paper-proof so disliked by common law justices. Affiants and deponents usually did not appear before the council, and so there was no occasion for cross-examination. Champions of the common law also objected to the *ex-officio* oath imposed by the council upon the defendant, who could in this way be made to testify against himself. The fact that the council could order torture was another reason for its unpopularity with common law justices and serjeants. But one important reason — and perhaps the real one — for the growing dislike of conciliar jurisprudence was its efficiency and adaptability: for the law courts it became a serious competitor.

It was the flexibility of conciliar procedure, on the other hand, that made it popular with civil litigants; but even in civil actions this might be to the disadvantage of at least one of the parties. The common law might be cumbersome; but conciliar jurisprudence was often arbitrary.

The council reached a decision in either a civil or criminal action by a general consensus rather than by a formal vote. In civil cases the council issued orders in the royal name requiring one of the parties to do or not to do something under penalty of a heavy fine. In criminal actions the council might impose a fine, with imprisonment for nonpayment. If more drastic action was called for, it had to turn over the results of its examinations to the regular courts for indictments and prosecutions. Although common law justices were later to rail against conciliar criminal jurisdiction, their own courts received business as a result of its exercise.

The appellate jurisdiction of the council derived from the old curia regis. At various times the council claimed that appeals, on law only, ran from the various courts through King's Bench, the Exchequer Chamber, to itself. This claim the peers hotly denied, saying that the council was only a truncated form of the true, full council — meaning themselves as the High Court of Parliament. In this they had the support of common law practitioners, who did not wish to see a body outside the common law and ignoring its procedures and precedents exercising final appellate jurisdiction over their courts. By the sixteenth century the peers and common law serjeants had established most of their claims; and the council's appellate jurisdiction was limited to appeals from overseas and, after 1534, from ecclesiastical courts. The former almost disappeared with the loss of Calais in 1558, but increased again not long after as Englishmen carried their laws with them to new colonies.

The merits and defects of conciliar jurisprudence were closely examined during the early seventeenth century, the arguments for and against being much the same as they were later with modern administrative tribunals and procedures.

Much of the council's jurisprudence would have been unnecessary if the common law courts had been willing or able to expand their remedies, but their failure to resist noble pressures forced the council into criminal equity. It might be argued that the king should have reinforced the regular courts, but that would be asking too much of medieval administrative practice: the council was at hand for the king, and he naturally used it to supplement the work of the law courts when the latter proved inadequate. There was not at first much rivalry between common law and conciliar adjudication, because the council usually acted only where the regular courts did not; and justices were frequently members of the council.

Nevertheless, although in some respects conciliar procedures were efficient and were in fact eventually adopted by the common law courts, the council was manned by household officials, who were peculiarly susceptible to royal pressures. This, in terms of broad justice, was the weakness of adjudication by council; all cases tended to be judged in terms of state policy of the moment. The council, whose members were primarily administrators, and frequently overworked, naturally handled cases in an administrative rather than a judicial context. Much has been made of the wisdom of the Yorkists and the Tudors in employing conciliar criminal jurisprudence only against great men — a policy frequently contrasted with the folly of the early Stuarts in extending this phase of conciliar jurisdiction to lesser men. But such a development was inevitable, because ultimately justice *is* the same for all men.

The Court of Chancery

For long the head of the royal secretarial office, the Chancellor came to assume judicial duties as well, allowing some of his secretarial functions to be taken over by the increasingly important royal private secretaries. In his original capacity the Chancellor had been responsible for the issue of writs and therefore the originator of actions at common law. In his later capacity he became an even more important figure in the judicial system of the country, and at the same time the fact that the Chancellor was an eminent ecclesiastic had its effect on his judicial work. He continued, as "keeper of the king's conscience," to see that the king followed his coronation oath to give justice to all.

It was his responsibility for the handling of petitions that led to the final emergence of the Chancellor as the head of the judicial hierarchy. He had been for some time the principal channel through which they passed to the king and council, and rules laid down by Edward I in 1280 [36] provided that those petitions which were not directed to other officials and courts and which needed the great seal on their answers, should be dealt with by the Chancellor himself. This was a vast area of jurisdiction, which grew while common law remedies remained fixed, until the king ordered the Chancellor and his Master of the Rolls, once the *magister scriptorii* [37] of the secretarial office, to settle such cases on the basis of right — or *equity*.

The emergence of the Court of Chancery followed. The Chancellor the Master of the Rolls were already an incipient court, even though they did most of their judicial work within the council. But as the feudal and manorial organization of society, with which the common law was equipped to deal, broke down, there were inevitably more and more cases which fell outside the scope of any common law writ. Some

[36] Above, p. 146.
[37] Above, p. 90.

sort of supplement to the law was therefore needed. It was during the reign of Edward III that the Chancellor and the Master of the Rolls became the *Court of Chancery*, and were called by that name in a statute of 1340. Either official constituted the court, although much of the work fell to the latter. The onetime clerks of the writing office rose with their superiors to become *Masters of Chancery*, with the duty of making preliminary investigations on petitions and sending recommendations on them to their employers. The court was intended to deal only in civil actions, largely those once handled by the full council. By the reign of Richard II it was fully operative, and a law of 1374 empowered the Chancellor to take security for costs incurred in his court and to award damages.

The Chancellor's procedure differed in a number of ways from that of the common law. In the first place, the Chancellor was not encumbered by a set of technical rules; he was able to act very much more on his own initiative, according to the dictates of his own conscience and to the merits of a particular case. He was not hampered by judicial precedent, and his own exalted and unassailable position as "keeper of the king's conscience" gave to his decisions as much authority as the common law derived from its dependence on tradition. The Chancellor did not proceed by writ, but by bill or decree, which again gave him much greater freedom of action; and as the Court of Chancery had no use for juries the Chancellor acted not only as judge of law, but of the facts. Inevitably, as time went on the procedure of the court became more systematized, but in its beginnings equity meant simply the various decrees issued by the Chancellor to settle cases for which the common law provided no remedy.

The rules of equity supplemented and occasionally contradicted the law. They were directed essentially at the *persons* joined to an action rather than its issues. This aspect remained even after equity rules came to rest in no small part upon issues. There was always in equity a strong element of the royal prerogative which was one reason why the Chancellor was able to enforce his rules by *personal control* over the parties to a case. The common law was no respecter of persons; it almost went so far as to profess ignorance of the individuals involved in an action. A law court ordered the sheriff to enforce its judgment *in rem*, indifferently of the persons concerned. The rigid application of law, however, might well be unfair for certain individuals in particular circumstances. The Chancellor had remedies in such cases, being in a position to pay much closer attention to the parties to an action until he issued his decree, or *rule*, and saw it enforced by his own *administrative* agents.

The overriding concern with persons permitted equity in its early history to ignore precedents. As business increased and as serjeants-at-law appeared in Chancery with pleas hearkening to its past decisions, equity began to take more notice of the *rem* of actions; but the court was still able to ignore all previous decisions and a rule of equity was certain only for the single case it governed. When Chancery came to invoke past rules in its decisions, it was to take *judicial notice* of them rather than to apply them in the rigid manner of stare decisis of the law.

Wardships, dowries, and property divisions came to equity as a result of the disintegration of feudal law. With regard to wardship, equity initially dealt only with the management of the property of minors, whose persons were for some time the business of Church courts and their canon law.[38] Dowries and the division of intestate property found equity dependent on canon law, with which the Chancellor as a churchman was well acquainted.

Prevention of wrongs and the enforcement of right conduct also fell to equity. The common law knew wrongs only as accomplished facts, capable of remedy in tort actions only. The Chancellor, however, as a prelate and as the chief adviser of the king on how to meet the obligation in his coronation oath to do justice to all, considered future sins. If investigation indicated that some person was contemplating an act which *would* be wrong, the Chancellor could issue a writ of *prohibition*, or injunction, a fearsome document enjoining that person from committing the act under heavy pecuniary penalties. Where justice demanded performance by an official of a duty laid upon him by law and he refused to act, the Chancellor took a very high tone in his order of *mandamus*, commanding in the royal plural that the person responsible for performing the duty do so at once under penalty of a heavy fine.

The prevention of frauds became the responsibility of equity. The common law did not "know" frauds, and by the fifteenth century there were people actually using the law to perpetrate them. A debtor, for

---

[38] When the Chancellor also became the guardian of the persons of minors, his problems soared, as he explained in *Iolanthe*, a brief but thorough survey of major equity duties by Sir William S. Gilbert and Sir Arthur Sullivan.

instance, might repay his creditor, only to find that by not returning the bond of debt the creditor could bring him into the Exchequer Court, where the barons would give judgment against the debtor on the strength of the bond, despite his pleas that he had paid. The only hope for the defendant, if he were not to repay the same debt over and over, was an order from the Chancellor to the former creditor to *cease and desist* from perpetrating this fraud.[39] Similarly, equity could undo forced or fraudulent property transfers.

In the field of contract, equity and common law competed for jurisdiction. When trade played but a small part in the life of the community, contract was of little concern to the common law, and by the time economic activity was increasing the rigidity of the law was such that it was unable adequately to cope with the novel issues arising from it. Apart from a general belief that trade should not be restricted and a reliance on the principle of *caveat emptor*, the common law had little to say about contract. The Chancellor, on the other hand, could issue a decree ordering a man to make good his *malfeasance* (a corrupt performance) or *misfeasance* (an injurious performance) of a contract; and, of course, the Chancellor's mandamus could deal with *nonfeasance* (non-performance).

By the reign of Henry VI, however, the common law courts had devised a way of dealing with questions of contract by the new legal action of *assumpsit*. This action rested on the simple theory that by accepting a *consideration* for the future performance of a duty, a man had *assumed* an obligation. Since this assumption of the obligation was a past fact, the common law had an interest in all issues arising from the promise, including the manner of its performance. The common law, however, required this element of consideration: otherwise it was powerless. But provided that it was there, the law could do nearly all that equity could. As a result many contracts became enforceable at law, although a large number were still controlled by equity.

The largest body of equity derived from the law of trusts, or, in medieval terms, the *use* of lands. The throttling of land alienation by the statutes of Mortmain and De Donis of Edward I [40] led to a practice whereby the possessor of the land alienated not its title but its *use* to

---

[39] Contrary to the general notion "cease" and "desist" are not synonymous, even legally. The one orders a person to stop whatever he is doing; the other tells him never to do it again. Obviously, both words are necessary to make an order of this type effective.

[40] Above, pp. 141–2.

another. In the eyes of the law, which saw only title, nothing had changed; to equity, however, everything had changed. The Chancellor regarded the transfer of the use of the land as a solemn obligation resting on the grantor *and* his heirs, who would inherit title to the land in question and nothing else. Heirs who objected were met with a stern decree from Chancery not to touch the use.

During the fourteenth and fifteenth centuries the doctrine of uses was elaborated. The person with title to land whose use was held by another was the *trustee,* obligated to uphold the rights of the *beneficiary,* or *cestui que use* (soon merely the *cestui*). This latter was one of that "happy breed of men" who by possessing only the use of land and not its title enjoyed its benefits without its burdens, such as feudal dues and taxes. Unlike the title-holder, the user could alienate freely, not the title (which he did not hold), but the use (which he did possess) to another. For the same reason the user, unlike the title-holder, could mortage his land-use. All this was possible because equity enforced the rights of the cestui against all comers, and particularly against the title-holder, who as time passed became an increasingly shadowy figure. More important, *all* issues arising from land held in use fell to equity and the Court of Chancery, not the common law and its courts.

In the mid-fourteenth century Chancery almost lost this lucrative jurisdiction by refusing to enforce a use beyond the lifetime of a single trustee; and if he somehow managed to transfer title, Chancery would not enforce the use against the new title-holder. Appreciating the implications of such a rule for the jurisdiction of his court, the Chancellor soon reversed this decision and decreed that true equity required Chancery to enforce a use forever and ever. Immediately, there was a rush to convert estates at law into estates at equity; the title-holder was virtually forgotten.

One person, however, had not forgotten: this was the king, who by the sixteenth century saw almost every acre in England held in use and so depriving him of wardships, escheats, and other servitudes lying on the title. Yet the doctrine of uses was so embedded in equity that even the royal prerogative could not help to remedy the situation. It was Henry VIII who cut this Gordian knot by his *Statute of Uses* in 1536.[41] This law immediately turned all holders in use into title-holders of their lands, which thereby ceased to be estates in equity and became estates at law. This meant that their holders at once became liable for

[41] 27 Hen. VIII, cap. 10.

the usual obligations of title-holders, and the statute restored to the common law the jurisdiction over land possession it had nearly lost.

In theory equity and law were complementary, but in fact a certain amount of conflict between them was inevitable. Those to whom the common law was sacred associated equity with capricious royal tyranny and in the seventeenth century attacks upon equity reached their climax. But the very existence of equity as a competitor forced the law to modernize itself in procedure and remedies during that century.[42]

Admiralty

Although the common law ultimately faced the facts of life for a nation increasingly interested in commerce, it did so only with regard to internal trade. The determination of issues arising from international trade found the law initially indifferent and later hostile. Special rules were necessary so that English and foreign merchants could work in mutual trust within a single body of jurisprudence. Since the common law had crystallized before this necessity was apparent and would not admit it even when it had become obvious, a separate body of jurisprudence was essential.

Mercantile codes had existed in the peaceful Mediterranean of the Roman Empire. After its disintegration much of the Roman law entered into codes developed by commercial centers, including those of Wisby, the Hanse, and Oléron — all having a good deal in common but with special variations to meet the conditions of a particular area. The very intimate political and economic connection between England and France after the Norman Conquest, a connection intensified with the Angevin Empire and Lancastrian holdings in France, made the *Laws of Oléron* the prevailing mercantile code for English foreign trade. With its rules often unknown, or running counter, to common law principles, the common law courts would not apply them, to the detriment of foreign and English merchants alike. The latter could scarcely expect foreign courts to invoke these laws in their favor, when their own national courts would not. The close connection between foreign trade and foreign policy impelled the council, therefore, to take on the duty of settling international mercantile disputes by applying these Laws of Oléron, with modifications to suit state policy.

The *Court of Admiralty* rapidly emerged from the council. Always

[42] Below, pp. 403-4.

overworked, the council naturally looked for an official to relieve it of this extra burden of adjudication. In Palestine the Crusaders had learned of the Saracen *al miral,* who commanded several ships and had regulatory powers over sea traffic. The rising power of the Genoese in the Mediterranean made such an official useful to them, and the office moved with their ships through the Pillars of Hercules to Gascony, where by 1295 there was an *admiral* in this then Angevin territory, with disciplinary powers over sailors in ports. Five years later the office came to the Cinque Ports of England.[43] Other English ports soon received admirals to regulate men and ships in their harbors. The naval requirements of the Hundred Years' War made it desirable to have an over-all commander of the fleet, the Lord High Admiral, or *the* Admiral, with disciplinary powers over the unruly crews in the naval service. As such, he was not superior to the admirals in port towns; but unlike them he was a member of the council. Acquainted with maritime affairs, it seemed to other members of the council that he might assist them in cases arising from the constant brawls between English and French sailors in the Channel and the Bay of Biscay. An Anglo-French treaty of 1339 formalized this practice by giving the Admiral power to deal with piracy in the Channel.

The Admiral originally exercised this jurisdiction within the council, but by 1357 there is positive evidence that he had his own Court of Admiralty. The court's jurisdiction was then narrowly limited to piracy, which both English and French merchants had reason to deplore. In 1361 the new court received a commission of *oyer et terminer* for criminal actions, which it was to handle by international maritime law.

The narrow *res* jurisdiction of the court was due to the violent hostility of common law justices, who weakened its authority further by supporting claims of concurrent jurisdiction by local port admirals. In 1389, moreover, Parliament limited the jurisdiction of admiralty courts to matters occurring at *sea.* Since a good share of international trade involved business on shore, this limitation was very serious. More serious was a statutory prohibition ten years later against admiralty courts dealing in issues of contract or wrecks. The most that this statute would concede to these courts was minor criminal jurisdiction below the last bridge before the sea.

[43] At that time consisting of Dover, Sandwich, Hastings, Hythe, and Romney; later expanded beyond these five.

Admiralty,[44] therefore, had only a limited competence, and it was not until the Tudors that it became fully centralized in the person of the Admiral, whose court was the only Court of Admiralty. The Court began keeping regular records in 1524. By 1585 the business of the court was so extensive and complex that the Admiral withdrew from it, leaving as its judge a doctor of civil (Roman) law, that law being basic to many principles of maritime jurisprudence.

Ordinary, or *instance*, Admiralty *jurisdiction* had three phases. By 1363 its *criminal* jurisdiction gave it sole control over crimes committed on the high seas by English subjects on any ship and by anyone on an English ship. This jurisdiction was transferred in 1536 to justices from King's Bench, sitting under special commissions to try such cases in Admiralty, but according to common law procedures.

Admiralty's *civil* jurisdiction came to include international bills of lading, harbor and wharfage rights, and everything to do with the salvage of vessels, although not of cargoes. Again, faced by the jealousy of the common law courts, which resented its civil law procedures, Admiralty lost most of this jurisdiction in the seventeenth century, and although it recovered it later, the law it dispensed had ceased to be international and had become common law.

The jurisdiction of *admiralty droits* was to protect certain prerogative rights of the crown in areas between the high tide mark and navigable water. Certain of these rights pertained to the sovereign as a person, such as that giving any *great fish* found in this zone to the king.[45] All beach *deodands* went to the ruler, as did *wreck of the sea*, goods washed ashore from shipwrecks. Goods left floating on the water, *flotsam*, went to the crown, as also goods jettisoned by sailors, *jetsam*. If the crew before hurling goods overboard tied buoys to them for future recovery, they still became royal property as *lagan*. Admiralty had the duty of seeing that these goods went to the sovereign or were sold for his benefit. Less personal was the droit of captured ships, both naval and merchants; but this last droit soon fell under Admiralty prize jurisdiction.

Prize jurisdiction existed only in time of war. It became completely separate from instance jurisdiction with a special procedure and

[44] Usage makes "admiralty" a body of law applied by "Admiralty," a court. Neither has the slightest connection with "the Admiralty," responsible for the administration and command of the Royal Navy.

[45] This is not as fantastic as it might seem because not infrequently a North Sea whale finds itself marooned in the Pool of London.

rules, *prize law*. So distinct was this jurisdiction of the court from its other phases that by the late seventeenth century special sessions dealt with it. Always closely connected with state policy, prize law tended to be more arbitrary in its exercise than the rest of admiralty jurisprudence. Initially, the council handled prize cases, particularly during the Hundred Years' War, when consistently adverse decisions for French merchants produced reprisals against English merchants abroad. In 1498 Anglo-French negotiators produced a treaty defining lawful prize in time of war and specifying what goods were exempt and therefore to be released by the captor nation. This first of innumerable "contraband" treaties constituted a phase of prize law, then being handled by the new Court of Admiralty, which also took notice of prize custom as codified by Italian and Dutch merchants and first published in 1589. This aspect of admiralty law, because of its relation to treaties and its acceptance of international custom, remained closer to international jurisprudence than its law of ordinary jurisdiction, which became largely English.[46]

The procedure of the Admiralty Courts differed, except in criminal cases, from that of the courts of common law. In its instance jurisdiction the procedure tended to lean heavily upon "paper-proof." The terms plaintiff and defendant were not used, instead it was "libellant" and "libellee," and they were not represented by serjeants or barristers, but by "advocates." Prize case procedure varied considerably from that of ordinary jurisdiction, being little concerned about fact, about which there was usually no question, but greatly concerned about law. Although common law pleaders could work in Admiralty criminal trials, advocates dealing in the other aspects of Admiralty's jurisdiction needed to know not only the common law, even after it had made large inroads into admiralty doctrines, but also Roman, civil law. The Admiralty bench usually had only one judge, but he could call upon advocates to assist him as "proctors" in judging cases.[47]

English admiralty principles became world-wide. English commercial and naval supremacy in the eighteenth and nineteenth centuries helped to spread them and former colonial countries continue to apply these principles. In the United States, the federal courts exercise their

---

[46] It may be noted here that the growing body of international air law rests largely upon treaties. What legal principles will govern interplanetary commerce is still to be seen.

[47] As David Copperfield discovered in his practice in the court with the silver oar in Doctors Commons.

monopoly of admiralty jurisdiction with an eye toward past and current English admiralty decisions.

The differentiation and refinement of government after Edward I involved the dominance of the crown and council, the latter co-ordinating and supervising the crown's numerous administrative duties. The obvious importance of the council made its control a vital matter to great nobles, who found in the new institution of Parliament a vehicle which might help them to secure this control. Parliament consequently ceased to be merely an agency of the crown and was sometimes able to stand apart from it. Parliamentary powers in finance were considerable, but not total. Legislative activity remained slight, but during the Lancastrian period there was greater parliamentary control over administration and policy than there had been in the past. In these last two areas Parliament overreached itself, but even during the Yorkist period the authority of Parliament was by no means negligible.

During this period the organization of Parliament became bicameral. Initially, an accidental result of social and economic forces, this bicameralism became formalized into a rigid convention. However, the presence of members of the same landed class in each House led to the further convention, which became law, that both Houses must approve measures before they could go to the king for his assent. The presence in only one House of mercantile elements with liquid wealth made it convenient, then conventional, and finally firm law, that fiscal measures had to begin in that House. These procedures in English bicameralism spread to nearly all later legislative bodies throughout the world.

The practical inability of Parliament to control local administration was agreeable to the knights of the shire, who preferred wide discretion in their numerous local administrative duties as justices of the peace. However, during the late Lancastrian period, lack of supervision could, for example, mean a local administrative system vulnerable to local pressures, particularly when the crown was weak.

Juridical differentiation occurred during this period. Although parliamentary legislation defined the crime of treason, Parliament, as the protector of the common law, was unable to prevent the rise of supplemental bodies of jurisprudence, as exercised by the council and its offshoots, the Courts of Chancery and Admiralty, with their special rules and procedures. Common law justices viewed these newer courts with misgivings, but judicial and parliamentary unwillingness to make

major changes in the common law meant that these courts and their rules were necessary.

READING LIST

ADAMS, GEORGE B. "The Origins of English Equity," *Columbia Law Review*, XVI (1916), 87.

BALDWIN, J. F. *The King's Council During the Middle Ages.*

CAM, HELEN M. *The Legislators of Medieval England.*

CLARKE, M. *Medieval Representation and Consent.*

HASKINS, G. L. *The Growth of English Representative Government.*

———. "Parliament in the Later Middle Ages," *American Historical Review*, LII (1946–47), 667.

HASTINGS, MARGARET. *The Court of Common Pleas in the Fifteenth Century.*

HOLDSWORTH, SIR WILLIAM S. *History of English Law*, Vol. V, Chaps. III–V.

LAPSLEY, G. T. *Crown, Community, and Parliament in the Later Middle Ages.*

PLUCKNETT, THEODORE F. T. *A Concise History of the Common Law*, Book I, Part I, Chaps. 4–5; Book II, Part III, Chap. 7; Part V, Chaps. 1–3.

7

THE NATIONAL MONARCHY

HENRY VII's victory at Bosworth in August 1485 put an end to the strife and chaos of the Wars of the Roses; it also put an end to much that had characterized the old medieval kingdom. In its place, under the efficient rule of the Tudors, there emerged the modern nation-state, monolithic and all-embracing, in which practically all the institutions inherited from the past, including that of the monarchy itself, assumed radically new forms.

"Tudor Despotism"

The policies and methods of the new dynasty have often been summed up in the phrase, "Tudor Despotism." It is an accurate enough description, so long as it does not carry implications of dark and capricious tyranny. It should be remembered that here was a group of rulers, whose problems were immense, whose crises were frequent and serious, and whose means of coercion were negligible — and who all died rulers, and in bed. The Tudor sovereigns played a vital part as individuals in the operation of government. And it was during the reign of Henry VII (1485–1509) that a significant change in the form of address for the monarch began to occur. No longer was it "IIis (or Your) Grace," which came to be reserved for dukes and bishops, but "His *Majesty*." The king represented the nation in his person.

Henry VII, whom Sir Francis Bacon was later to call "the best lawyer since Edward I," summoned a Parliament soon after his victory at Bosworth. To it he submitted an elaborate — but inaccurate — pedigree to support his claim to the crown, tracing his lineage back through his mother only and terminating with one of the bastards of John of Gaunt (fourth son of Edward III); their subsequent legitimization by Parliament had been with the clear proviso that neither they nor their descendants should have any claims to the throne. Apart from that, the mother through whom his claim ran was still alive at the time, and was in fact to outlive her son. Parliament, however, chose to ignore the whole matter of descent and simply declared Henry VII king. Ten years later the king had Parliament pass an act which was designed to comfort and encourage his supporters by stating that it was not treason to obey a de facto ruler, whatever the legal merits of his title, and that no harm could come to them if he were superseded.[1] Though illogical and of extremely doubtful validity, this act was characteristic of the practical, pragmatic Tudors. The policies of Henry VIII (1509–47) and Elizabeth I (1558–1603) often seemed to be dictated by mere opportunism; but in general they met with the approval of the people. Ruthless and autocratic though they were at times, they could not have achieved their goals if they had not been soundly backed by public opinion. In contrast, the policies of Edward VI (1547–53) and Mary I (1553–58),[2] though more clearly defined and more openly executed, ended in failure. Edward VI was a minor his entire reign, but Mary I ended her reign a failure in the eyes of herself, her contemporaries, and history.

However despotic their inclinations and however devious some of their policies may have been, the Tudor monarchs never believed that they were above the law or that the law was their will. They recognized and accepted the limitations on royal power, at the same time realizing that within these limitations there remained a wide area in which the king could act freely. These traditional restraints on the sovereign proved more lasting in England than on the Continent, where the "new monarchy" was moving in the direction of untrammeled absolutism. In England, although the king had sources of revenue apart from Parliament, no Tudor could collect a tax, as legally defined, without parliamentry sanction. The courts might apply royal ordinances and proclamations, but no Tudor could declare one of the solemn statutes without Parliament. Under ordinary circumstances men charged with crimes had to be tried publicly, with a jury of twelve having to agree unanimously before conviction was possible. If a verdict of guilty left

[1] In 1661 the regicides, on trial for their part in the execution of Charles I, invoked this law; but the judges would not accept this plea, declaring that Charles I was the lawful sovereign until his death.

[2] Although Philip and Mary upon their marriage were declared joint rulers, and statutes are cited as being those of Philip I and Mary I, the refusal by Englishmen to admit that Philip was king has become constitutional convention, and only his wife is referred to as a sovereign.

the convicted person with few grounds for appeal, one of acquittal left the crown with none. Any man aggrieved by a royal official could hale him into court on a tort action, where the common law was "no respecter of persons." The House of Commons could impeach any official and prosecute him in the House of Lords, from whose verdict there was no appeal. These limitations on royal power, even if they often remained potential rather than real, indicate how far the Tudor monarchy was from being a capricious absolutism.

Most important of all, the Tudors, in great contrast to their royal contemporaries on the Continent, lacked the instruments essential to a totalitarian regime. There was no standing army; in dealing with the frequent rebellions of the period, the government always had to appeal to the landed gentry and merchants — the classes making up the House of Commons — for its suppression. Since the king depended upon these classes it would have been fatal for him to adopt royal policies antagonistic to them. Again, for the implementation of their policies the Tudors had civil servants in the central government, but local administration depended upon unpaid justices of the peace, again drawn from classes supplying the House of Commons. Finally, the Tudors had no police force, either uniformed or secret.

These limitations on Tudor government were, in fact, so considerable that it is natural to conclude that those policies which enjoyed success did so because they were truly national. The eminence of the great men, the "overmighty subjects," who received such harsh treatment from the Tudor government, should not blind us to the vast number of people who never felt the heavy hand of government on their shoulders, nor its inquisitorial eyes over them.

Parliament

Parliament was essential for the Tudors, who gave it much important business to perform. It thus gained in experience and in self-confidence, and though the Tudors themselves were always able to keep it in check, by the end of Elizabeth's reign it was already showing signs of that independence and intractability that were to be the undoing of the early Stuarts. Henry VII devoted all his energies to restoring efficient government, and to increasing the royal authority in every possible way. He was determined to break the power of the old and fractious feudal nobility and to fill the royal Exchequer by every legal means that he could think of. And whereas in the past Parliament had often been used by dissatisfied magnates as a means for reducing or controlling the authority of the king, Henry VII made Parliament his ally. Far from being weakened by the alliance, he found that his greatest strength was derived from it and that the king-in-Parliament was immeasurably more powerful than the king alone. Henry VIII followed in his father's footsteps. The statutes passed by his Parliaments take up more physical space than those for all preceding reigns together: Henry was "modern" in his belief in legislation as the solution to all problems. He met the problem of uses and their threat to the common law by the Statutes of Uses and Wills.[3] The final incorporation of Wales into England, the first step toward the later legislative unity of the United Kingdom, came in statutes of 1536 and 1543. The religious settlement was the work of the king acting through Parliament,[4] and his successors were obliged to act in the same way if they wished to change it. In 1543 Henry frankly said, "We at no time stand so highly in our state royal, as in the time of Parliament; wherein we as head, and you as Members are conjoined and knit into one body politic . . ."

Parliament, however, did not meet at all frequently — at least not by modern standards. Henry VII summoned only seven Parliaments, all except a brief one in 1504 coming in the first eleven years of his twenty-four-year reign. Henry VIII summoned Parliament more often, and the one which separated the Church of England from Rome had sessions off and on for seven years. It was really the Reformation Parliament that established the principle that, though Parliament might not be "regular," it was "usual" for embodying great policy in legislative form.

Englishmen of the Tudor period agreed with the crown that Parliament should meet only for specific business requiring its attention. Lacking such business, there was no need for it to assemble. Since one of the usual items of business was taxes, most Englishmen were quite happy that Parliament did not meet too often. That it should gather regularly to legislate was quite a novel idea to most people, who still regarded legislation as something that should happen only occasionally, if it were to happen at all. Henry VIII's views, forced upon him by his own peculiar needs, were considerably ahead of his time.

[3] Above, p. 222; below, p, 273.
[4] Below, pp. 253–61.

Similarly, sessions tended to be brief. The idea that Parliament should be in session most of the time is a strictly modern one. Tudor Englishmen believed that Parliament should meet only for specific purposes; having considered those, it should go home. But in a brief session Parliament could nevertheless pass legislation of monumental importance.

The government summoned Parliament to perform precise items of business, prepared and placed before it by the king and Privy Council. Once submitted to Parliament, these items were watched over by the privy councillors there, and it was they who piloted the various measures through the Houses. It was taken for granted that the parliamentary agenda should be the work of the king and his ministers; for the only reason Parliament was in session at all was that the king had certain business for it to attend to. It was not for Parliament to decide what might or might not be discussed.

This arrangement worked well enough for most of the sixteenth century. Members of Parliament came from distant communities; they were not *au courant* with the business of state (in fact, they did not know the reason for their summons until the opening royal speech); and as yet they had little corporate sense. The briefer the session the more pleased they were, and they welcomed the royal statement of what was required of them and the guidance of the privy councillors in their midst so as to expedite their business.

But during Elizabeth's reign the temper of Parliament was beginning to change. Members, particularly in the Commons, were not always content with discussing only what was on the agenda. The fact that former Parliaments had dealt with great matters of state encouraged members to believe that they could discuss great issues, whether or not they had specific instructions from the crown to do so. To some parliamentarians this seemed a logical development of the privilege of free speech; from it there followed the right of individual members to bring up any subject they chose. The queen, however, angrily and contemptuously rejected this claim. In 1592 she told the Lord Keeper to inform the House of Commons through the Speaker that the privilege of free speech was "not as some suppose to speak . . . of all causes as him listeth, and to frame a form of religion, or a state of Government as to their idle brains shall seem meetest. She sayeth no king for his state will suffer such absurdities."

Despite such warnings, some members of the Commons continued to insist that freedom of speech implied the right to determine their own agenda. The queen would never permit the House to discuss the question of her marriage, but this, together with the succession, were matters of such anxious concern to members that they were unable to keep quiet about them. Time and again Elizabeth ordered the Speaker to terminate such debates. However, it was the queen's religious policies that finally caused the most friction. The growing Puritan group within the House, with its belief in a direct channel of command and duty between God and the individual, and the remembrance that Parliament had dealt hitherto with religious matters of the greatest importance, found it unreasonable that the queen should not permit them to introduce measures designed to lead the Church of England toward Calvinism. When she "impounded" (took away) such bills, they were galled, perhaps doubly so because of the refusal of the majority of members to support them.

In 1571 Walter Strickland introduced a bill to modify the Prayer Book along Puritan lines. Jolted by his temerity, the other members suspended his right to sit and did not object to his being questioned by the council. Hoping to forestall the royal wrath, the House asked leave to debate the bill, but to no avail. Although Strickland soon returned to the House, the other members gave him scant support.

Peter Wentworth, however, was too zealous a Puritan to ignore the plain call of duty. In 1576 a shocked House heard him attack royal prohibitions on religious bills, declaring that these commands violated the privilege of free speech. The dismayed House ordered him to sit down and sent him to the Tower for a month. Five years later his brother, Paul Wentworth, proposed a day of prayer without prior government sanction. The Commons apologized for his brashness. In 1587 he returned to the charge after seeing the House yield to the royal command not to debate a measure introduced by Sir Anthony Cope, providing for the replacement of the Book of Common Prayer by the Calvinistic Geneva Prayer Book and Discipline. In a series of leading questions to the Speaker, Wentworth again indicated that the control by the House of its agenda fell within its right of free speech. The only result of the gesture was the imprisonment of himself and Sir Anthony in the Tower, where Wentworth died.

The House of Lords, which received its name during the reign of Henry VIII, presented the crown with no problems. Until the religious changes the two archbishops, nineteen bishops, and thirty abbots gave the crown a steady ecclesiastical majority over the forty to fifty lay peers, who for their part, after the whirlwind of the Wars of the Roses, generally worked with the government also. After the dissolution of the monasteries [5] and the departure of the abbots from the House, the secular peers held the majority; but the crown had no serious problems in the upper House. Although the Tudors created peers, it was always for past services and never to build a royal "party" in the Lords.

During the Tudor period, however, the balance between the Houses shifted considerably in favor of the House of Commons. This does not imply that the House of Lords became unimportant; it did not. Certain privy councillors sat there as peers to explain and guide royal measures through the House. Individual peers controlled seats in the Commons so that they exerted influence in the lower House; and small "family interests" appeared, particularly after 1549 when heirs of peers were permitted to sit in the Commons, so that their later movement into the House of Lords found them with parliamentary experience. Nevertheless, the House of Commons became the more important; the word "Parliament" during the Tudor period sometimes meant only the lower House.

The Tudors turned to the Commons in part because they had reason to fear the nobility, some of whom had fair claims to the throne, and in part because changing social and economic conditions made the support of the gentry and merchants very much more rewarding. Tax measures had to begin in the Commons. Moreover, Tudor religious policy always needed to take into account the attitudes of gentry and merchants, and it was the Commons to which the king paid particular attention, through his privy councillors, during the great Reformation Parliament. The Tudor monarchs perceived that the "nation" with which they sought to identify themselves, was not the peers but the thriving gentry and merchants. Evidence of the rise of the House of Commons can be seen in the beginning of its *Journal* in 1547, with its first very simple entries which soon became complete reports on the business of the House.

The members of the House of Commons came from the 45 counties of England (including Wales),[6] each of which sent two members elected by all 40-shilling freeholders, and two from every borough, elected by a variety of franchises as set by each borough charter.

[5] Below, p. 262.
[6] Durham as a palatinate did not have representation until it became a county in 1660.

Counties were parliamentary creations, and Parliament did not increase their number. Boroughs, however, were the result of royal charters; and beginning with Henry VIII their number rose throughout the Tudor period. There were 298 seats in the first House of Commons of Henry VIII's reign, but there were 372 borough members alone in the last Parliament of Elizabeth. Clearly, the increase of boroughs by royal action provided the opportunity for packing of the House of Commons. During the reign of Edward VI, the Duke of Northumberland created boroughs where they would probably do him the most good. Mary too created boroughs in conservative, Roman Catholic regions, and Elizabeth in Protestant ones. All of the Tudors, beginning with Henry VIII, added to the boroughs in Cornwall, where the royal influence was at its highest. But there was also the hard fact, which Elizabeth I must have pondered as she contemplated the Wentworth brothers, who sat for Cornish boroughs, that a borough which began by sending co-operative members might soon be represented by men who were far from subservient. Often the royal creation of a borough came at the behest of some mercantile group or of some magnate who was the patron of one. Pressure of the latter type increased when boroughs during the Tudor period began to send gentry rather than merchants as their representatives. The practice was possible because of the flouting of the legal requirement that a member should be resident in his constituency,[7] and it increased the power of landed elements in the Commons and also that of peers, who had family connections with the gentry. This practice did not mean that mercantile interests were ignored by gentry members; usually it indicated the desire of the boroughs to have the "protection" of some noble. However, the tendency of Tudor boroughs to align themselves in this way with magnates meant that the royal influence in them was not as great as it might have been. In older and wealthier boroughs neither royal nor noble influence counted for much.

The "official" element in the House of Commons was not large, and its members had to stand for election like anybody else. Minor royal officials, ancestors of eighteenth-century "placemen" and forerunners of modern civil servants, constituted about one-fifth of the House, and their presence [8] there gave rise to some criticisms. Usually such men

---

[7] Above, p. 201.
[8] Although a bill of 1555 to bar them from the House of Commons failed to pass that House.

sat for small boroughs, often those where royal influence was dominant. Above them were the privy councillors, who had a direct responsibility to the crown for the management of the House. Although they could have sat for the same type of secure boroughs as the minor officials, proud and independent boroughs liked to be represented by men high in government. Both groups together, however, were only a small element of the Commons, and though they might hope to lead it, they could not dominate it by weight of numbers alone. The Speaker, although elected by the House, was really a royal nominee, and he was supposed to follow royal orders and keep members within the items of business presented to them by the crown. Elizabeth I was severe on speakers who failed in this duty.

Of far more importance in the Commons, for the administration of its laws, was the presence of many justices of the peace among the gentry sitting for both counties and boroughs. That men who had helped pass a law should administer it made for efficiency, but it also required the crown to consider the attitude of these administrators in the drafting of bills and during their passage.

In parliamentary elections the Tudors were unable in the majority of cases to exercise any great control over the electorate. Voting, of course, was open, which meant that there was ample opportunity for corruption and intimidation, but this was usually the work of local magnates rather than the government. In the counties, where the number of electors had been greatly increased when the Statute of Uses transformed many men into 40-shilling freeholders,[9] the government had very little influence. It was another matter in some of the boroughs, but here again royal influence was limited and irregular; the Treasury was not rich enough for it to be used in elections as it was in the eighteenth century, and there was no party organization in or out of Parliament to keep candidates and voters in line.

Thus, although the Tudors were interested in getting certain individuals into Parliament, outright royal interference in elections to get a favorable House of Commons was rare. It has been said that Thomas Cromwell "packed" the long Reformation Parliament from 1529 to 1536, but there is little evidence that he did more than bring pressure to bear at by-elections. He was more active in the general election of 1539, when he assured the king that he had so arranged things that "your Majestie had never more tractable parlement." It turned out to

[9] Above, p. 222.

be rather less tractable than he had anticipated. The most conspicuous evidence of royal interference on a large scale to secure a favorable House was the direction in 1554 by Mary I to the sheriffs to return men of a "wise, grave, and catholic sort" to the House; and her interference was sufficiently unusual for contemporaries to comment upon it. Elizabethan councillors worked for certain men, but not to "win a majority" in the House of Commons. In general, the Tudors had sufficient confidence in the acceptability of their policies or in the persuasiveness of their privy councillors, not to interfere unduly in parliamentary elections.

Any body of over 400 members requires direction. This the crown furnished and the bulk of the members welcomed it; had they not, had they resented such leadership, the Tudor system of government could not have worked. The managerial group of minor officials, privy councillors, and the Speaker could neither promise reward nor threaten reprisal. The government had no "party" over which to exercise discipline, no pension lists, no sinecures, and no contracts. There is no evidence that it ever attempted to bribe members. Ordinary M.P.s may have regarded high officials of state with some awe, and felt as amateurs in the presence of professionals, but they could not be dictated to or treated as mere puppets of the government.

Thomas Cromwell and William Cecil were masters of the art of directing members, marshaling them behind government measures, and turning them away from tricky subjects not on the agenda. In their management privy councillors had to listen carefully to members and bring to the monarch such views as they deemed worthy of his attention, particularly with regard to the wording of government bills. Henry VIII was the most amenable to suggested changes; Elizabeth I the least.

If the worst came to the worst and a bill went through Parliament over the objections of the crown, there was the remedy of the royal veto. Elizabeth had to use it toward the close of her reign on a religious issue. However, the royal veto was rarely needed, and the amenability of Parliament may be seen from the fact that it never rejected a major government proposal.

Although persistent opposition to the government was out of the question during the sixteenth century, a member of Parliament did not need to fear party discipline, and for him and others to insist on amendments to government measures did not raise issues of "confidence" or bring down the administration. He was also much more independent of his constitutents than his present-day counterpart, if only because the business he was expected to conduct was unknown to him until he actually arrived in London and took his seat in the House.

Parliamentry privileges were, in general, respected by the Tudors. Henry VIII, who had so much to gain from keeping Parliament in a good humor, always did his best to behave correctly in this respect and during his reign the enforcement of the privilege of *freedom from arrest* became a parliamentary monopoly. In 1512 the *Stannary Court* [10] imprisoned a certain Strode, a royal tax-collector and a member of the House of Commons. In his former capacity Strode was able to secure his release through the Exchequer Court. But the House of Commons was not satisfied and initiated a bill, which became law, declaring that the Stannary Court's action was void in that no civil process could issue against a member of Parliament during a session nor for 40 days on either side of it. The privilege of freedom from arrest was thus given a statutory basis, but its procedural implementation came only when the House of Commons took the initiative.

In 1543 one Ferrers, a member of the House and a servant in the royal household, was jailed for debt by King's Bench. When the House of Commons sent its sergeant-at-arms with the mace to demand his release, the London sheriffs and jailers physically resisted him. An angry House of Commons reported the matter to the Lords, which concluded that these officials had committed the gravest of contempts against Parliament; and the Lord Chancellor offered a writ ordering Ferrers's release. The Commons, however, insisted that its *warrant of the mace* be honored and sent off the sergeant-at-arms a second time. This time Ferrers went free, whereupon the House of Commons had the London sheriffs, the jailers, and the plaintiff in the action against Ferrers all thrown into the Tower, where they remained three days until the House released them upon the humble plea of the Lord Mayor. Henry VIII summoned the Chancellor, the Speaker, the judges, and some members of the House of Commons. Before this group the king warmly praised the House for its zeal in enforcing its rights, in the process making his famous recognition of the importance of Parliament to the crown: [11] "Whatsoever offence or injury during

[10] This little known court headed by the Vice-Warden of the Stannaries had jurisdiction over issues arising from the tin mines of Cornwall and Devon until its abolition in 1846.

[11] Above, p. 232.

that time is offered to the meanest member of the House is to be judged as done against our person and the whole court of Parliament. Which prerogative of the Court is so great . . . as all acts and processes coming out of any other inferior courts must for the time cease and give place to the highest." Thus fortified and vindicated, the warrant of the mace became the procedural device to implement the statutory guarantee of freedom from arrest; and there was no doubt about its validity when the House of Lords used it in 1572 to secure the release of Lord Cromwell.

The rigorous action taken by the House of Commons with the London sheriffs and jailers and Ferrers's adversary was an early exercise of the claim by the House (soon to be claimed also by the upper chamber) of the *power to commit* to prison persons committing "contempts" against it. Although the definition of these "contempts" was dangerously vague and rested solely on the will of the House, the power to punish for such offenses was essential if the Houses were to uphold their rights. For some time the Commons used the right to protect itself against royal wrath over the remarks of its more recalcitrant members. Thus in 1548 it committed such a member to the Tower, and in 1576 Peter Wentworth suffered the same fate for the same reason, and again in 1587 along with Sir Anthony Cope.[12] In 1581 the Commons expelled Arthur Hall, fined him 500 marks, and then sent him to jail for publishing a book which, among other things, said that honorable members were often drunk. The House was more lenient to a certain Bland, fining him only a pound for having uttered "contemptuous" words about it.

The privilege of *freedom of speech* was of particular interest to the House of Commons, where most members viewed it as the right to speak and vote as they saw fit on government measures. It was in this sense that Sir Thomas More as Speaker first presented the claim formally in 1523 for royal confirmation, saying that it was the right of every member "to discharge his conscience, and boldly in everything incident among us to declare his advice." Such a right was essential, said the Speaker, with his typical gentle wit, because "among so many wise men neither is every man wise alike."

Henry VIII confirmed the privilege and always listened tolerantly to the statements of members, some of which were at times highly critical of his policies. During the reigns of Edward VI and Mary I the

[12] Above, p. 234.

definition of the privilege remained in its customary form. Elizabeth was more cautious. In 1593 via the Lord Keeper she indicated her attitude, "God forbid that any man should be restrained or afraid to answer according to his best liking, with some short declaration of his reason thereon." This was little more than freedom of voting and fell considerably short of the freedom of speech confirmed and permitted by her father. In the same declaration she made clear that the privilege did not include the right of members to bring forward pieces of business without government approval.[13]

The right to *decide disputed elections* was also claimed by the House of Commons, though only infrequently, and it never became a serious matter under the Tudors. But in 1586 there was a question of irregularities in the Norfolk election. As in the past, Chancery investigated and decided on a new election, but the House of Commons objected. Despite orders from the queen to the Speaker, the House insisted on naming its own committee to investigate the election. When the committee upheld the results, the queen made one of her grand gestures and permitted the two members to take their seats. However, the House had yet to win a clear-cut decision that it was the sole judge of elections to it.

Financial matters concerned the Tudor Parliaments only when the crown had to ask for taxes, and all the Tudors were adept at tapping non-parliamentary sources of revenue. At the same time they had to face the steady decline in the value of money which was a consequence of the gold and silver from Spanish colonies pouring into western Europe. The Tudors found it increasingly difficult to make ends meet, and the problem was serious by the time of Elizabeth. The Tudors, who educated Parliament well with regard to legislation, did little to familiarize it with the facts of public finance, which required taxation for the regular maintenance of government. This was one reason why Parliament was so astonished and angry when the Stuarts repeatedly asked for taxes in peacetime.

When the Tudor Parliament had to vote taxes, for some time they took the form of the old "tenths and fifteenths." Originally fractions of the value of movables in boroughs and counties respectively, these terms in the Tudor period designated a sum of £32,000. In 1514 Wolsey, already the king's chief adviser and soon to be a great churchman and Chancellor, proposed a plan whereby the tax structure would

[13] Above, p. 233.

include an assessment of about 20 per cent on land and 14 per cent on personal property. This was bitterly resented by the Commons, which thereby earned Wolsey's undying hostility; but Parliament did finally approve these taxes as portions of a subsidy. Subsidies of ever increasing amounts were granted throughout the century, though usually in times of war or rebellion to meet extraordinary expenditure.

Parliament's main function under the Tudors was, however, legislation. In the past, Parliament had legislated only occasionally and then according to the theory that its statutes merely declared and clarified existing law. The Tudors, and Henry VIII in particular, adopted the radical theory that statutes could create new law on anything. Henceforth Parliament was to be primarily a legislative body, capable of making statutes superior to all other laws.

Tudor legislation dealt with all manner of subjects: basic land law, wills, treason, poor relief, and all the major phases of national religious policy after 1529. These great matters came to Parliament by royal direction; and it is little wonder that after dealing with them, Parliament, particularly the House of Commons, where much of this legislation was first introduced, became conscious of its power. The Privy Council drafted the bills, and its members presented them to Parliament, and piloted them through. But this procedure did not mean that Parliament always did what it was told. More than once Henry VIII found individual members outspokenly criticizing his policy, and as he could depend on getting his own way in the end he could afford to be indulgent with them. Unlike Wolsey, with his haughty contempt for representative institutions, Thomas Cromwell heard what members had to say, and it was the duty of privy councillors to get the "sense of the house" and report to the king. Cromwell, an astute parliamentarian, could usually "manage" the Commons, but he did not attempt to ignore the House.

The Commons was also entitled to prepare its own bills, but it was not until the latter part of the reign of Elizabeth I that private members attempted to initiate bills on great and often touchy matters, particularly religion; when they did, the queen was exceedingly irritated. Though she could always have recourse to the veto, there was the danger that before that stage strong passions might have been aroused in the House. She therefore occasionally "impounded" them, literally confiscating them and forbidding the House to discuss them further.

In 1539 Parliament passed the *Statute of Proclamations* (often called the *Lex Regia*). It provided that in an emergency, if Parliament could not assemble in time to deal with it, the king with the advice of a majority of the Council could issue proclamations having the force of law. This statute suggesting either extreme confidence in, or extreme subservience to, the king was not quite the surrender of Parliament's exclusive right to legislate as might at first sight appear; it forbade any proclamation, even one for the direst emergency, to derogate from the common law or from any statute. Even so, it was a dangerous precedent to have set and Parliament repealed it at the first opportunity after Henry VIII's death.[14]

Finally, Parliament retained its ancient right of determining the succession to the throne. It had recognized Henry VII as de facto king, just as the Anglo-Saxon Witan had recognized William the Conqueror, and Henry VIII in his various attempts to regulate the succession always saw that his wishes were sanctioned by Parliament. In 1534 Princess Mary, daughter of his first marriage, was denied the succession in favor of Elizabeth, and the next year Elizabeth herself fell under the same ban in favor of her half-brother, Edward. In 1536 Parliament, however, authorized Henry VIII to determine the succession by will; and, using this delegated power, Henry provided for the descent of the crown through Edward, Mary, and Elizabeth, and, failing issue from all of them, through the descendants of the marriage between his younger sister, Mary, and the Duke of Suffolk. When in 1553 the Duke of Northumberland persuaded the dying Edward VI, in the interest of the Protestant religion, to make a will to exclude Mary and Elizabeth and put Lady Jane Grey on the throne, Princess Mary successfully appealed to the nation that her brother's will, unlike that of her father, did not have parliamentary sanction.

Though Parliament may have done little more during this period than give formal statutory expression to the royal will, that it was called upon to do so in such weighty matters helped to define and consolidate its constitutional position. In 1559 a law was passed aimed at the supporters of Mary Stuart, making it high treason to deny the right of Parliament to decide the succession. Elizabeth, of course, deeply resented its interference in such matters and in her last hours set aside her father's will by verbally designating James VI of Scotland, descended from the marriage between James IV of Scotland and

[14] For the legal effect of the repeal see below, p. 248.

Margaret, elder sister of Henry VIII, as her successor. But James's first Parliament felt it desirable and necessary to close the legal gap by formally declaring him king. It may be argued that any institution able to name the head of state must be the ultimate authority in its constitution. This was hardly the case under the Tudors, except as an idea glimmering in the minds of one or two enthusiasts, but it was not long before Parliament was to put the idea into practice.

The Privy Council

The chief administrative agency of the Tudors was the Privy Council, a powerful, highly efficient instrument of the royal will. Its duties, like those of Parliament, were vastly increased by the Tudors, and the amount of work that it got through is amazing. Henry VII entrusted administrative and advisory duties to a small group of councillors, between twenty and thirty, who remained permanently in his service. He was charged with ignoring his true council for a secret, *privy*, council. This did not disturb him in the least, and although he did on a few occasions summon the older council, which had about 150 members, it had lost most of its significance and soon disappeared altogether.

The membership of the new Privy Council was determined entirely by the king. But Tudor policy of entrusting major administrative duties to the Privy Council made for a fairly stable membership; good administration is not encouraged by rapid and frequent shifts of administrators. Although some councillors were always with the monarch on his or her travels, again efficient administration required that administrators should remain with their voluminous records at Westminster. In 1496 the Lord President was appointed to preside over the council at Westminster during the ruler's absence, and in 1529 his office received statutory recognition. In 1540 the Privy Council began a new series of records for its proceedings and about the same time received a seal of its own, thereby marking the final stage of its emergence as a definite agency of government.

Contemporary usage mirrored the change. As early as Henry VII's reign "Council" and "Privy Council" respectively denoted the older, and now rarely summoned group, and the newer, constant, body. With Henry VIII "Council" for a brief time meant those members traveling with him, to be reabsorbed on their return to London into the resident

Privy Council. By the time of Edward VI, whose youth and infirmity perhaps hastened the change, as they prevented his traveling widely, "Privy Council" and "Council" were synonymous. Some of its members were at Westminster, some elsewhere; but all were of the same group.

The choice of councillors reflected Tudor policy. Beginning with the first Tudor, the men selected were for the most part commoners, named primarily for their administrative abilities — so that in some ways they resembled the senior civil servants of later times. Although some received peerages for their long services, they usually did not come from the old nobility that the Tudors so much distrusted; they were the "low-born men," about whom leaders of rebellions during the Tudor period invariably complained. They could be trusted to do the king's business and, unlike the great magnates of old, would not in their own self-interest do anything contrary to the royal will.

The relative importance of certain high offices changed during the Tudor period. The Treasurer was beginning to be superseded by the Chancellor of the Exchequer, who issued Treasury orders, and would eventually become the head of the financial system; it was not until early in the eighteenth century, however, that the office of Treasurer lapsed altogether. The Chancellor remained an important figure. After the fall of Wolsey the office was held by a layman, with the brief exception of Bishop Gardiner during the reign of Mary I. The Chancellor had his own court and usually presided over the House of Lords,[15] where he explained government policy. But gradually he ceased to be the chief adviser of the sovereign. In his place there appeared the royal secretary, whose public duties had been greatly increased by the enlargement of state interests. He retained his close contacts with the sovereign so that with his new public duties, particularly those relating to foreign affairs, he became important in the formation of state policy. So numerous were the duties of his office that in 1539 it was divided into two parts, each given to a secretary, although the post nominally remained singular despite its holders being plural. Their usually long tenure in office, particularly of William Cecil (Lord Burghley) and Sir Francis Walsingham during the reign of Elizabeth I, and her confidence in them, further enhanced the position

[15] It was usual for the Chancellor to be a peer, but not necessary because the woolsack where he sat was technically outside the confines of the House.

of the secretarial office. By the close of the Tudor period the Secretaries of State had emerged from the older secretarial position and had come to overshadow the Chancellor in the king's government.

The efficiency of the Council depended upon its being small, but there was a tendency for its membership to grow. The Council of Henry VIII had usually some twenty members, but under Edward VI it increased to forty,[16] and under Mary still more members were appointed. On her accession Elizabeth reduced the Council to eighteen, however, and did not permit it to go above twenty; indeed during her later years its membership had shrunk to twelve.

The preference of Henry VII for commoners as privy councillors early gave to the Tudor Privy Council its secular character. The Archbishop of Canterbury sat, but Henry VIII was suspicious of clerical members after Wolsey's debacle. Of the forty members at the death of Edward VI only four were ecclesiastics. Mary increased their number, but Elizabeth eventually made her Council entirely lay. Thus the long tradition of the intimate association of prelates with royal administration ended, even while the secular state was absorbing the Church.

Although Wolsey, More, and Cromwell were dismissed from the Council, such treatment was unusual. Normally, within a reign, appointments were fairly permanent. Even the supersession of Somerset by Northumberland did not produce a wholesale change in the Council of Edward VI. Northumberland appointed a number of new councillors of his own party, but the original members survived. Nor did a new monarch necessarily bring about any particular upheaval. Henry VIII took some of his Council from that of his father, and all the councillors of Edward VI had served under Henry VIII. Mary made considerable changes at her accession, both for reasons of religious policy and because all the councillors had only belatedly recognized her as queen after briefly accepting Lady Jane Grey. However, some of Mary's Privy Council had been with her father. Elizabeth named eleven councillors who had been with her sister (seven of them from the Privy Council of her brother and father) together with the seven she called to the board for the first time. Unlike her father she did not always attend meetings of the Council, where she was represented by her secretary, though this did not prevent her bullying and cajoling

---

[16] Henry's plan for a Council for the minority of his son envisaged one of sixteen members with twelve "assistants."

her councillors. She did not consider herself bound to accept their advice, though in practice she generally did, for she was served by her councillors with the utmost loyalty and conscientiousness.

Councillors might disagree violently with each other, but not with the sovereign. To do so meant dismissal — perhaps worse. At times one councillor was dominant over the others, but only because he had the particular confidence of the monarch. Thus Wolsey rode high until Henry VIII turned on him, and Thomas Cromwell experienced the same rise and fall. Edward VI's faith in his uncle, the Duke of Somerset, was a major reason why Somerset overshadowed his colleagues, although royal favor was insufficient to save either his office or his life once he had forfeited the confidence and respect of fellow councillors. Bishop Gardiner loomed large in the Council of Mary owing to her favor. The great confidence of Elizabeth in Burghley gave him a unique position in the government for nearly forty years, and after his death his son, Robert Cecil, became the leading figure in the Council. These devoted privy councillors received an annual salary of £100, plus any fees coming from their other offices, and meals in the Council chamber.

Faced by the ever increasing amount of business, Thomas Cromwell devised the method of *ad hoc* committees of the Council to deal with specific matters. If they lasted sufficiently long, these committees tended to become separate bodies, although their members continued to belong to the parent Council. The committees certainly got through a vast amount of work, though the burden on individual members was hardly reduced, for many served on several. Not all members needed to be present, however, for the Council to proceed; and a good deal of important work was done, especially under Elizabeth, by four or five of the more influential councillors, including of course the secretary, who were able to speak for the Council as a whole.

In addition to its executive functions, the Privy Council also acted as a legislative body. Its legislation was of two distinct kinds. Statutory orders filled in the details of laws passed by Parliament or else gave added weight or authority to them. Typical of such orders were those forbidding the importation of papal bulls and blessed articles, similarly forbidden by Parliament, during the reign of Elizabeth I. Statutory orders had to be in harmony with the principles of the laws under which they were issued, but they were equally laws and enforceable by the courts. The second type of order came in those areas where Parliament had never spoken, so that the sovereign theoretically retained a complete freedom of action, subject to the limitation that this second class of order could not contravene statute or derogate from the common law. The king could issue proclamations without consulting his Council at all, as Henry VIII frequently did, but the Elizabethan Council tended more and more to issue proclamations in the queen's name.

Orders of both types went from the Council to specific agencies and persons, the various administrative courts and justices of the peace; proclamations were addressed to loyal subjects generally. The Statute of Proclamations [17] had briefly regulated the competence of king and Council to issue proclamations, and its repeal in 1547 left the question of the proper sphere for proclamations somewhat confused. In 1553 the common law justices in an advisory opinion for Mary I repeated the earlier statutory limitations and added that neither proclamations nor orders could create new law or add to the jurisdiction of the recent administrative courts, whose competition the law courts were feeling. The most that the judicial opinion would concede to conciliar legislation was its ability to reinforce existing statutes. In fact, however, neither Mary nor Elizabeth closely observed these limitations, but neither did the justices in test cases, one reason being that administrative courts often received jurisdiction over matters dealt with by orders and proclamations, so that the law courts had no opportunity to rule on their validity. Parliament itself did not object to conciliar legislation during the sixteenth century. Not until the common law justices made a working arrangement with the House of Commons in the seventeenth century did Parliament complain about it.

In financial matters the Privy Council was responsible for the assessment and collection of the sovereign's extensive non-parliamentary revenues. These were not technically "taxes" which could be levied only by Parliament, for they were not direct obligations upon individuals. As the Tudors disliked asking for taxes except in emergencies, the financial responsibilities of the Council were great. It took all the ingenuity and efficient control of which it was capable to make ends meet during the sixteenth century when all the Tudors suffered from the decline in monetary values that was bedeviling governments everywhere in Europe. Such revenues were utterly inadequate for the prosecution of a war, and for people of that time only a war justified taxation; in peace the ruler like everyone else should "live of his own."

[17] Above, p. 243.

Not until long after the appearance of the national monarchy and the extension of state interests were people willing to accept the inexorable corollary that they should regularly maintain the government by taxes — and few people are happy about the idea to this day.

Like all monarchs, the Tudors had *hereditary revenues* from lands and rents, which Henry VII increased by resuming all lands granted by the Yorkists, since they had been usurpers. *Feudal dues,* although hardly what they had once been, came to the sovereign; and their revenues, along with the possibility of escheat of land to the crown, increased with the Statute of Uses.[18] *Fines* and *fees* went to the government, and Henry VII and Elizabeth I were particularly adept in working with the Council to uncover old laws to supply them. Both of these monarchs used distraint of knighthood, whereby a person had to accept the honor and pay fees, or refuse it and pay a fine; and the £20 annual land value, set by Edward I in 1278,[19] by the time of the Tudors included the lands of many.

More important, however, as trade boomed during the Tudor period, was the right of the sovereign, granted to Henry VII for life by his first Parliament, to levy *tunnage and poundage,*[20] on exports and imports. In setting specific duties in the *Book of Rates,* the Privy Council was really acting under a delegated parliamentary financial authority, which it exercised by charging what the traffic would bear, with certain advantages for English merchants, who therefore did not complain. It was not until the Spanish War, when trade slumped and the Elizabethan Council tried to get more for less by raising rates considerably, that for the first time there were complaints from the merchants and suggestions that export-import duties required parliamentary approval.

Henry VII and Henry VIII, and occasionally their successors, had recourse to *forced loans,* which, however, were repaid, and, even more invidiously, *benevolences,* supposedly free gifts from loyal subjects to their gracious sovereign. The Council might "suggest" the proper amounts from individuals, who if they did not pay might find themselves in prison. These benevolences were in violation of a statute passed under Richard III, which Henry VII dismissed as the work of the Parliament of a foul usurper. In 1495 he induced Parliament specifically to authorize his previous benevolences and the collection of those

[18] Above, p. 222.
[19] Above, p. 159.
[20] A "tun" was a unit of liquid measurement and a "pound" that for dry goods.

in arrears under penalty of imprisonment. Under this statutory authority the Privy Council became even more active in the assessment and collection of benevolences, the "voluntary" character of which was more than a little ironical. In 1525 Wolsey, desperately trying to raise money for the king, went too far. His "Amicable Grant" was a blanket benevolence, which demanded nothing less than one-sixth of the movables and incomes of the laity and twice as much of the clergy. Although this could not be regarded as taxation (Wolsey had not sought the consent of Parliament), opposition to the grant was immediate and widespread. The London merchants flatly refused to pay, and there was a threat of insurrection in East Anglia. The king had to climb down, protesting that he had not properly understood the severity of his Chancellor's demands; Wolsey was never forgiven by the people. Benevolences continued to be exacted, but the element of coercion diminished. Whether they were legal, however, remained a moot point; but if loyal subjects in a truly free manner wanted to give money to their sovereign, there was no legal reason why they should not.[21]

The religious changes wrought by the Tudors yielded large sums of money to the crown, though never enough to meet its needs for very long. Henry VIII exorted enormous fines from the Convocations of Canterbury and York of £100,000 and £18,000 respectively for having violated the law of praemunire by accepting Wolsey's special legatine judicial authority.[22] The confiscation of monastic and chantry property during the reigns of Henry VIII and Edward VI again brought vast potential wealth, but Henry soon sold the bulk of monastic properties to finance a war with France, and by the close of his reign only about one-third of these properties remained to the crown, bringing in £66,000 annually in rents. Sales continued during the reign of Edward VI, and the improvement in the royal finances following the confiscation of chantry property was similarly short-lived; members of the Council either sold the property or appropriated it to themselves and their friends. Even so, one may well ask what the Tudors would have done without this extra source of revenue, which finally amounted to about £136,000 annually from payments once made to the Church.

[21] In 1660 Chief Justice Hale gave judicial support for this right, and in the late eighteenth century Justice Blackstone viewed it with approval. In 1852 John C. Neild bequeathed £500,000 to Queen Victoria, who after increasing the legacies to the executors of his will and his servants, felt able to accept the residue in the absence of any relatives of Mr. Neild. As recently as 1926 Prime Minister Stanley Baldwin donated a sum to the Treasury.

[22] Below, p. 257.

Another way of raising money was by the sale of *monopolies* which conferred on the purchaser the sole right to produce or market certain commodities. The first two Tudors, combining fiscal and military interests, sold monopolies for the production of saltpeter and gunpowder. The legality of monopolies was, however, open to question. The common law forbade restraints of trade, which monopolies undoubtedly were. Yet there was also the right of the government to encourage production, as monopolies did. Elizabeth's grants and sales of monopolies in basic commodities were increasingly resented particularly by those who were thus barred from handling them. In 1597 and 1601 the House of Commons was extremely outspoken in its criticism of this practice, and the queen found it necessary to cancel a number of monopolies in order to placate its members; the majority, however, were left intact.

Yet for all these devices, the financial problem had become very serious by the time of Elizabeth. The queen was as niggardly and parsimonious as her grandfather, Henry VII, had been and with equally good reason. Her annual revenues without taxes simply would not meet all expenses of government which were her responsibility. But only by selling crown lands in the latter part of her reign could she meet her debts, which even so amounted to £400,000 on her death.

This was the crux of the Tudor financial problem, which the Stuarts inherited: the ordinary revenue was insufficient, and the ways and means of securing extraordinary revenue had been explored to the very limits. The Tudors did not in fact alienate their subjects, but they left to their successors an insoluble problem. That they failed to establish a sound financial basis of government was in part because neither the sovereign nor Parliament fully recognized what was happening. The increasing expense of government, rising prices, and the decline in the value of money were phenomena that took place gradually, imperceptibly. Men became familiar enough with their consequences, but it was not easy to see the causes. They did not come as a shock, compelling a radical change of old traditional ways; and by the end of the century the attitudes of Parliament and the crown toward the problem of national finance had become dangerously out of date.

Judicial Work of the Council

The *Book of Entries*, beginning in 1485 and enduring until the new Council roll in 1540,[23] indicates that about half the work of the early Tudor Council can be classed as administrative adjudication. Much of this business was passed on to administrative courts, and it is often difficult to determine whether the Council per se or one of these administrative tribunals acted in a particular matter, a difficulty not eased by their using the same Council roll. The Court of Star Chamber was often simply the Council acting in its judicial capacity and sitting in the star chamber in Westminster. At all events, these tribunals only partially reduced the work of privy councillors, because they usually comprised also the various administrative courts.[24]

The *original jurisdiction* exercised by the Privy Council was both civil and criminal. In the former the Council could act where neither the common law courts nor Chancery could. Thus at times the Council considered maritime disputes, until the clear emergence of the Court of Admiralty during this period.[25] Criminal justice was generally confined to investigations, which might involve the use of torture, the results of which were then placed before the law courts or the newer administrative courts. Only very rarely did the Council itself take further action in criminal matters. If it did hear and determine a criminal case, it could impose penalties only of fine and imprisonment, never death, which only the common law courts might inflict; and no criminal action could come before the Council for decision if it fell within the competence of the law courts. Conciliar jurisprudence was arbitrary, often ruthless, but the Tudor Council was nevertheless incorruptible and less likely to be swayed from its course by the machinations of the wealthy and influential than the common law courts.

The *appellate jurisdiction* of the Privy Council extended to cases heard by administrative courts and from overseas tribunals. The loss of Calais in 1558 briefly ended this latter phase of appellate work, which, however, was revived as Englishmen settled in the New World. After the subordination of the Church to the crown, the ultimate court for

[23] The actual *Book of Entries* has been lost so that our knowledge of its contents comes only from contemporary references to it.

[24] For the juridical aspects of the various administrative courts see below, pp. 274–80.

[25] Above, p. 224.

ecclesiastical appeals was the Privy Council,[26] and the Acts of Supremacy of 1534 and 1559 [27] gave to the Council the right to tender the oath of supremacy to persons suspected of denying that the king was head of the Church.

The National Church

The rules of William I had at least implied that the crown possessed the ultimate authority over the Church in England.[28] Every subsequent quarrel between English monarchs and the papacy had reinforced this principle. There was also a tradition of anti-papal feeling, visible as early as the thirteenth century and not confined to the laity. English ecclesiastics, with the exception of the monastic clergy (who recognized only the authority of the papacy and denied local episcopal control), had never accepted unlimited papal authority, and had sometimes toyed with the theory that above the papacy was the ecumenical council of the Church. Anti-papal feeling had shown itself in statutory prohibitions against appeals from English Church courts to the papal court in 1353, 1365, and 1393. Although the fact that they were repeated probably indicates that the prohibition had not been effective, such legislation by a body composed largely of laymen, but significantly including prelates in one of its houses, says much about contemporary attitudes. Equally significant, parliamentary legislation in 1351 and 1390 forbade any person to accept a direct appointment by the Pope to a position within the English Church. Again, the need to repeat the prohibition indicated that the law was often ignored by the crown, which found it easier to secure the prelates it wanted from the papacy than from cathedral chapters. Nevertheless, such legislation reflects the views of laymen and ecclesiastics in Parliament.

More widespread and deeply rooted than anti-papalism, however, was anti-clericalism in general. Abuses in the Church and deficiencies of character among the clergy were not new, but awareness and resent-

---

[26] The route of ecclesiastical appeals during the Tudor period was normally, although not invariably, from the particular archbishop's court through the *ad hoc* Delegates and thence to the Council, thereby resembling Admiralty appeals (above, p. 226). Since 1833 the ecclesiastical phase of the appellate jurisdiction of the Privy Council has been handled by its Judicial Committee (below, p. 515).

[27] Below, pp. 260, 266.

[28] Above, pp. 70–71.

ment of them were reaching a peak in the early sixteenth century. Reform was long overdue. The critical spirit, the sophistication of Renaissance humanism, could not tolerate a backward and corrupt clergy enjoying immense privileges. What Erasmus and Sir Thomas More expressed gracefully, many unsigned broadsides and pamphlets put more coarsely; such opinions were shared by the majority of the literate classes supplying Parliament. In 1515 the Commons delivered themselves of such strong anti-clerical sentiments in discussing the authority exercised by Church courts over laymen and the right of sanctuary that Cardinal Wolsey was appalled.

The personality of Wolsey is important in this context. From low social origins he had risen steadily to a high position in Church and state, acquiring enormous wealth and great arrogance in the process. To many men he came to represent a number of the things they liked least in the Church. The Duke of Suffolk, brother-in-law of Henry VIII, bluntly said what many felt, "It was never merry in England when we had cardinals among us."

Wolsey went just about as far as it was possible to go in those days before the formal severance of the English Church from the papacy. As Chancellor, he was second only to the king, holding in one hand the reins of government and administration: in the other hand he held the English Church, not as Archbishop of York, Bishop of Winchester, or his other numerous Church offices, but as papal legate *a latere*, a position according him not merely ambassadorial status but actual papal powers over the English Church. For Wolsey the only possible next step was to the papal throne itself, and he cautiously put out feelers among European churchmen with that end in mind. To the English clergy and laity alike Wolsey brought home very clearly the meaning of papal headship of the Church. English bishops had had little to fear from papal power when it emanated from distant Rome; when Wolsey exercised it in England for the first time, proud prelates mused over the advantages of an ecumenical council which would be superior to the Pope. English laymen with vested patronage rights in Church livings found them difficult to protect against papal powers wielded in England by a cardinal who hungered after still more Church offices.

Anti-papal and anti-clerical feeling were important; so too was the new spirit of nationalism in the country. They made possible the English Reformation in its early stages before any serious doctrinal changes were contemplated. But the overriding factor in bringing it about was the personal desire of Henry VIII himself. It was he who engineered the break with Rome for his own ends and, in alliance with Parliament, transformed the relations between Church and state in a few years of prodigious activity.

Of prime concern was the succession. This was vital to king and subjects. The vagueness of the original Tudor hereditary claims to the crown made it imperative that each Tudor sovereign in turn should have an heir with an unquestioned right to succeed him. Henry did not have such an heir. The only surviving issue of his marriage to his brother's widow, Catherine, was Princess Mary. Although English law did not explicitly prohibit a woman ruler, no woman ever had been a queen regnant (in contrast to a queen consort of a king) except Matilda, whose contribution to the anarchy of Stephen's reign set a sinister precedent. Moreover, if a woman could rule Henry VII had himself been a usurper, for his mother would have had prior claim to the throne. For both the king and the English people the Wars of the Roses were still a fearful warning of the possible consequences of a disputed succession; and there were other claimants who, though quiet now while Henry was alive, might claim the crown by hereditary right if Mary were to succeed.

Henry, of course, had also fallen in love with Anne Boleyn, and this fact, together with the growing conviction that the queen would not now bear a child,[29] persuaded him that he ought to marry again. In order that such a marriage and its issue should be of undoubted legality it was necessary to secure the dissolution of the present marriage by the Pope. Neither the king nor his Chancellor anticipated any great difficulties. Henry had only been permitted by special papal dispensation to marry his brother's widow. This was otherwise contrary to canon law, and if the marriage were now to be annulled, it would imply that the earlier dispensation had been illegal. Lutherans on the Continent were likely to make much of such a point, but Henry detested Lutheranism[30] and had always enjoyed good relations with the papacy. When in 1527 Henry entrusted Wolsey with the mission of securing a papal dissolution of the royal marriage, neither expected

[29] So serious was the succession problem for Henry that he toyed with the idea of declaring his bastard, the Earl of Richmond, his lawful heir, but abandoned the plan as being too open an admission of the weakness of the succession.
[30] One of the replies to the Ninety-five Theses of Martin Luther had come from Henry, who was an amateur theologian of some merit. In gratitude for the royal reply, the Pope had conferred upon Henry the title of "Defender of the Faith," still borne by English monarchs, although it is now a different faith to be defended.

rapid results, but they did not anticipate anything but ultimate success.

However, events on the Continent greatly complicated the situation. In 1527 Pope Clement was taken prisoner by the armies of the Emperor Charles V, who was the nephew of Queen Catherine of England and a man with considerable family feeling. Wolsey optimistically sought to acquire delegated authority to settle the matter himself while the Pope was in captivity, but the cardinals refused to grant it to him. It was not until after Clement's release, and when French successes over Charles in Italy had allowed him some respite, that the Pope authorized Wolsey to establish a papal court in England, composed of himself and another cardinal named Campeggio, who was also Bishop of Salisbury. Hopes were again high when news was received that the French army in Italy had been heavily defeated and the emperor was again at the Pope's side offering advice that could not safely be ignored. Campeggio was instructed not to proceed, and finally in 1529 the case was recalled to Rome, where no decision favorable to Henry was now likely to be given. Wolsey's diplomacy had failed and his fall was imminent.

Henry, however, was still determined to succeed in a matter that so vitally concerned him. The weapon he chose to fight with was Parliament; with the help of Parliament he gained his victory. In the course of five years he entirely changed the character of that institution, created a national Church, and transformed the constitution. Probably none of these things were in the king's mind when he summoned Parliament in 1529. But unable to get what he wanted from the Pope, he had resolved to settle the all-important question himself in consultation with his own people.

The participation of Parliament in the greatest enterprise of the reign meant that the final break with Rome produced a national Church, whose royal headship symbolized the congruency of Church and state. But in addition, Parliament's character also changed into that of a fundamentally legislative body with a very much stronger claim henceforth to share authority with the crown in major affairs of state.

The Parliament summoned in 1529 sat in seven sessions over a period of seven years. It is known as the "Reformation Parliament," though it hardly concerned itself with doctrinal or theological matters. There is no evidence that the crown took any special steps to secure a "favorable" Parliament, though the fact that it endured so long is evidence enough that Henry was well pleased with the services its members were rendering him. Though neither cringing nor servile, the Reformation Parliament was clearly amenable to royal influence and to the guidance of the king's secretary, Thomas Cromwell. In its first session it quickly began to remedy abuses in the Church, but when it recessed at the end of the year there had still been no question of a final breach with Rome. For another twelve months, during which time Parliament was not recalled, Henry continued to negotiate and plead with the Pope.

The moves toward separation were in logical sequence. In 1529 Parliament had enacted laws on mortuary and probate fees in ecclesiastical courts, as well as on the right of sanctuary, matters which had produced abuses which had been criticized by the new Chancellor, Sir Thomas More. In such laws was the implication that Parliament, a secular body, could regulate the internal affairs of the Church. Another law affirmed this even more clearly when it forbade nonresidency of clergy even with a papal dispensation. There was still a majority of spiritual peers in the House of Lords, and the government needed the support of at least some prelates to get these measures through the upper House. It is significant that though some objected to these statutes most did not, although the implication could hardly have been lost upon them. Nor, as Henry had hoped, was it lost upon the Pope. But the result was not a papal dissolution of the royal marriage but a protest against the laws, and against the anti-papal and anti-clerical sentiments expressed in the recent parliamentry session. With a mixture of guile and frankness, Henry replied that he, too, felt that some of the remarks were unfortunate but that the Pope should understand that in England the king dared not interfere with Parliament.

The papal protest, however, revealed that something more was needed if sufficient pressure were to be brought to bear on the Pope to persuade him to change his mind. After Parliament rose, Henry suddenly took the drastic step of having all the clergy indicted for praemunire for having accepted the special legatine authority of Wolsey. That the king had specifically authorized the cardinal to exercise it did not reduce the guilt of the clergy if they chose to submit themselves to juries in secular courts. In danger of imprisonment and forfeiture of all their goods, the clergy in the Convocations of Canterbury and York proposed expiation of their guilt by enormous fines of £100,000 and £18,000 respectively. The king refused to accept this solution until the two Convocations recognized him as head of the Church. With some members moved by fear and others by hope of reform under royal administration, the Convocations declared the king to be "Supreme Head" of the Church "as far as the law of Christ allows," a saving clause of considerable ambiguity. The clergy now recognized that future resistance to royal ecclesiastical policies could mean prosecution for praemunire as broadly interpreted by the crown. Yet significantly the royal demand revealed no member of the lower clergy willing to stand forth unequivocally for sole papal headship of the Church. The English clergy also had an anti-papal tradition; and they, too, were men of their times.

The papacy, never too certain of the English Church, was left without ecclesiastical supporters in England, except within the monastic orders. The completeness of the royal victory produced a gracious pardon for the clergy — but no papal dissolution of the royal marriage. Indeed the Pope had again specifically forbidden the king to remarry. In 1531 Henry again turned to Parliament. The recent pardon to the clergy was put on a statutory basis, and Parliament also demanded a similar protection for any layman guilty of praemunire. Henry's assent to a law for this purpose barred him from fining the laity as he had the clergy.

When Parliament met again in 1532, matters were approaching a climax. Privy councillors in Parliament encouraged its members to express their anti-clerical sentiments in a petition to the king, the essence of which was an attack on the authority of the Convocations. The attack rested on claims that ecclesiastical legislation was not valid because it lacked the royal assent and often ran counter to the laws of the realm. One of the rules of William I supported the parliamentary demand for royal consent to measures approved by the Convocations,[31] but the inference that canon law was inferior to secular law and must be in harmony with it was an utter denial of the medieval view that the two laws were incapable of conflict because of their separate spheres of action. The new radical notion that secular law, including parliamentary statutes, was supreme in all areas of human life jolted Sir Thomas More into resigning the chancellorship. The clergy, however, when confronted with the parliamentary petition and bullied and threatened by the king, gave way completely. They agreed to a review of all canon law by a joint parliamentary-ecclesiastical commission of eight peers, eight commoners, and sixteen clergy to decide which canons should be

---

[31] No measure of an ecclesiastical council to be valid without royal approval (above, p. 71).

retained and submitted for royal assent, henceforth necessary for all measures approved by the Convocations.

This surrender, known as "the submission of the clergy," was further proof of the power of Parliament and the irresistible authority of king and Parliament acting together. Although both the Convocations and Parliament were now instruments of the royal will, it was obvious that the latter was likely to be the more effective in determining the issue with the papacy. Parliament was no mere creature of the crown, however, as can be seen from the hot debates and narrow majorities during the passage of the *Act of Annates*, every line of which was a threat to the papacy. It slashed the customary payments to the papacy of "first fruits," the first year's revenues of a new incumbent in a Church post, to a paltry 5 per cent. New prelates might be consecrated despite the refusal of the papacy to approve their selection. But another provision delayed the operation of the law for a year pending royal negotiations with the Pope.

The Act of Annates marked the point where king and Parliament indicated their willingness to proceed to the ultimate step of separation from Rome should it prove necessary. During the next year the break became increasingly imminent. Late in 1532 Henry learned that Anne Boleyn was to have his child; the Pope ordered Henry not to set aside Catherine. The order was galling to royal and national pride and disastrous if obeyed, because Anne's child might be the long-desired son, whom Henry was determined should not be a bastard.

Henry could no longer afford to threaten; he had to move. In January 1533 he married Anne in secret. The marriage, obviously, was valid only if his marriage to Catherine were not. At the same time Thomas Cranmer became Archbishop of Canterbury by direct appointment of the Pope, who was glad to oblige Henry in something. In March Cranmer was consecrated, and in April Parliament passed the *Act in Restraint of Appeals*, forbidding ecclesiastical appeals to Rome. Despite its declaration that all ecclesiastical, like all secular judicial powers, derived from the king, the law did not provide appeals to him either in Council or in Parliament. Instead, ecclesiastical cases should terminate with the particular archbishop's court, except for cases involving the king which might go on to the bishops of the respective Convocations. The effect of the law when added to the others of the past four years was to substitute royal for papal headship over the English Church.

With the groundwork laid by Parliament, in May Cranmer and some

bishops, forming the highest Church court in the Province of Canterbury, declared Henry's marriage to Catherine never to have been legal
and his recent marriage to Anne therefore valid. In July, ignoring the
recent English law against appeals to his court, the Pope reversed this
decision and excommunicated the members of the court responsible for
it. The Pope gave Henry a month's grace before he fell under the same
ban, but the king was unmoved. So strong was his hold on the English
clergy that the Pope could find no prelate to "publish" the bill of
excommunication, which instead had to appear in the Netherlands.

And after all the rush and upheaval, in September 1533, Princess
Elizabeth was born.

However, there was no turning back; Anne might yet have a son. In
1534 Henry asked Parliament to take the final steps. Statutes ended all
payments to the Pope and barred his bulls and letters from the realm.
Some of the papal powers of dispensation went to the Archbishop of
Canterbury, but the papal power of direct appointments to Church
offices went to the king. Not satisfied with the submission of the clergy
by the Convocations, the crown had Parliament embody it in legislation.
Finally, the *Act of Supremacy* declared what had by this time become
the fact — the king was the "Supreme Head" of the "Church of England." The victory of the national, secular crown over a foreign, ecclesiastical power was complete.

How far the nation outside of Parliament wanted the victory is difficult to determine. At the final stages of its drive the government was
uneasy about a possible passive resistance by the clergy and secured a
law permitting direct royal appointment of bishops should cathedral
chapters refuse to act or not accept royal nominations to episcopal
vacancies. However, the royal *congé d'elire* (permission to elect) accompanied by the *letter missive* (giving the name of the person to be
elected) never encountered resistance from any cathedral chapter.
Bishop Fisher and some monks might be willing to lose their lives for
papal supremacy, but the mass of the English clergy preferred acceptance to martyrdom.

The government also received coercive weapons from Parliament in
the form of laws making it treason to refuse to take an oath affirming
the royal supremacy, or one declaring Henry's marriage with Anne to
be valid and their children entitled to inherit the crown. These laws
were terrible threats, but the government rarely invoked them. The
prominence of Fisher and More, whose willingness to swear to the suc-

cession but not in the form required by law cost them their heads, hides the vast number of men whose opinions the crown ignored.

A few reformers saw in the royal supremacy a vehicle for their plans to bring Protestantism into the realm immediately, and thereby guessed wrong. But the attitude of most people toward the religious changes seems to have been one of indifference, occasionally tinged with pride that "King Harry" had defied the Pope.

No doubt a major reason why the changes were so readily accepted was that to the ordinary man they made very little difference. The articles of his faith had been left untouched; as for the Pope or king, he had never seen either of them. The Church was now administered by the king's *Vicar-General,* an office filled by Thomas Cromwell. But this new administration had little effect on the parish, where the average man lived out his life. Doctrinally, the national religious policy was for the moment rigidly orthodox. The Act of Supremacy formally declared that the old faith was to be upheld in all details, including the Mass in Latin, the chief manifestation of religious faith for most men.

Henry never claimed that his headship of the Church entitled him to declare doctrine, even of the orthodox variety. But in 1536 the king, seeing the infiltration of Lutheranism, had Cranmer prepare a statement of faith, which the Convocations approved as the *Ten Articles* which made only baptism, penance, and the eucharist of the old seven sacraments essential to salvation. The next year Henry worked with the prelates in drafting another conservative statement of faith, the *Bishops' Book.* In 1539 Parliament set forth doctrine still on orthodox lines in the *Six Articles,* thereby making the faith of the national Church a matter of secular statute law. Little by little, however, Protestant tendencies were infiltrating from the Continent. In 1544 the government permitted some devotions in English, and so little did the Six Articles secure perfect orthodoxy that the next year the king sadly complained to Parliament that the Bible was being "disputed, rhymed, sung, and jangled in every alehouse and tavern."

Unknown to Henry his two major advisers on religious policy, Cromwell and Cranmer, had Protestant leanings; and indeed the king's own policies gave a fillip to Protestantism. His order that an English Bible be in every church and available to laymen placed in the hands of the nation the authority to which Protestantism made its appeal. Furthermore, the Six Articles themselves established the precedent that Parliament was competent to determine doctrine for the national

Church. When the literate and articulate elements of the nation became convinced that the Protestant position was correct, they could use Parliament to change doctrine in that direction. Henry, himself, seems to have recognized what was to come when he entrusted the education of his son and heir [32] to men with Protestant sympathies.

The dissolution of the monasteries and convents was the result of parliamentary action. Cromwell saw the religious orders as very wealthy and as supporters of papal authority. He had observed his mentor, Wolsey, confiscate some of the small monasteries; and in 1535 as Vicar-General he appointed agents to carry out a full-scale investigation of the monastic establishments. The agents probably knew what the government wanted to hear; but their reports, which went to Parliament the next year, repeated charges made in the past by such different observers as Wyclif and More. In the past religious orders had defied episcopal plans for reform, insisting that they were directly subordinate to the Pope, not the local bishop. The government, however, determined not on reform but on dissolution. Parliament would accept neither proof of efficiency nor of morality in arriving at its decisions; income was what counted, and those with less than £200 annual income were dissolved, their property going to the crown. The dissolution of the monasteries led to the sharp protest of the *Pilgrimage of Grace*,[33] and the failure of that rising virtually doomed the rest. Over the next three years some monasteries dissolved themselves; in 1539 Parliament put an end to those that were left.[34]

The dissolution of the monasteries ended the ecclesiastical majority in the House of Lords, from which the abbots departed, leaving the bishops a minority in the chamber. For the crown the expropriation of monastic property meant momentary enrichment, but most of the land was sold at reasonable prices to the English gentry, who thus acquired a vested interest in the religious changes, and good grounds for feeling a special loyalty to their sovereign king. When Mary sought to restore to the Church what it had lost, she was unable to do anything about the old monastic property, which was no longer in the control of the crown. Legally, the confiscation of the monasteries was a blow to

[32] The future Edward VI, born of the marriage between Henry and Jane Seymour, his third wife.

[33] Below, p. 276.

[34] Although there were inevitably tragic consequences, a number of former monks fared well, the government giving some abbots and priors appointments as bishops and cathedral deans, while pensioning others and finally permitting them to marry.

the common law doctrine of the sanctity of property rights, even those not supported by written charter although continuously exercised. It was now obvious that the Parliament of the nation-state could wipe out such rights by statute.

The subordination of the Church to the secular state had ramifications difficult for men to grasp. The new power of Parliament to legislate on anything was to men like Sir Thomas More utterly unreasonable. Sir Thomas had been willing to accept the first steps toward Church reform taken by Parliament; but that it was competent to legislate on canon law and doctrine he could never accept. This echo of Becket's position was fraught with danger. The Duke of Norfolk, warning More of the impending wrath of the king, received the reply, "Is that all, my lord? Then in good faith the difference between your grace and me is that I shall die today and you tomorrow." More might appeal to a "higher law," but once Henry's ecclesiastical policy had united Church and state, support for the former became the essential test of loyalty to the latter.

After the death of Henry VIII, Protestant reformers sought to introduce the doctrinal changes that the late king had always refused to countenance. The religious, as opposed to the political, Reformation was carried out during the reign of Edward VI (1547–53), who when he ascended was a mournfully precocious boy of nine. The royal minority meant that power was in the hands of the Council, the members of which had been named by Henry, but where the Duke of Somerset, uncle of the young king, quickly assumed a dominating position with the title of Lord Protector. Somerset was sympathetic to Protestantism but also showed a tendency toward toleration in religious matters peculiar in those days. In 1547 Parliament repealed the treason and heresy laws of the previous reign, as well as the Six Articles, thereby removing the statutory barriers to doctrinal innovations. Protestant enthusiasts took to destroying anything smacking of "popery," such as church ornaments, statues, stained-glass windows, and paintings. The government did nothing to discourage them. Indeed, in 1550 the Council ordered the removal of all altars from the churches. As part of the drive against superstitious practices, but also to fill the empty Treasury, the government ordered the dissolution of chantries, wealthy endowments for the saying of Masses for the souls of the dead, and expropriated their property under the laws abolishing monasteries.

If Somerset had hoped that the doctrine of the Church would be changed gradually and by general consent, the uproar during the early years of the reign quickly disillusioned him. But meanwhile the government continued step by step to make Protestantism the orthodox faith of the English Church. In 1548 Cranmer drafted a new communion service, Protestant in that it was in English and repudiated the doctrine of transubstantiation. The following year his first Book of Common Prayer was presented to Parliament. Written in magnificent English, it made concessions to both Catholics and Protestants in a noble attempt at compromise. The book was hotly debated and considerably modified by the peers before it was finally approved and all clergy required to use its services in the first *Act of Uniformity* in 1549. With the replacement of Somerset by Northumberland, the pace quickened. Iconoclasm and attacks against books and altars, encouraged by the government, increased. Northumberland dismissed clergy whom he regarded as deficient in "loyalty" — a rude shock to the medieval concept of the perpetuity of clerical status. In 1552 a second Prayer Book, clearly Protestant in tone, received parliamentary sanction in a second *Act of Uniformity*, requiring its use by all clergy in all services and compulsory attendance by laymen at them. Finally, Cranmer sought to fix the dogma of the Church of England once and for all in the strongly Protestant *Forty-two Articles* of 1553.

By the end of Edward's short reign, the government by drastic and decisive action had radically changed the doctrine and liturgy of the Church of England. Perhaps it had gone too far and moved too fast. Certainly the ordinary man, unfamiliar with the latest theologies from Switzerland, must have been confused and often resentful to see the ancient faith of his fathers being so much abused. At all events, as Edward lay dying, the whole achievement of these years was threatened. Northumberland made a desperate attempt to exclude the Roman Catholic Mary from the succession and put his daughter-in-law, the Lady Jane Grey, on the throne. With the failure of his plan, Northumberland was doomed, and so also were the hopes of introducing extreme Protestantism into the Church of England.

Mary I sought to restore Roman Catholic doctrine, complete with papal supremacy; she also wished to hand back to the Church its confiscated lands and properties. This, she realized, could only be done through Parliament, even though it would mean asking Parliament to reverse a good deal of its own legislation over the past quarter of a century. Her first Parliament offered little resistance to her proposal to repeal all the doctrinal laws of her brother's reign, but it resisted the attempts of her councillors to persuade it to make attendance at the restored Mass compulsory or to revive laws against heresy. Mary intervened actively in the elections for a new Parliament in 1554, at least to the extent of asking for the return of members "of the wise, grave, and catholic sort" to the Commons. Later in 1554 the new Parliament petitioned the joint sovereigns (against the advice of her councillors and the wishes of her people Mary had married Philip of Spain) to restore the Church to papal control, but made the reservation that this did not mean the restoration of former Church lands.[35] At the urgent request of the queen, Parliament restored the heresy laws, whereby Church courts tried the accused who, upon conviction, were given over to the secular government for burning.

The Pope was again head of the English Church, but Mary's victory was hollow. If there had been dismay about the rapid Protestant swing in her brother's reign, there was now opposition to the equally rapid reversal. Convinced Protestants went into voluntary exile or stayed to face martyrdom. Englishmen were not accustomed to the concentrated persecution conducted by the queen against the better judgment of the papal legate, Cardinal Pole, an Englishman, and even of her bigoted Spanish husband. About 300 persons died in the flames between 1555 and 1558, among them the popular preachers, Ridley and Latimer, and also Cranmer, who after faltering found courage at the last. Englishmen were appalled at the spectacle; and when Mary died, the mass of the people associated her religion with torture, foreign influences, and the other notable disaster of her reign, the loss of Calais.

A period of advanced Protestantism, followed by a reaction to strict Catholicism, had given more adherents to both parties, but the majority of people stood somewhere in between. It was on this assumption, at least, that Elizabeth based her religious policy. To her first Parliament of 1559, which appears to have been as freely elected as any during the Tudor period, her councillors submitted a program for a religious settlement that the council itself had devised without reference to the Convocations and without seeking clerical advice. By the Act of Supremacy, the queen became the supreme authority over the national

[35] Mary herself restored those former Church lands still in the possession of the crown, thereby weakening its financial resources.

Church, and the work of Mary's Parliaments was largely undone. By the Act of Uniformity, the 1552 Prayer Book of Edward VI, slightly revised, was adopted for use in all churches. These measures encountered the fierce opposition of the Marian bishops in the House of Lords; the Act of Supremacy was only passed after it had been several times revised, and the Act of Uniformity got through by a margin of only three votes.

The Act of Supremacy did not go so far as to declare the queen "supreme head" of the Church, in the formula used by Henry VIII and Edward VI. It described her instead as "Supreme Governor," a phrase intended as a concession to the Roman Catholics, for whom only the Pope could be called "head" of the church. All clergy and officials had to take the oath of supremacy to this effect. Failure to take the oath made a person liable to penalties ranging from dismissal from his post to death for treason. In 1563 this requirement was extended to teachers, barristers, university graduates, and members of the Commons.

The Act of Uniformity, requiring all clergy to use the services of the revised Prayer Book, was to be enforced by both the bishops and secular courts; it also authorized the Ecclesiastical Commission, which later became the Court of High Commission, for this purpose. At the third offence a cleric might be imprisoned for life; lay offenders who failed to go to church had to pay a fine of one shilling for each Sunday.

Constitutionally, the Elizabethan Settlement was statutory and secular. No part of it, even the revised Prayer Book, came from the Convocations. This was inevitable when the government wanted a quick "solution" to an extremely complex religious problem, a solution, moreover, which the Catholic clergy of the Convocations would never have drafted. Nevertheless, the need of Elizabeth at the outset of her reign for a parliamentary religious settlement prejudiced her later claim that her royal supremacy could be exercised equally in the Convocations or Parliament at her discretion.

The number of clergy who refused to accept the new religious settlement was estimated by a sixteenth-century writer as 177, and as 2000 by a twentieth-century Roman Catholic writer. Even if we were to accept the latter figure, it means that at least three-quarters of the clergy survived the change from the militant Catholicism of Mary to the doctrinal vagueness of Elizabeth. For laymen the government in the early years of the reign showed a marked disinclination to enforce conformity. Catholic families, especially in the conservative north, continued to hear the Mass as said by priests hidden in the priest-holes of great houses; and the government was lax in collecting fines for nonattendance at church. The position of such people would have been difficult had the government tendered them the oath of supremacy, but the queen's reluctance "to open windows into men's hearts" allowed many of them to live in peace during the first decade of the reign.

In 1570, however, the Pope placed English Catholics in an impossible situation by excommunicating Elizabeth. The papal bull declared that she was deposed and that anybody who continued to obey her would fall under the same ban. The already uneasy compromise that most English Catholics had been compelled to accept, reconciling as best they could their dual loyalties to the Pope and the "supreme governor," was shattered. Catholic recusancy — deliberately staying away from Anglican services — became a matter of grave concern to the government. Catholicism and treason had become identical.

In 1571 a law extended the definition of treason to include any attempt to execute the recent papal bull excommunicating the queen or to be "reconciled" to Rome. A decade later to convert or be converted to Catholicism became treason. Missionary priests not abjuring the realm were guilty of the crime, as were Englishmen presently studying abroad if they did not return to take the oath of supremacy. Since it was unlikely that they would return for this purpose, the statute declared that such failure to return should entail forfeiture of their property in England. To say or hear Mass became a felony punishable by fine and imprisonment, and the fee for nonattendance at church was put up to £20 monthly. The government made lists of all recusants, and a law of 1593 forbade their movement beyond five miles of their homes.

The severity of these laws reflected the attitude of many Englishmen that Catholicism was "foreign," a view gaining credence by the necessary location abroad of English Catholic seminaries and the fact that in all plots discovered against the state the Spanish government appeared to have been involved. Elizabeth, however, was prepared to apply the laws as sparingly as possible. During her 45-year reign she signed the death warrants for 200 people who were convicted, she insisted, not for their Catholicism but for their treason. Four persons, none Catholic, were burned for heresy. Parliament, particularly the House of Commons, at times criticized the crown for what it considered a dangerously lax administration of the recusancy laws, and would have gone further than the government in making new ones. Thus in 1571 Parliament passed a bill making participation in the Anglican communion compulsory, but the queen vetoed it. More than once she and the Council were a buffer between the Catholics and those who wished to enforce the letter of the law to the full.

The Catholics had been committed to a policy of subversion and rebellion; missionaries from the Continent were involved in efforts to overthrow the government out of their loyalty to the papacy. It was all very well for the Jesuit Edmund Campion to say proudly on the scaffold that his only treason was his religion and that he wished the queen "a long quiet reign with all prosperity"; many other Catholics would no doubt have shared his sentiments, had not the papal bull initiated a policy which, if successful, would necessarily have destroyed the queen and her government.

To treat Catholicism as treason was possible; to treat extreme Protestantism, with its dislike for the concessions made by the Elizabethan Settlement to the old faith, as treason was difficult. Regarding the queen as a bulwark against the return of "popery," this body wished to purge the Church of all traces of it. However, there was a wide divergency of opinion as to what changes were necessary to achieve this end, and the term "Puritan" described people with a variety of different aims. Most of them, however, were agreed that the Church should be a branch of the state and that the agencies of government were best able to "purify" the Church of its "Romish" remnants, such as kneeling in prayer, giving the sign of the cross in baptism, and the use of vestments.

In her determination to steer a middle course, the queen had always to be on her guard against the more extreme Calvinistic tendencies which continued to penetrate into England from the Continent. She denied the right of the Puritan clergy to introduce any modifications into Anglican services, as they were often tempted to do; and she made an arrangement with the bishops whereby each would support the power of the other and episcopal discipline was to uphold the Settlement at all points. In 1566 the Archbishop of Canterbury issued further detailed regulations on the conduct of the various services, and the bishops enforced them. When parish clergy were not amenable to episcopal directions, the crown used the Court of High Commission as an agency of the state to enforce these rules for its Church.

The alliance between crown and bishops made it impossible for the

Puritans to promote their interests through the Convocations where hitherto they had commanded a good deal of support. Instead, they turned to Parliament and soon found that the Commons was sympathetic to their cause. The queen, as a result, revived the theory that her ecclesiastical supremacy could be exercised at the royal discretion either in the Convocations or in Parliament. But the precedents established by Henry VIII and the regents of Edward VI were firmly laid, and Parliament would not readily agree to any reduction of its authority in ecclesiastical matters.

Clearly, a complicated constitutional issue was developing. Were the Convocations on the one hand and Parliament on the other two coordinate but independent legislatures for the Church, with the crown free to decide which it would use? Or did the statutory nature of royal supremacy require that to be binding the actions of the queen-in-Convocation had to be approved by the queen-in-Parliament? In 1563 the Convocations adopted the *Thirty-nine Articles*, a modified version of Cranmer's Forty-two Articles, as the basic doctrine of the Church. One or two clauses were extremely offensive to the Puritans, but Parliament was not consulted. Three years later, however, the Puritans introduced a bill to give them statutory force when suitably amended. The bill passed the Commons, but then the queen intervened and forbade the Lords to discuss it. She declared that the Articles were binding without parliamentary action, and that indeed Parliament had no right to discuss religious matters, which belonged to the royal prerogative. It was not until 1571 that the articles were finally given statutory authority in the *Subscription Act*, the offending clauses being omitted as a result of Puritan pressure.

The struggle between the queen and the Puritans in Parliament continued throughout her reign. When in 1572, Puritans boldly introduced a measure into the House of Commons to simplify services, she forbade the House to discuss it. Four years later when they presented a measure to change ecclesiastical discipline, now being exercised by the bishops against Puritan clergy, Elizabeth informed the Speaker that this subject was only for the bishops, the very authority the bill sought to circumvent. Her attitude was unchanged when the House of Commons had the support of the lower clergy for such a measure five years later. In 1597 she reiterated that the internal administration of the Church was a matter only for the crown and the clergy, not for Parliament.

Unable to bring about the changes in the Church through the Convocations or Parliament, some Puritans determined to hold their own meetings, or *conventicles*. As a result they, like the Catholics, became liable to fines for nonattendance at Church. The government refused to let the matter rest there. To Elizabeth the most heinous aspect of the attitude of these extremists was their refusal to conform outwardly after she had promised not to open windows into their hearts. In 1599 Martin Marprelate attacked the bishops with savage invective and ridicule in a series of pamphlets. He ran afoul of the government and also caused a general revulsion against Puritanism. The crown seized on this feeling to secure a severe law in 1593 against conventicles, with exile for attendance and death for return. Thus by the end of the century Puritans and Catholics, with nothing in common except their extremism, were equally victims of the Elizabethan compromise.

The inclusion of the Church within the purview of state-interest demanded adherence to the Church as a test of loyalty to the state. From this it followed that the state was responsible for checking religious "error"; Sir Thomas More's view that certain things were beyond the competence of the state to deal with received no sympathy from Henry VIII or his daughters — or from the mass of men, who accepted the Tudor idea that all things were now Caesar's.

Local Administration

Tudor local administrative changes were largely refinements of older practices, aiming at greater centralization of local government in the hands of the Council. So successful were the Tudors in this respect that their administrative arrangements endured in one form or another until the Parish Councils Act of 1894.[36]

The decline of some of the older units of local government facilitated this process. The hundred was moribund, although it was not formally abolished until 1867. The shire court was important only for selecting the two county members to the Commons. The sheriff remained primarily the executive officer of the royal courts, because the Tudors did not care to concentrate local power in one individual. In parliamentary elections the sheriff acted as a returning officer for the county meeting, but his tourn through the shire had died with its hundreds. The coroner continued his older functions, and a law of Henry VII encouraged him to fulfil them by fining him for not holding inquests

[36] See below, p. 506.

into suspicious deaths, and by paying him from the Treasury for doing so.

One new office, created by the Tudors by an act of 1557, was that of Lord-Lieutenant of the county. His responsibility was to supply military forces and leadership, without the danger inherent in the older practice of commissions of array.[37] By the Tudor period the government expected all able-bodied men to meet in the churchyard after the Sunday service and practice archery and to drill. The sheriff did not regain his duty of leading these public forces, which instead went to the Lord-Lieutenant. Although the office had only this specific military duty, its holder had general responsibility for law and order in his shire and was usually one of its justices of the peace.

The justices of the peace were the chief agents of Tudor local government. Traditionally drawn from the gentry, they were legally required until as late as 1906 to own land of £100 annual clear value; and their economic and social interests made them at one with the Tudor dynasty. By entrusting county administration to them as a committee, the Tudors avoided concentrating local power in one man.

The Tudors did not increase the judicial duties of these "J.P.s," as the justices were coming to be called; but the government greatly expanded their administrative duties, until they covered all aspects of county affairs. The remarkable thing is the efficiency with which these unpaid men, upon whom the local implementation of Tudor state policy depended, carried out their tasks. So successful were they that they continued to administer the shires until the County Councils Act of 1888.[38] The J.P.s checked on recusants, and administered the Elizabethan Statute of Apprentices and the poor law.[39] They encouraged the woolen industry by enforcing the law about wearing woolen clothes, even corpses requiring a woolen shroud. They saw to it that Protestant Englishmen ate fish on Fridays *and* Wednesdays so that the fisheries, that nursery of seamen, would prosper. Their reports on local matters, generally and specifically, went to the Deputy Keeper of the Rolls of the Council, which was constantly thinking of new burdens to impose upon them.

Despite their administrative character, the justices of the peace never became harrying and harried bureaucrats. With a strong sense of

[37] Above, p. 192.
[38] Below, p. 506.
[39] Below, pp. 272-3.

paternalism toward their people, whom they often knew also as their tenants, the J.P.s continued their pre-Tudor practice of assessing orders from the Privy Council in terms of local needs. The invariable participation of at least two of their number in the House of Commons (and possibly more with the tendency for the gentry to sit for boroughs) meant that they were familiar with the circumstances occasioning the passage of a particular law they were administering; and they did so in terms of local conditions. The Council wisely did not inquire too closely into the precise manner in which the justices of the peace executed statutes and orders, and there is frequently a hint in the terse reports of these agents to the Council that they had "improved" one of its policies.

The parish, hitherto an ecclesiastical unit with few secular functions, now became the basic unit for local administration. Prior to the Tudors parish government had consisted of a vestry, usually consisting of all adult males, and certain officials named by it. These, together with the parish priest, looked after the maintenance of the local church. After the religious changes of Henry VIII the crown used its new powers over the Church to reduce the vestry to propertied men, and by the seventeenth century most vestries were of this *closed* type. The vestry named the church wardens, who with the priest administered the ecclesiastical economy of the local church. Secular functions of the parish fell to officials similarly named. Public order was in the hands of the *constable*. Wandering animals were the responsibility of the *pound master*, while *hay* and *wood wardens* supervised communal meadow and timber rights. The vestry was to keep the parish free of noxious vermin, including foxes, after which the squires rode enthusiastically as part of their civic duties. Extremely minor *judicial* powers, largely over issues arising from common lands and woods, also belonged to the vestry.

The parish also became the unit for the administration of poor relief, after the dissolution of the monasteries. In 1543 it was required to give relief to paupers resident in it for three years. In 1597 the administration of poor relief became the responsibility of the justices of the peace of the counties, and four years later the *Elizabethan Poor Law* consolidated previous legislation in a form that was to last until 1834.[40] The policies decided upon by the J.P.s at their quarter sessions had to be implemented by the parish, which was responsible for the

[40] Below, pp. 479, 507.

actual distribution of relief. The vestry named *overseers of the poor*, including the *beadle* of the parish. The overseers had the duty of finding employment for able-bodied paupers, who if they refused to work were liable to whipping or expulsion from the parish. More important, the Poor Law of 1601 empowered the vestry to lay the poor law *rate* (not a "tax," as it was not imposed by Parliament) upon all parish property to supply funds for direct monetary relief, to be distributed by the overseers, to paupers unable to work by reason either of their age and infirmity or of the lack of jobs. Some vestries were adept at raising money "painlessly" for this purpose by naming as overseers men who preferred to pay the prescribed fine themselves rather than serve. Other men saw in the position a "good thing," as Oliver Twist discovered in the early nineteenth century. Nevertheless, the Elizabethan Poor Law worked fairly well until the eighteenth century.

The *Statute of Apprentices* (or Artificers) of 1563 was nothing less than an attempt to achieve the ideal of full employment, both for the benefit of individuals and for the social and economic health of the state. The law sought to ensure a proper ratio of workers among the various occupations and applied to all persons not already in a craft or engaged in agriculture. Justices of the peace received power to allocate labor among occupations, with agriculture having priority. Persons thus assigned had the obligation, and also the protection, of a contract for one year. The law did not attempt to fix a minimum wage, but left this to the justices of the peace who could decide it in terms of the local cost of living.

TUDOR JURISPRUDENCE

The Tudor period saw the emergence of administrative law and adjudication, and the growing hostility of common law justices toward them. Statute law extended its range and greatly increased in volume, at times overriding long-existent common law doctrines. On the other hand it also extended the scope of common law, often enabling it to act where hitherto it had been unable to. The Statute of Uses restored to the common law its vast jurisdiction over land, and the Statute of Wills extended its jurisdiction for the first time partially into the area of probate in 1540. Statute law could correct or simplify the common law. Thus, the common law definition of theft, like most definitions of crimes against property resting upon judicial decisions, included the essentials of the taking of money or goods from their lawful owner without his consent; and the common law had insisted that ownership meant actual physical possession. When a servant took five shillings from his master's purse without his permission, the law could move. If the servant collected five shillings rent and did not give it to his employer, the law was helpless. The person paying the rent had voluntarily parted with the money, and it had never been in the physical possession of the employer. Into the dilemma of the law stepped a statute of 1529 making the servant's action the crime of *embezzlement*.

Administrative Adjudication

During the fifteenth and sixteenth centuries the Council again produced a number of courts, as in the twelfth and thirteenth centuries, to deal with matters hitherto handled by the overworked parent body. Those who disliked the new courts and their law during the seventeenth century described them as "prerogative," intimating that they were illegal and agents of tyranny. Yet by strict definition it was the common law courts which were truly "prerogative," in that their origin was at royal command alone, and the law courts had few statutes supporting their existence. In contrast, the newer administrative courts had each been given a definite statutory basis for its existence. Nevertheless, their reputations grew steadily worse until they were eventually swept away by an angry and victorious Parliament in 1641.

Administrative tribunals were a development of conciliar jurisdiction. Some had existed before the Tudors, others appeared to adjudicate issues arising from Tudor policy. All existed because of the inability of the common law courts to meet certain problems, and until the seventeenth century there were invariably common law justices sitting on these administrative tribunals. Had they endured longer, they might have developed a body of precedent as rigid as that of the common law.

The *Court of Star Chamber* received a statutory basis in a law of 1487, which described its membership as consisting of any seven of the Council sitting in Star Chamber, with jurisdiction over cases of riots, overawing of justices and juries, and over livery and maintenance. Always including the Chancellor, two bishops, and a Chief Justice from one of the law courts, Star Chamber for some time was indistinguishable from the Council; and there is some doubt whether they were really two bodies, or the one body performing different duties in a different place. In 1527 the court received its own clerk, but he used the Council roll until 1540, when Star Chamber began its own. By that time the court had regular biannual sessions and no longer followed the traveling Council. Under Elizabeth it was clearly distinct from the Council in that it had quite different procedures and kept its own records, but all privy councillors attended its meetings, together with some common law justices, and peers who might be summoned by the crown to consider particular cases.

In its early days the court was particularly effective in dealing with great persons, who might be able to intimidate or bribe the common law courts but found Star Chamber incorruptible and beyond intimidation. Its activities increased during the sixteenth century; it could deal with all manner of cases, and all classes could apply to it if they felt that justice was not being done. Anything involving a breach of the peace, from rioting to the issuing of an "infamous libel" came within its sphere. Its justice was swift and often arbitrary, but its hearings were normally in public. It employed summary procedure, including "paper-proof" depositions and affidavits, inadmissible as evidence at common law, and it could also compel a man to testify against himself. The penalties it inflicted were as various as the cases it tried, though, like the parent Council, it could not impose the death penalty. Usually it ordered heavy fines, but whipping, branding, and various other forms of bodily mutilation could be ordered by its judges. Star Chamber had many admirers, including Chief Justice Coke in the seventeenth century, who did not as a rule approve of royal administrative tribunals, and it appears to have been popular. On the other hand, many practitioners of the common law resented it. It was bound by no precedents, and its actions, though swift, might be at the expense of basic individual rights. It might refuse counsel to the accused. That it was empowered to use torture and accepted verbal confessions cast a sinister light over its proceedings. That it was an instrument of government meant that its decisions might be determined by considerations of current state policy rather than of eternal justice. But on the whole, Star Chamber appears not to have abused its peculiar authority unduly, and its judgments were no harsher than those of the common law. Star Chamber also had *quasi-appellate* review over cases heard by other courts of criminal equity. From Star Chamber there could be an appeal to the Council, but as the two bodies consisted for the most part of the same men, such appeals were usually futile.

The *Council of Wales and the Marches* replaced the palatine jurisdiction of Chester. As that jurisdiction had disintegrated, the Council took over the responsibility for maintaining order in those turbulent parts, and by the time of Henry VIII certain members of the Council were specializing in this work. Statutory recognition was accorded to the court in 1542.

Similarly, the *Council of the North* partially replaced the palatine jurisdiction of Durham. The only Tudor administrative court without statutory basis or recognition, it came into being at the command of Henry VIII, after the Pilgrimage of Grace of 1536 had demonstrated the government's lack of control over the conservative north and its influential nobility. The court dealt in criminal and civil equity for the five northern counties. This latter jurisdiction did not go unchallenged by Elizabethan justices, who adopted the interesting position that while the crown could establish new *common law* courts without parliamentary action, it had to have parliamentary approval for any new "prerogative" tribunals!

The *Court of High Commission*, which received its name only in 1570, gave juridical expression to royal supremacy over the Church. Although earlier ecclesiastical courts remained, the crown needed a tribunal not bound by canon law to deal with issues impinging on the concept of royal supremacy, which meant a court working in *ecclesiastical equity*. Henry VIII, Edward VI, Mary I, and Elizabeth I (though for different reasons) had special commissions to enforce clerical conformity to their religious policies. Although brought into being by royal proclamations, these courts received a statutory basis in the Act of Uniformity of 1559, which authorized the crown to establish a commission for ecclesiastical *causes*, a very broad grant of jurisdiction.

Acting in terms of this statutory authorization, Elizabeth I created various *ad hoc* bodies, which gradually coalesced to form the Court of High Commission. Its first task was to compel the clergy to accept the Elizabethan Settlement. By the close of her reign this meant keeping a very close watch on the spread of Puritanism among the clergy and laity. The Puritans naturally resented the court and became increasingly critical of the other administrative tribunals as well. The Court of

High Commission was essentially secular in composition, with close links with the Council. Usually the court operated in panels of three members, one a prelate.

Like other administrative tribunals, but unlike older Church courts, High Commission employed summary procedures and even more than other administrative courts used written proof. However, common law justices and pleaders, seeing little danger to them from this administrative tribunal, firmly insisted that the statutory basis of the court gave it full powers to regulate religious opinion, subject only to the broad lines of doctrine set by Parliament.

Like other administrative courts, High Commission could use the procedure of the *ex-officio* oath. It also had sections traveling through the country whose principal function was to tender the oath of supremacy to all suspected of disloyalty and to report to the Council all refusals to take it. Like the Norman and Angevin *missi* [41] these traveling administrative agents employed the old inquest procedure from which had grown the jury of the common law. Any section of the court could swear in twelve men to answer questions about heresies, schisms, prolonged absenteeism from church, sedition, slander, and morality generally. Persons named by the inquests for such matters had to appear before the particular section of High Commission or the full body for further interrogation. This aspect of the court's work went far beyond its duty of securing clerical conformity.

The actual penalties permitted High Commission were limited. For clergy it could admonish, warn, fine, and occasionally imprison, or deprive the holder of a benefice. When dealing with laymen, the sectarians and their conventicles, High Commission often sent their victims on to Star Chamber for further action.

The *Court of Augmentations* was made necessary by the religious policy of Henry VIII. Purely administrative in its purpose of liquidating expropriated monastic properties, it was solely statutory in basis, resting squarely on a law of 1536. Under the direction of Cromwell, the court did its work swiftly.

The *Court of First Fruits and Tenths* adjudicated ecclesiastical payments due to the sovereign. Once paid to the papacy, these revenues were not as great as the crown had hoped, and the purpose of the court was to make sure that all those obliged to pay did so. The members of the court, knowing their duty and the king's financial plight, acquired

[41] Above, pp. 64–5.

a reputation for great avarice, and the court became the object of bitter criticism. It was abolished in 1641.

The *Court of Wards and Liveries* existed to ensure payment of feudal dues to the crown. Although these payments had declined with the disintegration of feudalism, the Tudors had no desire to see them disappear altogether. Wardship, one of the most lucrative of the various feudal incidents, Henry VIII made the responsibility of a Court of Feudal Wardships. It exercised feudal right of guardianship over minors and insane persons. Under a Master of Wards, the court had its own seal and was expected to exploit every possible advantage from the technicalities surrounding this incident of the all but dead feudalism. It became increasingly unpopular. It had the right to impose imprisonment summarily for failure to pay the amounts due to the crown from persons technically minor tenants-in-chief of the king, of whom there had been a considerable number since the legislation of Edward I.[42] Not surprisingly, the storm of 1641 blew away this court too; and the abolition of feudal military tenures in 1661 [43] precluded its re-establishment.

The *Court of Requests* was particularly abhorrent to common law supporters. This was the court which they had in mind when they subsequently flayed administrative courts as "prerogative" instruments of tyranny. Significantly, they dared not attack it directly, so great was its popularity, and it even survived the whirlwind of 1641 to live on, albeit in shadowy form, until 1873.

The court had its origins in the failure of Chancery to meet the needs of small men seeking equitable relief cheaply. Their custom of asking the Council to afford them such relief had received recognition in an ordinance of Edward III, which became a statute with Richard II. The overworked Council, however, could not cope with all these petitions and turned them over to the *Keeper of the Privy Seal,* who, like the Chancellors, until the appointment of Sir Thomas More was usually a churchman. His recommendations on these cases received a *pro forma* approval from the Council which soon permitted him to issue decrees on such matters under his own seal. The Chancellor did not object; his more lucrative judicial business and his greater proximity to the source of all equity, the king, removed any fears he might otherwise have had about possible competition from the Keeper of the Privy Seal.

[42] Above, p. 143.
[43] Below, p. 366.

The delegation by the Council of small equity business to this official had the usual result of producing a separate court under him. The process was completed when Henry VII reorganized the court. The Keeper became the *Lord* Privy Seal, and the king instructed other members of the Council to assist him on a *pro hac vice* basis in settling these small equity cases. About 1493 the court ceased to use the Council roll and began one of its own, and at about the same time it received the name of the Court of Petitions and Requests. Still very close to the royal person, it followed the king until 1516, when it came to rest at Westminster. However, the small traveling Council continued to act as a court of requests upon royal command, Henry VIII delighting in giving justice to his subjects by this means. Whether traveling or sitting, the court's personnel was closely linked with the Council, which continued to ratify its decrees, even if only as a formality, until 1516.

After 1516 the Court of Requests issued its own decrees. The volume of its business grew, and in 1550 it received two *Masters of Requests* to process cases and present their findings to the court for action. As a rule, however, the court merely ratified the findings of the masters, who thus became the functional court. Elizabeth named two additional masters, and by the reign of James I there were eight, technically still only assistants to the Lord Privy Seal and his colleagues from the Privy Council. But business was so brisk that any two masters could make recommendations, which amounted in effect to the decisions of the court.

It was at this point that the common law courts, or rather their justices and pleaders, realized that they were facing a potentially dangerous competitor. Like other courts before it, the Court of Requests had enlarged its jurisdiction and was giving remedies very similar to, but much cheaper than, those of Chancery. The common law courts had reason to fear such a court with these advantages to litigants, who might bring before it questions of land possession (particularly copyhold), usage of common lands, rights to tithes (possessed by certain laymen), and extents (the value of land). The court was also moving into cases of debt with speculation (bonds), executorships, what was left of villeinage, and water rights. It seemed but a little time before all civil cases would come into the Court of Requests, and common law courts would be empty, their justices and pleaders without fees.

The common law justices and pleaders of the Court of Common Pleas were particularly concerned. In 1590 Common Pleas began to issue writs of prohibition (injunctions) at the request of a respondent to a petition before the Court of Requests, forbidding its masters to process it. Since writs of prohibition were a monopoly of Chancery, the masters appealed those of Common Pleas to King's Bench, where the justices, however, supported their common law colleagues — and thereby extended the common law to include a remedy hitherto available only at equity.

In 1599 the justices of Common Pleas held, in the famous decision in Stephney v. Flood, that the Court of Requests could not enforce its decrees by imprisonment because it had never possessed proper jurisdiction over the case. This decision was a heavy blow to the Court of Requests. Again later, Sir Edward Coke, then Chief Justice of Common Pleas, ordered the release of a man from the Fleet Prison, lodged there for failure to fulfil a decree against him by the Court of Requests, on the grounds that the Court of Requests lacked the power to order imprisonment. Finally, King's Bench decided that false testimony in the Court of Requests was not perjury. Yet the Court of Requests was popular enough to survive even these attacks on its jurisdiction, and the masters did a large judicial business until the Civil War.

By the Restoration period judicial action had sufficiently reformed the common law [44] to make Requests, with its special concern for poor men, superfluous. The newly appointed masters found their chief business had become the processing of petitions from royalists claiming compensation for losses during the Civil War. When this work ended, there was little for the Court of Requests to do, and its masters became little more than clerks of Chancery. Thus, nearly forgotten, the Court of Requests lived on until its formal abolition in 1873.

It has been said that men charged with the administration of state policy are poor judges of issues arising from it; the state rather than the individual is placed first. The dangers inherent in Tudor administrative jurisprudence were clear to contemporaries trained in the common law, as they have been clear to historians since. But administrative adjudication was an expression of a new conception of government. The government believed that certain things had to be done for the good of the nation. The existing common law courts, rigidly bound by precedent in applying a law which often did not "know" these things, either could not or would not act. Therefore, the government created special bodies, manned by government administrators, conscious of the need for

[44] Below, pp. 403–4.

action. As administrators they were more interested in getting things done than in the niceties of legal speculation. Procedural forms meant little to them in their own courts, and they had no patience with the older formalities of the law courts which often served to defeat the ends for which their particular administrative court existed. The members of administrative tribunals saw in rigid procedural rules not protection for the individual, but barriers to the fulfillment of the greater needs of the nation, as these adjudicating bureaucrats conceived them to be.

The Tudor constitution was "modern" in its emphasis on the concept of "the state," which absorbed the Church and so was comprehensive. Such an emphasis on the administrative aspects of government was similarly modern. The dual control of crown and Parliament over the major facets of this state, however, precluded totalitarianism, while amateur, unpaid local administrators made central government dictation impossible. The modernity of the Tudor national constitution included the appearance of administrative adjudication and attacks on it by common law supporters, and the arguments for and against such administrative jurisprudence were similar to those of the twentieth century.

READING LIST

BEARD, CHARLES. *Justice of the Peace in England.*

ELTON, R. G. *The Tudor Revolution in Government.*

EVANS, F. M. G. *The Principal Secretary of State, 1558–1660.*

GASQUET, CARDINAL FRANCIS A. *Henry VIII and the English Monasteries.*

LEADAM, I. S., ed. *Select Cases in the Court of Requests* (Selden Society Publications, 1898, 1908).

NEALE, J. E. *The Elizabethan House of Commons.*

———. *Elizabeth I and her Parliaments, 1559–1581.*

PICKTHORN, K. W. M. *Early Tudor Government,* 2 vols. (Henry VII, Henry VIII).

PLUCKNETT, THEODORE F. T. *A Concise History of the Common Law,* Book I, Part II, Chaps. 7–8.

POLLARD, A. F. "Council, Star Chamber, and Privy Council under the Tudors," *English Historical Review,* XXXVII, 337, 516; XXXVIII, 42.

———. *Henry VIII.*

POWICKE, SIR FREDERICK M. *The Reformation in England.*

RICHARDSON, W. C. *Tudor Chamber Administration, 1485–1547.*

8

CROWN *VERSUS* PARLIAMENT

THE Tudor constitution, whether considering poor relief or setting forth the working relations between crown and Parliament, assumed a paternalistic direction by social superiors at the wish of subordinates. This assumption became unacceptable to many merchants and gentry; Sir Walter Raleigh in the early seventeenth century commented on a new type of man who had risen rapidly and was confident of his ability to do anything. Such a man resented paternal control and this fundamental social fact played an important part in the constitutional developments of the period.

The Constitutional Issue

The fundamental issue under the first two Stuarts turned on the relationship between crown and Parliament. In the past, no strong monarch had ever feared to summon Parliament — it enhanced his power. However, by the close of the Tudor period members of Parliament, especially those in the House of Commons, were very conscious of the role of Parliament in the nation-state; and it was precisely at this moment that the classes supplying the membership of the Commons found themselves in serious disagreement with the crown on policies of great concern to them. They were certain to use Parliament as a means of ,expressing, and if possible of redressing, their grievances. In doing so, they claimed for Parliament a much larger part in government than the Tudors had ever been prepared to allow. On both religious and financial policy Parliament was in almost constant opposition to the crown.

No large body of opinion in the early seventeenth century denied the right of the state to determine religious doctrine and practice for all of its members. This right, however, also involved the certainty that men with strong religious views would do everything within their power to gain control of the agencies performing this function. By the close of the Elizabethan period the crown was committed to preserving the *status quo* in the Church, and those who sought to advance to a more Protestant position could best hope to realize their ambition by using Parliament. From the conflict between these two positions large questions concerning the nature of the royal supremacy, and even concerning the position of the crown in the state, would arise.

Finance too was a permanent cause of discord. The Tudors had led the country out of the Middle Ages into modern times in most respects, but they had omitted to modernize their financial arrangements. The crown now found itself at the head of a prosperous modern nation-state, but with financial resources that were still essentially medieval. To supplement its income it was forced to adopt various devious and highly unpopular devices. The House of Commons sought to broaden the definition of a "tax," hitherto a direct levy upon individuals, to include any moneys paid to the crown. As it had long been accepted that only Parliament could levy taxes, this meant that the royal finances would have come completely under the control of Parliament. When the crown held to the older, narrower definition of a "tax," a second issue lay between it and its traditional supporters.

Religion and finance were vital questions, but in the end they came to be aspects of a still more fundamental issue — whether crown or Parliament was the ultimate authority in the nation-state, that new, all-embracing, all-powerful monolith. After the Tudors, neither crown nor Parliament could share power except to the extent that each was willing to delegate functions to the other, functions which the superior partner could always withdraw from its subordinate.

To view the conflict between crown and Parliament as one between royal tyranny and popular liberties is misleading. In the seventeenth century only a few men of wealth had the franchise and used it to return similar men to the House of Commons to represent their interests. It is, however, equally erroneous to consider the constitutional issue as being between a wise, far-seeing crown, imbued with a social conscience, and a few selfish men who saw in Parliament a means to further their anti-social ends. That James I and Charles I believed that they were ruling for the benefit of the entire nation, and that they were occasionally wiser than their opponents, cannot alter the fact that if successful their policies and methods would have led to royal absolutism on the Continental pattern. Similarly, that a few hard-faced men saw in

Parliament a vehicle to secure their own ends cannot obscure the fact that they developed certain concepts of parliamentary powers and individual rights, which if not initially forged for use by the mass of seventeenth-century Englishmen, proved essential for the full and free participation by their descendants in the twentieth-century state.

Appearance of Political Theory

The constitutional debate of the seventeenth century as to where the ultimate sovereignty in the nation-state was situated produced a spate of theories on the nature of the state, its government, and its proper concerns. Although much of this speculation was immature, particularly during the Interregnum, and had remarkably little influence even at the time, certain theories of the seventeenth century continue to influence men in the twentieth century.

The most popular political theory of the day was that of the Divine Right of Kings. It is necessary to make a sharp distinction between "liberal" and "popular" opinion, however, which rarely coincide. During the entire seventeenth century probably the majority of people did really believe that the king was more than other men. When as late as 1710, after the formal limitation of royal powers, the London mob surged into the streets to cheer a clergyman who denounced these limitations and to damn a government which prosecuted him for these views, it may be doubted whether the "common man" was a "liberal." Few people of the seventeenth century had any understanding of the modern English ideas of limited monarchy and popular sovereignty.

The theory of the Divine Right of Kings originated in the medieval conflict between popes and emperors. As the popes claimed supremacy by virtue of being the Vicar of Christ on earth, the emperors countered by saying that complete temporal power came to them by divine will. In the new nation-state, which in England had brought together temporal and ecclesiastical supremacy in the royal person, the occasion was even more propitious for the theory of the Divine Right of Kings. By the close of the sixteenth century many serious thinkers in Europe were supporting the theory as the ethical justification for royal absolutism.

One of the better expressions of the theory was the *True Law of Free Monarchies*, written by James VI of Scotland in 1598, as a protest against the pretensions by the Calvinistic clergy, as "godly and elect" men, to control state policy on the model of Geneva. Using their authority, the Bible, and the patristic literature of the Church, James sought to prove that monarchy per se was a divine institution. Therefore, (1) the person essential to the divine institution of monarchy, the king, was divinely chosen, and resistance to him was at least a sin against God; (2) in the exercise of his divinely ordained office, which had been divinely entrusted to him, the king possessed divinely bestowed powers, which could not be lawfully diminished by any mortal, not even by the king himself. To reduce, or attempt to reduce, these powers was thus an affront to God.[1]

No such affront, of course, had been committed by, or under, the Tudors; the great departments of state, the courts, the law, and equity were all extensions of the royal prerogative. The Tudors, whether they were interested in the theoretical basis or not, had actually acted as if by divine right — as the royal Scottish author saw clearly from across the border. When he jolted across it in 1603 on his southward journey to London, he anticipated no difficulties as James I of England.

Neither James I (1603–25) nor his son, Charles I (1625–49), an equally zealous believer in the theory, regarded it as justifying cruel and tyrannical rule; God would punish such a misuse of His gifts. Neither king believed that the theory allowed him to flout the law, either statutory or customary. When Dr. John Cowell, a Cambridge professor of civil (Roman) law, in his *Interpreter*, argued that the king was above the law, James I in 1610 ordered the suppression of the book as being false to the idea of the "marriage between the prerogative and the common law."

This self-denying statement echoed the Tudor, and particularly the Elizabethan, conception of the prerogative, saying that it operated in areas where the law was silent. The first Stuart was on a throne where for nearly half a century a dominant Tudor had exercised her prerogative in such a way that she had consistently turned to Parliament for statutes and for taxes; had used it for other matters (notably religious) at her discretion; but in all else had insisted that the crown could (and perhaps had to) act without Parliament. Certainly it never occurred to Elizabeth that it was possible for any agency to reduce the royal prerogative.

James I and Charles I adhered to this position at a time when the new

---

[1] J. R. Tanner, *Constitutional Documents of the Reign of James I*, 202. Henceforth cited as Tanner.

men described by Raleigh were seeking to use Parliament to make major changes in state religion and public finance. Elizabeth had barely managed, by a mixture of sternness and cajolery, to keep them in check. These men, with James I and Charles I, believed that God would punish wicked rulers; but unlike either monarch they believed, not in the discretionary right but the obligatory *duty* of "godly" men to insist that the king do "right." Although these people in the early seventeenth century would have shuddered at the idea of rebellion, their characteristic Puritan belief in a direct channel of communication and responsibility between God and the individual made them inject the element of moral judgment into the constitutional issues of their times. This ethical criterion reinforced their dislike of royal paternalism exercised through the prerogative when, in their opinion, it was used for "wrongful" ends. This same moral judgment impelled them inexorably from one step to the next until they were fighting a "righteous" war against Charles I, a "man of blood," whom they executed as an "act of grace."

The clergy of the Church of England, whose head was the king, had become vigorous supporters of his authority. One of the 141 canons submitted by the Convocations in 1604 to James I for his approval [2] enjoined obedience to the king by all true Christians. Bishops continued their tacit Elizabethan alliance with the Stuart crown, particularly during the reign of Charles I, whose leanings were toward the High Church doctrines of Archbishop William Laud. This alliance brought to episcopal thrones men whose only real hope of maintaining discipline over their clergy and laity lay in their own complete support of royal power.

The Church of England was not alone in supporting royal power. Despite the fears of James I, Calvinism per se was not opposed to monarchy, even strong monarchy. Resistance to the king by individuals found little approval in a theology which regarded most of them as predestined to eternal damnation. John Calvin had urged obedience to secular rulers. The chief exponent of Elizabethan Calvinism, Thomas Cartwright, would grant only to the Church as an institution the right to resist a wicked ruler, and denied utterly the right of individuals to resist. English Presbyterians, unlike their Scottish brethren, planned no theocratic state on the Geneva model, but were Erastian, aiming at a

---

[2] So that James met squarely what Elizabeth had evaded as to whether the crown could exercise its supremacy over the Church via the Convocations without reference to Parliament; see above, pp. 266, 269.

Presbyterian state church in which the ecclesiastical authority would be subordinate to the secular. English Presbyterians were so uneasy about resisting the king that at the very end of the tragedy of Charles I their representatives had to be expelled from the House of Commons before it could bring the king to trial.

At the close of the seventeenth century resistance to the monarch appeared to the mass of men the sin it had been at its opening. Sir Robert Filmer set down the traditional English view about obedience to the king in 1640, as the constitutional issue was approaching its climax. Although not published for another 40 years, his *Patriarcha* expressed the theory of Divine Right to the satisfaction of most seventeenth-century, Bible-reading Englishmen; God had given Adam and then Noah certain rights, which He then entailed through the Stuart crown. The appearance of Filmer's work in 1680, in the midst of the struggle to exclude James, Duke of York, from the throne, revived popular and traditional feelings about the sanctity of kingship and the divine rule of its descent by primogeniture.

William Prynne, whose *Sovereign Power of Parliaments* appeared in 1643, a year after the outbreak of the Civil War, took a different line, however. Looking back on English constitutional history, Prynne declared that Parliament was superior to the king and was therefore free, if it so wished, to replace him by another.[3] John Milton in *The Tenure of Kings and Magistrates*, 1649, went even further. He was attempting to justify to fainthearted Presbyterians the execution of Charles I,[4] and in doing so introduced theories of popular sovereignty which were several generations ahead of their time. Like Thomas Jefferson, he argued that the people could replace any regime with any other at their discretion, a view that has never been popular with any government at any time.

Growing Friction

Between the accession of James I in 1603 and the decision by Charles I in 1629 to rule without Parliament, several points of friction between crown and Parliament became dangerously heated. The various issues were all closely tied up with each other, and only the

[3] The work was in the form of a popular pamphlet.
[4] Milton's hints, however, of the "right" of rebellion against an unpopular government made his views of dubious merit to Interregnum regimes.

plea of clarity justifies their separate analysis. However, basic to them all was the refusal of Parliament to accept its Elizabethan role and the insistence of the Stuarts that it should do so.

The members of the House of Commons had benefited from Tudor commercial treaties, from the confiscation of monastic properties, and from the tacit encouragement of agricultural enclosure. By the early seventeenth century the wealth of these people was considerable, and the status and influence it gave them in the country were sufficient to provide the confidence needed for sustained opposition to the crown. The House of Lords, on the other hand, was much more submissive. The crown could create peers, and both James I and Charles I did so. There were 59 peers in 1603, about 150 in 1642; the presence of the upstarts was often deeply resented by peers who could trace their titles back for about two generations. Even so, the crown could not be certain of the Lords and received only intermittent support from them. The Lords often approved proposals from the Commons, and more than one peer carried on a covert opposition to royal policies through relatives and clients in the lower House.

Whereas the Tudors had manned their Privy Council with skillful professional politicians like Cromwell and Cecil, the Stuarts preferred their personal favorites, such as the Duke of Buckingham, who received vast patronage and dispensed it in a foolish and frivolous manner, harmful to the true interests of his royal patrons and ruinous from the point of view of efficient administration. Finding the door to preferment closed to them, the ambitious and hard-working politicians of the early seventeenth century expended their energies in the House of Commons, in opposition to the king.

The crown steadily lost control over the House of Commons. The early Stuarts were poor parliamentary managers. The Tudors had always seen to it that important members of the Privy Council had what would now be termed "safe seats" in the House of Commons; the Stuarts failed to do so. In part they suffered from the natural desire of faithful servants for peerages. Thus Sir Robert Cecil, the son of the great William Cecil, whom Elizabeth I had created Lord Burghley for his years of faithful service to her, had served that queen and James I well. It was natural he should want and the king grant him a peerage as the Earl of Salisbury, but the royal reward meant that the Lord Treasurer moved from the House of Commons to the upper House. Similarly, Sir Francis Bacon wanted and deserved to be Lord Chancellor, and the king gladly made him Lord Verulam; but again, a royal servant of real ability left the lower for the upper House.

To fill the vacancies left by such men in the House of Commons with men of similar caliber proved beyond the slender election resources of the Stuarts. The first elections of James I in 1604 saw the new men of Buckinghamshire turn aside Sir John Fortescue, a privy councillor, and elect instead Sir Francis Goodwin, an outlaw (by reason, however, of his contumacy in a civil, not a criminal, action). Chancery, which issued the election writs, examined their returns and invalidated Goodwin's election because of this outlawry. A new election writ from Chancery resulted in Fortescue's election. Here the matter might have ended, except that the House of Commons objected to the procedure used to invalidate the first election. When Parliament assembled, the House, as in the Norfolk election case of 1586,[5] protested and named a committee to investigate the merits of the first election. In 1586 Elizabeth had seen what was afoot and had let the two Norfolk members take their seats. However, in 1604, before James could act, the committee reported that Goodwin was not an outlaw (which he was); that even if he were, he could still sit (which he could not); and that at all events, the House was the sole judge of elections to it.[6] This, in fact, was the crux of the matter and the new king, unlike his predecessor, was forced to face it.

James first declared that Chancery as the writ-issuing agency was the sole judge of the returns, only to retreat from this legally strong position into a "compromise," whereby the House of Commons would have concurrent jurisdiction with Chancery over election returns. He then said there would be a third election in Buckinghamshire, with the understanding that Fortescue would be returned unopposed. The House of Commons accepted this plan, because it was a complete concession by the crown of a claim never conceded by the Tudors. The proposed concurrent jurisdiction between the House and Chancery was impractical; and the crown never again had Chancery examine returns, leaving the House of Commons with sole jurisdiction over disputed elections. The government was left with an acceptable member from Buckinghamshire and little control over future elections.

Without this reserve power of Chancery, the crown's slight election resources were insufficient to win elections, as James discovered

[5] Above, p. 241.
[6] Tanner, 202. Consistent with seventeenth-century freedom of spelling, "Goodwin" is frequently "Godwin."

after his strenuous efforts on the next occasion to win a favorable Commons. The result was the "Addled Parliament" of 1614. His election agents, *undertakers*, failed dismally to get a majority for the crown, and only succeeded in antagonizing local magnates with vested interests in seats. After this failure, the Stuarts made no further serious attempts to win elections.

The crown's loss of control of the Commons came from no lack of understanding of its importance, and the royal concession about disputed elections showed the desire of the new monarch to work with the House of Commons of his new kingdom. But once the "official" party of privy councillors had disappeared or proved itself inept, the management of the House fell into the hands of an "unofficial" group capable of wielding a similar influence. This group carefully planned its tactics on a sessional and even a daily basis, and much of the trouble of James I and Charles I with the Commons came from the ineffectiveness of its "official" element. The average member of the early Stuart Parliaments was no more familiar with public issues than his Tudor predecessor and wanted leadership. When the crown failed to provide it, he turned to this newer managerial group, whose members made it a point to keep abreast of public events. The few times during the early reign of James I that his privy councillors in the House insisted on formal votes, the official view had majority support; but these occasions were too infrequent to be of benefit to the crown and soon ceased. By the reign of Charles I the leadership of the House had passed to such antagonists of royal policy as Sir Thomas Wentworth and Sir Edward Coke, then to the more radical Sir John Eliot and finally to John Pym. The inability of the crown to defeat such men in elections was revealed when in 1626 the government named Wentworth and Coke sheriffs to render them ineligible for the forthcoming House of Commons.[7]

The new managers of the House of Commons changed its procedure to reduce crown influence still further. During the early seventeenth century the House began to give every bill three "readings," each followed by a vote to determine whether it should move on to the

[7] As returning officers, sheriffs were barred from the House. Heavy fines for refusal of the office caused Wentworth and Coke to accept it. With the death of Coke and the shift of Wentworth to the side of the crown (below, p. 307), the government did not repeat this tactic. After 1629 the personal rule of Charles I made it essential that only persons supporting him should hold the office of sheriff.

next. The first reading, in time to become a formality, was on the measure's subject; the second on its principles; and the third on the bill with such changes as had been made since its introduction. Previously, the "sense" of the House had suggested changes to its privy councillor members. During the reign of James I the unofficial leaders of the House interposed between the second and third readings the new stage of the *committee of the whole House,* later used also by the House of Lords. Though all members sat on "the committee of the whole," the royally-approved Speaker left the chair in favor of the *chairman of committees,* named by the House without reference to the crown. In the committee of the whole the crown's control over bills was lost; they might be altered drastically or even killed in committee simply by not reporting them out to the House as such.

Thus crown control disappeared over the agenda of the House of Commons, which the Tudors had correctly viewed as essential and which was the fundamental presumption underlying their management of Parliament. And soon the new leadership of the Commons actually drafted and introduced measures without consulting the crown.

The Issue of Religion

On religious matters James I and Charles I held to the Elizabethan position that such topics could come to Parliament only on the initiative of the royal head of the Church, who could operate equally through the Convocations. However, at the beginning of the reign of James I religious reformers were not rigidly committed to parliamentary action, and it was a matter of indifference to them whether Parliament or the king gave the Church a more Protestant orientation. As James bumped southward, he received the *Millenary Petition,*[8] claiming to express the views of over a thousand clergy, and asking for certain changes of a broadly Puritan nature in the Church. The king replied by summoning a conference between some bishops and Puritan clergy at Hampton Court in January 1604 to discuss the points of the petition. This action was consistent with James's attitude toward the royal supremacy, and in 1604 Puritan reformers had no real objection to it. James, who was unusually tolerant for his time and an amateur theologian of some merit, was not firmly committed to every aspect of the rituals or even of the doctrines of the Church. However, the

[8] Tanner, 56.

Puritan group was quite wrong in assuming that as a member of the Church of Scotland James would support changes of a Presbyterian nature in the Church of England.

James presided at the Hampton Court Conference, and all went smoothly until one of the Puritan clergy uttered the fatal word, "presbyter." Conditioned by his unhappy experiences in Scotland, James flatly declared that a Presbyterian system of ecclesiastical organization agreed with monarchy as well as the devil did with God; he ordered the Puritan clergy to obey their bishops, repeating "No bishop, no king," and abruptly ended the conference. Its only positive result, but that one monumental, was a new version of the Bible, the appearance of which in 1611 revealed one of the greatest achievements of Elizabethan English.

James met squarely the issue his predecessor had evaded in giving his assent to the canons submitted to him by the Convocations in 1604 without reference to Parliament.[9] When the House of Commons the same year touched on some of the matters raised in the Millenary Petition, James rebuked the members. Although the House in its subsequent *Apology* [10] claimed, among other things, the right to legislate on religious matters, Puritan reformers were not yet insistent on this point. If James and the new Archbishop of Canterbury, Richard Bancroft, insisted that the clergy use only the services in the Prayer Book and subscribe to the Thirty-nine Articles (thereby causing some 200 clergy to lose their posts), the crown by administrative action also dealt with some of the important grievances enumerated in the Millenary Petition. Pluralism (holding more than one Church post) was reduced, preaching by clergy was encouraged, and baptism by women was forbidden. These manifestations of a non-parliamentary royal supremacy satisfied many of the clergy and laity during the reign of James.

Those reformers not content with these changes were certain to turn from a crown which would go no further to Parliament, and thereby raise the question of its ability to initiate legislation for the Church without previous sanction by its royal head. This move, however, was tentative and incomplete during the reign of James. The Puritan group contained persons of such diverse aims that it lacked cohesion or a legislative program. Some men would have gone only a

---

[9] Above, p. 269.
[10] Below, pp. 301–2.

little way in the modification of ritual; some further. Doctrine concerned certain people but not others. Only a few at the time were
opposed to the episcopal organization of the Church; and only a tiny
segment — without sympathy from the mass of Puritans — argued for
a system of independent congregations, each having full control over
its belief and services. It was very difficult for these diverse groups to
agree on a single program, and James's own relative indifference to
the precise nature of the rituals of the Church kept Puritanism a vague
body of discontent during his reign. Though within a particular diocese
there might be conformity to the orders of its bishop, from diocese to
diocese there were variations in episcopal policy.

Charles I, however, introduced some cohesion and unity by making abundantly clear to the Puritans what they did *not* want. In supporting the High Church party, whose every attitude was anathema to
Puritans, he antagonized men of various faiths and brought them together on a common platform. Generally ignored by James I, the High
Church group, or "New School," under the direction of William Laud,
aimed at a *less* Protestant Church with more elaborate services and
doctrines which, to the Puritans at least, smacked of popery. From
the outset of his reign Charles I associated the royal supremacy with
this element, and Laud, even before becoming Archbishop of Canterbury in 1633, was advising the king on his selection of bishops. The
Laudian bishops, with royal support, compelled the parish clergy to
conform to High Church practices and employed the Court of High
Commission to achieve this goal. Parish clergy therefore either conformed or lost their posts. Country squires and urban merchants
saw the communion table removed from their midst in the congregation
to the far end of the church to become the altar, separated from
the laity by a rail. When from behind it a priest in elaborate vestments knelt in prayer, made the sign of the cross, and required them
to kneel at the altar rail while he delivered them the sacrament, they
were certain that Charles and Laud were leading honest, Protestant
Englishmen back to Rome by the back door.

Neither Charles nor Laud was, in fact, pro-Catholic, but each was
in an awkward position. Charles had a French, Catholic queen; and
the marriage treaty required him to relax penal laws against English
Catholics. Laud, although willing to have a rather wide variation in
belief among both clergy and laity — more than some of his Puritan
opponents would have allowed — emphasized that although the Church

of Rome was presently in regrettable error, it was equally with the Church of England a true descendant from the Church of the Apostles.

The alliance between the New School and the crown had inevitable constitutional results. The High Church clergy exalted the royal authority everywhere. Puritans, now fearful of popery, supported the full legislative competence of Parliament over the Church without regard to a royal supremacy, which seemed bent on returning to Rome. Thus the dichotomy of the religious settlement of Henry VIII and Elizabeth I came to stand forth clearly — royal supremacy meant control over the hierarchy, and so of all ecclesiastics; but Parliament had the strongest of Tudor precedents for acting on doctrine and so on any matter touching it, including ritual. Such an arrangement could only work when crown and Parliament were in essential agreement.

Between 1625 and 1629, when Charles I was trying to work with Parliament, each session saw gentry and merchants in the House of Commons protesting against "innovations" in the Church, only to be told that ecclesiastical administration lay solely with the crown. In 1625 Puritans in the House asked the king to improve the salaries of parish clergy, to allow more preaching, to reduce ceremony, and to concentrate on recruiting a better type of parish clergy. The crown was silent to these requests; but it made its position clear when a Laudian priest, briefly jailed by the House of Commons, was appointed a royal chaplain. In 1626 complaints from the House about the New School became louder, and by 1628 there was a growing belief that if the head of the Church would not save it from creeping popery, Parliament would have to.

The Problem of Finance

Neither James I nor Charles I solved the problem, bequeathed by the Tudors, of spiraling prices and fixed royal revenues; neither did Parliament. All Englishmen were reluctant to admit that the happy days, when Parliament taxed for a war but otherwise the king "lived of his own," had gone forever. The first two Stuarts, ignorant of the techniques of long-term and deficit public financing, found their financial difficulties steadily increasing; from 1603 to 1608 there was an annual deficit of £90,000. For its part Parliament felt that James I and Charles I were extravagant; and there was some truth in this charge for James, who, after a penurious youth, had become in his

new kingdom that fascinating specimen, as extravagant Scot, with a
splendid court cluttered with royal favorites to whom he acted with
great generosity. To the simple-living squires and businesslike merchants
in the House of Commons, there was something wrong about the constant royal need for money.

Like any executive, James objected to legislative efforts to reduce
his traditional sources of revenue. His first Parliament gave him the
right to levy tunnage and poundage for the duration of his reign; but
it also complained about purveyance, whereby, despite no less than
36 statutes against it, the crown was still taking goods and paying for
them at its own rates. Some merchants raised the issue of monopolies,
the sale of which had been an important source of revenue for the
Elizabethan crown. James might have explained that to abolish these
financial resources of the crown would entail taxes to replace them.
But instead he adopted an Elizabethan tone, that did not so well become
him, and ordered the House of Commons, which had been discussing
religious matters and its privileges generally, to return to its officially
prepared agenda. The reply of the House of Commons in its *Apology* [11]
gave the king little financial consolation.

The attitude of the mercantile element toward prerogative sources
of revenue was revealed after Parliament rose. A certain Bates refused
in 1606 to pay a 6d duty on some Levantine currants on the grounds
that it had been imposed by the Council (as in the past), whereas it
was a tax and as such could only be levied by Parliament. This novel
idea was dismissed by the Exchequer Court, which held that the duty
was not a tax and that the king had the right to impose such duties as
part of his prerogative with regard to foreign affairs. Although the
justices were in fact uncertain whether the crown could lay such
impositions for general revenue purposes as well as for regulating
foreign trade, the decision of the Court was encouraging to the king.
On the strength of it, James boldly increased old imposts and added
new ones. Resultant revenues were still not nearly sufficient to meet
royal needs, however, and in 1610 the king called Parliament.

When Parliament met, the merchants introduced into the Commons
a resolution deploring the decision in the Bates Case; but a bill to
abolish such conciliar impositions failed in the House of Lords. The
merchants then persuaded the lower House to propose a typical commercial bargain, whereby the crown would surrender its rights to

[11] Below, pp. 301-2.

feudal dues, purveyance, and impositions in return for an annual sum of £200,000. In his response to this *Great Contrast*,[12] James equivocated. Under the careful supervision of Salisbury, the first two items were now producing £115,000 annually, and revenues from impositions had been rising since the Bates Case decision. At the next session James demanded a further £100,000, parliamentary opposition stiffened, and eventually the Great Contract was dropped.

James then decided that the House had no right to discuss impositions which were part of his prerogative by divine will and also sanctioned by judicial decision. This brought forward the whole issue of free speech, and the House stopped working until the king removed his prohibition. Tempers began to fray; and as the session moved into 1611, it became obvious that no agreement would be possible. Finally, in a fit of rage, James dissolved Parliament.

When his next Parliament met in 1614, James again heard mercantile complaints about impositions and with them questions about the definitions of taxes and royal powers generally. When, despite royal warnings, the House of Commons continued to debate these topics and even passed a resolution against conciliar levies, James again dissolved Parliament, whose labors of a bare two months had produced only squabbles.

For the next seven years the crown tried to do without taxes, which was not an impossible task. Prerogative revenues, now that they included the increased customs, permitted the government to operate if it husbanded its resources. James also sold titles and honors, with a definite price for each rank in the peerage. For those unable to afford a peerage, there was the new rank of baronet, an hereditary knighthood. More distressing for his subjects was the revival of benevolences, last employed during the reign of Henry VIII. Twice called for by James between 1614 and 1621, benevolences now provoked vigorous criticism, which the Star Chamber punished with fines.

By 1621, with war against Spain and probable intervention in the Thirty Years' War imminent, the government was again compelled to summon Parliament. Parliament was in favor of war and voted a token grant as a sign of its good intentions; whereupon it turned to debate high policy and how best to conduct the war, matters which James, like Elizabeth, felt were quite outside its competence.[13] The

[12] Tanner, 345.
[13] Below, p. 299.

Commons also irritated James by again attacking monopolies, passing a resolution declaring them to be illegal. Later in the session the House passed a measure abolishing them, but the peers took no action on it. Nevertheless, the crown did cancel some of the more irritating monopolies. When the Commons, however, continued to discuss policy instead of voting money for the war, relations between the House and the king again deteriorated, with the Commons presenting its *Great Protestation*,[14] and the king replying by dissolving Parliament.

In 1624 Prince Charles and his friend, the Duke of Buckingham, returned from an unsuccessful wooing in Spain to demand immediate war with that country. James again summoned Parliament, which upon hearing his promise to give a full account of the futile negotiations with Spain, voted a large grant and promised as much as was needed to prosecute the war.

With their generosity, however, the leaders of the Commons forced through Parliament a measure, to which James gave a reluctant assent, abolishing monopolies for private persons except those granted by open (patent) letters from the crown for the exploitation of inventions; and these last were to be limited to twenty-one years.

James I died in 1625. His son, Charles I, was faced with war with Spain and also soon afterwards war with France. As Parliament had been warmly in favor of both these enterprises, Charles reasoned that it was its duty to provide the funds to prosecute them successfully. When instead, in 1625, Parliament debated the conduct of Buckingham and the recent "innovations" in the Church, the king was irritated and dissolved Parliament before it voted money. Another Parliament the next year acted similarly and suffered the same fate.

Without funds from Parliament, the crown could hardly conduct a vigorous war. The king took such undignified actions as mortgaging the crown lands and pawning the royal jewels, but these were futile gestures. When he attempted to raise a benevolence, it was a complete failure; and there was a significant refusal by the justices of the peace to press people to pay. Charles, thereupon, tried a forced loan, with individuals to subscribe amounts equal to their assessments had Parliament voted five subsidies, about £350,000. When Chief Justice Crewe doubted the legality of the demand, he lost his post; but there was passive resistance to the loan on a large scale, and in 1628 Charles was compelled to try Parliament again.

[14] For a further discussion of the Great Protestation, see below, p. 303.

Parliamentary Control of Policy

After the experiences of the past year, Parliament assembled in an ugly humor. The conflict between crown and Parliament over religious and financial issues had brought forward a third issue, the right of Parliament to exercise control over royal policy. This came to a head when Parliament pressed the crown to make large changes in its foreign policy. With the possible exception of the Lancastrian period, Parliament had not participated actively in the formation of policy, except indirectly by its ability to grant funds. For policies whose implementation did not require parliamentary grants, the crown could, and usually did, operate without reference to Parliament. There was some historical support for the view of James I that great policy of state was "king's craft" and not a fit topic for parliamentary discussion; and every executive down to the present has always been unhappy when the legislature has turned its hand to policy formation.

Although not part of their original program, the rising class of new men came to regard parliamentary control of royal policy as essential, because they disagreed with James and Charles in religion, finance, and now foreign policy. The mechanics for such control, however, hardly existed. The king selected his Privy Council, whose opinions might not bind, but certainly influenced him. The suggestion in the *Apology* [15] that the king should listen to the opinions of the Commons in framing policy was actually little more than the hope that the Tudor practice of having privy councillors in the House to relay its "sense" to the king should continue. Certain of the more able of James's councillors, notably Sir Francis Bacon and Salisbury, urged the king at least to consider the views of the Commons.

By 1621, the new leadership of the House had little faith that the crown would act in this manner, and it turned on those advisers of the king who seemed to be encouraging him to flout the views of the House of Commons. When this unofficial leadership revived the process of impeachment against these men, it acquired a very dangerous weapon. Two notorious monopolists were accused and condemned by the Commons, and their decision was upheld by the Lords. This success encouraged the leaders of the lower House to turn on the second officer

[15] Below, pp. 301–2.

of the state, Lord Chancellor Verulam, better known as Sir Francis Bacon. He was charged with corruption, with having accepted gifts from suitors in the Court of Chancery. He admitted the charges, though he claimed that he had never allowed such gifts to influence his decisions. No doubt many members of Parliament were genuinely shocked to discover corruption in so exalted a personage. But he had also given offense to Parliament, both by his views on the relations of the law courts with the crown and Chancery and by persuading James on occasion to ignore the demands of some of the more truculent spirits in the Commons. When the king tried to save his most able councillor with a suggestion that a mixed commission of peers and commoners selected by the crown should try Bacon, the House of Lords asserted its sole right to try impeachments. The Lord Chancellor, however, was spared the ordeal of trial by pleading guilty. He was fined £40,000 by the House of Lords, barred from holding office, and forbidden to come near any place where a court was sitting, lest he contaminate it.

Meanwhile, much to the alarm of English Protestants, Catholic forces in Germany were sweeping all before them in the first stages of the Thirty Years' War. Among the victims was the former Elector of the Palatinate, James's son-in-law. In 1621 the Commons wanted war with Spain for both religious and commercial reasons. The Spanish ambassador, who was making every effort to keep England neutral, lulled James into believing that his royal status would permit him to mediate between the belligerents. Flattered, and essentially a man of peace, James began negotiations for a marriage between Prince Charles and a Spanish princess. The House of Commons boldly demanded war with Spain and a Protestant wife for Charles; James, as was to be expected, denied its right to deal in such great matters.

The reaction of the House of Commons was to demand royal confirmation of its privileges, including that of free speech, which by now implied the right of the House to determine its own agenda. When James answered that undoubtedly the House had this and other privileges, but that they emanated from the crown, he may have been historically correct, but tactically he was making a bad mistake. The situation called for Elizabethan tact, not Jacobean didacticism. Not having received royal blandishments, but a lecture, the House of Commons retorted with its *Great Protestation*,[16] the very name of

[16] Below, p. 303.

which indicates how things had changed in the seventeen years since the House had presented the *Apology*. James dissolved Parliament.

James, in his last Parliament of 1624, in spite of his cherished hopes for peace, allowed Prince Charles and Buckingham to put forward their plans for a war with Spain. When Lord Treasurer Middlesex resisted them, the prince and Buckingham connived with the House of Commons to impeach him, technically for corruption, really for his pro-Spanish attitude. He was convicted by the Lords. James, wise in his old age, warned his son that he would soon get a "bellyful of impeachments."

Only two years later, Charles was dissolving Parliament to save Buckingham from impeachment. Sir John Eliot pressed charges against the duke for the disastrous expedition to Cadiz the previous year. When the Commons voted the impeachment, and Eliot and Dudley Digges appeared in the House of Lords to prosecute the charges, Charles ordered the two members jailed and had the case transferred from the jurisdiction of the House of Lords, despite its protests, to Star Chamber, where Buckingham was acquitted. When the Commons with the support of an angry House of Lords declared that there had been no true impeachment trial and refused to vote funds until there was one, the king dissolved Parliament.

As a method of controlling crown policy, let alone participating in its formation, impeachment was peculiarly sterile, almost negative, a locking of the door after the horse had gone. Although it might be a warning to privy councillors not to persist in policies unpopular with the Commons, it scarcely gave that body a share in shaping future royal policies. England went to war against Spain and then France less because of the attitude of the House of Commons than because Charles and Buckingham wanted war. The Parliament which impeached Middlesex, was unable, despite formal petitions from both Houses, to prevent James from negotiating a marriage for Charles with a French, Catholic princess in a treaty committing the government to relax anti-Catholic laws, which was subsequently to be a cause of embarrassment to Charles and of grave misgivings to Parliament.

At the close of the second Parliament of Charles in 1626, the new leadership of the House of Commons had remarkably little to show in the way of positive achievements. Its design to use Parliament to create a truly Protestant Church had not merely been checked by royal supremacy, but had received a considerable set-back from the Laudian

New School. The hope of broadening the definition of taxes, and thus parliamentary control over finances, had been in vain and had acquired no judicial sanction. Efforts to control or initiate policy had met with no success.

Parliamentary Privileges

If the new men were to play a larger role in government, there had to be some radical changes in the traditional definition of parlia mentary privileges. Some steps had already been made in this direction. James had conceded the entire claim of the House to decide *disputed elections* in 1604,[17] and in the same year had approved a bill ensuring the privilege of *freedom from arrest* in civil actions. This issue arose out of the refusal of the Warden of the Fleet Prison to release Sir Thomas Shirley, a member of the House lodged there for debt, on the grounds that anyone releasing Shirley would become liable for his debt. The House of Commons successfully appealed to James to order the warden to free Shirley. Parliament then passed, and the king assented to, a statute declaring that the privilege existed during the session and forty days on either side of it.

Certain attitudes had been advanced also by the *Apology* of 1604. This not only expressed Parliament's fears that its privileges were being ignored or abused, but announced the program of changes that the Commons felt were necessary for the well-being of the realm. Thus the *Apology* suggested that certain small changes might be made in some Church services without much harm and perhaps with great bene fit by removing points of contention. It went on to claim that only the king in Parliament could make these or any other modifications in the Church. When it came to the privilege of freedom of speech, the *Apology* took up a position it was to maintain over the next forty years — the privileges of the House of Commons represented the essential liberties of the people of England. Only the respect owed by all members to Parliament, which included the two Houses and the king as a single entity, limited their freedom. In using this phraseology, the *Apology* borrowed from James's opening speech to his first Parlia ment, but it used his words to imply that the king could not interfere in debates. Here was a new departure. No monarch had ever believed for a moment that the crown could not intervene in parliamentary pro-

[17] Above, p. 289.

ceedings whenever it chose. It was also at this point that the *Apology* made another break with the past by claiming that the privileges of Parliament thus detailed were the unique possession of the House of Commons by inherent right and not by any royal grant. However erroneous historically this claim might be, if the House succeeded in winning it, henceforth the definition of its privileges and their extent would be entirely in its own hands.

Neither James I nor his Privy Council seems to have been greatly disturbed by the *Apology*, and indeed it is doubtful whether it was in fact ever presented to the king. But the statement had been made, and though the Commons might in future be preoccupied with specific issues as they arose, rather than with the general principles underlying them, it had defined its privileges to its own satisfaction and left a document to which it could always refer.

The *Apology* did not define precisely the privilege of freedom from arrest, with the result that both James and Charles were able to adhere to the traditional definition, now embodied in statute, that the privilege meant freedom only from civil arrest. After the brief Parliament of 1614 James jailed certain members who had spoken sharply about his prerogative. Since Parliament was not in session, it could not enforce the privilege, even assuming that it had been violated. In 1621 James, acting on the Tudor principle that the crown could commit members for contemptuous remarks, ordered the Earl of Southampton of the Lords and Sir Edward Sandys of the Commons to be imprisoned for encouraging opposition to royal policies. Both Houses threatened to do no work until their members were released and demanded that the king should admit that only the particular House concerned could punish for contemptuous remarks made in it. James released both men, but emphasized that he did so only as an act of grace and not out of any recognition of the claim by the two Houses.

Five years later, with Parliament in session, the House of Lords freed the Earl of Bristol, jailed by Charles I for attacks on Buckingham, by threats of a legislative strike. But although Parliament was far from acquiescent, as it had often been under Elizabeth, and was willing to enforce the privilege of freedom from arrest against the crown, it was still only able to do so while in session. The moment Parliament rose, the crown could deal harshly with members who had opposed it regularly during the session. Thus, following the dissolution of Parliament in 1626, the king sent Sir John Eliot and Dudley Digges to the

Tower for daring to initiate the abortive impeachment against Buckingham. The two men remained imprisoned until royal orders freed them.

Such highhanded actions were an infringement of Parliament's privilege of free speech, if that privilege were interpreted as the right to discuss anything, and not merely what the king had placed before it. But the actions of James in 1614 and 1621 in jailing members, obviously for their opposition to royal policy, indicated that he still upheld the traditional Tudor interpretation. In 1621, after James had rebuked the House of Commons for meddling in foreign policy, the members asked him to confirm their right of free speech, which the king did in the traditional manner. Such a confirmation did not satisfy the leadership of the House of Commons. In much stronger terms than the *Apology*, the Commons now defined the privilege of free speech as being the right of any member to speak on any matter of concern to the realm; this momentous declaration was entered into its Journal as the *Great Protestation*. Yet for the moment it did no good. James dissolved Parliament, sent for the Common's Journal, and tore out the offending page. He then imprisoned Sir Edward Coke and two other members for the part they had played in encouraging this impertinence, and John Pym was placed under house arrest.

James, however, was not consistent. Only three years later, hostility to Spain giving him for once something in common with his Parliament, the king tacitly admitted the broader interpretation of the privilege by not merely promising Parliament to reveal what had occurred in the negotiations with Spain, but urging members to speak freely on foreign affairs. This concession was eagerly grasped and exploited by both Houses in the session of 1624, so much so that although Charles I did his best to return to the narrower definition of the privilege and imprisoned members both during and after sessions, it was to no avail. The House of Commons pointed to the precedent of 1624 and could not be kept quiet.

The Liberty of the Subject

The framers of the *Apology* had said that the rights of Parliament were the liberties of Englishmen. Whatever their intentions, therefore, the Stuarts' refusal to accept Parliament's definition of its own rights would henceforth be regarded as an infringement of the liberties of the subject. The guilt of violating these liberties, however, was not that of the Stuarts alone: their opponents were by no means innocent. In 1621 the House of Commons jailed a certain Floyd, a Catholic, who had publicly rejoiced at the expulsion of the Protestant Frederick of the Palatinate (son-in-law of the king) from his realm by Catholic troops. When it was objected that the Commons lacked the power to commit Floyd, who was not a member of Parliament, the leaders of the House passed the case to the House of Lords, whose judicial functions scarcely extended to punishing outsiders for remarks of this nature. Undaunted by this, the peers ordered Floyd fined, branded, pilloried, and imprisoned. Obviously, parliamentary concern about "free speech" ended abruptly at the doors of Westminster.

As early as 1614 royal devices for raising money caused Star Chamber to fine country gentlemen for refusing to contribute to a benevolence. The forced loan of 1626 presented the issue of the liberty of the subject more sharply. Although many justices of the peace refused to act administratively on the loan — and thereby revealed a fundamental weakness of the Stuarts, who unlike the Bourbons had no class of professional administrators on the local level — the government ordered the imprisonment of persons refusing to contribute. Among those jailed were five knights, itself an indication of the folly of Stuart policy, which meant alienating these traditional supporters of the crown. From their cells the five knights, technically there for debt, petitioned in 1627 for a writ of habeas corpus.[18] This was to raise an enormous question. Habeas corpus was then a prerogative writ, and the knights were in jail by prerogative order. Thus, said the crown pleaders before the puzzled justices of King's Bench, the prerogative could not undo what the prerogative had done. Counsel for the petitioners replied that the chapter of Magna Carta forbidding imprisonment of any freeman except "by judgment of his peers and the law of the land," [19] governed the exercise of the prerogative with regard to imprisonment; the crown was, therefore, now bound to undo what its prerogative had done. Between the two pleas the justices wavered. They finally declared that persons jailed by special command of the king could not be admitted to bail; but they postponed the larger question of the issuance of the writ by saying that they would have to con-

[18] Usually cited as Darnell's Case, the subsequent action is better called the Five Knights' Case, although even that name is not too accurate, in that Darnell, one of the five, lost his nerve and withdrew his request for the writ during the course of the actions. See p. 328.

[19] Chapter 39 of the 1215 version of the charter; above, p. 116.

sult precedents before they could decide. Judicial timidity thus left the five knights in jail and the basic rights of the person at the mercy of the principle of reason of state. Charles released the five knights two years later, before the justices had made up their minds, but he did so only as an act of grace.

The liberty of the subject also became an issue as a result of the financial weakness of the crown. The troops it dredged up from the scum of society for a war with France in 1627 had to be quartered in private homes rather than in barracks, which the government could not afford. The soldiers misbehaved themselves disgracefully in the homes of their unwilling hosts, and at Dover and other ports of embarkation brawled with citizens. The government tried the remedy of martial law for both soldiers and civilians in port towns, and proud merchants faced courts-martial. By the time Charles I had to call Parliament in 1628 to get money for the war, angry gentry and merchants were beginning to realize that the liberty of the subject transcended all other questions. Ignoring the royal request for money, they turned to dispose of this crucial matter in the *Petition of Right*.[20]

The Petition of Right was entirely the work of Parliament. Technically, it was not a statute, nor was it strictly legislative. Its framers, fearing a royal veto if it were presented in the form of a bill, turned to a legal form used by persons asking for special royal grace for the redress of particular grievances. The assent which Charles, unable to dissolve Parliament because of his financial needs, eventually gave to it was in the phrase usual in replying to such requests, "Soit droit fait" — rather than the legislative, "Le roi le veult." By convention, however, the Petition of Right has come to be regarded as a statute.[21]

The first major constitutional document since Magna Carta, the Petition of Right dealt with immediate grievances and, like the charter, insisted that no innovations were contemplated but only a return to the old and better ways of the past. Unlike Magna Carta the Petition of Right was very brief, a mere four sections, all dealing with royal powers, and all significantly couched in negatives. No person should be required to pay a tax or benevolence without parliamentary approval. No person should be imprisoned without cause being shown, with the royal command *not* to be sufficient cause. No troops should be

[20] Samuel Rawson Gardiner, *Constitutional Documents of the Puritan Revolution*, 66. Henceforth cited as Gardiner.
[21] And is cited as 3 Car. I, cap. 1.

quartered in private homes without the consent of and compensation to their owners. Finally, the crown should issue no commissions for proceeding by martial law.

These few terse negatives were significant as an expression of parliamentary self-confidence and determination; no Tudor Parliament would have thought of addressing the sovereign in such terms. Yet they also point to the essentially moderate position of Parliament in 1628. Except for benevolences, against which there had been numerous unsuccessful statutory prohibitions in the past, the Petition did not touch prerogative financial powers. If royal orders by themselves did not justify imprisonment, the crown could still jail persons under cover of criminal charges. The quartering of troops remained a problem until the eighteenth century, when Parliament finally laid out money for barracks, although so strong was the revulsion against arbitrary quartering of troops in private homes that the prohibition of the practice in the Petition of Right entered the United States Constitution.[22] The prohibition against martial law would soon be ignored during the Civil War, while during the Interregnum the government of the Protectorate placed the entire realm under martial law.[23]

Strictly speaking, Charles was right in denying that the Petition's limitations on royal financial powers extended to tunnage and poundage, a levy increasingly irksome to the merchants. Previous Parliaments had authorized monarchs to impose and collect these dues for life. The first Parliament of Charles, however, had given him this right only for a year; and in the storms over Buckingham in 1626 Parliament had not extended the time. Charles maintained that the statutory time limit was contrary to ancient custom and continued to collect tunnage and poundage. In 1629, the faction in the Commons headed by Sir John Eliot attacked the practice, not on the basis of the statutory time limit (where there was a case), but in terms of the first section of the Petition of Right (where there was none); for Eliot maintained that tunnage and poundage were taxes. Obviously, the Eliot group was trying to accomplish by way of interpretation what the Petition had failed to achieve in its formulation. Eliot lost the support of the House of Lords; and some members of the Commons, notably Sir Thomas Went-

---

[22] As the Third Amendment, forbidding quartering troops in private homes in time of peace without their owners' consent and requiring that in time of war such quartering be done only in a manner prescribed by law.

[23] Below, pp. 350–51.

worth, who until now had been highly critical of royal policies, began to have doubts about Eliot's leadership. A test case in the Exchequer Court produced the legally correct decision that tunnage and poundage was not a tax but part of the prerogative, so that Parliament had no interest in it, a judicial dictum supporting the royal view.

Eliot was impulsive and tactless, and by trying to press the Commons too far too quickly failed to take advantage of the successful Petition. By his claim that tunnage and poundage were taxes, Eliot and his friends cost the merchants dear and prejudiced their entire case against the royal financial power. Seeking to retrieve their shaken position in the Commons, they turned to attack the two men always most likely to arouse the passions of the House, Buckingham and Laud. Charles had had enough and prepared to prorogue Parliament, whereupon Eliot and his men took the unprecedented line that the king could not prorogue either House without its consent. When the Speaker attempted to adjourn the House at the royal command, there was a great outcry. The Speaker was held down in his chair (so that the House was technically still in session), while in the midst of the commotion three resolutions were hurriedly passed. Against the Laudian New School, one resolution denounced as a "capital enemy of the realm" anyone making "innovations" in religion to bring in popery, and two other resolutions placed in the same category all persons advocating tunnage and poundage, and all people paying it, without parliamentary approval.[24]

As the House of Commons broke up in tumult in 1629, the moderates who had witnessed this scene felt more than a little uneasy. Under the leadership of the fiery Eliot, the Commons had demanded wars with France and Spain and then refused to provide the money to pay for them; it had actually rejoiced in the assassination of Buckingham in 1628; it had proposed "novel" theories about taxes and limitations on royal prorogations. It had alienated the House of Lords with which it had worked so successfully at the time of the Petition of Right. If this was how extremists were planning to use Parliament, moderates were prepared to do for a time without Parliament. Such was the reasoning of Sir Thomas Wentworth, at least, who now offered his great abilities to the king, in implementing the royal plan to rule without Parliament.

[24] Gardiner, 82.

Crown without Parliament

The experience of Charles with his Parliaments, particularly the last, made him determined never to have another. Although later historians, particularly in the nineteenth century, represented the eleven years during which the king ruled alone as a time of royal tyranny, with the people of England now defenseless against him, this was not exactly the case. As has been seen, moderate men regarded Eliot and other extremists with considerable misgivings. To the average man, the summoning of Parliament had usually meant new taxes and few, if any, tangible benefits. However, by the end of this period of royal rule, many Englishmen were beginning to realize that frequent and regular Parliaments might well be necessary if they were to preserve what freedom they had.

Charles I was not a capricious tyrant. He considered himself a model king who was trying to raise the condition of all his subjects, only to be thwarted by a minority which had perverted the true functions of the House of Commons for selfish ends. The obvious answer was to rule without Parliament, a policy which until Charles's failure, had not necessarily been considered the mark of a tyrannical ruler. However, this policy presumed a Privy Council of men with great administrative ability; and this was not the case.

The most able of the royal advisers was the new recruit, Sir Thomas Wentworth, who had come to the conclusion that only strong, "thorough" government was workable. Such a government could never come from Parliament, he thought, only from a strong crown. Wentworth, created Earl of Strafford in 1629, had genuine administrative ability; but the king had so few similar men that he had too often to employ Strafford's talents outside the Privy Council, first as President of the Council of the North and, after 1633, as Lord Deputy of Ireland. In both positions the "thorough" methods of Strafford brought order and some prosperity to these usually troubled regions. In his attitudes, his zeal for efficiency, his very doctrine of "thorough," there is a ring of twentieth-century totalitarianism about Strafford.

Nearly as able an administrator as Strafford was Laud. However, Laud's own brand of "thorough" was mostly devoted to enforcing conformity within the Church, and he spent most of his time on ecclesiastical rather than secular matters. Like Strafford, however, and unlike Charles, Laud was a realist. He recognized that while administration could do much, it required direction, which from the very nature of Charles's system could come only from the king himself.

Charles had little interest in the details of administration. Even if he had been prepared to devote himself to it, however, by the seventeenth century the complexity of royal administration was such that it would have defeated a much greater man than Charles. What he lacked in clear-sightedness and diligence, he attempted to make up for with stubbornness and a faith in his divine right. He made the grave error, moreover, of believing that since he had come to love his wife her ideas must be sound. She was a French, Catholic princess with no patience with Parliaments, and still less with the English theory of legal limitations upon royal powers. She pointed to the example of her brother across the Channel, who wasted little time on malcontents, but by *lettres de cachet* gave their ardor an opportunity to cool in prison for as long as the royal will desired. However, the queen was not responsible for administration; the king was. And in the course of eleven years, this kindly, obstinate, and rather stupid man doomed forever the possibility of royal, personal nonparliamentary government in England.

One of the first problems he had to face was that of local administration. In trying to run the Tudor administrative system, Charles was dependent on the justices of the peace, who were drawn from the very classes most irritated by certain of the royal policies, notably finance and religion. Inevitably these unpaid local administrators lacked enthusiasm. By the close of the period of personal rule these squires were virtually sabotaging royal policies. When the queen pointed to the example of her brother, she forgot that his local administrators were *intendants*, named by, responsible to, but above all paid and promoted by the crown. Lacking such a professional body of administrators, Charles's government rested on very insecure foundations.

Finance too was a grave, though not an entirely insoluble problem. Though Charles had to forgo taxes and benevolences in view of the Petition of Right, it should also be remembered that Parliament had never been particularly generous. In time of peace the larger share of crown revenues had come from non-parliamentary sources. Since these were now to be the government's only revenues, it was as well that Charles was able to bring to an end the wars with France and Spain. The government then exploited every possible source of nonparliamentary revenue, and inevitably in the process infuriated a number of important groups. The London merchants and others of the rising entrepreneur-capitalist class resented the *sale of monopolies* to companies, which were still legal, though many of the companies were merely dummies. Law officers searched for old laws that might bring in further revenue; none that they found were calculated to please the people affected, but all were of undoubted legality. One, for example, was the use of *distraint of knighthood*, resting on a statute of Edward I,[25] which had been employed by Elizabeth when, despite the doubling of the original £20 figure, many country gentlemen came under its provisions. When Charles now invoked the law, which would bring in money by virtue of the fees required for knighting, many gentlemen who would have proudly accepted an honor freely given by their king refused it, preferring to pay the fine rather than purchase the title.

More serious to landed groups was the revival of the *forest laws*, which among other things forbade alienation of forests without royal permission. Over the centuries the borders of the royal forests had become blurred, and the crown had alienated large parcels of forest land. Charles had titles closely searched, and persons holding lands once part of the royal forests had to pay heavy fines to retain their land or else see it revert to the crown. This method of raising money alienated great landholders, hitherto strong supporters of the crown.

These sources of revenue were unimportant compared with *ship money*, which came to be the major guarantee to the crown of an annual revenue sufficient to meet its needs. The royal navy as such had been the creation of Henry VII; and all the Tudors had continued the prerogative right of mobilizing private shipping in times of crisis. The duty of furnishing ships and crews naturally fell on the port towns, which, however, with royal permission could commute this duty by a payment determined by the crown. With merchants naturally wanting their ships for trade, most port boroughs, except in time of actual threat of invasion, preferred monetary commutation. In the years between 1625 and 1627, the crown had called for ship money three times for the war against Spain; and the payment was thus an accustomed one. In 1634 Attorney-General William Noy suggested that ship money be treated as general revenue. The realm

[25] Above, p. 159.

was then at peace, although the usual pirates in the Channel had been kidnaping Englishmen from their shores. After dismissing Chief Justice Heath, who had doubts about the legality of ship money in time of peace, Charles received a favorable judicial opinion for it; and the writs went out to the port towns. The merchants grumbled but paid. Only the Puritan-mercantile stronghold of London declared the demand illegal, but even London paid. Encouraged by such meekness, the crown in 1635 demanded ship money from the entire kingdom. There were complaints about this extension of the levy to inland regions, but the realm paid the full amount set by the government. When in 1636 the government again called for ship money, it was obvious that this prerogative source of revenue had replaced parliamentary taxation. John Hampden, a very wealthy gentleman from the inland county of Buckinghamshire, which had a tradition of Lollardy, Quakerism, and nonconformism in general, refused to pay his one pound assessment on the ground that if the king could take twenty shillings from him without parliamentary sanction, "He can take all that I have" in the same manner. Never was a constitutional issue so neatly stated.

When the Hampden test case came before the Exchequer Court in 1637, its barons (justices) felt that the legal questions involved were sufficiently large to warrant their sending it at once to the common law justices in Exchequer Chamber,[26] for a general decision on the legality of ship money. Hampden's counsel argued before the twelve justices that the crown could not raise money for one purpose (to build or buy ships) and spend it on another (general administration). Crown counsel replied that there was not a single common law precedent to support this argument, but that there were many upholding the right of the crown to use money, not specifically appropriated by Parliament, as it saw fit.[27] The justices already partly committed by their earlier opinion in favor of the legality of ship money, now divided on the question. Only two flatly declared ship money in time of peace to be illegal. Three others said that Hampden

[26] It is probably unnecessary to recall the difference between the Exchequer Court, dealing with financial cases, and the Exchequer Chamber, composed of all common law justices, sitting to decide a point of law.

[27] In terms of budgetary practice after the younger Pitt (q.v., below, p. 450) the argument of crown counsel was better than that of Hampden's. It might also be noted that the crown did use a large part of ship money to build up the navy, most of which went over to the parliamentary side in the Civil War.

(and by inference all like him) was not liable to pay ship money in that he did not live either in a port town or a coastal county. A majority, the other seven justices, citing numerous precedents, held that the royal duty of defending the realm gave to the prerogative such powers as were necessary to fulfill this duty. Ship money being one such power, the crown might call for it at its discretion, compel its payment by all subjects, and disburse the proceeds as it saw fit.[28]

The prerogative had won a great victory in the crucial field of finance, and until 1639 the government called for ship money annually. The problem of revenue seemed solved.

Charles and his advisers were not deliberately seeking to impose a tyrannical regime, but their need to get money and to hold the line obliged them to deal rigorously with persons objecting to their policies. The first blow fell on nine leaders of the late House of Commons, including Sir John Eliot, whom Charles particularly blamed for the assassination of Buckingham. On royal orders the nine were imprisoned for contempt against the crown, an action typical of the narrow "legality" of Charles's policies. Although the royal charge was based on remarks made by the nine men during the last session, Parliament was now dissolved, and its privileges of freedom of speech and freedom from arrest were no longer effective. Nevertheless, the nine men in their petition for a writ of habeas corpus insisted that both privileges protected them and refused to plead on the contempt charge before anybody except Parliament, which alone, they claimed, could punish for contempts alleged to have been committed in it. In addition, they appealed to the statute of 1512,[29] which they claimed made their present detention illegal.

The justices of King's Bench, barred by the Petition of Right from accepting the plea of a royal order as justifying imprisonment, nevertheless in 1630 found for the crown by the simple, if remarkable, decision that the law of 1512 applied only to the Stannary Court, whose action had occasioned it. The court then fined all nine heavily and remanded them to prison until they had purged themselves of contempt by admitting it and had found sureties for their future good behavior. Five of the nine gave way. Four, including Eliot, would not. After ten years one of these had escaped, and Charles released two more on the eve of another Parliament. He could not release Eliot;

[28] State Trials, III, 826.
[29] Above, p. 239.

he had died in prison in 1632, a martyr to the sanctity of parliamentary privileges.[30]

One reason why Charles determined to do without Parliament was the sharp criticism by the leadership of the Commons of Laudian attitudes. After Parliament dispersed in 1629, Charles promised to safeguard the Church equally against popery and schism. The former promise rang hollow for many in view of the king's support of High Church ritualism. Laud, himself, was neither a bigot nor cruel as his enemies said; and in doctrine he was more tolerant than some. However, his devotion to "thorough" in the Church blinded him to the fact that its real strength lay in its presenting different avenues of worship to different men. Laud's ideas on ritual were not entirely anathema to everyone, but he insisted that everyone accept them in every detail. Along with Richard Neale, Archbishop of York, whose co-operation was essential and is too generally forgotten, Laud sought precise and rigid conformity to every phase of High Church ritual by clergy everywhere.

In enforcing their ideas Laud and Neale relied on episcopal authority, which they exalted, and which was increasingly exercised by High Churchmen as the crown filled vacant bishoprics. Puritans, who had never liked the episcopal organization of the Church, came to detest episcopacy when it was used to enforce ideas which to them meant a return to popery. When episcopal sanctions were insufficient, High Commission forced the clergy either to conform or lose their posts. Puritan preachers, many not ordained clergy, fell afoul of Star Chamber, which punished them savagely. Laud's opponents, both clerical and lay, were certain that he was ramming popery down their throats. Many a country gentleman who was horrified at the notion of resisting royal authority discovered that he was even more horrified by popish vestments, kneeling in prayer, and the sign of the cross.

Yet the English reaction was mild compared with that in Scotland. The Scottish Church, or *kirk*, with its Calvinistic theology, had never accepted the idea of royal headship and had made such a conception quite impracticable by its Presbyterian organization, whereby local congregations elected presbyters to administer the local church and to select its minister. These presbyters in turn elected synods, the members of which named the Assembly of the Church. This system of indirect election thus gave a considerably larger lay participation in the Church

[30] In 1667 the House of Lords as the highest appellate court reversed the decision of King's Bench upholding the royal order. See below, p. 368.

of Scotland than in the Church of England, while the Assembly of the Kirk was more of a "national" institution than the oligarchic Estates, the Scottish Parliament.

James VI of Scotland had little love for Calvinistic clerical pretensions, but though he succeeded in introducing bishops into the Scottish Church, he was prudent enough not to push things too far, knowing "the stomach of that people." Charles I was not so prudent. In 1633 he was crowned King of Scotland by Laud in Edinburgh, and the elaborate ritual scandalized the Scots. The ultimate blunder came in 1637, when the king and Laud decided the Church of Scotland should use a service similar to the English Book of Common Prayer. When on a July Sunday morning the Bishop of Edinburgh attempted to read services from the new Prayer Book in St. Giles Cathedral, an old woman threw a stool at the bishop and the service ended in a riot. Hatred of popery and hatred of foreigners, two deep-seated Scottish passions, came furiously to the surface.

The result was the *National Covenant*,[31] to which virtually all Scots subscribed. They protested their loyalty to their king, but they also swore to resist to the death any innovations in religion and any changes in their kirk not approved by its General Assembly. The Assembly of the Church of Scotland then rejected the new Prayer Book, ejected the bishops, and acted as the national legislature in defiance of the Estates. Charles could not ignore these plain challenges to royal authority. When negotiations failed, he tried force and scraped together a wretched army, which the Scots quickly defeated. The Scots, however, had no wish to fight their king and consented to a truce in 1639. In the subsequent parleys Charles insisted on the restitution of the Scottish bishops and denied the right of the Assembly to supersede the Estates. When the Scots remained obdurate on both points, he decided to renew the war.

This meant that he must raise a new army capable of waging it, which in turn meant that he needed more revenue than nonparliamentary sources could provide. Laud urged Charles to call Parliament to get money for this "crusade." Strafford, recalled from Ireland by the king for his advice, urged the same thing but for a different reason, the need to institute "thorough" government in the northern kingdom. And so the writs summoning Parliament went out in England. The ship of royal personal rule had foundered on the rock of Scottish Calvinism.

[31] Gardiner, 124.

The Drift into War

The Short Parliament of 1640 accomplished nothing. Most of its members did not regard the Scots as foreign invaders so much as defenders of the faith against popery. The grants to the crown of £180,-000 from the Irish Parliament, and of £120,000 from the Convocations were insufficient for a successful prosecution of the war; the king now asked for £840,00 from Parliament. The House of Commons was indifferent to the request, and its merchants and gentry demanded redress of grievances before they voted any money or supplies. When the Lords asserted that exactly the opposite principle should apply, the Commons angrily reminded the peers that money measures could originate only in the lower House and proceeded to engage in bitter debates about the royal policies of the past decade. Charles, against the advice of Strafford, offered to surrender ship money if only the House would vote the £840,000; but the king would not surrender his prerogative revenue for a shilling less. With no satisfactory response from the Commons, Charles, without consulting Laud or Strafford, suddenly dissolved Parliament, a bare three weeks after it had assembled.

Dissolution was no solution. Charles still needed money and for the moment could only resort to desperate measures: he seized the Spanish bullion stored in the Tower, debased the coinage. A miserable army of unpaid conscripts finally marched north against the Scots, was promptly defeated, and the king was forced to agree to an armistice; by this the Scottish army occupied the northern English counties, with the Scots carefully providing that the English government should pay the cost of this military occupation.

Only money could save Charles. But rather than summon Parliament, he revived the feudal Magnum Concilium, a council of peers. In terms of Magna Carta he asked this body to consent to an additional "aid." [32] The peers, however, were not inclined to revert to feudal "legality" and advised instead that the king should summon Parliament. Though fearing the worst, the king realized that he had no alternative. His slender chances of getting a favorable House of Commons were further reduced by the vigorous electioneering of John Pym. When the Long Parliament met in November 1640, the king had no party in it to withstand those members who were determined to reduce the power of the crown.

[32] According to cap. 12 of the 1215 charter; above, p. 113.

In a single session Parliament stripped the crown of those attributes and instrumentalities which had permitted it to operate without Parliament, which was now regarded by its members as vital for the maintenance of their financial, religious, and personal interests. Henceforth the crown would have to act as Parliament determined. When they had finished this work, they left a crown which was subordinate to Parliament; and it was around this limited crown — not the Tudor-Stuart prerogative crown — that a royal party later rallied, for which the Cavaliers rode forth, and which was restored in 1660.

Fortified by the presence of the Scottish army in the north, Pym prepared his program. Its first item was the removal of the most able, and so most dangerous, of the royal advisers, Strafford, who had told Charles to give Parliament one more chance and then, if it again failed to vote funds for the Scottish war, to dissolve Parliament and *rule*. Pym had the House of Commons impeach Strafford for high treason in planning to bring in an Irish army to crush Parliament. Whether Strafford actually had advised the king along these lines was unimportant from a legal point of view, for treason could be committed only against the king, who had complete confidence in Strafford. The managers of the House of Commons, headed by Pym, argued before the House of Lords that since Magna Carta had placed the king below the law, any councillor, even one in the royal confidence, who advised illegal measures was guilty of the highest treason, which was against the realm. But the chances of proving Strafford's guilt seemed remote and while the peers were hesitating, the Commons decided to abandon the impeachment and introduced a bill of attainder instead. A group in the House appears on this occasion to have acted independently of Pym and to have piloted the bill through the Commons. Strafford was extremely unpopular, as a renegade from the parliamentary party of 1628 and as the chief exponent of the policy of "thorough." It was a time of great nervous tension. There were rumors of army plots, still fears that the Irish army might arrive. In London the mob was on the move. The Lords, in a bitter and rancorous session, accepted the bill, and only the king could now save Strafford from death. Charles had sworn that he would never allow harm to come to his friend, but as the mob closed in round the palace in Whitehall he thought of his wife and children, and surrendered the one person perhaps capable of saving him, into the hands of Parliament.[33] On the same day Charles placed himself still

[33] Gardiner, 156.

further at the mercy of Parliament by approving a law forbidding its dissolution without its consent.[34] As a result this became the "Long Parliament," "legally" in existence until 1660, when after many vicissitudes it finally dissolved itself. The immediate effect of the act, however, was to guarantee the parliamentary reformers time to put through their program.

In a stupor of grief over the death of Strafford, Charles gave his unthinking assent to the reformers' measures. A *Triennial Act* [35] reflected the experience of the past decade by requiring that Parliament should assemble at least once every three years, and struck again at prerogative by empowering sheriffs to call elections should the crown fail to issue the necessary writs. However, the real enforcement of this law came from another act, which so extended the legal definition of taxation that the king would have to summon Parliament. Henceforth, ran the act, the crown might not compel the payment of any money without specific parliamentary sanction,[36] thereby making the crown utterly dependent upon parliamentary revenues. The power of the crown to implement policies independently of Parliament by means of administrative tribunals disappeared with the abolition of Star Chamber, Council of the North, and High Commission. The Council of Wales lost much of its jurisdiction, and the Privy Council retained only ecclesiastical and overseas appellate jurisdiction.[37] Only the Court of Requests escaped the fury of the storm.[38]

By the summer of 1641 the first part of its program was complete, and Parliament negotiated a peace settlement with the Scots; the forces which had protected the early labors of the Long Parliament were withdrawn. Many members were now willing to stop, confident that in future the crown would be compelled to co-operate with Parliament. But in fact the movement for reform had by this time gained so much momentum that it was no easy thing to stop. Reformers had become extremists and extremists revolutionaries. Moderate or conservative men who now began to find the pace too swift turned their eyes once more to the crown, in its sadly depleted glory.

To begin with, the spectacle of Parliament acting in an executive capacity, a role played since time immemorial by the king and his

[34] Gardiner, 158.
[35] Gardiner, 144.
[36] Gardiner, 189.
[37] Gardiner, 176, 186.
[38] Above, p. 280.

councillors, was in itself unnerving to more timid citizens. The Scottish peace was negotiated by parliamentary commissioners, acting in the name of an otherwise impotent crown. By the time of the second session of the Long Parliament in October 1641, a serious rebellion in Ireland had changed the question of how far Parliament could act executively from a somewhat academic issue into one of deadly urgency. There was general agreement that this religious and nationalistic revolt had to be crushed and that only a good army could do it. Pym and his colleagues did not dare to give such an army to Charles, who might also use it against Parliament. They therefore proposed that the command of this force should be exercised by men selected by and responsible solely to Parliament. To many members it was a sad and dismaying thing to find that the king, who had always been the head of the national armed forces, was to be so no longer.

Similarly, religious considerations drove these same moderates toward support of the new limited crown. When the Long Parliament had assembled, it had promptly impeached Laud, who was confined to the Tower.[39] His High Church policies had no support in either House, but within Parliament a deepening cleavage appeared over future religious policy. The more extreme elements, disliking episcopacy as a heritage from Rome and hating it for its enforcement of Laudian policies, desired its abolition and replacement by a Presbyterian organization, and demanded doctrinal changes of a Calvinistic nature in the Church. The drastic Root and Branch Petition, which sought to abolish episcopacy altogether, revealed that in the generations since the Elizabethan Settlement what had started as a coolly calculated religious and political compromise had found a warm place in the hearts of many Englishmen. In the debates on the Petition in the House of Commons both supporters and opponents were in favor of a strict enforcement of religious penal laws, but the moderates obviously liked the pre-Laudian Church with its mild episcopacy, comfortable services, and doctrinal vagueness. Faced by the Root and Branch men, these moderates were beginning to feel that their faith might best be protected by the crown after all.

They were by no means reassured by a proposal, passed by a small majority in the Commons, that bishops should be barred from the House of Lords. As the peers ignored this, the Commons, led by Pym and

[39] He was not executed until 1645, three years after the outbreak of the Civil War.

Henry Vane, set to work preparing the *Grand Remonstrance*,[40] a constitutional document of the utmost importance. Beginning as a statement of grievances in 119 clauses, it went on to claim for Parliament — more particularly the House of Commons — various executive functions, including the direct appointment of civil and military officials. It also proposed changes in religion, the details of which were to be determined by Parliament and a synod of clergy. Though clearly designed to win popular support and reclaim those moderates who were on the brink of forming a royalist party, the Remonstrance still seemed to some members an almost treasonable attack upon the king. Sir Edward Hyde,[41] for instance, who had helped reduce royal powers and who detested Laudian ideas, felt that it went too far. After a bitter and furious debate, the Grand Remonstrance was passed by a majority of only eleven votes in the Commons. The king was persuaded that he had after all a party in the House, even if its ideas were somewhat different from his own about both Church and crown. He replied in a conciliatory tone to the Remonstrance; and had he now accepted the role of limited monarch and consented to a non-Laudian Church, he might have commanded sufficient loyalty from his subjects to be able to hold out against any further demands from the radicals.

But instead he promptly prejudiced his position by an ill-advised attempt to arrest Pym and four of his lieutenants for "subverting the fundamental laws of the realm." Although the charge had some possible merit, albeit Pym's declared aims were to preserve them, the refusal of the Commons to commit the five members on these charges should have warned Charles that its membership was jealous of its privileges. Instead, Charles committed the folly of personally appearing in the chamber of the House to arrest the five members, who had been warned and were absent. Whatever differences there might be among members, they were at one in deploring this royal threat to the privileges of the House. Amidst jeers, the king was obliged to withdraw from his embarrassing situation, the last English sovereign ever to enter the House of Commons.[42]

[40] Gardiner, 202.

[41] Later the Earl of Clarendon and Lord Chancellor of Charles II.

[42] Naturally, the heir to the throne may attend debates of the lower House, although the consort of the sovereign has not always been welcome, the most famous case being objections by some members to the presence of Prince Albert, husband of Queen Victoria, in the gallery of the House. Prior to the occupancy by the members of the House of Commons of their new chamber, built to replace the one blitzed in World War II, George VI by special permission of the

The king tried to recover the ground he had lost by dropping his
charges against the five members, but his foolish invasion of the House
caused it to reintroduce the bill barring bishops from the House of
Lords, and the peers themselves now accepted it. Still seeking to placate
his own party, Charles gave his approval to this obvious first step toward the total abolition of episcopacy.[43] The Pym group pressed its
momentary advantage to drive through Parliament, albeit by narrow
majorities, the *Militia Bill*, giving Parliament control of the armed
forces. When the king refused his assent, Pym, still riding the crest of
parliamentary resentment against Charles, persuaded both Houses to
pass the measure again, this time as an *ordinance*.[44] Hitherto, ordinances
had emanated only from the king-in-council. For many men the trans-
ference of such power to Parliament seemed dangerous, and the provision in the Militia Ordinance that disobedience would be punished by
Parliament as contempt against it was further proof that reform had
begun to sap at the very foundations of the constitution.

Once again, the moderates in Parliament gravitated toward the king
as, ironically enough, the only guarantor of the limited crown, moderate
episcopacy, and individual liberties. Neither these moderates nor the
extremists, however, could compromise any longer. In June 1642 the
small majority that Pym was able to command in the Commons approved his *Nineteen Propositions*,[45] demanding the royal surrender to
Parliament of control over all government appointments, over the militia, and over the Church, which Parliament was to reform without
further reference to the crown. Charles returned a reply [46] so reasoned
that there must be doubt as to his authorship of it. Instead of invoking
Divine Right, as might have been expected, the royal answer was an
early expression of the theory of *mixed government*, which was to
permeate England in the eighteenth century and receive elaboration in
Blackstone's *Commentaries*, and a further trans-Atlantic refinement in

members toured the empty room, which technically was not yet the House of
Commons until the members sat there. The House of Lords has never had this
prohibition against the presence of the sovereign, and it might be constitutionally
impossible to exclude him from the debates of the peers. However, the last ruler
to attend them was Charles II (1649–85), who declared them better than a
play.
[43] Gardiner, 241.
[44] Gardiner, 245.
[45] Gardiner, 249.
[46] John Rushworth, *Historical Collections*, IV, 731–2, as reprinted in Robert
Livingston Schuyler and Corinne Comstock Weston, *British Constitutional History since 1832*, 98.

the theory of checks and balances from the members of the American Constitutional Convention.

Monarchy, he explained, was only one of three types of governments, each with strengths and weaknesses. Monarchy gave a focal point for national unity, but could lead to tyranny; aristocratic regimes secured the best men for government, but also led to factions among rival aristocrats; democracy meant individual liberty, but ran the danger of violence as people struggled for power. It was the great fortune of England to have a constitution combining the elements of these three major types of government in such a manner as to have the benefits of all without the dangers of any.

Thus the king had executive functions, including the conduct of foreign affairs, the creation of peers, the appointment of members to his Council and of all civil and military officials. Should the monarch abuse these powers or his councillors give evil advice, the remedy lay with the elective House of Commons. Its sole power to initiate money bills (and Charles inferentially admitted that all crown revenues now came from such measures) and to impeach officials would check the monarch and return him to proper policies. Between the monarchical and democratic elements of the constitution stood the aristocratic House of Lords, which tried impeachments and had to concur in all legislation, including finance bills.

Each element of government thus had a definite part to play. For one to encroach upon another would be fatal to the delicate balance in the constitution, and so to the happiness of the realm and the liberties of the people. In the present instance, the Nineteen Propositions aimed at transferring to Parliament powers which historically it had never possessed, thereby reducing the strength of monarchy, and so the rallying point for national feeling, even while simultaneously stimulating factionalism (the inherent evil of aristocratic government), first in the Lords and then in the Commons. Nor would this be the end, continued the royal reply with remarkable prescience; the possession by Parliament of complete executive powers would soon produce conflicts between its two Houses, where the House of Commons, as the elective House, would have a growing advantage over the Lords, until the elective body would obliterate the aristocratic element of the constitution, leaving itself with total legislative and executive power. Since the size of the Commons precluded its acting effectively as a continuous executive, it would have to entrust executive powers to a few men who in a short time would become utterly irresponsible. Meanwhile, as the new tyranny grew, the people would have to be lulled into acceptance by skillful appeals to liberty and the complete equality of all men, to the point where they would believe that they were the masters of government and would wipe out even this powerful House of Commons, the lone remnant of the ancient constitution, leaving a barbarism where neither life nor property would be safe. And so Charles, like the barons at Merton in 1236, concluded his reply, "We do not want the laws of England changed." [47]

The king's answer to the Nineteen Propositions was an obvious bid for the support of the large moderate block in Parliament. Pym, however, correctly saw it as an indication that the king would fight rather than accept any further radical changes in the constitution. When the king issued commissions of array, empowering loyal men to raise forces to defend the constitution, the Commons ordered that a parliamentary force should be enlisted.

The constitutional question as to the ultimate authority in the nation-state had reached its crisis. Neither side could afford to let the other win this glittering prize, and in the summer of 1642 each appealed to the arbitration of arms.

The Appeal to Force

The lines of division in the Civil War cut through social classes, even through individual families. Generally, the mercantile element in the large urban centers and the gentry in the south and east supported the parliamentary army. Most rural people in the north and west, and most peers, were on the royalist side. Puritan and Anglican clergy naturally were opponents. But even to these generalizations there were numerous exceptions. Many people, of course, stood aloof; and individuals who did support one of the contestants thought long before deciding which one. Furthermore, the determinant factor for one man in his decision for king or Parliament might not have had much meaning to another man who had reached the same decision. If there were "war aims," the Cavaliers of Charles I were fighting for the limited crown and moderate Church created by Parliamentary action prior to the summer of 1641; while the Roundheads of Parliament were fighting for Pym's program after that date. Both sides, however, assumed that a

[47] Above, p. 139.

monarchy of one sort or another would survive; only at the very last did a small, desperate minority turn against it.

The defeat of the Royalists did not by any means solve the constitutional question. Having allied themselves with the Scots in 1643 in the *Solemn League and Covenant*,[48] the parliamentarians had virtually committed themselves to establishing a Presbyterian state church. On the other hand, the army was strongly for an Independent, congregational religious system, with some degree of toleration. With the king finally at its mercy, it is not surprising that Parliament had no clear idea what to do with him. This was the royal opportunity, and Charles exploited it with more skill than might have been expected of him. Playing off his opponents against each other, he eventually maneuvered himself into a position where his enemies were virtually offering to restore him to his pre-1641 position if only he would guarantee the particular wish of that faction. Victory, to the army's dismay, had solved nothing. Still no agreement could be reached. Then came the Second Civil War, with the Scots now fighting on the royal side. The army under Cromwell first defeated the Scots and then turned to deal with the man it held responsible for renewing the war.

After the final victory, the Presbyterian members of the House of Commons, who were still prepared to negotiate with the king, were rudely expelled from the House by Colonel Thomas Pride at the head of a detachment of troops, an action which made Charles's attack on the five members seem mild in comparison. Pride's purge left a mere 90 members in this *Rump* of the Long Parliament, out of its original 504. Of the 90 in the Commons only about half usually attended, and it was a small House of 46 which, by a mere six votes, passed an ordinance naming 135 members as an *ad hoc* administrative tribunal, the High Court of Justice, to try Charles Stuart.[49] When the moribund House of Lords rejected the ordinance, the same 26 members of the lower House declared the ordinance to have full force of law; the sovereign power of the people was expressed in the House of Commons and its measures did not require the approval of either the peers or the king.[50]

Over half of the persons named in the ordinance refused to sit on the court (among them Lord Fairfax, nominal commander of the army), whose members like those of the administrative courts abolished in 1641

[48] Gardiner, 267.
[49] Gardiner, 357.
[50] Gardiner, 357.

were judges equally of law and fact, but unlike them had competence over an issue of life and limb. Brought before the court, the king denied its competence and refused to plead. The proceedings went on, however, and after evidence had been heard of his participation in the Civil War, the court found him guilty and condemned him to death for being "a tyrant, traitor, murderer, and a public enemy to the good people of this nation." [51] Even then it was only with difficulty that members of the court could be persuaded to sign the death-warrant. But on 30 January 1649 Charles I went to his death, "a martyr for the people," as he said, and the people themselves shuddered when they saw in the cold light of day the terrible thing a few men had done.

At the same time the Rump abolished the monarchy and the House of Lords and declared England a *Commonwealth*.[52] The break with the past was almost complete, and indeed a new calendar was ordered to emphasize the fact. Year I began with the execution of Charles I.[53] The only constitutional link with the past was the remains of the House of Commons.

THE "VICTORY" OF THE COMMON LAW

In struggling to control the nation-state, the common-law lawyers were in partnership with Parliament, against the attempts of the crown to sustain the prerogative and against the various administrative courts, which competed for jurisdiction with the courts of common law. Parliament did indeed abolish much of this administrative jurisprudence, but it also came to assert its own supremacy over the common law.

The Parliamentary-Common Law Alliance

The alliance between Parliament and the common law was anything but "natural." It rested on some very weak assumptions by both parties to it, and by the time Charles I died there were signs that it was disintegrating. Even Parliament's belief that the common law supported its claims to a share in sovereignty was very much open to question.

[51] Gardiner, 377.
[52] Gardiner, 384, 387, 388.
[53] Thereby anticipating the similar action by the makers of the First French Republic. Like Napoleon after him, Cromwell refused to use the new calendar.

Each of the parties to the alliance was, in fact, to some extent deceiving the other. Only their momentary need of each other can explain their marriage of convenience in the early seventeenth century. When the common lawyer declared the king to be "below the law," he meant the "law," not Parliament; if pressed, he would also have placed Parliament below the law. Parliamentary leaders might claim that the "law" supported their views, but they did not know that the champions of this "law" saw neither crown nor Parliament as the ultimate authority in the state, but the common law courts, which would arbitrate between them as to their proper spheres. The parliamentary idea, carefully fostered by common law supporters, that the common law set limits for the prerogative had remarkably little basis in fact. Prior to the Stuarts the common law not only assumed the existence of the prerogative, but admitted its ability to do what the law could not. By this doctrine neither prerogative nor law was superior to the other. In the early test cases of the seventeenth century, justices were indeed uncertain what the limits of the prerogative were. By 1640, Parliament had given up hope that the common law could limit the prerogative and prepared to do so itself by legislation.

Both parties, however, shared a common dislike of administrative jurisprudence. To the common lawyers it was a competitor, to the parliamentary leaders it was an agency of the prerogative. With both groups attacking administrative courts, even if for quite different reasons, an alliance between them was possible and was signalized in 1610 by the repetition by common law justices of the judicial opinion of 1553, that conciliar legislation could only reinforce common and statute law, but could not enlarge the jurisdiction of Star Chamber and similar tribunals.[54]

This opinion had little effect upon the first two Stuarts, but it was an indication that the common law would generally tend to support Parliament. The alliance was strengthened when a judicial decision seemed to place the law courts at the mercy of Chancery; their pleaders and justices then became anxious to have parliamentary protection.

The comforting theory that Chancery and the law courts could never conflict, because one handled only equity and the other law, two entirely different things, began to break down when Chancery extended its equity reliefs, to the great concern of common law justices and

[54] Above, p. 248.

pleaders. The issue of the relationship between Chancery and the law courts came to a head in *Glanville's Case* in 1614.[55] Sir Edward Coke as Chief Justice of King's Bench had given a decision based upon testimony, which, unknown to him, was perjured. When the losers of the case discovered the perjured nature of the testimony, they found that they had no remedy at law, so certain was the common law that no one would dare swear falsely in its courts. They therefore turned to Chancery for relief. After satisfying himself that the facts alleged in the petition for relief were true, Lord Chancellor Ellesmere issued an injunction forbidding the lying winners in King's Bench to enforce its judgment in their favor. Angry at having been fooled, and no lover of Chancery anyway, Coke was furious at this unwarranted interference in *his* court and persuaded the successful litigants to defy the injunction and collect damages according to his original judgment. Ellesmere retorted by fining them heavily for contempt. Coke countered by having the losers in his court indicted for praemunire in their refusal to abide by its judgment — even if based on false testimony.

Into this delicate situation stepped James I, who had been accustomed to the more logical system of Roman law in his native Scotland and could not understand how there could be conflict between *royal* courts. The king referred the matter to a committee under the chairmanship of Bacon, the Attorney-General. The committee upheld Ellesmere and, more important, the right of the Court of Chancery to enforce its decrees even if they were directly opposed to the results of litigation at law. The decision was a grave blow to Coke and the common law, and one more reason to turn to Parliament in search of a protection that the common law apparently could no longer give its own courts.

From this time onward the Court of Chancery was fair game for any disgruntled member of the House of Commons, where Sir John Selden bitterly complained that its equity varied with the length of the Chancellor's foot. The court thus became a symbol of the tyranny of the prerogative; and although it weathered the storm in 1641, it did not long survive the king, being abolished by the Rump Parliament shortly after the death of Charles I.[56] Restored with Charles II in 1660, Chancery did not fully recover until the late eighteenth century.

[55] From the affair dated Coke's implacable hatred of Bacon.
[56] Below, p. 403.

The Arbitration of the Bench

When supporters of either parliamentary or crown claims appealed to the law, they had to bring test cases before the common law courts, which thereby in the view of such an ardent upholder of the common law as Coke, performed their proper duty of delineating the spheres of crown and Parliament. This procedure was to bring forward the entire issue of *judicial review*, which was to become of little importance in Great Britain but which in the United States allowed the courts to determine whether national and state legislation was in harmony with the Constitution.[57]

Whatever the sympathies of the lawyers were, the common law itself generally favored the crown. This was not surprising in a law which originated in remedies initially designed by the king and applied by his justices in his personal courts for his benefit. That these remedies had become the common property of all his subjects was due to their being able to do what the remedies of other courts could not. But the origins of the common law and its courts gave the crown an advantage when it called upon them to arbitrate between Parliament and itself. Thus by applying rigid common law doctrines in the Bates Case of 1606, the justices accorded the prerogative an important victory in the crucial matter of finance. The essential sympathy of common law judges in the early Stuart period toward royal prerogative was shown in *Calvin's Case* in 1608. Having failed to persuade the English Parliament to accept a legislative union with his northern kingdom, James I turned to the law, and not in vain. The government found a young Scot, born in Scotland shortly after James's accession to the English throne, and bought land in his name in England. English law forbade alien ownership of land; but in the resultant collusive action, the judges, including Sir Edward Coke, unanimously held in their *post-nati* decision (heavily overlaid with prerogative) that subjects of the king born in either of his kingdoms after his accession to the English throne owed him allegiance in the other, and hence were aliens in neither. In 1629 the Exchequer Court, in *Chamber's Case*, refused to restore the

[57] How far the arguments of the seventeenth century about judicial review have traveled can be seen in Robert H. Jackson, *The Struggle for Judicial Supremacy* (New York, 1941), written while he was Attorney-General of the United States. Interestingly, Justice Jackson of the United States Supreme Court later seemed to forget at times what Attorney-General Jackson had written.

goods of a merchant who had lost them by an order of Star Chamber for refusing to pay tunnage and poundage. Two years later in *Vassall's Case* the court extended its earlier decision in the Bates Case regarding the prerogative right to lay impositions. During the years when Charles I ruled without Parliament the courts consistently upheld his various devices to raise money, including distraint of knighthood and ship money.

Although it is true that the king dismissed judges whose decisions he resented, and appointed judges whom he expected to act as servants of the crown, it is also true that these decisions upholding prerogative financial devices rested, according to stare decisis, on earlier decisions, including the crucial one in Bates's Case, in which Coke had participated. Faced with these judicial decisions, Parliament could do nothing in 1641 except change the law and prohibit enforced payments to the crown without legislative approval by statute.

Similarly, the common law was able to do little to protect the liberties of the subject against the prerogative. Darnell's Case proved this limitation clearly,[58] and even where parliamentary privilege was involved, as in the case of the nine members of the Commons, the justices of King's Bench could see no way under the common law to issue a writ of habeas corpus.[59] When in 1641 the House of Commons tried to overthrow this latter decision, the Lords significantly took no action.[60]

The Independence of the Bench

The modern attitude, that no honorable government will touch the freedom of its judicial agencies and that any tampering with the sanctity of the bench is the most heinous of crimes, derives from the experiences of Englishmen during the seventeenth century. Until that time the independence of the judiciary had not been an issue.

The bench had been independent before the seventeenth century, although, like all officials, royal justices held their positions at the royal pleasure. Once named to the bench, however, they had in practice security of tenure. Royal intervention in cases under adjudication, *sub judice*, was rare because unnecessary, and the devotion of justices to stare decisis made them apply a law which rarely ran counter to royal interests.

[58] Above, pp. 304–5.
[59] Above, p. 312.
[60] The Lords did however reverse in 1667. See above, p. 313, note 30; below, p. 368.

With the seventeenth century, however, the situation changed. Common law cases came to involve important questions of state policy. With both crown and Parliament appealing to the law for support, each side brought test cases to the courts; their decisions were now important not so much for their determination of the particular issues under litigation as for their influence on the formulation of state policy, and especially for any light they might throw on the fundamental questions of parliamentary privilege and the royal prerogative. This was precisely the role that Sir Edward Coke believed the common law ought to play, but he was unable to realize that neither contestant could afford the luxury of impartial judicial arbitration. Each had to control the arbitrator, and it is significant that true judicial independence and permanency of tenure came only after 1688. Until that time, however, the advantage generally lay with the crown.

The crown insisted that to rule on a test case merely by a rigid application of precedents, without considering the possible consequences any decision might have for the state as a whole, was unrealistic and unwise. The fact that justices viewed only the specific issues of each case and decided it strictly according to precedent had been one of the main reasons why the administrative courts had been necessary. There remained, however, a variety of cases capable of adjudication at law, where the justices could at least inhibit state policy by a rigid application of stare decisis.

Every executive in a governmental system where judicial review has operated has echoed Francis Bacon's words, that justices should be "lions, but lions under the throne." To James I, as to Andrew Jackson or Franklin D. Roosevelt, the thought that major state policy might turn upon the decision of a judge, based upon narrow precedents, in an isolated case between private parties, was extremely displeasing. James argued that where cases did touch on public policy, justices should consult the executive and so become acquainted with the reasons behind such policy. And every strong American president from George Washington to Franklin D. Roosevelt has had exactly the same idea, just as every strong justice from Sir Edward Coke through John Marshall and Charles Evan Hughes has resisted it as a threat to the independence of the bench.[61]

[61] However, the Supreme Court of the Dominion of Canada must upon the request of the government render advisory opinions as to the constitutionality of proposed policies, although the law and justices have been equally firm in denying that these opinions in any way bind them in actual future cases. A similar situation exists for eleven state supreme courts in the United States.

In the early seventeenth century, however, the common law courts were the king's courts, its justices "the king's justices," royal servants whom the king could appoint *and* dismiss. If the courts were to be used as arbiters between king and Parliament, it was unlikely that the former would tolerate unfriendly royal servants on the bench. For such a man as Sir Edward Coke to believe that the king would remain passive while his justices undercut the prerogative was less than realistic.

Sir Edward Coke was the most wholehearted believer in judicial independence. He has been canonized by later generations for the stand he took, but many people today, including lawyers, would find his views difficult to reconcile with the facts. His devotion to the mystique of the common law was comparable with the devotion of the first two Stuarts to the theory of Divine Right. For Coke "law" consisted solely of writs, pleas, and precedents, combined in a mystical entity incapable of modification either by the crown or Parliament. His idea that the common law and its justices were superior to executive and legislature alike was completely at variance with modern English legal doctrine which makes a statute the ultimate authority on any subject. Even during his own lifetime not many of his colleagues were prepared to go as far as he did in a policy which would have endangered their alliance with Parliament. Carried to their logical conclusion, Coke's views would have made the law unresponsive to any pressure for change, modified only by the halting and minor alterations that a supreme and irresponsible judiciary might have grudgingly made. Although Coke was later to be a leader in the Commons against the prerogative, he never envisaged the modern English concept of parliamentary supremacy and would have resented bitterly any parliamentary intervention in the common law, which, no doubt, he would have regarded as illegal. Coke had been notorious as a particularly severe Attorney-General under Elizabeth I and James I, and it is as well to remember that the man who spoke so grandly of the supreme majesty of the common law never did so in terms of the liberty of the subject. His prosecution of Sir Walter Raleigh was extremely vindictive and ferocious.

In 1606, for his past services Coke received from James I, who had no reason at that time to regard him as a problem, the post of Chief Justice of Common pleas. The later quarrels between himself and the king did not so much concern the extent of the prerogative; Coke, as is not surprising in a man so saturated in case law, chose to disagree with the king initially on legal technicalities. He became a tower of strength for his brethren on the bench in resisting rival jurisdictions, attacking both the Courts of Request and Chancery, and blaming on Sir Francis Bacon his failure to wreak the havoc he had intended; and Bacon thus became one of his bitterest enemies. The king, baffled by the spectacle of courts all supposedly operating under his authority and competing with each other, proposed to resolve the conflicts by hearing cases himself. Coke in 1608 denied that he was competent to do so. When James sought to arbitrate between King's Bench and High Commission, Coke from Common Pleas explained to him that he had no such right. In 1609 the Chief Justice of Common Pleas went further and informed the king that in any judicial conflict between the law courts and administrative tribunals it was the royal duty to support the former. *Bonham's Case* in 1610 is of particular interest, not only from a medical point of view, but because it reveals Coke's real views about the relationship between common and statute law. Dr. Thomas Bonham held a medical degree from Cambridge and by statute could practice anywhere in the kingdom. He decided to settle in London, where the Royal College of Physicians also trained and licensed doctors under another statute, which empowered the president and censors of the college as the governing board to summon and fine unauthorized persons practicing medicine without the collegiate license — half of the fines going to the board. The two statutes together plainly meant that the Royal College of Physicians was to license all medical practitioners in the city, except those trained by the universities, who could practice there or anywhere else without further authorization. However, the president and censors took the illogical and somewhat petty view that by act of Parliament no one, not even the holders of university medical degrees, might practice in London without their license.

When Bonham chose to defy this self-allotted monopoly by practicing in London without a license from the college, the president and censors summoned and fined him. He paid, but still did not ask for a license and continued to practice, with the result that the board summoned and fined him a second time. Bonham now refused to pay and went to jail, from whence he petitioned for release on a writ of habeas corpus.

The hearing on the petition was before Coke. It was clear that two statutes, one of national and the other of local application, could not be in conflict, that the action of the governing board of the Royal College of Physicians was illegal, and that Bonham ought to be released. This indeed was the decision Coke reached, but for reasons that were by no means immediately obvious. Instead of construing the two statutes in their natural relationship, he seized upon that part of the second statute giving the president and censors of the college half of the fines they imposed. That made them both prosecutors and judges, which was contrary to a basic principle of common law. That this power of the board was statutorily conferred did not deter Coke, who declared in a decision which no modern English jurist would render, "It appears in our books, that in many cases the common law will controule acts of parliament, and sometimes adjudge them to be utterly void; for when an act of parliament is against common right or reason, or repugnant, or impossible to be performed, the common law will controule it and adjudge such act to be void. . . ." It was Bacon who recognized the real threat in those words — that the common law, as interpreted by Coke, should "controule" all. In 1613 Bacon advised the king to "elevate" Coke to the chief justiceship of King's Bench, where he would be mostly engaged on criminal business; at the same time Coke became a privy councillor, and all seemed well.

But first came Glanville's Case, in which Coke and the common law were worsted by Chancery,[62] and then in 1615 there was a case concerning a certain clergyman named Peacham, who had been imprisoned and finally defrocked by High Commission. While in "durance vile," Peacham was questioned closely about his political views and his house searched by crown agents who found notes for a sermon, which if delivered would have been incitement to treason according to the law of that time. However, the sermon had not been given. Nevertheless, the Council wanted Peacham indicted for treason and sought a judicial opinion that his preparation of the undelivered sermon was "constructive treason," a doctrine much favored by Coke. Vast issues were at stake, for Peacham's views were not untypical of those of other clergy of Puritan tendencies. Great, therefore, was the irritation of James and the Council when the justices refused to give an opinion until they had consulted together alone. Suspecting the hand of Coke, James demanded that they give their views immediately and individually. Coke objected to this on the grounds that royal majesty might influence, if not overwhelm, a single justice. However, eleven justices gave way and answered the crucial question affirmatively. Coke stood fast, refused to give an opinion, and later sent one in writing to the Council in the

[62] Above, p. 326.

negative, objecting at the same time to consultation of justices by the crown.[63]

The next year, in 1616, James and Coke clashed again on the right of the crown to intervene in cases already *sub judice*. The practice was not uncommon, but Coke had objected to it. In the present case, however, the crown was certain to intervene, as vital issues were at stake. Bishop Neal of Litchfield had received from the crown a parish living to hold along with, *in commendam*, his not very lucrative episcopal post. Such plural livings by bishops were common, despite complaints of absenteeism. However, the ecclesiastical issue was not in dispute. It was something infinitely more important — the patronage rights of two gentlemen who had lost their right to name to the parish when the royal head of the Church had given it to Bishop Neal. The two gentlemen appealed to the law, in the knowledge that since the days of Henry II the royal courts had consistently upheld such private prescriptive property rights of advowson by the dictum of *darrein presentment:* "Let him who presented last present again." [64] Could the king as head of the Church override private property rights? Could the prerogative act in this way?

The importance of the case brought it before all the justices in Exchequer Chamber, where Coke expressed doubts, but not a formal ruling, as to whether the prerogative right to issue such a *commendams* could supersede private property rights. Coke's views were having such obvious influence upon his colleagues that the king instructed Attorney-General Bacon to ask Coke to delay a decision until the king and Council could explain the implications of the case to them. Coke was no friend of Bacon; he also disliked royal intervention in cases *sub judice;* above all, he was opposed to royal consultation with justices. The result was a blistering reply to the Attorney-General, in which he alleged that the request violated the independence of the bench. Instead of complying, Coke urged his colleagues to reach a decision immediately. The other justices hesitated just long enough for James to summon them all to the Privy Council, where he categorically insisted that in any case touching the prerogative or state policy they were always to consult with the king and Council, "else you may wound the king through the sides of a private person"; this expressed neatly enough

---

[63] The case ended in an anticlimax. Using the opinion of the eleven justices, the crown secured an indictment for treason against Peacham, but the trial jury could not agree on a verdict.

[64] Above, p. 107.

the executive's dislike of any judicial determination of government powers and policy on the basis of a single private suit. Confronted by the royal wrath, eleven justices promised that in such cases they would consult with the king and Council; but Coke argued. James then consulted with each justice individually, to the displeasure of Coke, who correctly feared that his colleagues were of less stern stuff than himself. Again eleven said that they understood the crown's position; Coke declared that he would do what a justice should. The result was a decision by the Exchequer Chamber against the bishop, but one carefully leaving the royal prerogative intact. Coke strongly dissented.[65]

James had endured enough from this thorn in his side and in November 1616 dismissed Coke from the bench.[66] The dismissal brought common law justices sharply into line, and their decisions in later test cases were clearly influenced by their awareness that, in a very real sense, they held their posts at the royal pleasure.

Consequently the crown won its cases, but it did so under a shadow; the bench had been tampered with, and Coke had seen to it that that fact should not be overlooked. Charles I followed his father's precedent in dealing with Chief Justice Crewe of King's Bench in 1627, after the latter had expressed doubts about the forced loan, which subsequently his successor and the other justices upheld.[67] In 1630 when Chief Baron Walter of the Exchequer was uncertain whether the king could levy and collect tunnage and poundage after the time limit set by Parliament had expired,[68] Charles replaced him with a more amenable justice; and the court later ruled that tunnage and poundage was a matter solely for prerogative action.[69] In 1634 Chief Justice Heath went the same way, because he doubted the legality of the forthcoming ship money writs, and the justices who heard the Hampden case had not forgotten his

[65] Tanner, 192.
[66] Coke frantically sought to regain the royal favor. Over the objections of his wife he had his daughter marry the idiot brother of the Duke of Buckingham, but she fled from her distasteful husband. By 1617 Coke was back on the Privy Council and participating in Star Chamber. In 1621 he entered the House of Commons for the royal borough of Liskeard so that his opposition to royal policies during the session was thus doubly galling to the king. He did succeed in "getting" Bacon (above, pp. 298-9), but after his imprisonment following the session, he retired from public affairs until his death in 1634. Coke's Institutes on the common law still occasionally appear in citations in pleading and judicial decisions, although some of their doctrines cannot be supported by precedents prior to their time of writing.
[67] Above, p. 297.
[68] Above, pp. 327-8.
[69] Above, p. 328.

fate.[70] Charles himself cast a further doubt on the merit of that decision and on the impartiality of the courts as arbitrators between king and Parliament when to the Short Parliament of 1640 he offered to have the result of the Hampden Case reversed by the House of Lords on a writ of error if only Parliament would vote funds.

By this time, however, parliamentary leaders were seeking means to control appointments to the bench themselves. In 1641 Parliament resolved that justices might hold their posts for good behavior, but by the spring of 1642 the Nineteen Propositions envisaged Parliament's appointing justices together with other officials and made no mention of their tenure for good behavior. Parliamentary leaders were hardly more disposed than the crown to have a truly impartial bench, which would be possible only when one of the rivals had won a clear-cut victory over the other.

The rivalry between the elements controlling crown and Parliament in the early seventeenth century took the form of disagreements over religious and financial policy. To these issues was added the fundamental one of the liberty of the subject. Neither side intended, nor wished, armed conflict from the rivalry; but in the end the reality of the contest — nothing less than control of the nation-state — found both willing to appeal to arms. Constitutionally, the outcome of this Civil War was a denial of the traditional constitution except for a truncated House of Commons, the apparent victor in the struggle.

In the course of the struggle to control the nation-state, both sides appealed to the common law courts, so that control of judicial personnel was added to the other constitutional issues. Common law supporters, fearful of rival administrative justice, turned to Parliament to protect their law from its rival.

READING LIST

ALLEN, J. W. *English Political Theory, 1603–1640.*

CHEYNEY, E. "Court of Star Chamber," *American Historical Review*, XVIII, 222.

EUSDEN, J. D. *Puritans, Lawyers, and Politics in Early Seventeenth Century England.*

FIGGIS, J. *Divine Right of Kings.*

[70] Above, p. 311.

JUDSON, MARGARET A. *The Crisis of the Constitution.*

NOTESTEIN, WALLACE. *The Winning of the Initiative by the House of Commons* (Proceedings of the British Academy, 1924).

PLUCKNETT, THEODORE F. T. *A Concise History of the Common Law*, Book I, Part I, Chap. 7.

RELF, F. H. *The Petition of Right.*

TANNER, J. R. *English Constitutional Conflicts of the Seventeenth Century.*

WORMUTH, F. D. *The Royal Prerogative, 1603–1649.*

9

THE IMPERFECT SOLUTION

THE YEARS between the execution of Charles I in 1649 and the return of his son, Charles II, in 1660, are called the *Interregnum*. Legally, all that occurred during that time was void by reason of the absence of the king. What was restored in 1660 was the limited monarchy, very much in the form envisaged by the first session of the Long Parliament in 1641. The most complete break with the constitutional past was during the first four years of the Commonwealth. After that there was a general inclination to return to older and more familiar forms of government.

The Flood of Theories

The execution of the king came as a profound shock not only to all those ordinary people who must subsequently have gone in fear of divine vengeance, but also to intellectual people, to whom it presented fundamental questions about the nature of society and of political authority. The unsettled times, too, gave rise to a spate of political theories. All gradations of political thought were expressed, from the pessimistic conservatism of the great Thomas Hobbes to the democratic radicalism of the spirited John Lilburne. Some of these theories made only a slight impression on Englishmen, but they were taken up and played their part in the more fluid social conditions on the other side of the Atlantic.

Perhaps the most primitive form of political thought during this period was that expressed with some success by the *Fifth Monarchy* men. They found proof in Holy Writ that there had been four great empires in the past, and the wondrous victory of the righteous over the royalists convinced them of the nearness of the fifth, the Kingdom of God. During the brief delay before its arrival they, as godly men, should rule, to the exclusion of such sinners as the members of the Rump Parliament, and Oliver Cromwell in particular.

The Fifth Monarchy zealots annoyed all "sensible" men. So also did the *Levellers,* under the leadership of John Lilburne, whose radical notions were, however, acceptable to many army officers. Lilburne was one of the first believers in popular sovereignty ever to achieve any sort of political influence in modern times. He called for a legislature elected by universal male suffrage, beggars and servants excluded, with limited powers as fixed in a written constitution, which would guarantee individual rights and liberties. He hated any form of tyranny and called for equal justice to all; to say that Parliament had more authority than the people, he argued, was as absurd as to say that an ambassador had more authority than the prince who sent him. The proposed constitution, the *Agreement of the People,*[1] put forward by the victorious army, was based on the political philosophy of the Levellers.

A more extreme group still, calling itself *True Levellers,* although generally known as *Diggers,* was interested in a return to the pastoral simplicity of the Old Testament. Some of them under Gerrard Winstanley, whose *Law of Freedom* in 1651 ascribed the fall of man less to Eve and the apple than to commercial activity, tried a sort of agrarian communism. Again, however, the Diggers are interesting more for showing how the break with the past presented an opportunity for social experiments than for any practical influence they had in their own time, or indeed in later years.

It may be said, however, that the Levellers and the Diggers were the party of the people, in so far as the people were in any sense politically conscious. But the Civil War had been won by the middle classes, the merchants and gentry, and they had no wish to see their victory undermined by democratic government, which they could not distinguish from anarchy. These solid citizens, of whom Cromwell was fairly representative, believed in a franchise based on property, and government by men of wealth and substance. Persons of this type did not need to theorize about an "ideal" government; they had become, according to some basic principle that had survived the Civil War, the ruling class, and that being so, it was in their interests to preserve the status quo. Theories of sovereignty were clearly subversive. They were opposed equally to lower-class radicalism and to that unquenchable royalism that lingered among the masses, as among the aristocracy.

[1] Below, p. 342.

Thomas Hobbes had witnessed the Civil War and had also come to the conclusion that its aftermath was anarchy. He wanted stability and sound government; in their absence he drew a picture of the state which can be summed up in the title of his major work, the *Leviathan*. A materialist, he rejected any theocratic basis for the state, thus antagonizing both Laudians and Calvinists. The state was a necessity, forced on men by fear, for in a state of nature life was "nasty, brutish and short." Consequently men had made a compact, a contract, with the state, to which they had surrendered certain individual rights in return for its assuring them security in life and possessions.

To place the state on the secular basis of contract was to make it understandable to middle-class people; and there was some historical justification for his assertion that the state had come to encompass all other social groupings and their activities, which it could thus regulate as it chose, including religious faith, in the same manner as it collected revenues or maintained roads. Writing in a time when there seemed to be no authority, Hobbes hotly refuted, in terms of the middle-class value of sanctity of contract, all theories, such as those of Milton, which sought to justify rebellion. Having voluntarily surrendered certain rights to the state, individuals could have no right under any circumstances to break this contract by rebellion. As a practical argument against rebellion, Hobbes maintained that every rebellion, particularly if successful and thus an encouragement to future ones, returned men just that much closer to the anarchy from whence they had sought escape by making their contract with the state. By inference, at least, Hobbes thus denied the legality of the Civil War; and his idea of the state had in fact something in common with that envisaged by Strafford and described by the word "thorough." But so great was his desire to be allowed to live in peace and quiet under the protection of a strong government that it was a matter of indifference to him whether Oliver Cromwell or Charles II actually *ruled*, provided that he did so efficiently and carried out his side of the contract.

Sir James Harrington dedicated his *Commonwealth of Oceana* of 1656 to Cromwell, then Lord Protector.[2] Oceana was the ideal state, its government enjoying stability by virtue of its close relationship with the distribution of property. Here Harrington approached the eighteenth-century Whig view that government should be by men with a "stake in the country" and that conversely, all persons of that category

[2] The dedication is interesting in view of Harrington's friendship with Charles I.

should be able to participate in government. The fact that some men of this type had been unable to do so in the early Stuart period had caused them to turn to Parliament and challenge the traditional powers of the crown. Harrington, however, would have gone further than either these men or their eighteenth-century descendants in defining those with a stake in the country. In Oceana all men elected the lower house of a bicameral legislature, and the senate, composed of and named by men of wealth, acted as a brake upon unbridled popular passions. Harrington's arguments for this type of bicameralism were echoed in the debates in the American Constitutional Convention of 1787, when that part of his plan of government which called for the replacement of a third of this senate at each election was actually adopted.[3]

Harrington considered that stable government was possible only if it were based upon the socio-economic fact of the unequal distribution of property. He wished to avoid, however, a concentration of property, particularly of land, which he viewed as the stabilizer of society, in the hands of a few persons. He would have forbidden individuals to own land above £2000 value in England or £300 in Scotland. To avoid accumulation of property above these values by marriage or inheritance, the law of Oceana limited dowries and replaced primogeniture descent of property by partage (equal division) among all children.

Harrington's plan had much to recommend it, though the governments of the Interregnum could hardly have dared to let every man vote for the lower house, because it would have been overwhelmingly royalist. Harrington's ideas, however, influenced other "planners" of government, including John Milton, whose *Ready and Easy Way to Establish a Free Commonwealth* appeared in 1660, after it was all over and the Stuarts about to land.

The Commonwealth Phase

When in 1649 the Rump Parliament declared England a "Commonwealth and Free State," its few members believed that a new day had come. That new day to them, however, did not mean an opportunity to erect an ideal society but rather the chance to perpetuate their own power.

Parliament legally was sovereign during the Commonwealth. Yet to call the truncated House of Commons "Parliament" was ridiculous. No

[3] Constitution of the United States, Article I, Section 3–2.

member represented the Anglican mass of the nation, its few Catholics, nor even the Presbyterians. London, the stronghold of English Puritanism, had one member. Only the insistence by its few members that they were Parliament had made it such by convention. Like all revolutionary assemblies, this small House of Commons drew to itself all functions of government and delegated only a limited exercise of them to specific agencies, which it supervised minutely and suspiciously. Constitutionally, the Commonwealth was thus the ultimate in parliamentary sovereignty, particularly since the members of the Rump had no intention of consenting to their dissolution as required by the law of 1641. But in the midst of an overwhelmingly hostile nation, this small body was able to govern only so long as it had the support and protection of the army. Within four years of the execution of Charles, however, it had antagonized the army and was doomed.

As envisaged in the Nineteen Propositions of 1642, which the Rump still regarded as having been a statement of its war aims, Parliament acted executively, naming all civil officials and military commanders — including Oliver Cromwell, who replaced Fairfax when the latter refused to participate in the trial of the late king, as commander of the army. Although rarely more than sixty members were present in the Rump, it was too large for co-ordinating daily administration. This was made the duty of the *Council of State*, which was composed largely of members of Parliament holding their posts at its pleasure, and with a few army leaders forming a small minority. Parliament, moreover, was so fearful of any potential rival that initially the Council was allowed no president, and later when this proved inconvenient, one was named for a single month's term. The close check by Parliament on the Council, whose members were unwilling to move on their own, was not calculated to improve administrative efficiency. Civil government compared unfavorably in this respect with the military administration, which was in the hands of Cromwell and the Army Council, and highly efficient.

The legislative activity of the Rump was considerable. Severe laws dealt with violations of the sabbath and the observation of Christmas. A rigorous poor law reflected the essential Puritan belief that somehow a pauper had fallen from divine grace. Laws forbade cock-fighting and made adultery a capital crime, although juries often refused to convict. In 1651 a navigation act expressed prevailing mercantilist principles and the desire of the merchants to break the Dutch hold on the carrying trade of goods of other countries. The importation of goods into England except by ships of the country of their origin or in English bottoms was forbidden. This eventually provoked a war with the Dutch; but the port towns and ship owners were very much in favor of the act and it was the only law of the Interregnum to be re-enacted after the Restoration.

Local administration, however, was inefficient. Although the class responsible for it had sabotaged some Stuart policies, the sharp revulsion of feeling that fatal January day in 1649 had made many of the gentry politically "unreliable" for the Rump, which like its royal predecessors discovered that legislation without efficient administrative implementation was a barren thing. Parliament had to turn to "outsiders" from Kent to administer its laws in Sussex. Hampered by their invidious status, similar to that of the carpet-baggers in the post-Civil War Southern United States, and the unpopularity of the regime they served, these officials were hamstrung by detailed instructions and constant interference from the Rump.

The army had hoped that the Rump would dissolve itself and give way to a more representative body. Politically conscious "Agitators" moved among the troops,[4] and in 1647 had persuaded the army to accept a constitution for a republic, known as the *Agreement of the People*. This was the nearest that lower-class radicalism, as preached by Lilburne, came to taking over the government. Calling for the voluntary dissolution of the existing Parliament, the draft constitution proposed to replace it by a single house, elected by all persons paying local taxes, or "rates," in districts of equal population. It was to sit for a fixed term of two years, but with a *maximum* annual session of six months, with all parliamentary powers exercised in the interim by a Council of State named by Parliament. There would be a Puritan state church, but with toleration extended to all sects except Anglicans and Catholics.

The Agreement of the People did not equate political democracy with parliamentary sovereignty; and the limitations on parliamentary powers and the duration of sessions reflected the army's weariness with the Rump and ought to have served as a warning to that body. Some of the more extreme radicals in the army wanted to impose the proposed constitution by military force, but Cromwell disliked the use of

---

[4] There is an obvious similarity between these Agitators and the *représentatives en mission* and the political commissars in the French and Soviet revolutionary armies.

force in the establishment of any government. His great prestige allowed him to persuade the army that the best method of putting the proposed constitution into operation was for him to present it to his colleagues in Parliament for their approval.

But members were still in no hurry to dissolve themselves. Moreover, as the army was engaged in operations in Ireland and Scotland until late in 1651 its influence at Westminster was necessarily limited. It was not until after the Battle of Worcester in September 1651 that it was free to take a closer interest in the central government. Then Parliament, recognizing that Worcester required some gesture in return, undertook to dissolve itself within three years. Only with difficulty did Cromwell restrain his troopers.

Democratic ideas had strongly influenced the army's lower ranks, somewhat to the concern of the higher echelons, but both were agreed on a number of points with which the politicians at Westminster had little sympathy. Like most soldiers, those of the Puritan army had a better opinion of the enemy than of their civilian superiors. When in answer to army demands the Rump passed an amnesty act for royalist troops, Puritan soldiers were disgusted by its many and broad exceptions. The hopes of the army for a religious settlement along Independent lines, with a degree of toleration at least for Puritan sects, was frustrated by a Parliament which still toyed with the idea of establishing a Presbyterian state church with no toleration beyond it.

Cromwell found it ever more difficult to persuade the army that Parliament would dissolve itself. His dual position as commander of the forces and as a parliamentarian was not a happy one and caused him to hesitate. Finally, in April 1653, he was able to report to his men that Parliament at last was going to fulfill the requirement of 1641 and dissolve itself, only to discover that its plans for new elections did not include the present members, who were to retain their seats so that their constituencies would not vote in the elections. When despite his warnings the Rump persisted in this plan, Cromwell decided to end the farce. On 20 April 1653 he summoned a troop of soldiers and dispersed the remnant of the Long Parliament; later the same day he dismissed the Council of State. The Long Parliament had finally been destroyed by its own creation, the army.

Cromwell tried to evade the implications of his own position. A complex personality, he was almost unique among dictators in his dislike of dictatorship and his striving after government by consent.

His tragedy was that such consent was impossible when so many men were still stubbornly royalist. In April 1653, having overthrown the Commonwealth, Cromwell shrank from the consequences, and on the advice of Major-General Thomas Harrison entrusted the government of the country to a group of "godly" men. After his experience with the sinners of the Rump, Cromwell was willing to try this Fifth Monarchy alternative and ordered all Independent congregations to submit the names of such men to the Army Council. The Council then selected 190 of them, including six from Ireland and five from Scotland, to constitute Parliament, which met in July 1653.

The Little Parliament was the first legislature to represent the entire British Isles. It was, however, "Parliament" only by courtesy, representing neither the communities of the realm, as had the historic Parliament, nor the people, as would the modern one. At best, it represented only the Independent faction of the Puritan minority. Called derisively the "Barebone's Parliament," after one of its members named "Praise God Barebone," it did not represent government by consent, but government by the elect.

Although influenced by Fifth Monarchy ideas, the Little Parliament was not so certain of the imminence of the Second Coming that it proposed to do nothing. Its legislation dealt with public responsibility for the mentally ill, permitted civil marriage, and established a national register of vital statistics for marriages, births, and deaths. Educational reforms were attempted, but at once came up against the religious problem. The religious settlement was the bugbear of the Little Parliament, for a small majority, on the basis of their Independent background, favored a church without tithes or endowments, supported instead by voluntary contributions. The minority, including Cromwell, thought that the plan was impractical. Debates on the proposal revealed that the Independents had little interest in, and not much sympathy with, the other major elements of English Puritanism, the Presbyterians and Baptists, and still less with the numerous small nonconformist sects. When it became obvious that the majority was determined on this "voluntary" church, the minority rose early on the morning of 12 December 1653, and in an action reminiscent of some of the "legal" coups and putsches of the twentieth century, came to the house to form a quorum and surrendered all power to Cromwell.

The Protectorate Phase

The second phase of the Interregnum, the Protectorate, saw a steady, and often deliberate, reversion to the traditional constitution. But first the army generals, anxious to invest the new regime with an appearance of legality and to disguise the fact that it rested on military force, drew up *The Instrument of Government,* the first and last written constitution that England was ever to have.

Its military drafters had had quite enough of theories of government by consent and by the elect and wanted only stability, which they hoped to achieve by setting down in a single document a complete statement of the structure and powers of government. The commanders believed in a strong executive, independent of parliamentary control; Pym's idea of an executive subordinate to Parliament was abandoned, together with that expressed in the Agreement of the People for a co-ordinate executive-legislative relationship. Instead there was a rigid separation of powers between Parliament and the executive, with most real powers in the hands of the latter.

The executive was to consist of the *Lord Protector* and a *Council of State,* and the Instrument of Government named Cromwell as Lord Protector, and his fellow generals of the Army Council, together with some civilians, as his colleagues in the Council of State. Members of the executive held their positions for life and filled vacancies in their number from a list to be compiled by Parliament, from which the Council would pick two names, with the Protector making the final selection. Parliament, however, would have no part in naming Cromwell's successor, which was a matter solely for the Council of State.

The Council of State was the key to the entire constitution. Although the Lord Protector was the commander of the armed forces, except when Parliament was in session (a concession without meaning in terms of military actualities), he had to exercise his other powers with the approval of the Council of State, including the conduct of foreign affairs. The Council and the Protector could issue ordinances, providing that they did not contravene this constitution or parliamentary legislation. The executive could also veto any measure passed by Parliament within twenty-one days if the Council considered the bill unconstitutional. Yet although the Lord Protector's position may have been envisaged as *primus inter pares* with his councillors, Cromwell's authority was undisputed; whatever the constitution might say, he was recognized as the head of the state.

To protect this plural executive against legislative coercion the constitution gave it what no English monarch had ever possessed or ever would enjoy — nothing less than the authority to raise money annually *without* parliamentary sanction for the maintenance of an army of 30,000, a navy, and £200,000 for civil administration. This astounding provision struck from Parliament its power of the purse and cancelled the law of 1641 which had forbidden any enforced payment to the crown without parliamentary approval.

Parliament was theoretically co-ordinate with and independent of the executive, though in practice it was neither. The military authors of the constitution no longer thought in terms of parliamentary sovereignty and did not want the executive to be hampered as it had in the past by parliamentary interference. Continuing the legislative union of the British Isles, they provided for a unicameral body of 460, with Scotland and Ireland each sending 30, roughly distributed by population but elected by the "right people." Borough franchises were laid down in charters to this end, and the county suffrage was raised from the 40-shilling freehold qualification, which had returned the shire representatives to the Long Parliament, to that of the ownership of land or chattels of £200 value. Such a franchise clearly intended a House of Commons (with a membership qualification the same as for the franchise) consisting of wealthy, conservative Puritans.

Parliament had to meet at least once every three years (thereby continuing the law of 1641)[5] for not less than five months, and had power to legislate (although not so as to alter the constitution or contravene it) and to vote funds beyond those conferred by the constitution on the executive. Apart from compiling the list from which the Council filled its vacancies, Parliament had no part in selecting the executive. It had to ratify executive appointments to the higher administrative and judicial positions, but this was little compared with its recent power actually to make such appointments. Furthermore, the financial independence of the executive meant that under normal circumstances it would probably summon Parliament only every three years, and would thus have ample opportunities to make what appointments it wished in the meantime.

The legislative function granted to Parliament by the Instrument of

[5] Above, p. 317.

Government revealed a serious flaw in the political thinking of its authors and was to be the source of great friction between Parliament and the executive. The latter was in no sense part of the legislature, and did not share in its activities as privy councillors had in the past; but its veto of "unconstitutional" measures might block legislation, *unless,* and herein lay the entire difficulty, Parliament overrode such a veto by a simple majority.

The commanders had done their best to erect a strong and independent executive, but in fact they had left both the executive and the constitution itself at the mercy of a parliamentary majority. According to the constitution the executive had no members in Parliament, and consequently little control over its legislation. Since no measure would ever come before the executive for a decision regarding its constitutionality without having had the support of a majority in Parliament, the Protector's veto at best could only delay the transformation of a bill into law, even one drastically altering the constitution or even abolishing it. Cromwell's fear of just this sort of legislation lay behind his poor relations with Parliament during the Protectorate.

A bill of rights further limited both the executive and the legislature, but it was in this part of the Instrument of Government that the widest gulf lay between the idea and the reality. The enumeration of such rights as personal protection against arbitrary searches and seizures, arrest without cause, and the guarantee of speedy trial by jury did not prevent the violation of all of these rights by the government. Parliament was less guilty here than the executive, which found, as had James I and Charles I, that certain policies committed it to arbitrary action against those people opposing them, particularly now in a revolutionary situation where most people felt little or no loyalty to the regime.

In applying the guarantee of religious liberty, except for Anglicans and Catholics to whom it was specifically denied, the government moved in the opposite direction, however. Both of these excluded groups received practical toleration from Cromwell, the government disregarding Anglican services and asking only that English and Scottish Catholics should not plot against it, although it was very much more severe on their Irish co-religionists. Parliament, on the other hand, demanded savage action against Quakers for their denial of any secular authority and against Unitarians for their denial of the Trinity. Cromwell invariably commuted capital sentences imposed on these people, and when Parliament protested, he drily replied, "Notions will hurt none but them that have them." More acceptable to Puritans, with their Old Testament orientation, was Cromwell's readmission of the Jews, barred from England since 1290, when Edward I had found it simpler to expel them than to repay what he owed them.[6]

Cromwell accepted the new constitution late in 1653, and the first Parliament of the new government met the following year. It was at once apparent that its wealthy and self-confident members were not prepared to see Parliament retreat from its former position and accept a subordinate role. A few radicals, who had been elected despite the narrow franchise, pressed for a revision of the constitution, which all members had sworn to uphold. When Cromwell reminded them of this oath, which likewise bound him, they retorted in phrases reminiscent of the Great Protestation to James I. The executive's answer was to elucidate a doctrine of "fundamentals" and "circumstantials" with regard to the constitution, only the latter being susceptible to legislative alteration. This left the executive to decide into which of the two categories a constitutional issue fell, which did not at all please the radicals. But the Protector demanded a pledge from all members not to legislate on "fundamentals," and expelled from the House some 30 members who refused to give it. Parliament, however, continued to discuss proposals whereby it should name the Lord Protector and his Council and have sole control over all revenues. The executive naturally argued that these were "fundamentals," as were parliamentary demands for a reduction of the army to its constitutional maximum of 30,000; Cromwell refused to reduce the size of his forces until he felt it was safe to do so. When he later made the reduction, he insisted that it was at his own discretion. With relations between the executive and the Commons hardly better than they had been during the reign of Charles I, Cromwell suffered Parliament for the five months laid down in the constitution and then dissolved it.

He undoubtedly would not have summoned it again until the expiration of the constitutional three years, had it not been for a war with Spain late in 1654, the expenses of which demanded parliamentary grants. Despite the restrictive franchise and the active intervention by the major-generals in charge of local administration,[7] the elections of 1656 returned a Parliament in which at least a quarter of the members

[6] Above, p. 167.
[7] Below, pp. 350–51.

was actively hostile to Cromwell. The Council of State met this embarrassment by applying the constitutional requirement that members
of the Commons be men of "integrity, fearing God and of good conversation"; about a hundred of them did not answer to these criteria and
were forcibly prevented from taking their seats. When it became evident that the majority of members was prepared to accept this affront
to the dignity of Parliament in a spirit of meek subservience, a further
50 members absented themselves from the House in protest. But even
among those who remained there was a core of anti-militarist feeling
and a general tendency to hanker after older and well-tried forms of
government. By 1657 this tendency was sufficiently strong to produce
a *parliamentary* revision of the constitution, which could not in theory
be amended at all. In this Parliament had the active approval of Cromwell, who was himself anxious to broaden the basis of government and
escape from his dependence on military force.

The *Humble Petition and Advice* aimed at restoring the situation of
1641. In framing it, and the later *Additional Petition and Advice*, the
members of Parliament were certainly dealing with the "fundamentals"
of the constitution, but Cromwell this time did not demur. Parliament
first of all called upon Cromwell to become king, but the Protector,
knowing that the army was against it, after some hesitation refused the
crown. He did, however, become Lord Protector for life with the
right to name his own successor, instead of the Council of State.
Members of the latter were to be nominated by the Protector and
approved by Parliament, and they could be removed only if Parliament
agreed. These alterations in the government greatly reduced the position of the Council of State, now to be known again as the Privy
Council, and revealed Cromwell's real desire to have a parliamentary
basis for government, although the executive still possessed financial
independence for its ordinary expenditures.

Part of Cromwell's willingness to allow Parliament to play a larger
role in government came from his assurance that he would be able to
check opposition in the House of Commons by the new "Other
House." This body was to consist of between 40 and 70 members
nominated by himself. The return to legislative bicameralism was an
obvious effort to restore the past, and what now existed was "King,
Lords, and Commons" in everything but name. Installed as Lord Protector with all the pomp of coronation except the actual crowning,
Cromwell became "His Highness" and dropped the republican signa-

ture of "Oliver Cromwell" for the quasi-royal "Oliver, P" (in emula-
tion of "Charles, R"). Yet the very closeness of the constitution to
that of 1641 inspired in the mass of the people a feeling of so near and
yet so far; things could not be right again until the king "came into
his own."

The revised constitution worked badly. The coldness of the nation
toward the regime denied it the basis of assent for which Oliver had
hoped. However, confident that he could control the new "Other
House," he did not interfere in the elections to the House of Commons,
which met in early 1658, and even permitted strong republicans, who
regarded him as a traitor, to take their seats. Once there, these republicans promptly returned to the task of modifying the constitution still
further in the direction of parliamentary sovereignty, to be exercised
by a unicameral body. With the war against Spain still on his hands,
Oliver asked for money and received from these republicans savage
attacks on his "Other House." Fearful that the ideas of the radicals
would spread to the lower ranks of the army and despairing of getting
funds from this Parliament, Oliver dissolved it as angrily as had ever
James I or Charles I. Once again he was forced to rely on military
force as the basis of government. Worn out by his labors and disappointments, in September 1658 he died, to the relief of republicans
and royalists alike.

Local Administration

Protectorate local administration was efficient and for that reason unpopular. The unreliability of the traditional local administrators made it
necessary to send special agents from Westminster for the performance
of specific duties, particularly the assessment and collection of taxes to
supply the extra-parliamentary revenues of the executive allowed by
the constitution. The tax burdens under the Protectorate were heavy,
and many a Puritan squire had reason to wonder why John Hampden
had ever complained about a ship money assessment of 20 shillings
levied by a prerogative crown.[8]

In 1655 a royalist rising caused the government, in defiance of the
Petition of Right, to place the entire nation under martial law.[9] For the
next two years local administration was under the direction of major-

[8] Above, p. 311.
[9] Above, p. 348.

generals, each responsible to Cromwell for the administration of his district. Although lifted in 1657 as part of the "liberalizing" of government that year, martial law left memories of really efficient, inflexible, highly centralized local administration by military commanders with no feeling for local interests.

The real measure of the government's insecurity can be seen in its interference in the boroughs, which were always regarded before the Civil War as Puritan strongholds. The central government now purged their electorates and councils for "safety." During the two years of martial law, mayors who protested against these practices went to jail by order of the local general.

The local administration of the Protectorate thus helped to drive the Puritan gentry of the counties and the merchants of the boroughs back to the principles of monarchy. The religious settlement of the Protectorate also converted many of the same people to Anglicanism.

The Puritan State Church

The religious policy of the Protectorate pleased no one. Both the Rump and Barebone's Parliaments had run aground on the issue of the Puritan state church. The Protectorate constitution provided for a state church supported by tithes, but the actual religious settlement was by executive fiat. Cromwell and the Council of State issued an ordinance for a "comprehensive" Puritan state church embracing the three major Puritan groups: the Independents, Presbyterians, and Baptists. Government commissioners assigned the appropriate clergy to a district according to which of these three denominations was dominant there. In each locality only one of the three groups would be in possession of the "official" pulpit, although all Puritan sects were tolerated by the constitution. However, it was a matter of great concern to each of the three major groups to get as many of its clergy as possible into state church pulpits, for only their occupants received the tithe; other Puritan churches in the area had to depend upon voluntary contributions.

Like all previous attempts to arrive at a religious "settlement," this was a compromise. It sought to placate all three major groups of Puritan clergy, but only succeeded in irritating each of them. The Presbyterians, who regarded themselves as socially superior to Independents and even more to Baptists, were particularly dissatisfied. None of the three denominations liked their enforced association with each other in the state church, and the Presbyterians went so far as to intrigue with the dispossessed Anglican clergy for another kind of "comprehensive" church. The religious settlement of the Protectorate revealed that the only common element among the Puritans had been a detestation of Laudianism. But the average man was an Anglican and now identified that faith with his loyalty to the Stuarts.

The tithe was the bane of the Puritan state church. Members of the two Puritan denominations not holding the official pulpit resented having to support themselves by voluntary contributions, while at the same time having to pay the tithe to a religious competitor. Members of other Puritan sects not officially recognized in the settlement were even less enthusiastic about a tithe which they had no hope of receiving. Above all, the tithe was unpopular because of the efficient way in which it was collected. The old Anglican tithe had often been in the hands of laymen who gave what they wanted to the actual upkeep of the local church. Whether in lay or ecclesiastical hands, however, its incidence had been haphazard and its collection inefficient. Neither condition applied to the tithe of the Puritan state church, whose clergy insisted upon a full and regular collection of one-tenth of all people's incomes and crops, and who did not hesitate to call upon government agencies, including the army, to achieve these ends. Many a Puritan squire must have thought almost kindly of Archbishop Laud as he watched troopers cut down exactly one-tenth of his grain and cart it off to the minister's barn. By the close of the Protectorate most of the gentry had become defiantly Anglican, and borough merchants, after seeing the Puritan tithe in operation, were at least having second thoughts.

The Disintegration of the Protectorate

The death of Cromwell proved how necessary he had been to the existence of the Protectorate; within two years of his death, Charles II was back in Whitehall. But his return need not be regarded as inevitable. Although the trend since 1654 had clearly pointed toward a restoration of the monarchy, it was weak leadership that doomed the Protectorate after 1658, rather than any particular action on behalf of the Stuarts. A regime which, despite the constitutional modifications of 1657, depended for its operation upon executive action could not survive without a strong personality at the helm. Richard Cromwell, eldest son of Oliver, became Lord Protector, supposedly on his father's nomination. He enjoyed the confidence of neither the army nor the Puritan clergy, but if he had possessed qualities of leadership, he might have ignored them both and taken advantage of the wide popular desire to return to the "good old days" and become Richard IV. Instead, Richard, a pleasant and ineffectual man but without training for his post, was helpless among the struggling factions.

His first Parliament met in 1659, and the radicals promptly renewed their demand for control of the army. When the generals forced Richard to dissolve Parliament, it was clear who were the real rulers. Their action was a signal for the resurgence of that political and social radicalism that the Protectorate was intended to restrain. In the confusion Richard left for France,[10] leaving the generals to cope with a deteriorating situation. Englishmen before they were soldiers, and disillusioned with the results of their victory over the king, the generals were no longer prepared to take a firm stand. They did not appoint another Protector to take the place of Richard Cromwell; instead they chose another expedient. They summoned the remnant of the Rump.

The surviving 49 members had learned little since Cromwell had dispersed them, and it was not long before General John Lambert became wearied of the spectacle of their debates and prepared to disperse them again. The members forestalled him by dissolving themselves in early 1660, and so at last fulfilled the statutory requirement of 1641. However, their voluntary dissolution left a complete vacuum of civil power, and only the army had any authority. Using this authority, General George Monk and his Coldstream Guards marched in. Monk called for a "free Parliament," and the wishes of the people could at last be heard.

The Convention Parliament completed the return to 1641. So-called because its summons had not come from the king, the Convention Parliament had a House of Commons elected under writs issued at the orders of Monk and specifying the suffrage of 1641. The peers, with the exception of the bishops who were still barred from the upper House,[11] came together on their own initiative. The two Houses joined in declaring that "According to the ancient and fundamental laws of this kingdom, the government is and ought to be King, Lords, and Commons." When the last two elements, already present, invited Charles II to supply the first, the Interregnum was over and the possibilities of a limited monarchy envisaged in 1641 could be explored anew.

[10] He returned after the Restoration to be ignored by the royal government, so unimportant did everyone regard "Tumble-Down Dick."
[11] Above, p. 320.

The Results of the Interregnum

The positive results of the Interregnum are difficult to assess, partly because of the deliberate effort after 1660 to cancel out that decade in which the country had been without a king. Charles II's reign was said to have begun in 1649; nothing connected with that period had any legal existence. Some of the ideas to which the Interregnum had given birth made a trans-Atlantic passage, particularly to New England, which had supplied ministers and officials for Interregnum governments. After 1660 many of these people returned to New England, where in different conditions Puritan political ideas, in the form of written constitutions and bills of rights, flourished. In England, however, the kingless decade was for the moment regarded as an aberration, as something best forgotten. But so violent a break with the past could not be forgotten for long, and its consequences were bound to be far-reaching.

The monarchy restored in 1660 was almost exactly in the form that had been envisaged for it in the legislation of the first session of the Long Parliament. Then the plan for a limited monarchy had had no time to work before the country drifted into Civil War. The results had not been parliamentary sovereignty but military dictatorship, as the drafters of the Humble Petition and Advice had tacitly recognized in 1657. Now in 1660 Englishmen could give limited monarchy a fair trial. It had felt strange without a king, and they were glad to welcome him back. At the same time they realized that they had once proved too strong for the king and if necessary they could be so again. These things they knew; so also did Charles II. When James II, a less astute ruler, made an obvious effort to remove the limitations of 1641 on the crown, the reaction was swift and decisive.

The Restoration of 1660 also saw the restoration of Parliament to its historical role. During the Interregnum, Parliament had ceased to be either popular or representative; its authority had been based upon armed force. When the Rump tried to exercise its theoretical sovereignty beyond a certain point, the army, its sole protector, turned on it. While it might be possible for the Rump to claim descent from the historic Parliament, or at least its House of Commons, not even such a strained interpretation could thus dignify the Little Parliament. The early Parliaments of the Protectorate aspired to the dignity of the name, but significantly the Parliament of 1657, in its efforts to recover its former position, felt it necessary to restore bicameralism. The narrow basis of both Houses and their dependence upon the executive for protection against mass royalist feeling, meant that Protectorate Parliaments had less power than the Parliament of 1641.

In 1660, Anglicanism was restored as the state religion, but it was no longer possible to establish it as the *national* religion. The Puritan revolution could not be undone, and no amount of legislation could eradicate Puritanism after more than a decade as the state church, with its various sects enjoying official toleration. Though harsh laws were passed against Protestant dissenters, as they were called after 1660, they remained numerous and active. It was gradually realized that the Church was no longer the nation and that adherence to the one could not be a test of loyalty to the other.

Another generation was to pass, however, before there was legal toleration for all Protestants,[12] and in 1660 the association of Puritanism with rebellion was such that it seemed reasonable to insist that public offices should be held only by Anglicans. Successive laws, beginning at the local level and finally affecting all departments of government, enforced this policy, which in time came to apply also to the crown itself. The Anglican monopoly of government was not broken until 1828, when legislation ended it for most offices, but the monarch is still legally obliged to be Anglican.[13] Even after the abolition of the monopoly, social attitudes going back to the Civil War and Interregnum left most offices in the hands of Anglicans throughout the nineteenth century.[14]

Another consequence of the Interregnum was that Englishmen were henceforth highly suspicious of standing armies. The success of a body of trained and zealous men, in their time the superior force of all Europe, in making and unmaking governments and imposing them on the people, made Englishmen wonder whether a standing army was compatible with their personal liberties. A distinct niggardliness was manifested by later Parliaments in their treatment of the army, so that in contrast to the Royal Navy, which was not considered a menace to popular rights, Great Britain always tended to enter each of its wars with insufficient manpower and equipment in the land forces.

The over-all results of the Interregnum were, therefore, negative. The crown should *not* be supreme; *neither* should Parliament, at least

[12] Below, p. 400.
[13] Below, p. 395.
[14] Not until 1916 did a non-Anglican, David Lloyd George, become Prime Minister.

in law. Religious tests were *not* feasible for determining loyalty to a government, and there should *not* be a standing army. But though negative, these nevertheless represent achievements of the greatest importance. The positive consequences of this episode in English history can be better observed in subsequent developments in the United States.

The Menace to the Common Law

Ironically enough, the time when the common law stood in real danger was not during the sixteenth century, when Continental rulers were "receiving" Roman law and the Tudors were sharpening administrative jurisprudence in England — while simultaneously upholding the common law and its courts. The gravest threat to the common law came when its supposed ally, Parliament, included in its claims to supremacy the ability to legislate fundamental law. The result was an end to the alliance between the common law and Parliament.

Legal "Reform"

By the close of the Civil War this tacit alliance was already beginning to dissolve. By that time, although Parliament had been convinced by the lawyers of the evils of Chancery, it was also beginning to take a somewhat critical interest in the common law itself, which upon investigation appeared far from perfect.

The abolition of the Court of Chancery was the final action of the alliance. Both allies, even if for different reasons, had hated the court. During the Commonwealth Chancery was moribund. The Rump embarked on a general reform of the law, of which the abolition of Chancery and equity was to be one part in a larger program for drafting a uniform code of law for all contingencies. This larger project had not progressed far when Cromwell dispersed the Rump, although it had had time to abolish pleading in law-French, with the idea that pleading in English would bring the law closer to the people and so break the monopoly of lawyers, who came in for some severe criticism by the Rump for their love of technicalities, which often defeated the larger ends of "justice."

This broader "justice" was the concern of the Little Parliament, which hoped to be able to frame a broad, but simple, and uniform legal code. Thus these men abolished the Court of Chancery, and with it much of equity. However, the lack of equity reliefs revealed that the law was by no means the perfect, judge-made thing which Coke had proclaimed. It simply did not provide certain reliefs, and the members of the Little Parliament decided that they would have to "reform" it by legislation. The awkwardness of the situation may have been a reason why the Little Parliament, having abolished Chancery, did not take similar action against the Court of Requests with its equitable reliefs.[15]

Parliamentary attempts to draft a single, perfect code were frustrated by the inexperience of members and the enormous complexity of the task. Slight progress was made by the Little Parliament. Cromwell, himself, hoped that legal reform would include some modification of the savage criminal law, and he expressed this hope to the successors of the Little Parliament. But their attempts to codify and rationalize the law were also unsuccessful.

The re-establishment of the Court of Chancery marked the end of the effort to legislate legal reform. Significantly, it was the first Parliament of the Protectorate which recognized the limitations of the law and so resurrected the court, the procedures and fees of which were to be carefully watched. The re-establishment of an equity tribunal, however, was an admission of the practical impossibility of formulating a single code where judicial action would be merely *pro forma*. Although the ideal of codification remained, the major interest in Protectorate Parliaments was a restoration of parliamentary control over the executive, and this diversion of parliamentary interest saved the common law from drastic legislative revision. It was no accident that among the chief movers for a restoration of old forms of government in the Humble Petition and Advice were lawyers, who grasped what parliamentary supremacy could mean for their law. After the Restoration talk of legal reform by legislation was unpopular, since it was connected with the Interregnum.

"Constitutional" Law

The Interregnum saw the brief appearance in England of the concept of "constitutional" law — law so fundamental that all other laws had to be in harmony with it. The concept had some historical basis in England. Statutes were the ultimate law, which overrode all others, al-

[15] Above, p. 278.

though Coke would have subordinated even statute to common law.[16] But statutory law actually spoke on few subjects. Conciliar ordinances also were of limited applicability. The judge-made common law, therefore, was often the only law available. The requirement that nonstatutory law should not conflict with statutes was in consequence relatively easy to meet. While jurisprudence recognized the various gradations of law, it also assumed that each was operating in an essentially different area and complementary to the other. But it was equally possible, once the concept of a supreme or fundamental law was allowed, to assume that the law set forth in a written constitution was fundamental and superior to all other law, which would have to be in harmony with it. With a written constitution actually in existence under the Protectorate, the opportunity was there for an application of the theory of constitutional law.

The question immediately arose, however, of which agency should apply the criterion of constitutionality to subordinate law. The constitution, itself, appeared to favor the executive, but at the same time rendered its vetoes nearly meaningless by permitting Parliament to override them easily.[17] The executive was determined, however, that the courts should not pronounce on questions of constitutionality and dealt hardly with justices presuming to do so.[18] To the common law, the application of the doctrine of constitutional law was another threat. Did the common law have to be in active or passive harmony with it? Was the law to interpret the constitution — or the constitution to interpret the law? Whatever the answers, their implications made common law supporters uneasy. After the Interregnum they were glad to return to the older concept of different grades of law having different areas of operation.

Silent Leges Inter Arma

A major reason why the concept of constitutional law received only a limited application during the Interregnum lay in the fact, presented to Englishmen of the seventeenth century and discovered by later generations of Europeans, that a revolutionary situation, in which the government essentially exists only by military force, does little good for the rule of law. If the Restoration was of king, Lords, and Commons,

[16] Above, p. 330.
[17] Above, p. 347.
[18] Below, p. 359.

so also was it of law, which could operate only in the traditional frame
of government and when the government was accepted by the people,
so that the regime was not under the necessity of violating fundamental
law to protect itself.

Juridical weakness was obvious during the Interregnum. The interest
in legal reform was not accompanied by a desire for a strong and independent bench; such a bench was hardly necessary when only the
automatic application of the provisions of a code were anticipated.
Furthermore, like all revolutionary bodies representing only a minority
and at the same time becoming increasingly radical, the Rump went in
fear of a counter-revolution. The result was the introduction of a savage
treason law and of another requiring all people to swear loyalty to the
new government. In cases in any way touching on its powers, even
when already *sub judice*, the Rump did not hesitate to intervene. Justices
who resisted such intervention in the spirit of Coke were dismissed. The
judiciary was constitutionally subordinate to both the executive and
the legislature under the Protectorate, though in practice it was the
former that exercised the control. Judicial tenure at the pleasure of
Parliament meant in fact at the pleasure of the executive, which denied
the right of courts to test the constitutionality of its ordinances in cases
between private parties, and still less when the government was a party.
Two justices lost their posts because they denied the competence of the
Protector and Council to issue a treason ordinance, saying that this
power lay solely with Parliament.

The liberty of the subject inevitably suffered. No regime estranged
from the nation can afford to be oversensitive about individual rights,
and the Commonwealth and Protectorate regimes proved no exceptions.
During the Commonwealth the Rump had an administrative court,
the High Court of Justice, which dealt with its suspected enemies in a
manner resembling that employed by the later Revolutionary Tribunal
in France, and similar administrative tribunals of the twentieth-century
dictatorships. In this way, Charles I and three peers after him were sent
to the block, and others were jailed; the provision in the Petition of
Right against imprisonment solely on the royal order [19] did not apply
to Parliament and its courts.

The Protectorate bench was hardly more concerned with individual
rights when "need of state" was involved. During the period of martial
law the courts operated only at the pleasure of the military, which did

[19] Above, p. 305.

not hesitate to use courts-martial for the trial of civilians, whenever commanders thought them desirable.

Due process of law, therefore, was impossible so long as government rested essentially on military force. Had Cromwell been able to establish a government by assent, as he always wished, the rule of law could have been resumed. But lacking this essential condition, law had to be subordinate to reasons of state.

The Interregnum had major negative effects upon later English constitutional developments, but its positive contributions were nil. The lack of mass popular acceptance of kingless government meant that the various regimes of the Interregnum had to rest upon armed force, a force which ultimately came to end the Interregnum and restore Charles II. Disillusionment about "planned" government extended to common law supporters, who discovered that their law was in far greater danger from Parliament than it had ever been from royal administrative jurisprudence.

READING LIST

ABBOTT, W. C. *Oliver Cromwell.*

GOOCH, G. P. *History of English Democratic Ideas in the Seventeenth Century*, 3rd ed., edited by H. J. Laski.

HOBBES, THOMAS. *Leviathan.*

JENKS, L. *Constitutional Experiments, 1649–1660.*

SMITH, G. "The Reform of the Laws of England, 1640–1660," *University of Toronto Quarterly*, X, 469.

10

PARLIAMENT OVER THE CROWN

In 1660 the king returned to his own, with all the pageantry and pomp due on such an occasion. Charles II looked and acted the part. But in fact the role he was playing was fundamentally different from any for which his predecessors had been cast. He was to be a constitutional monarch. And though for many centuries the monarchy in England had been considered "limited," it was so now in the very special sense defined by the Parliament of 1641. During these years of the Restoration period, the executive had to work with the legislature on all important issues, and in no case where royal policy encountered firm parliamentary opposition did it prevail. Nor was the will of Parliament, even when contrary to royal wishes, ever frustrated.

Political Theory

The doctrine of the Divine Right of Kings had survived many brutal refutations during the past decade, at least in the popular mind. But after the Restoration those theorists who were inclined to think in such terms tended to dilute the doctrine in the theory of *Non-Resistance*, or *Passive Obedience*. Whereas Divine Right had declared the person and powers of the monarch divinely ordained and so beyond the interference of any human agency, Non-Resistance spoke in a lower key, merely saying that all Christian men owed the king obedience. Such a view had nothing to say about existing limitations on royal authority, neither denying their legality nor proposing their removal. Even Filmer's *Patriarcha*,[1] with its extravagant Divine Right sentiments, was silent on that point.

The clergy of the Church of England and its intellectual center in the University of Oxford adhered to the doctrine of Passive Obedience,

[1] Above, p. 287.

but on the assumption that the crown would maintain the fundamentally Protestant character of the Church and defend it equally against Protestant and Catholic dissenters. In due course this assumption proved to be unfounded, and the theory of Non-Resistance, when put to the test, was seen to have flaws. Faced by James II's popish tendencies,[2] the Church had either to honor the theory and become Catholic or forsake the theory and remain Protestant. Bishop Sanderson argued that if an individual were certain that a royal command was wrong, he had the right to disobey it. Although he sought to mitigate this by saying that under no circumstances was an individual permitted to resist actively, the theory of Passive Obedience could not in practice survive the policies of James II. After 1688, the only persons true to it were those clergymen of the Church of England who preferred to lose their posts rather than accept William and Mary,[3] and with their disappearance this muted echo of the theory of Divine Right disappeared also.

During this period, political theorists concerned themselves more with things as they actually were rather than with "ideal" states or "ideal" constitutions. Though liable to be damned as "republican" by their opponents, they did in fact tacitly recognize that no government could have general acceptance, and so be limited, unless it were first monarchical.

Henry Nevill, a pupil of Sir John Harrington,[4] accepted the monarchy in his *Plato Redivivus* of 1680, but argued that the shift of property away from it to the upper and middle classes had left it unable to perform its duties efficiently. Nevill's remedy was to keep the existing powers of the crown but to entrust their exercise to men having the confidence of Parliament. This may seem to anticipate the later cabinet, but it was actually closer to the Nineteen Propositions of Pym [5] and to Sir William Temple's position of 1679.[6] In 1680 Nevill's ideas earned him a cell in the Tower, but he was no radical. He believed that government should be in the hands of men of property, who would have a real interest in performing efficiently what Nevill considered the first duty of any government — the protection of life and property.

Hardly more radical was Algernon Sidney, scion of a proud family, whose "republican" ideas brought him to the block in 1683. His *Dis-*

[2] Below, p. 391.
[3] Below, p. 401.
[4] Above, p. 339.
[5] Above, p. 320.
[6] Below, p. 385.

courses Concerning Government was not printed until 1698, in the more favorable climate of post-Revolutionary times. The book reveals a man very concerned about the type of government best qualified to protect life and property. Sidney angered the more rabid royalists by his assertion that no one form of government was perfect. Government was "good" only to the extent that it rested on social facts and could fulfil its duties of guaranteeing life and property and of promoting the general welfare. Such duties emphatically did not mean democratic government to the young aristocrat, who believed democracy to be effective only in the smallest units in government; the "natural" leaders of a country were its aristocracy.

In the bitter party conflicts during the Restoration period one man secretly praised moderation. Denounced by both extremes as a "trimmer" for his middle position in the struggle between 1678 and 1680 over the Exclusion Bill,[7] the Marquis of Halifax proudly accepted the title in his *Character of a Trimmer,* which in 1683 he cautiously circulated privately. His book emphasized the importance of people like himself in keeping the ship of state trimmed to the violent shifts of wind and wave, and thereby keeping it afloat.

For Nevill, Sidney, and Halifax, there was nothing sacred about any particular form of government; it could be judged only by its success in ensuring the safety of life and property. Such an uncommitted view made them appear radical for their times, and for that reason they had little influence upon the mass of their contemporaries. But their views showed how the intellectual minority was coming to see government as a means, not an end, the virtues and vices of which could be rationally assessed.

John Locke appealed to the "reason," to the "common-sense" of his readers, unfolding a theory of "logical" government, based upon "natural law," and confirmed by the Glorious Revolution of 1688. In his *First Treatise on Civil Government* (1690), Locke set out to refute doctrines of monarchical absolutism and in particular the Divine Right theories expressed in Filmer's *Patriarcha.* But Locke's *First Treatise* only buried what was already dead. It was the *Second Treatise on Civil Government* which was of the greater importance for English political thought, on both sides of the Atlantic. In that work Locke accepted and developed the contractual explanation of government, and in so doing set Anglo-American political thought on a course that has often run

[7] Below, pp. 386–7.

counter to Continental theories of the state. He distinguished between the state and government. Although he accepted in outline Hobbes's conception of the origins of civilized societies, he did not share the latter's views on the brutish nature of man in his raw state. It was not, therefore, necessary to surrender absolute authority to anybody; in a state of nature man had not been ignorant of natural law, that is to say completely without moral sense, but he had been compelled to be his own interpreter of these laws and inevitably his views had clashed with those of other men. For that reason men had required an arbiter among them for the protection of their lives and property. As "reasonable" creatures men had recognized this need and had created this arbiter by delegating certain (but no more) of their individual rights, not to the state, but to *government*.

This distinction enabled Locke to make one highly significant point — that men could change their government without endangering social stability, as Hobbes had feared. Locke maintained that, as in any contract, rights and duties were precisely stated; men allotted to government precise powers in order that it might perform its functions of protecting life and property. Powers not needed by government to perform these duties were not included in the original contract and so might not be lawfully exercised by government. Where a government did exceed its contractual powers or failed to perform its contractual duties, it had broken the contract between itself and the governed. A broken contract was no contract; therefore the basis for government ceased to exist; and therefore there was no government. The conclusion was inexorable. In this situation, even as on the first day of the original contract, natural law gave to men as creatures of reason the right to make a new contract with a new government which would observe its terms. Thus Locke justified the Revolution of 1688 and at the same time his readers could look at that Revolution as proof of the validity of the theory, in particular that government, as distinct from the social entity of the state, could be changed without endangering the latter.

None of Locke's contentions about the origins of government were any more capable of proof than those of Hobbes, but Locke's views seemed "reasonable" to men of the eighteenth century. For Englishmen in North America his justification of revolution had real meaning. When in 1776 one of them was called upon to draft a statement as to why some people in North America were going to have a new government, he virtually paraphrased a part of Locke's *Second Treatise:*

We hold these Truths to be self-evident . . . That . . . Governments are instituted among Men, deriving their just powers from the Consent of the Governed, That whenever any Form of Government becomes destructive of these Ends, it is the Right of the People to alter or to abolish it, and to institute a new Government . . .[8]

Locke's proposals that in the exercise of its limited powers government should operate through three independent, co-ordinate branches — legislative, executive, and judicial, each checking the other — never had real application in England, although such diverse figures of the eighteenth century as Blackstone and Montesquieu believed that it did. Locke's ideas, however, received direct and conscious application by the framers of the United States Constitution.

After 1688, Englishmen did not again experience the need for revolution as a technique of constitutional change. But in the light of Locke's theory there was always before the government its obligation to meet as best it could the needs of the people. Though governments might often err, and though for Locke and men of his class the "People" were those with wealth, holding a "stake in the country," the principle survived. There were always those, including some politicians, ready to regard the government as the servant of the people, with its functions determined by the terms of the original contract. The men who directed the Revolution and who reaped its benefits for most of the eighteenth century were certainly no democrats and feared what they called "the mob." Yet the definition of the "People" was eventually extended, and its sovereign role in a democratic society was granted.

The Clarendon Phase

From 1660 to 1667, while Charles II played the part of a "merry monarch," his Lord Chancellor, the Earl of Clarendon, was the leading figure in the government. As Sir Edward Hyde he had helped impose the parliamentary limitations on the crown in 1641. As the Earl of Clarendon he found the limited monarchy difficult to operate.

With the exception of the Council of Wales and the Court of Requests, the work of which had rapidly declined, the crown had no administrative courts to apply its policies, and the narrow appellate jurisdiction of the Council had no administrative utility. More important, the crown was utterly dependent upon Parliament financially. Although

[8] *Declaration of Independence.*

Parliament voted Charles II tunnage and poundage in 1661, and gave him a tax on malt and beer to replace the few remaining feudal dues which disappeared with the statutory abolition of military tenures the same year, these revenues were insufficient for the ordinary expenses of government and totally inadequate for the extraordinary expenses of war. In 1662 the government was so pressed financially that it sold Dunkirk, which had been captured by Cromwell's army, back to France. As Charles saw clearly enough, the only way he could do without Parliament was to gain freedom from this dependence upon its monetary grants. For him, the solution was to become a pensioner of Louis XIV of France, and this foreign, extra-constitutional source of revenue permitted him to rule without Parliament for the last five years of his reign. But it was a dangerous and unpopular policy, and in general Charles II always moved with great circumspection. The memory of a successful rebellion could not be erased, and when he joked that he did not "want to go on his travels again" he seriously meant what he said.

A further limitation on the royal power had been self-inflicted by Charles. In the Declaration of Breda,[9] issued from his last port of exile in 1660, rather than assume the responsibility himself, he promised that the four most pressing issues of the moment should be determined by Parliament: the size and payment of the *army*, the issue of *royalist lands* lost during the Civil War and Interregnum, the extent of *pardon* for offenses against the lawful ruler during this period, and the *religious settlement*, although in this last Charles expressed the hope that Parliament would respect differences of religious opinion. He thus bound himself on this occasion to accept any parliamentary action on these subjects, an undertaking which Parliament regarded as of permanent applicability.

It was not easy for the crown to assert its influence in Parliament; Clarendon simply did not have the means to do so. Bribery of members was occasionally resorted to, but it was an admission that the crown had no other means at its disposal, and in any case, as a man bought once had to be repurchased constantly, the crown lacked the money even to do this. The failure of the crown to control Parliament was particularly apparent in 1667 when, upon the impeachment of Clarendon by the Commons, the king advised him to flee rather than face trial by the Lords.

The king might have packed the House of Lords with new peers, but

[9] Douglas, VIII, 57–8.

Charles actually created few. Experience showed that once created, a peer was not inevitably a king's man — as witness Ashley Cooper, who as the Earl of Shaftesbury led his supporters against royal policy. The bench of bishops, supporters of the doctrine of Non-Resistance, restored to the House of Lords by statute in 1661,[10] was the only group in the upper House on which the king could confidently rely. But even here, his religious policies [11] enjoyed little episcopal support.

Charles II was no more able than his father and grandfather to find "safe seats" in the House of Commons for his leading advisers, who therefore were inevitably peers. Without a managerial group in the Commons, the crown lacked control over its business. In 1667 Charles tried to remedy the situation by the creation of new parliamentary boroughs, which traditionally was his prerogative. However, his first new borough charter produced such wrath from Parliament that he had to withdraw it. No further attempt was made to revise the parliamentary constituencies until Parliament itself did so in 1832. The composition of the Commons was proved to be really in its own hands. The incident was also proof that the social elements represented in Parliament were not going to permit the royal prerogative to operate against their own interests.

Parliament had developed a strong sense of its own corporate strength. The Convention Parliament of 1660 was succeeded by a regular Parliament elected under royal writs in 1661. If the members of this "Cavalier" Parliament were more "royalist than the king and more Anglican than the bishops," it was not so much because of their admiration for either Charles or the bishops, but because they believed that the institutions they represented were bulwarks against radicalism and guarantees of a social order in which they would be dominant. It indicated no want of self-importance on their parts and they were ready to challenge the policies of Church and crown whenever these threatened their own fundamental purpose of controlling the nation. Although Charles promised the members of this Parliament, most of them comparatively young men, that he would keep them until they had beards, his relations with them became increasingly uneasy as the years passed. By 1679 he had to dissolve the Cavalier Parliament to prevent its passing the Exclusion Bill, barring his brother, James, Duke of York, from the throne.[12]

[10] Above, p. 320; Douglas, VIII, 208.
[11] Below, pp. 372, 376.
[12] Below, p. 384.

Members were jealous of their privileges, which Charles was sensible enough not to touch. In 1667 a concurrent resolution of the two Houses denied the validity of the decision of 1630 by King's Bench upholding the royal imprisonment of members for contempt.[13] To give the resolution legal force, the House of Lords as the highest appellate court reversed the decision of King's Bench on a writ of error. With this ultimate judicial sanction for their sole right to punish members for contempt, both Houses felt that their long-sought privilege of freedom of speech had at last been fully assured and were not slow to take advantage of it. The only recourse the crown had was either prorogation or dissolution.

Relations between the two Houses were complex. The undoubted institutional superiority of the House of Commons, particularly in view of its sole right to initiate money bills and the royal dependence on parliamentary grants, obscured the dominance of the House of Lords at other levels. During the Restoration the internal, unofficial management of the Commons, which had baffled the early Stuarts, gave way to management from outside the House by great magnates in the House of Lords, a control which was to last until 1832. This development did not benefit the crown, however. The peers kept a close watch on their supporters in the lower House, made up of their sons, relatives, and friends. Local influence and bribery of voters by the magnates permitted a few of them to possess considerable voting strength in the Commons, and a few such peers concerting their forces could thus manage the Commons where the crown with its slender resources could not. Even so, there was friction between the two Houses during the Restoration period.

Parliamentary sessions were frequent. The difficulty the crown had in dealing with Parliament, however, usually made them short. In 1661 Charles asked Parliament to repeal the Triennial Act of 1641, requiring a parliamentary session at least once every three years and providing for the automatic holding of elections by sheriffs in the absence of a royal summons.[14] Although still in the first flush of enthusiasm for the restored ruler, Parliament refused. Three years later Charles declared that he would never give his assent to any bill passed by a Parliament assembled under the alternative method. Parliament went so far as to repeal the act of 1641, but only with the rider that Parliament must

---

[13] Above, p. 312; Douglas, VIII, 165.
[14] Above, p. 317.

still be summoned at least every three years. Without machinery to implement this requirement, the prerogative was left in an apparently
stronger position, but the royal need for money made it an empty victory for the king.

Parliamentary control of finance was obvious but not specific. The
need of the crown for parliamentary grants did not mean that Parliament assumed any minute control over royal expenditures. In 1665 and
1666 it did vote funds specifically for the Dutch war, but such precise
appropriations were rare. On that occasion it named commissioners to
audit the disbursement of the funds, and when they discovered that Sir
George Carteret, Treasurer of the Navy, had paid out money without
warrants, Parliament insisted on his dismissal. The House of Commons
also summoned the Clerk of the Acts of the Navy Board to its bar to
justify the whole administration of his office, a task which, as that official modestly confided to his famous diary, he performed like another
Cicero. However, such detailed parliamentary inquiries into expenditure were exceptional and usually a result of general dissatisfaction with
the administration. Normally, Parliament voted money in general terms,
but this made the crown no less dependent upon it.

While Clarendon remained in power, Parliament's role in directing
policy was perhaps more real than apparent. But the Lord Chancellor
knew the limitations of the monarchy only too well and realized that
the king would often have to assent to measures widely at variance with
royal policy. After Clarendon, parliamentary control over crown policy
was exercised more openly by a combination of squires, merchants, and
a few nobles; but even from the start Parliament legislated on important subjects without regard to royal wishes, beginning with the matters cited in the Declaration of Breda.

First Parliament paid off and disbanded Monk's army, a source of
constant uneasiness, although Charles would have been willing to keep
it. Then, in dealing with the issue of former royalist lands, it was agreed
that those actually confiscated by Interregnum governments should be
returned to their former owners or their heirs, but that lands sold by
royalists under economic or political pressure should not be restored.
Some of the purchasers sat in Parliament. Again, the Cavalier Parliament
might have dealt harshly with people who had legally committed treason
since 1641 in supporting the enemies of the king. However, neither Parliament nor Charles could proceed very far here. Certain members of
Parliament had left the Protectorate ship only when it was obviously

foundering, and Charles had been restored by nearly the same elements which had overthrown his father. Only some fifty names were listed as exceptions to the general Act of Indemnity. The body of Oliver Cromwell was dug up and hanged in chains at Tyburn, and a few regicides were condemned to death; but on the whole there was but little retaliation and an attitude of unusual clemency.

It was the ecclesiastical settlement, however, which struck most directly at the royal prerogative. Charles, who had no great religious feeling himself and whose tolerance of differences of belief among others extended in particular to Roman Catholics, had tied his hands in the Declaration of Breda. For the next few years he had to assent to bills which placed the responsibility for the national Church securely in the hands of the social groups represented in Parliament. Dispossessed Anglicans and dissatisfied Presbyterians had restored Charles, the latter largely because of their desire to disassociate themselves from Independents and Baptists and to be included, together with the Anglicans, in a new state church. Conferences between Anglican and Presbyterian clergy at Savoy House in 1661 fell through, however; the Presbyterian policy of "comprehension" was severely exclusive, being as violently hostile to other Puritan sects as to Roman Catholics. But to the Cavalier Parliament of 1661 the Presbyterians appeared to be as guilty as any other Puritan sect for the crimes of the past twenty years. The members of Parliament were resolutely Anglican, identifying that faith with a social order wherein their interests would be safe. They therefore reaffirmed the old policy which made adherence to the official faith the criterion of loyalty to the regime. Puritanism was regarded as *the* cause of the Civil War and the attendant social upheavals, and four laws were passed in an attempt to eradicate nonconformity. Wrongly termed the "Clarendon Code," for the Chancellor, and still less Charles, would not have gone so far, these measures initiated a period of bitter persecution. They were also a striking denial of the Elizabethan view that the royal supremacy could be exercised without reference to Parliament.[15]

Parliament sought to break the Puritan control of borough government by the *Corporation Act* of 1661,[16] requiring all borough councillors and mayors to swear allegiance to the king, and admit his ecclesiastical supremacy; to take another oath denying the right of resistance to him; and to abjure under oath the Solemn League and Covenant, by

[15] Above, pp. 266, 269.
[16] Douglas, VIII, 375–6.

which the Puritan Parliament had enlisted Scottish assistance during the Civil War in return for promising to establish an English Presbyterian state church. This last was a blow to Presbyterians, and the additional provision in the law that all borough officials must take the sacrament only by Angelican rites made it impossible for sincere Puritans any longer to hold office in local government.

What the Anglican rites for the sacrament and other services would be was still in doubt in 1661, because a committee of bishops was revising the Prayer Book. In 1662, although their work was not completed, the *Act of Uniformity* [17] declared that only the services of the revised Prayer Book should be used in the Church. All clergy, university fellows, and teachers had to swear to abide by these services and use no others. When the new Prayer Book appeared, over a thousand clergy could not accept its services and gave up their livings. The law thus seemed to have achieved its purpose of driving Puritanism out of the Church.

In 1664 Parliament sought to end Puritanism outside the Church by the *Conventicle Act*,[18] forbidding under heavy penalties services other than those of the Prayer Book, where over five persons were present, except for family worship. In some counties this statute was rigorously enforced, but where Puritanism had retained the loyalty of the squires its enforcement was sporadic. Intended to deprive urban Puritanism of its spiritual leaders, the *Five Mile Act* [19] of 1665 completed the Clarendon Code. It forbade any person failing to make the necessary declarations under the Act of Uniformity to come within five miles of any borough where he had once been employed.

Constitutionally, the religious settlement was parliamentary, even as Charles had promised in the Declaration of Breda. But he had also then promised toleration, and now he tried to break through the parliamentary settlement — and failed. In 1661 he asked for statutory authority to dispense with the operation of the Corporation Act for safe persons; Parliament refused. The next year, the king on his own prerogative issued a proclamation, designed to fulfil his promises at Breda, suspending all religious penal laws.[20] Charles was thinking less of Puritans than of Catholics. The House of Commons, however, denied that the provisions of the Declaration of Breda entitled the king to act independently of

[17] Douglas, VIII, 377–82.
[18] Ibid. 384–6.
[19] Ibid. 382–4.
[20] Ibid. 371–4.

Parliament. This denial of royal ecclesiastical supremcy and prerogative Charles did not dare challenge, and with his own hand he tore the Great Seal from the proclamation. The next year he and Clarendon attempted to put through a bill permitting the crown to dispense with the Act of Uniformity in certain individual cases; again the bill failed. Thus the parliamentary nature of the ecclesiastical settlement was now clear. It was equally clear that Parliament was determined, and furthermore was able, to set rigid limits to the royal prerogative, which could operate only in those areas which Parliament was willing to entrust to it; and in the most vital issue of the day Parliament refused to let it act.

The Clarendon Code did not eliminate Puritanism, or nonconformism, as it came to be called. Barred from all government offices, nonconformists turned their attention to other matters: to business, banking, or manufacturing. Deep Puritan religious feeling was never to be eradicated amongst the humbler classes, despite persecution. The distinction between Anglican and nonconformist, between "church" and "chapel" people, came to imply profound social, political, and economic differences, and it was this permanent division of English social life that was the most important consequence of the Clarendon Code.

Administration

The day-to-day work of administration was carried on by the king and his ministers. Parliament tended to be even less concerned with its details than it had been in earlier reigns. After 1660, moreover, the Privy Council ceased to be the center of administration, and this in turn meant that Parliament was not enlightened on administrative matters by its councillors in either House. The size of the Privy Council after 1660, never less than 50 members, made efficient control of administration impossible; its membership grew steadily until by the close of the seventeenth century it was an honor without much responsibility. Charles II continued to meet with it, but he conducted little important business there. He preferred to work directly, often secretly, with individual advisers. If they headed administrative departments, they conducted them without reference to the full Council. The Lord Treasurer, the Lord High Admiral, the Southern and Northern Secretaries of State responsible for diplomacy with southern and northern European states, and a number of boards and committees conducted the business of government. Charles also gave Irish administration to the

Northern Secretary and at times used both Secretaries to deal with domestic matters.

The decline of the Privy Council and the restored predominance of the crown in the central administration was a matter of concern to those who feared that this would lead to a reduction of Parliament's power. An attempt was made to reinvigorate the Privy Council and to define its relationship to Parliament.[21] But the Privy Council was beyond help, and the crown continued to extend its administrative advantage.

Local administration became more autonomous and more completely in the hands of the justices of the peace. Without a small, vigorous Privy Council there was no effective supervisory agency of the central government over them. With such an arrangement any absolutist tendencies manifested by the crown were doomed to frustration at the local level. Certainly some of the local squires were themselves capable of petty tyranny over people who were often also their tenants; but there were many others, like Sir Roger de Coverley, who could protect them against all government except their own paternalistic kind. The influence of these country gentry and of the manor house on the village life of England during these years was incalculable.

The fall of Clarendon was brought about by parliamentary action. Clarendon was the last of the administrative Chancellors, and his ideas of government, based on the Tudor model of a powerful Chancellor working with the Privy Council, conflicted with the new style of administration through departments, the heads of which felt responsible only to the king. Clarendon found it difficult to control the policy for which Parliament held him responsible. Dogmatic, hard-working, and somewhat old-fashioned, he was not popular with Parliament, nor indeed with the king who owed him so much. His difficulties increased during the Dutch War of 1665–67, of which he had never approved. The merchants in Parliament had desired the war but had been reluctant to vote the money for it. The war revealed royal administration to be inefficient, particularly in the navy, where lack of funds forced the government to lay up the fleet. The Dutch burnt part of it in the lower Thames. Clarendon was not responsible for the lack of funds or for naval administration, but this humiliating and calamitous episode on an English river demanded a scapegoat, and Parliament and the king both selected Clarendon. The former held him responsible for the sale of Dunkirk, the royal marriage (despite the inclusion of Tangier and

[21] See the plan of Sir William Temple, below, p. 385.

Bombay in the otherwise barren bride's dowry), and the mismanagement of the Dutch war; the latter had grown weary of this man from
his father's generation with his notions of duty and honor. When in
1667 the House of Commons impeached Clarendon, Charles, unlike his
father, refused to identify himself with an unpopular minister, and advised him to flee. Clarendon took the advice and went to France, where
he died. With his departure, the office of Chancellor, although still important, ceased to be the dominant one in the government.

The Cabal

From 1667 to 1673 Charles II took the first steps toward royal absolutism, carefully screening his moves by using five principal advisers.
Collectively known as the Cabal, they owed their relationship with the
king to their position in Parliament. Until his plans were ripe, Charles
had to work with Parliament, which meant that he had to discover a
means of managing it, as he had failed to do in Clarendon's time.

The word "cabal," from the Spanish, had been used previously in
England with connotations of intrigue and secret dealing, but the word
seemed peculiarly apt for these five advisers because of the initial letters
of their names:

> Clifford — Lord Treasurer
> Arlington — Secretary of State
> Buckingham — Master of the Horse [22]
> Ashley (Earl of Shaftesbury)—Lord Chancellor
> Lauderdale — Secretary for Scottish Affairs

Each of these men was a close adviser of the king, not because of his
membership in the Privy Council, nor even because of his office, but
because of his ability to control votes in Parliament, more particularly
the Commons. The offices they held were entrusted to them by the king
in return for their votes.

The Cabal had a number of resemblances to the later cabinet, but in
fact their collective name implies a unity among them which did not
exist. Initially all were anti-Dutch, but this common bond soon dissolved. Clifford, a secret Catholic, and Arlington, an incipient one,
wanted religious toleration in order to prepare the way for a restoration
of Catholicism. Shaftesbury and Lauderdale were fiercely anti-Catholic

[22] Son of the favorite of Charles I.

and wanted toleration only for Protestants. Only Buckingham seems to have believed in toleration for all faiths. Unlike the later cabinet, the Cabal had no single leader. Each of its members dealt directly with the king, who consulted such of them as he chose and played them all off against each other. They, in turn, jockeyed for a favored position and in frequently changing factions tried to gain an advantage over men they regarded not as colleagues but as rivals.

Disunity among the Cabal played into the king's hands. Exploiting the mutual rivalry of its members and their common dislike of the Dutch, Charles was ready by 1670 to enter into the French alliance he had been seeking for some time. Acting as his own negotiator, but with the approval of all members of the Cabal, the king concluded the *Treaty of Dover*,[23] which bound England and France in an offensive alliance against the United Provinces of the Netherlands, with Louis XIV of France obliged to pay part of the English expenses in the forthcoming war. Unknown to members of the Cabal, except Clifford and possibly Arlington, the treaty had secret clauses. Louis was to give Charles a subsidy and reduce his dependence on Parliament; and Charles at a time to be chosen by himself would declare himself a Catholic, with the assurance that French troops would deal with any English opposition to the royal conversion.[24] Charles, like many of his contemporaries, had been dazzled by the glorious achievements of Louis XIV, *le roi soleil;* a monarchy, absolute, nonparliamentary, and Catholic, had become his aim. None of the members of the Cabal, except Clifford, wanted such a regime; but Charles calculated that when the time came for him to establish it, they would be unable to check his plan. As an intelligent man, it is extraordinary that Charles should have been blind to the effects of his policy, once it became known, on public opinion.

In 1672 the public part of the Treaty of Dover was put into effect by the declaration of war on the Dutch. Almost at once, without the prior knowledge of any of the Cabal except Clifford, Charles issued his second *Declaration of Indulgence*,[25] suspending the operation of all penal laws against dissenters, Protestants and Catholics alike. Charles hoped that English dislike of the Dutch would make them accept the religious consequences of the treaty. Instead, the classes represented in Parliament

[23] Douglas, VIII, 863–7.

[24] The secret, religious clauses of the treaty were there because of Charles's insistence; the French doubted their desirability and feared that their implementation might wreck the alliance.

[25] Douglas, VIII, 387–8.

discovered that they hated the Dutch less than they feared Catholicism. Parliament was not in session when the king made these moves, but unfortunately for him the war required more money than the French were willing to pay. This meant summoning Parliament in early 1673, and its members immediately expressed their fears of a French, Catholic hegemony over Europe. In the space of a year Parliament had cancelled both the secret and public portions of the Treaty of Dover.

The House of Commons formally denied the ability of the prerogative to suspend *any* laws, a much broader assertion than that of a decade previously when members had said no more than that the royal promises at Breda could be effective only by statute. After this expression of the "sense" of the Commons, Shaftesbury, who now suspected the existence of secret provisions in the treaty, took the lead in the House of Lords and put through the *Test Act*.[26] This law extended the requirements of the Corporation Act [27] for borough officials to all holders of any office, who in addition had to deny under oath the Catholic doctrine of transubstantiation. Catholics could not possibly take the Anglican sacrament or such an oath.

Charles, at last recognizing the danger signs, assented to the Test Act, which he never attempted to evade, still less have repealed. The law flushed a covey of Catholics from government, including Clifford and the Duke of York, Lord High Admiral, and more important, heir to the throne. The discovery of these Catholics in high places increased Parliament's suspicion of royal policies, and within a year Parliament had forced the king to reverse his anti-Dutch policy, which the Cabal had originally sanctioned.

Bitter criticism in Parliament of the "evil councillors" who had persuaded the king to take this line was a sham, as parliamentary leaders knew; Charles had been his own foreign minister. Constitutionally his prerogative undoubtedly included the conduct of foreign affairs; but in Parliament it was being suggested that if the Dutch war was an example of how the prerogative managed foreign affairs, it was time for Parliament to take over. Members also viewed coldly the recent marriage of the Duke of York, now revealed as a Catholic, to an Italian Catholic princess; any male heir would be Catholic and have precedence in the succession over James's two Protestant daughters by his first marriage.

[26] Douglas, VIII, 389–91.
[27] Above, pp. 370–71.

Above all, there was the insistence in Parliament, carefully nurtured by Shaftesbury, who had much to hide here, that the Dutch war should end. Parliament had the means to enforce this demand; it threatened to stop providing funds for *any* purpose unless it was clear the Dutch were actually refusing to negotiate. The shrewd burghers gladly entered negotiations. Charles, admitting to Louis that he had no choice, made peace with the Dutch in early 1674.

The Cabal disintegrated. Never a united group, it was shattered by the events of 1672 and 1673. Clifford, as a Catholic, had had to resign office, and his religion made him suspect in Parliament and so of little use to the king. When the Commons threatened to impeach Arlington and Buckingham, Charles dared not let either go to trial and reveal the royal plans; to forestall parliamentary wrath he transferred the former to the comparatively unimportant office of Lord Chamberlain and dismissed the other outright. Shaftesbury, who while putting through the Test Act had spoken mysteriously about "plots," lost his post. Only Lauderdale survived the wreck, and his parliamentary following by itself was too small to be of value to the king.

Charles was in a delicate position. The attacks in Parliament against evil advisers were transparent fictions, as he knew. He had moved too openly, too soon. He still needed Parliament, and the great peers who controlled vital votes were violently Anglican, anti-Catholic, and anti-French. Charles faced the realities. Henceforth, he recognized that Anglican support was essential if he were to make any progress in the direction of absolutism; also for the time being, he needed Parliament as well.

The Rise of Parties

Much of the operation of the modern British constitution assumes and depends upon the existence of well-organized political parties, one controlling government, the others contesting for it and ready to take it over at any time. British voters support "party" government and rarely elect a nonparty man to Parliament.

Modern British parties have an ancestry stretching back to the post-Cabal phase of the Restoration, from 1673 to 1681, when they appeared for the frank purpose of controlling government. For a long time prominent British leaders deplored "party" as the worst sort of factionalism, and the early history of the parties certainly supported this charge.

However, they were an essential part of the growth of democracy, which to date has found no other way to express itself on the national level.

Parliamentary groups had first appeared when the early Stuarts lost control of the House of Commons, and Pym had had at his disposal the makings of a political party when the Civil War interrupted this development. The downfall of the Cabal provided the next occasion. One of its members, the Earl of Shaftesbury, whose physician and private secretary was John Locke, realized that so long as ministers had independent control over separate blocks of votes in the House of Commons, the king could play off these advisers against each other in his own interests. If, however, a parliamentary leader enjoyed the loyalty of a majority of the Commons both by patronage *and* by the election machinery outside Parliament, that leader would control the government, including the king, who would be unable to get any measure through Parliament without him. Another man reasoned in exactly the same way as Shaftesbury — Charles II, who had to find a parliamentary leader now to protect his very crown. The result was the Whig and Tory parties.

The Whigs were the political heirs of the Puritan opposition to Charles I. The enemies of Shaftesbury compared his supporters with Scottish robbers who killed their victims before plundering them — Whigs, a badge of shame, which Shaftesbury's men came to accept with pride in preference to their first name of the "Country Party." Although leaders in the party were necessarily Anglicans, they had the support of many Protestant dissenters, who if they could not hold office, could vote if they met franchise qualifications. Thus the major sources of party strength, financially and electorally, lay in boroughs where Puritanism had been strong. In London, the center of the party, Shaftesbury's Green Ribbon Club organized voters and kept them in line by all the tactics known to later political bosses, including favors and outright bribery.

The Whigs had certain principles, although their leaders, in the manner of practical politicians, soon learned to rise above them. If they had any central principle, it was fear and detestation of Catholicism, which their leaders skillfully exploited. Everything else was subordinate to keeping England Protestant. Translated into practical politics, this principle committed the Whigs to an Anglican monopoly of government and toleration for Protestant dissenters. The few great lords, the merchants who underwrote the party, and the mobs organized by the Whigs to bawl "No popery or wooden shoes" were not anti-monarchical; but given a choice between a Protestant republic and a Catholic monarchy there was no doubt as to their preference.

This was certainly the view of Shaftesbury, who like many party leaders combined in himself great altruism with the worst sort of self-aggrandizement. He was convinced that Charles II was trying to restore England to Catholicism and knew that his brother and heir was a Catholic. The Whig leader was determined to thwart the aim of the one and the succession of the other. Though unable to attack the king directly in view of popular feeling about the monarchy, his program committed the Whigs to a further limitation of royal power and an outright exclusion of James from the succession.

The Tories stood for the Restoration settlement, which they equated with monarchy and the Anglican church. The gentry, the clergy of the Church of England, and a number of peers, saw in these two institutions the guarantee of the kind of social order they wanted, and they were naturally unwilling to see any changes in either of them for fear of unloosing the forces which had appeared during the Civil War and Interregnum. Their party thus had certain principles, which its leaders, like those of the Whigs, could ignore when occasion required. For the Whigs these principles were anathema, and they likened those upholding them to Irish cattle thieves who hamstrung their prey — Tories. Again, the appellation was accepted by those whom it was intended to insult, and they dropped their earlier name of the "Court Party."

The fundamental principle of the Tories was the crown, to which they attached a certain mystique. It was the crown, however, as envisaged in 1641 and as it had been during the first years of the Restoration, which the Tories assumed would have the last word. Unlike the Whigs, they were unwilling to allow, whatever happened, any further interference with the crown, for fear of another internal conflict and dictatorship. The Tories thus expressed the deep national sentiment surrounding the monarchy and gave political expression to the theory of Passive Obedience.

Closely connected with this was the party's devotion to Anglicanism. Even more than the Whigs, the Tories believed in the Anglican monopoly of government, and in addition would have eradicated all other religions, particularly Puritanism, which they held solely responsible for the mid-century upheavals. It was here, however, that the party faced a dilemma. Although it could maintain that Charles II was an Anglican, it could not possibly do so with his brother and heir. How could the party's insistence on Anglicanism be reconciled with the principle of loyalty to the crown when the ruler was a Catholic? The Tories might have preferred to ignore this embarrassing contradiction, but it could not be ignored for long. Before the issue came to a head, they argued that the Catholic person of the monarch could not affect the Anglican nature of the crown. But in fact, they wished to accept unconditionally the monarchy as they now knew it and were as averse as the Whigs to unrestrained royal absolutism. If the monarch were to be Catholic as well, some way out had to be found; and Tory leaders had every reason in view of the devious policies of Charles II and the known Catholicism of his heir to compromise with their own stated principles.

Charles II preferred the Tory party as the lesser of two evils. But with both parties assuming parliamentary ascendancy over a limited crown, from his point of view there was little to choose between them, except that the Tories were committed to keeping the existing powers of the crown intact. Having sensed the temper of the nation as it expressed itself in the Test Act, he delivered himself into the hands of the Tory, Sir Thomas Osborne, soon to be the Earl of Danby.[28] He had succeeded Clifford as Treasurer, and relieved the crown of some of its most immediate financial worries by introducing long-term government financing, a novelty known at its inception as the *Stop of the Exchequer*.[29] For two years the government paid nothing on its debts and then announced that beginning in 1674, it would meet their annual interest but would repay their principal when it chose. This new financial technique ruined some of the older lending agencies, such as the London goldsmiths, and the Treasury had to turn to the rising mercantile-banking community of London. If the technique marked the beginning of a permanent national debt, it also placed a further restraint on crown policies, for the crown could not antagonize groups with liquid capital when it dealt with them as businessmen any more than it could when it met them in Parliament.

The selection of Danby was an admission of the king's weakness. In spite of his achievements as Treasurer, for which he was rewarded with

---

[28] Danby became Viscount Osborne, then Earl of Danby, Marquess of Carmarthen, and finally Duke of Leeds.

[29] There is disagreement as to whether the Stop of the Exchequer began in 1672 or the previous year with Clifford. For the technique, see Douglas, VIII, 352-3.

a peerage, and although as a Tory he was devoted to hereditary monarchy, Danby also believed in the monarchy as defined in 1641, and
was against both toleration and the French alliance. For the king to
have selected such a man to save him from further inroads upon his prerogative was a confession that his plans had gone awry and that only
the uncompromising Anglicanism of Danby could check Shaftesbury's
drive for further limitations on the crown.

Danby's financial methods assumed that the crown would secure parliamentary grants at the proper time to meet the interest payments. This
presumption, to be valid, required an effective control over Parliament,
and Danby sought to achieve this by presenting a strong Anglican policy
and by systematically bribing its members, particularly those of the
Commons, hoping thereby to detach them from their various noble
patrons. Danby made the office of Lord Treasurer the most important
in the government. He also identified his position with that of head of
the party to which he belonged, but in which he had subordinates not
colleagues. He and not they had direct access to the king, who in turn
was less interested in communicating with them since they were subordinate to Danby in the party. In sum, Danby had a strong resemblance
to the later Prime Minister, who with few exceptions has remained connected with the Treasury ever since.

In one important respect, however, Danby differed from the modern
Prime Minister. Charles insisted upon acting as a free agent in the prerogative area of foreign affairs, and Danby could only acquiesce. Here
the king continued a policy of subservience to Louis XIV, still hoping
that French funds would make him independent of Parliament and
therefore of any party or leader. According to modern conventions,
Danby should have resigned when the king persisted in policies with
which he disagreed. But Danby was not Prime Minister on those terms.
He did not act with the assurance of a majority in the Commons behind
him when presenting policies to the sovereign who, even if he did not
care for them, would still accept them in the knowledge that the Prime
Minister commanded that majority. On the contrary, Danby considered
it his duty to do everything possible to convince a majority in the House
that the king was right in pursuing a policy he had already embarked
upon. This not only distinguished him from most modern prime ministers, but led him into grave embarrassments.

Party warfare was bitter and unscrupulous. With Danby enjoying
royal favor, and his position at the Treasury allowing considerable scope

for bribery, Shaftesbury had to build up a party of sufficient strength in and out of Parliament to counteract and displace him. Party conflict and the ambition of leaders meant that in the last five years of its life the Cavalier Parliament spent itself in short, acrimonious sessions, with the king proroguing Parliament just when the Whigs seemed on the point of carrying the day. Shaftesbury talked darkly of Catholic plots; his Green Ribbon Boys, the Whig party militia, were given "Protestant flails" with which to beat the Catholics. This "scare technique" was certainly effective; the suspicion that the Catholics were plotting to take over the country was lodged in many breasts. The Whig leader hoped that Danby's followers would finally desert him out of sheer panic, leaving the king the choice of either dismissing Danby or calling for a new election, in which Shaftesbury believed his superior party organization would defeat the Tories. So confident was he that in a misguided moment he urged dissolution on the abstruse, antiquarian grounds that the House of Lords was illegal, and had been since a long obsolete statute of Edward III. His fellow peers deeply resented this aspersion and in 1677 committed the Whig leader and some of his lieutenants to the Tower. In the cool of his cell Shaftesbury recognized that the judicial decision of the Lords a decade earlier, whereby each House had the sole right to punish its members for contempt, barred him from appealing to the courts.

The absence of the Whig leaders from Parliament in 1677 gave Danby an obvious, and at first sight overwhelming, advantage. But to such an extent had he lost control that Parliament voted funds only for an "actual war" with France, a condition which made the grant worthless to Charles. He prorogued Parliament after a sharp lecture on the prerogative nature of foreign affairs reminiscent of his predecessors. At once Shaftesbury and his friends petitioned for a writ of habeas corpus, alleging that the committing authority, the House of Lords in Parliament, no longer existed. In a decision which is still a ruling precedent, the justices held that the power of each House to commit did not extend beyond the session and that it therefore followed that the end of a session ended the detention of any persons it had committed.

That the king and Danby could still avoid a dissolution and a new election was infuriating to Shaftesbury, who was now committed to war with France. Danby, on the other hand, no longer dared to meet Parliament again on the same platform of benevolent neutrality toward France. The French subsidies to Charles were never enough to meet expenses, and Danby could pay them only with money from Parliament. In the autumn of 1677 financial considerations forced him to insist on a reorientation of royal policy; Parliament's control over foreign affairs, despite the royal lecture of the last session, could not be ignored. In November 1677 Princess Mary, Protestant daughter of the Duke of York, married William of Orange, the Dutch leader of the coalition against Louis XIV. A month later an Anglo-Dutch alliance bound both countries to enforce peace upon France.

Charles realized that the reversal in policy was due to his dependence upon parliamentary funds, and he ordered his ambassador to France to plead for a subsidy of such size that he might do without Parliament for three years. In return, he would see that France received favorable peace terms. This was less than the benevolent neutrality for which Louis had already been paying, and he can hardly have felt much sympathy for a king who allowed himself to be put in so humiliating a position. But once again, resigning himself to the peculiarities of the English constitution, he increased the subsidy to Charles.

Charles was engaged in duplicity of such danger that none of his ministers would countersign his recent secret agreement with France. The Whigs, however, were also receiving grants from Louis, who wanted to keep the English political cauldron boiling. Shaftesbury himself was bitter at the apparent change in foreign policy, which he had advocated but which had brought him no closer to office. Members of Parliament, when they assembled in the spring of 1678, were no longer so impressed with his dark hints when the government was showing great activity in preparing for a war with France. They were thus dumbfounded when the king in his opening speech announced that there was soon going to be a general European peace and that the fleet was to be laid up.

Members were frustrated. Was Shaftesbury right about there being a plot to prevent England helping European Protestants? The Whig leader returned to the charge and again persuaded Parliament to vote funds for a war with France, but nothing happened. There was tension and suspicion everywhere and men were on the brink of violence. At that moment two remarkable men appeared upon the scene, "Dr." Titus Oates and Israel Tonge, both of them scoundrels, the former a pathological liar. Between them they concocted the Popish Plot and drove the country into a fit of madness.

The Whigs used the Popish Plot for their own political advantage; it was indeed exactly what they wanted. As described by Oates and Tonge, both clergymen of the Church of England, with a wealth of contradictory detail and barefaced lies, Catholics were going to assassinate Charles, replace him with James, and make England Catholic, massacring English Protestants in the process. Shaftesbury seized upon this "plot" to whip parliamentary fears into a frenzy. Charles, knowing the true plot, dared not intervene to save the innocent victims of the false one, who went to their deaths after trials which will for ever be a stain on English justice. Whenever passions seemed to be subsiding, Oates recalled further horrific details about the plot. Those who refused to believe Oates, the Whigs asserted, must themselves be involved in the plot. However, the Whigs were able to use the terror to extend the requirements of the Test Act to members of Parliament, with the significant exception of the Duke of York.

In due course Danby himself became involved. The former ambassador to France, Ralph Montague, suddenly disclosed to the Commons certain letters from Danby, in which he had instructed the ambassador to negotiate subsidies from Louis. That Danby had always been hostile to France and that he had written thus only as a servant acting on royal orders was a matter of indifference to the Whig leaders; they behaved as if they had found at last the true villain of the piece — the Lord Treasurer Danby, who for five years had given the king false counsel. The revelation lost him control of the Commons, where his bribery could not match the furious terrors inspired by the Whigs. He was impeached. Charles, aware that the next move might be directly against himself, dismissed Danby. It was a major victory for the Whigs, and once again the House of Commons had given an impressive demonstration of its strength by forcing out a royal adviser.

The king did not dare to let Danby come to trial, and perhaps reveal all his own secrets; but at the same time and for the same reason the Whigs were determined that he should. In desperation Charles offered Danby a pardon for any crimes he might have committed. In reply the Commons, now following Shaftesbury, resolved that a royal pardon was no bar to impeachment and committed Danby to the Tower. Much as Charles disliked the idea of dissolving Parliament and the inevitable election which would follow in view of his need for funds, he dared not keep the present one now that it was under Shaftesbury's control. In the early summer of 1679 the king dissolved the Cavalier Parliament.

The election of 1679 was fought between the parties. Although Pym had electioneered in 1640, this had been an exception to the general rule by which magnates managed elections and secured seats in the Commons for their clients. In the 1679 election, however, the party organizations went to work in the constituencies. The Whigs with their better machine and their hold on the boroughs, which returned most of the seats, already had an advantage over the Tories, and the Tories were still further handicapped by having a leader in the Tower, charged with complicity with French popery. In winning votes, the royal funds available to the Tories could not match the contributions of wealthy merchants and bankers available to the Whigs. Although the Tories appealed to the widespread popular feeling for the monarchy, the Whig cry of "no popery" was for the moment the more compelling slogan. The result was an overwhelming Whig victory and for Shaftesbury a solid majority in the House of Commons.

The king changed his advisers to reflect the Whig victory. Wanting now only to save his crown, Charles called Shaftesbury and his friends to office on the basis of Sir William Temple's plan for reinvigorating the Privy Council. Sir William, accepting in principle the theory of government put forward by Neville,[30] proposed a Privy Council with a maximum of thirty members selected by the king according to the strengths of various parliamentary groups. These thirty and the king should formulate the policy upon which the king was to act. Temple's plan accepted the existence of the parties and also assumed that Parliament already did, and should, control the crown. Its weakness however lay in the assumption that a king like Charles II would act on the advice of such a Council, particularly since its multi-party composition would make it unlikely that it would ever formulate a single line of policy.

Charles again named Shaftesbury Lord Chancellor and appointed fourteen of his followers to the new Privy Council, but he balanced them by fifteen officials not in Parliament. Financially, the new arrangement worked well; the men controlling the Commons presented money bills to the House, and for the first time for many sessions generous parliamentary grants were made to the crown. Within the new Council, however, there was little harmony between the two factions; the king himself was only placating the Whigs until he could rid himself of them, while Shaftesbury planned to use his control of the Commons to force the Whig program upon the king. Once in power, Shaftesbury was in no hurry to bring his fallen rival, Danby, to trial, although the

[30] Above, p. 362.

new Whig House of Commons wished to do so immediately. He saw the advantages of leaving him in the Tower while holding a possible trial in reserve to threaten the king.

The main object of Whig policy was the anglicanization of government at all levels. This policy had already been accomplished except at the very highest level, that of the sovereign. Time was now running short. Shaftesbury had no doubt that once James was king he would seek to end Parliament and Protestantism in England. The Whigs therefore introduced into the lower House their *Exclusion Bill*, which enunciated the principle that Parliament could determine the royal succession and provided that on the death of Charles the crown should pass to his nearest Protestant heir. The latter was not identified, because the Whigs disagreed among themselves about who the heir should be. It might be Princess Mary, but her marriage to a Dutchman made her unacceptable to some of the Whigs. Her Protestant sister, Princess Anne, was truly a "weak woman." The ideal choice for many of them would have been the Duke of Monmouth, a son of Charles and a Protestant, but unfortunately he was a bastard. No matter how firmly the Whigs believed in the principle of parliamentary regulation of the succession, they could hardly overrule the principle of legitimacy. The Whig majority in the Commons easily carried the bill through two of its three stages; and to forestall its certain passage Charles was again compelled to dissolve Parliament.

Shaftesbury was indignant, but, as the king had anticipated, some of his supporters were prepared to regard the matter rather less emotionally. The "trimmers," represented in the Council by Halifax,[31] would have accepted the succession of the Duke of York if sufficiently close statutory restrictions were made upon his powers. Charles did not like the proposed "compromise," but he encouraged these "trimmers" against the extremist Whigs in the hope that they would cancel each other out in the forthcoming election which, according to the calendar of the royal financial requirements, was due in the latter part of 1679. Shaftesbury, although now isolated in the Privy Council, believed that the election would once again give his Whigs control of the Commons. His followers continued to reject the Duke of York under any circumstances and even tried to persuade the nation that Monmouth had been born in wedlock. Not even Charles's assurance that Monmouth was his bastard quite dampened the enthusiasm of these Whigs.

[31] Above, p. 363.

In the autumn elections, their power in the boroughs gave the Shaftesbury Whigs a majority in the Commons. But the moderate Whigs and
Tories assumed control of the upper House. In this position the king
felt strong enough to dismiss Shaftesbury from his office and from the
Privy Council. This meant the end of Sir William Temple's short-lived
scheme for a reinvigorated Privy Council, which again fell into decline.

The dismissal of Shaftesbury killed the Temple plan but left the
crown without any effective means of managing the Commons. Despite
the king's promise in his opening speech in 1680 to do anything Parliament thought necessary to protect the Church of England, the Commons refused to vote him funds and passed the Exclusion Bill.[32] Only
the efforts of Halifax, by bringing together moderate Whigs and Tories
in the House of Lords, were able to stop it. To forestall any more action
on the Exclusion Bill, even in modified form, Charles dissolved Parliament.

The Whigs in their anger now began to threaten violence. It was an
unwise thing to do. For one thing they thereby denied their own belief
in parliamentary supremacy and what had to be a basic principle of
party government. No party proposing to use Parliament as a vehicle
for winning control of the government may appeal beyond it except to
the electorate; the moment a party threatens force to achieve what
Parliament and the voters will not give, it has excluded itself from the
constitution. Moreover, the king knew that Whig threats of civil war
were as disturbing to the nation as the Popish Plot had been two years
previously. Using Lawrence Hyde, he appealed to the Anglicanism of
the gentry and sought to reidentify the crown with social stability. He
also made it clear to Louis XIV that English neutrality was possible only
if the English crown were rid once and for all of financial dependence
upon Parliament. The result was another large grant from Louis.

Strengthened internally and externally, Charles planned to allow the
Whigs enough rope with which to hang themselves and called for a
new Parliament early in 1681. The Whigs again won a comfortable majority, but their open threats of rebellion should their Exclusion Bill
again fail alarmed the nation. Charles prudently changed the meeting
place of Parliament from London, where the mob was the organized
Whig sounding board, to Oxford, the intellectual center of High Anglican Toryism. Undismayed, the Whigs in the Commons again urged the
Exclusion Bill. The king gave the Whigs a week to reveal their intentions

[32] Douglas, VIII, 113-14.

to a country now fearful of going over the brink into civil war; then he dissolved Parliament. Some defiant Whigs wanted to remain in session, but most of them had come to realize the abhorrence in which the country held their plans to juggle with the crown and their threats of war. The seemingly omnipotent party had received a severe setback; as Whig members rode away from Oxford, it might almost have appeared to have disintegrated altogether. For Charles it was a considerable victory. With Louis XIV's help he enjoyed for the remaining years of his reign what he had so long wanted — a realm without Parliament. He had saved what remained of the prerogative and the historic principle of legitimacy in the succession. He could not increase the powers of the crown, nor did he attempt to do so, and he had succeeded in escaping from direct parliamentary control only by becoming a pensioner of the King of France. But he had escaped the Whig danger and prevented any further inroads upon the royal power and dignity.

The intensity of party conflicts under powerful leaders offering definite programs cut deep cleavages in the electorate and Parliament which could not be erased. Even if deplored as selfish factionalism, political parties had entered the constitution and had come to stay. The House of Commons was now a prize of such value that every tactic, ethical or corrupt, was worth using in order to win control of it.

Parliament in Abeyance

From 1681 to his death in 1685 Charles II ruled without Parliament. Even so, his dependence on the support of the Tories meant that even in its absence Parliament's influence had not entirely gone.

The temporary debacle of the Whigs gave the Tories their opportunity. They were now able to make peace with France and end a war which few but the Whigs had wanted. It was, of course, essential for the king to have peace if he were to avoid another Parliament. Again, Whigs had received strong nonconformist backing; the Tories persuaded the crown to enforce the Clarendon Code. Danby remained in the Tower,[33] but at the instance of Tory councillors a number of Whig leaders were charged with treason. Some went to the block or gallows, but the grand jury of Middlesex, part of the London Whig stronghold, refused to

---

[33] To be released in 1685 by James II, against whom he intrigued so vigorously that subsequent to that monarch's ejection he made his later advances to his ultimate dukedom.

indict Shaftesbury. He left the country and died, only a few weeks later, in Holland.

The strength of the Whigs in the boroughs had long been a thorn in the side of the Tory party. After three successive election defeats, they were determined to do something about it. The freeing of Shaftesbury by the grand jury of Middlesex was also a characteristic example of how royal and Tory wishes could be frustrated by the municipal corporations. The crown, therefore, instituted *quo warranto* proceedings against the boroughs, calling their charters into question before the courts; on close investigation it was not difficult for a subservient bench to find grounds for declaring them invalid. In 1683 London forfeited its charter. The government issued new charters, carefully framed in an effort to ensure Tory control of borough government, and so, it was hoped, of borough representation in Parliament. The Whigs appeared to be ruined. Their leaders were either dead or in exile and their borough strength seemed to have vanished.

During the last year or two of his life, Charles appeared stronger, was certainly beset by fewer anxieties, than at any other time during his reign. Royal power had not in fact increased; he did not, nor did he attempt to, undo what Parliament had done; he was tied to Louis XIV abroad and to the Tory party at home. But after the alarms, the factions, and the narrow escapes of the previous twenty-five years, the wonder is that he survived so long and emerged at the end with all the appearances of success. It was not only the most sanguine who believed in 1685 that Charles was leaving to his successor the enviable inheritance of stable government and a prosperous and loyal realm.

The Proof of Parliamentary Superiority

A monarch of great perception coming to the throne of England in 1685 might have observed that there were still considerable powers available to the king, still much he could do, provided he remembered two golden rules. One, to do nothing to offend that class of landed gentry, merchants, and financiers which had decided that its interests were best served by limited monarchy of the kind it had already known. Second, to do nothing to upset the deepest religious feelings of the people. If he ignored the former, his reign would end in failure; if he ignored the latter too, it would also be short. The man who came to the throne in England in 1685 did not have great perception. Instead, he was stupid and egocentric. No doubt he was sincere, but this virtue hindered him as much as his vices.

James, not a recipient of a pension from Louis XIV, had to call Parliament upon his accession. Thanks to the remodeling of the boroughs by his brother, he had a Tory House of Commons to work with Tory peers. As Tories and Anglicans, the members welcomed James as proof that the principle of hereditary monarchy was still viable after all the Whigs had tried to do to it. The efforts by the Dukes of Argyle and Monmouth, in Scotland and western England respectively, to place the latter on the throne, caused Parliament to attaint both and to give the crown a large army to crush the rebellion, the last popular rising in England. James emerged from the threat with loyalty to the crown enhanced and a standing army maintained with funds voted by Parliament, something his brother and father had never enjoyed. He was also voted for life the annual revenue enjoyed by Charles II. The first session of Parliament had been satisfactory for James.

But very soon his Catholic policy was causing the opposition to be heard. In the second session, Parliament refused to repeal the Habeas Corpus Act of 1679 [34] and the Test Act. It offered a large grant but only on conditions; James would give no assurances on religion and refused the grant. Before long James and his Parliament had reached such an impasse that he prorogued the Houses and never called them again. Instead, he sought to accomplish his ends, especially his religious policy, by prerogative action.

Royal religious policies were blatantly Catholic. James used the royal headship of the Church, in which as a Romanist he could not believe, to exercise control over ecclesiastical appointments. Unwilling to wait for bishoprics to fall vacant, he established the *Court of Ecclesiastical Commission*, which bore a sinister resemblance both in name and in fact to the Court of High Commission, abolished in 1641,[35] except that the new court was solely prerogative, without any statutory basis. Headed by Lord Chancellor Jeffreys, the new administrative tribunal enforced clerical conformity, not to Anglicanism but to Catholicism.

James next directly contravened the Test Act by giving an army commission to Edward Hales, who as a Catholic could not take the statutory oaths. Hales's coachman, Godden, brought a collusive action against him; and in the resultant action the issue was the relationship of the pre-

[34] Below, p. 409.
[35] Above, p. 317.

rogative to statute law.[36] Hales's counsel argued that the king had the right to *dispense* with the operation of statutes in specific instances. When the justices accepted this plea in their decision, James felt free to name Catholics to any post. Some Catholics entered high office, but for the moment the king moved carefully, because he was also trying to win the support of another group with every reason for wishing to see an end of Anglican dominance.

The bid for Protestant nonconformist support was a shrewd enough move. If James could persuade these victims of persecution that royal absolutism would mean toleration for them, his position would be considerably strengthened. Using the decision in the Hales case, in 1687 the king issued his first *Declaration of Indulgence*, which *suspended* the operation of all religious penal laws. The reaction of the nonconformists was mixed. They were glad to be free from persecution, but on the other hand they could not help being uneasy about the king's Catholic policies. Furthermore, it could be guessed that what the king had given so easily he could as easily withdraw when it suited his interests. These Protestant dissenters were more interested in suggestions being made by the now worried Anglicans that if James would only call Parliament, they would support statutory religious toleration for Protestants — something much more difficult to cancel than a royal proclamation.

On 7 May 1688, James issued a second *Declaration of Indulgence* and an order that the clergy of the Church of England should read it in their pulpits on an appointed Sunday.[37] Obedience would mean that the Church might cease to be Protestant; disobedience was counter to its teachings. Seeking a way out of their dilemma, seven bishops, headed by the Archbishop of Canterbury, petitioned the king to withdraw, not the declaration, but the order to read it. James made no reply, waiting to see what the parish clergy would do. On the fatal Sunday some clergy, among them the Vicar of Bray, read the declaration, but the overwhelming majority did not. Outraged by this unexpected resistance of the "non-resisting" clergy, the king ordered the seven bishops tried for seditious libel. The nation gasped; then it groaned. On 10 June the king had a son.

Until that time fearful English Protestants had been willing to endure much from James, because his heir was Princess Mary, Protestant and

[36] For the juridical-legal aspects of the case, see below, p. 405.
[37] Douglas, VIII, 83–4, 399–400.

married to William of Orange, champion of Continental Protestantism. The birth of a prince dashed their hopes and presaged a future of Catholic, absolute monarchy. James's policies had been drawing Whigs and Tories together. Now their leaders began to toy with the idea of asking William of Orange to force an early succession for his wife. However, these politicians had to have some sign that there would be support for their plan. They soon received it in the trial of the seven bishops. The bench divided, at first the carefully selected jury failed to agree, but then came the triumphant verdict of "Not Guilty." [38] James stood apart from the nation and was doomed. Whig and Tory leaders now realized that their plan had a chance of success, and on the day of the bishops' acquittal they dispatched their invitation to William of Orange to save their religion and their liberties, an amazing admission by proud men that they could not do these things by their own efforts.[39] When William landed, James stood alone in the realm, without a hand raised to help him — except to escape. The aristocratic leaders of the Revolution had won completely and bloodlessly.

The Revolutionary Settlement

As one of his last blunders, James had sent his new son with his mother to France. Had that child been in England, the politicians probably would have had to accept him, although they would have made him a Protestant.[40] His absence, however, and James's own flight had left a vacuum, and Whig and Tory leaders advised the Prince of Orange, an alien with absolutely no legal authority in England, to summon a Convention Parliament. When it met in early 1689, the Whigs had recovered ground in the boroughs and won control of the House of Commons; the Tories held a majority in the Lords. The first issue to arise between the parties concerned the question of whether the throne was vacant or not. The Whigs were anxious to declare that it was; the Tories most unwill-

[38] For the legal aspects of the case see below, p. 406.
[39] The bitter disappointment over the birth of a son to James combined with national reverence for the crown to produce a tale to justify the Revolution, to the effect that the child was an impostor, a London foundling smuggled into the palace in a warming pan. Careful research by cooler heads has shown that the child was a bona-fide prince. However, the absence of important officials from the queen's lying-in helped the story for a time and resulted in measures to ensure their presence at all future royal births, the duty now falling to the Chancellor, the Home Secretary, and the Archbishop of Canterbury.
[40] And, considering the aims of the political leaders, the Revolutionary Settlement would have been about the same.

ing. They first proposed a Protestant regency under Princess Mary, for her "absent" father. When this suggestion failed, however, the Tories finally agreed with the Whigs that the throne was vacant, but for completely different reasons. The former argued that by advice of "jesuits and other wicked persons" James had fled and had thus "voluntarily" abdicated; the latter argued that he had broken the contract between himself and his subjects. Either way the throne was vacant, and the two parties planned to seat only Mary on it. The refusal by both Mary and William to accept this scheme forced the politicians to offer the crown to them jointly, but not unconditionally.

To its offer the Convention Parliament attached specific conditions, consisting of short statements denying the legality of particular attempts by James II to undermine the Restoration constitution. These, said the framers of this *Declaration of Rights* like those of Magna Carta before them, were illegal because they were *innovations*. Like the barons at Runnymede, the authors of the Declaration were thinking in terms of their own experience, and the constitution which they declared they were "restoring" was based on Restoration practice, in turn based upon the constitution envisaged in 1641. Thus the Declaration denied the "pretended" right of the king to dispense with or suspend laws, and a new coronation oath bound the sovereign to govern according to acts of Parliament. The recent Court of Ecclesiastical Commission, and all like it, were and always had been illegal.[41] The Declaration repeated the statutory prohibition of 1641 against enforced payments to the crown without parliamentary sanction,[42] and in a section of dubious historical validity, but understandable in view of the recent fear that James's army might come to his assistance, announced that standing armies in time of peace without parliamentary approval had always been illegal. It had always been proper to petition the king, so that prosecution of petitioners had been illegal and should cease—and this guarantee of the right of petition entered into the Bill of Rights of the American Constitution.[43]

Other sections of the Declaration were to be adopted in the United States Constitution. The fear of a Catholic army when James was king now produced a guarantee to all Protestants to possess arms, a provision extended in the American Constitution to include all citizens.[44] Prohibi-

---

[41] For the juridical meaning of this statement see below, p. 410.
[42] Above, p. 317.
[43] Amendments, Article I.
[44] Amendments, Article II.

tion against excessive bail, fines, and cruel and unusual punishments tacitly left their definition to the courts, and the interpretations of these terms during the eighteenth century was such that Americans later insisted on the inclusion of the identical words in their Constitution.[45] The framers of the Declaration reaffirmed the right of parliamentary free speech, thereby giving it a statutory basis which entered the American Constitution; [46] and then made a general reaffirmation of all other privileges claimed by Parliament.

Every ruler was to swear to uphold the Church of England as by law established, emphasizing its parliamentary basis after 1660, and to deny under oath the dogma of transubstantiation. Thus the principle of the abortive Exclusion Bill [47] finally entered the law. It was also added that no one owed allegiance to a sovereign who was Catholic or married to one. Finally, the Declaration determined the succession to the throne in some detail: first it was to go to William and Mary jointly (with the actual administration in the former's hands), next to the survivor, thence to their issue, and failing such issue to Princess Anne (thereby ignoring her drunken husband), her issue, and lacking such issue, to descendants by another marriage of William should he survive Mary.

When William and Mary accepted these conditions of the Declaration of Rights, the Convention Parliament declared them William III and Mary II.[48] Then it passed a bill transforming itself into a regular Parliament, to which the joint sovereigns assented. This Parliament re-enacted the Declaration of Rights as the *Bill of Rights*,[49] and the joint royal assent made it a statute.

Yet when all this was done, one highly significant fact remained: the Bill of Rights, the foundation of the entire settlement, was illegal. The Convention Parliament was no Parliament, and no matter how much it sought to legalize itself, whatever it did, was, to the purist, legally void. Historically, Parliament was an agency of the crown, summoned by the sovereign, or at least in his name, as with the Parliaments which had forced out Edward II and Richard II.[50] The Convention Parliament of 1689 had *not* been summoned in any king's name, but by an alien. It bore no resemblance to the Convention of 1660, which had merely asked the

---

[45] Amendments, Article VIII.
[46] Article I, Section 6–1, which also includes freedom from civil arrest.
[47] Above, p. 386.
[48] William III had the same regnal designation as Stadholder in the Netherlands; he was also William I of Scotland (below, p. 402).
[49] Douglas, VIII, 122–8.
[50] Above, pp. 181, 194.

legal ruler to return to his own. But the Convention Parliament of 1689, without legal status, legislated the alien who had summoned it into king; and he then assented to a measure transforming the Convention into a regular Parliament. For legal purists all this was impossible.

The practical politicians of the Revolution, however, had no time to quibble about such niceties; they had to secure their victory as quickly as possible and at the same time prevent its going any further, for in revolutionary situations there is always the danger of radicalism — a thing abhorrent to the men who directed the Glorious Revolution of 1688. They therefore attributed to "Parliament" per se an existence apart from the sovereign, and the capacity to do certain things independently of him. By its actions of 1689, Parliament finally demolished the theory of Divine Right and changed the whole mystique of monarchy. What now existed was truly a limited, constitutional monarchy, a creation of the legislature.[51]

This was emphasized by the *Act of Settlement* in 1701,[52] when Parliament had to supplement its earlier entail of the crown. By this time Mary II was dead, and William III, who had not remarried, was dying. By the Bill of Rights Princess Anne would succeed him, but she was unlikely to add to her numerous progeny, all of whom had died in infancy. In 1689 everyone had ignored the "warming pan" baby; now he was in the minds of everyone, with some people regarding him as the "lawful" successor of Anne, and others already calling him James III.[53] His Catholic faith, however, made him unacceptable to party leaders; and in 1701 a Tory Parliament further entailed the crown by declaring that on the death of Anne, it should pass to her distant Protestant cousin, Sophia, widow of the Elector of Hanover, and her heirs. The law also required that not merely must the sovereign be Protestant, but he must also be a member of the Church of England — William had not been — as well as have a Protestant consort. At the same time certain lessons learned from the experience of having William as king gave rise to another series of clauses in the Act: a foreign-born monarch was not to take England into war to defend his Continental holdings, as the Tories declared William had done, without parliamentary approval; he was not to

---

[51] Not such a clear precedent was the parliamentary action in 1399 in creating Henry Lancaster Henry IV and ignoring primogeniture (above, p. 194), in that this Parliament was summoned in the name of his predecessor.

[52] Douglas, VIII, 129–34.

[53] These people argued that James II, who was to die in 1701, had forfeited his crown, but that his son was his lawful successor.

be absent without permission from England, as William had been frequently and for long periods; foreigners would not be accepted as members of the Privy Council — William had appointed a number of his Dutch advisers.

The Act of Settlement, the work of a Tory Parliament, was the final ratification of the Revolution of 1688, and in its pronouncements on the succession it frankly ignored the comforting illusion of "legality" which some people still cherished. These people had said that after all Mary II was the "true" heir of James II and that William III was king because he was her husband,[54] which was not impossible logic and had the precedent of Philip I and Mary I.[55] The theory became a little more strained with Anne (1702–14), who if she was a lawful heir of James II also had a husband, who was not king because Parliament had not mentioned him in the entail of 1689. However, to move the succession to Sophia in 1701 could not be justified on such grounds; it was an outright assertion that Parliament was free to decide the matter as it thought best. Although Sophia never benefited from the new entail, dying shortly before Anne, her son George, Elector of Hanover, became George I of Great Britain [56] by this Act of Parliament, *and for no other reason*. His successors based their titles on this law, which was subject to legislative modification at any time.

By the twentieth century this concept of a legislative crown included the corollary that a person receiving it by parliamentary entail could not be rid of it except by action of the entailing authority. Edward VIII (1936) remained king a full day after his own instrument of abdication, until Parliament gave it legislative effect by amending the Act of Settlement to allow the crown to pass to George VI (1936–52) and his heirs, so that the title of Elizabeth II (1952–) rests on the amendment of 1936 to the Act of Settlement.[57] The position of sovereign and a public housing project are thus equally the results of legislation, and the nation can deal with an unsatisfactory sovereign as it deals with other problems — by legislation.

The gentlemen of England recovered their control of Parliament, which had been threatened by the autocratic experiments of Charles II

[54] In addition, he was a grandson of Charles I.

[55] Above, p. 230, note 2.

[56] By that time England and Scotland had united as Great Britain (below, p. 402).

[57] For the effect of the Act of Settlement and its amendent in 1936 see the genealogical table on p. 567.

and James II. Their confidence that they were now the ruling class was expressed in their high claims for Parliament and in its ascendancy over the crown and the executive. To ensure that they maintained their position, it was necessary that they should have full control in parliamentary elections and that Parliament should meet frequently.

The Bill of Rights declared that parliamentary elections ought to be "free" — meaning free from royal interference — and that the Commons had the right to decide disputed elections, a privilege upheld by the House of Lords in 1689. Seven years later this judicial basis for the privilege received statutory expression, thereby ensuring aristocrats "free" parliamentary elections.

The statement in the Bill of Rights that Parliament should meet "frequently" came to mean annual sessions. After 1689 parliamentary grants to the crown, although not always minutely specified as to purpose, were for the period of a single year. At the end of that time the crown had to call Parliament for new grants.

The military needs of the crown also ensured annual sessions. In 1689 it seemed certain that James II would try to recover his realm with French military assistance and so an army was needed to repel him. Parliament and the oligarchs who controlled it had reason to suspect standing armies, and their legality in peace time without specific parliamentary approval was denied in the Bill of Rights. With James about to launch his attack, Parliament reluctantly had to agree with William III that the defense of the Revolution required an army in readiness when hostilities broke. As the law stood, since the Petition of Right had forbidden martial law,[58] the discipline of this force was under the common law, which regarded desertion as breach of contract, a tort, and striking a superior as simple assault, but which did not "know" the crime of mutiny or any kind of trial except by jury. The common law, therefore, was of little use for the maintenance of military discipline.

Faced with these facts, in 1689 Parliament grudgingly passed the *Mutiny Act*,[59] authorizing the crown to raise an army and to maintain it by martial law under Articles of War to be issued by the government, but only for six months. Parliament hoped that after this period the need for the law would have ended. Instead, England was in the midst of a war, so Parliament renewed the statute for a year, then another, and

[58] Above, pp. 305–6.
[59] Douglas, VIII, 812–13.

another. The war ended, but the Mutiny Act continued to be renewed annually, for politicians had come to realize that this was one sure way of having annual sessions — so long as the crown wanted an army.

The Mutiny Act thus gave Parliament indirect control over the army. It was also the first important parliamentary delegation of legislative authority since the Tudors. Subject to the broad provisions of successive Mutiny Acts, the crown prepared Articles of War, listing crimes and punishments and providing trial by courts-martial for persons made subject to those articles by the Mutiny Act itself. These Articles of War became the model for the early ones in the United States.[60]

The Mutiny Act received annual renewals until 1881, when it became the Army Act, similarly enacted annually. In the twentieth century this law became the Army and Air Force (Annual) Act.[61] Although these annual renewals may appear perfunctory, they serve the useful purpose of reminding any government of its ultimate dependence upon Parliament.

Once having secured annual sessions, the aristocrats were confronted by the danger that over a period of years the crown, by judicious patronage and bribery, might lure their parliamentary supporters away from them. To preclude this possibility was the purpose of the *Triennial Act*,[62] which in 1694 set the *maximum* term of Parliament at three years, although it might be dissolved sooner. Nothing so indicates the volume of water which had flowed over constitutional dams and under bridges than a comparison of this law with the similarly named one of 1641, requiring Parliament to meet at least once every three years.[63] Each law, if in an opposite manner, cut royal prerogative; but where the earlier had explicitly provided machinery for elections once every three years, the act of 1694 said nothing about an election after a dissolution of Parliament or the expiration of its term. Annual appropriations and the renewals of the Mutiny Act made such an election inevitable and

[60] However, the division of powers in the American Constitution, which gave command of the armed forces to the executive but entrusted their raising and maintenance to the Congress (except that appropriations for them might not be for over a two-year period), required legislative enactment of the American Articles of War (since 1950 the Uniform Code of Military Justice) as part of the federal statutes.

[61] The discipline of the Royal Navy reflects seventeenth- and eighteenth-century attitude that it was no menace to parliamentary liberties in that not until 1866 was naval discipline a subject for legislative action, which then took the form of a *permanent* statute, which with amendments is still in force.

[62] Douglas, VIII, 159–60.

[63] Above, p. 317.

therefore no mention of it in law was required. The act of 1694 also established the principle that Parliament should set its own term, a principle employed by it in 1716 to raise the maximum to seven years and in 1911 to reduce it to five.

Like all seventeenth-century governments that of England licensed printing presses, and printers producing material offensive to the government lost their licenses. This procedure had been on a statutory basis since 1662, but in 1695 a quarrel between the Houses on quite a different matter caused the statute to lapse. There was an immediate surge of political pamphleteering. But now neither party would support a renewal of the government's licensing power, an attitude which showed considerable political maturity. The changed position of the crown made the courts unwilling to punish for mere criticism of the government, the complexion of which, as the judges knew only too well, could change. The result was that the English press enjoyed a degree of freedom that, compared with the rest of Europe at that time, was astonishing. Writers, editors, and printers were still subject to laws of libel, sedition, obscenity, and blasphemy; and courts at times might rigidly interpret these terms. But there was still scope for plenty of free criticism, and party leaders were not slow to exploit it. Though some of the pamphlets might be scurrilous, malicious, and prejudiced, for the first time the English press did have the opportunity to educate public opinion on political issues.

Party leaders also received legal protection. The savage political warfare of the Restoration had seen Whigs and Tories hustling each other's leaders off to block and gallows after treason trials which had been travesties of justice, the accused laboring under heavy procedural disadvantages and the common law doctrine of "constructive treason" serving the crown well. After the Revolution political leaders realized that they would have to let live in order to live. This was the purpose of the *Treason Act* [64] of 1696, which abandoned the doctrine of constructive treason by requiring two witnesses to the same overt *act* of treason, or one witness to each of two separate treasonable acts, requirements repeated in the United State Constitution,[65] before conviction was possible. Other sections of the law put the accused and the crown precisely on the same plane in court,[66] thereby reflecting the original principle

[64] Douglas, VIII, 89–92.
[65] Article III, Section 3–1.
[66] For the legal aspects of the act see below, p. 411.

that even in dealing with persons seeking to overthrow it the government places limits upon itself.

Protestant nonconformists at last received toleration by the *Toleration Act* [67] of 1689, which did not, however, extend political rights to Protestant dissenters. The law specifically denied toleration to Catholics and Unitarians. But William III had learned from his experiences in the Netherlands that full toleration was in the national interest; moreover, the upper classes, which supplied the political leaders, were beginning to regard religious persecution as old-fashioned. The groups statutorily denied toleration did in practice receive it. John Locke would have gone further. In his *Essay on Toleration*, he argued that the government had more than the passive duty of "not persecuting"; it had also the active obligation of penalizing individuals who were intolerant. Locke's idea that the state might coerce the intolerant into tolerance has reappeared in twentieth-century American fair employment codes aimed at preventing racial discrimination.

Despite the limitation in the Toleration Act, some Protestant dissenters began to enter political life, meeting the requirements by taking the Anglican sacrament occasionally, normally once a year. These people were usually Whigs, and the Tories objected to such *Occasional Conformity*. By a law of 1711, they denied that it qualified a person for office.[68] Three years later their *Schism Act* [69] sought to end nonconformity with the present generation by requiring all education to be in Anglican hands. Soon afterwards, during the same year, the Whigs returned to power and promptly repealed these measures. During the eighteenth century the tolerance of the Whigs toward Protestant dissenters was such that the party passed annual acts of indemnity, as a result of which even those nonconformists who had not "occasionally conformed," presumably because of "oversight" or "ignorance," were still able to hold office.

Significantly, however, after 1689 party attitudes on religion turned on political advantage and not the protection of the state. The Toleration Act was an admission that a religious test was not valid as a test of secular loyalty. It also reflected an even larger principle, that although the state may be potentially the Hobbesian monolith, it voluntarily denies itself the right to operate in certain areas of human existence — in this instance, religious opinion — and thus becomes a limited state.

[67] Douglas, VIII, 400–403.
[68] Ibid. 406–8.
[69] Ibid. 409–10.

The Church of England itself became more flexible. The Revolution had saved the Church from the consequences of exalting the crown until James II had been able to threaten its very existence. Even so, the doctrine of Non-Resistance was not entirely discredited and some 400 *nonjuring* clergy, headed by five of the bishops whom James had prosecuted for libel, preferred to lose their posts rather than swear allegiance to William and Mary. Their departure left a large number of vacancies, which the crown filled with broad, "latitudinarian" men, whose ideas enabled the Church to move with the times and absorb some of the urbanity and enlightenment of eighteenth-century civilization.

Around the whole of their Revolutionary Settlement the gentlemen of England wove the binder of vested financial interest. The Revolution coincided in time with a surge of liquid capital available for investment, and the government now offered a sound investment opportunity in its technique of long-term financing by government bonds, whose interest the government would pay annually, but their principal only at a time of its choosing. This resurrection of the Stop of the Exchequer was dignified by the title of the *National Debt* in 1692. In 1694 a group of Whig financiers took up all of a government bond issue in return for a charter allowing them to issue stock for a bank, which should have a monopoly of rediscounting commercial paper and issuing bank notes, which should be legal tender. Stockholders in this *Bank of England* and holders of government bonds might drink the king's health over the water, but they fervently wished him to remain there.

The technique of long-term bonds permitted the government to finance the long wars with France for the next century and a quarter, but there was no weakening of parliamentary control over finance. In contrast to the annual and usually unspecified grants to the crown were the statutes authorizing the issuance of government bonds, which narrowly specified the purposes of the proceeds realized from their sale.

England and Scotland

Though English and Scots had had the same sovereigns since 1603 and though they possessed common citizenship, relations between the two countries were not particularly amicable. Both were glad to see their enforced association during the Interregnum end in 1660.[70] But with

[70] Above, p. 353.

the Revolution the two kingdoms began to move toward each other. The Scots took the initial and very significant step when in 1689 they forsook their ancient, national dynasty. The Lords of Convention at Edinburgh followed the English lead exactly and replaced James VII by William I and Mary II.[71]

Scottish nationalism still remained vigorous, and negotiations for an actual merger of the two kingdoms were for long hampered by it, also by the reluctance of the English to make the necessary trade concessions. But the Act of Settlement made the issue suddenly of vital concern. Scots could accept Anne as a true Stuart, but the German succession provided by the English Act of Settlement had no appeal for them. The Scottish Estates, in great contrast to their action in 1689, passed an *Act of Security*, declaring that on the death of Anne without issue, the Scottish Parliament would decide what measures should be taken. This cryptic statement clearly held out the possibility that James VIII might be invited to return to Scotland, from whence he might easily become James III of England. English leaders now showed every consideration for the Scots, and in 1707 the Parliaments of both kingdoms passed the identical measure, the *Act of Union*,[72] fusing the two kingdoms into the single kingdom of Great Britain. The Scots received equal trading rights with the English and forty-five seats in the House of Commons in the Parliament of Great Britain, to whose House of Lords the Scottish peerage would elect seventeen of its number for the parliamentary term. The Church of Scotland remained established; and while the new Parliament might modify Scottish public law, it could change Scottish *private* law only with Scottish consent. In return the Scots agreed that the English Hanoverian succession should apply to the new kingdom.[73] Despite their initial doubts, the union was to the

---

[71] Over the protests of Claverhouse, who called out the Bonnets of Bonny Dundee.

[72] Douglas, VIII, 680–95.

[73] Whether a sovereign body, the Parliament of Great Britain, is bound by the limitations of the law calling it into existence is a very knotty question. Most Scottish legal writers have argued cogently that the Parliament of Great Britain as the creation of identical laws passed by two independent legislatures is incapable of modifying any phase of that law which called it into being. Typical of this interpretation is T. B. Smith, "Scotland's Law under Two Queens," *South African Law Journal*, LXX (1953), 355–68. An opposite opinion is that of Charles A. Povlovich, Jr., "Scottish Juridical Institutions and Practices under the Impact of the Union with England" (unpublished doctoral dissertation, University of Southern California, 1953), although he admits that there are strong arguments to the contrary (p. 2, n. 2). In practice the question is not too important. By standing orders of each House of Parliament all measures relating solely to Scotland before their

advantage of both peoples. During the eighteenth century, as Dr. Samuel Johnson noted with irritation, Scots streamed down the road to London and from there made the British Empire their business domain.

LAW AND PREROGATIVE

The Restoration freed the common law from the imminent threat, during the Interregnum, of large-scale parliamentary intervention, while also giving it an opportunity to act in fields once covered by administrative adjudication. During the Restoration the subservience of justices to the prerogative ultimately caused parliamentary intervention in a few, but crucial, areas of the law.

The Expansion of the Law

The fallen administrative tribunals had left vast areas bereft of jurisdiction, and the task of the common law was in consequence greatly extended. After 1660 there was a steady improvement in its remedies and procedures, as it equipped itself to deal with its increased responsibilities. Equity, a possible rival of the common law, was however hampered by the fact that the Court of Chancery was not able to remove the stigma stamped upon it by early seventeenth-century parliamentary leaders. Even such powerful men as Clarendon and Shaftesbury used the office of Chancellor primarily for political rather than judicial purposes. A more serious rival to the common law courts was the High Court of Parliament, increasingly known by its legislative name of the House of Lords. But its claim to original jurisdiction in the areas once controlled by administrative jurisprudence was rebutted by a judicial decision in 1666.

In their adjudication of matters formerly under administrative tribunals, the law courts borrowed heavily from the remedies and procedures of their fallen rivals. Much of this borrowing was necessary, because the common law was now dealing in matters which until recently it had not "known." It was inevitable that justices should seek to find what administrative courts had thought about these matters; and

second reading go to the Scottish Committee, composed of all members of the House having Scottish constituencies or members sitting as Scottish peers. This arrangement practically precludes any measure strongly objectionable to the Scots from becoming law.

in consequence remedies, and particularly procedures, of the dead administrative courts filtered into the older areas of the common law. The result was a vast improvement for the common law in both its substantive and procedural phases; by their decisions justices reduced the possibility of large scale parliamentary legal "reform."

In contrast to Parliament's doubts about royal powers, and the purposes to which Charles II and James II put them, was the readiness of the judiciary to uphold and enhance these powers. The justices were dealing in a law which had originated in courts which had begun as royal personal agencies, and which therefore could not be hostile to prerogative. Justices also remembered the recent threat during the Interregnum of a major intervention in the law by Parliament; they preferred the prerogative, the intervention of which in law would, they believed, be occasional and brief, and leave its essential fabric untouched. Finally, the tenure of justices for the royal pleasure was unlikely to produce a bench which would deny the royal prerogative in any case where the king had a direct interest.

Judicial decisions during the Restoration were in fact promising to give the crown an opportunity to meet Parliament on equal terms and might have done so had not the Revolution intervened. In 1680 two unfortunate printers, Carr and Harris, were brought before Chief Justice Sir William Scroggs of King's Bench. He delivered himself of the decision that it was illegal in common law to publish anything about the government without its consent, and he permitted the jury to decide only the fact of publication, reserving to the bench the sole determination of the truth or falsity of the libel.[74] Although the crown did not rely solely on judicial decisions to control the press, the common law, at least as interpreted by the bench, was no defense for freedom of the press until after the Revolution.[75]

A more fundamental assertion of prerogative was the judicial acceptance of the power of the king to dispense with the operation of statutes. In 1674, just a year after Parliament had forced Charles II to withdraw his second Declaration of Indulgence,[76] the common law justices in Exchequer Chamber gave a significant decision for the prerogative in Thomas v. Sorrel. The latter was a London tavern keeper, who contrary to a statute of 1660 sold wine without a license. His coun-

---

[74] Although common usage makes "libel" synonymous with falsehood, the legal definition of the term is merely any published matter without reference to its veracity.

[75] Above, p. 399; below, p. 412.

[76] Above, p. 376.

sel entered the plea that James I had given a dispensation to London vintners to ignore a similar Elizabethan law and argued that this dispensation governed all subsequent similar legislation, including that of 1660. When the justices upheld this contention, although with many reservations about the validity of rights exercised continuously under such a dispensation, they dealt a severe blow to the competency of statute law. Moreover, their decision, although the justices did not quite say so, gave the crown a nearly unlimited dispensing power over statutes creating *mala in legem*, although not over statutes reinforcing prohibitions against *mala in se*.[77]

From the decision in Thomas *v*. Sorrel it was a short distance to the much clearer judicial support for the dispensing power of the prerogative in Godden *v*. Hales, heard by the four justices of King's Bench in 1686. The action, a collusive one, tested the ability of James II to give Catholics army commissions (and by inference, any office) contrary to the Test Act.[78] As arranged, Godden in the role of a common informer sued Hales for £500 for accepting a colonel's commission without taking the oaths required by the statute, which, as a Catholic, Hales could not do; the king therefore had dispensed with this requirement in his case. No issues of fact thus lay before the court, only issues of law.

Indicative of the strong position of the prerogative in the common law by this time was the refusal of Godden's counsel to attack the dispensing power itself. Instead, the plaintiff argued that the royal power could not operate to the detriment of private persons, in this instance Godden, who stood to gain £500 if Hales had done wrong. Hales's counsel, brushing this flimsy argument aside, defended the principle of dispensation as part of the prerogative, which, he argued, was as much the law of England as any statute. This plea ignored the historical fact that prerogative had operated only where statute was silent. A stronger argument, supported by judicial precedents of some length, was that the king did have the right to dispense with a statute creating *malum in legem*. In this case Parliament had passed the Test Act creating such *malum* in the belief that a certain class of people (Catholics) were a danger to the realm. However, the king did not apprehend this danger with Hales; for him the law had no application and therefore the royal dispensation was completely legal.

This was to exalt prerogative over statute, but the justices of King's

[77] Above, p. 196.
[78] Above, p. 391.

Bench did not flinch. After consulting their other common law colleagues, they entered a unanimous decision remarkable for its implications concerning the future relationship of prerogative and statutes.
They began by asserting, on extremely doubtful historical grounds,
that English sovereigns were absolute monarchs. The justices also took
the more plausible, but dangerously narrow, view that statutes were the
king's law and that the king could therefore dispense with them; in this
they rejected the opinion of medieval common law serjeants that the
king could withdraw his assent to statutes only in the place where he
had originally given it, that is, in Parliament, which would thus have to
pass a repealing measure.[79] Finally, the decision closed with the statement that no statute could reduce, still less abolish, this royal dispensing
power, which the decision had already made effectively superior to
statute law.

The justices thus not merely decided in favor of Hales; they dealt a
mortal blow to statute law and so elevated the prerogative that it could
be exercised quite irresponsibly. It is not surprising that the Convention
Parliament made the first two items of its Declaration (later Bill) of
Rights a legislative reversal of the "pretended" royal right to dispense
with or suspend laws.[80]

The Hales case decision permitted James II to dispense with all laws
creating religious disabilities in his two Declarations of Indulgence.[81]
With the second came the order for the clergy to read it and the petition
of the seven bishops requesting withdrawal of that order. When in 1688
the bishops faced King's Bench for trial for seditious libel, there was
again no question of fact; the prelates freely admitted their action. Technically, the legal issue was not the royal dispensing power; King's Bench
had already upheld it. The issue was whether the petition was seditious.
Actually, the exercise of the royal dispensing power in the area of
religion made that power the real issue at trial, and opposing counsel
found themselves speaking on it. Two justices summed up entirely for
the crown, holding that the dispensing power was unlimited and opposition to its exercise illegal. Another justice wavered in an opinion which
said little. The fourth justice, however, ignored the Hales decision and
denied the competence of the king to dispense with any statute.[82]

With the bench thus divided, the jury received the case, nominally to

[79] Above, p. 197.
[80] Above, p. 393.
[81] Above, p. 391.
[82] Douglas, VIII, 84–5.

decide whether the bishops had presented their petition in good faith as loyal subjects or with malice as seditious ones. The real issue before the jurors was the royal policy of giving posts to Catholics in defiance of acts of Parliament. When the carefully selected jury, one member of which was the royal brewer, finally brought in a verdict of acquittal, the bishops went free, and the royal right to dispense with statutes stood repudiated by "twelve, reasonable, prudent, and careful men." The right of petition, however, was not clearly stated until Parliament included it in the Bill of Rights, forbidding the prosecution of petitioners.[83]

The only way in which the justices did anything to reduce prerogative was by their insistence on freedom of juries. Since the Tudors, the crown had been likely to fine juries for returning verdicts of acquittal; threats of such fines were freely expressed by crown counsel and justices, and the average juror could not afford to ignore them. In 1667 a resolution of the House of Commons protested about the fining of juries,[84] though this had no legal effect. Three years later an irate justice fined a jury for acquitting William Penn and some fellow Quakers of the charge of violating the Conventicle Act. One of the jurors, Bushnell,[85] an "average, careful, and prudent man," preferred jail rather than pay the fine, and thereby won a well-deserved fame in having a leading case named for him. From his cell Bushnell petitioned for a writ of habeas corpus, which Chief Justice Vaughan of Common Pleas granted. In the resultant hearing [86] before his court Vaughan guided his three colleagues and wrote their unanimous decision, which, while not directly denying the legality of fining juries, put an end to the practice. The crown's contention that Bushnell was in jail for not paying a fine imposed by a justice for participating in a verdict contrary to the evidence, Vaughan blandly brushed aside, saying that the crown had not submitted any of this evidence in the present hearing in Common Pleas so that the court could not rule on this point. Getting to the heart of the issue, he pointed out that if the common law made justices the sole determiners of questions of law, it likewise made juries the sole judges of fact. A jury swore to reach the answer to a question of fact honestly; thus any verdict was its honest view and therefore, since the jury was the sole judge of fact, valid. Bushnell went free and with him all future jurors wherever the English common law runs.

[83] Above, p. 393.
[84] Douglas, VIII, 85–6.
[85] Also spelled "Bushel."
[86] Douglas, VIII, 86–91.

Appointment of justices for the "royal pleasure" was no mere formula; it was literally the case. The crown did not hesitate to dismiss justices who displeased it, with even the violent Scroggs losing his post in the end. It is not surprising therefore that they showed a certain deference to the king's wishes and were generous in their interpretations of his prerogative. Justices like Scroggs and Jeffreys, however, gave the Restoration bench a bad name by acting as the agents of the crown in criminal cases, particularly treason trials. Yet this was the traditional role of the criminal trial justice; and that champion of common law, Sir Edward Coke, as Chief Justice of King's Bench, had been a terror to criminal defendants. Some of the vials of wrath poured so liberally on Scroggs, for his conduct of the Popish Plot trials, and on Jeffreys, who as a reward for his conduct of the Bloody Assizes after Monmouth's Rebellion, received the office of Chancellor, might be saved for the nameless men on the juries who convicted the victims of these judicial murders. Had they dared to acquit, all the fury of Scroggs and Jeffreys would have been for naught. The framers of the Bill of Rights recognized this when they required that jurors in treason trials be freeholders of the county where the trials took place and be properly impaneled, so that their names would be known then and for all time.

Parliamentary Intervention

Parliament had always been reluctant to tamper with the common law; it had sometimes done less than it might have done. With the notable exception of the Statutes of Uses and Wills,[87] when Henry VIII had prevailed upon it to change the common law, there had been but little legislation affecting the fundamental law of the country. The Interregnum Parliament's designs for a major legislative overhaul had come to nothing. Changes by judicial action itself had reduced the need for much legislative intervention in the common law, but in one or two vitally important respects there was still work to be done by Parliament.

First, habeas corpus was put on a statutory base. The action was well known to the law, but the writ of that name initiating it was solely prerogative, so that the justices in hearing the resultant action, or return of the writ, were liable to be influenced by prerogative considerations. It was a basic dictum of the common law that detention of the person was *prime facie* illegal and required justification to be otherwise. The

[87] Above, pp. 222, 273.

writ was the remedy for a person detained, commanding his jailer to *have his body* before the court issuing the writ so that its bench could determine whether sufficient reason existed for his detention. While leaving the burden of justification on the detaining authority, usually the crown, judicial decisions on the sufficiency of reason rested on precedents which were very much in favor of the crown. In 1628 the Petition of Right had to forbid justices from accepting the plea of a royal order as a sufficient reason, as they had done in effect in the Five Knights Case.[88] The justices had evaded this prohibition in the case of Sir John Eliot and his friends in 1630,[89] and the subsequent reversal of that decision had been in terms of the parliamentary privilege of free speech and not of the common law doctrine concerning habeas corpus.[90]

Decisions by Restoration justices made it highly questionable whether this common law remedy for arbitrary imprisonment, so vital for the liberty of the subject, was sufficient for its purpose. Justices expressed doubts whether a single judge could issue the writ or hear its return during the courts' vacation. The bench on more than one occasion upheld crown pleas that essential witnesses against the prisoner having been absent at the last assize, the accused had to remain incarcerated. The crown often charged persons with misdemeanors so that the writ of habeas corpus, applicable only to treason and felony charges, did not lie. The government moreover evaded the consequences of the writ by moving prisoners to locations technically outside the realm, notably the Channel Islands, where the writ did not run. In 1679, while the Whigs were in power, Parliament therefore finally gave the action a statutory basis in the *Act of Habeas Corpus*,[91] which reduced judicial discretion on the issuance of the writ and the decisions on its return. Justices and jailers not complying with the statute or removing prisoners beyond the writ's reach were liable to heavy fines.

The act empowered, and also required, a single justice to issue the writ upon petition by a prisoner and to hear its return at any time. The statute then required that in his decisions on the return the justice should admit all persons accused of misdemeanors immediately to bail. All persons charged with treason or felony but not indicted at the assize following their detention likewise had to be admitted to bail unless the crown could *prove* the unavoidable absence of witnesses whose testi-

[88] Above, pp. 304, 305.
[89] Above, p. 312.
[90] Above, p. 368.
[91] Douglas, VIII, 92–6.

mony would have caused the grand jury to indict. Only if the crown could thus satisfy the justice, could he remand the petitioner to jail. After the next assize all persons previously admitted to bail and not yet indicted had to be released unconditionally. Those previously remanded to jail but still not indicted now had to have bail, and therefore if not indicted at the succeeding assize, would likewise have to be released.

It is impossible to overestimate the importance of the Habeas Corpus Act. By it, an important part of the prerogative power disappeared; it became futile for the crown to bring ill-founded charges against a person, and detention on the grounds of "need of state" became impossible. It is not altogether surprising that James II asked for the statute to be repealed, or that Parliament refused.[92] Henceforth, limitations on habeas corpus could come only from Parliament, which in times of crisis was willing to suspend the writ but only for carefully limited periods. In the United States Constitution, the suspension of the writ of habeas corpus was prohibited except during rebellion or invasion,[93] and American courts have ruled that even in such circumstances suspension could be made valid only by legislative action.[94]

The Bill of Rights further reduced the influence of the prerogative in the common law. It denied the dispensing or suspending power of the crown and clearly affirmed the right of petition,[95] which the common law had failed to do during the Restoration. The prohibition against the Ecclesiastical Commission and all similar tribunals without parliamentary sanction [96] afforded a protection to the common law courts against a revival of administrative courts.[97] This they had been unwilling to grant themselves. The denial of the legality of "grants and promises of fines and forfeitures" prior to conviction recalled the effort of Charles II to save Danby in 1679,[98] and the use of that method by both that king and James II to bar the prosecution of other individuals.

---

[92] Above, p. 390.

[93] Article I, Section 9-2.

[94] Notably in *Ex parte* Merryman (1861), occasioned by the suspension of the writ by President Lincoln's proclamation. In this case the detaining authority refused to obey the judicial order for Merryman's release. Subsequently, the Congress passed legislation indirectly sanctioning the executive action in suspending the writ, but also implying that only this legislation made the suspension legal.

[95] Above, p. 393.

[96] Ibid.

[97] This limitation, however, has meant that modern administrative jurisprudence, which common law supporters dislike as heartily as ever (see below, p. 556), has statutory sanction, making it difficult to attack.

[98] Above, p. 384.

The Treason Act of 1696 was a major parliamentary intervention in the common law. That law's doctrine of constructive treason and its procedural disabilities for the accused had produced terrible travesties of justice during the Restoration. The accused did not know the specific charges against him until he entered court, he had no counsel except for arguing narrow points of law, and he could not compel the attendance of witnesses, who might be fearful of guilt by association if they appeared at his request. Moreover, their testimony was not under oath and would carry less weight with the jury than that of the sworn witnesses for the prosecution. Against the accused stood the full power of the crown, armed with an indictment drawn up by its law officers conducting the case, and supported by the sworn testimony of subpoenaed witnesses.

Since the common law could do nothing to change the situation, Parliament intervened in 1696 with this statute. It first restricted the substantive law of treason to that defined in the statute of 1352,[99] and abolished the doctrine of constructive treason by repeating the requirements of the statute of 1547,[100] which the common law had forgotten during the seventeenth century: there must be two witnesses to the same overt *act* of treason, or one each to two or more *acts* of treason, not "imagining the death" of the sovereign.

Procedurally, the Treason Act placed the accused and the crown on precisely the same level, a situation not to be completely duplicated for other crimes until 1836. The accused had to see the indictment at least ten days before trial, for which he should have counsel for all phases, and to which he could subpoena witnesses who would testify under oath. For treason trials of peers the crown had to summon *all* peers, and not a carefully selected few, to the Court of the Lord High Steward, which in consequence never met again.[101]

The modern substantive law of treason is still based on the statute of 1352, and procedural law depends upon the act of 1696. Judicial doctrines of treason must comply with these laws, including the latter's denial of constructive treason. During the post-Napoleonic period of reaction there was a brief statutory expression of the doctrine of constructive treason, but it was soon repealed. In the Anglo-Boer War and World Wars I and II judicial rulings refined the "adhering" category of

[99] Above, pp. 209–10.
[100] Above, p. 263.
[101] This last provision of the statute ceased to operate in 1948, with the abolition of trial of peers by peers (q.v. below, p. 551).

treason as declared in the law of 1352. Thus for a British subject to become a citizen of the South African Republic during the first conflict
was "adhering" to the enemy, and so treason. For Sir Roger Casement in
World War I to raise an Irish brigade in German prison camps to fight
for Irish independence was treason. William Joyce (Lord Haw-Haw)
committed treason by broadcasting for the Nazis during World War
II. In the Joyce trial the judicial view, largely resting on the seventeenth-
century writings of Sir Edward Coke, was that an alien status (Joyce
being an American citizen) would not bar prosecution for treason if the
accused had secured protection from the sovereign in a manner usually
extended to his subjects, in the case of Joyce, by a British passport.[102]
Indeed, by judicial dictum an enemy alien domiciled in Great Britain
and owing allegiance to his own country may nevertheless commit
treason by assisting it, in that he is temporarily enjoying the protection
of the British sovereign.

Parliament also intervened in the common law in several other ways.
The Mutiny Act barred regular courts from hearing appeals from
military tribunals, except to inquire whether they had possessed the
necessary *personam* jurisdiction in the case. The refusal of Parliament
to renew the licensing statute after 1695 brought the press under the
jurisdiction of the common law, which in the post-Revolutionary era
could no longer adhere to the doctrine of Scroggs that the permission of
the government was necessary for any material printed about the government. In the law of libel, however, it was still maintained that the
jury could determine only the fact of publication and that the sole decision as to truth or falsity must be left to the justices. It required an
act of Parliament later in the eighteenth century to limit this common
law principle.[103]

Finally, the Act of Settlement of 1701, which left judicial appointments in the hands of the crown (unlike the United States, whose Senate must confirm judicial appointments), placed judicial tenure at the
parliamentary rather than at the royal pleasure, by providing that the
crown could remove justices only upon a joint address from both
Houses of Parliament.[104] Although this provision guaranteed judicial in-

[102] Almost the same situation applied to Louis Riel, who between his first and
second Métis Rebellion in 1870 and 1885 in Canada had lived in the United States
and had become an American citizen. His counsel, however, did not plead this
citizenship as a bar to prosecution for treason.

[103] Below, p. 457.

[104] Whether upon such an address removal is permissive or mandatory is not clear,
because since 1701 there has been no occasion for a ruling on this question.

dependence of the crown, it was certainly no guarantee of independence of Parliament. The position of justices after 1701, holding their posts at the "pleasure of Parliament," meant that for the common law the chief result of the Glorious Revolution was its subordination to statute law. This did not mean the replacement of common by statute law; vast areas existed where the silence of statute gave the common law free play. Even after the flood of legislation during the nineteenth and twentieth centuries the common law still has large areas which it alone "knows." Common law principles and judicial precedents also govern the interpretation of statutes. But the supremacy of acts of Parliament meant that although Englishmen might still speak of a "higher law" and a "law of nature" during much of the eighteenth and nineteenth centuries, the courts knew the highest law to be acts of Parliament, which they applied without hesitation.

The advantage of Parliament over the crown widened during the Restoration and was assisted by the rise of parties, which used Parliament for their own purposes. The only way Charles II could avoid this parliamentary control was to become a French pensioner, and even so, he had to accept parliamentary policy in the basic areas of religion and foreign affairs. When James II tried to upset this Restoration constitution in the crucial area of religious policy, his failure was sudden and complete. The aristocratic framers of the Revolutionary Settlement used the vehicle of Parliament to ensure their control of a crown created by and subject to Parliament.

In contrast to the aims of parliamentary leaders during the Restoration, the courts invoked and devised common law doctrines to support royal prerogative. The result was several major legislative interventions in the common law to ensure that it and its courts would uphold statutes, which thus became the supreme law.

READING LIST

Abbott, W. C. "The Long Parliament of Charles II," *English Historical Review*, XXI, 21, 254.

———. "The Origins of English Political Parties," *American Historical Review*, XXIV, 578.

Bosher, R. S. *The Making of the Restoration Settlement.*

Brown, P. H. *Legislative Union of England and Scotland.*

FEILING, SIR KEITH. *History of the Tory Party, 1660–1714.*
GOOCH, G. P. *English Political Thought from Bacon to Halifax.*
LOCKE, JOHN. *Treatises on Civil Government.*
MORGAN, W. M. *English Political Parties and Leaders in the Reign of Queen Anne.*
TREVELYAN, SIR GEORGE M. *The English Revolution, 1688–1689.*
TURBERVILLE, A. S. *The House of Lords in the Reign of William III.*

11

THE ARISTOCRATIC CONSTITUTION

FOR OVER a century after the Glorious Revolution the aristocracy of England, landed and mercantile, acted as the trustee of the constitution for the nation. England was very far from being a democracy in the years between 1689 and 1832; the administration was frequently corrupt and usually inefficient. But it was a period during which an oligarchic system of government established once and for all the principle of parliamentary supremacy in the constitution and during which a new relationship between Parliament and the executive emerged.

The Crown

The Bill of Rights, as has been seen, directly reduced the powers of the crown, but nevertheless those powers remained substantial. No politician could afford to ignore the wishes of the sovereign. Whether he belonged to the government or opposition, his success was likely to depend on royal favor. The appointment of ministers was the unquestioned right of the crown. Parliament paid remarkably little attention to foreign and colonial affairs and to administration generally; and the conduct of these matters was in terms of the royal prerogative. The prerogative of mercy was completely untouched by Parliament. The king was statutory head of the Church and supreme commander of the armed forces. Legally, the sovereign had sole control over the appointments to his Privy Council, and his veto remained intact.

However concerned with preserving the Revolutionary Settlement, Parliament showed no inclination to reduce these attributes of the prerogative. But it was confident, too, that in the exercise of the prerogative the crown would never act contrary to basic parliamentary opinion. So long as Parliament protected the Protestant succession and the permanency of the other phases of the Revolutionary Settlement (including those involving regular interest payments to government bondholders), the men controlling it were quite willing to leave the prerogative untouched.

The position of the sovereign is easily oversimplified. The nineteenth-century view was that Great Britain owed its unique constitution, not shared by "less happier lands," to the unpopularity of William III, the stupidity of Anne, and the beneficent indifference to English affairs of the first two Hanoverians. Such a view would have surprised the politicians of the day who had to work with these sovereigns and who knew better than to leave the royal temper out of their own political calculations. William III (1689-1702) regarded his ministers as his servants; he certainly did not consider himself bound to accept their every view. In foreign affairs he acted largely on his own initiative, without seeking ministerial advice and often without keeping his ministers informed. Anne (1702-14) on occasion successfully resisted her ministers, for whom she entertained considerable contempt; she once refused her assent to a parliamentary bill (the last time that the royal veto was exercised) and she regularly presided at meetings of the Council. Her breach with the Duchess of Marlborough wrecked the Duke's political career. The ministers of George I (1714-27) were unable to prevent him from dipping into post-office funds, and always tried to avoid his displeasure. Those of George II (1727-60) went through elaborate gyrations to keep him from learning what he already knew — that he was being run by his amiable queen and Sir Robert Walpole. For his part, Sir Robert, a most shrewd and practical politician, rarely ignored the whims of either of the first two Georges.

The sovereign, therefore, was no mere figurehead in the aristocratic constitution. But after 1689, though the prerogative remained untouched, it gradually came to be understood in a different way. During the eighteenth century the term "crown" developed a wider meaning. It no longer referred only to the person of the sovereign, who was only one part of it — and as the events of 1688 had demonstrated, an easily replaceable part. The "crown" was the executive, monarch and ministers. Their precise relationship varied with personalities and with changes in party groupings, but by 1830 no one believed that the king alone could exercise any real authority.

The decline of the prerogative in the conduct of foreign affairs was very rapid. Where William III had been his own foreign minister, Anne's physical and mental shortcomings prevented her from acting in this capacity, and consequently her ministers had to assume the responsibility. Although she welcomed the Tory moves which culminated in the Treaty of Utrecht in 1713, she played no part in the negotiations. George I and George II understood foreign policy in terms of Hanoverian interests. However, if British foreign policy after 1714 took Hanoverian considerations into account, there is no evidence, except in the charges of disgruntled politicians, that these interests influenced British diplomacy to any real extent. In fact, the connection benefited Great Britain by providing a Continental listening post and ally. The crown union between Great Britain and Hanover endured only until the accession of Queen Victoria in 1837, since Hanoverian law barred women from the throne.

Although the prerogative right of the veto, which William III had employed several times at his discretion, lapsed after 1707, when Anne used it for the last time, many years were to pass before ministers felt able to sponsor legislation personally unpalatable to the sovereign. Walpole recognized this fact; and in 1801 the refusal of George III (1760–1820) to countenance Catholic emancipation was sufficient to make the younger Pitt resign with the promise that he would not press the issue in Parliament. Upon his return to office in 1804 he repeated the pledge. When Pitt died in 1806, the king was able to wring a similar commitment from the Fox-Grenville ministry.

In place of the formal royal veto, applied after Parliament had acted, there was therefore an informal, but quite effective restraint which could be applied in advance. The effectiveness of this informal veto rested on the ability of the sovereign to manipulate the parties to his advantage. If he lacked this ability or if the state of the parties was such that they could not easily be manipulated, the veto was almost impossible to apply. In 1829 George IV (1820–30) attempted to wield the same influence as his father on the question of Catholic emancipation. But by that time the fluidity of the parties was much less than it had been in the past, and in spite of the king's protests his ministers introduced a bill for Catholic emancipation [1] which was passed. Rather than assent to the bill the king threatened not the royal veto, but abdication — a threat which made little impression on his ministers, who rightly assumed that he would eventually give his assent and remain on the throne.

Though the sovereign selected his own ministers, he was not in practice free to choose anybody he wished. His choice was limited to those

[1] Below, p. 468.

men who could manage Parliament. William resented this, and both he and Anne disliked changing ministers simply in order to comply with changes in the party representation in Parliament. They felt it outrageous that Parliament should react differently to legislative proposals merely because one set of ministers and not another presented them. Nevertheless, William and Anne found themselves obliged to change ministers to correspond with shifts of party strength in Parliament simply in order to get things done.

By the time of George I and George II, the choice of ministers had been still further narrowed; these monarchs selected only a few of the most important ministers, who then selected their own colleagues. Even so, with the major appointments still in their hands, the first two Hanoverians were assured of the deference of politicians and for better or for worse were able to make their presence felt. The antipathy of George II to the elder William Pitt kept that statesman out of high office until the crisis year of 1756. Pitt's political fortunes reveal the forces and counterforces at work in the aristocratic constitution. With the Newcastle ministry exposed by Pitt as utterly incompetent in its direction of the war with France, Newcastle at first defied his critic, but a surge of popular feeling beyond Parliament demanded that he should be replaced. George II very unwillingly accepted his resignation and called Pitt to office, whereupon the king and Newcastle proceeded to hamstring him by their control of the House of Commons. After five months the king dismissed Pitt, but the violence of public opinion made it impossible for another figure, even Newcastle with his control of blocks of seats in the Commons, to form a ministry. After three months Pitt returned to office, but only after making a deal with Newcastle on patronage, so that Pitt would have the votes of his henchmen in the House of Commons.

With growing Whig disunity in the later eighteenth century George III was able to make the most of his right to select ministers. Even the existence of a large majority in the Commons supporting the Fox-North coalition in 1783 did not deter him from dismissing that ministry and naming the younger William Pitt as Prime Minister. Pitt accepted office on the royal assurance that the full resources of the crown would be used to secure a majority for him in an election in the near future. When this was achieved the next year, Pitt soon learned that the ultimate loyalty of this majority was to the king.[2] In 1788 he and his Whig rival, Charles James Fox, were equally sure that should the latter's friend, the

[2] Below, p. 449.

Prince of Wales, become regent with unlimited powers during the insanity of his father, Fox would replace Pitt as Prime Minister.[3] As late as 1827, both Canning and Wellington believed that the decision as to which would become Prime Minister lay with George IV.

Control of patronage lay with the crown. The number of government posts, including many sinecures, and government contracts was sufficiently large for their distribution to give the crown real power; it was the reason why politicians regarded royal favor as an essential condition for office. In the allocation of this patronage the relationship between the two aspects of the crown, between sovereign and ministers, was subtly worked out. The extent to which the ruler was willing to allow a politician to allocate jobs and contracts made all the difference in the world to the loyalty he could command from his supporters, to his power as a parliamentary manager, and hence as a minister. Without royal confidence, therefore, a politician had little hope of building a following in Parliament to support his claims to office.

William and Anne gave limited amounts of patronage to their ministers. George I and George II were quite generous with Walpole after he had won their confidence. Just how far George III retained control over patronage is a matter of disagreement, but it is significant that Whig politicians thought that he was not "playing the game" — at least by the rules they had previously known.

By eighteenth-century political standards (and for that matter, by modern ones) there was nothing reprehensible about using patronage for political purposes. Nor did a change of ministers necessarily mean a wholesale sweep of office-holders. An office, even a sinecure, or a contract was property; and the eighteenth century was very sensitive to property rights. A new ministry had to build up its own opportunities for patronage gradually, by waiting for offices to fall vacant, and not by "throwing out the rascals."

The ancient right of the crown to dissolve Parliament entirely at its own discretion began to disappear. Although the Triennial Act of 1694 [4] and the Septennial Act of 1716 [5] had reduced the royal prerogative in this respect by setting maximum terms for Parliament, within these limits the crown retained the right of dissolution. William III and Anne insisted that the exercise of this right was for their personal determina-

[3] Below, p. 421.
[4] Above, p. 398.
[5] Above, p. 399; Douglas, X, 150.

tion. But, while the former was able to maintain this position, the latter, to her great chagrin, found it increasingly difficult to dissolve Parliament unless her ministers were of a like mind. With George I and George II this became the conventional procedure; within a parliamentary term the king would dissolve Parliament only at the request of the Prime Minister. This did not mean irregular terms for Parliament, which normally ran close to its statutory maximum, but rather that the Prime Minister set the precise date of dissolution as the time limit approached. The action of George III in 1784 in dissolving a Parliament with nearly three years left of its term to run was a striking demonstration that dissolution could still be a matter of royal personal prerogative. On that occasion, however, the actual dissolution was on the assurance of John Robinson, the Treasury election agent, that everything was prepared for an election to give the Pitt ministry a majority. Because of the king's satisfaction with Pitt, and because of his own subsequent mental decline, such arbitrary behavior was not repeated, and in future the dissolution of Parliament remained a matter for the Prime Minister to decide.

The one exception to this procedure occurred on the death of the sovereign. Historically Parliament was an agency of the crown so that the death of the ruler terminated a Parliament. The danger of a Jacobite reaction after the Revolution produced legislation in 1696, extending the term of the last Parliament summoned by the king for six months after his death.[6] Clearly if Prince James returned, he might well not summon Parliament at all. To cover this contingency another statute in 1707 provided for the automatic assembling of the last Parliament on the death of the monarch.[7] These statutes underlined the inference in the Bill of Rights that Parliament could exist apart from the ruler.

One gap still remained; it was possible that the monarch might die between the dissolution of one Parliament and the assembling of the next. This would produce the odd, and possibly illegal, situation of having a Parliament summoned by one ruler assemble for another. In 1797 a statute closed the gap by providing that in this situation the last Parliament of the former sovereign should meet according to the law of 1707 with an extended term of six months, unless dissolved earlier by the new ruler.[8]

[6] Douglas, VIII, 160–61.
[7] Ibid.
[8] 37 Geo. III, cap. 127.

Just as Parliament had claimed the right to determine the royal succession, so in the eighteenth century it established its right to settle the problem of regency. William III had named Lords Justices to exercise his powers during his frequent absences from the realm, and on the death of Anne in 1714 the great lords in the Privy Council named similar Lords Justices to administer the kingdom until the arrival of George I. The same device was used during that monarch's frequent sojourns in Hanover and during those of his son. This was consistent with traditional practice. Normally, when his heir was a minor, the sovereign had designated a council for him and given it regency powers, as did John for Henry III and Henry VIII for Edward VI.[9] In 1689 the Tories first suggested that Parliament might be competent to act in such matters when they recommended that a council should act for the absent James II.[10] During the eighteenth century Parliament passed various regency laws, to meet the possibility of the heir succeeding as a minor, in which close relatives were named as a collective regency.

In 1788 a crisis arose when the temporary insanity of George III demanded a regency. The Fox Whigs wanted the Prince of Wales to be regent with full regal powers, while the Pitt government did not and presented a regency bill narrowly restricting his powers.[11] The recovery of the king removed the need for the measure, in which for entirely political reasons Whigs and Tories had reversed their usual attitudes toward the prerogative. In 1811, when George III sank into his final insanity, Parliament conferred a limited regency upon the Prince of Wales. But as soon as the Tory government discovered that his sympathies were no longer with the Whigs, it withdrew these limitations.

Royal personal funds were securely under parliamentary control. The old and congenial theory that except for the extraordinary expenses of war the king should "live of his own" in meeting the costs of government could not survive after 1660. In 1698 Parliament distinguished between funds for public purposes and those granted to the king as personal money. It placed in the former category only the funds for the upkeep of the armed forces and made the remaining *Civil List* responsible for the costs of the entire civil administration, as well as for the upkeep of the royal household.

Parliament gradually reduced the public burdens on the Civil List,

[9] Above, pp. 120, 263.
[10] Above, p. 392.
[11] *Parliamentary History*, XXXVII, 706.

which, while retaining this name, became increasingly a personal fund for the sovereign. In 1760 George III relinquished certain hereditary revenues and crown lands in return for a fixed annual grant of £800,000, which Parliament had to increase in 1784 to take care of his large family. George IV complained that his annual grant of £850,000 was insufficient for his own needs after he had paid the salaries of officials still carried on the Civil List. In 1830 Parliament relieved the List of all public salaries, except those of justices, and then reduced it to £510,000 for William IV (1830–37), who found it difficult to make ends meet. With the accession of Victoria in 1837, Parliament made the Civil List responsible only for the royal maintenance and cut it to £385,000, divided into the categories of the privy purse, salaries of royal household servants, jewels, entertainment, and unappropriated — the last to supplement the amounts in other categories as required. In practice, only the first category of the privy purse belonged to the sovereign personally. The same procedure continued with Edward VII (1901–10) and George V (1910–36), each of whom had an annual Civil List of £470,000. The bachelor status of Edward VIII (1936) reduced this amount, but George VI (1936–52) received only £410,000. Elizabeth II (1952–) has a Civil List of £475,000, but only £60,000 goes into her privy purse, the rest being allocated for the expenses of the royal establishment. Other members of the royal family receive much smaller grants from Parliament.

The Best Club in England

Parliament regarded itself as the guardian of the Revolutionary Settlement, whose sanctity was inviolate for most Englishmen and which had become the new test of "loyalty." Within the broad limits of such a test there was room for urbane gentlemen to agree to disagree. The flirtation of the Tory Bolingbroke, in the last days of Anne, with the Pretender gave to his party a tinge of "disloyalty," an impression assiduously cultivated by the Whigs during their dominance from 1714 to 1760. During those years the word "Tory" was rarely used, and indeed party names had little meaning during much of this period of aristocratic rule; they certainly did not indicate any broad differences on basic principles. During the years of the Whig monopoly of government, factions within the party contested bitterly for power but never with quite that savagery that had characterized Restoration politics. The failure of the

impeachment against Walpole after his fall in 1742 [12] practically ended
reprisal as a political tactic. The rehabilitation of the Tory party by
1760 did little to clarify party divisions, which was possibly a reason why
the tradition of tolerance toward opponents continued. The younger
William Pitt, who was a "Tory" only to his enemies (indicating that unpleasant connotations were still attached to the word), at one time considered having Charles James Fox of the Whigs tried for treason, but
wiser counsels prevailed. By 1830 tolerance of opposition elements in
Parliament had given rise to the happy phrase, "His Majesty's Loyal
Opposition," indicating a body of men opposing the government and
yet safe to be entrusted with it, which performed the essential duty of
keeping ministers truly responsible to Parliament. In 1937 the *Leader of
the Opposition* received statutory recognition, with a public salary [13]
for his important duty of organizing attacks on the government and
being prepared to replace it at any time with his own supporters.

Aristocratic government was not of a kind to give rise to any burning
constitutional issues. Much of the business of Parliament consisted of
little more than jockeying for office and favors. However, as ministers
knew, Parliament could intervene directly at any time in their exercise
of the prerogative of the crown; and they had to bear in mind the fact
that the Commons regarded hostility toward the executive as an essential part of their heritage. Fortunately for the government, however,
Parliament rarely debated foreign policy, and showed remarkably little
interest in colonial matters, even while relations with the North American colonies were worsening. Nor was administration of much interest
to members, who knew that too close an inquiry into its details could
mean only embarrassment to themselves and their friends. When Walpole urged members to "let sleeping dogs lie," he was sympathetically
understood.

The importance of the House of Lords during this period was considerable. It was a small compact body of some 220 peers, twenty-six of
whom were bishops. So great was the wealth and power of some of the
peers with their vast estates and great influence in the country, that no
minister could afford to ignore or alienate them, either as individuals
or as members of a great legislative assembly and the highest court of
appeal in the land. In all governments of the period there were more
peers than commoners; and although the authority of the Commons was

very much greater than that of the Lords, the fact that individual peers controlled votes in the Commons makes it difficult, during this phase of aristocratic government, to say just where ultimate power resided.

In 1711 the Tory ministers of Anne had created twelve Tory peers in order to ensure a majority in the Lords for their peace policy.[14] After the Whigs returned to power in 1714, an attempt was made to prevent any repetition of this incident by the *Peerage Bill*,[15] which would have greatly reduced the prerogative of the crown and made the Lords virtually a closed body; the peerage of England and Great Britain was to be fixed at six more than its existing number. The bill was supported warmly by the Lords, but failed in the House of Commons, where Sir Robert Walpole warned of the constitutional danger of having one house of Parliament closed to new membership, and so irresponsible. However, in his castigation of the evil of depriving country gentlemen of the hope of reward from a gracious sovereign for loyal services, Sir Robert gave some indication of his true reasons for opposing the measure, and of the new role he and others like him envisaged for the House of Lords. Politicians had enough to do in dealing with the Commons and should not have to worry about the House of Lords; membership there should be the reward for faithful followers who could (and would) deliver votes in the Commons. Obviously, to gain a large number of supporters in the Commons by dealing with a few peers was only sensible. Yet Walpole's formal reason for opposing the bill on constitutional grounds was vindicated in 1832 and again in 1911, when the House of Lords passed the Reform Bill and Parliament Acts only because the government had threatened to create new peers if it failed to do so.[16] Had the Peerage Bill become law such threats would have been futile.

In the creation of new peers, certainly one of the most important considerations was that a man should control votes both for and by members of the House of Commons; after 1783, the younger Pitt bestowed peerages on such men quite openly. Most of the 90 peers created during his first administration between 1783 and 1801 owed their coronets to the seats they "owned" in the Commons. His successors continued his policy until the House of Lords, which had begun in 1714 as an exclusive Whig club, ended as a Tory stronghold of some 400 members.

Among the 400 peers of 1830 were the 28 lay Irish peers, who took

[14] Actually, only eleven accepted the proffered peerages.
[15] Douglas, X, 151-4.
[16] Below, pp. 470, 531.

their places in the upper chamber at Westminster in 1801.[17] Unlike their sixteen Scottish counterparts, who were elected for a single Parliament, the Irish representative peers were elected for life. Some came from old Irish families; others were Englishmen whose services had not been considered of sufficient caliber to win them peerages of Great Britain. Usually the 28 Irish lords temporal supported the ministry of the day for practical reasons of reward, for themselves and for their families.

One element of the peerage rested its nobility on merit, the *law lords*. Although appointments to judicial posts might be affected by considerations of patronage, most went to leading members of the bar. The Chief Justices of the common law courts invariably received peerages; and the Lord Chancellor, who presided over the upper chamber, despite his ministerial position, was usually a former barrister of ability. The law lords were of the greatest importance when the House of Lords acted in its judicial capacity. As the supreme court the Lords enjoyed great prestige and performed its functions with the most impressive dignity and ceremony. During the eighteenth century, moreover, the law lords also assisted the development of the procedure for *private bills*, not to be confused with private member bills (measures introduced by members of Parliament not in the ministry).

Private as opposed to public legislation authorized specific persons, both real and artificial, to take certain actions as provided in the private act of Parliament. The acceleration in land enclosures during the eighteenth century brought numerous petitions to Parliament requesting legislation to permit the petitioners to combine individual holdings. These petitions, increasingly in the actual form of the desired legislation, went to the Lords, where a quasi-judicial procedure of hearings and testimony evaluated their merits. If the peers found them good, they approved them and sent them to the House of Commons, which usually passed them without debate. The subsequent royal assent transformed these petitions into private acts of Parliament. Although they gave little comfort to small landholders, who often lost their acreage in the process of enclosure, the method served larger owners well. Canal and turnpike companies, which burgeoned in the later eighteenth century, as well as numerous private associations performing what would later be considered functions of local government,[18] made use of private legislation. With modifications, the procedure is still employed: private bills are

[17] Below, p. 437.
[18] Below, p. 452.

always initiated in the House of Lords, heard by the peers, and passed
automatically by the Commons.

The House of Commons represented property. Its members stood
not so much for a collection of individual voters as for certain areas of
interest; the knights and burgesses had in fact never represented people
but socio-economic groups. When parliamentary reformers later argued
that there was no relationship between the allocation of seats and the
distribution of population, they were quite right; but this was outside
the context of parliamentary history and to aristocratic politicians of the
old school largely irrelevant. They accepted the historic role of the
House as representing *communities*, social and economic; and the Whig
idea that men "with a stake in the country," those with wealth, should
have their *interests* represented in the House was thus within the historic
frame of reference of the Commons.

The long-standing idea that only gentlemen, by definition substantial
landowners, should be members received statutory expression in 1711
from a Tory Parliament, which in hopes of injuring the Whigs, whose
strength lay in the boroughs, enacted the requirement of *ownership* of
land of £600 and £300 clear annual value by county and borough members respectively.[19] Although these were large sums, to the Tories' dismay the Whigs proved able to meet the requirements, which had been
careful not to state that the land to be owned must be located in the
constituency of the member. The law thus enhanced the general tendency toward nonresidency of members in their constituencies, until in
1773 Parliament repealed the law requiring such residency which had
been ignored for so long.[20] Another effect of the 1711 law was to increase the tendency of landed men to sit for both counties and boroughs,
although as merchants and businessmen bought land in order to acquire
social status for their children, if not for themselves, it was difficult to
say whether a member's interests were primarily in land or in trade. The
statutory abolition of the residency requirement for members in 1773
also ended it for voters.[21] An individual, therefore, might exercise his
suffrage in every constituency where his property gave it to him. *Plural
voting* was not easy in a time of poor transportation, but with the polls
open for several days, energetic campaign managers could work won-

[19] This requirement could easily be evaded. It was often met by land transfers
within families, and it did not *continue* to apply to a member after taking his seat.

[20] Above, p. 201.

[21] Actually, in the absence of registration of voters, residency was almost impossible to enforce.

ders in getting voters to every constituency where they were qualified.

The propertied basis of the franchise easily led to the view that a man's vote was itself his property, which he could therefore dispose of in the same way as any other of his possessions. Consequently, anyone wanting the use of his vote had to pay for it. This simple principle of property law underlay those aristocratic practices which reformers would later call corruption.

Whatever the source of his income, a member of Parliament could point to his seat as proof of his being a "gentleman." Although some looked to the main chance, the average member was poorer for being in the House. Living in "town" for the session in the midst of the expensive London "season" meant heavy expenses beyond those already incurred in a member's election.

The House of Commons in the Tory Parliament of 1711, which had given the statutory definition of a gentleman, had recently increased its membership by the 45 seats from Scotland to a total of 558, a number which remained constant until the addition of 100 more members from Irish constituencies in 1801.[22] Thus the 513 English seats (including the 24 from Wales) comprised over 90 per cent of the House prior to 1801 and over three-fourths of it after that date. Arithmetical considerations alone meant that politicians thought largely in terms of English seats. There were also the four seats in the House belonging to the Universities of Oxford and Cambridge, whose respective degree holders elected two members for each. University representation was not abolished until 1948.[23]

Nearly three-fourths of the House prior to 1801, and still over 60 per cent of it after that date, consisted of the 417 English borough seats (again including those of Wales). Five boroughs had only one seat, London had four, but all the other boroughs each sent the traditional two members. There were certainly many anomalies in the borough representation, as reformers were later to point out. London, for example, returned only four members, as compared with the 42 returned by 21 Cornish boroughs, none of which had an electorate of over 200. In the eighteenth century, however, the fact that this was anomalous was not immediately apparent. There were sound historical reasons why the representation should be as it was; small boroughs in southern and western England returned 230 members because commercial activity had

[22] Below, p. 526.
[23] Below, p. 433.

developed early in those parts. But in any case, these members were thought of as representing not people, but property interests of some sort. To the aristocracy of England it did not seem strange that Gatton had only six houses and yet sent two members to Parliament; that Dunwich was falling into the sea but still providing two members; or that Old Sarum (which had excited some comments by James I) was no more than an open field. It was not until toward the close of the century that reformers began to point to these peculiarities of the electoral system as abuses.

Borough franchises varied with the specific provisions of each borough charter. In 1760, these different franchises gave the vote to about 85,000 people, with some 15,000 of them electing over half of the borough members. The several franchises fell into five broad legal categories. The narrowest suffrage was in the some 40 *burgage boroughs*, whose charters gave the vote only to owners of specific parcels of property cited in them. In the *corporation boroughs*, also about 40, the borough council, or corporation, named the members. Members from the 80 *freemen boroughs* had a constituency of people holding the formal status of borough freemen, often on an hereditary basis. About 40 boroughs had an electorate of people paying the ancient parish levy of *scot and lot*. A dozen boroughs had charters giving the vote to nearly all residents.

This leaves rather more than 100 boroughs unaccounted for. In these boroughs there were combinations of the various formal categories of franchise, and there was often a blurring of the precise category into which a borough fell. To politicians, however, the legal definition of these franchises was of small importance. For all practical purposes, they fell into three further functional categories. The *pocket boroughs*, nomination or close boroughs, belonged to some patron as much as the watch he carried in his pocket; he owned the two seats of the borough and could dispose of them freely. The men he selected were to vote as he directed, and certainly never against his interests. Should they be unable to meet these obligations, they were bound in honor to vacate their seats. Obviously, the smaller a borough's electorate, the better chance the borough had of falling into this category, where nomination by the patron was tantamount to election. In fact, most burgage boroughs were pocket boroughs in that patrons owned all or most of the property giving the franchise in them. The most famous such borough was Old Sarum, which for some time was the property of the Pitt family. It was, however, possible for a borough to have a wide franchise legally and yet to be a pocket borough in fact. Thus Gatton had the very generous qualification of mere residency, but such a paucity of residents that its electorate usually amounted to about six people, who as renters of Sir John Colebrooke did his bidding.

But even the size of the electorate was no sure indication of the actual status of a borough. The 32 members of the corporation of Bath had a tradition of fierce independence in their selection of members of Parliament; on the other hand, the 1000 voters of Bedford faithfully did what the Duke of Bedford desired of them. Local traditions and family influence might more than outweigh simple numerical considerations. In 1760, politicians estimated that about 100 people, 51 of them peers, either owned or had overwhelming influence in elections to over 190 seats. By the early nineteenth century, reformers were charging that 155 persons, most of them now peers due to the policy of the younger Pitt in raising to the peerage men who controlled sure seats, either owned or effectively dominated 307 seats.

Such a situation suited the politicians admirably. It permitted them after a few deals with borough patrons to secure good-sized blocks of votes in the House of Commons, and in aristocratic opinion such arrangements were quite proper. One man possessed property in a borough seat which another wished to use; obviously, the one had the right to expect, and the other the obligation to make, payment of some kind. Cash payments were considered rather crude, and the preferred mode was favors and sinecures. Nevertheless, the doubling of the normal life expectancy of the House of Commons by the Septennial Act in 1716 [24] increased the price of seats. In 1724 the Duke of Newcastle became Secretary of State, and for the next 38 years was willing to pay the owner of a borough seat £1500 for the right to name a member to it. Newcastle was able to use secret service money, for which he did not have to account to Parliament, in this *borough mongering*, although his enemies and later reformers greatly exaggerated the amounts. Most of his funds came out of his own considerable private fortune or from private contributions, often from people wanting seats. After his departure from office there was an inflation in prices for pocket-borough seats, which by the early nineteenth century had reached the astounding figure of £7000. By that time the traffic in pocket boroughs was being denounced as vile corruption by the reformers.

[24] Above, p. 399.

Rather different from the pocket boroughs was the second functional category, the *rotten boroughs*. Whatever the franchise arrangements were legally, the actual electorate was relatively small. A few corporation boroughs frankly sold their seats to the highest bidders, but this was unusual. Normally, voters of a rotten borough offered the seat to some aspiring politician on the understanding that he would contribute to various civic enterprises, such as paving and street lighting,[25] and also give to local charities. Expenditures for these purposes could be very large, but whether they were corrupt is open to question. They resemble those incurred by modern candidates in "nursing constituencies" in the intervals between elections, when they know that they are expected to give toward the local war memorial and ensure the success of the annual flower show.

True corruption flourished in the third type of boroughs, which had a comparatively *large electorate*. There the voters expected to be wooed with beef, ale, and cash by the gentlemen of England, and in such boroughs as London, Bristol, Westminster, and Liverpool, expenses might be astronomical. In Liverpool in 1830, the two candidates for its single seat together spent over £100,000, with the heavier spender losing! Elections in these boroughs were truly riotous. But it is perhaps as well to remember that in the whole of eighteenth-century Europe only in England did gentlemen find it necessary to woo the people at all.

Professional politicians, particularly those in the government, refused to assume the financial burdens and risks of elections in the boroughs with large electorates. They much preferred making "arrangements" with borough patrons and corporations, with the result that during the eighteenth century the number of actual election contests in boroughs with small electorates declined. However, political managers could not be certain about the permanency of these arrangements. Deals with pocket-borough patrons had a way of breaking down; and still worse, the impossible occasionally occurred when a pocket borough inexplicably slipped from one pocket into another. Rotten boroughs would have sudden spasms of civic virtue. Finally, in their competitive efforts to build an "interest" in the House of Commons rival politicians might find that they had created an equilibrium of strength among their blocks of borough seats.

In this situation the votes of the 92 county members from England and Wales became important. Some of the 92 called themselves Inde-

[25] Below, p. 452.

pendents, some Tories, in protest against Whig political jobbery, not from any doubts about the sanctity of the Revolutionary Settlement. Their independence, like those of certain borough members with very large constituencies, came from the size of the county electorate, which made mongering in county seats unfeasible.

In contrast to the varied borough franchises, the county franchise was uniform and defined by Parliament, having been set by statute in 1430 as the *ownership* of land of 40 shillings clear annual value.[26] Originally, this 40-shilling *freehold* qualification had been restrictive, but the subsequent decline in money values had made it rather generous, particularly when in the eighteenth century it was interpreted to include men possessing *life leaseholds* and *mortgages* on land of this value. Thus the county franchise at the middle of the eighteenth century gave the vote to about 170,000 people. Although the number in each county varied, the average figure for all shires was about 4000.

It was the large size of the average county electorate, far larger than that of the great majority of boroughs, which made professional politicians unwilling to enter county elections — not the independence of county voters. Indeed the voters, far from standing forth boldly as independent yeomen, life tenants, or mortgagees, were usually in the grip of the great landlords, and very often the land giving them the vote was less important to them than the land they rented on short term leases. Landlords expected these tenants, who were 40-shilling freeholders only incidentally, to vote "right," and with open voting it was an easy matter to see whether they did so.

The landlord class itself was divided into the squirearchy with broad acres and the aristocracy with acres still broader. Just where the line lay between the two groups was impossible to state, though nobody living in a county could be in much doubt about it. The squires, country gentlemen, often called themselves Tories, occasionally because of Jacobite sympathies, but usually because of their dislike for the Whig aristocrats. But in the face of the enormous expenses involved in country electioneering it was often desirable that two groups of landlords should sink what differences there might be between them and make informal arrangements whereby each would nominate an unopposed candidate. Often, therefore, county voters had no opportunity to vote. However, such arrangements could disintegrate under the impact of a local squabble or a feud between great families, and the resultant election contests

[26] Above, p. 200.

would then be fierce, with expenses rising to as much as £100,000. Understandably, professional politicians stayed clear of county elections; and with the exception of Middlesex, which was under the influence of the London merchants, the counties were the preserve of the landlords. County representatives were expected to vote in their interests, but where measures did not impinge upon those interests they enjoyed a good deal of independence.

It was in winning the votes of independent members, whether from the counties or the few boroughs with large electorates, that the great orators of the eighteenth century were of importance. The classical style, the stately eloquence, and the rolling perorations, moved men in the eighteenth century very deeply, and speakers able to present their arguments in the grand style could sway the votes of independent members. Political managers tried to attach these invaluable orators to their "interest"; but it was often not easy to do, for the great orators themselves were frequently independent members.

Management of the House of Commons required very considerable skill, as it had done since the time of the Tudors. It is true that at first sight it may appear that a few crafty politicians manipulated their puppets in the Commons and that election results during the eighteenth century reveal consistent ministerial victories. But on closer inspection this turns out to have been not entirely the case. The Whig ascendancy until 1760 obscures the fact that the eighteenth-century Whigs were less a party than a group of factions with little in common except a belief in the Revolutionary Settlement and a thirst for office. The reappearance of the Tories after 1760 did nothing to clarify party divisions; indeed they became still more confused. When George III summoned the younger Pitt in 1783, the Whigs damned him as a Tory, but neither he nor the "friends of Mr. Pitt," as his followers significantly called themselves, considered that he was heading a party. The very name of "party" during the latter part of the eighteenth century was better avoided, for there was felt to be something invidious about it. When Pitt used the French Revolution to terrify the Portland Whigs and make them join the Tory party in 1794, "Whig" and "Tory" had more meaning; but by modern standards party lines were still very obscure. What existed during the aristocratic phase of government were "interests," composed of members who were clients of a patron, either out of duty or from hope of reward. This meant that though the politicians might command blocks of votes in the Commons, they could never be assured of the kind of majority that the backing of an organized political party could give them. The situation in the Commons was always fluid; there was always an element of unpredictability in spite of all the efforts to manage and manipulate the House into docility.

Ministers, of course, had an advantage over their opponents in that they owned a number of pocket boroughs and were able to lease others from their patrons in return for favors and occasionally cash. The 42 Cornish borough seats "belonged" to the government, and the Treasury and Admiralty "owned" others. In them sat men who owed favors, contracts, and even jobs to the government, which could thus depend upon them. Opposition elements constantly denounced these *placemen*, who often held sinecures, but who also were frequently acting as incipient civil servants in the actual work they did. Revenue officers were expected to campaign in the boroughs and support the government in the House. Holders of government contracts also occupied these seats, especially from the Admiralty boroughs; and a recalcitrant "independent" member for a borough was often more sympathetic toward the arguments of the government when they were accompanied by a contract for victualing ships or the offer of a sinecure. Men who owed so much to the government and yet voted against its measures could lose contracts, sinecures, and even commissions in the armed forces for their ingratitude.

The 45 Scottish members also usually supported the ministers of the day, if only in protest against the frequently harsh remarks made by English members about their country. After 1801, 100 members from Ireland, actually representing only a tiny Anglican community in that unhappy island, were also hungry for patronage, and so again usually followed the government. These non-English seats, a minority of the House but very useful for any government, were thus a constant factor in political calculations and required little management. The advantages all seemed to lie with the government, which before 1801 could apparently muster 280 votes in a House of 558, and after that date 380 in one of 658.

Yet in spite of these facts and figures the ministers of the day did not find it so easy to maintain a majority in the Commons. They had no means by which they could consistently hold their followers in line. Favors, even actual bribery, were in fact admissions by the leaders of the various factions that they lacked any other way of keeping their supporters loyal. The most reliable supporter might become rather less dependable as time passed, and sooner or later the day would come when he would inquire of ministers just what they had been doing for him lately. Patrons of boroughs became less willing to keep them under the government standard as government patronage dwindled. An equilibrium of forces could appear suddenly, so ministers were in desperate need of orators to win over the independents, particularly the county members. There were frequently frantic last-minute attempts by placemen on the floor of the House to bring in a majority for the government. Edmund Burke scornfully compared these buttonholers to the whippers-in of the hounds at hunts and, like other terms originally intended as derogatory, "whip" survived to become an honorable name for an essential functionary in the modern House of Commons.

Meanwhile opposition elements would nibble at the government's strength, intrigue with borough owners, canvass county members, and try to create dissension among ministers in the hope that several would cut themselves and their followers out of the ministerial pack. If their efforts appeared likely to succeed, a worried government might try to short-circuit the opposition by taking some of its leaders into the ministry. This only worked if it suited the purposes of the opposition leaders to join the government. If they were bent on bringing it down, however, they might mobilize enough strength to be able to dissolve what had seemed the firmest of ministerial combinations. Newcastle, who throughout his career was beset by many neurotic anxieties, had good enough reason to fear losing a majority in the House of Commons. Thus Walpole, ablest of parliamentarians, eventually lost control of the House in 1742 and fell from office. In 1756, the Duke of Newcastle, with all his resources of patronage, was ousted by Pitt, and the latter, despite his popularity in the country, could not muster enough support in the face of Newcastle's opposition to survive for more than a year. The dangerous impasse reached in 1757, when the country was deeply engaged in the Seven Years' War, could only be resolved by the unlikely combination of Pitt and Newcastle in a joint ministry, with the former prosecuting the war effort and the latter busying himself as usual with the bestowal of patronage and the delicate manipulation of the Commons.

The work of the House of Commons was not arduous during this period. Although most legislation began in the House, it was usually drafted by ministers; and the total amount of legislation was not great. The leisurely pace of business permitted the House to look upon itself and refine its procedures. Speaker Onslow, who for thirty-three years after his election in 1727, showed exemplary independence of character, had the House embody much of its customary procedure into formal *standing orders*, which with occasional amendments reflected the "gentlemanly" tone of the House. These orders were sufficient to get the business of the House done until the 1880s, when they were deliberately misused by Irish Nationalists to tie the House into procedural knots and had to be revised.

The main concern of the House of Commons was with taxation, a subject about which the gentlemen of England could quickly lose their urbanity. The long unwillingness of Parliament to tax for public purposes of an ordinary nature, even when it became obvious that such taxation was necessary, produced the convention, which in turn became a standing order, that only ministers of the crown might introduce measures relating to taxation. This order, still governing financial bills in the Commons, precluded "pork-barreling," but it also put ministers on the defensive. All taxation proposals, unlike other bills, had to go to the Committee of the Whole House before their first reading. Again this provision, which is still effective, put ministers in an anxious position; a critical House would watch the Chancellor of the Exchequer open his bag, or *bougette*, or budget as it came to be called, and lay before it proposals which were unlikely to bring satisfaction to anybody.

The relationship between members of Parliament and their constituents, like that between Parliament and the general public, was variously interpreted during the eighteenth century. At one extreme was Edmund Burke, who denied to the voters of Bristol that he had any responsibility to them for any action that he took in the House, or that they could bind him by instructions. He held that voters gave a full power of attorney to their member to vote as he deemed best. At the other extreme was the constituency of a member for a pocket borough — its owner — who usually held the member closely accountable. In general, however, under the aristocratic regime of the eighteenth century few members felt it necessary to go out of their way to court popularity, and apart from Wilkes and such eccentrics who formed the "popular" party, only Pitt, the Great Commoner, seemed anxious to take the public into his confidence.

The House of Commons was, in fact, generally unwilling to admit any responsibility beyond its doors and dealt severely with people reporting its debates. In 1681, not without misgivings, the House had consented to its Votes and Proceedings being printed from its Journals, but these gave only the action of the House on a particular matter and did not indicate how individual members had voted or report any of the debates. Thus information about these matters prior to 1688 must be gleaned from the surviving diaries of members. After the Revolution, however, the clerks of the House developed a thriving news service, distributing quite full reports of the work of a session to private subscribers. But in 1694 the Commons expressed its displeasure, declaring that newsletters should not deal with debates in the House. In 1738 it went further and made such reporting a violation of its privileges and punishable as contempt. Although the order was generally ignored, the government was liable to invoke it when the House was required to debate an unpopular measure or when secrecy seemed to be to its advantage. In 1770 Burke suggested, rather oddly considering his views on the responsibilities of members toward their constituents, that the Commons should print division lists on all motions and bills. The House, however, rejected the idea and did not start to print them until 1836.

In 1771 John Wilkes, the most persistent and disturbing agitator of his day,[27] with a number of his colleagues defied the order and started printing the debates in full. His colleagues were jailed, though Wilkes on this occasion was allowed to escape. When his allies re-emerged from the Tower, they found themselves heroes; but the Commons solemnly reaffirmed the illegality of reporting debates, and the government continued to exclude reporters when publicity seemed undesirable. By 1803, however, there was a reporters' bench in the gallery, and William Cobbett was busy recording the proceedings in shorthand. Nine years later T. C. Hansard took over the duty of reporting the debates, a task which he and later his sons did so well that they gave their family name to the published debates of every Parliament in the modern Commonwealth. Thus unwillingly, the House of Commons had to admit that, even as the elder Pitt had said, there was a sovereignty of the nation beyond the House. Nevertheless, the reluctance of the House to give way was reflected in the private reporting and printing of the debates until 1908, when Parliament finally took over the duty.

Relations between the two Houses were usually harmonious. Peers controlled seats in the lower House, wherein sat their heirs, younger sons, relatives, and clients; above all, they were men from the same social classes as themselves, who thought essentially as they did. For members of both Houses politics tended to be an aristocratic game, with deals

---

[27] For his other challenges to the existing order see below, pp. 446-7.

and counter-deals the essence of the sport. The interests of members became at times dangerously partisan and narrow, yet the prestige and authority of Parliament remained unweakened. Ministers of the crown, responsible for the day-to-day administration of the country, for the conduct of foreign affairs and the building of a great empire, had to face the disagreeable fact that their efforts ultimately depended upon the support of this wayward, perverse, but fortunately for long periods corruptible body of men.

Aristocratic techniques of government achieved the union of Great Britain and Ireland.[28] Until 1782, although technically a separate kingdom, Ireland had a Parliament subordinate to the British government by legislation beginning in 1495. In 1782, as one result of Yorktown, the Irish Parliament became an independent body; but the officials of the Irish government, the "Castle Gang," were not responsible to it. The Irish Parliament was remarkable for the few interests it represented. Until 1768, its term was for the life of the sovereign, when it was reduced to eight years. At most, it spoke for the tiny Anglican landlord clique. In 1793, the Pitt administration forced the Parliament in Dublin to give the franchise to all 40-shilling freeholders, regardless of religious faith. However, the law did not affect the Anglican monopoly of membership; but it did permit landlords to "create" 40-shilling freeholders, who were otherwise still their tenants, for election purposes.

The French Revolution echoed in Ireland as uneasiness and rebellion. In 1799, Pitt had the British Parliament pass the necessary legislation for the union of the two kingdoms, but the Irish Parliament rejected this plan for its demise. In 1800, the British government "persuaded" the Irish Parliament to pass the measure by means which were rather direct (including cash payments) even for the time.

The resultant Act of Union of 1800, effective 1 January 1801, created the United Kingdom of Great Britain and Ireland, whose Parliament would have 100 members in the Commons and 28 peers, elected for life by the Irish peerage, in the Lords, along with four prelates from the misnamed Church of Ireland, the church of the small Anglican group in Ireland. The Act of Union continued the monopoly of government by this element, with neither the considerable Presbyterian minority nor the overwhelming Catholic majority permitted to sit in the United Kingdom Parliament for Ireland. The failure of the statute to grant such representation, particularly for the latter group, made the old Irish sore fester still more deeply.

[28] Douglas, X, 683, 686, 697, 701; XI, 674, 197.

The Emergence of the Cabinet

The greatest accomplishment of the aristocratic oligarchy was to develop the cabinet system of government in the British constitution. So successful was it that it spread into British territories overseas and was consciously emulated by nineteenth- and twentieth-century liberals on the Continent of Europe. Like most developments in the British constitution, however, it came about haphazardly and informally, and those present at its birth did not know that it was being born.

Even today the cabinet is a rather mysterious phenomenon. It has no legal status; the law knows only the Privy Council, to which all members of the cabinet belong.[29] In the late eighteenth century Blackstone in his famous *Commentaries* did not recognize the existence of a cabinet, and not until 1937 did a statute give recognition to someone called a "Prime Minister," who was usually First Lord of the Treasury. By law the ministers of the cabinet have no collective responsibility to the House of Commons, but are individually responsible solely to the sovereign, whose pleasure determines their tenure in office. That this legal situation is utterly at variance with the true position of the cabinet serves to demonstrate its *parvenu* status in the constitution. As late as the early nineteenth century the actual workings of the cabinet were not at all clear to the politicians most intimately concerned with them. No English statesman explained the cabinet system until Sir Robert Peel did so in 1841.

Essentially, the cabinet is a joint committee of both Houses of Parliament; its members are the ministers in charge of executive departments, except in the rare cases when they are ministers without portfolio. Most of these ministers are members of the Commons, although the Foreign Secretary is often a peer. One is the *Prime Minister*, who, like his cabinet colleagues, owes his position in the government to his position in the party, in his case that of party leader. The cabinet exists because its members control a majority in the *House of Commons*. The word "control" is important, because in practice the membership of the Commons has never determined cabinet personnel except indirectly. From the eighteenth century onward it has been the members of the cabinet whose individual and collective control of seats has given it a majority

[29] If not already members of the Privy Council, ministers are sworn in at the time of their appointment.

in the Commons, so that ministers can carry their measures. This was even more obvious in the eighteenth century when men who could consistently deliver blocks of votes in the Commons had strong claims to ministerial posts. Furthermore, with the exception of about thirty-five years after the Reform Act of 1832, the cabinet has employed increasingly vigorous means to control its majority.[30]

The ministers in their dual capacities as heads of departments and as members of Parliament make the cabinet the point where legislative and executive functions meet. For this reason a particular group of ministers in a cabinet has the *sole* right, through the Prime Minister, to advise the sovereign, who will act *only* according to that advice on any matter. This principle shelters the monarch from criticism and gives a new twist to the old saying that the king can do no wrong; it also assumes the willingness of the sovereign to act in all public matters only as his ministers advise. This assumption is essential, for legally the sovereign is everything and the cabinet nothing.

The cabinet retains this position until it loses control of a majority of the House of Commons, whereupon it resigns and is replaced by one able to control such a majority; *unless* the defeated cabinet gambles on winning a majority in an election and has Parliament dissolved. This alternative, which is really an appeal from the Commons to the voters, has become the usual course in modern times; and there is thus reason to doubt whether the cabinet is not in fact responsible to the electorate rather than to the House of Commons.[31]

A rudimentary cabinet began to appear in the seventeenth century. As early as James I the practice of consulting only some of his Privy Council in his private "cabinet" had provoked criticism on the grounds that the king should consult all his Privy Council — even as critics had deplored the use by Henry VII of a Privy Council instead of the old full Council.[32] Clarendon used the term "cabinet," with connotations of intrigue, in speaking of the advisers of Charles I prior to 1641. The Cabal of Charles II continued the tradition of an inner group within the Privy Council,[33] and despite all complaints, committees of the Council continued to operate for the remainder of the seventeenth century. The Temple plan to reinvigorate the Privy Council[34] thus proved abortive;

[30] Below, pp. 493–4.
[31] Below, p. 538.
[32] Above, p. 244.
[33] Above, pp. 374–5.
[34] Above, p. 385.

and the only part of the scheme, and that inadvertently, which found its way into the cabinet system was the principle that royal advisers should be office-holders. However, as Charles II had discovered, his selection of ministers had to take into account the prevailing attitude in Parliament.[35] After the Revolutionary Settlement, the sovereign was still less able to ignore men who had "interests" in the Commons. Variable franchises, pocket and rotten boroughs, provided politicians and the monarch with the basis for the cabinet system of government, which was the creation of both partners in the dual crown existing after 1689.[36] If the cabinet was a committee of Parliament, like Parliament it began as a creation of the crown, even though the nature of the crown was very different from that which had created the older institution.

The nascent cabinet almost died in 1701, when the framers of the Act of Settlement, in an effort to keep members of the Commons loyal to their aristocrat patrons, included in that law a prohibition against any member of the lower chamber (significantly not the upper) accepting any office under the crown. Had this prohibition continued, no member of the Commons would have been in the cabinet, which, therefore, might have never developed. In 1705 "West's Expedient" allowed a member of the Commons to accept an office if he immediately stood for re-election. Although the expedient applied only to offices existing prior to 1705 (to prevent the crown from tempting members with newly-created ones), practical politicians quickly adopted the convenient fiction that the device applied to *all* offices. Thus men with crass motives saved the embryonic cabinet system.

Two routes thus led to the cabinet; one taken by the professional politicians, the other by the king. By the beginning of the Hanoverian dynasty in 1714 the routes were beginning to converge. A politician having a fairly large and reasonably reliable group of supporters in the Commons expected a government post in return for directing them to vote for government measures. The sovereign, for his part, found himself obliged to appoint just such men as his advisers, and having given them ministerial positions, he had to strengthen their hands by allowing them patronage with which to attract and hold their supporters in the House. Even William III, who had hoped to rule independently of the parties and to choose his own advisers irrespective of their parliamentary position, found in the end that in order to get government measures

[35] Above, p. 385.
[36] Above, p. 419.

through Parliament he was compelled to give high office to the men who could manage it. He drew the line, however, at changing his advisers whenever there was a change in the balance of parties in Parliament. But within a few years, Anne found that this too was necessary if she were to retain the confidence and co-operation of Parliament. Her ministers, moreover, tended to meet apart from her and to work out a definite line of policy before presenting it at a formal "cabinet" meeting for her approval. Anne still presided at these meetings, though not invariably, but the fact that ministers were beginning to operate apart from the sovereign indicated that a new technique of government was emerging.

There appeared at that time to be no less than three bodies trying to advise the ruler. The oldest, largest, and least effective was the *Privy Council*, which embraced the other two. The legal ability of any three members of the Council to exercise the powers of the full board was an admission that the traditional Privy Council had ceased to have any real importance. When George I landed in England, the ministerial group actually in charge of affairs was the *Committee of the Council*, an informal body operating in Parliament, forming policy, and generally acting as if it were the full Privy Council. But within this smaller group there was appearing a still smaller *Cabinet Council*, composed of men actually managing Parliament and directing the work of the Committee of the Council. However, the distinction between the two latter groups seemed so unreal to contemporaries that they used their names interchangeably. Not until the administration of the younger Pitt after 1783 did the smaller cabinet group stand apart clearly from the Committee of the Council, which then ceased to have any importance.

Politicians in the early days of the cabinet knew only that certain men among them were closer than others to the machinery of government because of their relationship to the House of Commons *and* to the monarch. Neither George I nor George II was indifferent to English affairs, but each recognized that he was sovereign only by act of Parliament and that the exiled Stuarts still exerted a fascination for many men. The new rulers, therefore, had to work with Parliament, a none too easy task for men unaccustomed to any comparable institution in their native kingdom and who were appalled by the corruption needed to manage such an institution. George I found men he could trust to do this dirty work. Initially he shrank from giving so much power to a single man and divided it among several ministers. They were Whigs, because the Whig party had supported his succession, and he selected them for this reason. But neither he nor his ministers believed that they owed their offices solely to the possession of a majority in the Commons. Instead, the Whigs had received certain resources of patronage from the king to enable them to get such a majority. It was plain that the minister with the most patronage at his disposal was the one most likely to amass the largest block of votes in the Commons and so dominate his colleagues in the cabinet.

It was during the reign of George I that the sovereign ceased to attend cabinet meetings. With the king not understanding English, and his minister speaking no German and little French, there was little profit in such discussions. George II, though not handicapped in the same way, followed his father's example. It was an important precedent to set. It meant that the cabinet could debate and decide on policy with much greater freedom, and that the king was presented only with ministerial decisions without being acquainted with the alternatives.

It was Sir Robert Walpole who came to the fore as Prime Minister, though at the time he deemed it inadvisable to describe himself by such a title; it was his enemies who used this term. But because he controlled a majority in the Commons that was his actual role. His ability to dispense patronage and his astute managerial sense made him the head of his party, such as it was. Thereby appeared one of the basic principles of cabinet government, which if occasionally ignored during this period of aristocratic rule, triumphed in the end: the head of the party having a majority in the House of Commons *must* be Prime Minister, and *only* he can be Prime Minister.

Walpole, himself, preferred to exercise his control directly in the Commons. But the structure of political life was such that it was possible for the leader of the majority party in the Commons to control it from the House of Lords. Most of the prime ministers during this period were peers, and though some of them were merely titular prime ministers with the real power in the hands of Commoners,[37] this only emphasized the importance of peers in the practical politics of the day. As late as 1902 there was a Prime Minister in the House of Lords.[38]

[37] Examples of this type of Prime Minister were the Duke of Devonshire, who in 1756 was the nominal head of the elder Pitt's short ministry; the Duke of Grafton, the figurehead for Lord North and the Earl of Shelburne in 1767; and the Duke of Portland, who in 1783 was the cover for the Fox-North coalition.
[38] The ability of ministers to appear only in the House of which they are members creates problems, which other Commonwealth states (except Canada) have tried to reduce by allowing ministers to speak in both Houses, although naturally voting only in their own.

The principle that it was his position in the party that should determine the sovereign's choice of the Prime Minister was accepted only gradually. In 1727 George II, who in traditional Hanoverian fashion had quarreled with his father, dismissed Walpole on becoming king and named Sir Spencer Compton in his place. The results were swift but not nearly as decisive as later Whig writers tried to show. Without talents for party management, Compton floundered and gave up; but Walpole did not rely on his position in the Commons alone to regain office. He cultivated Queen Caroline and promised the king a larger parliamentary grant than his rivals dared to do. Although the king recalled Walpole, the incident revealed that though the Commons could prevent a minister's remaining in office, the majority could still not force its choice upon the king. Walpole continued in office until 1742, but he considered good relations with the king, or more precisely his queen, as important to him as a majority in the Commons.

During his years of power Walpole laid down the first principles of cabinet government. He alone consistently had *direct access* to the sovereign, whom other ministers saw only with his approval. That this was a sensible arrangement became evident later, when "joint" ministries led to hesitant and confused policies, and when George III encouraged individual ministers to consult him without the knowledge of their chief. The obvious merits of Walpole's practice were eventually recognized; by 1803 the younger Pitt was insisting in the face of Addington that there could be only one first minister, and that dual headship of the cabinet was impossible.

During his years of dominance Walpole insisted on *cabinet unity*, a second basic principle of cabinet government, which again received acceptance only grudgingly. Ministers disagreeing with cabinet policy were free either to remain in the cabinet and be silent, or to resign; but they were not to be in the government and oppose its policies. After he was forced to drop the Excise Bill in 1733, Walpole had the king dismiss those ministers who had attacked it. Although, as his enemies charged, partly due to pique, Walpole's action came from the realization that the cabinet's only strength before a stubborn monarch or a restive Commons was the appearance of unity. His colleagues did not abide by this principle when Walpole himself was forced from office in 1742; they remained in the cabinet of his successor, and his successors were much less insistent than he had been on the principle of unity. Again, however, it was the younger Pitt who successfully established the principle when he demanded that the king should dismiss Lord Chancellor Thurlow in

1792 for his intrigues with Fox and his opposition to ministerial policy in the House of Lords.[39]

Walpole's *resignation* also established one other principle for his successors. By 1741 his enemies were able to win the elections, so that the next year Walpole faced a consistently hostile majority in the Commons, whose threats not to renew the Mutiny Act or pass the annual appropriations were not idle. Rather than wait for the debacle, Walpole preferred to resign from the government, even though he still retained the support of the House of Lords and the king. This was the principle that when the Prime Minister loses his majority in the *Commons*, he must resign. Disapproval of him by the Lords, on the other hand, is not so important; if necessary, the sovereign can always create a favorable majority for him there. Walpole, however, did not resign upon his first defeat in the Commons; it was only after experiencing a series of them that he realized that the opposition majority was firm. During most of the eighteenth century prime ministers followed his example, waiting to see whether the hostile majority of today might not have changed by tomorrow — and often it had. Later, prime ministers were more sensitive and resigned after a few defeats. In modern practice the first defeat of a Prime Minister is usually his last: he resigns immediately. When Walpole resigned in 1742, moreover, his colleagues did not feel in any way committed by his action. It was only much later that the resignation of the Prime Minister came to mean the resignation of his entire cabinet.

Walpole also began the convention, although it was not consistently followed until much later, of directing the cabinet from the post of *First Lord of the Treasury*. Upon the death of Anne in 1714, the office of Lord Treasurer had gone into commission among several "lords," and the Chancellor of the Exchequer took over the financial aspects of government completely. Walpole found the post of First Lord the best office for dispensing patronage and spending money on party management. The departmental duties of the office were negligible, so that it became increasingly popular with prime ministers. Although some of them did hold offices with departmental obligations, all discovered that they were too onerous to permit the effective direction and co-ordination of the government. Walpole's choice and the increasing preference of his successors finally received statutory recognition in the Ministers

[39] The ultimate expression of this principle came from Lord Melbourne, Prime Minister, 1834-41, who once told his colleagues that it did not matter a bit what they said as long as they said the same thing.

of the Crown Act of 1937, the first mention in law of the office of Prime Minister, which was thereby joined to the post of First Lord of the Treasury.

Walpole is usually considered the first Prime Minister, although this is to ignore the significant position of Danby during the reign of Charles II. Yet in many ways Walpole and his immediate successors were quite different from their twentieth-century descendant. In their choice of colleagues they were often more influenced by the sovereign than by the House of Commons, for the king had vast resources of patronage at his disposal. Walpole and his successors also lacked what the modern Prime Minister has, a well-organized party behind him. Walpole knew factions, but not parties, except in the broadest sense of men supporting or attacking the Hanoverian succession. It was only when parties were more than the personal followings of politicians and represented large sections of national opinion, that they became vital in the workings of the constitution, providing the basis for strong ministries and for the cabinet in its modern form.

The Reign of George III

In an unsettled political situation and with the cabinet and its workings so hazily understood, it was not difficult for George III (1760–1820) to intervene directly in government. Contemporaries regarded his close interest in politics as a nuisance, but not as unconstitutional. Furthermore, George III conducted his entire program within the framework of the Revolutionary Settlement, particularly that portion emphasizing the supremacy of Parliament. He was no doubt the first Hanoverian capable of understanding the practical realities of English politics, and he used his patronage resources shrewdly enough to persuade political leaders that they should look to their sovereign if they cared for their futures. His intention was to cleanse the government of all taint of corruption and to inaugurate a new era of virtue. He was quickly to find that this was not so easy. Though free to make what ministerial changes he wished, he was confronted by a depressing lack of alternatives. There were to be many momentous events throughout George's reign, but in none of them did the king play quite the part that he could have wished to play, or that Whig historians were later to accuse him of having played. Although it may be true that the power of the crown revived for a time during his reign, the resources at his disposal were no longer sufficient for him to assume a leading part in the political developments of his day.

One of the first problems that George III had to contend with, and one of the first intimations that times were changing, was John Wilkes. Wilkes was a man of profligate character, who damaged his cause by his rather conspicuous personal vices, but his was the voice of a growing radicalism which in that dominantly aristocratic age had few means of expression, and which therefore demanded major changes in the establishment. At first, the king chose to regard Wilkes as his personal enemy, but actually Wilkes was the enemy of all professional politicians, not merely the king. He found little support among the "gentlemen of England," but the crowds were with him and "Wilkes and liberty" became a popular slogan in the City of London.

As a Whig member of Parliament, Wilkes opposed the government's policy of making peace with France after the elder Pitt's resignation. In 1763, in his newspaper *North Briton,* he attacked the royal speech approving this policy at the opening of Parliament. He emphasized that he was attacking not the king but the ministers, since everyone knew that it was they who were responsible for the royal speech. However, as Wilkes also knew, George III had participated actively in the peace policy and in the drafting of the speech. The king demanded that the ministers should have Wilkes punished for his temerity. The government had the offending number of the *North Briton* seized and ordered Wilkes's house searched under the authority of a general warrant.[40] Using patronage power, control over government borough seats, and making much of his bad reputation, the ministers persuaded the Commons to withdraw the parliamentary privilege of freedom from arrest from Wilkes. He was then charged with seditious libel, but he avoided trial by leaving for France.

Important constitutional issues were at stake: parliamentary privilege, and beyond that, the liberty of the subject. Wilkes, who was declared an outlaw because of his failure to appear for trial, seemed to be a martyr to popular liberties; and his expulsion by the Commons, technically because he was an outlaw, seemed to point to one weakness of the aristocratic constitution — its failure to take account of non-aristocratic interests. The implication was that such outsiders had no

---

[40] For the large legal issues involved in the use of general warrants see below, p. 454.

business playing the aristocratic game of politics, and should be punished for their temerity in daring to think that they could.

Four years later Wilkes returned and succeeded in having the outlawry charge quashed; but he was sentenced to twenty-two months for seditious libel. Nothing daunted, and reveling in his role as a rebel against the whole aristocratic "system," Wilkes stood for Parliament for Middlesex. Three times the Middlesex voters elected him; three times the government had the House of Commons declare the Middlesex election invalid. The fourth time the House declared Wilkes's opponent, who had received only a handful of votes, duly elected. More responsible leaders such as Chatham, who detested Wilkes personally, declared that Parliament was acting like a mob toward him. Wilkes, in fact, made a real challenge to prevailing political practices, but there was at that time no way for him, or for those who shared his views, to make a truly effective protest — except by mob violence which only discredited their efforts.

In 1776 Jeremy Bentham's *Fragment on Government* was published. It argued that the true duty of government was not so much to secure property as to achieve the greatest good of the greatest number. This view, so often repeated since that it has become a platitude, was at the time not easy to assimilate; to the average member of Parliament it did not fit in with what he had always been taught to believe. For over half a century, Locke's conception of government had been unquestioned; when Bentham appealed for legislative action to achieve this goal, he seemed to be alone. A number of aristocratic politicians were prepared to admit that existing arrangements were not perfect, even Lord North venturing this view. But it was dangerous to make changes, they argued; no one could tell where they would end.

This conservatism persisted until after the end of the century. Certain changes were necessary, it came to be admitted, but the time was not yet ripe for them. As England changed from an agrarian, rural nation to a land of mills and factories, the reluctance of the *ancien régime* to bestir itself became increasingly serious. Radicals were pointing out that the interests of new men with a "stake in the country" were not receiving representation. But the aristocratic defenders of the eighteenth-century constitution had vested interests in the anomalies which prevented the new wealth from finding expression in Parliament.

The debacle of British arms in North America eventually wrecked the ministry of Lord North, in which George III had misplaced his trust, and brought in a Whig group headed by Rockingham, pledged to overhaul a system which had failed to meet the crucial test of war. Criticism of the government had led to criticism of the crown. Unpopular as Lord North had become, it was the king who had chosen him and must share the responsibility. In 1780 John Dunning placed his famous resolution before the House: "The influence of the crown has increased, is increasing, and ought to be diminished." It was carried by 233 votes to 215 in the Commons. The vast patronage that the king could command, which was greater in times of war than in peace, was becoming increasingly resented. Parliament realized that as long as sinecures, contracts, and secret service money were at the disposal of the crown, members would yield to temptation and the king or the oligarchs would be able to buy a majority in the House of Commons. The Rockingham reformers, who included Edmund Burke, took the view that the first essential for efficient government was a truly independent Parliament. To this end, in 1782 the government placed before Parliament, which was in a thoughtful mood after Yorktown, measures to abolish many sinecures, to bar holders of government contracts from the Commons, and to disfranchise revenue officers, postmasters, and masters of ships of the Royal Navy.[41] It was hoped that without the sinecures and without these officials in the Commons, the king would be willing to work with the House rather than attempt to manipulate it.

However, the Rockingham ministry was not yet ready to deal with the problem of the allocation of parliamentary seats and variable franchises; too many vested interests were at stake. The younger William Pitt proposed that certain pocket boroughs should be abolished, their owners being duly compensated and the seats going to the newer urban, industrial areas. But the Commons rejected the plan.

In 1783 Fox and North sank their long antagonism to form a coalition with a large majority in the Commons; the king, who had lost confidence in North and had always hated Fox, was repelled by this unnatural alliance, so much so that for nearly six weeks he refused to recognize it. When he was eventually compelled to do so, it was a striking victory for the ministers; under the nominal leadership of the Duke of Portland, the government of Fox and North was independent of the king and had a majority in the Commons that was all its own. The most important measure introduced by the coalition was the

[41] Douglas, X, 155-8.

India Bill, which transferred political patronage in India from the East India Company to Parliament. After long debates, the bill passed the lower House; but the king, deeply hostile to the measure, authorized Lord Temple to circulate a card in the Lords saying that he would consider all who voted for the bill as his enemies. In consequence, it was defeated in the Lords by a narrow majority. It was an extraordinary assertion of the royal power, and was quickly censured as a breach of privilege by the Commons. But the king had already decided to dismiss Fox and North and to make a fresh start with the younger Pitt. He had been assured by Robinson that in a general election Pitt would win a substantial majority. Such an assurance was needed, for, faced by a hostile and self-assured majority in the Commons, Pitt was at first consistently defeated. But he refused to resign and the king refused to dismiss him. Gradually, the followers of Fox and North saw that Pitt was the man to whom the king had entrusted patronage, and one by one they moved to his side. Fox and North had threatened not to renew the Mutiny Act, and twice the House voted representations to the king protesting against his refusal to dismiss his ministers. But the opposition majority steadily declined. On the day that the hostile majority in the Commons was down to a single vote, Fox allowed the Mutiny Bill to go through, and the king dissolved Parliament, although it had three years left to run of its normal term.

The election of 1784 was a triumph for George III. No government in the eighteenth century lost an election, but none won an election quite so decisively as this. Later writers claimed that it resulted from a popular revulsion against the old gang headed by two crafty and corrupt politicians, and a national surge of feeling for the lonely young man who had flung himself into the breach against them. This spirit did not reveal itself in the election campaigns themselves. The election was managed by Robinson in the usual way; he came to terms with the borough patrons, the corporations, and the small electorates. Much money was spent on it and the Treasury influence was as decisive as ever. But probably no election before this time had aroused public opinion to quite the same extent. More than 150 supporters of Fox's lost their seats. To at least some contemporaries the result appeared as a victory of the royal prerogative over the House of Commons.

The Decline of the Crown

Despite the victory in the 1784 election, the political power of the crown did inevitably decline as its resources shrank. The abolition of many sinecures in 1782 was the starting point for a series of similar laws. By 1819 Lord Liverpool, then Prime Minister, was complaining that he had no means by which to influence the House of Commons.

The mental instability of George III was another factor in the decline of royal power. After his recovery in 1788, the king frankly told Pitt that henceforth he could not be so active in public affairs. When he finally sank into insanity in 1810, the Prince of Wales, who acted as regent for his father for ten years, failed to maintain the influence of the crown; he never showed the same understanding of English politics that his father had possessed.

It was ironically enough Pitt, who had benefited from the crown's resources in 1784, who was largely responsible for reducing them. His *financial reforms* ended the system whereby revenue from different sources had paid different expenses of government. Instead, all revenue went into the *consolidated fund,* out of which came all appropriations. This budgetary reform meant greater publicity for government expenditures. After 1785 commissioners of public accounts reported to Parliament on ever-widening areas of expenditures. By the early nineteenth century only the secret service funds were beyond their scrutiny. The pension list was analyzed and reduced. Pitt's method of letting government contracts publicly deprived the crown of a very effective means of influencing politics. The swarms of minor officials, or placemen, followed the government contractors out of the Commons. Slowly but surely over the years, Pitt rooted out corruption and extravagance in the government, and accomplished what had from the beginning been his main objective — efficient administration.

The decline in the political power of the crown reduced its value to aristocratic politicians. Whether controlled by the king or by the politicians, crown patronage had been an essential part of the aristocratic system of government, and the reduction of crown resources inevitably meant its decline. Even before the close of the Napoleonic Wars there was a body of floating members in the Commons which the ministry could not reach with the means at its disposal. After Waterloo their numbers increased, to the despair of Lord Liverpool. In 1822 he had to include the reforming Tories, Huskisson, Canning, and Peel, in his ministry in order to placate the Commons.

In the election of 1830, made necessary by the death of George IV and the accession of William IV (1830–37), politicians were still working on the assumption that the government could always win an election and that only subsequently might the opposition bring down the ministry by making deals in the Commons. But times had, in fact, changed. Wellington's cabinet in 1830 could not use the Treasury as John Robinson had done in 1784. For the first time, the government of the day lost the election. It was proof that the dominance of the old aristocracy had come to an end and had passed into constitutional history.

Local Administration

The justices of the peace continued to administer local government, with very little supervision from above. Usually drawn from the squirearchy, they tended to be Tory and until 1760 disliked the central administration because it was in the hands of the Whigs. But whether Whig or Tory, the central government preferred to interfere as little as possible at the local level. The cabinet did not take over from the moribund Privy Council the function of co-ordinating and supervising the work of the justices of the peace, who were therefore left with considerable local autonomy.

This did not result, however, in a wide variation of policy from county to county. Men with the same social backgrounds tended to approach local problems in much the same manner in Sussex as in Devon. The Speenhamland decision of 1795 is an interesting example of their tendency to see eye to eye on matters of local administration. It was the justices of the peace of Berkshire, faced by the duty of providing poor relief which had been laid upon them in 1601 and which had become in recent years a more acute problem than ever, who met in quarter session at the manor of one of their number at Speenhamland. There they agreed that the Berkshire parishes should disburse cash relief to paupers and to those whose wages were below a certain level at a rate based on the price of bread. In a few years this policy spread all over England, as if, said its opponents, it was the *Speenhamland* "*Act*" of Parliament.[42] The economic and social consequences of this

[42] Douglas, XI, 414.

well-intentioned "act" were not all beneficial, but from the constitutional point of view it is curious to see the squires of England determining national policy without any reference to the central government.

Borough government was generally of an oligarchic nature. The franchises in the charters issued by Charles II after the *quo warranto* proceedings [43] were restrictive in aim. With the decline of population in the older boroughs and the appearance of the new industrial centers, the suffrage was usually limited to a few. In many of them the corporation co-opted vacancies, so that it was a self-perpetuating body. These oligarchic governments often had little interest in meeting new public needs nor, it must be added in fairness, funds to do so. For the new owners of factories, who either could not vote in the boroughs or whose plants were located outside the existing borough limits (and therefore under the county administration of justices of the peace), local administration was far from satisfactory.

The new middle class tended more and more to meet the problems of local administration by private initiative. By the late eighteenth century businessmen were forming voluntary associations, to which they subscribed generously, and which performed functions neglected by local government, but nonetheless necessary. Fire protection, sanitation of sorts, street surfacing and lighting were the principal purposes of these private, extra-constitutional associations. Far from meeting the needs of the new middle classes, however, such associations merely whetted their appetite and convinced them that these things should be done by public agencies and funds. The neglect of local administration by the ruling aristocracy of the eighteenth century was increasingly resented. By the early nineteenth century a middle-class radicalism, more concerned with drains and street lighting than with any abstract political theories, was beginning to make itself felt. But even these interests found expression in the philosophical and political doctrines of "utilitarianism."

THE YEARS OF THE JUDGES

The appointment of justices lay solely with the crown, and in an age when birth and family connection counted for so much, the fact that these appointments were almost invariably based on merit is remarkable. Although governments naturally named barristers of the

[43] Above, p. 389.

same political persuasion as themselves, most judicial appointments were from leading members of the bar, many of whom had quite ordinary social origins and who had made their way by their ability to win cases. Once on the bench, a justice was beyond the control of any government. The result was a succession of such powerful figures as Camden, Mansfield, Stowell, and Eldon.

Judicial Prestige

Security of judicial tenure was an accepted principle. By the Act of Settlement the crown could remove a justice only on the request of both Houses of Parliament, and no such request was ever made. So strong was the concept of an independent bench that although commissions lapsed with the death of a sovereign, the judges were invariably reappointed by the new monarch. There were, however, doubts whether the justices might act during the interval between the lapsing of their old commissions and the issuance of their new ones. In 1760, therefore, a law was passed whereby the commissions of justices did not terminate with the death of the sovereign; [44] it was not until 1901 that any other offices came under the same provision.

The House of Lords depended upon the justices for the performance of its judicial duties. The Lord Chancellor, although he presided over the court of Chancery, had usually been trained in the common law and his judicial influence in the House, where he also presided, was great. Lord Eldon as Chancellor was a dominant figure, whose word the peers would normally accept on any legal issue. Usually the Chief Justices of King's Bench and Common Pleas were also peers. In addition, the lay peers invariably called on all justices to advise them in the exercise of their appellate and original jurisdiction. Although there is something a little incongruous about a body of legislators acting as judges, in fact the House of Lords in its judicial capacity depended almost entirely on the common law bench.

Judge-Made Law

Free of their obligation to arbitrate between the crown and Parliament, the justices after the Revolutionary Settlement acted independently of both. In general, their decisions tended to reduce the executive

[44] Douglas, X, 247–8.

power and to be sensitive to the liberty of the subject. When in 1763 Wilkes fell foul of the government,[45] a general warrant, issued by a Secretary of State, ordered the sheriffs of London and Middlesex to seize the "authors, printers, and publishers" of the offending *North Briton*. Under the authority of this warrant, which like all general warrants did not specify any reason or any particular individual, the sheriffs entered Wilkes's house, searched it, and seized some of his papers, and then jailed him and forty-eight others. None of this was new; officials had been employing general warrants for some time. What was new was the reaction of Wilkes. He sued out a petition for habeas corpus, and alleged that the failure of general warrants to state specific charges and persons made them illegal. Chief Justice Pratt of King's Bench in the resultant hearing ordered the release of Wilkes and his friends and severely criticized the use of general warrants, although he did not rule on their legality.[46]

Two years later, in spite of this decision against the government, Pratt became Lord Camden. He then took up the question of general warrants again in the case of Entick *v*. Carrington.[47] Crown counsel had argued their legality on grounds of "state necessity," but Camden rejected this plea and declared that officers of the government had to show specific legal authority for all their actions. "If it is law, it will be found in our books. If it is not to be found there, it is not law." General warrants had no such specific mention in the law and therefore were illegal. He also denied that "need of state" had any standing in law and uttered the immortal words, "Political policy is not an argument in a court of law."

The same independent spirit was also manifested by Lord Mansfield, who although detesting Wilkes, nevertheless quashed the outlawry charge against him in 1768.[48] Mansfield also defied the government six years later in Campbell *v*. Hall, when he held that once a colony had an elected legislature the crown could no longer legislate for it by orders-in-council.

The younger Pitt, alarmed by the events of 1793 in France, hoped to be able to use the courts to stifle the reform movement in England. But conservative justices upheld the principles of Camden and Mansfield against him. Political policy was no argument in a court of law, and

[45] Above, p. 446.
[46] Douglas, X, 256–7.
[47] Ibid. 258–63.
[48] Above, p. 447.

the bench duly instructed juries that the law of England made treason an *act*, with the result that men like Thomas Hardy and Horne Tooke, radicals who in Pitt's eyes were a danger to the state, were acquitted. The government had its way out. It put through legislation to deal with "sedition," and Parliament suspended habeas corpus in what appeared to be an emergency. But these actions were legislative, not judicial.

The formal abolition of slavery in Great Britain was a result of judicial action. Although this did not affect slavery in the colonies, it established a principle that Parliament had shown no willingness to assert — that a slave enjoyed all the rights of a free subject so long as he was on English soil. In 1772 after long frustrations, Granville Sharp, an anti-slavery leader, persuaded Chief Justice Mansfield to rule in the *Somersett Case*,[49] a habeas corpus action brought by Sharp in the name of a slave he had befriended. Sharp maintained that English law recognized only the servitude of serfdom, now long past, which had required a contract (either oral or written). Somersett, naturally, had no such contract. In a lengthy decision Mansfield ordered his release on the grounds that slavery was so odious that only positive prescriptive law could justify it. There being no such law in England, Mansfield applied the Camden dictum and declared that there could be no slavery in England.

Chancery, after its various setbacks during the seventeenth century, discovered a new lease of life. The undoubted supremacy of Parliament after 1689 meant that it was less open to attack as an instrument of royal tyranny, and during the eighteenth century common law barristers increasingly practised also on the Chancery "side." They brought to it the common law forms of fixed pleading and the concepts of stare decisis, which began to penetrate equity.

Chancery thus developed a procedure which became as formal and rigid as that of the law courts. Its basis in equity was almost forgotten, and by the early nineteenth century a huge backlog of cases had accumulated. What had originally been a court with almost summary procedures became notorious for its slowness and delays. Finally, it was the monstrosity described in all its horrors by Dickens in *Bleak House*. Neither the barristers in Chancery nor the chancellors saw the need for reform, and Lord Chancellor Eldon clutched to his bosom all the stultifying formalities of *his* court and defied all attempts to change them.

[49] Douglas, X, 263–4.

Statute Law

Parliament had little interest in dealing with the basic law, believing that as it stood it was well-nigh perfect. Most of its statutes were private acts required for land enclosures, and statutory intervention in the common law was usually only to confirm it.

But the maintenance of public order in unsettled times did however require statutory action. Without effective police agencies, boroughs were often at the mercy of mobs, which might riot for sheer joy, or on the orders of their leaders, who received pay from agitators for their services. The common law was uncertain about the legality of using force against mobs. In 1714, the government, fearing that the Jacobites might have recourse to mob violence to overthrow the newly established Hanoverian dynasty, passed the *Riot Act*.[50] This law empowered a justice of the peace, sheriff, or mayor to "read the Riot Act" to any group of twelve or more persons riotously assembled, ordering them to disperse. Failure to obey the order in one hour made all members of the mob guilty of a felony and authorized the official who had read the act to use any means, including the use of troops, to disperse the rioters. The law made it clear that any injury or death inflicted on rioters during such a dispersion was not a crime. Although giving a wide discretion to local authorities, for it was for them to decide when the act should be read, the statute remains the ultimate legal basis for the maintenance of order. By itself, however, the law was ineffective in achieving this end. In 1780 the savage penal laws against Catholics, which had been mercifully ignored for nearly a century, were repealed. A hare-brained noble, Lord George Gordon, stirred up the London mob over "popery," and the resultant riots, which got completely out of hand, wrecked portions of the capital, and deeply alarmed all law-abiding citizens. The city magistrates stood by helplessly, misinterpreting the Riot Act, which had never intended to say that once violence had broken out no action was possible until the Act had been read. It was the king who in the end ordered drastic action. The Gordon riots revealed the dark passions which seethed beneath the veneer of eighteenth-century urbanity and also the lack of any authority, except the military, to keep public order.

The law of libel, which permitted the jury to decide only the

[50] Douglas, X, 271–5.

question of publication, with the truth or falsity of the statement determined by the bench, was modified by the *Fox Libel Act*[51] of 1792. This permitted the jury, in addition to its verdict as to the fact of publication, to return one simply of not guilty, without reference to the fact of publication. Such a verdict precluded a ruling from the bench, although it indicated indirectly that the jury accepted the truth of the statement published. However, as the jury could still return a verdict on publication alone, it often meant that the bench continued to rule on the veracity of the statement. Defendants in libel actions frequently found themselves prevented from proving the truth of their printed statements, and during the years of the French Revolution when respectable Englishmen went in terror of "dangerous" ideas, justices almost rebuilt the common law doctrine of libel.

Perhaps the most important piece of legislation during this period was that which abolished the slave trade. After many years of agitation both in and outside Parliament, the slave trade (though not slavery) was made illegal in 1807, the law becoming effective the following year.[52] The penalties the law carried, however, were insufficient to deter people from engaging in such a lucrative trade; it was worth taking the chance when all the trader had to fear was a fine or at worst the confiscation of his ship. In 1811, however, the *Slave Trade Felony Act* finally put an end to the British slave trade. Any British subject who engaged in the trade in any capacity became liable to transportation or imprisonment.

The traditional common law prohibition against restraint of trade received statutory reinforcement in the *Combination Acts*, which beginning in 1799, forbade the organization of trade unions as aiming at such restraint under heavy penalties. Interestingly, the lack of centralized control over local administration actually meant a sporadic enforcement of these statutes.

The savage criminal law of the eighteenth century was largely the result of enactments in Parliament. English criminal law had rarely provided the penalty of imprisonment because it was expensive and there were few prisons. Imprisonment was usually only for debtors or for persons awaiting trial. Conviction consequently tended to mean either a fine, some form of corporal punishment, or hanging. Ever since the Norman Conquest the list of capital crimes had been steadily

---

[51] Douglas, XI, 363.
[52] Douglas, XI, 803.

increasing. During the Interregnum Cromwell had urged Parliament to modify the criminal law,[53] but nothing had happened; as men of property, members believed that only hanging would deter potential criminals. After the Revolution such an attitude received further statutory expression and by the close of the eighteenth century over two hundred crimes carried the death penalty.

The reform of the criminal law, therefore, was already long overdue before any substantial body of opinion began to campaign for it. Even then it seemed more effective to advocate reform not on humanitarian grounds but by an appeal to the self-interest of property owners, on which the harsh criminal law rested. It was pointed out that the very severity of the laws and the inconsistency of their application defeated the ends for which they were intended. In 1819, for example, over 14,000 capital cases came before juries: 5000 persons, many of whom were guilty, were acquitted simply because jurors shrank from bringing in a verdict of guilty when the penalty for such minor crimes was so drastic. Of the 9000 sentenced to death, all but a few were saved from the gallows by the royal prerogative of mercy; the alternative was usually transportation to Australia.

Those who upheld the severity of the laws argued that their inconsistency of application was a virtue, for royal clemency could save people worth saving, while the existence of the laws deterred criminals. Reformers claimed, however, that the facts pointed in quite the opposite direction. By the early nineteenth century the reluctance of juries to convict forgers and so send them to their death was notorious; in consequence, forgers were thriving. The criminal law reformers, notably Sir James Mackintosh and Sir Samuel Romilly, won their first important supporters when the bankers themselves pleaded that the penalty for forgery should be reduced. Similarly, merchants came to doubt whether the death penalty for stealing goods worth five shillings or over served any useful purpose when juries so often found the accused guilty of stealing merchandise worth four shillings, a crime which the law did not "know." By the close of this period the groups which had demanded that their property should be protected by such savage laws were beginning to think in terms of their modification.

The rules of evidence and pleading in criminal trials rested on judicial decisions, and procedure was hardly affected by statute law. Appeals for a convicted defendant were possible from the assize court to King's

[53] Above, p. 357.

Bench only on legal errors revealed in the trial record. This record, however, consisted of little more than jottings by the trial justice and contained neither evidence, summations by opposing counsel, nor even the justice's directions to the jury. From King's Bench a similar appeal on points of law ran to the Exchequer Chamber, and from thence to the House of Lords. In practice, therefore, criminal appeals were infrequent.

During the eighteenth century trial barristers developed new pleas. Justices hesitated to rule on them and instead *reserved* their ruling while the case continued. If the jury acquitted the accused, there was no judicial ruling on these pleas. However, if the jury convicted, the trial justice, after passing sentence, took these reserved pleas with him back to Westminster, where he consulted his colleagues and ruled on them. If the ruling upheld these pleas, the conviction was quashed.

This informal practice became institutionalized in the nineteenth century. In 1848 the *Court for Crown Cases Reserved* was created by statute: it consisted of any five justices, including one Chief Justice, who were to hear and rule on such pleas.

The aristocratic constitution, based on the Revolutionary Settlement and on the sanctity of property, emphasized the supremacy of Parliament, whose control by landed and mercantile aristocrats made them willing to leave large powers in the possession of a subordinate crown. The meshing of crown and Parliament came in the cabinet system of government, whose early years presumed the control by a few men of blocks of votes in the House of Commons. Although challenged by George III, the aristocratic control of government continued until it became clear that it no longer embraced all substantial property interests. The rising industrial ownership thus felt a peculiar sympathy toward theories challenging the *status quo*. This feeling was strong on the local level, where the autonomous control exercised by landed J.P.s singularly failed to meet the needs of the new factory wealth. By the early nineteenth century the aristocratic constitution had thus lost much of its vigor.

The emphasis on *status quo* by the aristocratic constitution included the law, whose administration by strong, independent justices did not produce major changes in it. Parliamentary intervention in the law was infrequent, but included a major modification in the law of libel and

the abolition of the slave trade. The same criticisms leveled at aristocratic government came to include the law, which reformers found
illogical by the close of the aristocratic constitution.

READING LIST

BARNES, DONALD G. *George III and William Pitt.*

FEILING, SIR KEITH. *History of the Second Tory Party, 1714–1832.*

FOORD, A. S. "The Waning of the 'Influence of the Crown'," *English Historical Review,* LXII, 484.

HOLDSWORTH, SIR WILLIAM S. *History of English Law,* Vols. X–XII.

LASKI, H. J. *English Political Thought from Locke to Bentham.*

NAMIER, L. B. *The Structure of Politics at the Accession of George III,* 2
vols.

PARES, R. *George III and the Politicians.*

PLUCKNETT, THEODORE F. T. *A Concise History of the Common Law,* Book
I, Part I, Chap. 8.

PORRIT, E., and A. G. PORRIT. *The Unreformed House of Commons.*

ROBERTS, M. *The Whig Party, 1807–1812.*

TURNER, E. R. "The Development of the Cabinet, 1688–1760," *American
Historical Review,* XVIII, 751; XIX, 27.

WALCOTT, ROBERT. *English Politics in the Early Eighteenth Century.*

WIGGIN, L. M. *The Faction of Cousins: A Political Account of the Gren-
villes, 1733–1763.*

WILLIAMS, BASIL. *The Whig Supremacy, 1714–1760.*

WILLIAMS, E. T. "The Cabinet in the Eighteenth Century," *History,* XXII,
240.

12

THE CONSTITUTION OF "REFORM"

FOR SOME sixty years after about 1820, the concept of "Reform" dominated constitutional developments. Before this period changes had come
about in a largely pragmatic manner, as part of the day-to-day business
of government. But in the age of "Reform" constitutional changes reflected certain *a priori* attitudes toward the function of government and
were conceived in terms of a general revision and reconstruction of the
existing political system. This is not to say that there was "planning" in
the modern political sense of that word: laissez-faire and a belief that the
state should interfere as little as possible in the lives of its citizens were
generally accepted principles. But the political and constitutional
changes for which the reform movement was responsible were of
fundamental importance.

The Social and Philosophical Background

The intellectual background of the reform movement may perhaps
be traced back to the publication of Jeremy Bentham's *Fragment on
Government* in 1776. This and subsequent writings by Bentham and
his followers, though very far from revolutionary in tone, assumed the
necessity of change: as the existing order was fundamentally resistant
to change, it followed that there was an element of radicalism in
Bentham's moderate theories: the old aristocratic system would have
to give way before anything could be accomplished. The only valid
criterion of government, as the Benthamites saw it, was *utility*. And
by utility they meant the greatest happiness of the greatest number.
Bentham's standard of utility was so simple, so much a matter of
ordinary common sense, that once stated, it soon came to appear as a
self-evident truth. It was certainly a highly practical philosophy, and
the reforms which the Benthamites sought were entirely sensible

— the elimination of injustice and abuses in the law, the achievement of peace and prosperity and public order, and in general the promotion of pleasure rather than of pain. By the early nineteenth century, Bentham was meeting his friends and followers regularly at the Political Economy Club. Such men as James Mill, David Ricardo, and Thomas Malthus would listen to each other's essays on society and government and discuss what needed to be done. All insisted that utility was the only possible standard for anything and that it could be determined quite simply on an entirely rational basis: actions tending to pleasure were good, actions tending to pain were bad.

Once having accepted this principle, utility could be achieved, as Bentham argued in his *Theory of Legislation*, which also appeared in 1776, by the simple expedient of legislating it into being. Bentham and his followers regarded government as a necessary evil; they wanted as little of it as possible. Yet the essential importance of Parliament in achieving their ends was never disputed. During the eighteenth century there had been very little legislation: all was for the best in the best of all possible worlds, the aristocratic politicians believed; or if they did not, they were haunted by the possibility that changes might do more harm than good. The Benthamites, the Philosophical Radicals, the Utilitarians, as they were variously called, wanted to start the wheels of the legislative machinery turning again. The purpose of government was not merely to protect life and property, as Locke had declared. It was to promote "the greatest good of the greatest number," and in the light of this definition it was clear that much needed to be done.

The Philosophic Radicals were not democrats; they had little faith in the common man's ability to apply the "hedonic calculus" of pleasure and pain. Initially, they had no strong views about the franchise, except that they believed that it should be uniform throughout the country. But the theory of the greatest good of the greatest number inevitably gave rise to certain questions. What was the greatest good? Who was to decide what would bring the greatest happiness to the greatest number? James Mill, of the generation after Bentham, supplied the answers most acceptable to the utilitarians. The lower and aristocratic classes, he argued, were equally isolated at either end of the social scale, and so not competent to determine the greatest happiness for the greatest number. The class capable of deciding this matter was the one between the two extremes — the middle class. In consequence, the Philosophic Radicals not merely failed to call for universal suffrage but actually feared it.

Apart from the intellectuals, the new industrial owners were the most vigorous members of the middle classes, a term used to distinguish them from the older landed and mercantile wealth on the one hand and rural and urban wage earners on the other. Eager for a share in government themselves, these men had little interest in political theories, but in assessing the merits of any government they would be likely to judge it in terms of "business efficiency." They were primarily concerned with such things as the reduction in the cost of poor relief, the establishment of limited liability for company stockholders, the simplification of the fantastically complex trade regulations, and the control of borough government. Under the old aristocratic regime, these representatives of the new wealth had little opportunity to make their presence felt. Both the variable franchises and the distribution of seats in the House of Commons made it difficult for wealthy cotton mill magnates and iron "kings," for instance, to find any effective representation for their interests. Industry had mushroomed in the midlands and the north, but in those areas there were few boroughs. The county franchise, the ownership of land worth 40 shillings annually or a life leasehold or mortgage on land of that value might, however, be beyond the reach of these factory owners, absurd as it may seem. Owners of smelters and power looms had far more than 40 shillings in capital investment in their plants, but they did not own the land on which they were built. English law with its entail provisions made the acquisition of outright ownership of land very difficult, and factory owners usually leased land for factories for either less than their lives or for periods far in excess of them (such as the famous 999 years). Either way, factory owners were not life leaseholders and so were unable to meet the county franchise requirements. Thus very wealthy men with urban and industrial interests were being denied their true place in the community and being forced to depend upon others, usually with a rural and agrarian background, to protect their interests.

In the second decade after Waterloo, these men found support in the theories of the Philosophic Radicals. Like the intellectuals in the Political Economy Club, they had no desire to see universal suffrage; like aristocrats and intellectuals they feared the "mob." Factory owners had been inclined to agree with the aristocrats that the French Revolution had proved that after a certain point of constitutional change it was impossible to prevent the mob's taking over — and just where that point lay no one could say. But still, a franchise that excluded themselves from any say in government was clearly too narrow, and certain moderate changes were called for. Voteless themselves, they could still exercise some influence in politics by investing in candidates for the House of Commons who supported "Reform," which more and more was coming to mean parliamentary reform. Local *political unions* also received financial assistance from factory owners in their sponsorship of such candidates. When the French middle class in 1830 showed that it was possible to stop a revolution at the point where the middle classes had control of it, English mill owners, confident of their ability to do the same thing in a better "English" manner, hesitated no longer. In the election of 1830 industrial money was solidly behind the reform candidates, and they at last won their majority in the Commons.

Fortunately for the Radicals and industrial owners, the political situation after Waterloo permitted them to use an already existing party to achieve their ends rather than construct a new one. The Whigs, for long dominated by the great aristocratic families and deeply reluctant to take anybody except the highest born into their midst, had been in the political wilderness since the war. Indeed, they had been out of office more or less continuously since 1760. As a party they had no particular connection with the reform movement. But the time had come when the party badly needed an infusion of new blood; and it was clear that at whatever sacrifice of principle their best hope of winning their way back into office lay in embracing "Reform." Their traditional belief that men "with a stake in the country" should be represented in Parliament was, however, about all they had in common with the Radicals and factory owners.

The Political Economy Club acted as liaison between the theoretical Radicals and the practical politicians, and Lord John Russell, scion of a great Whig family and a member of the House of Commons, embraced them both. Russell was friendly with the Radicals in the club, and in an ideal position to represent their ideas in the stately homes of England, explaining to the aristocracy what electoral reform as advocated by the Radicals would mean in practice. By the close of the first decade after Waterloo the Whigs were ready to accept an infusion of reform for the sake of the party. They had, however, no intention of accepting more than was necessary to get back into office, as the Radicals eventually discovered.

It was not an easy partnership. Neither the intellectuals, nor the businessmen, nor the great magnates who traditionally directed the fortunes of the Whig party, had much confidence in each other. But for the time being they worked together and were extremely successful. They were helped by a fundamental weakness that was by this time beginning to show in the ranks of the enemy.

By the early nineteenth century, the constitution was failing to provide what it required of itself — the representation of all substantial property interests. In the Revolutionary Settlement, the property interests of the day, then largely landed and mercantile, had been adequately provided for. But by the early nineteenth century there was this other wealthy group in the country, which had not existed in 1689, and for which the aristocratic constitution in the course of the eighteenth century had found no place. Smelter owners and cotton-mill kings certainly had a "stake in the country," and yet they were denied any opportunity to participate in government. There had been a certain mystique attached to the Revolutionary Settlement, a belief that the *status quo* was sacred and change iniquitous, and the events of the French Revolution confirmed this view; once allow change into the body politic and chaos and destruction followed. Edmund Burke's *Reflections on the French Revolution* of 1790 contrasted the unnatural excesses in France with the natural, harmonious, and evolutionary developments in England in 1688; violent breaks with tradition were necessarily evil, and governments which preserved existing institutions, reflecting the "peculiar genius" of the people, were essentially good. Such a view died hard. But by 1820 Burke's *Reflections* carried less weight than the opinions of the Political Economy Club; the fact that important property interests were not being represented could no longer be ignored.

The Acceleration of Reform

Although for political reasons the Whigs finally accepted parliamentary reform as the most important part of their program, already by 1823 the government had been forced to take in three "reforming" Tories. Canning at the Foreign Office was pursuing Castlereagh's policies to their logical end; Peel as Home Secretary had taken up penal law reform;[1] and Huskisson as President of the Board of Trade had begun to nibble at the mercantilist system of trade which the new wealth had come to find so irksome. Thus "Reform" had spokesmen in the government for almost a decade before the Reform Act modified the basis of parliamentary representation.

[1] Below, pp. 508-9.

The repeal of the Combination Acts [2] indicated a partial recognition of the principle of laissez-faire. Philosophic Radicalism with its insistence on the inexorable laws of economics, particularly the "iron law of wages" as described by David Ricardo, saw no reason why Parliament should interfere, even if it were only in support of common law prohibitions against restraint of trade. Radicals like Joseph Hume argued that even if workers were free to organize, they would find trade unions useless against the law of wages. Skilled workers under the direction of Francis Place, a master in the formation and manipulation of pressure groups, wanted the repeal of the Combination Acts for precisely the opposite reason — that free combinations of workers would be able to bargain with employers for higher wages. Huskisson was influenced primarily by the first argument, and he sponsored legislation in 1824 to repeal the laws without any clear idea as to the results or any previous consultation with his Prime Minister, Lord Liverpool. A Parliament composed largely of landed aristocrats passed the repeal,[3] whereupon there was a wave of strikes; in consequence, legislation was passed the following year to curb the unions. But reform had shown sufficient strength to do away with the Combination Acts once and for all.[4]

Legislation to improve the banking facilities for the new industrial owners was also badly needed. Big financial institutions outside the City of London were required, but the stockholders of the Bank of England, who belonged to the governing oligarchy, had always done their best to prevent legislation for joint stock banks in the "provinces," where only small, individually owned country banks were therefore able to operate. Financial disquiet in 1825 finally proved the need for joint stock banks in the new industrial regions, and the following year a law permitted their establishment beyond a radius of 65 miles from London.[5] One section of the governing class, that representing the older financial interests, had lost a part of its vested interest in the aristocratic system.

The reform movement took a further step forward with the removal of political restraints on Protestant nonconformists. All three members of the reformist alliance denied the validity of religious tests for office. During the eighteenth century these tests had really ceased to apply to Protestant dissenters, who engaged in occasional conformity or were

[2] Above, p. 457.
[3] Douglas, XI, 758.
[4] For the legal effects of the repeal, see below, p. 513.
[5] A limitation removed in 1833; below, p. 478.

THE CONSTITUTION OF "REFORM"

covered by annual acts of indemnity for not practising it.[6] Thus the Corporation and Test Acts themselves had had little meaning for these people. But the fact that Protestant dissenters generally belonged to the lower social classes meant that few could enter office, particularly at the national level. The property qualifications in land for membership in the Commons [7] barred the mass of nonconformists, and many of them lacked the property qualifications for the suffrage, for which there was no religious test. With the rise of the Wesleyan movement, however, which steadily gained converts among the class of new factory owners, Protestant dissent acquired wealth and social importance for the first time in a century. Such an "anomaly" between formal law and actuality was anathema to the Radicals, and in 1828 Lord John Russell of the Whig opposition introduced a measure to repeal these laws as they applied to Protestants.[8] Russell argued that this would merely make the law conform with what was actually the case, and this argument satisfied the Whigs and those Tories calling themselves Canningites; but the Wellington Tory ministry feared that the bill was only a prelude to proposals for Catholic emancipation. Again, the Radicals had sufficient influence in both parties to carry the bill through. But, as Russell said, it changed nothing.

Catholic emancipation came the next year.[9] The fears of the government about Russell's act proved correct, though this had nothing to do with the small group of English Catholics, who asked only to be let alone, and indeed were.[10] The issue was brought to a head by the Irishman Daniel O'Connell, who had founded the Catholic Association, a pressure group designed to bring about the dissolution of the union between Ireland and Great Britain. In the election of 1826 O'Connell had hinted at the strength of his association by defying landlords in two constituencies and securing the election of Protestants opposed to their interests. Two years later it became clear the aristocrats had lost control over the Irish voters when Vesey Fitzgerald, having accepted the Presidency of the Board of Trade, was obliged to stand again for his Irish seat for County Clare. The government anticipated no difficulty. Fitzgerald was a popular Protestant landlord, and it seemed that O'Connell

[6] Above, p. 400.
[7] Above, p. 426.
[8] Douglas, XI, 674.
[9] Douglas, XI, 787.
[10] The long unenforced penal acts against them had been repealed formally in 1780 (above, p. 456).

by setting himself up as a rival candidate was being no more than quixotic; as a Catholic he was in any case ineligible for Parliament. With these facts before them, the voters of Clare as members of the Catholic Association, under the eyes of their landlords and their agents, elected O'Connell. It was clear that what had been accomplished in a by-election could be repeated in a general election: Ireland, always precariously situated, could be brought to the brink of civil war.

The issue of Catholic emancipation roused the deepest emotions. After 1801 Grattan had vainly tried to secure in the United Kingdom what the Act of Union had failed to give — the right of Catholics to sit in Parliament. After him Plunket had taken up the cause. Both Whigs and Tories had shied away from the issue. Now in 1828 Irish Catholics forced it on a Tory government, headed by Wellington and including Peel and Eldon — all politically and personally opposed to Catholic emancipation.

In the face of O'Connell's unspoken threat of civil war, the government withdrew. The Irish leader had asked only that Catholics should have the right to sit in Parliament; the government, however, put through a law [11] which threw open all offices to Catholics except those of the sovereign, Lord Lieutenant of Ireland, Lord Chancellor of Ireland, and Lord Chancellor of England.[12] It was the end of the old order in Ireland. No longer could the ministry depend upon landlords there to provide them with 100 faithful "Irish" members. But at the same time the government changed the Irish county franchise from the 40-shilling "freehold" (often by courtesy) to a bonafide £10 freehold. No doubt it was hoped that this greatly reduced electorate, composed of substantial men, would not support O'Connell; for Catholic emancipation was not retroactive, and the Irish leader had to stand again in Clare. Yet the £10 freeholders did re-elect him.

The death of George IV in 1830 necessitated a parliamentary election. The Whigs stood for reform, the middle class poured out cash, and the government lost. Despite the variable franchises and existing distribution of seats, the reformers won a small majority in the Commons. Wellington announced in the Lords that he doubted whether he could devise as perfect a constitution as now blessed England. But faced by the reformers and the Whig regulars in the House of Commons, the

---

[11] Douglas, XI, 311.
[12] Catholic clergy, like clergy of the Church of England, remained ineligible for the House of Commons.

government was in a minority and resigned. Its place was taken by the Whig cabinet of Earl Grey, pledged to the reform of parliament — whatever that meant.

The Reform Act of 1832

In 1820 Earl Grey had been uncertain about parliamentary reform; and when he asked Whig members of Parliament for their views, he found no overwhelming support for it. It had taken the efforts of Lord John Russell to show the older leaders of the party the practical advantages of parliamentary reform. Grey's cabinet of 1830 consisted almost entirely of aristocrats, but by that time they were ready to embrace parliamentary reform both for party reasons and because, unlike the Tories, they had finally come to realize that public opinion would have to be conciliated.

The passage of the Reform Act was a long and bitter affair. An inner group of the cabinet drafted the measure along the lines which were to govern later reform bills, considering the distribution of seats and the franchise. Only with the latter did the aristocratic authors of the bill apply the Radical ideal of uniformity, and then only partially. In framing the measure, the inner cabinet shrewdly estimated how much radicalism was necessary to serve the Whigs effectively.

Russell introduced the bill into the House of Commons in March 1831; and the bill passed its crucial second reading by one vote. In the committee stage enough Whigs broke ranks for the Tories to be able to mangle the measure. When he heard of the crippling amendments, Grey asked the king to dissolve Parliament, and thereby the Whig leader committed his party even more rigidly to parliamentary reform than in the previous year. In the election of 1831 the issue was "the bill, the whole bill, and nothing but the bill." Despite the existing franchise and distribution of seats, the Whigs, thanks to middle-class political unions and money, increased their majority.

A new bill, slightly modified, was passed in the House of Commons without difficulty in September 1831. The next month the House of Lords, now a Tory stronghold, rejected it.[13] The ministry replied by bringing the bill a third time into the House of Commons, where it

[13] How much party considerations governed attitudes on the bill can be seen in the opposition of 21 bishops (named by Tory ministries) to it. If they had supported it, the bill would have passed.

was again passed. This time the peers passed the measure through its second reading and then began to cut it up in committee. With a minority in the upper House, Grey asked William IV to create fifty peers. When the king refused to go beyond twenty, Grey resigned, in May 1832; and the king requested Wellington to form a government.

Wellington had only contempt for the mob, but he shuddered at the spectacle of sober middle-class people now grimly drilling. He was willing to pilot the bill into law, but he could not command the support of the Whig majority in the Commons, which passed a vote of confidence in Grey; so Wellington advised the king to recall the Whig leader. Upon his return to office, Grey received the king's word that he would create enough peers to ensure that the Lords would pass the bill in the form approved by the Commons. Confronted by this threat, a number of Tory peers at Wellington's suggestion stayed away, and the Whigs were able to pass the bill unchanged through the upper House. On 7 June 1832 the Reform Act received the royal assent.

The provisions of the Reform Act [14] were all in favor of the Whigs, which in itself explains Tory bitterness. In allotting seats the Whigs kept the membership of the House of Commons at 658 but about one-fifth of the seats, all from England, were changed. Fifty-six boroughs under 2000 population, most of them Tory strongholds, lost their parliamentary representation; and another thirty with populations between 2000 and 4000 each lost one member. One combined borough had its seats halved from four to two. The framers of the law thus had 143 seats to place.[15] Eight of them went to Scotland and five to Ireland,[16] but the 130 remaining seats went to English (and Welsh) constituencies.

The allocation of these seats reveals much about the plans of Whig leaders. Exactly half went to the *counties*, where the new franchise arrangements strengthened landlord control of the electorate. Twenty-

[14] Douglas, XI, 341.
[15] The odd number came from the disenfranchising of one borough with a single seat. The original bill had proposed to take away parliamentary representation from 60 boroughs and halve that of 47 others, giving a total of 166 seats for redistribution.
[16] Separate Reform Acts in 1832 dealt with Scotland and Ireland along the same general lines as that for England (Douglas, XI, 341, 353, 357). Scotland had its representation increased from 45 to 53 (30 in the counties); and although its county franchise was unchanged, the narrow burgh franchises gave way to one giving the vote to householders occupying premises of £10 annual value. Irish representation, raised from 100 to 105, rested on the county franchise of the £10 freehold, established in 1829 and not changed in 1832, and upon a £10 householder qualification in the boroughs.

two urban centers, most without previous representation, each received two seats and became parliamentary boroughs, as did another twenty-one new boroughs which each received a single seat. Although the law gave new industrial centers, such as Manchester and Birmingham, parliamentary representation, the counties made a gain of 70 per cent in their representation.

The concern for landed interests was obvious in the franchise requirements, which provided for two distinct and uniform franchises — county and borough. The old county qualification of the 40-shilling freehold remained, but the law made clear that it had to be possessed by actual occupancy or inheritance, not by mortgage or life lease. Persons holding either life leaseholds or leases of sixty or more years on land of a clear annual value of £10 gained the vote. These new voters would be fairly independent, as would also those leasing land of £50 annual value for a minimum of twenty years. But those who also now gained the county franchise because they rented land of the same value, but as tenants-at-will on a yearly basis, were in a much weaker position. This group was not included in the original bill and was only brought into the final law by an amendment in the Commons by the Marquis of Chandos, who was certainly not influenced by democratic considerations. His amendment was designed to improve the position of the landlords, who would be able to control more votes in their constituencies. The Whigs did not resist the amendment.

In the boroughs the franchise was also made uniform and given to borough freemen, if residents, and 40-shilling freeholders. It now included, however, persons either residing in the borough or living within seven miles of it, who had paid its rates, and owned or rented within it a house, warehouse, counting-house, or other building which with the land it occupied had a clear annual value of £10. Through this qualification the owners of the new industrial wealth at last received the vote.[17]

A third phase of the Reform Act dealt with the problem of impersonation of voters, now made considerably more acute by the addition of over 200,000 new ones to the electorate. The law provided for the *registration of voters*, with the responsibility for registration laid on the voter, who had to pay a shilling to have his name entered in the registry

---

[17] The Reform Act actually disenfranchised some borough voters, such as the pot wallopers (those who had the vote by virtue of cooking in a borough) and those paying scot and lot (above, p. 428), suffrages which the law of 1832 did not continue.

of the constituency. No person, even if otherwise qualified, could vote without being on such a registry. From this provision of the Reform Act came the growth of party organizations outside Parliament, because Whigs and Tories formed registration societies, which "helped" potential party supporters to register.

The passing of the Reform Act was celebrated joyfully throughout the country, but its political consequences hardly justified the first jubilation of the populace. The chief result of the act was to tighten the grip of the Whigs, and to consolidate their power; their party was still predominantly aristocratic. From 1832 to the next extension of the franchise in 1867, the Whigs were only out of power for five years; and they shared a coalition with the Tories for three. Thus for twenty-seven of the thirty-five years between the two franchise laws the Whigs were in the government and could thank the authors of the Reform Act for having served their party well.

For the Radicals, however, the result was disappointing. Despite Wellington's prophecy that "no gentleman will want to sit in the House of Commons," gentlemen emphatically did. The first election after the Reform Act, in 1833, sent some 500 members who were of the landed interest to the House, and of these 200 were heirs of peers or of baronets. Only a few Radicals reached the House in 1833; their influence proved to be slight and short, and none achieved real political prominence after 1832. One reason why they reaped so few benefits from the law was because it enlarged the English electorate by only 217,000 — though with increasing prosperity this figure would steadily rise. Prior to 1832 one man in ten had the vote; afterward the ratio was one in six. The Radicals had hoped for something better. The new voters, moreover, were for the most part wealthy businessmen, who had wanted certain things from Philosophic Radicalism but had had little interest in its ideological aims. As businessmen they were still prepared to leave politics to landed aristocrats, who, in the words of Lord Palmerston, "no longer played to the royal box but to the public galleries." The owners of industrial wealth acquired a share, but only a small one, in the government; but a more striking development was the movement of the landed aristocracy into business, particularly after 1840. The heir of the sponsor of the famous Chandos clause saw his father go bankrupt on the land; he then retrieved the family fortunes by investing in railways. There were many examples of this kind. It was the workings of economic and social processes, rather than the Reform Act, which steadily increased middle-class influence in government.

One way of considering the Reform Act is to see what it did not do. Most importantly, it did not reform Parliament, only the House of Commons, and that only in part. It ignored the House of Lords altogether. The threats of creating new peers in 1832 no doubt carried weight and may have been the reason why for nearly thirty years the peers were willing to accept legislation from the Commons with only occasional and slight modifications. But a more important reason was the continuing basic community of interest between the bulk of the membership of both Houses, so that it was unlikely that one would pass measures unacceptable to the other. Although "management" of the Commons after 1832 was far more than making "deals" with individual peers, such arrangements were still possible. Some peers exerted a very large political influence. Of the thirteen ministries between 1832 and 1867, in eight the Prime Minister was in the upper House. Of the remaining five, two were headed by Lord Palmerston, an Irish peer,[18] and one by Lord John Russell, son of the Duke of Bedford.[19] Only the two Tory cabinets of Sir Robert Peel had a Prime Minister with a genuinely middle-class background.

One reason for the continuing harmony of basic interests between the two Houses was the failure of the Reform Act to abolish qualifications for members of the Commons. Even if the owners of the new wealth had the inclination to enter Parliament, their wealth was in smelters, cotton looms, and steam engines — not land, of which a borough member still had to own £300 worth and a county member £600. In 1838 the requirement was modified by allowing these amounts to include chattels as well as land, but there was still little change in the type of man who stood for Parliament. The abolition in 1858 of property qualifications for membership in the House of Commons did not change the essential upper-class character of its members. Whether payment of members would have changed this situation is an open question. Lord Blandford proposed such payment while the Reform Bill was moving through the Commons, but the House rejected his amendment.

The Reform Act did not touch plural voting. A Radical amendment

[18] Sitting for an English constituency, as permitted by the Act of Union of 1800 (above, p. 437).
[19] Russell headed his first ministry as a commoner, but his second as a peer, having accepted a peerage in 1861.

to reduce it fell through, without a Whig or Tory supporting it. Plural voting generally helped the landed interests, for until after the period of reform most businessmen had their business premises and their homes in the same constituency. Landlords, on the other hand, often owned real property in several constituencies.

The law did not abolish every pocket and rotten borough, and the influence of patrons continued to be great in many constituencies. It certainly did not end corruption, and by enlarging the electorate it actually extended practices of the sort observed by the traveling section of the Pickwick Club in the contest at Eatanswill.[20] The additional voters also meant that election costs remained high. As late as 1857 those for an ordinary borough contest ran a candidate between £200 and £300, while expenses for a large borough or a county were around £1000. Financially conscious businessmen might well hesitate about standing for Parliament.

The Reform Act did not provide for the secret ballot as a remedy for corruption; this suggestion was, indeed, defeated on the grounds that secret voting would make it more difficult to prove corruption! Furthermore, said opponents, freeborn Englishmen should be proud to state openly their choice for their member of Parliament. And behind these openly expressed criticisms was the further objection that £50 tenants-at-will were useful to landlords only if voting were open.

Yet although the Reform Act failed to do so many things and left the power of the landed magnates almost untouched, it is nevertheless a landmark in the constitutional history of England.

In the first place, the way in which it was passed revealed that the old aristocratic system of government was already, in one important respect, outmoded. Although the Whig party leaders responsible for seeing the measure through were themselves aristocrats — with the exception of Henry Brougham — when Grey had Parliament dissolved and elections held in 1831 on the specific issue of the Reform Bill, he denied the concept of the supremacy of Parliament, on which the aristocratic system of the eighteenth century had always insisted. Previously, ministries when defeated in the Commons had either meekly suffered

---

[20] The official opening date of the Pickwick Papers, 1827, does not so much fix the date of the Eatanswill election as the reference in the pertinent chapter (XIII) to the famous Schedules A and B of the Reform Act, respectively abolishing and halving the representation of boroughs on these lists. Thus plainly, the election occurred after that law. The relation of this chapter to the action of Bardell v. Pickwick, which is probably Norton v. Melbourne (1836), would seem to place the Eatanswill affair in or near the general election of 1835.

or had resigned. When, instead, Grey went to the country, he gave effect to Chatham's dictum that beyond Parliament was the ultimate power — the electorate. He was also setting the pattern to which later ministries would increasingly conform, until it became the usual ministerial response to a defeat in the Commons.[21]

Secondly, it was during the passage of the bill that party lines became much more clearly defined. When the Whig majority in the Commons categorically refused to accept Wellington, even with his promise to drive the bill into law, the aristocratic constitution was indeed dead; only five years earlier Wellington might have been able to carry it through. By 1832 the heat of debates and the election of 1831 had produced a sense of party unity which denied him office. Although party lines were far from sharp after the Reform Act, they were much clearer than when Whigs, Canningites, and Tories had all merged.

Again, the registration provisions of the law itself meant that the party divisions spread throughout the whole electorate. By the close of the reform period, the societies which had been formed simply to register voters had become highly organized, well-disciplined national party organizations.

Beyond these things, in determining the composition of the House of Commons, the Reform Act had several other important constitutional implications. It began by denying the principle, embodied in previous plans for parliamentary reform, that public funds should compensate "owners" of any seats which might be abolished. The Reform Act took away 143 seats from their former constituencies without compensation, and thereby declared that seats in Parliament "belonged" to none except the nation. The franchise provisions of the law also marked a radical break with the past. Parliament had set the county franchise in 1430,[22] and its enlargement of the county electorate in 1832 thus applied the traditional principle that Parliament — not the crown — should set county suffrage requirements. But not so the boroughs. Parliament had never had any say in their creation or their franchises; these were matters solely for the crown. Now in 1832 Parliament determined the allocation of seats among boroughs, in the process creating some new boroughs and taking away from others what the crown had once given them, and then bestowing a uniform franchise upon all boroughs. Although the Tories thought of their immediate interests

[21] Below, p. 498.
[22] Above, p. 200.

when they attacked the borough sections of the Reform Act, they were correct in describing them as revolutionary.

The Reform Act did not finally put an end to the power of the crown, but it did reveal that by that time the crown was no longer able to control political events. A generation previously, Wellington would have received enough patronage resources to command a majority in the Commons. By 1832, however, the sovereign and his ministers simply did not have the resources upon which Pitt and Fox had reckoned in 1788 in their struggle over the regency measure.[23] With the passage of the Reform Act, the enlarged electorate made it even less possible for the limited patronage of the crown to have any effect upon politics. This became quite obvious in 1834, when William IV dismissed the Melbourne Whig ministry and called on Peel to form a Tory government. After several major defeats in the Commons, the new Prime Minister in 1835 appealed to the country, but the elections went in favor of the Whigs. All that the king could do was to recall Melbourne;[24] he had been unable to do for Peel what his father had done for Pitt.[25] When Peel did form a stable Tory cabinet in 1841, it rested on a solid majority in the Commons, given by the voters.

The Reform Act also rejected the traditional principle that Parliament represented "communities"; representation in the House of Commons came to depend upon population, even though for the time being imperfectly. If Parliament represented the people, why should exceptions be made: why should it not represent all people? It was here that the Whigs were wrong and the Tories right in interpreting the meaning of the bill. Lord John Russell insisted that the measure did not violate the fundamental aristocratic principle that the House of Commons represented the interests of men with a "stake in the country." He emphasized that the people to be enfranchised were just such men, and that if for a moment he had thought that the bill might be the starting point for further franchise extensions, he would have dropped it; this bill was final. But "Finality Jack" lived to urge further suffrage extension and to see a much larger one in 1867.[26] Because, as Lord Eldon gloomily declared in the upper chamber, the bill inaugurated a new policy of modifying the franchise in order that people presently unable to exercise it might do so in the future. Eldon foresaw demands from men unable

[23] Above, pp. 418–19.
[24] Below, p. 500.
[25] Above, p. 449.
[26] Below, p. 484.

to meet the franchise as it stood for still further changes in it. And so it proved. The old franchises had not been logical, but they were defensible in the historic framework of Parliament. The new franchises were rather more logical, but quite indefensible in terms of the "logic" beloved by Philosophic Radicalism. If a £10 householder could vote in a borough, why not a £9 one? The answer could be only as Eldon prophesied — further legislative measures lowering suffrage qualifications, until ultimately it would reach a point that Eldon even in his worst moments never anticipated: not merely every man, but every woman had the vote.

Some credit for the Reform Act does perhaps belong to the Tories. They heard the mobs bawling and saw the middle classes drilling in support of the measure, and their answer to both groups might have been to sanction the use of armed force. That at least was possible, for Tory feeling was strong in the officer class of the army. But the aristocratic constitution for nearly a century and a half had insisted upon the principle of parliamentary supremacy and, within it, tolerance toward political opponents. By its close these attitudes were so strong among politicians that the answer of "a whiff of grapeshot" never occurred to Tory leaders.

Like the various portions of the Revolutionary Settlement, the Reform Act was ordinary legislation, capable of repeal at any time by normal legislative processes. Yet the Tories, after fighting the measure bitterly, never indicated the least interest in its repeal. They accepted the new frame of reference and won office within it. As in so much else of English constitutional history, the door opened only one way.

The Momentum of Reform

For half a century after 1832, both political parties were committed to a policy of "Reform" in one way or another. The popular political and constitutional issues to which they lent their support were of various kinds, but all reflected the general reformist tendencies of the age.

The campaign for the abolition of slavery had been fought in and out of Parliament for many years, but although slavery had enjoyed no protection in England since 1774,[27] and the slave trade had been illegal for British subjects since 1808,[28] slavery itself existed in various British

[27] Above, p. 455.
[28] Above, p. 457.

colonies, notably in the West Indies and the Cape Colony. When the Anti-Slavery Society pressed for the abolition of slavery throughout the Empire by act of the British Parliament, there arose again the constitutional issue which had helped disrupt the Empire in 1775. West Indian slave owners argued, as the Boston merchants had in the past, that Parliament had no power to legislate on internal colonial matters. Unlike the North American colonies, however, the West Indies had only a small resident European population to lend weight to the argument, and in 1833 the British Parliament passed a measure abolishing slavery throughout the Empire.[29]

The authors of the law tried to avoid the constitutional issue by appealing to the colonies with elected legislatures (those without them were no problem) to indicate their *consent* to the British abolition measure by repassing it as their own. If they failed to do so, however, they would not receive any of the £20 million appropriated by that law as compensation to slave owners. Faced with this dilemma, the various colonial legislatures duly passed the British act, which was really a forced sale by slave owners of their human chattels to the British taxpayer, whose Parliament had already declared them free.

In economic policy the principles of laissez-faire were only partially accepted. In 1833 the Bank of England lost its fiscal monopoly within the 65-mile radius of London;[30] and various measures eased the formation of companies, culminating in a law of 1844 which permitted the registration of a company with a government registrar as the equivalent of incorporation by the older method of a royal charter. Such registration gave to stockholders the benefits of *limited liability*, whereby each was responsible for the liabilities of the enterprise only to the extent of the par value of his shares in it.

Middle-class voters had to accept another kind of economic legislation, proving that neither they nor the exponents of pure Philosophic Radicalism dominated the post-1832 scene. The passage of the *Factory Act* of 1833 [31] marked the entrance of the state into a new and enormous area. The law dealt with children and young people in textile mills: no child under nine was to work in these mills, and hours were set for the others, both on a daily and weekly basis. The law also applied state

[29] Stephenson and Marcham, 726.
[30] Above, p. 466.
[31] Douglas, XII-Pt. One, 949.

compulsion in education for the first time by requiring all children in factories under thirteen to attend school two hours a day.

In its requirements, which were to be extended considerably in the next few years, the law seems mild enough, but it produced anguished outcries from cotton factory owners. This was in part because it was clear that this law, in contrast to earlier factory acts, would be enforced. It provided that inspectors, named by and responsible solely to the central government, should supervise its administration and report violations to the government. Furthermore, in its denial of the right of employers to hire persons of certain categories (in this instance, children under nine) and their right to work persons in other classifications as they would, the Factory Act of 1833 marked the beginning of the state's claim to control basic industrial policy. Nine years later the *Mines Act* extended the principle and that of enforcement by government inspectors. Industrial legislation continued to occupy Parliament, and by the close of the reform era the right of the government to determine industrial policy in terms of state needs and interests had ceased to be an issue.

Similarly, the *Poor Law* of 1834 [32] obliged the government to assume further social responsibilities. Middle-class voters tended to regard the problem of poor relief from two points of view: first, it cost too much; second, poverty was in any case a sin, or at least the consequence of sin. The result was a law sweeping away all previous statutes on poor relief and their interpretations, such as the "Speenhamland Act," [33] and removing the responsibility for it from the counties and their justices of the peace to the central government. There were to be three poor law commissioners, with wide powers to effect a uniform administration of the basic principles set forth in the law. The commissioners, however, became extremely unpopular. Their attempts to reduce the cost of poor relief, largely by building workhouses for paupers unable or unwilling to work, caused great bitterness among the lower classes, one expression of which can be seen in Chartism.[34] Laissez-faire and the middle-class principle of self-help appeared to be triumphant.

The long-term effect of the Poor Law was, however, quite the opposite. It ended, in the first place, a major function of local government,

[32] Douglas, XII-Pt. One, 849.
[33] Above, pp. 451-2.
[34] Below, p. 480.

and thus much of the local autonomy which had characterized both county and borough administration since the mid-seventeenth century. Not only did its methods presage those of the welfare state, its actual provisions laid the foundations for the modern social service state. The law gave the first Treasury grant for education, even if only for pauper children. In time it led to better housing, sanitation, and medical care for the lower orders. In 1848 came the first *Public Health Act* in which, rudimentary though it was, a further responsibility of government was recognized. In 1871 all functions for poor relief went to the new Local Government Board,[35] which in this and other matters increased the central government's social services and its control over local administration. And in 1875 a Conservative ministry made local authorities responsible for public housing by the Artisans' Dwelling Act. By that time, laissez-faire as a principle of government policy was dead. Ironically, the Poor Law of 1834, conceived in the spirit of laissez-faire, set Britain on the road toward the modern welfare state.

The reform movement, as has been seen, did not envisage the participation of the lower classes in government, and in most cases those who described themselves as Radicals were wary of the "masses" and of the implications of popular sovereignty. And the lower classes might have remained silent, allowing the middle class to lead them, had it not been for the new poor relief policy. This aroused the most violent opposition, which was expressed in the *People's Charter*, from which the word Chartism derived. The charter laid down six principles: *universal* (manhood) *suffrage*, the *secret ballot, constituencies of equal population, no property qualifications* for election to the House of Commons, *salaries* for members, and a *one-year term*. Each one of these points marked a sharp break with parliamentary history, except the last; each eventually became law, except the last.

None of the other five points became law, however, during the period within which Chartism flourished. The movement was at its most vigorous in 1839, it revived again in 1842, and after a last convulsion in 1848 disappeared without having won any of its points. Chartist leaders did everything wrong. Although their supporters wanted a quick repeal of the Poor Law, they insisted that all six points had to be achieved before this was possible. They quarreled with trade unions, which as a result relied upon economic, rather than direct political action. The Chartists also had a remarkably blind spot about the House

[35] Below, p. 506.

of Lords, which formed no part of their program. Probably this omission was due to their recollection of the surrender of the peers in 1832, and their acquiescent attitude subsequently toward bills from the Commons. The assumption of the Chartists, however, that the Lords would continue this role in dealing with measures from the kind of Commons they desired was not realistic. But the worst error of the Chartist leaders was to threaten violence. On this ground reform, with its emphasis on "respectability," which in the early nineteenth century was permeating all classes, met and defeated Chartism.

The repeal of the Corn Laws was itself a later result of the Reform Act, and the pressure group methods the Anti-Corn Law League employed became a model for many later campaigns by other bodies. Facts and figures were poured out to prove the economic fallacy and the ethical immorality of grain tariffs. In 1845 a potato famine in Ireland forced the Peel Tory ministry to suspend the tariffs there; the League could claim that all its contentions were proved. The next year Peel split his party by sponsoring legislation repealing the Corn Laws. With Whig support the measure passed the Commons, and in the House of Lords the Duke of Wellington grimly carried the bill through. Three years later the repeal of the remnants of the Navigation Acts underlined the social and economic consequences of the Reform Act.

During the 1850s, because neither party had supporters clamoring for specific items of reform, the movement lost some of its force. But the death in 1865 of Palmerston, a Whig defender of the *status quo*, and the drastic franchise extension of 1867 [36] together with the formation of the first Gladstone government the next year, brought about its revival. Gladstonian Liberalism aimed at equality of opportunity, so that the old Radical ideal of free competition could truly operate. The first area where Gladstone applied this theory was in Ireland, as part of his program to pacify that island.

The Church of Ireland was for a tiny Anglican minority, and its established position symbolized English control of Ireland. The great bulk of the Irish understandably resented having to pay tithes to it. In 1869 Gladstone brought in a bill [37] to remove all government connections with Irish religious groups, which should all become voluntary and have exactly the same legal footing in 1870. The measure passed the Com-

[36] Below, p. 484.
[37] Douglas, XII-Pt. One, 89–94; 32 and 33 Vic., cap 42.

mons and, thanks to the intervention of Queen Victoria with the Arch-bishop of Canterbury, the Lords. The *Church of Ireland* was disestab-lished and disendowed, and its prelates left the House of Lords; the *Presbyterian Church* in Ulster lost the *regium donum*, which it had received for supporting William III; and *Catholics* likewise lost the *Maynooth Grant*, given by the government to an Irish seminary of that name for training priests. Although the law contributed little to the solution of basic Irish problems, it created a constitutional precedent for the disestablishment of the Church of England elsewhere.

Where the principle of equality of opportunity made the government sever its connection with Irish religious bodies, the same principle caused the Gladstone ministry to apply the state directly to the cause of education. Private voluntary schools (often sponsored by religious groups, particularly the Church of England) were meeting the needs of only half of the children of elementary school age. The *Education Act* of 1870 made the government responsible for elementary education. Where voluntary schools were meeting local needs, they continued. Where the government felt them insufficient, locally elected school boards provided schools for the education of children up to the age of thirteen. The central government gave grants to elementary schools; the school boards in addition could levy rates for their schools; and parents, if financially able, paid fees. This last source of revenue for board schools disappeared in 1886. The law did not make elementary education compulsory, but it permitted local school boards to do so; and as a result of Treasury policy, most boards did.[38]

At the other end of the educational scale the government had to con-sider the fact that an Oxford or Cambridge degree was essential to a man in many professions, including the new type of civil service.[39] The colleges of Oxford and Cambridge were private foundations with power to regulate their own affairs, including requirements for admissions and degrees. The two universities and their constituent colleges had con-sistently denied that the government had any interest in them. Until 1854, only persons subscribing to the Thirty-nine Articles of the Church could enter Oxford. Cambridge permitted nonconformists to enter its colleges but not to receive its degrees. In 1854 and 1856 statutes put an end to religious tests for both universities for entrance and for bachelor degrees, except those in theology. However, higher degrees, scholar-

[38] Below, p. 507.
[39] Below, p. 491.

ships, and fellowships, along with faculty positions at both universities, remained Anglican monopolies. In 1871 public law dealt with the internal policy of private institutions by forbidding the imposition of any religious tests for any honor or post at Oxford or Cambridge except those in theology.

Further extensions of the franchise followed inevitably from the Reform Act. As the intellectual basis of "Reform" broadened from the somewhat rigid Philosophic Radicalism of James Mill to the more humanistic Utilitarianism of his son, John Stuart, the father's "logical" inclusion of the middle class in the suffrage became in the mind of the son the equally and inexorably logical conclusion that it should include all men. Although reform had fended off the Chartists' demand for universal manhood suffrage, it was not long after that Lord John Russell, now influenced by the younger Mill as he had once been by the elder, began to argue in favor of the enfranchisement of the "better sort" of artisans. Russell's plan was indifferently received by the Whigs, as was Benjamin Disraeli's by the Tories, and their task of persuading their respective parties was made more difficult by the indifference of the people they proposed to enfranchise. Whereas the middle classes had themselves fought for the franchise in the early nineteenth century, skilled workers in the 1850s, organized in strong unions, believed that collective bargaining with employers was sufficient for their needs.

Indifference on all sides led to the failure of franchise proposals in 1852, 1858, 1860, and 1865. With the death of Palmerston in 1865, Russell, who had been in the Lords since 1861, formed a ministry of which Gladstone was the driving force in the Commons; and it was he who was the principal author of a new franchise measure in 1866. The bill planned to give the vote to some skilled artisans, but it split the recently named "Liberal" party, with Robert Lowe heading a group which from its "Cave of Adullam" sneered at the "lower orders." The government resigned, and the Conservatives took over, nominally under the Earl of Derby, but actually directed by Disraeli in the Commons.

The Conservative cabinet was in a minority in the House and dependent upon the Adullamite Liberals, whose slurs on workingmen had finally stung trade unionists into demanding, at gigantic meetings, the vote. Convinced that some kind of franchise bill was necessary, Disraeli introduced a very moderate one in 1867. It would have given the vote to skilled workers but would have cancelled the effect of this grant by "fancy franchises," whereby people with special qualifications (such as deposits in savings banks) would have cast an additional vote in any constituency where they already had the suffrage. These fancy franchises (different from plural voting, in that the latter permitted persons to vote once in the various *different* constituencies where they were qualified to do so [40]) would largely have benefited the middle classes.

Gladstone was furious at what he considered a typically cheap, political, insincere, Disraelian trick; and he tried to embarrass the government by radical amendments. His recently divided Liberals closed ranks behind him to pour coals of fire on the government to prove its insincerity. As the Conservative leader blandly accepted one Liberal amendment after another, the Liberal proposals became more and more extreme. One of the few amendments not accepted was that by John Stuart Mill to give the vote to women on the same terms as men, a proposal shouted down by a hilarious House.

The upshot was an almost complete rewriting of the bill on the floor of the House of Commons, where both parties cast principles aside and worked in terms of immediate tactical advantages. When the measure reached the Lords, the fancy franchises were gone; and Derby and the Conservative majority there were dismayed by what their Leader of the Commons had accepted for a bill which they could not disavow. When the bill became law in 1867, many agreed with Derby that it was a "leap in the dark," and pessimists shared the view of Thomas Carlyle that it was like "shooting Niagara."

The law, the *Reform* (or Representation of the People) *Act of 1867* [41] proceeded on the same lines as that of 1832, shifting seats and extending the suffrage. The number of seats in the Commons remained at 658, but they were redistributed according to population. Where Gladstone's bill had proposed to transfer 30, and Disraeli's original measure 45, the final law took 52 seats away from boroughs with less than 10,000 population. Seven of these went to Scotland,[42] leaving 45 for England. Of these, 25 were given to the counties, although the growth of industry since 1832 made them less a gift to the landlord class than they would have been in that year. Urban areas, most of them new boroughs, re-

---

[40] In 1861 John Stuart Mill in his *Treatise on Representative Government* had proposed additional votes in the same constituency for persons with greater education.

[41] Douglas, XII-Pt. One, 181.

[42] Separate measures in 1868 dealt with Scotland and Ireland, whose seats respectively were 60 and 103, leaving England with 495. The franchise provisions of the Scottish and Irish acts roughly paralleled those of the measure for England.

ceived fifteen; and, in a radical move, the parvenu University of London received a member to be elected by its degree holders.

During the debates on the measure there had been a vain proposal by Mill to replace the traditional method of representation by the Hare system of proportional representation.[43] The final law misapplied the theory of proportional representation by giving Manchester, Leeds, Birmingham, and Liverpool three members, but allowing their electorates to vote for only two. The idea that this device would give minority representation proved illusory, particularly after Joseph Chamberlain and his Liberal caucus in Birmingham had hired a mathematician to demonstrate how they could capture all three of its seats.[44]

Even more than in the Reform Act of 1832, it was the distribution of seats in the 1867 law which tore holes in the traditional idea of the corporate representation of boroughs and counties by two members. It was not this which alarmed Conservatives, however, so much as the franchise provisions. Although franchises for counties and boroughs remained distinct, Liberal amendments had greatly broadened them. In the counties the 40-shilling freehold qualification continued, and landlords could still influence £50 tenants-at-will. But all other male occupiers of land of £12 assessed (not rental) value could now vote. The various types of tenures which in 1832 had given the vote at £10 annual value, now did so for £3. Taken together, the county franchise provisions of the 1867 measure gave the middle classes control in the counties, where only rural workers and miners now lacked the suffrage.

In the boroughs the law nearly doubled the electorate (indeed it tripled it in Birmingham and quadrupled it in Leeds) by giving the franchise to every man occupying (not owning) a house on which rates had been assessed for one year. Since even the worst shacks were assessed for these local taxes, every man occupying a dwelling in a

---

[43] The system of proportional representation, often called simply P/R, had been devised by Hare in 1859. According to this, voters listed their first, second, and so forth choices of candidates. If a candidate had a majority by virtue of first choices, he was elected. Candidates not having such a majority might receive one on the basis of second choices. This process, known as the single transferable vote, continued until all posts were filled. The system was more personal than the List System of P/R used on the Continent, where voters cast ballots for an entire party slate, with the individual candidates on it elected according to the ratio of votes their list received *and* their place on it. However, criticism of the Hare system was strong because it required several posts to be filled in a single constituency, and because it encouraged minority political factions, which could hope to get at least one of their candidates in on the basis of the alternative choices of voters.

[44] Below, p. 493.

borough received the suffrage. In addition, men renting an unfurnished room of £10 annual value had the vote. This lodger vote, however, did not prove to be of much importance, except in London, for most lodgers were transients and thus unable to meet the qualifications for registration, which the 1867 law maintained.

It was the vast enlargement of the borough vote which frightened Conservatives in 1867 and made the franchise changes of that year more significant than those of 1832. Then the electorate had risen by about 47 per cent in England (including Wales), and most of the new voters had been men of substance. In 1866 Gladstone's bill would have added about 474,000 voters; but the final law of 1867 increased it by 938,000, thus raising the electorate by 89 per cent. More important, these new voters belonged for the most part to the lower classes. The middle class may have taken over in the counties, but this was of less significance now than it would have been in 1832. By the mid-nineteenth century middle-class people in the counties were consciously striving to become "gentry" and cultivating the attitudes, including the political ones, of that class. Furthermore, county seats were still a minority in the Commons after 1867. Most seats continued to come from the boroughs, where electorates were now predominantly working class and so large that they cancelled the effects of plural voting, which the law did not touch. If these lower-class people came to the conclusion that the extension of state activity in a particular field would be of benefit to them, both parties — for the sake of seats in the Commons — would be likely to lend their support. Henceforth, parties were in fact bidding for the votes not of substantial people with a "stake in the country," but of those voters without substance, whose interests had never been previously represented in Parliament. Considered socially, economically, and politically, therefore, the franchise extension of 1867 was vastly more important than that of 1832.

Even more than the Reform Act of 1832 the franchise extension of 1867 rendered its limitations indefensible, particularly since it barred people from the suffrage who would have possessed it had they lived in boroughs instead of counties. It was not agricultural laborers and miners, however, who compaigned for their own enfranchisement, but the radical section of the Liberal party, under the leadership of Joseph Chamberlain, which in 1884 forced the Gladstone ministry to bring in a bill extending the suffrage to these people in the counties. Unlike the Reform Act of 1867, but like that of 1832, the measure led to a collision between the two Houses. It passed the Commons easily enough, but the House of Lords turned it out. Gladstone refused to have an election on the issue and reintroduced the bill into the Commons, while privately warning Queen Victoria that the attitude of the Lords would inevitably raise the issue of its place in the constitution, something which neither he nor she wanted. With the Prime Minister's approval, the queen intervened with the Conservative leader, Lord Salisbury, and the *Reform Act of 1884* was eventually passed.[45]

This law applied to the entire United Kingdom, and the electorate rose from 3 million to 5 million,[46] which meant that practically every man could vote — thereby fulfilling Lord Eldon's doleful prophecy half a century earlier. The 1884 law could not lower borough qualifications much further, but it extended the £10 annual value for premises to include possession of land of this value without buildings. A new borough franchise gave the vote to domestic servants, who legally were not occupiers. The law then made all these borough qualifications applicable to the counties, where in addition, the £12 occupation qualification fell to £10, and the £50 short-term lease qualification disappeared. Only the old 40-shilling freehold qualification for the county franchise remained from the past. None of the values for either the borough or county vote were high in 1884, and already the Rand in South Africa was beginning to reduce money values by swelling the world's gold supply. Although the suffrage after 1884 still legally rested on property, a man was in effect voting because he was a British subject.

The law of 1885 [47] redistributing seats, gave twelve more members to Scotland, to raise the total of the Commons to 670 members. It also ended the anomaly whereby the average borough member had represented about 78,000 people, while one for a county spoke for about 40,000. Of 79 boroughs under 15,000 each lost its single member, while another 36 dropped from two to one member each. In allotting these 115 seats and the new ones for Scotland, the law first combined them with all other seats and then, with the exception of a few boroughs of between 50,000 and 165,000 and the universities, which retained the historic two seats, divided the entire realm into

[45] R. K. Gooch, ed., *Source Book on the Government of England*, 18 (henceforth cited as Gooch).

[46] Most of the 1,300,000 new voters came from England; Scotland supplied 250,000 and Ireland 450,000.

[47] Stephenson and Marcham, 805.

single-member districts of about 54,000 population. The futile plan of
1867 whereby certain boroughs had three members, but their voters
were limited to two choices, was abandoned. Thus after 1885 the bulk
of the Commons represented neither boroughs nor counties, but simply
people. The failure of the distribution act, however, to provide for an
automatic redistribution of seats as the need arose without further parliamentary intervention meant that a generation afterward the distribution of seats was again in need of attention.

The extension of the vote in 1832 had also extended corruption, as
experience in the old wide franchise boroughs might have led the reformers to expect. Bribery of voters after 1832 was common, but it was
difficult to prove. Intimidation, especially by landlords over short-term
tenants, was frequent but almost impossible to prove. In 1854 Parliament defined bribery in elections and made it a criminal offense; [48] but,
with election disputes still decided by the Commons on a partisan basis,
the law had little effect. The Reform Act of 1867 brought to the polls
a mass of new voters of a sort particularly susceptible to bribery and
threats, and in the election of 1868 corruption flourished.

The same year the House of Commons forced on unwilling courts
the duty of deciding election disputes,[49] but justices found that the
definitions of improper practices were so loose that they were of little
value to them in ruling on such cases. It was the revelations of widespread corruption during the 1868 elections that finally led to the
Ballot Act of 1872,[50] whereby the ballot was made secret. Although this
reduced the opportunities for corruption and intimidation, however,
there remained certain practices which reformers considered improper.

In 1883, therefore, the *Corrupt and Illegal Practices Act* tried to establish what amounted to an election code.[51] Corrupt practices, such as
bribery and intimidation, were criminal and carried heavy penalties,
including the disqualification of the guilty candidate from a seat in
Parliament for seven years. Illegal practices were those running counter
to an extremely detailed set of election regulations, which were to
become more complex over the years. Thus a candidate might not
spend over £100 himself during the campaign and had to have an agent
through whom all expenditures were to be made and reported to the
Commons. No money might be spent on door-to-door canvassing or

[48] Douglas, XII-Pt. One, 143.
[49] Douglas, XII-Pt. One, 184; Gooch, 259.
[50] Douglas, XII-Pt. One, 186.
[51] Gooch, 261.

door to poll transportation of voters. The rules certainly reduced campaign costs. But they did not do so to the point where the average man could afford to stand for Parliament. They did not apply to the intervals between elections, when potential candidates might spend any amount of money for any purpose in "nursing constituencies." However, a major and immediate effect of the law was to create that special figure in British politics, the professional *election agent*, who was both a campaign manager and an expert in election law, which became so complex that candidates had to defer to their agents lest they inadvertently violate some rule.

Business Efficiency

The Reform Act of 1832 brought into political life voters who set great store on efficiency in business and who therefore expected to find it also in government. Moreover the extension of state interest required changes in the administrative machinery of the government, which had to be equipped to perform tasks never before expected of it.

Although Prime Ministers usually held the office of First Lord of the Treasury, it was the Chancellor of the Exchequer who was ultimately responsible for the nation's finances. After 1832 he tightened his control over the spending of departments headed by his cabinet colleagues, seeing that each department got the most for its money and spent no more than was absolutely necessary. In 1834 a new method to control expenditure, obviously copied from private business, required that all requests by departments to spend money had to pass the scrutiny of the *Comptroller-General*, who was ineligible for Parliament but enjoyed the same status as justices, being removable only by an address from both Houses. The Comptroller checked on whether departmental requests fell within the purposes set by parliamentary grants and also whether they were necessary. Only if he approved the request, did the Treasury release the stipulated amount to the particular department. At the close of the fiscal year his counterpart, the *Auditor-General*, reviewed all expenditures in terms of both their legality and necessity in a report to a joint committee of Parliament, which reported to the respective Houses. In time this committee review of expenditures became nominal, but by then the Treasury had made its influence paramount in government; its officials were in every department to check on spending and to co-ordinate it with Treasury policy. Sir Robert

Peel, who came from a business family, initiated the procedure when he was Prime Minister whereby departments submitted estimates for the coming fiscal year to the Treasury. Treasury officials then compared them with anticipated revenue and generally urged the various departments to lower their sights. If a departmental head felt aggrieved, he might appeal to the Chancellor of the Exchequer, and then possibly to the Prime Minister and the full cabinet. But such appeals were rare. It was not accidental that, as the Treasury came to be the dominant department in government, the ministerial bench in the Commons was often called the "Treasury Bench." The Chancellor of the Exchequer, invariably in the Commons, rose to rank just below the Prime Minister, if the latter himself did not hold that post; and co-operation between them was essential for any success in a ministry.

The reform of the civil service was also made necessary by the growing responsibilities of government, and by the new conceptions of business efficiency. In the old days, the Tadpoles and Tapers (as Disraeli called the more futile members of aristocratic families) had usually entered government service because they enjoyed political "pull," and frequently because they were unfit for anything else. As long as recruitment of officials lay with individual department heads, it was difficult to establish adequate standards for the appointment and promotion of civil servants.

The merit system for appointments and promotions had been forced on the East India Company in 1833; in 1854 a committee of the Treasury looked at the results of this system and found them good. The committee, therefore, recommended that the appointment of government civil servants should be on the basis of competitive examinations in subjects — largely classical — taught at Oxford and Cambridge. Recruitment for the Indian civil service, the committee argued, had shown that men with good records in university subjects were capable of subsequent training in any specialized administrative work. Gladstone, as Chancellor of the Exchequer, accepted the committee's recommendation; and in 1855 the Civil Service Commission under the Treasury began to give such examinations and issue certificates of competence.[52] With the exception of "mature persons" and those with highly technical qualifications, only persons with such certificates were eligible for appointments by department heads. Four years later legislation limited retirement pensions to persons who had entered the civil service with certificates.

[52] Douglas, XII-Pt. One, 578.

The adoption of the merit system of civil service recruitment was finally completed in 1870, when an order-in-council [53] made competitive examinations the only way to enter the service, unless the Treasury and its Civil Service Commission agreed to make an exception, which came to mean that only the Foreign Office selected its officials without them. The order emphasized that examinations were to be open to all comers on equal terms, although in practice only a man well grounded in the classical studies of Oxford and Cambridge had much of a chance.

Once certificated, a successful candidate went to a particular department, as the Treasury directed, for training in its work. After six months of satisfactory performance, the new civil servant had security of tenure (barring convictions for felonies or treason) and the guarantee of a substantial pension at retirement. In return for this security a civil servant had to eschew all political activity, except voting. Although the Treasury might move him to another department, such interdepartmental changes were rare and considered wasteful.

Promotion remained a departmental matter and raised difficulties. Not every bright young man entering the civil service would close his career as the Permanent Under-Secretary of a department. Departmental promotion committees of higher civil servants and a Treasury representative determined promotions up to a point, but the minister was ultimately responsible, especially for promotions to the upper reaches of a department.

Civil service reform reduced ministerial departmental responsibilities. In the days of the Tadpoles and Tapers, ministers had to devote much of their time to supervising administration, knowing that they could not trust such unqualified subordinates. But with the growing complexity of government, the average minister, who owed his post to his political position, had reason to appreciate an honest, efficient civil service, performing its work equally well for ministers of every party. The amateur minister had to lean heavily on these permanent experts, who had no political responsibility. If they persuaded a minister to adopt a policy which subsequently was unpopular with Parliament or the public, his was the responsibility, the theory being that he had been free to accept or reject the advice of his expert permanent officials. In effect, however, these officials often dominated a department, even to the point of forming policy. This meant that, except for the largest issues exciting public opinion, a change in government did not necessarily involve any

[53] Douglas, XII-Pt. One, 603.

drastic changes in over-all policy. Behind the changing ministerial figures were the faceless civil service experts, who looked on complacently as ministers came and went, while they continued to run the government as usual.

The New Role of Party

The development of the party system had important consequences for the constitution, notably in regard to the relations between the House of Commons and the cabinet. Before the Reform Act of 1832 local political organizations had existed here and there during the brief periods of elections, but "party" really meant the *parliamentary party*. Neither Whigs nor Tories were highly organized, nor did they possess a national organization beyond Parliament. Both were predominantly aristocratic, drawing their support from similar social groups.

Until as late as the fierce conflict over Irish Home Rule in 1886, the social division of the two parties was not horizontal but vertical. Aristocrats were quite as evident and important among the Whigs, and later the Liberals, as among the Tory or Conservative parties. If middle-class voters tended to prefer Whigs to Tories, neither Peel nor Disraeli of the latter had a landed background. The Liberals won the new lower-class voters in 1868, but the Conservatives successfully wooed them in 1874, and in 1880 the Liberals won them back. Five years later, on the eve of the Home Rule struggle, both major parties shared the support of various social classes about equally.

The rise of nonparliamentary party organizations, the registration societies, after the Reform Act of 1832, served to consolidate party divisions in Parliament. Originally the societies operated independently of each other and of the parliamentary party, but in 1852 Disraeli began to take steps to bring the various Tory societies into line. Fifteen years later the National Union of Conservative and Constitutional Associations took over the duty of co-ordination. Its time was too short, however, before the 1868 election, which cost the Conservatives the government. After this disaster, Disraeli took a step essential to the English party system by establishing the Central Office, which had a permanent staff and linked the two phases of the party, parliamentary and nonparliamentary. More important, operations of the Central Office were under the direction of party leaders *in* Parliament. With the bulk of contributions to the party going to the Central Office, party leaders were in a position to exercise control over local organizations and prevent their becoming rivals to the parliamentary party, which selected the party leader.

The completed party structure gave party leaders real discipline over their followers in the Commons. Those who followed party discipline received financial assistance from the Central Office, and local associations liked to have a candidate with such backing. Members who did not were deprived of Central Office funds and also encountered rival, "regular" candidates of their own party who were enjoying its financial assistance, and so were more likely to be "adopted" by the local party association.

Liberal party organization began somewhat differently but had the same end result. In 1867 Joseph Chamberlain changed his Birmingham Liberal Association, a typical registration society, into a caucus along American lines. Any Liberal upon paying a small fee, a requirement soon eliminated, could join the caucus. Hoping to capture all three seats allotted to Birmingham in 1867,[54] the caucus was divided into ward committees, and Liberal voters were taught how to cast their two votes so as to elect three members for Birmingham. The success of this method in the 1868 election made the Birmingham Liberal Caucus a model for other local Liberal organizations. They remained independent, however; and Chamberlain attributed the 1874 Liberal defeat to the lack of a national organization. Three years later he created the National Liberal Federation. It was Chamberlain's personal vehicle, however, and the credit it received for the Liberal victory in the 1880 election gave him a claim to cabinet office which Gladstone had to meet. To counter Chamberlain's party machine, the Liberal Central Office under the party leaders began operations. When Chamberlain split with the Liberals in 1886 over Irish Home Rule, the Federation merged with the Central Office, which thus became exactly the same sort of organization as that of the Conservatives.

In 1831 candidates had offered themselves as Whigs or Tories, occasionally as Independents. Whatever their "label," however, they had owed no rigid allegiance to an over-all party program, and had usually issued their own manifestoes to the voters. That of a party leader might set the "tendency" of a party, but no more. Thus the address of Sir Robert Peel to the voters of Tamworth in 1834 appeared to commit the Tory party to a policy of moderate, judicious reform. But in fact Sir

[54] Above, p. 485.

Robert spoke only for himself; he did not and could not bind other Tory members of Parliament. Successful candidates felt that their obligation was primarily to their constituents and only afterwards to their party. As a result individual members enjoyed a considerable degree of independence in the Commons; but this also led to unstable majorities in the House, and to frequently changing ministries.

The electoral reforms of 1867 and 1884 changed the relationship between candidates and constituents, and the change was already apparent in the 1868 election. With more voters determining his fate, a candidate needed a more efficient organization if he was to reach them. He and the local party organization needed funds to meet the greater expenses of campaigning in a much larger electorate. And such funds were available from the Central Office, *if* candidates were acceptable to it. Only wealthy local party groups — which were few — could afford to ignore, still less to flout, the Central Office, which could make things very difficult by sponsoring an "official" party candidate against an irregular one. Thus the candidate became the local spokesman for a national party, with a detailed program and intensive organization, determined and controlled by the party leaders through the Central Office. The speeches of party leaders were no longer directed toward their own constituents so much as to the national electorate, and the issues presented by candidates in each district were at most minor variants of a national program.

In 1865, Gladstone was calculating government strength in the House in *approximate* terms; in 1868 he knew precisely. Members of the party were expected to vote "regular," on pain of expulsion from the parliamentary party, and such an exile might well ruin their chances of re-election. There had been a decline in the independence of individual members of the Commons; firm party alignments had been laid down and, therefore, there were stable ministries from one election to the next. Above all, the position of the party leader had been enhanced. Chosen by his parliamentary party, he had to be able to work with his chief rivals to the post or lose his leadership. Lesser lights, the "backbenchers" of the party, had of course to be considered. Nevertheless, a party leader with a strong personality, such as a Palmerston, Gladstone, Disraeli, or Salisbury, could wield more authority over his party than a Melbourne or an Aberdeen. It was indeed the personalities of such men that more than anything else brought their parties into power. Palmerston carried the Whig party victoriously through the elections of 1857,

1859, and 1865, and his own personal authority in the party steadily increased in consequence. After the Liberal defeat of 1874 Gladstone temporarily retired from active politics, but his Midlothian campaign of 1879–80, when he took the voters into his confidence on matters of high state policy, had plainly so much to do with the Liberal victory that he again became party leader and Prime Minister. It was as much Gladstone or Disraeli that the electorate was voting for as Liberal or Conservative.

The "Reformed" Parliament

For thirty-five years after the Reform Act of 1832, the House of Commons enjoyed more independence than it had known since the early seventeenth century; and significantly, as during that period, usage often equated "the House of Commons" with "Parliament." [55] After the extension of the franchise in 1867 and the creation of a national electorate by 1884, there were signs that parliamentary dominance had reached, and perhaps passed, its peak. The franchise extensions of 1867 and 1884 did not, however, lead to any immediate changes in the composition of the House of Commons. So long as middle-class voters were busy making money and lower-class voters were without the funds to fight an election, they were unlikely to acquire seats in the House.

The privileges of the House of Commons were unquestioned — that battle had been fought and won. So certain was the House of its position that in 1868 it surrendered its right of deciding *disputed elections* to the courts.[56] The privilege of *freedom of speech* for both Houses received further statutory confirmation after the case of Stockdale *v.* Hansard.[57] The latter, as the parliamentary printer, had published a report of a committee of the Commons containing material offensive to Stockdale, who sued Hansard. On orders of the House, Hansard pleaded the parliamentary privilege of free speech; but Queen's Bench denied that it extended to printed matter and gave damages to Stockdale. The Commons retorted by jailing Stockdale, his counsel, and the sheriffs who executed the court's judgment. Queen's Bench refused to intervene on the ground that the House was the sole judge of what constituted contempt against it. However, the decision against its printer made the

[55] Above, p. 291.
[56] Above, p. 488.
[57] Stephenson and Marcham, 794–8.

Commons take the lead in extending the privilege of free speech in the *Parliamentary Papers Act* of 1840, which barred suits for libel against the publishers of papers printed by order of either House.

The Commons was also partly responsible for determining the *qualification of members*. The oath they had to take included the phrase, "on the true faith as a Christian." In 1858 the Commons approved a new oath omitting these words, but the Lords would not agree to it. The lower House then passed, and persuaded the peers to accept, a bill, whereby each House might modify the actual wording of its oath. Under this law the Commons took out the phrase, in order that Jews might take their seats in the House. In 1866 a statute, along the lines of the one proposed in 1858, allowed non-Christians to sit in either House. Two years later another law permitted Quakers and other people, who had religious scruples about swearing an oath, to make an affirmation instead. In 1880 Charles Bradlaugh, a self-professed atheist, also claimed the right to affirm. For the next six years the House debated this question, and Bradlaugh was expelled and re-elected several times. In 1886 the Speaker ruled that no member had the right to question the right of another either to affirm or to take the oath.

The House of Commons also reformed its procedure, adapting it to the needs of members anxious to get down to business, rather than to engage in the leisurely debates favored by the eighteenth-century aristocracy. In reforming its procedures, the Commons showed little consideration for the government, which for a long time after the Reform Act could be sure of only two days a week for the transaction of its own business. Anything else came to it as a favor of the House. Many of the ideas for procedural reform originated with the clerk of the House, Thomas Erskine May. It was he who suggested the elimination of many technicalities and who, as a labor of love, compiled the *Treatise on the Law, Privilege, Proceedings and Usage of Parliament*, which immediately became the authority for the Commons on procedure. From time to time the House had new orders on procedure and Speakers' rulings incorporated in *May*, which like *Hansard* ultimately ceased to be regarded as a person and instead became an institution, the ultimate authority on parliamentary procedure for Parliaments of the Commonwealth.

The House of Commons generally held the initiative in directing Parliament. After 1832 all measures of any importance originated in the lower House, only private and ecclesiastical bills being first introduced in the Lords. Private bills, approved by the peers, usually received the blessing of the Commons. Ecclesiastical measures, however, came in for sharp scrutiny at times from the "lower" House.

But on the whole relations between the two Houses were usually harmonious. An important reason for this was the similar social background of the members of both Houses. Sons of peers were in the Commons, which meant that most peers had at one time been in the lower House. With both parties composed of essentially the same type of people, neither had occasion to use one House to thwart the other. Usually the Whigs held the Commons, and the Tories the Lords; but this did not inhibit the legislative process. The basic harmony between the two Houses was evident in the repeal of the Corn Laws in 1846 by a Tory Prime Minister, who in carrying the measure through the Commons split his party. When the bill reached the Lords, instead of seizing on the repudiation of the government by much of its own party and rejecting the measure, the Tory majority followed the Duke of Wellington and passed the bill, even though it was contrary to landed interests. Finance and industry were already luring the peers away from their traditional economic preserve.

In 1867 Walter Bagehot, the journalist and writer on the constitution, predicted that the recent extension of the vote to the lower classes might produce a situation in which the Commons would pass legislation directly contrary to the interests of the peers, who would have to move with great circumspection if serious clashes with the lower House were to be avoided. There were signs of the imminence of such conflicts. The need for royal intervention in 1884, to resolve differences between the Conservative majority in the Lords and the Liberal majority in the Commons on the franchise and redistribution bills,[58] revealed the possibility that parties might use their control of the different houses to thwart each other. By the end of the period, a situation of some delicacy had in fact come to exist between the Commons and the Lords.

Not only did the House of Commons hold the initiative over the Lords, it was also, for at least three decades after the first Reform Act, able to assert its supremacy over the cabinet. Ministries rose and fell according to the fluctuating opinions of members; it was not until after 1867, and the emergence of a mass electorate and an organized party system, that the Commons began to lose its grip. It was during the period between 1832 and 1867 that the "classical" writers on cabinet

[58] Above, p. 487.

government formulated their views. To them it appeared that the Commons, which by withdrawing its support could bring down the ministry, was the central factor in the cabinet system, and so of parliamentary government. During these 35 years, there were ten changes of government. On three occasions, this was due to the result of an election; on the other seven occasions it was because the House had changed its mind during the intervals *between* elections. The convention was that a Prime Minister whose cabinet had lost its majority in the House should resign. Only four times did a Prime Minister appeal from a hostile House to the voters, or "go to the country" — Peel in 1835, after constant defeats in the House; Melbourne in 1841, following a defeat on the budget and a formal vote of no-confidence by the House; Palmerston in 1857, upon a similar vote of censure; and Derby in 1859, having wearied of being in the majority one day and the minority the next. Only the appeal of Palmerston was successful. It was natural to assume, therefore, that the Commons controlled the fate of cabinets.

After 1867, however, the situation began to change. Between 1867 and 1885, there were four changes of government. All but one came from electoral decisions against the existing ministry; and in no case was the election due to a ministerial appeal from an unfriendly majority in the Commons to the voters. Instead, each election was close to the expiration date of the parliamentary term, with its exact date selected by the government in terms of possible advantage. The fourth instance of a change of government during this period was the last, in 1885, and was admittedly merely a temporary arrangement until the election that year.

To the classical writers on the cabinet, election results were less important than the shifting tides of opinion inside the Commons. Between 1832 and 1867 only three ministries which won an election remained in power until the next one; as a rule, an election triumph guaranteed no security to the successful party. Thus the Whigs won the election of 1833, only to be in opposition a bare year later; and they entered the 1835 election lists in that role. In 1841 the Tories gained a solid majority of seats at the polls. Peel optimistically formed a government. Five years later the Tories split over the Corn Laws, and Russell formed a Whig ministry, which won at the polls in 1847, only to be supplanted by a Tory cabinet in 1852. The subsequent 1852 election was indecisive and between it and the next one in 1857 there were successively Tory, Coalition, and Whig cabinets — all without reference to the electorate and due solely to changing groupings in the Commons. In 1857 Palmerston's appeal from an unfriendly majority in the House to the country gave him a good majority; the next year he was out and a Tory government in power. That ministry lost the 1859 election to the Whigs, who were able to remain in power until the 1865 election, which they also won. However, the next year the Whig-Liberals split over franchise extension, and the Tory-Conservatives were in office until the 1868 election. The last word still lay with the House of Commons.

After the 1868 election, however, it began to be clear that the last and almost the sole word lay with the voters. Changes in government came only because of their action at the polls, and the party which won there formed a government, which kept its majority largely intact until the next election. Thus the Liberals formed a ministry in 1868 on the basis of their election victory and remained in power until the Conservative triumph at the polls in 1874. Six years later the ballots returned the Liberals to office, where they remained until 1885, when, owing to a shift in loyalties of the Irish Nationalists, Gladstone resigned. On that occasion Salisbury formed a caretaker Conservative ministry until the elections later that year. But this was an exception.

Before 1867, even if a cabinet had obviously lost an election, it always met the new House of Commons and suffered formal defeat there at the hands of the new hostile majority before resigning. In 1868, however, Disraeli began the convention that the Prime Minister of a government defeated at the polls should resign immediately and his victorious rival form a cabinet before the new House of Commons met. Behind the new convention, which Gladstone followed after the Liberal defeat in 1874, and Disraeli (now Lord Beaconsfield) again honored in 1880 when the Conservatives lost, lay the fact that, as political leaders recognized, the new party organizations had created a discipline sufficiently rigid for there to be little chance of winning individual members of the Commons away from their leaders and persuading them to "cross the floor" of the House. Election results would determine the role of parties in the Commons until the next election.

The "Reformed" Crown

The Reform Act of 1832 emphasized the impossibility of reviving the political power of the monarch, which had virtually disappeared with George III's sanity. Grey as Prime Minister was not on good terms with

William IV, but in the end it was the monarch, not the minister, who gave way on the crucial matter of creating peers to ensure that the Reform Act went through. The Radicals said in 1834 that William IV had "dismissed" the Melbourne ministry, but in fact Melbourne himself, wearied with their pressures and intrigues, had asked the king to send for Peel. The monarch could no longer dictate to his ministers; at best he could only hope to influence them by drawing on the ancient traditions of respect for royalty.

The accession of Victoria in 1837 brought to the throne a girl of eighteen, who found a father-figure in Lord Melbourne, who for his part carefully instructed her in the constitution as it was understood by aristocratic Whigs. She was so fond of him that in 1839 she made things very difficult for Peel, who was attempting to form a Tory ministry and trying to persuade the young queen to replace her Whig ladies-in-waiting with Tories. Failing to do either, he gave up the attempt; and Melbourne returned. But such a resolution of this "Bed Chamber Crisis" was possible only because Melbourne was able to patch up his cabinet. Two years later his party's defeat in the election meant that the queen had to accept Sir Robert and to compromise over her ladies-in-waiting.

By this time Victoria was falling under the influence of her new husband, Prince Albert. The Prince Consort believed that monarchy should take a more active interest in government, but there would have been little danger of his interfering in an unconstitutional way had not he and Victoria been excessively provoked by Palmerston.[59] As Foreign Secretary Palmerston was likely to act not only without consulting his sovereign, but even without consulting the cabinet. Several times Victoria urged Russell to dismiss him, and often the Prime Minister would have been only too relieved to do so, had he not realized that Palmerston was indispensable. In a famous memorandum of 1850, inspired by Albert, the queen stated that the sovereign had the right to expect that the Foreign Secretary would state precisely what he proposed to do in a particular matter, so that "she may know distinctly to *what* she has given her Royal sanction"; and that having given "her sanction to a measure, that it be not arbitrarily altered or modified by the Minister." Failure by him to act along these lines could "justly be visited by the exercise of her Constitutional right of dismissing that Minister."

There was certainly the implication in this that the queen believed

[59] Douglas, XII-Pt. One, 71–5.

she had some particular responsibility for foreign policy, which had of course belonged to the royal prerogative in the past. Palmerston did not openly disagree, but he carried on very much as before, and in 1851 he finally went too far. Two days after the *coup d'état* of Louis Napoleon in France, Palmerston on his own initiative gave it his approval. This caused an outcry in the cabinet, and Russell, to the great satisfaction of Victoria and Albert, asked him to resign. But four years later, in spite of the protests of the royal couple, there was no way in which they could prevent his becoming Prime Minister.

Walter Bagehot described the rights of the monarch in these terms: he (or she) was "to be consulted, to encourage, and to warn." This more or less described the true relationship between the queen and her ministers by 1867, when the withdrawal of the monarchical crown from practical politics received statutory recognition in the abolition of the rule that the term of Parliament should end with the death of the sovereign. Henceforth, the life of each would be independent of the other. It was in the exercise of this neutral role that monarchy was to gain its greatest strength. A sovereign with a reign of any duration — and Victoria reigned for 64 years — outlasted most ministries and became a vast repository of experience, upon which ministers, if they were wise, drew. The real value of monarchy came to lie in its neutrality, in its position not so much between, as above, the contesting parties. Ministers could safely invoke royal intervention, as did Gladstone in 1869 over the Irish Church bill [60] and the 1884 franchise measure,[61] in the certainty that neither party would gain from it. The intervention was at the request of the Prime Minister, and it was he who was responsible to the House of Commons for invoking it. Far from reducing the monarch's responsibilities, this role, if conscientiously taken, increased them considerably. It was necessary to know all about the drift and flow of politics, while remaining apart, so that party leaders could safely accept the mediation of the sovereign.

Relations between the sovereign and ministers were usually through the Prime Minister. This convention became established during the period in which Melbourne was Victoria's guide and mentor. After his resignation in 1841, Peel was uneasy about the continued correspondence between the queen and the Whig leader. But Peel, with the help of

[60] Above, pp. 481–2.
[61] Above, p. 487.

Prince Albert, eventually communicated his disapproval to the queen and her correspondence with Melbourne became perfunctory. For a time the royal couple dealt directly with ministers other than the Prime Minister, but had little or no effect on cabinet policy. In the new electoral situation ministers knew the folly of intriguing against their party head. Ministers receiving royal commands for consultation thus always informed their chief and actually met with the sovereign only with his approval.

After Albert's death in 1861 the queen for some time was in a self-imposed *purdah* and saw only the Prime Minister. Disraeli's flattery brought her out again, but also turned her against Gladstone, whom she tried to avoid as Prime Minister in 1880, 1886, and 1892. Her letters of complaint about Gladstone to other ministers and to opposition leaders would have been very serious had they been effective. However, in the new political circumstances after 1867, and with universal manhood suffrage after 1884, no political leader thought that he could ride to power on royal approval. Thus opposition leaders failed to act on the queen's complaints; they knew that office would come to them only at the polls — not in the royal closet.

Relations between the sovereign and the Prime Minister could be very formal or extremely easy. Grey and Melbourne patronized William IV. Victoria enjoyed being a daughter to Melbourne and was never quite happy with Peel. Russell, Palmerston, and Derby all tended to be formal with the queen. Until the close of his first administration she had warm feelings for Gladstone, but the interlude of Disraeli from 1874 to 1880 turned her against the Liberal leader. However, the personal relations between Prime Minister and sovereign might make the former's tasks easier or harder; but they could not seriously affect matters, although Victoria nagged all her ministers after Melbourne.

At the beginning of the reform period "ministry" and "cabinet" were nearly synonymous; but as the responsibilities of government increased, new officials appeared who were political figures, responsible to the Commons, but not of cabinet rank. The ministry became larger than the cabinet, which formed an inner group of ministers. Minor political officials were in the outer circle of non-cabinet ministers, to which also belonged the *Parliamentary Under-Secretaries*. Unlike the Permanent Under-Secretaries of departments, who were civil servants, the new Parliamentary Under-Secretaries were politicians and members of Parliament. Originally, they represented a minister in the House of which he was not a member.[62] Later, they eased his burdens in his own chamber also. Unlike ministers, the Parliamentary Under-Secretaries did not form policy but merely helped to explain it to the House.

A ministry might not have the approval of the sovereign, but it had to have that of the House of Commons. The construction of cabinets aimed at securing a stable majority in the House. Ministers rarely owed their offices to their prior knowledge of a department's work; instead, their offices came to them by virtue of their representing groups in the Commons, whether they themselves were members of the lower House or not. Groups in the Commons were not adverse to having peers as leaders, and peers and commoners shared about equally in every ministry. The strength of a politician's claim to ministerial office was in direct ratio to the size and cohesiveness of his following in the Commons. The general independence of members between the first and second Reform Acts meant that a man with a permanent loyal following had to have office. Russell's vain effort to do without Palmerston in 1851 proved this necessity. Men who could win votes in debates were likewise in a good position to achieve ministerial status.

But as party discipline and stability increased within the House of Commons, the leader of the majority party had to think less about building strength in the House and more about satisfying the claims of prominent party figures and pleasing the electorate. Satisfactory performance of these obligations was a challenge to the abilities of any Prime Minister, who also had to consider the fact that certain leading personalities did not work together in that harmony which was essential to any government.

The cabinet consisted of those ministers summoned regularly by the Prime Minister to decide on government policy and discuss tactics. The actual ministers in the cabinet varied and their number ranged from twelve to sixteen during the reform period. The Chancellor of the Exchequer, Lord Chancellor, President of the Board of Control (after 1858, Secretary of State for India), and the Home, Foreign, Colonial, and War Secretaries, along with the First Lord of the Admiralty, were regularly present. The offices of Lord President of the Council and Lord Privy Seal were at times held by sufficiently prominent politicians for them to be of cabinet rank. But other offices varied. As some of them declined in importance, they went to lesser political figures and so ceased

[62] And so unable to appear in it to speak, in contrast to certain Commonwealth Parliaments (above, p. 442, note 38).

to be of cabinet rank, while others grew in importance and came to be represented in the cabinet. Thus the Master of the Mint, Master of the Ordnance, and Paymaster of the Forces were invariably in the cabinet at the beginning of the period, but gradually they disappeared and were replaced by others. In 1859 the President of the Poor Law Board (later President of the Local Government Board) gained a seat; and in 1885 the general preoccupation with Irish affairs caused Lord Salisbury to include the Lord Chancellor of Ireland in the cabinet, although he never again appeared there.

During the first thirty years after the Reform Act the Prime Minister's relations with cabinet colleagues reflected the independence of members of the Commons, their loyalty to certain men, and so the changing majorities in the House. Grey and Melbourne found that their colleagues were also their rivals. Peel had a more subservient cabinet until the rebellion over his repeal of the Corn Laws. Relations between Palmerston and Russell, regardless of which was Prime Minister and despite their basic agreement on policy, were always delicate. The Derby-Disraeli combinations and the Aberdeen coalition did not lend themselves to much more than a nominal headship of the government by the Prime Minister. After 1859 Palmerston's outstanding ability, especially for winning votes, gave him more control over his colleagues, but even so he had Gladstone to contend with.

The elaboration of party organizations enhanced the power of the party leader, and the Prime Minister was able to direct cabinet policy more successfully than had been possible hitherto. He was, of course, far from being absolute. In cabinet meetings he tried to secure a consensus, reached after free discussion; he might direct the talk, but he could not dominate it. But the personality of the leader, and the fact that he could command votes in the country, made him the more indispensable to his colleagues; they would certainly hesitate before rejecting his leadership.

Peel and Gladstone assumed, in their first and second administrations respectively, in addition to the post of First Lord of the Treasury, the departmental post of Chancellor of the Exchequer. Both found the burdens of the department too much, along with their duty of coordinating and directing the government and the party. In 1885 Lord Salisbury took on the Foreign Office, an unprecedented step, and appointed a party subordinate to the post of First Lord of the Treasury, which was really a bestowal of a cabinet post without portfolio. Although the ministry was responsible to the Commons, during the reform period seven members of the Lords became Prime Minister as opposed to five from the Commons.[63] Russell and Disraeli (Earl of Beaconsfield) were Prime Ministers as both commoners and peers.

Prime Ministers in the Lords, however, found the direction of the cabinet difficult at times. As early as the ministry of Earl Grey, such a Prime Minister had to share direction of the government with the *Leader of the House of Commons,* usually the Chancellor of the Exchequer. The Leader of the Government was liable at times to overshadow his chief in the Lords. One reason for Melbourne's desire to leave office in 1834 [64] was that the succession of Viscount Althorp to his father's peerage as Earl Spencer deprived Melbourne of the only Leader he felt he could trust. During the three Derby-Disraeli ministries, the latter's role grew with each of their administrations, until early in 1868, after he had been forced to accept Disraeli's Reform Act, Derby resigned in favor of Disraeli as party leader, and so as Prime Minister. Russell, after his experience as Prime Minister in the Lords from 1865 to 1866, retired from politics. Disraeli had effective control over his cabinet until he became the Earl of Beaconsfield, when he had serious problems with it. In 1885 Lord Salisbury hesitated to take the office as a peer, particularly since ministerial responsibility now was to a House of Commons resting on universal manhood suffrage. Salisbury's doubts in his own case proved unfounded in any of his three governments, but he was the last peer to be Prime Minister.

The Merging of Central and Local Government

The extension of state interest on the one hand, and the Radical ideal of uniformity on the other, tended to obliterate the old distinctions between central and local government. Although the principle of elected local government agencies was accepted, and there was an increase of popular representation in local government, the authority of these agencies declined as they came to exist more and more for the purpose of carrying out the orders of central departments.

The elective principle made its appearance in borough government

---

[63] The five from the Commons included Viscount Palmerston, an Irish peer sitting for an English constituency in terms of the Act of Union of 1800 (above, p. 472, note 18).
[64] Above, p. 500.

with the *Municipal Corporation Act* of 1835.[65] This swept away all the various forms of borough government which royal charters had created and established a single, uniform type — only the ancient City of London being an exception. All borough residents paying rates (a somewhat more generous suffrage than that given for the borough parliamentary franchise) elected a council for a three-year term, one-third retiring annually, with the exception of a third designated by the council as aldermen. These served six years, one-third retiring every two years. The borough council exercised all the functions of borough government and selected one of its number to act as mayor, with a term of one year.

The efficiency and honesty of the new borough government led to the elective principle being adopted for other units of local government. In 1888 the *Local Government Act* [66] established elective *county councils* for the new *administrative counties*, whose boundaries were similar to, but not identical with, those of the historic shires. The law also raised boroughs of 50,000 or more to the status of *county boroughs*. One of the more important of the latter was that of London, where the London County Council (with the City of London retaining a special status within it) took the lead in extending the functions of local government in the area of metropolitan London.

The councils of the counties and county boroughs took over most of the remaining administrative duties of the justices of the peace. Six years later *district* and *parish* councils, each equally secular, completed the scheme of elected local councils.[67] But even then, centralization was reducing local autonomy, and these newest units of local government found their revenue-raising capacities insufficient to allow for any sort of independent action.

The extension of state interest into the field of social welfare also tended to reduce local autonomy. Reformers, doubting the sympathy of justices of the peace for their plans, depended upon national legislation, applied by new agencies with specific duties. The new Poor Law of 1834, which gave wide power to the three commissioners, provided for the implementation of their orders by *poor law unions*, composed of several parishes, and each having a *board of guardians*, elected by persons paying the poor rates, in turn levied by the board. The

---

[65] Douglas, XII-Pt. One, 628.
[66] Stephenson and Marcham, 808; Gooch, 473.
[67] 56 and 57 Vic., cap. 73.

guardians were responsible for the administration of poor relief in the union in terms of the parliamentary statute, including the management of the union workhouse, *and* under such orders as the commissioners issued from Whitehall. These directives proved more important than the law authorizing them, and they provided a uniform administration of poor relief by local guardians. This tendency toward centralization increased when the commissioners gave way to the Poor Law Board in 1847. In 1871 the Local Government Board [68] took over the direction of poor relief as part of its duties of supervising ever-increasing aspects of local administration which dealt with social affairs. By 1919, when this board was replaced by the *Ministry of Health,* the tradition of local autonomy had almost disappeared under the flood of directives from Whitehall.

Centralization was also a consequence of the state's interest in education. The Poor Law of 1834, in providing Treasury assistance for the education of pauper children, gave the commissioners some control over their instruction. The Education Act of 1870 formally made elementary education a local matter, including the determination of compulsory attendance, which the law left to each school board. However, school boards did not want to levy heavy education rates and looked to the grants from the Treasury, as provided in the law, to ease their financial load. The Treasury officials, however, tended to pay by results, and in order to get money from the Treasury, most school boards used the power bestowed upon them by the Education Act and made elementary education compulsory in their districts. It was in any case made compulsory everywhere by the Act of 1880.

Similarly, the *Artisans' Dwelling Act* of 1875 [69] allowed local councils to "borrow" from the Treasury for the purposes of inspecting, condemning, demolishing, and rebuilding housing for workers. The gigantic *Public Health Act* [70] of the same year gave similar "loans" to local authorities to build and maintain sanitary establishments. However, in order to receive these grants-in-aid, since the "loans" were never to be repaid, local governments had to construct housing and sanitary facilities according to precise specifications set by Treasury civil servants; and these specifications were, in effect, as binding on a local council as any act of Parliament.

[68] 34 and 35 Vic., cap. 70.
[69] 38 and 39 Vic., cap. 36.
[70] 38 and 39 Vic., cap. 55.

The Local Government Board was responsible for more and more aspects of local government. Established in 1871, the board consisted of the Lord President of the Privy Council, all the Secretaries of State, the Chancellor of the Exchequer, and the President of the Board and its Secretary. The pressure of work on the other members of the board meant that only the last two, who sat in Parliament, were active in carrying out the co-ordinating function of the board over local government activities. Initially, the Board was concerned only with public health, police,[71] and poor relief, but it steadily increased its control. By the time it disappeared in 1919, its duties were innumerable. During its own lifetime the board and the Treasury together really controlled local government.

The justices of the peace had, by the end of this period, lost most of their administrative functions and a good many of their judicial ones. With the electorate supporting policies that could only be carried out with the help of central government experts, the justices of the peace fell into the background. Minor judicial work and the licensing of pubs constituted most of their work. They had ceased to be buffers between their own localities and the central administration.

THE LAW "REFORMED"

The supporters of reform found the inconsistencies and confusions in the law obvious targets for attack. The belief by reformers in the efficacy of legislation to achieve utility was particularly strong for legal reform, which they believed would never come from judges bound by precedent. In fact, those things in the law most galling to reformers often rested on statutes, so that only further legislation would correct them.

Criminal Law Reform

The most dramatic legal reforms during the nineteenth century were in criminal law. The number of capital crimes was greatly reduced after Sir Robert Peel became Home Secretary in 1822. During the next few years Peel secured the abolition of the death penalty for over a hundred offenses. By 1856, only treason, murder, and burning the

[71] For the techniques of central control over local police see below, p. 509.

royal warehouses remained as capital crimes — and they were to remain so for another century.[72] Despite the misgivings of such distinguished lawyers as Lord Eldon, and of many bishops, the rate of crime declined. Juries, moreover, were now more ready to convict when the penalty for a crime was no longer so drastic.

The organization of a regular police force also helped to reduce crime. Theoretically, the old institution of *hue and cry* [73] still survived, but for centuries the parish had actually had the duty of keeping public order. Vestries named constables, usually to keep them off poor relief, for this purpose. The constables were tolerated, as harmless, by the criminals. Somewhat more efficient were the Bow Street Runners, who armed with warrants from that magistrate's court in London pursued criminals — but also were often in league with them. In 1829 Peel laid the foundations of the modern British police in a law authorizing a metropolitan London force under a commissioner named by the Home Secretary. From the beginning this force operated solely on a merit basis, and it was so quickly effective that criminals found it advisable to emigrate from the capital to the "provinces." In 1839 a commission, though it did not suggest a national force, did recommend the transfer of police from one district to another as required. The suggestion assumed uniform standards of training and performance, which did not exist at that time. In 1856 Parliament authorized the Home Office to "inspect" local police forces outside London.[74] Using this power of inspection, as opponents of the law had predicted, the Home Office by administrative action gradually centralized under its metropolitan police commissioner the determination of standards for police recruitment, training, and promotion. The result was a truly national force, functionally, if not formally. When the Local Government Board took over the duty of supervising local police in 1871,[75] it continued to work closely with the Home Office in this duty.

Criticism of such a centralized police system, and the idea that a special force was dangerous, did not long survive. Instead of being "spies," bent on encroaching on the "liberties of the people," the police were members of the people, thanks to the wise rule, begun by Peel and continued after him, that the police should live in their homes, not in barracks. Moreover, a jealous Parliament, and a group of higher

[72] Below, p. 552.
[73] Above, p. 41.
[74] Douglas, XII-Pt. One, 641.
[75] Above, p. 508.

police officials as saturated in English traditions as anybody, ensured that the police went unarmed except for truncheons, and if these were drawn, a full report was required by their superiors. By the close of the century the police had ceased to be the suspect "Peelers" and had become the more likable "Bobbies."

A change in the procedure of criminal trials admitted the defendant's evidence. The common law had only slowly come to accept testimony of any sort and had stood firm against any by the accused, originally because the law had assumed he would lie,[76] but by the nineteenth century because it formed a protection for him. As long as he could not enter the witness box, the prosecution could not cross-examine him and thus force him to testify against himself. Disagreement arose as to whether this common law rule really protected the interests of the defendant. In 1898, in one of its few interventions in procedural law, Parliament passed an act [77] permitting the defendant to testify if he desired. Trial barristers pointed out that the new situation was not a complete blessing for a defendant and often gave him an invidious choice. If he testified, he was subject to cross-examination. If he did not, the jury, knowing his ability to do so, would be prejudiced against him. Furthermore, while the law forbade the prosecution from commenting on his failure to testify, it specifically allowed the presiding trial judge to do so in his summing-up to the jury. For defense counsel the choice was almost impossible.[78]

Another change was that the defense of insanity was recognized, although severely limited. The common law had always presumed the full responsibility of all men (but not women) for all their actions, including unlawful ones. But in the more rationalistic climate of the eighteenth century, justices had mitigated this common law dictum and dealt mercifully with people who had committed crimes while in a condition of mental instability.[79] The legal definition of insanity, how-

[76] Above, p. 149.

[77] 61 and 62 Vic., cap. 36.

[78] So much so that one of the greatest criminal trial barristers of the late nineteenth and early twentieth century, Sir Edward Marshall Hall, refused to make it and insisted that his clients state in writing whether they wanted or did not want to give evidence in their own behalf.

[79] One of the most famous examples of the application of this modified rule was in the case of Mary Lamb sister of the literary figure, Charles, who in 1796 killed her mother while in a seizure of what would now be termed hysterical mania. Her obvious mental derangement at the time of the killing caused the justices to remand her to her brother's custody; so that we may thank the bench for *Tales from Shakespeare.*

ever, remained hazy until 1843. In that year Daniel McNaughton,[80] with a fancied grievance against Sir Robert Peel, planned to shoot him, but by error killed his secretary instead. Such a mistake was no defense, the common law being clear that the accidental killing of one person with the intent to kill another was still willful murder. McNaughton, however, was so obviously paranoiac, although the word had yet to appear, that his counsel raised the issue of his sanity; and the justices instructed the jury that should it find McNaughton insane (a term which they did not define), it should acquit him. The jury pondered this question of fact and found McNaughton not guilty, whereupon the justices remanded him to an asylum at Her Majesty's pleasure.

The instructions from the bench and the resultant verdict in this prominent case raised such a storm of protest that Lord Chancellor Lyndhurst summoned the common law justices before the House of Lords, as the High Court of Parliament, to advise the peers on the precise definition of insanity. In answering the questions, framed by the Lord Chancellor and some judicial peers, the justices, themselves living in the milieu of Victorian attitudes about individual responsibility and long before Freud and Jung, formulated the *McNaughton Rules*, which until 1958 determined the validity of a plea of insanity and which still have great influence.[81] The basic rule was that the defendant carried the burden of proof for rebutting the common law presumption of his sanity. In order to rebut this presumption successfully, he had to show that at the time of the crime (invariably murder) he did not know what he was doing, *or* that he was conscious of the act but did not know it to be wrong. This judicial *opinion*, not a decision — even its name being misleading in that it did not apply to the McNaughton case, which was now closed — quickly became part of the stare decisis of the common law.[82] The peers indicated that they would apply these McNaughton rules in deciding the legal correctness of trial justices' instructions to juries about insanity in any criminal appeal coming to the House of Lords. The rules were accepted in other courts in British overseas territories, *and* in American courts, which used British judicial rulings in formulating their definition of insanity.

---

[80] Variously spelled "MacNachten" and "MacNagten."
[81] Below, p. 552.
[82] *State Trials*, New Series, IV, 847.

Civil Law

Legislative intervention in the civil side of the common law had always been rare and justices interpreted statutes along traditional common law lines. Even during the reform period, Parliament was disposed to interfere only very infrequently.

The law of libel, however, required parliamentary attention. The Fox Libel Act [83] had become heavily overlaid with judicial dicta which nearly defeated its purpose, and defendants found it of little use so long as they were unable to plead the truth of the alleged defamatory matter. In 1843 *Lord Campbell's Libel Act* permitted the defendant to do this; but libel, unlike other common law actions, placed most of the burden of proof on the defense. Judicial decisions and instructions to juries kept the English law of libel considerably more stringent than that of other jurisdictions, including those of the United States.

Law and equity drew more closely together as a result both of judicial and legislative action. Barristers practising on "both sides" had caused a reciprocal transfer of law and equity doctrines during the eighteenth century. Probably the law benefited by the transfer more than did equity, the workings of which became clogged with new requirements for formal pleadings and a greater regard for precedents. The law, on the other hand, became somewhat more fluid in procedure and more flexible in its reliefs. The *Common Law Procedure Act* of 1854 recognized the similarity between law and equity procedure; and four years later *Lord Cairn's Act* permitted the common law courts to issue injunctions and apply certain other equitable reliefs, and allowed Chancery to rule on such questions of law as might arise in actions before it and also to award damages to aggrieved parties.

Law and equity were thus merging into each other when in 1873 the *Supreme Court of Judicature Act* [84] completed the process by empowering any of the divisions of the new High Court of Justice to apply such remedies of the others as were needed in any case before it — although an action still fell within the jurisdiction of a particular division according to the principal remedy sought. When the statute went into effect in 1876, law and equity became nearly in-

[83] Above, p. 457.
[84] For the effects of the statute on the court structure see below, p. 516. Douglas, XII-Pt. One, 547.

distinguishable parts of a single body of jurisprudence, which also determined the rulings of the new Court of Appeal and the House of Lords.[85]

The same road had already been taken across the Atlantic, when in 1848 New York joined law and equity in a system of *code pleading*. At present 31 state jurisdictions, distinguished by such pleading, permit courts to combine legal and equitable reliefs in a single judgment. In thirteen states and the Federal jurisdiction, legal and equitable actions are separate but are handled by the same courts, which take judicial notice of decisions rendered on their "other side," so that there is in effect a single body of jurisprudence in these jurisdictions. Only six states retain separate courts for law and equity. Even here, however, there are no insurmountable problems of pleading; because all twenty jurisdictions without code pleading permit a rapid transfer of an action to or from law or equity if the court rules that the case should be on the "other side."

Trade union legislation brought about fundamental changes in the basic law of the country, although it was a long struggle for the unions to achieve recognition. The repeal of the Combination Acts in 1824 [86] did not give them legal status, in that the law did not "know" them as persons, and further legislation in 1825 placed severe limitations on trade union activities. The common law courts even ruled that embezzlement of their funds by dishonest officials was not a crime, for the unions were not legal persons. But by 1871 the *Trade Union Act* declared that unions should not be deemed an illegal restraint of trade and gave protection to their funds; yet at the same time, the *Criminal Law Amendment Act* imposed rigid restrictions on such trade union techniques as boycotting and picketing.[87] It was angry trade unionists who voted in the Conservative ministry of Disraeli, which in 1875 passed legislation [88] declaring that actions which were legal when done by an individual were equally legal when done by groups of individuals. The government also modified the master and servant law to make breach of contract (possible in a strike) a civil rather than a criminal action.

Union leaders believed that these laws were sufficient for their purposes. However, they left unanswered the vital question as to whether trade unions were legal persons. They were unincorporated,

[85] Douglas, XII-Pt. One, 550.
[86] Above, p. 466.
[87] 34 and 35 Vic., caps. 31, 32.
[88] 38 and 39 Vic., cap. 86.

but they possessed many of the other attributes of corporate bodies. In the early twentieth century trade unions suddenly had to face the dangers of their ambiguous legal position.

Reform and the Courts

When the forces of reform looked at the court system in the early nineteenth century, they stood in awed horror before a jungle of tribunals with overlapping jurisdictions and yet with anachronistic gaps still existing between them. Legislation had created the confusion and only legislation could end it, though to begin with reformers themselves only made matters worse by believing that still more courts were needed to fill the gaps.

Chancery, Common Pleas, and King's (or Queen's) Bench had jurisdictions resting largely on old judicial rulings, partially repeated in statutes. The Exchequer Court had had its jurisdiction fixed by Edward I.[89] Admiralty operated in an area defined by statutes and orders-in-council. When Parliament created new courts, it determined their jurisdictions precisely. In 1831 the Bankruptcy Court began operations. In 1857, the Probate Court and the Court of Divorce and Matrimonial Causes were created, taking from the ecclesiastical courts most of their jurisdiction and leaving them with little except doctrinal issues to consider. All of these courts were concerned with one particular aspect of the law and no more. Any involved case which needed different remedies had to have its issues severed and given to different courts; this procedure complicated adjudication and made litigation very expensive. In addition to all this there were also those half-forgotten courts, such as that of the Stannaries for issues arising from the Cornish tin mines, or the Common Pleas at Lancaster and Durham.

The lack of a single final appellate court made the confusion even worse. Civil appeals from the three common law courts lay to the Exchequer Chamber, composed of all common law justices, and from thence to the House of Lords. Appeals from Chancery went directly to the peers, however, until 1851, when an intermediate court of the Chancellor and two Lords Justices of Appeal began to act on appeals from Chancery, which then might continue to the Lords. The few criminal cases appealed went either to the Court of Crown Cases Reserved or via the Exchequer Chamber to the House of Lords.

[89] Above, p. 146.

Admiralty and ecclesiastical appeals went to *Delegates,* appointed *ad hoc* until 1832, when a law was passed transferring these appeals to the Privy Council, or rather to its Judicial Committee which was created the following year. Probate appeals flowed directly to the House of Lords, but those from the closely related Court of Divorce and Matrimonial Causes went first to a special court composed of the Chancellor, all common law justices, and the justice of the Probate Court (who had already heard the case as judge of the Divorce Court). Only if this intermediate court upheld the dissolution of a marriage, did further appeal lie to the House of Lords.

The creation of the *Judicial Committee of the Privy Council* by legislation in 1833 was the first attempt to simplify this situation. The Committee was composed of the Lord Chancellor, Lord President, former holders of these offices, all present and previous high-ranking justices, and two other members named by the crown. Any four (later three) of the committee might hear appeals belonging to the Privy Council. Normally, five members of the committee acted on cases, and their decisions, in the name of the full Privy Council, took the form of advice tendered to the sovereign, as fountain of justice, to issue an order-in-council embodying the decision of the committee.[90]

Improving the competence of the House of Lords to act as a final court of appeal proved more difficult. Legally, every peer could sit in the High Court of Parliament, and as late as 1783 "lay" peers had participated along with "law lords" (peers presently or previously holding high judicial office) in determining appeals. What could happen in these circumstances became clear when in 1844 Daniel O'Connell appealed his conviction for sedition from Queen's Bench (in Dublin) to the House of Lords. A large number of lay peers, who wanted to "get" O'Connell, appeared in the chamber, ready to vote against his appeal. The justices, summoned by the peers to give their opinion, advised that the conviction was legally sound, whereupon Lord Chancellor Lyndhurst put the question. The vote indicated a majority against O'Connell. But Lyndhurst was embarrassed by what might be construed as a

[90] The committee's jurisdiction over appeals from overseas territories more properly belongs to imperial rather than to English constitutional history and is therefore not considered here. Although the committee often imported judicial figures from colonies to assist in the hearing of the appeals, their implication of lack of sovereignty of the overseas territories caused the independent members of the Commonwealth to prohibit or very narrowly restrict them. In determining these overseas appeals, the committee often kept an eye on their political implications for intra-imperial relations.

naked display of partisanship in a judicial matter, and although he was himself opposed to the appeal, he refused to announce the result of the vote. Lord Wharncliffe, a lay peer with some sense of proportion, suggested that all of his kind withdraw and leave the decision to the five law lords, who voted three to two (Whig against Tory) to reverse O'Connell's conviction. But it remained a matter of chance whether there were enough peers with judicial experience in the Lords, and this problem was not solved for another thirty years.

The Supreme Court of Judicature Act of 1873 made sweeping changes and momentarily put an end to the House of Lords as an appellate court. It abolished all courts except the ecclesiastical and the Judicial Committee of the Privy Council, and made a fresh start by establishing the *Supreme Court of Judicature*, composed of the *High Court* and the *Court of Appeal*. The former consisted of the three divisions of Queen's (King's) Bench, for all common law, civil and criminal, cases; Chancery for equity; and Probate, Divorce, and Admiralty as a single court for these subjects, which although they might seem to have nothing in common, all depend on the Roman-civil law in some manner. Each of the divisions, however, could apply the remedies of the others as required in a case; and justices could sit in any of the divisions, although they usually remained in one. From the divisions of the High Court civil appeals on issues of law lay to the Court of Appeal, consisting of the Master of the Rolls and the Lords Justices of Appeal, usually sitting in divisions of three. If appellate business were pressing, the Chancellor might enlist the help of his own predecessors, former Lords Justices of Appeal, and any present or past justice of the High Court. Normally, however, these additional persons were unnecessary.

As critics of the law pointed out, different rulings by trial and Appeal Court justices required a third ruling. In 1875 a statute, effective the next year, restored the appellate jurisdiction of the House of Lords. It guaranteed a constant judicial element within the House, and for all practical purposes separated the House of Lords as an appellate court from the chamber as one of the legislative houses. Although the law did not forbid lay peers to act in appeals, it presumed (and correctly) that they would not, by requiring that at least three law lords should hear such cases and by empowering these law lords thus to act when Parliament stood prorogued or even dissolved, times when there was no legislative House of Lords in being.

The measure added to the traditional definition of law lords as being the present and previous Chancellors, along with other peers holding, or having held, high judicial office by incorporating the principle, rejected by the Lords in 1856, of life peerages, which went to the *Lords of Appeal in Ordinary*. Initially two in number, but subsequently increased gradually to nine, these Lords of Appeal in Ordinary were actually appellate judges, receiving salaries as such. Invariably, at least one was an expert in Scottish law, which he explained to other law lords in deciding cases coming to the House of Lords on appeal from Scottish courts.

With two separate final courts of appeal, the House of Lords and the Judicial Committee of the Privy Council, there was still the possibility of conflicting decisions on the same issue of law. However, after 1876 all law lords, if not already on the Judicial Committee, received appointments to it.[91] Thus the same faces appeared in both courts, and this fact was useful to the House of Lords as an appellate court. The Lords were (and are) bound by their decisions; the Judicial Committee was (and is) not. Thus the House of Lords as a court could take "judicial notice" of modifications of their decisions by the Judicial Committee and apply these modifications so as to change precedents of the High Court of Parliament.

Local courts came under the scrutiny of reformers. The assize courts continued, although the reforms of 1873 made them more efficient. Justices of the peace handling minor criminal matters, either singly or in petty sessions (two or more justices), operated by rule of thumb. By laws of 1839 and 1840 boroughs might hire *stipendiary magistrates* from the ranks of barristers to deal with minor criminal cases. The old *coroner's court*, elected by freeholders, was overhauled in 1888, when the new county and the older borough councils gained the right to appoint the coroner. Although their selections were usually sound, legislation of 1926 limited them to barristers, solicitors, or physicians. The court continued its duty of investigating suspicious deaths and also of holding inquests into treasure trove to ensure that the crown received its share of the find.

Probably the largest single change in local courts came in 1846 with the establishment of *county courts* [92] for minor civil actions, largely small torts and debt cases. Despite their name, they were not the

[91] Gooch, 395.
[92] Douglas, XII-Pt. One, 529.

descendants of the old shire courts and were for districts whose boundaries rarely coincided with those of the historic counties, some of which had several such courts. The new courts were very popular, and in 1888 they received some minor equity jurisdiction. Their jurisdiction continued to expand considerably in the twentieth century.

The achievements of the age of reform were manifold, and it was an age which saw in legislation the solution to most of its problems. Such legislation ended religious discrimination, sought to create equality of opportunity, and by 1884 had given the vote to nearly every man in Great Britain. Although the original reformers had believed in laissez-faire, their legislative activity, notably in regard to poor relief and industrial legislation, laid the basis for the modern welfare state. Legislation, in creating a mass electorate, also led to the development of organized parties with rigid discipline over their members in the House of Commons. By the close of the period, there was less control by the majority of the Commons over the cabinet than there was ministerial control over the majority.

"Reform" aimed at uniformity and more popular participation in local government. Legislation seemed to secure these goals, but other laws which transferred former local government functions to agencies of the central government greatly reduced local autonomy. By the close of the reform era local governments depended upon the central government for the performance of many of their functions, notably in social service, so that in turn, these functions were controlled by the central administration.

Juridically, "Reform" meant a merger of law and equity and a simplification of the central court structure. "Reform" also touched the local courts, including that of the coroner, and established the new county courts.

READING LIST

BAGEHOT, WALTER. *English Constitution*, 3rd ed., with introd. by Earl Balfour.
BRINTON, C. C. *English Political Thought in the Nineteenth Century*.
CHRISTIE, O. F. *The Transition from Aristocracy*.
———. *The Transition to Democracy*.
DICEY, A. V. *Law and Public Opinion in England*.
GASH, NORMAN. *Politics in the Age of Peel*.

HOVELL, MARK. *The Chartist Movement.*

KEITH, SIR ARTHUR BERRIEDALE. *The Constitution of England from Queen Victoria to George VI,* 2 vols.

MILL, JOHN STUART. *Political Economy,* 6th ed.

SEYMOUR, C. *Electoral Reform in England and Wales, 1832–1885.*

SMELLIE, K. B. *A Hundred Years of English Government,* esp. 1832–1870.

VEITCH, G. S. *Genesis of Parliamentary Reform.*

WEBB, SIDNEY, and BEATRICE WEBB (Passfield, Lord and Lady). *English Local Government,* 4 vols.

13

THE ENLARGEMENT OF THE CROWN

DURING the reform period it became increasingly clear that the term "crown" was indicating two quite different things, and this duality could no longer be doubted in the twentieth century. At one and the same time "crown" referred to the sovereign and to the government; and although legally, the latter belonged to the former, realities declared otherwise. Each aspect of the dual crown enlarged itself markedly beginning in the late nineteenth century — the monarchical crown subtly, the governmental crown obviously.

The Dual Crown

The kings and queens of England, good, bad, mad, or indifferent, had left behind them by the end of the nineteenth century an institution that was almost above criticism. In spite of the vicissitudes it had suffered, it represented stability, continuity, tradition. It was expected to represent too the hopes, aspirations, and morality of the nation as a whole. In the two World Wars, George V and George VI identified themselves with the nation and commanded the personal loyalty of millions. In peace, the coronation of Elizabeth II inspired the people with visions of the dawn of a new Elizabethan age. Perhaps in no other country has so much of the sheer glamor of royalty survived — except, of course, vicariously in certain republics. Deprived at last of all political power, the monarchy remained essential to the constitution, if only because the people insisted upon it. The monarch need no longer bully, cajole, or manipulate the House of Commons; as a symbolic figure, he or she was above all politics and party differences, in a sphere of serene neutrality. The relics of political influence such as the power to dissolve Parliament or to select the Prime Minister, all disappeared. Relations between the Prime Minister and the sovereign are confidential, so it is, of course, difficult to say to what extent the crown can still make itself felt by giving advice or by the influence of the royal personality. Edward VII (1901–10) was friendly toward each of his three Prime Ministers. George V (1910–36) had close relations with Asquith, Lloyd George, and Mac-Donald. His dealings were more formal with Baldwin, with whom Edward VIII (1936) had little rapport. Speaking to the Commons on the abdication, Baldwin said that he had told the king "all I thought he should know." Churchill and George VI (1936–52) worked closely together during World War II, but there is no evidence that the king influenced the conduct of the war except to prevent Churchill from taking part himself in the Normandy invasion. The sovereign was a figurehead, treated by politicians of both parties with the utmost respect, but only because the sovereign knew his place so well. The tercentenary of the execution of Charles I in 1949 was the occasion for the expression of royalist, rather than of parliamentary, sentiment.

But while the crown in the sense of the royal person ceased to be politically active, the crown of the ministry steadily increased its powers. In this sense the "crown" was the "government," which unlike the royal crown was the object of constant criticism. The law did not "know" the ministry as the government; it recognized only the Privy Council. But any three members of the Council could act for the full number, which was now over 700. If a minister were not already a Privy Councillor, he was made one; and it was his oath as a Privy Councillor which made his relations with ministerial colleagues and with the sovereign confidential.

New ministerial posts were created and existing offices fluctuated in importance, so that the composition of the cabinet was always changing. As the welfare interests of the state increased, such offices as Minister of Pensions and Minister of Health achieved cabinet rank. During World Wars I and II an inner *war cabinet*, the members of which had few departmental duties but were mainly concerned with co-ordination, naturally overshadowed the regular cabinet. But in 1937, the *Ministers of the Crown Act* [1] did something to rationalize the position of the cabinet; it named fifteen ministers who were to receive salaries of £5000, and by implication these were the men who could

[1] 1 Edw. VIII and 1 Geo. VI, cap. 38.

be expected to hold cabinet posts. The Chancellor of the Exchequer, the Secretaries of State, First Lord of the Admiralty, and Lord Chancellor, were specifically allotted this salary. Other offices had salaries of £3000 and would remain in the outer ranks of the ministry, unless their holders were chosen by the Prime Minister to make up the fifteen who were to receive £5000, in which case they would join the cabinet. This act also recognized, for the first time in law, the office of Prime Minister and specifically joined it to that of the First Lord of the Treasury. The Prime Minister thus became something more than *primus inter pares* among his colleagues, for his salary was double theirs.

The relationship of the Prime Minister to his colleagues was subtle and changing. Generalizations on his position are dangerous, for his actual power varied according to personal, party, and political factors. Of the holders of the office after 1885, unquestionably the one with the most power was Churchill during World War II, with Lloyd George a very close second — again in wartime. But the Prime Minister could not ride roughshod over his colleagues. He and they owed their places to decisions taken by their parliamentary party, which had other leaders and was, above all, concerned about the next election. Gladstone discovered that, when it came to a basic disagreement with his colleagues in 1894, it was he and not they who left office. Balfour did not try to arbitrate between the tariff and free trade members of his cabinet, but instead attempted to ride both horses, only to fall between them. The Prime Minister needed either infinite tact and a readiness to compromise, or else a personality so dominating that opposition simply withered away.

Melbourne's dictum that what ministers said was of no account so long as they said the same thing contained an important truth. But cabinet discussions, reaching toward a consensus rather than a formal vote, often left individual ministers very vague as to just what had been said and just what the position of the cabinet was on a certain issue. This vagueness could lead to contradictory ministerial statements in Parliament and before the public. Some ministers tried to take notes, but Prime Ministers, beginning with Disraeli, generally ruled that no notes might be taken at cabinet meetings.

World War I made a more systematic way of conducting cabinet business essential. In 1916 the inner war cabinet began a secretariat, which was little more than the private secretarial staff of Prime

Minister Lloyd George pressed into duty. The secretariat was criticized, but it remained after the war. The members of the secretariat, headed by the *secretary to the cabinet,* had from the outset a peculiar position. They were not civil servants, but neither were they personal employees of cabinet members. Named as needed by the Prime Minister, they usually remained in spite of ministerial changes. The secretary often held the same post in other more or less formal committees, such as the Committee of Imperial Defence and the Economic Advisory Council.

Members of the secretariat, particularly the secretary, had a highly confidential and delicate relationship with ministers. Upon call by the Prime Minister, the secretary sent notices of cabinet meetings, with their agenda and related papers, to other cabinet members. Initially, the secretariat kept fairly full accounts of cabinet meetings; but the inherent danger in this procedure of leakage of information to unauthorized persons reduced the records to skeleton statements as to the matters discussed, the points raised, and the conclusions reached. The secretary submitted the last to all cabinet members, but other ministers received only abstracts of the conclusions, only what the Prime Minister believed they needed to know. Even the skeleton statements and abstracts of them, however, were confidential among the persons receiving them; and the secretariat had the duty of keeping inviolate the records of one cabinet from the members of another!

Like the Prime Minister, the Leader of the Opposition also received legal recognition in the Ministers of the Crown Act, which acknowledged the vital part played in parliamentary government by the "shadow cabinet" when it gave the Leader of the Opposition a salary and so a legal status. When there was more than one opposition party, the leader of the largest received the salary. The provision for the Leader of the Opposition was a recognition that he and his lieutenants provided an immediate replacement for the existing ministry, which meanwhile it was doing its best to undermine by questions and debate.

In 1905 Sir Henry Campbell-Bannerman established another constitutional principle when the Balfour Conservative ministry resigned between sessions of Parliament. Although his party was then in a minority in the Commons, when asked by the king to form a ministry, the Liberal leader immediately undertook the task, on the ground that a party refusing office when asked did not deserve the support of voters. This convention means that under normal circumstances the opposition must take office upon the resignation of the government, and if in a minority in the existing Commons, must appeal to the country for a mandate before meeting Parliament, as Sir Henry did in 1906.

Electorate and Party

The nearly universal male franchise of the late reform period had provided a broad base for the exercise of party discipline by leaders. When that base widened to include all adults, the force of party discipline increased proportionately.

The first victory in the battle for women's suffrage came in the field of local government. If ratepayers, they were eligible to vote for poor law guardians in 1834, borough councils in 1869, and school boards (on which they might also sit) the next year. In 1894 they could vote for district and parish councils, and were also eligible for membership on them. In 1907 a similar arrangement applied to county and borough councils. Progress had been rapid, but the way to the parliamentary franchise was long and hard.

The elections of 1906 revealed a tendency for voting by class, and politicians, in their belief that women would vote as women, did not want to complicate their electoral calculations by adding them to the electorate. Bills to give a modified parliamentary suffrage to women failed in 1910 and 1911. In 1912 hopes of women suffrage leaders were dashed by the rejection of an amendment to a bill, giving the franchise to all men, for the same grant to women. In 1913 a similar amendment to a similar measure was ruled out of order by the Speaker as not relating to the subject of the bill. In the face of repeated disappointments some women became militant "suffragettes" engaged in campaigns of violence or passive resistance, which exasperated rather than persuaded their enemies.

Their cause was saved by the war. It changed the economic and social status of women, and their activity in war work made many of the objections to woman suffrage seem absurd. In 1917 a Speaker's conference of representatives of all parties drafted a new franchise bill and endorsed the principle of woman suffrage. In 1918 this multi-party measure became the *Representation of the People Act*.[2]

The law first gave the vote to all men at the age of 21 and then to all women at 30, the age differential being set to avoid a preponder-

[2] Stephenson and Marcham, 827.

ance of women in the electorate after the heavy losses of men during the war. With its avowed purpose of creating a truly democratic franchise, the law reduced the maximum number of votes per person to two and required that one be cast in the district of residence. Persons entitled to vote in other constituencies had to indicate in which they would vote, and their actual casting of the additional vote became more difficult by virtue of the law's limitation of polling to one day. Plural voting, therefore, ceased to have much meaning, except for the university constituencies, where a degree-holder could cast his second vote by mail. The slogan of "one man, one vote" was, however, accepted into the law in 1948,[3] when university representation was abolished and the last trace of plural voting disappeared. The law also shifted responsibility for registration from the individual voter to the government, first the Ministry of Health, and after 1921 the Home Office having the duty of compiling election registers.

Although woman suffrage leaders had not originally insisted on the right to sit in Parliament, preferring to concentrate all efforts on the franchise, another act of 1918 allowed women to sit in the House of Commons, and "Hon. Gentlemen" soon encountered ladies on the green benches. In 1919 a private member bill became the *Sex Disqualification (Removal) Act*,[4] which swept away sex distinctions for all offices and professions. Women appeared as cabinet ministers, jurors, justices of the peace, barristers, on the bench of the High Court, and even eventually in the House of Lords.

In 1918 the government had explained its reasons for limiting women to the House of Commons on the grounds of an imminent general reform of the upper House. Lady Rhondda, one of the few peeresses in her own right,[5] waited for four years; but nothing happened. In 1922 she claimed that the removal of sex distinctions for any office or position entitled her as a "peer" to take her seat in the House of Lords, the more so because as the holder of a peerage she could not vote and therefore had no representation, despite her paying taxes. Although these arguments appeared sound, the Lords rejected her claim on the grounds that the chamber was about to be drastically reformed, being careful not to add that they felt that there ought to be one place left in the British Empire which a man could call his own.

[3] 11 and 12 Geo. VI, cap. 65.
[4] Stephenson and Marcham, 830.
[5] That is actually possessing a peerage and not having a courtesy title by virtue of marriage to a peer.

But the Lords could not hold out for long. In 1957 the peers approved a government resolution proposing to strengthen the House of Lords by life peerages, to be bestowed upon both men and women. In 1958 Parliament passed a law to this effect,[6] and four of the new life peerages went to women, who took their seats in "their lordships' house." [7]

The age differential in the franchise between men and women began to appear more and more illogical after World War I, particularly as politicians discovered that women (like men) did not vote as a sex, but according to their individual social, economic, and intellectual attitudes. Ten years after women received the parliamentary franchise, the age differential ended, with all women as well as men able to vote at twenty-one.[8] And so the worst fears of Lord Eldon back in 1832 were not only realized but surpassed.

The Representation of the People Act of 1918 set the membership of the Commons at 707, and with the exception of the university constituencies made the single-member-district the basis for parliamentary representation, with each member representing a district of about 70,000 people. Like its predecessors, however, the 1918 measure failed to provide for the redistribution of seats as needed. When the Irish Free State was established in 1922, the number of seats in the Commons dropped to 615, but this did not affect the electoral ratio in what was now the United Kingdom of Great Britain and *Northern* Ireland.[9] By the close of World War II the constituencies of members had again become disproportionate. In 1948 the same measure which ended plural voting and university representation fixed the membership of the Commons at 630 and transferred the function of delimitation of seats from Parliament to a judicial commission, which was to act after each census.

It was a matter of democratic principle that members of Parliament should be paid. Despite the abolition of property qualifications for membership in the Commons, the lack of salaries precluded men without independent means from entering the House. Any political action by the trade unions, for instance, was seriously hampered by this.

[6] For a further discussion of this act see below, p. 533; 6 and 7 Eliz. II, cap. 21.
[7] Among them, the persistent Lady Rhondda.
[8] Gooch, 23.
[9] After the creation of the Irish Free State the number of representative Irish peers sitting in the Lords for life gradually declined as vacancies were not filled by the Irish peerage, to which no more additions were made.

After the failure of bills in 1893 and 1895 to give such payment, the unions tried to solve the problem by paying any of their working-class candidates who won seats themselves; but this was condemned on the grounds that a member of Parliament should not feel obligated to a certain set of interests. The new Labor party, formed from the Labor Representation Committee in 1906, retorted that without these payments its members could not afford to be in the Commons. In 1909 the House of Lords, however, pronounced on the *Osborne Case*, the law lords declaring that the use of trade union funds for political purposes was illegal.[10]

Labor supporters of the Liberal government continued to insist on legislation for the payment of members. Anticipating the rejection of such a bill by the Lords, the government preferred to proceed by having the House of Commons adopt, in 1911, a standing order authorizing the Treasury to pay its members an annual salary of £400. This amount was just enough to keep body and soul of the average member together. Usually he had to be his own secretary or put his wife to work with his correspondence. Wherever possible, members tried to find work in London during the session as journalists, barristers, teachers, and doctors. This meant that the important business of the Commons began only after the London working day ended. Gradually, the salary of members rose, but always lagging behind the London cost of living. In 1957 it was £1500, hardly in itself a sufficient incentive to persuade a man to stand for Parliament.

As descendants of the feudal curia regis, members of the House of Lords were obliged to attend the sovereign on his summons, although there was no legal way to enforce their attendance. None of the peers thus received remuneration, except the Lords of Appeal in Ordinary, who had salaries as judges. But in 1957, hoping to encourage attendance, the Lords voted its members an "allowance" from the Treasury of three guineas (£3 3s.) for each day on which they put in an appearance. This did little to solve the problem of the absentees, which was the subject of serious debate by those peers who were present during the session of 1958.

The organization of the parties continued to become more complex and more efficient. At the base were *local associations*, composed of zealous amateurs, who kept the embers of enthusiasm alive between elections and reported the prevailing attitudes of their constituencies

[10] For the legal aspects of the case, see below, p. 545.

to their member, or hoped-for member, in the Commons. These associations sent delegates to the *annual party conference*, which was usually held at some resort. The conference was designed to whip up enthusiasm among the faithful and to give national publicity to the party, rather than to form policy. Its attitudes and resolutions might guide party leaders, but the last word was theirs. At the summit of the party structure was the *parliamentary party*, chosen by the voters. Its members ranged in importance from the newest backbencher to the Prime Minister, or alternatively, the Leader of the Opposition. Among party leaders, backbenchers, and the party organization outside Parliament, no one element could entirely dominate the rest. But the parliamentary party, having won the confidence of the electorate, was normally entrusted with the formation of policy and party tactics. The party leader himself, chosen by the parliamentary party, often because of his manifest popularity with the electorate, had to lead and listen simultaneously.

Linking the parliamentary leadership and the faithful beyond Westminster was the Central Office, controlled by the party leaders. Such control gave them much power over their party in Parliament, but if to the rank and file their policies seemed unlikely to meet with support in the country, backbenchers would warn their whips, who in turn would warn the party leaders. In their own interests they would then be likely to modify their line of action.

The Attack on the House of Lords

The increase of political democracy inevitably raised the issue of the place of the House of Lords in the constitution. Just as inevitably, the resolution of that issue was in democratic terms, but the major constitutional result of the reduction in the powers of the Lords was an increase in the power of the ministerial crown.

The similarity in social background and attitudes between the members of the two Houses, which in the past had usually been sufficient to ensure harmonious relations between them, had begun to disappear by 1885. By then men were entering the House of Commons whose interests and backgrounds were far removed from those of the Lords, and friction could no longer be avoided. The party system, moreover, tended to exacerbate it. The party with a minority in the Commons had little chance of resisting government policy successfully. If it could command sympathy in the Lords, however, there was a great temptation to use the Lords to frustrate the party controlling the Commons.

The fierce struggle over Irish Home Rule caused a significant realignment in the social groupings within the parties. Previously each party had included elements from all social classes, but with the Liberal split in 1886, some Radicals, and most of the wealthy and aristocratic elements of the party, joined the Liberal Unionists, and from there inevitably gravitated to the Conservatives, who changed their official name to the Unionist party. The enlarged Conservative party for the first time had a monopoly of the upper classes, socially and economically. This left the Liberals largely a middle-class party, but strongly bidding for lower-class supporters to replace those lost over Irish Home Rule. The Conservatives thus found themselves confronted by unacceptable lower-class demands, to which the Liberal party became increasingly committed. Thus whenever the Conservatives did not control the House of Commons, where rigid party discipline made it impossible for them to win votes away from the Liberal government, they naturally thought of the House of Lords, which they did control.

In 1893 the Lords rejected the second Irish Home Rule Bill, which the Commons had passed. And for the remainder of Gladstone's administration, and for that of Rosebery, the Conservatives used the Lords to wreck the Liberal program. Although Gladstone threatened at times, his party took no action against the upper House. With the defeat of Rosebery in 1895, Salisbury formed a Conservative cabinet, and the issue was shelved until the Liberals returned to power in 1905.

There was a considerable difference between the situation of the 1890s and that which the Conservative leaders now faced. The new Liberal government had a good majority in the House, and had been elected on the strength of a specific program. For the Leader of the Opposition in the Commons, Arthur Balfour, to use the Lords to thwart the enactment of this program was imprudent and doomed to failure. Balfour believed that voters would lose faith in a government which could not get its bills through the Lords and would therefore replace it with one which could. But he misread the temper of the times, and the Conservative majority in the Lords contributed to its own undoing by agreeing to follow the orders of the party's leadership in the Commons. It either rejected, or amended to a point which could not be allowed by the Liberal majority in the Commons, measures abolishing plural voting, modifying the education law, dealing with small-hold-ings, and reducing the number of pubs. Liberals were naturally in-dignant, for they had an election mandate and therefore a responsibility to the voters for these bills. They were quick to point out that these projects touched on some of the vested interests of the aristocracy of the Conservative party. In contrast, the Lords had passed the radical *Trades Disputes Act,* which made trade unions immune from damage suits, because the landed aristocracy of the Conservatives had few dealings with unions.

Matters came to a head with the budget of 1909, introduced by the Chancellor of the Exchequer, Lloyd George. To pay for the new social services and naval expansion the budget raised taxes generally and also incorporated certain principles of a bill which had previously been rejected by the peers. Death duties rose, and there was a tax on the "unearned increment" of land values (those which had risen through no effort by their owner). Compared with post-World War I budgets that of 1909 was mild, but in that year it was revolutionary; and the Chancellor of the Exchequer made no secret of his belief that changes in the tax structure could drastically alter that of society.

After bitter debates the budget went through the Commons to the taunts of Conservatives that it would never become law, and so the constitutional crisis came. The undoubted right of the Commons to initiate money bills had come to mean that the Lords always passed the budget, although legally they could amend [11] and even reject it. In 1909 the Conservative leadership made the fatal mistake of ordering the House of Lords to reject the budget.

Radicals were by no means displeased by this, for it meant that at last the government would be compelled to accept the challenge. Fortified by a vote of confidence from the Commons, the ministry went to the country in early 1910. The results were less than decisive. By declaring that only an unfettered House of Lords could prevent the passage of an Irish Home Rule measure, the Conservatives raised their strength in the Commons almost to the level of the Liberals, who stayed in power only because of Labor and Irish Nationalist votes in the new House.

[11] The resolution of the House of Commons in 1671 (above, p. 368) notwith-standing; since this did not have the force of law, although the Lords after that date refrained from amending money bills.

The House of Lords now passed the budget and hoped that the storm would not break. It did because Labor and Irish supporters of the government insisted on a measure to cut the veto power of the Lords against socialistic bills and Irish Home Rule. Under this pressure the government drafted legislation which became the issue of a second election in 1910. The election results almost duplicated those of the earlier ones, and the cabinet went ahead with the bill. Fierce debates marked its passage through the Commons. Although the Liberal ministers emphasized that this was like any other measure, capable of repeal by ordinary legislative procedures, the Conservatives knew that they would never dare repeal it, should it become law. When the measure reached the Lords, some Conservative peers were for fighting to the end; but the cabinet's threat to have peers created *en masse* caused enough Conservative lords to stay away or vote with the ministry, and the *Parliament Act* became law in 1911.[12]

The Act dealt only with the powers not the composition of the House of Lords, though it was stated in the preamble that there would soon be a general revision of its personnel. Conservatives did not object to this statement, or to the reduction by the law of the maximum term of Parliament to five years. There was more doubt about the provisions relating to money bills, defined as those being certified by the Speaker as concerned only with financial matters.[13] These money bills, the act declared, should become law thirty days after passage by the House of Commons, regardless of any action taken by the Lords.

The Conservatives fought the Parliament Act most savagely on its sections relating to non-money bills, where the law embodied a plan suggested by John Bright in the nineteenth century to resolve conflicts between the Houses. Such bills would become law after passage by the House of Commons in three successive sessions (regardless of any possible intervening election), no matter what action the Lords took on them, providing a minimum of two years had elapsed between their first introduction and final passage, *and* that in their final form they were *exactly* the same as when first introduced.

The Parliament Act reduced the powers of the upper chamber and at the same time made it virtually impossible that it should ever

[12] Gooch, 329.
[13] Speaker James William Lowther, who presided over the bitter debates in the Commons on the Parliament Act, as Viscount Ullswater in *A Speaker's Commentaries* (2 vols., London, 1925) declared that the 1909 budget, which occasioned this law, would not have met its criteria for money bills (II, 103).

recover them. At first the peers did delay bills unpalatable to them for the maximum period. Thus the Irish Home Rule Act of 1914 and the measure disestablishing the Church of England in Wales took the full time to become law. The former was suspended for the duration of World War I, and by that time events in Ireland had made it a dead letter. Immediately after the war the peers also held up a measure aiming at reducing the number of pubs in Scotland.

But in every case the delay was in the end futile. The government began all controversial bills sufficiently early in the term of Parliament for them to pass through the Commons three times before the next general election. Under ordinary circumstances these measures would not become election issues except as statutes; and it might prove difficult for those who had opposed them, assuming they won the next election, to repeal such statutes. Not until after the formation of the Labor government in 1945 did the peers again try to delay a bill. They then selected the highly controversial measure nationalizing the iron and steel industry, for which the ministry had a dubious mandate from the voters.

The answer of the government was to use the procedure of the Parliament Act of 1911 to pass the *Parliament Act of 1949*,[14] which reduced the number of successive sessions for the passage of non-money bills by the Commons from three to two and the minimum time from two years to one. Then, rather than try and pass the Iron and Steel Bill under the terms of the new Parliament Act, which would have left insufficient time before the 1950 election, the government stated that the Parliament Act of 1949 meant that the Iron and Steel Bill, having already met its provisions, was *already* law!

The peers lost their effective power of amending bills. Under the Parliament Act of 1911, and even more so under its modification of 1949, the ministry could have its supporters in the Commons quite safely reject amendments by the Lords in the knowledge that the upper chamber could not insist upon them. The only time when the cabinet had to take amendments from the Lords seriously was when immediate legislation was required. Thus at the opening of both World Wars I and II the government had to have its majority in the Commons accept amendments by the peers to war power bills, which somewhat reduced government war powers.

The Parliament Act, however, reduced not only the power of the

[14] 12, 13, and 14 Geo. VI, cap. 103.

House of Lords but that of the Commons too. Legally, as those objecting to it pointed out, the act produced something close to unicameralism, with the House of Commons supreme. In practice, however, it tended to subordinate the Commons still further to the ministry. Not only could the cabinet ward off amendments by the Lords to its measures, but it could prevent such amendments coming from its own majority in the lower House, merely by pointing out that any changes in a bill would render it ineligible for passage by the procedure of the Parliament Act, should the Lords object to it. In consequence, once the ministry had introduced a measure into the Commons it usually went through unchanged; the only thing likely to alter it was the government's fear of an adverse reaction by voters at the next election.

Reform of the House of Lords came slowly. After 1911 there were numerous proposals to implement the promise of the preamble to the Parliament Act. The need for bicameralism was generally accepted, even by the Labor party. The most serious proposals came in 1918 from a multi-party commission headed by Viscount Bryce, the eminent political scientist. All members agreed that a second chamber had value in delaying controversial legislation for reconsideration; in debating important matters of policy without regard to party considerations; in amending details of measures passed by the Commons; and in initiating noncontroversial measures. But the commission could not agree on how the Lords could be reformed so that it might best serve in this role. Any modification of the hereditary principle was likely to strengthen the upper House; and politicians in fact preferred not to have to consider a second chamber's reactions to their policies. The public was for the most part quite indifferent, and no party felt much need to include reform of the House of Lords in its program. It was not until 1957, that any action was taken by the government. Then the House of Lords approved the principle of life peerages, which had hitherto applied only to the Lords of Appeal in Ordinary. Despite Labor denunciations of the plan as a Conservative plot to thwart the will of the people, the Macmillan government proceeded to implement the plan by legislation in 1958. While not forbidding the creation of peers of the usual hereditary type, the law authorized the crown to grant fourteen life peerages. Later that year the new life peers, four of them women, took their seats.

The Parliament Act had the effect of limiting the selection of the

Prime Minister to members of the Commons. In 1923 the Conservatives passed over Viscount Curzon for Stanley Baldwin. In 1940 Viscount Halifax immediately rejected the suggestion by Neville Chamberlain that he should succeed him as Prime Minister on the grounds that he was in the House of Lords. Also the heirs of peers were likely to be frustrated if they cherished political ambitions, for they might be called to enter the House of Lords at any time. In the early twentieth century the heir of Viscount Astor, himself then in the Commons, proposed that heirs of peers should be permitted to waive their rights of succession, but the other members of the Commons were indifferent. Nearly forty years later Quentin Hogg, then also in the lower House, found its members had no sympathy with his efforts to avoid becoming Viscount Hailsham. And Anthony Wedgewood-Benn had to face a similar problem in 1961, when despite heroic efforts, he duly became Viscount Stansgate.

Party and the House of Commons

The last time a cabinet lost its majority and another took over without appealing to the country was in 1895, when the Rosebery Liberal government was defeated on a snap division in committee and replaced by the Salisbury Conservative ministry. Even on that occasion, however, the new Prime Minister quickly called for a general election to secure a dependable majority in the House. Occasionally a government might resign because of differences within the party, without reference either to the Commons or the electorate. Thus in 1905 Balfour, with a cabinet divided over tariffs, but still controlling a majority in the House, resigned in the hopes of embarrassing the Liberals. But he miscalculated. Campbell-Bannerman formed a Liberal ministry, which, however, did not meet the old House of Commons. It appealed to the country and won a majority in the elections. Again in 1915 the Asquith Liberal government, under severe criticism for its conduct of the war, gave way to a coalition of all parties except the Irish Nationalists, without having suffered a formal defeat in the House. In 1922 the decision of the Conservative parliamentary party to fight the general election the next year as a separate party, and not as part of the coalition, caused Lloyd George to resign the same evening without meeting the House of Commons, where the coalition was still in existence. The result was an immediate general election, because the new Conservative Prime

Minister, Bonar Law, needed a party majority in the Commons before he met it. In 1931 a Labor government, kept in power by the Liberals, gave way to a coalition national government solely on the basis of consultation among party leaders, who presumed (though wrongly in the case of Labor) that their respective parliamentary parties would swing in behind them. But the House of Commons, as such, had not demanded such a shift. Instead, it was confronted by a new ministry. In the midst of the worst crisis in British history the Chamberlain government in 1940 beat down a Labor motion of censure by 81 votes. The most that some of his disciplined Conservative supporters dared do to show their disapproval of his administration was to abstain from voting. But the possibility that in time abstentions might become opposition votes, and the refusal of Labor to enter a coalition government headed by Chamberlain, caused him to resign and Churchill to form a coalition ministry.

On none of these occasions was the government actually defeated in the Commons. Sir Anthony Eden resigned because of disagreements within his own party over his Suez policy and because of ill-health; but the Conservative majority remained intact, and Harold Macmillan was able to form a new Conservative cabinet without appealing to the country. Party discipline had become such that ministers no longer needed to fear the Commons, except in so far as their behavior there might affect the voters at the next election. And if unpopular measures were put forward early in its term, there was a good chance that the government might live them down by the end of its five years. The chief danger of defeat occurred when a government was returned with so slender a majority that it might be brought down almost by accident. This was the danger for both the Labor government of 1950, which had a majority of only eight, and the Conservative government of 1951, which could muster a majority of no more than sixteen.

The reality and meaning of party discipline in the House of Commons was revealed in the practice with the significant name of the *free vote*, when party leaders, particularly those in the government, announced that they did not regard a particular issue as having "party" connotations, so that individual members might vote as they saw fit. The existence of such a practice demonstrated the realities for voting on most other matters. On the other hand, the practice also indicated the limits of party discipline in that party leaders at times had to permit their followers to vote as they wished.

The House of Commons also lost much of its actual control over finance, to which in the past it had owed its dominant position in Parliament and its power over the king. During the nineteenth century cabinets still regarded the budget votes as crucial tests of their strength in the House. Yet it is now over a century since the House of Commons last rejected a budget. The government can now be virtually certain that the House will approve it *in toto*, and this has led to the convention that any changes in taxes announced in the budget are effective the next day, although the Commons do not pass the final stages of the appropriation measures until the last day of the session.

Standing orders of the House of Commons also tended to favor the government. Reform of procedure constantly sought to keep up with the ever increasing amount of business which Parliament had to get through in the limited time at its disposal; and certain rules, like that of the "guillotine closure," which allowed the Speaker to end debate on any section of a bill, or on an entire bill, and put the question to the vote, could seriously curtail debate and prevent the full hearing of an issue. More drastic was the "kangaroo closure," by which the Speaker selected the sections of a measure which could be debated. Both guillotine and kangaroo closures also operated in the Committee of the Whole House, where the Chairman of Committees exercised them.

The general effect of standing orders was to give most of the time of the House to government business. Naturally, during World Wars I and II there was no private member time, but it is significant that in the twentieth century, instead of two days a week being allotted to government business as after the first Reform Act, two days a week came to be allowed for private member bills. During these two days members who had won by *drawing lots* brought up their legislative projects, which, if they ran counter to government policy or convenience, would receive no more time.

Standing orders gave the government control over the agenda of the House in a manner quite as effective as that exercised by Elizabeth I and her ministers. Each Thursday a committee of the cabinet met with the Speaker and prepared the subjects for debate the next week. Individual members did not object, as they had during the reigns of Elizabeth I and James I; for the crown was now a group of party leaders with real control over their majority in the Commons.

The rule that ministers must stand for re-election upon accepting office became increasingly inconvenient, especially when the Prime Minister was trying to form a new cabinet after a general election victory over the former ministry. In 1919 a statute allowed members of the Commons to accept office within the first nine months of a new Parliament without standing for re-election, and seven years later Parliament abolished the requirement of re-election for new ministers entirely.[15]

The various proposals for the reform of the House of Commons were usually aimed at winning back control over the executive, or at least at curbing the excessive growth of its powers. One such proposal was *devolution*, either functional or geographical, or both, and it had some vogue in the 1920s. Geographical devolution seemed feasible after the establishment in 1922 of a local Parliament for Northern Ireland, which, however, still sent representatives to Westminster. But the Parliament at Belfast handled local matters, and so reduced the burdens on the Parliament at Westminster to some extent. Devolutionists therefore proposed similar regional parliaments for Scotland, Wales, and for several major areas in England, and would have left only defense, foreign policy, and "broad social policy" to the central Parliament. By definition "broad social policy" was national; and it was possible that the central Parliament would define it in a manner unacceptable to the majority of a regional Parliament. The proposition was not very practicable and did not command wide support. During the 1920s and 1930s the Labor party put forward the suggestion that social and economic matters should go to an Economic Parliament for the entire realm, leaving only political questions for the older Parliament. Again, however, because of the impossibility in the modern state of distinguishing between the two, the suggestion did not meet with much success.

The American congressional system inspired various schemes for making greater use of *committees*. The House of Commons had five standing committees: A, B, C, D, and the Scottish Committee. The last, composed of all members representing Scottish constituencies, examined and reported to the House on all bills relating to Scotland before their second reading. The other committees had a membership determined by the Chairman of Committees without regard to party; only rarely did they reflect the proportional strength of parties in the House.

It was sometimes urged that there should be proportional representation for the parties in each committee and that more work should be

[15] Gooch, 155–6.

given to the committees "upstairs" (those which met on the floor above the chamber of the House). Under existing rules of the House, ministers sent such matters as they wished "upstairs," and a single committee dealt with them irrespective of the subject. But it was argued that certain committees should have specific subjects to examine and that bills should be presented to them after the second reading in the House, when the basic principles had been laid down. The standing committees would then hammer out the details, and thus lessen the burden of the Committee of the Whole House. The House would still have to approve the work of the committee and also the third reading of bills, and would therefore retain control of the legislative process. On the other hand, it was argued that such an arrangement would undermine the principle of ministerial responsibility. The cabinet could not be made responsible for bills after they had been through the committees, where each chairman might himself become a little prime minister. And there was also the example of the French *rapporteurs,* who had wrested the initiative from ministers. Furthermore, it was difficult to decide what was meant by "details," which actually might profoundly change the meaning of a bill.

Suggestions that the government resign only on a formal *vote of no-confidence* rested on the theory that party discipline would be operative only for such a vote and would not bind members in other matters. Opponents of the proposal, however, pointed out that many so-called "details" of legislation were vital to its principles, on which the government had definite pledges to voters. If members were not bound to those details, the opposition could wreck the ministry's pledged program by capricious amendments and by refraining from moving such a formal no-confidence motion.

But on the whole the parliamentary system escaped serious criticism. Whatever the faults of the highly organized party system, it did produce stable government and permitted the electorate to assess responsibility for it. Though the government was not itself responsible daily to the House of Commons, it could not ignore the warnings of its backbenchers, or disregard the general "sense of the House." Moreover, party discipline was an assurance to voters that a party's promises would be honored if they voted it into power. If it failed to redeem its pledges, the remedy was obvious.

The Welfare State

The "welfare state," created by no one party, nor during a single period, grew by sheer force of circumstances and may perhaps be said to have begun in the sixteenth century when the government began to concern itself with poor relief. There is little new in the principle of the twentieth-century welfare state, but the very size of its operations gives to it a particular constitutional significance.

By the close of the nineteenth century the government, regardless of the party in power, had become interested in industrial conditions, housing, and the alleviation of poverty; and the burst of social legislation in the early twentieth century, termed the "New Liberalism," quickly ceased to be the unique characteristic of one particular party. In 1908 a law guaranteed a 5-shilling weekly *old age pension* to all persons (but only 7s. 6d. to a couple) who had previously earned under 10s. weekly at the age of seventy.[16] The old age pension was not insurance, because it automatically went to those meeting its requirements as of right. The insurance principle was embodied in the *National Insurance Act* of 1911,[17] which aimed at the reduction of poverty due to unemployment and sickness. Employers, employees, and the government contributed to an insurance fund, which provided benefits for employees during unemployment and assured them medical treatment when they were sick. Initially, the law applied only to industries where employment fluctuated, but later measures steadily increased its coverage.

After World War I both the pension and insurance plans were extended. The fund of the latter was deeply drawn upon during the Great Depression, and the government supplemented insurance payments by the dole. It had already undertaken to find work for people by means of *Labor Exchanges*, which were first established in 1909.[18] Local exchanges, operating through a central exchange, listed employment opportunities for specific trades. If a man could qualify for a job in a different locality but was unable to pay for his transportation to it, his local exchange advanced him the money. Under the direction of William Beveridge, the Labor Exchanges were soon getting qualified men

[16] 8 Edw. VII, cap. 40.
[17] Stephenson and Marcham, 824.
[18] 9 Edw. VII, cap. 7.

into jobs. The government's *industrial census* showed what types of
industry there were in the country, their location and size.

Though large employers were strictly regulated by law on the conditions in their factories, in the sweat shops, where a few workers
labored in very bad conditions for low wages, there was at first very
little supervision. The *Trades Boards Act* of 1909 [19] set up local boards
to investigate conditions and wages in these small enterprises, whose
employees were rarely union members. Wherever a board found sweat
shop conditions, it was empowered to set minimum standards as to
conditions and pay and enforce its orders as law.[20]

Government economic planning increased during and after World
War I. In 1919 the government embarked on the *National Grid* system [21] for the transmission of electric current, which went into operation
in 1926 under the Central Electricity Board, a semi-detached agency of
the Ministry of Transport. Owned by local government units, which
had always owned local generating plants, the National Grid gave
uniform electric power through the entire kingdom.

Agricultural production, encouraged by the government during the
war, received further government assistance in the 1920s and 1930s by
the use of marketing schemes and agricultural mortgage loans. The
government was also active in elaborate housing projects, providing
loans to local authorities and subsidies to private builders.

Planning was the order of the day, and in 1932 the Chancellor of the
Exchequer, Neville Chamberlain, announced in the House of Commons
that the government could not permit unrestricted competition where
it was socially deleterious. Simultaneously the ministry announced that
if two-thirds of the producers in a section of industry or agriculture
agreed on a marketing plan, the cabinet would have it enacted into a
law binding all such producers.

Even more, World War II increased state controls. Production, distribution, employment, and the allocation of food and clothing were all
solely in the hands of the government. During the war, Prime Minister
Churchill promised that the government would rebuild any home or
business destroyed by the blitz. For many people these government
controls meant an increase in living standards. After the war, the welfare
state was carried to its logical conclusion, with the state still increasing

[19] 9 Edw. VII, cap. 22.
[20] For the legal significance of this power see below, p. 555.
[21] 9 and 10 Geo. V, cap. 100.

its powers and its responsibilities, particularly during the period of Labor government after 1945.

In 1945 both Labor and the Conservatives had campaigned on the issue of full employment, which had real meaning to those voters who remembered the slump following World War I and the bleak years of the Depression. The two parties differed only as to the means to achieve full employment. Both promised to rebuild property destroyed by the war on the basis of individual need.[22] The Conservatives promised large government subsidies to private ownership to give full employment according to government directions. Labor proposed nationalization of basic industries.

The Labor victory brought nationalization, which took the form of the public corporation, the leading previous example of which had been the Port of London Authority, which since 1908 had exercised wide powers over the management and development of one of the greatest commercial areas of the world.[23] Most of the industries transferred from private to public ownership after 1945 were those which had previously been subjected to close government regulation. Former private stockholders in these enterprises received Treasury certificates with a guaranteed annual interest in place of their shares. Thus socialism in Great Britain created a class of people with a vested, capitalistic interest in it!

The managerial staffs of the enterprises became government officials and ran the businesses as before, with the object of profit, which, however, now went to the Treasury after first taking care of capital improvements in the particular venture.

The Bank of England had experienced increasingly strict control by the Treasury, which in 1946 took over the shares of its former private owners.[24] The nationalization of the coal mines in the same year [25] proved to be scarcely more than a change in the wording of a measure of 1938, which had left their nominal private owners with little more than the pit-head equipment. The National Coal Board and its Minister of Fuel and Power now had the unenviable task of increasing production in a long laggard industry. Railways and air transport had been regulated by the government since World War I, so that their formal nationaliza-

[22] Subsequently under this plan one of the last residences to be repaired was Buckingham Palace.
[23] 8 Edw. VII, cap. 68.
[24] 9 and 10 Geo. VI, cap. 27.
[25] 9 and 10 Geo. VI, cap. 59.

tion changed little.[26] The Ministry of Transport naturally took over the former, whose real management, however, was by the Railway Executive of the British Transport Commission. Air transport, previously regulated minutely by the Department of Civil Aviation, now became a public corporation.[27] The Post Office had long run domestic telegraph and radio services (including the British Broadcasting Corporation) and now added overseas cable and radio communications. Public ownership of gas and electricity production, which went back to the "municipal trading" of Joseph Chamberlain, was now moved from the local to the central level of government. Treasury certificates went to the former "private" owners of these industries. A gas board,[28] under the Ministry of Fuel and Power, had responsibility for the production and distribution of this fuel. The Central Electricity Board became the National Electricity Authority under the same ministry.[29]

Nationalization of trucking and of the iron and steel industry met with the strongest opposition, because in these private ownership had operated with considerable profit. The Conservatives, as they had pledged, denationalized both of them in 1952.[30] However, this did *not* mean automatic return to their former owners, who had already received compensation in Treasury certificates. Rather, the government sold these properties to the highest bidder. The Conservative cabinet did not touch other phases of nationalization, which like so many other doors in English constitutional history seemed to open only one way.

The welfare state raised certain constitutional problems. From the late nineteenth century onward it was clear that Parliament could not effectively debate technical social legislation and had to leave much of its detail to administrative agencies.[31] The only way in which Parliament could exercise any control over these agencies was by asking questions in the House and by nagging ministers if dissatisfied with the replies.

It can hardly be said, however, that the ministers themselves were in a position to control the agencies of the welfare state except by setting policy in the broadest of terms. Civil servants really operated independently of ministers in the administration of the welfare state, and it was

[26] 11 and 12 Geo. VI, cap. 49.
[27] 9 and 10 Geo. VI, cap. 70.
[28] 11 and 12 Geo. VI, cap. 36.
[29] 10 and 11 Geo. VI, cap. 36.
[30] 1 and 2 Eliz. II, cap. 13; and 1 and 2 Eliz. II, cap. 15.
[31] For the legal and juridical effects of this delegation of legislative powers by Parliament see below, p. 555.

this phase with which people constantly came in contact. Ministers might be responsible to Parliament, more particularly the Commons, but much of the legislation relating to the welfare services of government was not drafted by them, but was the product of the civil service, which was not responsible to Parliament at all. Ministers might refuse to sponsor such legislative measures, or modify them before doing so; but they hesitated in their amateur status to do either.

However, the civil service had only limited control over public corporations, most of which were not governed by civil service regulations and whose managerial staff and technical employees were only by the widest definition "civil servants." Thus the Minister of Fuel and Power and his permanent civil servants had to give the National Electricity Authority a free hand in the actual operation of the National Grid. The Postmaster-General legally headed a department of which the British Broadcasting Corporation was one part, but it would be a brave Postmaster-General who interfered in any way with the Third Programme of the B.B.C., which reflects high cultural and intellectual interests. Such a diffusion of responsibilities sometimes made it difficult to know where to attribute blame when things went wrong. Voters with unfortunate experiences on British Railways might feel inclined to blame the government, might vote against it at the next election. But all this would achieve would be a new Minister of Transport. The technical experts of British Railways, the people who were actually running the railways, carried on as usual.

The welfare state and its operation of basic industries made the *Leviathan* of Hobbes a minnow by comparison. The new state at times almost seemed to be a creature apart from the people who composed it, and only the most rigid and continuing scrutiny of every aspect of state activity could protect the rights of the individual, which the British proudly believed was the first concern of their constitution. No one could say how this enormous problem would be met, except that the British would meet each of its aspects as it arose in their usual empirical fashion.

LIBERTY AND LAW

There were those who argued that individual rights were in the gravest danger in the welfare state, and others who said that only the welfare state could protect the true interests of individuals. In any event, the relationship between the state and the individual is fundamentally a question of law.

The Enlargement of "Persons"

Legislation broadened the common law definition of "persons" to the benefit of women and trade unions. The common law had in effect denied that women could own property, which until their marriage belonged to their fathers, then it went as dowry to their husbands. The married woman was thus incapable of owning property, and few spinsters did. In 1870 there was a slight statutory modification of this common law doctrine,[32] and in 1882 the *Married Women's Property Act* [33] emphasized that property acquired by them both before and after marriage remained in their separate ownership. Enlarged further by statute in 1893, the new legal doctrine made husband and wife separate persons for the purposes of property acquisition and disposition. In turn, the new principle made it possible for husband and wife to steal and embezzle from each other so that the law, which otherwise held that as "one person" marriage partners were incapable of testifying against each other, in these cases required them to enter the witness box.

Trade union legislation of the nineteenth century had avoided saying whether unions, like corporations, were persons, even while giving them many of the attributes of persons. Whether a union was or was not a person ceased to be an academic issue when, following a successful railway strike, the *Taff Vale* Railway Company sued the union for physical damages and for loss of revenue suffered by it during the strike. Obviously, the action would lie only if the union were a person and so capable of suing and being sued. The trial justice ruled that the union was a person and gave the case to the jury, which awarded heavy damages to the plaintiff. The union naturally carried the case to the Court of Appeal, which held that without formal incorporation, no association, including a union, was a person.[34] Just as naturally, the company brought the case on to the House of Lords (that is, its law members), which in 1901 held that their numerous personal attributes made unions persons despite their being unincorporated.

[32] Douglas, XII-Pt. One, 537.
[33] 45 and 46 Vic., cap. 75.
[34] Law Reports [1901] A. C., 426.

The Taff Vale decision, which cost the union very heavily, came as a profound shock to the trade union movement. It received another blow in Quinn *v*. Leatham, which made unions liable to damages suffered by an employer from a boycott sponsored by them. Trade union leaders demanded legislation to remedy the legal situation created by these judicial decisions, and a royal commission made certain recommendations to this effect. However, before the existing Conservative government could act on them, it went out of power. The new Liberal ministry, under Campbell-Bannerman, adopted as a government measure a private member bill from the new Labor party, which stated simply that no court should entertain a tort action against a trade union.

As opponents pointed out, the bill placed unions practically above the law, to which even the crown was subordinate. Even the sovereign himself could be sued under the procedure of a petition of right, in which the petitioner requested permission to sue and the royal reply "Let Right be Done" permitted him to do so. Nevertheless, the bill became law in 1906 as the *Trades Disputes Act*.[35]

Equally delicate was the issue as to the right of unions to use their funds for political purposes. Union officials usually placed these funds at the disposal of the Labor party, which, however, was (and is) far from having the support of every individual union member. In 1908 W. V. Osborne, secretary of a local branch of a railway union, which disliked the forced payments imposed on the branch by the union's national officers for the support of Labor candidates, applied for an injunction against the practice. Unlike the Taff Vale case, there was consistency in the various judicial rulings in the *Osborne Case*.[36] A justice in Chancery granted the injunction on the ground that the purposes of a trade union did not legally extend to securing parliamentary representation. Later that year the Court of Appeal unanimously upheld the decision, and the next year the House of Lords agreed.

The Labor party was disturbed by the decision, because it quickly became apparent that voluntary contributions would never be able to compensate for the loss of the compulsory levies. After 1910, the Liberal cabinet needed Labor support in the Commons and hoped to secure it by providing for the payment of members of the House. But this was not enough. The Labor party wanted legislation to supersede the

[35] Stephenson and Marcham, 817.
[36] Law Reports [1909] 1 Ch., 163; [1910] A. C., 87.

Osborne decision, and the result was the *Trade Union Act of 1913*.[37] This provided that if a majority of a local union favored using its funds for political purposes, the local branch could then earmark a portion of the dues from *all* members for such purposes, *except* the dues of those members who specifically indicated that they did not want their dues so used. Critics pointed out that this "contracting out" provision of the law gave little protection to the minority of a local union in view of the great pressures for union "solidarity."

Following the 1926 General Strike, the *Trades Disputes and Trade Union Act of 1927* [38] reduced union legal immunity and reversed the principle of political contributions. After forbidding civil servants to join unions which were affiliated with others, the law made unions engaging in sympathetic strikes liable to tort actions. Unions continued the method of voting on the question of using their funds for political purposes as provided in 1913, though a favorable vote now permitted them to use only the dues of those members who specifically indicated that they wanted them devoted to political ends. The substitution of "contracting in" for "contracting out" made the Labor party pledge itself to repeal this law. In 1929 Labor formed a government, but the coolness of its Liberal allies toward a repeal prevented the ministry from taking any action.

Thus when Labor won an independent majority in 1945, one of the first items of their legislative program was the *Trade Disputes and Trade Union Act of 1945*,[39] which with almost brutal directness and brevity repealed the 1927 act and all orders issued under it. The repeal thus restored the laws of 1906 and 1913.

Criminal Law

Both judicial and legislative modifications of the criminal law reflected the general desire to protect individual rights and at the same time a growing concern for the reformation of criminals rather than for punitive justice. However, certain criminologists and penologists felt that the criminal law remained far from ideal.

The grand jury virtually disappeared. The return of indictments by

[37] 2 and 3 Geo. V, cap. 30.
[38] Stephenson and Marcham, 835.
[39] 9 and 10 Geo. VI, cap. 52.

it during the twentieth century increasingly became a *pro-forma* approval of charges prepared by government authorities. Though occasionally the grand jury may have saved the innocent from unnecessary trials by rejecting such "bills," there were strong reasons for saving the time and expense required by grand jury action on accusations. In 1933 a statute provided that indictments by grand juries should be only on charges of treason committed outside the realm, violations of the official secrets laws, and oppressive acts by governors of colonies.[40] With these exceptions, indictments were now to be returned by an examining magistrate after what amounted to a preliminary hearing on the charges, and in a few instances, by coroners' juries, and by judicial officers for charges of perjury.

The Judges' Rules protected the accused prior to trial. Without legislative action, the justices of the High Court formulated an extremely complex code of procedure covering all aspects of the processes of arrest, detention, police interrogation, and examination by magistrates. The general tenor of these rules was to protect the accused at every point, and the justices made the rules effective by dismissing charges against persons when they discovered that there had been any violation of these rules.

It was this anxiety to protect the accused that made the bench very doubtful about the admissability of fingerprints as evidence, because a man's fingerprints were self-incrimination, which the common law forbade unless the accused gave testimony. In 1952 legislation permitted the police to take fingerprints of a suspect if he were over fourteen and if authorized by a magistrate upon the request of a police inspector. However, if the suspect were subsequently freed, either by the police, examining magistrate, trial jury, or appellate court, the police had to destroy the fingerprint card.

The right of appeal in criminal cases was extended. The Judicature Act of 1873 had actually reduced the scope of criminal appeals by abolishing the Court of Crown Cases Reserved. The Court of Appeal established by the law had only civil jurisdiction, so that during the brief time the House of Lords was without appellate functions, there was actually no criminal appeal from Queen's Bench. The restoration of the House of Lords as a final appellate court in 1876 again permitted criminal appeals on points of law from the rulings of trial justices.

[40] Gooch, 397.

The same argument which had restored appellate jurisdiction to the House of Lords in civil cases applied also to criminal cases, in that the trial justices and the law lords might rule differently on the same issue of law and thereby raise the question as to which was correct. To most people, however, this argument in favor of an intermediate criminal appeal court had little meaning until the sensational Adolf Beck cases of 1896 and 1904, which resulted in his being convicted of different crimes actually committed by another man. As the law then stood, Beck had no issue of law on which to bring an appeal, and there was no appeal for questions of fact in criminal law. Only the royal prerogative of mercy was available to him, and it did not come to Beck until after much personal anguish and expense.

On the basis of a royal commission report, in 1907 a statute provided for as many courts in the criminal appellate hierarchy as there were for civil cases. The law established the *Court of Criminal Appeal*,[41] composed of three justices, or a greater uneven number, from King's Bench,[42] other than the trial judge of the appealed criminal case. A convicted defendant, never the crown, might appeal to this court on any question of law, and with the leave of the trial justice, on a mixed issue of law and fact, or on one of fact only. If the trial justice refused such leave, the Court of Criminal Appeal might grant such leave. The defendant could also appeal the severity of his sentence, unless it was specifically fixed by law. These provisions gave the Court of Criminal Appeal a very wide jurisdiction, which became even larger by virtue of its ability to receive an appeal on "any other ground" appearing adequate to it.

In exercising its broad appellate criminal jurisdiction, the new court had large powers, including the very unusual one, for an appellate tribunal, of being able to receive new evidence discovered since the trial, although the court was very careful about exercising this power. If it were satisfied with the conduct of the trial and the jury verdict, the Court of Criminal Appeal "dismissed the appeal," that is, affirmed the judgment of the trial court. If, however, the court found that the verdict was "unreasonable," or not supported by the evidence, or if it found errors in the rulings of the trial justice, or that "on any ground there was a miscarriage of justice," the court could "allow the appeal,"

[41] Gooch, 390.
[42] The usual composition of the court was the Chief Justice and two other justices from King's (Queen's) Bench.

that is, quash the conviction; *or* reduce the severity of the sentence, if this had been the grounds for appeal. The word "could" is to be noted; because the statute made clear that the court, even if it found the point raised in the appeal could be decided in favor of the defendant, might still dismiss the appeal if it felt that "no substantial miscarriage of justice had actually occurred."

The court also received the duty of advising the Home Secretary, at his request, on the exercise of the royal prerogative of mercy, though not in capital cases.

Unlike most American appellate courts, the Court of Criminal Appeal lacked the power to remand a case for retrial. Such a retrial began the case *de novo*, as if the original one had never occurred, so that the defendant again was innocent until proven guilty. Those who argued that the Court of Criminal Appeal should have this power pointed to its unwillingness to accept new evidence, wisely perhaps, because, unlike the jury, it had not actually *heard* other testimony. However, opposed to this view was the opinion that a new trial increased expenses for the litigants, which was no great problem for the crown, but which might be very serious for the defendant. In 1948 the Court of Criminal Appeal received the power to return cases for retrial, one of the few powers it had not previously possessed.

The act of 1907 provided that from an adverse decision by the Court of Criminal Appeal the defendant might appeal to the House of Lords on a point of law, only if the Attorney-General certified that such a further appeal was in the "public interest." This was a very broad phrase, and became really even broader by the provision that no legal process might compel the Attorney-General to grant or to withhold such a certificate. This feature of the 1907 law was perhaps even more remarkable than the sole discretion accorded by the Parliament Act of 1911 to the Speaker in deciding what were, or were not, money bills; because the Attorney-General was the chief law officer of the crown, which had formally prosecuted the case, and might himself have appeared for the crown in the trial and appeal courts. Significantly, there was little criticism of this section of the act, or of its actual exercise by Attorneys-General, who issued very few of the certificates necessary to bring a case from the Court of Criminal Appeal to the House of Lords, and then usually to clarify the law as to just what and how much of what kind of evidence was necessary to sustain a conviction. In cases exciting public interest a great deal of pressure might be brought to bear on the Attorney-General. F. E. Smith (later Lord Chancellor Birkenhead) refused a certificate to Sir Roger Casement after his unsuccessful appeal to the Court of Criminal Appeal from his conviction for treason in 1916, although many felt that considering Smith's strong Ulster, anti-Irish Home Rule feelings prior to World War I, he might have been wiser to have given one. On the other hand, in 1946 Sir Hartley Shawcross issued such a certificate so that William Joyce (Lord Haw-Haw) could appeal his conviction for treason to the House of Lords, which then held against him.

The Criminal Justice Act of 1948,[43] based largely on the work of a commission which sat before and during World War II, extended certain procedures of the juvenile courts to adults convicted of noncapital crimes carrying statutory penalties of two or more years' imprisonment. In such cases a panel of experts, including a criminologist, a psychiatrist, and any other person desired by the court, investigated the case and made recommendations to the trial judge. On the basis of these recommendations, if he felt that an alternative to a prison sentence would reform the person and yet also deter crime, the justice might order *corrective training* for from two to four years. The first part of this training, which could be psychiatric, educational, vocational, or anything else embodied in the order of the court, was institutionalized. However, if at any time the authorities of the institution felt it desirable, they might release the person under conditions to be observed by him for the remainder of his original period of corrective training.

At the other end of the scale, the law dealt with the problem of the habitual adult criminal. Upon his fourth conviction as an adult of a crime carrying a statutory penalty of two or more years of imprisonment, the trial judge, instead of imposing the statutory penalty for the fourth crime, might sentence him to *preventive detention* for seven to fourteen years. The only limitations on judicial discretion in such cases was that the convicted person had to be over the age of thirty and that the judge, himself, had to be satisfied that such preventive detention was in the public interest. Actually, preventive detention was the same as imprisonment, and there was a question as to whether its preventive aspect was designed to protect the prisoner or society from any further crime by him; and critics said that this phase of the 1948 law was an admission of failure.

In the course of the passage of the Criminal Justice Act, the House

[43] 11 and 12 Geo. VI, cap. 58.

of Lords succeeded in what it had failed to do in 1937; it ended the trial by peers of peers indicted for treason and felony. For centuries it had been argued that this placed burdens on peers unknown to commoners charged with such crimes. The peer had no right to challenge his triers, there was no requirement of unanimity in verdicts, and there was no appeal — the first court for peers being the nation's last. In 1936 the House of Lords had passed a resolution declaring that the procedure had outlived its usefulness, and the next year it passed a bill abolishing it; however the Commons had not then acted on the measure. Now in 1948 the peers inserted an amendment in the Criminal Justice Bill, which the lower House accepted.

The growing public distaste for capital punishment became politically effective after World War II, when a group of backbenchers from both sides of the Commons campaigned for its abolition. By 1948 their pressure was sufficient to cause the Labor ministry to allow free votes on two amendments to the Criminal Justice Bill. One, abolishing the death penalty, failed; but the other, suspending it for five years, passed the Commons. When the Lords rejected the amendment, the government, by pointing out that the amendment had rendered the bill incapable of passage without the approval of the upper House in terms of the Parliament Act,[44] was able to have its majority drop the amendment and pass the measure in the form approved by the Lords.

In 1955 the Conservative cabinet had to permit a similar free vote on a resolution condemning capital punishment, which passed the House of Commons after the sensational announcement by the former Home Secretary of the recent Labor cabinet, that he was convinced that he had permitted an innocent man to go to his death. Impressed by the passage of the resolution, the Home Secretary of the existing government began to commute most death sentences to life imprisonment, though the Lord Chief Justice saw in this practice something like the suspension of the law which was forbidden by the Bill of Rights. On the other hand, there had never been any statutory limitations on the royal prerogative of mercy.

In 1956 a bill, abolishing the death penalty except for a few cases, passed the House of Commons, only to be rejected by the Lords. Under the terms of the Parliament Act of 1949, however, the multi-party group sponsoring the measure could make it law by a second passage through the Commons the next year.

[44] The bill no longer being in the same form as when introduced; above, pp. 531, 533.

At this point the ministry intervened and forced its majority in the Commons to accept a government compromise, which became the *Homicide Act*[45] in 1957. This law while not abolishing capital punishment, sharply reduced the possibility of its application in murder cases by creating the classification of "capital murder," which was for any *second* conviction of murder in Great Britain; or for any *first* conviction if the killing were committed in the furtherance of theft, by resisting arrest, or escaping from custody; or of police or prison officials; or by shooting or causing an explosion. For all other murders, including felony-murder other than theft, there was a penalty of life imprisonment. The law further reduced the possibility for conviction of either type of murder by throwing over the McNaughton rules and importing from Scottish law the provision that where the defendant proved mental abnormality so as to "substantially impair mental responsibility" at the time of the killing, the jury should return a verdict only of manslaughter. Critics of the statute grumbled that persons contemplating homicide would do well to consult their solicitors. In actual trials the chief difficulty in applying the law lay in its use of the doctrine of "diminished responsibility," which English juries (unlike their Calvinistic Scottish counterparts) found as puzzling as the former "right-wrong" test of the McNaughton rules. Where juries refused to find such mental impairment and convicted of murder (of either type), defence counsel asked the Court of Criminal Appeals to so find; but the justices took considerably more convincing on this issue of fact than did the average jury.

The interests of the state raised questions of personal rights. The *Official Secrets Acts* of 1911 and 1920[46] made it a criminal offense to disclose information of a confidential nature injurious to the interests of the state. Plainly, these laws constituted potential threats to individual freedom. The government, which under these laws had wide powers of search, also had the power to compel the disclosure of the source of the confidential information. This might possibly lead to the silencing of any criticisms of government policy. On the other hand, the right of the state to protect itself from potential enemies, who could learn much from the improper revelation of classified information, was incontestable. As the trials for the violation of these laws were necessarily held in secret, the problem became even more difficult.

[45] 5 and 6 Eliz. II, cap. 11.
[46] 1 and 2 Geo. V, cap. 28; 10 and 11 Geo. V, cap. 75.

In 1938 a member of the House of Commons, who held an army reserve commission, gave facts and figures in the House to show that the government's rearmament program was deficient in anti-aircraft defense. Prime Minister Chamberlain did not deny the figures, instead, he threatened a prosecution under the Official Secrets Acts. This, of course, threatened the sacred parliamentary privilege of free speech; and a special committee of the Commons rebuked the ministry in a report which was accepted by the House. At the same time the House of Lords resolved that no provision of the Official Secrets Acts applied to any statement made in its chamber. But the average man, who was not a member of Parliament, had to depend upon the self-discipline of the government, and the degree to which public opinion could be brought to bear on it, for his protection against prosecutions under these laws.

Legal costs were always a serious problem for defendants. Although the accused enjoyed various privileges against the government in criminal actions, the law was silent on a matter which was of the greatest importance to many people — the power to secure competent counsel to cross swords with the expert talent employed by the government, known as *Treasury counsel*, although they were usually private barristers.

The truly poor man had a less serious problem than the person of average means. Trial courts had assigned counsel to poor persons charged with serious crimes; and in 1930 magistrates received the same authority for minor criminal cases. In 1949 magistrates were required to resolve any doubts about the ability of defendants to hire counsel in their favor. The person of average income, however, had no such protection against legal costs, which might be ruinous for himself and family, and very likely the most desirable counsel was the one least within the defendant's means. A not particularly successful effort to deal with the problem was the provision in the Criminal Justice Act of 1948, permitting (but not requiring) justices on the trial or appellate levels, in the event the accused went free, to order payment of his legal costs from county or borough funds. Even where justices chose to make such orders, the amounts were far below the fees charged by leading solicitors and barristers.

A special branch of the law came to be concerned with juvenile crime. Hitherto common law, with its emphasis on *rem*, had seen only the crime, not the status of the person committing it. As early as 1857,

however, it was beginning to be recognized that such an attitude was
fallacious, and a statute was passed empowering the Home Secretary to
remove children guilty of juvenile offenses from criminal environments.
By the twentieth century various laws made the treatment of juvenile
crime different from that of the common law. They were codified and
extended in the *Children and Young Persons Act* of 1933.[47] The law first
sanctioned the old legal doctrine, derived from canon law, that no child
under the age of eight could under any circumstances be guilty of any
crime. Between eight and fourteen the juvenile, still legally a child,
continued to receive the protection of that status, except that the crown
might rebut it with evidence. From fourteen to seventeen the "young
person" was presumed legally capable of committing crimes; but he
was under the jurisdiction of a special magistrate's court, the juvenile
court.

Invariably closed to the public, the court naturally first determined
the guilt or innocence of the accused, who was entitled to counsel. But
the court could not "convict" him; it could only "find" that he had
broken the law. Likewise, the court could not "sentence" him, but only
make an "order" for special attention. Under no circumstances might
the crown in a court proceeding against the person as an adult bring
forward his contacts as a juvenile with agencies of the law or of the
juvenile court.

As far as possible the court's order for a juvenile was for probation.
If this method were not possible, the order usually provided adequate
training and education in special centers, the most famous being those
of the Borstal system, run like the public schools, even to the point of
having a school tie. Again, under the Criminal Justice Act of 1948, the
juvenile court could not order any person under twenty-one to prison
— and this, too, was a recognition of previous practice — or sentence
anyone eighteen or under to death. The last provision gave a statutory
effect to the old judicial practice which first condemned such people
but only on the assumption that the crown would commute the sentence
to detention at the sovereign's pleasure.

Administrative Jurisprudence

The enlargement of state activities gave the crown new legal and
juridical functions and powers. Similar to those of the Tudor and early

[47] 23 and 24 Geo. V, cap. 12.

Stuart periods, these functions and powers produced the same disagreements about administrative jurisprudence as they had done in former times.

Parliament tended to delegate more and more legislative powers to agencies of the crown, or to the government. Social legislation was of great complexity and demanded a considerable amount of flexibility in administration. Parliament was simply unable to provide more than the broad outlines of policy in a statute, which itself had very often been drafted by civil service experts, and hardly changed in the course of its passage through the Houses. Parliament authorized specific executive agencies to implement this legislation. It was like the way Parliament had delegated business to the Privy Council in former times, but now the business was very much greater.

Provisional orders did require parliamentary confirmation, but this simply meant that orders lay on the table of each House for ten days.[48] If no member objected to them, Parliament confirmed them by *provisional order confirmation acts*, the passage of which was perfunctory, although they made all of these orders acts of Parliament.

Statutory orders, of course, had the force of law in that the statute providing for their issuance gave them this status, as in the Trades Boards Act of 1909. In this way administrative legislation was speeded up and became steadily more popular with government agencies. The crown thus gained wide legislative powers, which in the view of the critics was a serious challenge to the legislative competence and power of Parliament. But for those who supported such administrative legislation it appeared to be dictated by necessity. Parliament could not legislate minutely on complex social and technical matters; it had neither the time nor the knowledge. Even if it did, to embody these matters in statutes would make the administration of such laws much less flexible, and it was important that they should be as flexible as possible. Parliament, it was pointed out, could always refuse to confirm any provisional order and could quickly repeal a statutory one. Yet the existence of such powers by members of Parliament, who were so often amateurs, subject to party discipline, was no guarantee that they would ever exercise them.

Administrative adjudication of executive legislation raised the same issues as it had in the sixteenth and seventeenth centuries. The individual

---

[48] Actually, they did not lie on the table of the House at all but in the library of each House.

could easily find that he had inadvertently violated the "law" of statutory orders and confirmed provisional ones. When he did so, he went not before the law courts, but before administrative tribunals. There he discovered that the "legislators" were also his judges, using procedures unknown to the law and liable to change with very little warning.

As in the days of the Tudors, it was argued that the regular courts and their law had little relation to the complexities of the present time. Their very devotion to precedent made them poor arbiters of rules issued to refine already complex social and technical legislation on such matters as public health and electric current generation. Thus although in the past common law courts had possessed the power to declare orders-in-council *ultra vires,* statutes delegating legislative power to executive agencies increasingly forbade the common law courts from taking any cognizance of issues arising from such administrative rules.

The old arguments were also employed on behalf of the other side. Departmental experts, it was said, thinking only in terms of their particular services, issued rules binding upon people whose parliamentary representatives had no really effective control over them; and the specific rules were not matters for regular judicial action. The average person simply could not hope to know every rule issued by a single department, let alone by all departments. Yet these rules had the force of law, and contravention of them meant trial.

Trial, however, was administrative, by departmental administrative tribunals which applied the specific regulations. Procedures, as before, were summary and flexible — an advantage, said their supporters; a terrible danger, said their critics. Appeal from a departmental trial tribunal was within the hierarchy of that department, and it was difficult and often legally impossible for a litigant to carry his appeal from an administrative tribunal into a common law court. On the one side it was argued that only experts were qualified to review the judicial work of departmental experts; on the other it was pointed out that experts always agreed with experts.

And so the English again wrestled with administrative legislation and adjudication, the needs of state and society still at odds with the rights of the individual; the ghosts of Bacon and Coke were still walking over the land.

The extension of political democracy and the demand for state social action created a situation where the ministers of the crown by virtue of their being party leaders often dominated the House of Commons. The sharp reduction in the status of the House of Lords enhanced this ministerial power so that the Commons often merely followed the ministerial lead in such crucial matters as finance and foreign policy. This situation perturbed many people; and various solutions were proposed, none very satisfactory. Others argued that as long as a democratic electorate expressed its opinion of government policy at regular intervals, the danger of tyranny was less than imagined.

Legal developments endeavored to protect the rights of the individual, but the enlargement of the welfare state once again produced administrative jurisprudence with all of the old arguments for and against it.

The English obviously did not find their constitution perfect, but they could be expected to improve it by the pragmatic, piecemeal methods of the past. Thus the constitution would never achieve perfection — as few human institutions do.

READING LIST

BOOTH, A. H. *British Hustings, 1924–1950.*

CAMPION, LORD, ET AL. *Parliament, A Survey.*

DALE, H. E. *The Higher Civil Service in Great Britain.*

GILES, F. T. *The Criminal Law.*

GROVE, J. W., and W. J. M. MACKENZIE. *Central Administration in Britain.*

HEWART, LORD. *The New Despotism.*

JENNINGS, SIR (W.) IVOR. *Cabinet Government.*

———. *Parliament.*

MORRISON, HERBERT. *Government and Parliament A Survey from the Inside.*

OWEN, A. D. K. *The British Social Services.* "Report of the Committee on Administrative Tribunals and Enquiries," *British Parliamentary Papers,* 1957, House of Commons, Cmd. 218.

ROBSON, W. A. *Justice and Administrative Law.*

WHEARE, K. C. *The Civil Service in the Constitution.* "Who Governs Britain?" *The Twentieth Century,* CLXII, 291.

APPENDIX I

Sample Original Writs of Henry II [1]

WRIT OF NOVEL DISSEISIN

The king to the sheriff, etc. A hath complained unto us that B unjustly and without judgment hath disseised him of his freehold in C within 30 years last past, and therefore we command you that if the aforesaid A shall make you secure to prosecute his claim, then cause that tenement to be reseised, and the chattels which were then in it, and the same tenement with the chattels shall be in peace until the first assize when our justices shall come into those parts, and in the meantime cause twelve free and lawful men of that visne [neighborhood] to view that tenement, and their names to be put into the writ, and summon them by good summoners, that they be before the justices aforesaid, at the assize aforesaid, ready to make recognizance thereupon, and put by gages and safe pledges the aforesaid B, or, if he shall not be found, his bailiff, that he may be then there to hear that recognizance, etc. And have there the summoners, the names of the pledges, and this writ, etc.

WRIT OF MORT D'ANCESTOR

The king to the sheriff of S greeting: If A shall make you secure, etc. then summon etc. twelve free and lawful men of the neighborhood of N that they be before our justices at the first assize, when they shall come into those parts, *or* before our justices at *Westminster* on the octave of etc. *or* before our beloved and faithful D and E and those whom we have associated unto them, at a certain day and place, whereof they the said D and E shall give you notice ready to recognize by oath, if W father of the aforesaid A or mother, sister, brother, uncle or aunt was seised in his (or her) demesne as of fee of one messuage with the appurtenances in N, the day whereon he died, and if he died after the coronation of lord king Henry [I]; and if the same A be his next heir; and in the meantime let them view the said messuage and land, and cause their names to be put in the writ, and summon by good summoners B who now holds the aforesaid messuage and lands, that he may be there to hear that recognizance; and have there the summoners and this writ. Witness, etc.

---

[1] The English translations of these writs are those given by George Booth, *The Nature and Practice of Real Actions in their Writs and Processes both Original and Judicial*, 1st American ed. (New York, 1808), 91, 95, 206, 210, 221, 225.

WRIT OF DARREIN PRESENTMENT

The king, etc. to the sheriff greeting: Command A that justly, etc. he permit B to present a fit person to the church of N which is vacant, and belongs to his gift as he says. And whereof he complains that the said A unjustly hinders him. And unless he will do it summon by good summoners the said A, that he be before our justices of Chester, at Chester, on the first day of the next session of the county court of Chester, to be held at Chester, to shew whereof he has not done it. And have there the summoners and this writ. Witness.

WRIT OF UTRUM

The king, etc. If A, parson of the church of D shall make you secure, etc. then summon, etc. twelve free, etc. of the visne of D, that they may be before our justices at the first assize, etc. or before our justices on such a day prepared to recognize under oath whether one messuage etc. in E, is frankalmoign, appertaining to the church of said A of D, or the lay fee of S, etc. and in the meantime let them view the land, and summon etc., the aforesaid S who holds two acres thereof B (and others holding thereof) that they be then, etc.

WRIT OF THE GRAND ASSIZE

The king to the sheriff, etc., greeting: Summon by good summoners, four lawful knights of your county, that they be before our justices at the first assize, when they shall come into these parts, to elect twelve of the lawful knights of the neighborhood of N, who may better know and will speak the truth to make cognizance of our great assize between A demandant, and B tenant, of one messuage with the appurtenances in N, whereupon the same B who is tenant, hath put himself upon our great assize, and hath prayed that cognizance may be made, whether of them hath greater right in the messuage aforesaid, and summon by good summoners the aforesaid B, that he be then there to hear that election; and have you there the names of the aforesaid knights and this writ.

WRIT OF RIGHT

The king to the sheriff, etc. command A that justly etc. he render unto C one messuage with the appurtenances in M which he claims to be his right and inheritance, and whereof he complains that the aforesaid A hath unjustly deforced him, and unless he will do this, and the aforesaid C shall give you security to prosecute his suit, then summon by good summoners the aforesaid A that he be before our justices at _____ , on the _____ day of the [ecclesiastical season], to show why he will not do it; and have you there the summoners and this writ. Witness, etc. Because I, the chief lord of the fee, hath thereupon remitted to us his court.

APPENDIX II

Sample Entries from the Year Books [1]

ACTION OF UTRUM — (Pleas in Easter Term, 1306)

§ En une "jure de utrum" le priour de Bradestoke voucha le priour de Wandragese par reson des eschanges des tenements dela la mer qil dona pur meyme les tenements qe sunt en demaunde, e monstra chartre qe ceo testmoigne, e la chartre le Roy qe testmoigna ces eschanges.

—*Toudeby* [pleader for plaintiff]. La chartre en sey suppose estre fete hors de roialme, par quei &c.

—*Malmesthorpe* [pleader for defendant]. Vous nel poez dedire, car la chartre le Roy testmogne les eschanges, e les ratefie; par quei &c.

—BEREFORD [justice]. Veistes le plee entre le Roy de Escoce e un B. ou une chartre ne poeit estre dedit pur ceo qe la chartre le Roi fust mis avant en testmoignance de ceo fet, auxi com ore?

—*Toudeby*. Quant les eschanges se pristrent nous lui liverames touz les monumenz qe nous avioms de ces tenements, e par queux monumenz nous duissoms voucher; par quei garantir ne devoms. Estre ceo il ount une chartre de nouse qe William le Conquerour nous fist, par la quele il le puet barrer; jugement &c.

—BEREFORD. Ceo est vostre folie demene.

—*Toudeby*. Solom les eschanges entroms en la garantie.

—*King* [for defendant]. Nostre predecessour seisi en temps le Roi qe ore est, e aliena, e prioms la Jure.

—*Toudeby*. Les eschanges se pristrent en temps le Roi Henri, par quei nous prioms aide de ceo qe fust dist einz ceo qil nous voucha e si ne avoit il rien dist.

—*Warr* [for defendant]. De pus qe la persone ad suffert le voucher qe est plus [omission] de sa accion, nentendoms mie qil deive aver la Jure de plus bas temps qe nostre seisine ne fust.

—Et non allocatur [ruling by court].

[1] From Alfred J. Horwood, ed. & trans., *Year Books of the Reign of King Edward the First. Michaelmas Term, Year XXXIII and Years XXXIV and XXXV* (London, 1879; vol. XXXI, pt. 5 of *Rerum Brittanicarum Medii Aevi Scriptores*, or *Chronicles and Memorials of Great Britain and Ireland during the Middle Ages*), 52–5, 222–5, 184–6, 442–5, 198–9. Both the law-French and English translation are given for the utrum pleading; for the other entries only the English version is given in the Appendix.

—*Toudeby*. Nous prioms qe la Jure soit examine sur la forme del primer
doun.
—Et concessum fuit [action by court].

ACTION OF UTRUM — Translation (Pleas in Easter Term, 1306)

In Jure de utrum the prior of Bradstoke vouched the prior of Wandragese
by reason of exchanges of tenements beyond the sea which he gave for the
same tenements which are in demand, and he showed a charter witnessing
this, and the King's charter which witnessed the exchanges.
—*Toudeby* [for the plaintiff]. The charter supposes by itself that it was
made out of the realm, wherefore &c.
—*Malmesthorpe* [for the defendant]. You cannot deny it, for the King's
charter witnesses the exchanges and ratifies them; wherefore &c.
—BEREFORD [justice]. Have you seen the plea between the King of
Scotland and one B., where a charter could not be denied because the King's
charter was put forward in evidence of that deed, just as now?
—*Toudeby*. When the exchanges were effected we delivered to him all the
muniments of those tenements which we had, by which muniments we ought
to vouch; wherefore we ought not to warrant. Moreover, they have from
us a charter which William the Conqueror made to use, by which he can
bar him; judgment &c.
—BEREFORD. That is your own foolishness.
—*Toudeby*. According to the exchanges we enter into warranty.
—*King* [for the defendant]. Our predecessor was seised in the time of the
present King, and he alienated; and we pray the Jury.
—*Toudeby*. The exchanges were made in the time of King Henry, where-
fore we pray aid of what was said before he vouched us, and as if he had
said nothing.
—*Warr* [for the defendant]. Since the parson has allowed the voucher which
is more [omission] of his action, we do not think that he ought to have the
Jury from a lower time then our seisin was.
—And it was not allowed [ruling by court].
—*Toudeby*. We pray that the Jury may be examined of the form of the
first gift.
—And this was granted [action by court].

ACTION OF NOVEL DISSEISIN — Translation (Pleas in Hilary Term, 1307)

§ STAUNTON [justice]. Philip, son of Elis, brought the assise against
William de la Bere &c and complained &c. *William* said that there ought
not to be an assise, for he said that one Henry le Fevre acknowledged the
right of the tenements &c. to belong to John de law Bere, whose heir
William is, by fine &c. and granted that the tenements which ought to revert
to him after the death of one Emma &c. should remain to him in fee simple;
and so he entered after the death of the said Emma: and he prayed judgment

if in opposition to that fine there ought to be an assise. And Philip said that one Emma (she who held for term of life) enfeoffed him of these tenements in fee simple by her charter, which he produced, and put him in seisin, and so he was seised until William and the others tortiously &c. The ASSISE said that Henry le Fevre to whom the fee and the right of these tenements belonged granted them to John de la Bere brother of William &c. whose heir &c. and by fine &c.; but that Emma who was tenant of the free hold for term of her life did not ever attorn to John; but they said that Emma held only for life by lease from the said Henry, which Emma, after the grant and acknowledgement which the said Henry had made to the said John, enfeoffed the said Philip in fee simple of the said tenements, and put him in seisin, which seisin he continued until William &c. ousted him. The court doth adjudge &c. and that Philip do recover his seisin of that estate which he first had, and let William have his recovery out of the note &c. if he please &c.

ACTION OF MORT D'ANCESTOR — Translation (Michaelmas Term, 1305)

(Although not so indicated in the entry, the action, both by external and internal evidence, is plainly in King's Bench.)

Before the King.[2] A judgment in an assise of Mordancester [sic] reversed.[2]

ROUBYRI [justice of King's Bench].[2] John son of Avelyne brought a writ of Mordancester before Sir RALPH DE HENGHAM [Chief Justice of Common Pleas],[2] on the death of John the clerk, his uncle, against Edmund of London, warden of the house of St. Thomas of Acre; and Edmund came and said that there ought not to be an assise; for he said that this is a writ which is to be brought on the death of the person last seised; and he said that after the death of John the clerk, there entered on those tenements one Avelyne, mother of the said John who brings &c., as sister and heir of the said John the clerk, and was seised, on whose death this John son of Avelyne might make use of the writ, and he prayed judgment of the writ; to which exception it was answered that Avelyne, after the death &c. did not enter and was not seised. And thereupon the Assise came and told this story — that after the death of the said John the clerk, the said Avelyne, while the corpse was in the bier, entered and took possession, claiming as heir of John, and for half an hour in the day remained there, until, on the corpse being carried away, she still wishing to keep possession, came the Edmund and ousted her. And because it appeared to the said Sir Ralph and his companions [Court of Common Pleas][2] that that small seisin and at that time was nothing, they considered that, notwithstanding that abatement &c., the said John of Avelyne might on the death of John his uncle well employ this writ, and they adjudged that John should recover his seisin. And because we [King's Bench] see, as the verdict &c., that Avelyne, claiming &c., entered after the death of John and was seised until &c., on which seisin she might have employed the assise &c. and her heir after her

[2] Evidence that the entry is for an action in King's Bench.

death might have employed a writ of Entry founded &c., and thus the exception of the said Edmund is affirmed by the verdict of the Assise; and the cause of the judgment was the short time &c., and as to that we think that a mere placing of the foot conferred seisin on the true heir, — this Court adjudges that Edmund do have again his seisin &c. and his damages, and that John may have his recovery by another way if he will.[3]

ACTION OF DARREIN PRESENTMENT — Translation (Easter Term, 1306)

§ An Assise of Darrein presentment was brought against the Dean of Lincoln, who said that he had nothing in that church except jointly with the chapter who were not named in the writ, and he prayed judgment.
—*Willuby* [pleader for plaintiff]. You are the sole deforceant, ready &c.
—*Herle* [pleader for defendant]. That which they call a church is a chapel appendant to our deanery; and we have nothing in the deanery except by the election of the chapter, without whom &c., and we pray aid of the chapter.
—*Passeley* [pleader for plaintiff]. We shall recover damages because you deforce us &c., which is a personal act as far as on as in a Quare impedit; wherefore &c.
—BEREFORD [justice]. And if a Mordancester were brought against the Dean for tenements, and he were to say that he found his church seised and his predecessor before him seised, should he not have aid? (intimating that he should) So (said he [BEREFORD]) in this case.
—And he [the Dean] had the aid [action by court].

ACTION ON WRIT OF RIGHT — Translation (Trinity Term, 1306)

§ One A brought a writ of Right against Gilbert de Gaunt, and demanded the manor of Honewardby. And the case was that part of the demesne, which was in the seisin of the ancestor of the demandant, was alienated, to be holden of Gilbert, and so charged with services. Gilbert said that he could not render the entire manor, because such an one holds so much, and such an one so much, to wit certain parcels alienated.
—*The demandant*. You hold the manor wholly in demesne as in demesne, in service as in service.
—*The tenant*. As before.
—And upon this there was an inquest.
—And the tenant saw that he had unadvisedly joined the Jury, and he came before the Jury, and disclosed the case, and that he did not hold the entire manor as it was in the seisin of the ancestor of the demandant; and he prayed that the other side might understand that he had put himself upon the jury in that form.
—*The demandant*. We are at a certain issue; wherefore you can not replead.

[3] John, son of Avelyne, undoubtedly will be back in Common Pleas since King's Bench has practically told him outright the proper writ for him to buy.

—And the Inquest gave verdict against the tenant, whereby the demandant recovered. And then Gilbert caused the record and the process to come before the King, to redress the error therein, in that the Court had received that issue by averment of the jurors, whereas the parties were not opposed in the issue; for it might well be that Gilbert de Gaunt held the entire manor in demesne as in demesne, in service as in service, on the day when the writ was purchased, as the demandant said, and yet that of the same manor according to the state in which it was in the seisin of the ancestor of the demandant, such an one held so much, and such an one so much, on the day when the writ was purchased, those parcels having been alienated as the tenant says.

—And afterwards Gilbert died, the error not being corrected.

THE LEGISLATIVE ENTAIL OF THE CROWN

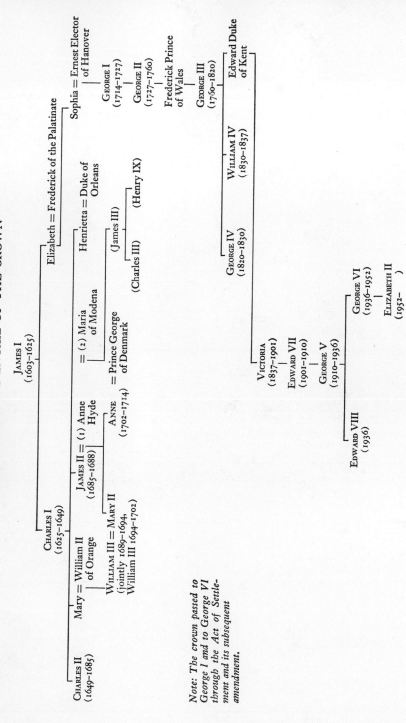

Note: The crown passed to George I and to George VI through the Act of Settlement and its subsequent amendment.

INDEX

Aberdeen, Earl of, 494
Acton Burnell, Statute of (De Merca-
    toribus), 133
Additional Petition and Advice, 349
administrative adjudication and courts,
    85–91, 252
    abolition in 1641, 317, 323, 325; effect
    of Bill of Rights, 410; Tudor and
    Stuart, 274–6; twentieth century, 555–6
Admiral, 224, 372 (see also Admiralty,
    First Lord of)
Admiralty
    appeals prior to 1873, 515; Court of,
    223–7, 514; droits, 225; First Lord of,
    503, 552; merger into High Court,
    516
adulterine castles, 61
advowson, 871
    disputes to be settled in royal court,
    96, by Assize of Darrein Presentment
    (q.v.), 107
Agreement of the People, 338, 342
agricultural planning, 540
aids
    customary, 58; other additional, 158
air force, 398
air transport
    government regulation, 541; national-
    ization, 542
Albert, Prince Consort, 500, 501, 502
Alfred the Great
    Laws of, 13, 36; and regicide as capital
    crime, 8, 13
allodial ownership, 18
Amiens, Mise of, 128
Angevin administrative-juridical innova-
    tions, 85–91
Angevin empire, 83, 84
Angles, 3, 8 (see also Jutes and Saxons)
Anglo-Saxon Chronicle, 51
Anglo-Saxon government, 5, 9–17 (see
    also king and Witan)
Anglo-Saxons, 3–8

Annates, Act of, 259
Anne, 395, 402, 416, 418, 419, 421, 441
Anne Boleyn, 255, 259, 260
annual party conference, 528
Anselm, 72, 75
anti-clericalism, 192, 253–4
Anti-Corn Law League, 481
anti-papal feeling, 253
Apology of the Commons, 292, 294, 295,
    298, 301–2, 303
appeal (accusation by individual), 109
    relation to impeachment, 186
appeal
    admiralty, 515; common law, late thir-
    teenth century, 145–6, late fourteenth
    century, 213–14, late eighteenth cen-
    tury, 459, nineteenth century prior to
    1873, 515, nineteenth century subse-
    quent to 1873, 516–17; Court of, 516,
    547; Lords Justices of, 515, 616
Appellant, Lords, 192
Apprentices, Statute of, 271, 273
Argyle, Duke of, 390
Arlington, Earl of, 374
Arms, Assize of, 88
army
    Council, 345; dissolution, 366, 367;
    dominance, 354; Militia Ordinance,
    320; and Parliament, 340, 342–3; pro-
    curement, 318; subsequent to 1688, 390,
    393, 397–8; Tudor lack of, 231
Army and Air Force (Annual) Act, 398
arraignment, 42, 148
arrentation, 131
Articles of Stamford, 179
Articles of War, 397–8
Artificers, Statute of (see Apprentices)
Artisans Dwelling Act, 480, 507
Asquith, H. H., 521, 534
Assembly of the Church of Scotland, 314
assize courts, 517
assizes, 86 (see under specific assizes)
    effect on land law, 105

CITED CASES

Amalgamated Society of Railway Servants, Osborne *v.*, 527, 545
Bates's Case, 295, 327, 328
Beck, R. *v.*, 548
Bonham's Case, 331
Bushnell, *ex parte*, 407
Calvin's Case, 316, 317–18, 327
Campbell *v.* Hall, 454
Carrington, Entick *v.*, 454
Casement, R. *v.*, 550
Chamber's Case, 327
Darnell's Case (*see* Five Knights' Case)
Eliot's Case, 312
Entick *v.* Carrington, 454
Five Knights' Case, 304–5, 328
Flood, Stephney *v.*, 280
Fortescue, Godwin *v.*, 289
Glanvil's Case, 326, 332
Godden *v.* Hales, 390, 405
Godwin *v.* Fortescue, 289
Hales, Godden *v.*, 390, 405
Hall, Campbell *v.*, 454

Hampden's Case, 311–12, 335
Hansard, Stockdale *v.*, 495–6
Joyce, R. *v.*, 550
Leatham, Quinn *v.*, 545
McNaughton, R. *v.*, 510
O'Connell, R. *v.*, 515–16
Osborne *v.* Amalgamated Society or Railway Servants, 527, 545
Peacham's Case, 332
Quinn *v.* Leatham, 545
R. *v.*
  Beck, 548; Casement, 550; Joyce, 550; McNaughton, 510; O'Connell, 515–16; Seven Bishops, 391, 392, 406–7
Seven Bishops, R. *v.*, 391, 392, 406–7
Somersett, *ex parte*, 455
Sorrell, Thomas *v.*, 404
Stephney *v.* Flood, 280
Stockdale *v.* Hansard, 495–6
Taff Vale Case, 544, 545
Thomas *v.* Sorrell, 404
Vassall's Case, 328
Wilkes, *ex parte*, 454